HARVESTING THE SEA IN SOUTHEASTERN ARABIA

Cambridge Semitic Languages and Cultures

General Editor: Geoffrey Khan

This is the first Open Access book series in the field; it combines the high peer-review and editorial standards with the fair Open Access model offered by OBP. The series includes philological and linguistic studies of Semitic languages, editions of Semitic texts, and studies of Semitic cultures. Titles cover all periods, traditions and methodological approaches to the field. The editorial board comprises Geoffrey Khan, Aaron Hornkohl, Esther-Miriam Wagner, Anne Burberry, and Benjamin Kantor.

You can access the full series catalogue here:
https://www.openbookpublishers.com/series/2632-6914

If you would like to join our community and interact with authors of the books, sign up to be contacted about events relating to the series and receive publication updates and news here:
https://forms.gle/RWymsw3hdsUjZTXv5

Harvesting the Sea in Southeastern Arabia

Volume 1: Regional Studies

Edited by
Janet C.E. Watson, Miranda J. Morris, and Erik Anonby

https://www.openbookpublishers.com

©2025 Janet C.E. Watson, Miranda J. Morris, and Erik Anonby

This work is licensed under an Attribution-NonCommercial 4.0 International (CC BY-NC 4.0). This license allows you to share, copy, distribute, and transmit the text; to adapt the text for non-commercial purposes of the text providing attribution is made to the authors (but not in any way that suggests that they endorse you or your use of the work). Attribution should include the following information:

Janet C.E. Watson, Miranda J. Morris, and Erik Anonby, *Harvesting the Sea in Southeastern Arabia: Volume 1: Regional Studies*. Cambridge, UK: Open Book Publishers, 2025, https://doi.org/10.11647/OBP.0409

Further details about CC BY-NC licenses are available at
http://creativecommons.org/licenses/by-nc/4.0/

All external links were active at the time of publication unless otherwise stated and have been archived via the Internet Archive Wayback Machine at
https://archive.org/web

Any digital material and resources associated with this volume will be available at
https://doi.org/10.11647/OBP.0409#resources

Semitic Languages and Cultures 32

ISSN (print): 2632-6906
ISSN (digital): 2632-6914

ISBN Paperback: 978-1-80511-331-7
ISBN Hardback: 978-1-80511-332-4
ISBN Digital (PDF): 978-1-80511-333-1

DOI: 10.11647/OBP.0409

Cover image: Unloading goods from the mainland on al-Ḥallāniyah island.
Photo © Miranda Morris, 1980.
Cover design: Jeevanjot Kaur Nagpal

The fonts used in this volume are Charis SIL and Scheherazade New.

TABLE OF CONTENTS

Abbreviations and Symbols xi

List of Figures xiii

List of Tables xvii

List of Maps xvii

Main Contributors xix

Janet C. E. Watson, Erik Anonby and Miranda J. Morris
Harvesting the Sea in Southeastern Arabia:
Introduction.. 1

   1. Ecosystems, Cultures, and Languages in
      Southeastern Arabia 1

   2. The Present Compendium 2

   3. Purpose and Scope 4

   4. The Structure of This Study 7

   5. Translanguaging 11

   6. Authors, Sources and Data 15

   7. Phonological Inventories and Transcription 18

   References 24

Part I: Harvesting the Sea on the Musandam Peninsula 27

Erik Anonby and AbdulQader Qasim Ali Al Kamzari
A Typology of Fish Names in Kumzari 31

Acknowledgments 31

1. Introduction 32
2. Fish and Fish Species 40
3. A Typology of Kumzari Fish Names 50
4. Fish Names in Wider Linguistic Context 58
5. Conclusion 68

Appendix: Explanatory Lexicon of Kumzari Fish Types 69

References 85

Christina van der Wal Anonby
Mṣaww wa Maḥḥar: The Sea in Kumzari Poetry 91

1. Introduction 91
2. Sea Poem from *Sōntyō* 93
3. Geography 95
4. Tides and Weather 97
5. Excerpt from *Sōntyō* 98

6. Sea Creatures and Plants 100

7. Natural and Supernatural 102

8. *Sōntyō*'s Destination 104

References 105

Erik Anonby and Simone Bettega
Three Arabic Fishing Songs from the Musandam Peninsula 107

1. Introduction 107

2. *Ayāllā* 'O God' 115

3. *Xəbbāṭ* 'Little Kingfish' 126

4. *Lā Ramētə* 'I Will Not Give It Up' 150

5. Conclusion and Reflections 155

References 159

Part II: Harvesting the Sea among the Bəṭāḥira 165

Miranda J. Morris
Harvesting the Sea among the Bəṭāḥira 169

Acknowledgments 169

1. Introduction 172

2. The Bəṭāḥira 173

3. Harvesting the Sea 180

4. In Conclusion 251

5. Baṭḥari Texts: Introduction 254

6. Texts 257

Part III: Harvesting the Sea in Central Monsoon Dhofar and al-Mahrah 337

Janet C. E. Watson, with Miranda J. Morris, Alec B. M. Moore and Said Baquir

Harvesting the Sea in Central Monsoon Dhofar and al-Mahrah 341

    Acknowledgments 341

    1. Introduction 341

    2. Fieldwork 343

    3. Climate 344

    4. The Cultural Value of Fishing 345

    5. Fish Types and Uses 347

    6. Names 354

    7. Fishing Methods and Tools 360

    References 363

    8. Texts 365

Part IV: Harvesting the Sea in Soqoṭra 423

Miranda J. Morris, Mubārak ʿĪsa Walīd al-Soqoṭri and Aḥmad Saʿd Taḥkí al-Soqoṭri

Harvesting the Sea in Soqoṭra 427

    Acknowledgments 427

    1. Introduction 429

    2. Soqoṭra, Trade and Island Fishermen................... 433

    3. Traditional Fishing: Fish 454

    4. Traditional Fishing: Non-Fish............................... 509

    5. The Craft of Soqoṭra... 552

    6. Sea Products for Consumption and for Export 571

    7. Conclusion.. 595

    References 597

    8. Texts... 601

Index... 723

ABBREVIATIONS AND SYMBOLS

ᴬ	Arabic (following single Arabic word; preceding and following Arabic phrase)	ELAR	Endangered Languages Archive
ᴬᴰ	Arabic dialect (in texts)	emph.	emphatic (ejective or pharyngealised)
alv.	alveolar	Engl.	English
Ar.	Arabic	f.	female
ArD	Arabic dialects	GAr	Gulf Arabic
B	Btahret (Bathari) (bəṭaḥrēt)	H	Hobyot (hobyōt)
Bl	Balochi	ᴴ	Hobyot (in texts)
Bn	Bandari	Ḥ	Harsusi (in texts)
br.	breathed	ʰC	pre-aspirated consonant
C	consonant	imm.	immature
Ç̣	emphatic (ejective or pharyngealised) consonant	K	Kumzari (kumẓārī)
		lg.	large
Cʸ	palatalised consonant	lit.	literally
cf.	confer, when referring to similar material	m.	male
		med.	medium
coll.	collective	M	Mehri (mahri)
dim.	diminutive (associated with small size, affection, or contempt)	ᴹ	Mehri (in texts)
		Mn	Minowi (Minabi)
		MP	Middle Persian
		MSAL	Modern South Arabian languages

MusAr	Musandam Arabic	vd.	voiced
n.	noun	vl.	voiceless
P	Persian	1	first person
pl.	plural	2	second person
ś	Shehret (in texts)	3	third person
sg.	singular	*	hypothetical or historical form
sgv.	singulative		
sm.	small	<	coming from
Sh	Shehret (śḥerēt)	>	changing to
so.	someone	+	exhibiting a feature
sp.	species (sg.)	-	not exhibiting a feature; morpheme break
spp.	species (pl.)	~	in variation with
Sq	Soqotri (sɔ́ḳóṭri ~ sāḳáṭri)	/	alternating with; end of text division
sth.	something		
SwIr	Southwestern Iranic (Iranian)	//	phonemic representation
trade	term used in commercial contexts	[ ]	IPA phonetic transcription; omitted segments (texts); omitted words (glosses)
v.	very		
V	vowel	( )	optional; variable
ᵛ	epenthetic (inserted) vowel	‿	connection of separated syllables in a word
V̄	long vowel	' '	gloss (meaning)

LIST OF FIGURES

A Typology of Fish Names in Kumzari

Figure 1: Musandam Peninsula
Figure 2: *Li kūkū* 'gillnet' fishing with Hakim, Yusuf and Hassan al-Kumzari
Figure 3: Fish catch from *li kūkū* 'gillnet' fishing

Mṣaww wa Maḥḥar: The Sea in Kumzari Poetry

Figure 1: Kumzari *lenj* (dhow), Strait of Hormuz

Three Arabic Fishing Songs from the Musandam Peninsula

Figure 1: Musandam Peninsula in the context of Arabia
Figure 2: Habalayn in late afternoon, in the shadow of the mountain to the west
Figure 3: Xōr Ḥabalēn (Habalayn Inlet)
Figure 4: Muḥammad Salūm al-Ḍhuhūrī, consultant for this study

Harvesting the Sea among the Bəṭāḥira

Figure 1: Camel pack saddle
Figure 2: Gāt watering place with cave shelter
Figure 3: Women fetching water in goatskins, Al Jazir
Figure 4: Unloading goods from dhow to dugout
Figure 5: Cutting and shaping leather
Figure 6: Early morning among the goats, upper plateau

Figure 7: Plaiting wild date-palm fibre
Figure 8: The *Nannorrhops* desert palm, with edible fruit
Figure 9: Twisting fibre into cordage
Figure 10: Working *Nannorrhops* fibre with a bodkin
Figure 11a: Former living quarters at Mingiy
Figure 11b: Former living quarters at Mingiy, with Maḥmūd Mšaʿfi Al-Baṭhari (used with permission)
Figure 12a: Former living quarters at Warx, with graves
Figure 12b: Former living quarters at Warx, with cave shelters behind
Figure 13: Goat drinking dewdrops
Figure 14: Night quarters for fishermen near Mingiy
Figure 15: Warx and lagoon with former shark pits in foreground
Figure 16: Tanning a goatskin
Figure 17: Leather and wood cradle, back view

Harvesting the Sea in Central Monsoon Dhofar and al-Mahrah

Figure 1: Old fishing boat, eastern Dhofar
Figure 2: Drying sardines, Mḥayfīf, al-Mahrah
Figure 3: Drying sardines, al-Muġsayl
Figure 4: Dried shark, al-Ġayḍah
Figure 5: Drying abalone, Ḥadbīn
Figure 6: Shark liver, al-Ġayḍah
Figure 7: Sea lemon, Ḥāsik
Figure 8: Shellfish meal, Sadḥ
Figure 9: Boys with broken fish trap, Mirbāṭ

Figure 10: Traditional fish traps, eastern Dhofar

Figure 11: Modern fish trap, Sadḥ

Figure 12: Hauling in sardines, Salalah

Harvesting the Sea in Soqoṭra

Figure 1: Wild monsoon seas and fishing settlement, east coast

Figure 2: Fishing dhow nearing Soqoṭra, *talbīs* raised

Figure 3: Old boats, north coast

Figure 4: A fisher home, east coast

Figure 5: Seasonal fishing settlement with stone-built boat shelters, a variety of fishing boats, shark-liver oil drums and gulls, east coast

Figure 6: Conches freshly harvested, east coast

Figure 7: Modified dugout, on rollers, with outboard engine wrapped in sacking, Mōmi

Figure 8: Dugout recently treated with shark-liver oil, east coast

Figure 9: Dugout shelter among date palms, north coast

Figure 10: Old stitched boat, south coast

Figure 11: Rubbing salt into slashed fish, eastern tip of Soqoṭra

Figure 12: Storing dried and salted fish in shade, Mōmi

LIST OF TABLES

Table 1: Continental MSAL consonant inventory
Table 2: Soqotri consonant inventory
Table 3: Kumzari consonant inventory
Table 4: Musandam/Gulf Arabic consonant inventory

LIST OF MAPS

Map 1: Languages of southeastern Arabia
Map 2: Musandam Peninsula
Map 3: Dhofar and adjacent areas of al-Mahrah
Map 4: Soqoṭra and neighbouring islands

MAIN CONTRIBUTORS

Erik Anonby is Professor of Linguistics and French at Carleton University in Ottawa, Canada. He has spent extensive periods of fieldwork in partnership with language communities in Arabia, north-central Africa, and Iran. His interdisciplinary research focuses on the importance of linguistic diversity in individual human experience and collective heritage. His publications include *A Grammar of Mambay* (2011), *Adaptive Multilinguals: Language on Larak Island* (with P. Yousefian, 2011), and *Bakhtiari Studies* (with A. Asadi, 2 volumes, 2014, 2018). He is co-director of the Endangered Knowledge and Technology (ELK-Tech) research group at Carleton University, and an active contributor to Janet C. E. Watson's research group on Language and Nature in Arabia at Centre for Endangered Languages, Cultures and Ecosystems (CELCE).

Miranda J. Morris is an independent researcher whose interests focus on the Modern South Arabian Languages, Soḳoṭri, Hobyōt, Bəṭaḥrēt, Śḥerēt, Mehri and Ḥarsūsi, and the traditional cultures of those who speak them. She has lived and worked with MSAL-speaking communities in Southern Arabia and the Soqotra Archipelago over several decades, and has worked on a variety of projects, with the Darwin Initiative, UK; the Global Environment Facility; the European Union; and the Royal Botanic Garden Edinburgh. Her publications include *Plants of Dhofar, the Southern Region of Oman: Traditional, Economic and Medicinal Uses* (with A. G. Miller, 1988); *Oman Adorned: A Por-*

trait in Silver (with P. Shelton, 1997); *Ethnoflora of the Soqotra Archipelago* (with A. G. Miller, 2004); *A Comparative Cultural Glossary across the Modern South Arabian Language Family* (with J. C. E. Watson, D. Eades et al., 2019); *The Oral Art of Soqotra: A Collection of Island Voices* (with Ṭ. S. Di-Kišin, 3 volumes, 2021), and *Ethnographic Texts in the Baṭḥari Language of Oman* (2024). With Fabio Gasparini, she is currently completing *A Grammar of the Bəṭaḥrēt Language of Oman* for publication by Harrassowitz.

Janet C. E. Watson is currently an Honorary Professor at the University of St Andrews and a Visiting Researcher at Sultan Qaboos University, Muscat. She was elected Fellow of the British Academy in 2013. Her current research areas are on Modern South Arabian, and the language–nature relationship. Her main research interests lie in the documentation of Modern South Arabian languages and modern Arabic dialects, with particular focus on phonetic and theoretical phonological and morphological approaches to language varieties spoken within the southwestern Arabian Peninsula. Her publications include *The Phonology and Morphology of Arabic* (2007), *The Structure of Mehri* (2012), *A Comparative Cultural Glossary across the Modern South Arabian Language Family* (with M. Morris, D. Eades et al., 2019) and *Language and Ecology in Southern and Eastern Arabia* (co-edited with J. C. Lovett and R. Morano, 2023). She is co-director of the Centre for Endangered Languages, Cultures and Ecosystems (CELCE).

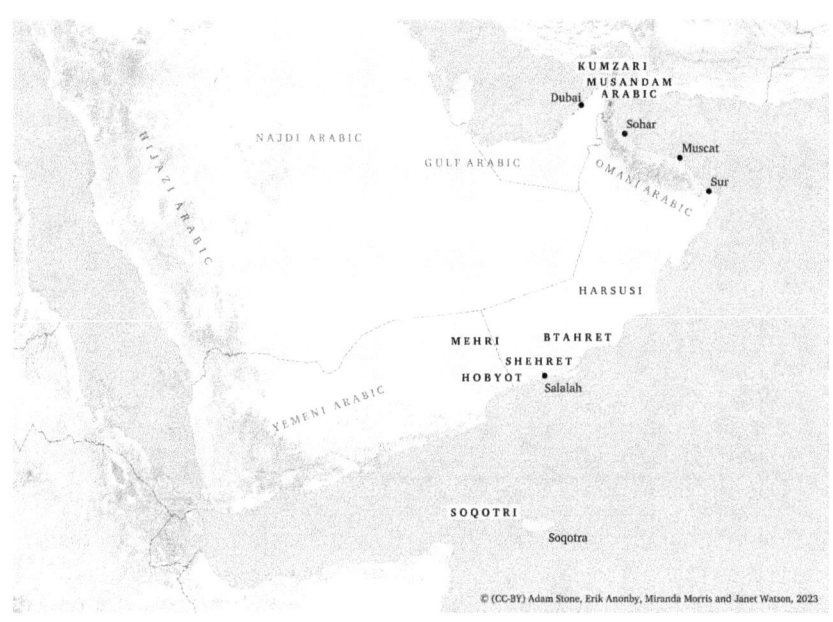

Map 1: Languages of southeastern Arabia

Languages featured in this volume are shown in bold.

HARVESTING THE SEA IN SOUTHEASTERN ARABIA: INTRODUCTION

Janet C. E. Watson, Erik Anonby and

Miranda J. Morris

1. Ecosystems, Cultures, and Languages in Southeastern Arabia

Perhaps no corner of our world—whether land or water—is now untouched by human hands, but relationships between people and their environments vary profoundly from one place to another. And wherever people live, our coexistence with the environment evolves, allowing us to shape our surroundings through the same living impulse that enables us to survive.

The strength of our societies lies in their diversity, but a rift is emerging between the present and the long past. As technology moves humanity toward a single, interconnected civilisation, the foundations of this civilisation are crumbling: resilient, diverse, and infinitely innovative societies are separated from long-standing means of subsistence through a cycle of loss of traditional knowledge, loss of connection to the environment and, eventually, loss of the sustaining environment itself. Yet, as cultural homogenisation and extractive practices enabled by current technologies put collective survival at risk, there is increasing awareness that these disappearing ways of life may well hold the keys of tomorrow, both locally and globally.

Fundamental to what it means to be human, language links our cultures with the ecosystems we inhabit. Each language, in a unique way, allows us to name the elements of the natural world that we depend on for life, and to negotiate and pass on knowledge of the activities through which we can accomplish this. Ironically, with technological magnification of communication between individuals and language communities and the imbalances that accompany these relationships, linguistic diversity—like the diversity found in the cultures and ecosystems that nourish it—is fading away.

2. The Present Compendium

Harvesting the Sea in Southeastern Arabia brings together and investigates relationships between these three facets of human existence: ecosystems, cultures, and languages. We focus on four regions of southern and eastern Arabia: Musandam Peninsula, the Bathari seaboard opposite the al-Hallaniyyat Islands, Dhofar and al-Mahrah, and the island of Soqotra. These are regions in which indigenous, non-Arabic languages are spoken and in which we have worked over many years. There is scope for similar work to be conducted in the region between Dhofar and the Musandam Peninsula, and we hope that such work will be carried out by others in the not-too-distant future.

At the meeting point between the sea and some of the harshest terrestrial environments, the shorelines of Arabia have given rise to a wealth of communities. Strung like jewels along the coasts of the Peninsula, and once thriving against all odds through the harvesting of the sea and trading its produce, these communities are changing rapidly. Over millennia, their languages—the Modern South Arabian languages, Kumzari, and many Arabic varieties—held their place clear and vibrant, but are now at risk of falling silent. Our work tells part of the story of these communities, and of their worlds, through the voice of their disappearing languages.

A decade ago, as a continuation of their work on Modern South Arabian languages, Miranda J. Morris and Janet C. E. Watson began joint research toward two major works: a comparative cultural glossary (Morris and Watson 2019), and a comparison of traditional fishing methods and terminology across the Modern South Arabian-speaking communities of southern Arabia, which led to our proposing and working on this book.

On the same Arabian coast, a thousand kilometres to the north, Christina van der Wal Anonby and Erik Anonby were carrying out work with the Kumzari language community of Musandam Peninsula, beginning in 2006. Meeting with Morris and Watson for the first time at the Arabian Seminar in London in 2013, van der Wal Anonby, and later Anonby, became part of a circle of researchers focussing on minority languages in Arabia hosted by the University of Leeds and connected to the Centre for Endangered Languages, Cultures and Ecosystems (CEL-

CE). It was soon evident that the wealth of marine-related materials collected for Kumzari would fit well as a geographical counterpoint within a comparative linguistic account of harvesting the sea in southeastern Arabia.

Since 2017 the work has taken shape through a series of AHRC-funded workshops on *The Symbiotic Relationship between Language and Nature in Southern and Eastern Arabia*, organised by Watson. From 2020 to 2022, when it became impossible to meet due to COVID-19, our collective research was furthered through online workshops, also organised by Watson, on *Language and Nature in Southern Arabia*. Finally, through an intensive writing process that is spanning more years than any of us would have imagined, this work has become a reality.

3. Purpose and Scope

The purpose of this collection of studies is to document and compare traditional knowledge of harvesting the sea among the traditional cultures of Musandam, southern Oman and neighbouring areas of Yemen, and Soqotra. We explore this topic through discussion of culture and language, with a focus on oral literature and comparative glossaries of marine terms. Our work examines four marine-rich peripheral regions of the southern Arabian seaboard where harvesting the sea has traditionally played a critical role in culture and livelihood: the mountainous Musandam Peninsula at the far northern reach of eastern Arabia; the Bathari seaboard opposite the al-Hallaniyyat Islands in southern Oman; the intermittently lush and dried-out region of coastal Dhofar, with mentions of areas extending to the eastern

Yemeni province of al-Mahrah; and the island of Soqotra, located 380 kilometres off the Arabian coast but culturally bound to it. These areas are home to indigenous peoples at the periphery of the dominant Arabic-speaking mainstream population of the Arabian Peninsula. The languages spoken in these regions include members of the Modern South Arabian language family—unmistakably Semitic but only distantly related to Arabic—as well as the mixed Semitic-Indo-European language Kumzari and the distinctive Arabic dialects of Musandam.

Since the 1970s, the languages and marine cultures in Oman and in Yemen have been under considerable pressure, and the way of life of the fishing communities is becoming rapidly unrecognisable. Threats come from both benign and malignant forces—the unification of Oman under Sultan Qaboos (ruled 1970–2020) brought with it alternative livelihoods, education, infrastructure and access to oil-based wealth that had not been previously available. All these factors led to traditional coastal communities no longer needing to rely exclusively on harvesting the sea for their survival. An increased standard of living has supplied means to hire migrant workers from south and east Asia to do most of the work of fishing. A new, wealthier generation has abandoned the fishing knowledge and skills of their forefathers. Imported goods mean that fishers no longer have to produce their own equipment from natural resources. Threats to marine livelihood come also from an increase in trawler fishing throughout the Arabian Sea. This has led to a significant decrease in traditional fish stocks, with coastal fishers seeking their catch further and further out at sea. For these reasons, we believe we are at the last point in history when the ages-old expertise of these communities can be documented through the words of those who used traditional methods to harvest the sea.

Harvesting the Sea in Southeastern Arabia contributes to research on the documentation of the Modern South Arabian languages (henceforth MSAL), with a focus on Shehret (autonym: *śherēt*), Hobyot (*hobyōt*), Mehri (*mahrī*), Btahret (*bəṭāḥrēt*) and Soqotri (*sɔ́ḳótri ~ sāḳáṭri*). One remaining MSAL language, Harsusi (*ḥərsáyyət*), is spoken only inland, on the desert plains of central Oman. The livelihood of Harsusi speakers was not closely tied to the sea; their connection to marine livelihood was essentially restricted to the purchase of dried fish from local markets. For this reason, Harsusi does not fall within the scope of this study. However, the region in focus extends northward along the Arabian coast—beyond MSAL-speaking regions—to include Kumzari (*kumẓārī*) and Arabic varieties of Musandam Peninsula (pronounced locally *ārabī* or *ʿārabī*). (For a geographic overview of these languages in the regional context of Arabia, see the 'Languages of southeastern Arabia' map at the beginning of this volume.)

This work therefore takes its place among linguistic studies on the languages of the region, collections of annotated texts, research on the traditional cultures of the southeastern Arabian seaboard and Soqotra, and research on the exploitation of marine fauna in the region. For MSAL, these sources are inventoried in a regularly updated bibliography by Watson and Morris (2013–present). Key resources on Kumzari are van der

Wal Anonby (2014a, 2014b), Anonby (2011, 2020), Anonby and Yousefian (2011), and Anonby, A. Al Kamzari and Y. Al Kamzari (2023). Musandam Arabic has been sketched out in Jayakar (1902) and Bernabela (2011), and is currently being studied by Anonby, Bettega and Procházka (2022) and Bettega and Gasparini (2022).

4. The Structure of This Study

Harvesting the Sea in Southeastern Arabia is a series of interrelated studies based entirely on fieldwork conducted over many years. All parts of the book are framed by ample linguistic and cultural data. Each section is based on collection and analysis of linguistic data, whether organised vocabulary lists or oral texts—transcribed, translated, and annotated, and where possible accompanied by audio or audio-visual texts. The authors have had differing research priorities and have adopted different methodologies. This presents alternative models for future researchers to follow or adapt.

This work is divided into two volumes. **Volume 1** contains this general 'Introduction' and four regionally themed sections.

Here in the 'Introduction', we have set out the purpose and scope of the work and shown how it fits within the literature on the endangered Kumzari and MSAL language groups of the region and their distinctive cultures (sections 1.–3.). Following this overview of the structure of this study (4.), there is an explanatory section devoted to 'translanguaging' (5.), which helps situate some complexities in the data with respect to the interaction of language communities characteristic of the region. We conclude by presenting an overview of our data and information sources (6.), along with explanations of phonological inventories and transcription conventions for the languages studied here (7.).

This 'Introduction' is followed, within this first volume, by four main sections:

Part I: 'Harvesting the Sea in Musandam'
Part II: 'Harvesting the Sea among the Bəṭāḥira'
Part III: 'Harvesting the Sea in Central Monsoon Dhofar and al-Mahrah'
Part IV: 'Harvesting the Sea in Soqoṭra'

These sections, rich in illustrative oral texts, deal with fishing from the viewpoint of indigenous fishers and explore the cultural significance of a variety of marine fauna within the different communities, shedding light on ways of life that are threatened or already lost.

Part I: 'Harvesting the Sea in Musandam', is divided into three chapters. It opens with Erik Anonby and AbdulQader Al Kamzari's typology of fish names in the Kumzari language. This chapter provides a systematic account of fish names, with insights into their linguistic structure and cultural significance. It is also instructive in the account it provides regarding the fieldwork process, as an example of how data were collected for other sections of this series—in particular the comparative lexicon. Christina van der Wal Anonby's chapter then moves from linguistic analysis of Kumzari lexicon into oral literature, focusing on the role and depiction of the sea in Kumzari poetry.

Working through a poem in the folktale *Sōntyō* 'The raft', she touches on geography, tides and weather, and sea creatures and plants. The study concludes with reflections on the characterisation of relationships between the natural and the supernatural on the one hand, and nature and human agency on the other. The section on Musandam is rounded out with a presentation of three Arabic fishing songs from the peninsula, by Erik Anonby and Simone Bettega. This chapter makes a valuable contribution in two ways: it is the only study here that treats fishing songs, and among the other studies in this book, it is unique in its focus on regional Arabic.

In Part II: 'Harvesting the Sea among the Bəṭāḥira', Miranda J. Morris gives an overall impression of how this once marginal but profoundly resourceful community eked out a livelihood with few resources other than the sea. The study also discusses some of the strategies developed by this small community to ensure fair distribution of these resources.

Part III: 'Harvesting the Sea in Central Monsoon Dhofar and al-Mahrah' is written by Janet C. E. Watson, in collaboration with Miranda J. Morris, Alec B. M. Moore and Said Baquir. This study focusses on the central coastline of Dhofar, with some mention of al-Mahrah in eastern Yemen, since it shares the monsoonal climate of Dhofar. It is based on fieldwork with Shehret and Mehri speakers conducted between 2014 and 2019, and is told through the voices of fishers and through Watson's diary and field notes. Topics covered include fieldwork methods; the climate of Dhofar and al-Mahrah; the cultural value of fishing; fish types and uses; the naming of marine fauna; and fishing methods and tools.

Part IV: 'Harvesting the Sea in Soqotra' is co-authored by Miranda J. Morris, the late Mubārak ʿĪsa Walīd al-Soqoṭri, and the late Aḥmad Saʿd Taḥkí al-Soqoṭri, with input from many other members of the Soqotri language community. This study gives a rich and extensive overview of how marine resources used to be exploited on the island before the commercial development of the fisheries in the 1990s. This part has five core sections: trade and island fishermen on Soqotra (2.); traditional fishing: fish (3.) and non-fish (4.); marine craft of Soqotra (5.); and the consumption of fish and their processing for export (6.).

Volume 2 is a comparative lexicon of marine organisms across the six main languages featured in this study: Soqotri, Shehret, Hobyot, Mehri, Btahret and Kumzari, and is further subdivided into two parts. It is co-authored by Miranda J. Morris, Erik Anonby, and Janet C. E. Watson, and benefited from consultation with a large body of speakers of the languages studied, as well as participation in fieldwork and checking of biology-related information by Alec B. M. Moore, Uwe Zajonz and Friedhelm Krupp. Part I organises the lexicon according to a western scientific taxonomy, to the degree possible. In Part II, marine species terms are indexed alphabetically and accompanied by notes on meaning, origins, and other descriptive characteristics of these terms, as well as the significance and usage of particular species in each culture. Terminology related to marine organisms is also featured.

5. Translanguaging

One particular topic relevant for all of the language communities featured in our work is the idea of 'translanguaging', coined by Cen Williams (1980) on the basis of the Welsh term *trawsieithu* and further developed by Ofelia García to describe situations where multilingual speakers use multiple languages in communication. Since translanguaging relates to intersections between language communities, and even regions, it is necessary to treat it separately here. Further, this discussion helps to provide a better understanding of variability in the linguistic forms that people use, and grounds our analysis of other complexities typical of the various language situations across the wider area.

Southeastern Arabia is a region in which a certain level of multilingualism has long been the norm: coastal and mountain dwellers led a symbiotic relationship, with coastal people moving inland during the monsoon period when the seas were 'closed', and people of the interior coming down to the coast to barter animal and other products in return for dried sardines for their livestock, and for imported goods. Among fishers and fish traders there has long been movement along the Arabian coastline. These recurrent movements of individuals and communities have resulted in a considerable degree of translanguaging in southeastern Arabia. For certain prized fish, fishermen would travel great distances. Askari Hujayran, Watson's consultant in al-Ghaydhah, described travelling overland as a young man more than a hundred miles from Hawf to eastern Dhofar during the abalone season, as abalone were not found as far west as

Yemen. (For an overview of the locations mentioned here, see the 'Dhofar and al-Mahrah' regional map at the beginning of Part II of this volume.) At Hasik in eastern Dhofar—known as a good place for shark and where a certain amount of fishing was possible even during the monsoon months—fishers were attracted from across the wider region. Many also travelled to the fish markets and interacted with people from different language communities, transporting fresh fish to the Mirbat and Salalah markets of southern Dhofar or—once the technologies became available—trucking fish in cold storage tanks to markets in Muscat and the Gulf, and delivering processed and salted fish to the markets of the interior. Such movement of fishermen and traders led to many important commercial fish being known by specific names across a whole area, regardless of which languages were spoken in that area. Consequently, there is considerable sharing of fish terms across the MSAL, and between the MSAL and various Arabic dialects. Thus, in the Salalah market a particular kind of fish could have the same name, generally based on Arabic, as this same type of fish in the market at Sur on Oman's central coast.

On the Musandam Peninsula of eastern Arabia (see Anonby and Al Kamzari's chapter in this volume), we find a similar translanguaging space extending throughout the Gulf and to the east along the Makran coast of the Eurasian mainland. Many Kumzari fish names resemble those found in the Arabic, Bandari, and Balochi varieties of the wider Strait of Hormuz region. In some cases, a single term for a particular type of fish is used among all of the languages in the area, and it is not always possible to determine where the term originated. Some Kumzari terms are even shared with the MSAL, hundreds of miles to the south, thanks to the larger translanguaging space of coastal Arabia as a whole: for example, certain types of mackerel are known as *xubbaṭ* in Kumzari and *xabbāṭ* in Shehret; the remora (suckerfish) is known in Kumzari as *lāẓuq* and in the MSAL as *ləẓāḵ* (Shehret) or *ləṣāḵ* (Btahret), presumably all of which originate in *lāṣaq*, an Arabic word meaning 'adhesive'.

In the case of shark in particular, the principal traders were from the great Omani port of Sur, and they plied the coasts of southern Arabia, East Africa and the Gulf buying up marine products. As a result, a majority of MSAL terms for commercially valuable cartilaginous fish are in fact Arabic or adapted from Arabic. Examples across the MSAL community include *bū maṭrakəh* and *bū ḱáṭaʕ* for the hammerhead shark, *maṭlūṭ* and *marbūʕ* for different sizes of the larger sharks, *ḏəmāwi* for blacktip shark types, and variable names for the smoothhound shark—*bū ḥanak, bū ḥanákə, bū ḥanēka, bū ḥnēk, baḥának*—all of which are clearly based on the regional Arabic term, *bū ḥanak*. In some cases, there is alternation between the original MSAL *ś* and its Arabic reflex *š*, for example in the term for a variety of large grey sharks known in Mehri as *śaṣyət~šaṣyət*—used alongside the actual Arabic term *šīṣa*. Kumzari shark terms that exhibit a clear Arabic source include *ab dēnō* 'silky shark' (lit. 'father of the ears'), *namarānī* 'shark sp. with light spots' (cf. Ar. *namir* 'leopard; tiger' and Musandam Arabic [MusAr] *nimr* 'leopard'), *manqab* 'shark sp. including hardnose shark' (MusAr 'beak'), and *laqmit sūd* 'shark sp. with a black dorsal fin tip' (lit. 'black morsel', cf. Ar. *laqma* 'morsel', Ar. *aswad* and MusAr *swəd* 'black'). The whale shark is known by similar terms across southeastern Arabia, from regional Arabic (*karr*), Soqotri and Shehret (*kɛr*), Mehri (*karr*) and Btahret (*ker*) to Kumzari (*kōr*).

In regions where fishermen from different MSAL communities fished together, a Btahret or Shehret term may be shared with Mehri, admitting lexical terms or phonemes not typically attested in the borrowing language. Among Mehri fishermen in eastern Dhofar, for example, *sīźōb* (with the voiced lateral fricative, /ź/, otherwise not attested in Mehri) is the Mehri equivalent for Shehret *sīźób* 'rabbitfish'; *xolxól* with non-Mehri short /o/ is adopted to denote types of grouper; *xśum* with non-Mehri short /u/ occurs alongside *xśōm* to denote sweetlips; and *ḳayṣ́ər ḏ̣ə-rōnəm*, imitating the Btahret term for 'sea' (*rawnə*), occurs alongside *ḳayṣ́ər ḏ̣ə-rawrəm* for one kind of moray eel. Conversely, Shehret fishermen adopted certain terms from Mehri, as ʿ*abádyət* from Mehri *ābadyət* for guitarfish species—a form which exhibits intervocalic /b/, otherwise unattested in Shehret.

In other cases, MSAL terms have been maintained in local contexts, even when an Arabic term used by fish traders dominates in the markets. Examples include Arabic-based ʿ*aḵāma* 'barracuda' alongside the indigenous Shehret ʿ*oḵū́t* (pl. ʿ*ayḵúmtə*); Arabic *bū ʿayn* for all sorts of large-eyed fish, which can be compared to Shehret *baʿlit aʿayʰn* denoting a small grunter; Ar. *bū ṣayf* alongside indigenous *baʿl əšḵay* for the sawfish, elicited from Mehri fishermen; *ḥōmər*, related to Ar. *aḥmar*, 'red' for reddish-coloured snappers, alongside Shehret *saʿd ʿófer* and *merēt*; Ar. *sulṭān ibrāhīm* for goatfish spp.; and *bint an-nōxəḏəh* (lit. 'the captain's daughter') for the double-bar sea bream as alternatives for Shehret *ṣīrór* or *sbīt*, Hobyot *ṣəbíjiš*, Mehri *bər ṣəmīrūr* and Btahret *ṣīrór* or *kētəb*; and Arabic-based *miśaṭ* or *bū mšiṭ* as alternatives for the MSAL terms *miśerék̲* and *məśrék̲* for sicklefish and butterflyfish (all with the literal sense of 'comb').

In many cases, including the terms mentioned already, degrees of structural modification take place. One example of morphological restructuring is *ṣāllət* in all MSAL from Arabic *ṣāllah* for various trevally spp., and phonological modifications are evident in Shehret *ɛrsēsɛ́* and *ersāsa*, based on the Arabic *bū rasās* for a pompano species. Such borrowing and cross-fertilisation continue today, with borrowing from languages other than Arabic: for example, *blēwud* (< Engl. 'plywood') for the flat, rather two-dimensional Indian threadfish, and *filibīnī* (< various languages 'Filipino'), or *dīsko* (< Engl. 'disco') for large, multi-coloured parrotfish.

6. Authors, Sources and Data

This compendium is edited and primarily authored by Miranda J. Morris, Janet C. E. Watson, and Erik Anonby, with contributions by Christina van der Wal Anonby, Said Baquir, Simone Bettega, AbdulQader Qasim Ali Al Kamzari, Alec B. M. Moore, Mubārak ʿĪsa Walīd al-Soqoṭri, and Aḥmad Saʿd Taḥkí al-Soqoṭri. Data for all parts of this work come from primary sources, and we gratefully acknowledge the contributions of the many people who shared their expert knowledge.

Especially in earlier years of fieldwork, most of Morris' data were recorded as handwritten notes made while living with fishing families, as well as recordings made on a UHER reel-to-reel recorder. More recently, Morris' and Watson's audio and Watson's video recordings were produced *in situ* and transcribed, translated and annotated by the authors in collaboration with colleagues from the language communities. Photographs were taken by the main authors, including a number from Morris' collection dating from the late 1970s and 1980s. Further details on our methods and information sources are provided in each of the volume's chapters.

Most of the data for Anonby's contributions on Kumzari in the present work were collected while accompanying Christina van der Wal Anonby during her work on the language between 2006 and 2009. He gathered additional data on Kumzari and Musandam Arabic during a further field trip to Musandam in 2018 and extensive virtual consultation with speakers since then.

The initial focus of our research was on language and culture rather than on marine biology, but we encountered all sorts of marine species in the course of fieldwork. In identifying species, we have benefited from—to varying degrees—living with fisher families, joining fishing crews, taking part in discussions at fish markets, and reading through the literature on marine species with a focus on Arabia. With fisher consultants we examined field guides and photographs. However, this sharing of drawings and photographs was not very helpful, especially as regards older fishers: these experts need to see and feel a marine organism to be confident in naming it.

Where possible, we have attempted to identify and provide technical English equivalents for all species, either by consulting the literature or with the assistance of traditional fishers and marine biologists. The English terms are for the most part those proposed by the FAO (Food and Agriculture Organization) of the United Nations (FAO Fish Finder / Field Guides) as codified in *FishBase* (Froese and Pauly 2023), but for the sake of wider usability we have also incorporated additional, common terms encountered in published sources.

For the state of the art in marine species classification and labelling, we consulted the marine biological specialists Alec B. M. Moore, Uwe Zajonz and Friedhelm Krupp. We are very grateful for all their help. In 2014, Alec B. M. Moore accompanied Miranda J. Morris and Janet C. E. Watson on a field trip to Dhofar and the identifications that resulted from this fieldwork are the most reliable. Otherwise, for the purposes of identification, these specialists had only our non-expert descriptions or details provided by our fisher consultants—whose criteria for identification differ greatly from those of a marine specialist trained in western taxonomic conventions. However, our work is not aimed at marine specialists, so rather than attempting to be scientifically rigorous according to the taxonomic systems of ichthyology, we have aimed at a compromise which we hope makes identifications more accessible to the general reader and non-marine expert.

7. Phonological Inventories and Transcription

The transcription conventions applied in this book follow those of the *Journal of Semitic Studies*. Here, to provide further context for the transcriptions, we also provide phonological inventories of the languages under investigation.

7.1. Consonants

For MSAL of the Arabian mainland, the consonantal inventory is provided here:

Table 1: Continental MSAL consonant inventory

	labial	dental	alveolar	post-alv.	palatal	velar	uvular	pharyngeal	glottal
plosive (+br.)			t			k			
(-br., emph.)			ṭ			ḳ			
(-br., vd.)	b		d			g			ʔ
fricative (+br.)	f	ṯ	s	š/s̃			x	ḥ	h
(-br., emph.)		ḏ̣	ṣ	ṣ̌/ṣ̃					
(-br., vd.)		ḏ	z	ž/ž̃			ġ	ʕ	
lateral (+br.)			ʰl	ś					
(-br., emph.)				ṣ́					
(-br., vd.)			l	(ź)					
nasal (+br.)	ʰm		ʰn						
(-br., vd.)	m		n						
rhotic (+br.)			ʰr						
(-br., emph.)			(ṛ)						
(-br., vd.)			r						
glide (-br., vd.)	w				y				

Where continental languages differ in the articulation of certain consonants—for example, while Mehri has a palato-alveolar emphatic /ṣ̌/, Shehret has a labialised (outrounded) alveo-palatal /s̃/—the articulation most common in the languages is provided first, followed by a slash (/) and the less common articulation. Phonemes presented in parentheses in the table have a low functional load: the emphatic rhotic /ṛ/ contrasts weakly with its plain counterpart, and the voiced lateral fricative /źֿ/ in Shehret most frequently appears in complementarity with /l/. Regarding the categories and structure of the table, note that in addition to alveolar /s/ and palato-alveolar /š/, Shehret has a labialised (outrounded) alveo-palatal /s̃/, placed here for reasons of space in brackets in the post-alveolar column. Other systemic considerations are as follows: Mehri, Btahret and Hobyot palato-alveolars /š/, /ž/, and /ṣ̌/ correspond to Shehret alveo-palatals /s̃/, /z̃/, and /ṣ̃/. In some dialects of Shehret, the reflex of historical *g is a palato-alveolar affricate, transcribed in the texts and lexicons as /j/. The emphatic interdental, which varies in its voicing, is transcribed in this work using the symbol /ḏ̣/.[1]

---

[1] In her work on Mehri and Shehret, Watson transcribes this phoneme as /ṯ̣/. In those two languages, it is typically voiceless in utterance-initial and utterance-final position, but may be voiced or partially voiced between vowels. In Btahret and Hobyot, voicing generally extends to initial position as well. There is further variation in the patterning of voicing between individual speakers. In any case, as described in the following paragraph, this phoneme is specified for a primary 'breathed' vs. 'unbreathed' distinction rather than for voicing. In order to maintain consistency across this work, we decided to use the symbol /ḏ̣/ for this phoneme for all MSAL.

In contrast to most earlier work on MSAL, the consonants are organised in these two tables into 'breathed' and 'unbreathed' categories (based on Heselwood and Maghrabi 2015; Watson and Heselwood 2016; Morris and Watson 2019; Watson et al. 2020), due to the phonetic and phonological patterning of these consonants in the languages. 'Breathed' (in the tables, '+br.') consonants include what for English are termed 'voiceless' consonants, such as /t, ṭ, k, s, š/, which involve degrees of pre-aspiration and aspiration or the release of audible breath on their release. There is also a series of breathed, pre-aspirated sonorants /ʰl, ʰm, ʰn, ʰr/ in central and eastern varieties of Shehret, and a post-aspirated glide /yʰ/ in Soqotri. 'Unbreathed' (in the tables, '-br.') consonants do not involve aspiration on their release. In MSAL, these are consonants that are canonically voiced (in the table, 'vd.')—i.e., they involve vibration of the vocal folds—as well as the emphatics (in the table, 'emph.'), which typically do not involve vibration of the vocal folds. In alphabetical order, the 'breathed' consonants in MSAL (including Soqotri; see below) are:

f, h, ḥ, k, ʰl, ʰm, ʰn, ʰr, s, š/s̃, ś, t, tʸ, ṭ, x, yʰ

And the 'unbreathed' consonants are:

ʔ, ʕ, b, d, ḏ, ḍ, g, gʸ, ġ, l, m, n, r, ṛ, ṣ, š/s̃, ṣ́, ṭ, w, y, z, ź,
ž/z̃

For Soqotri, we depend on Kogan and Bulakh's (2019) analysis of the consonantal inventory, supplemented by further notes from Leonid Kogan (pers. comm. 2021). With permission from Leonid Kogan, we have reformatted the table here to align with our analysis of breathed and unbreathed consonants, as well as the conventions for transcription adopted in the present work. Soqotri consonants are as follows:

Table 2: Soqotri consonant inventory

	labial	alveolar	palato-alv.	palatal	velar	uvular	pharyngeal	glottal
plosive (+br.)		t		(tʸ)	k			
(-br., emph.)		ṭ			ḳ			
(-br., vd.)	b	d		(gʸ)	g			ʔ
fricative (+br.)	f	s	š			x	ḥ	h
(-br., emph.)		ṣ	ṣ̌					
(-br., vd.)		z	ž			ġ	ʕ	
lateral (+br.)			ś					
(-br., emph.)		(ḷ)	ṣ́					
(-br., vd.)		l						
nasal (-br., vd.)	m	n						
rhotic (-br., vd.)		r						
glide (+br.)				yʰ				
(-br., vd.)	w			y				

The segments in parentheses here, *tʸ* and *gʸ*, are likely distinctive palatal or palatalised allophones of /k/ and /g/ (cf. Kogan and Bulakh 2019, 283). Superscript ʸ is occasionally used to mark allophonic palatalisation of other consonants as well, such as *kʸ* and *rʸ*. The emphatic lateral /ḷ/ is marginally contrastive. The fricative uvulars /x/ and /ġ/ are preserved in Western dialects, but lost elsewhere on the island (except in recent Arabisms). The voiced non-emphatic lateral ź, resulting from palatalisation of /l/, is non-phonemic.

Table 3: Kumzari consonant inventory

	labial	alveolar	emphatic alv.	palato-alv.	palatal	velar	uvular	pharyngeal	glottal
plosive (vl.)	p	t	ṭ	č		k	q		ʔ
(vd.)	b	d	ḍ	j		g			
fricative (vl.)	f	s	ṣ	š			x	ḥ	(h)
(vd.)			z̧				ġ		
nasal	m	n							
rhotic		r							
lateral		l	(ḷ)						
glide	w				y				

The Kumzari consonantal system resembles those of nearby Arabic dialects of the Gulf (cf. the description of Musandam Arabic immediately below), as well as languages from other families represented in the region. Noteworthy regional characteristics include absence of a dental/interdental series, presence of the voiceless pharyngeal /ḥ/ but absence of its voiced counterpart /ˤ/, a robust emphatic series with secondary velaropharyngeal articulation (Anonby 2020), and presence of the additional phonemic obstruents /p, č, g/. The emphatic sibilant /z̧/ has no plain counterpart in Kumzari. A chart of Kumzari consonants, adapted from Anonby (2011) and van der Wal Anonby (2014a), is as above (with phonologically peripheral consonants given in parentheses).

Table 4: Musandam/Gulf Arabic consonant inventory, as appears in the texts in this volume

	labial	alveolar	emphatic alv.	palato-alv.	palatal	velar	uvular	pharyngeal	glottal
plosive (vl.)		t	ṭ	č		k			
(vd.)	b	d	ḍ			g			
fricative (vl.)	f	s	ṣ	š			x	ḥ	h
(vd.)		z					ġ	(ʕ)	
nasal	m	n							
rhotic		r							
lateral		l							
glide	w				y				

The phonological system of Musandam Arabic was cursorily described in Jayakar (1902), but one variety was treated in more depth by Bernabela (2011), and it is the subject of current research by Erik Anonby, Simone Bettega and Stephan Procházka. Since the varieties differ significantly, we provide a consonant inventory here based on the texts—three songs—featured in the Musandam Arabic chapter in this volume. As Anonby and Bettega note there, the phonology of these songs more closely reflects a generalised Gulf Arabic phonology than it does the dialects of Musandam. This is a clear example of translanguaging in the Musandam region, complementary to the situation described in detail for Dhofar above (section 5.).

7.2. Vowels

In all of the languages treated here, there is a basic distinction between long and short vowels. The long vowels for all languages are transcribed with a macron, as in: /ā, ē, ɛ̄, ī, ō, ɔ̄, ū/. Nasalisation on vowels in Shehret is denoted by a tilde above the vowel, as in: /ɔ̃, ĩ/. Stressed syllables for languages in which stress is not predictable from syllable weight are marked with an acute accent on the stressed vowel, as in Soqotri *láxīm* 'shark'.

References

Anonby, Erik. 2011. 'Illustrations of the IPA: Kumzari'. *Journal of the International Phonetic Association* 41 (3): 375–80.

Anonby, Erik. 2020. 'Emphatic Consonants Beyond Arabic: The Emergence and Proliferation of Uvular-Pharyngeal Emphasis in Kumzari'. *Linguistics* 58 (1): 275–328.

Anonby, Erik, AbdulQader Qasim Ali Al Kamzari, and Yousuf Ali Mohammed Al Kamzari. 2023. 'When Water Shapes Words: The Kumzari People of Musandam Peninsula and the Language of the Sea'. In *Language and Ecology in Southern and Eastern Arabia*, edited by Janet C. E. Watson, Jon C. Lovett, and Roberta Morano, 81–104. London: Bloomsbury.

Anonby, Erik, Simone Bettega, and Stephan Procházka. 2022. 'Demonstratives in Musandam Arabic: Distinctive Archaisms and Innovations'. *Arabica* 69: 675–702.

Anonby, Erik, and Pakzad Yousefian. 2011. *Adaptive Multilinguals: A Survey of Language on Larak Island*. Uppsala: Acta Universitatis Upsaliensis. https://urn.kb.se/resolve?urn=urn:nbn:se:uu:diva-162008, accessed 1 September 2021.

Bernabela, Roy S. 2011. 'A Phonology and Morphology Sketch of the Šiħħi Arabic Dialect of əlǦēdih, Musandam (Oman)'. Master's thesis, Leiden University.

Bettega, Simone, and Fabio Gasparini. 2022. 'A Musandam Arabic Text from Lima (Oman)'. *Kervan: International Journal of Afro-Asiatic Studies* 26: 201–25.

Froese, Rainer, and Daniel Pauly (eds.). 2023. *FishBase*, version 10/2023. Online at www.fishbase.org.

Heselwood, Barry, and Reem Maghrabi. 2015. 'An Instrumental-Phonetic Justification for Sībawayh's Classification of *Ṭā'*, *Qāf* and *Hamza* as *Majhūr* Consonants'. *Journal of Semitic Studies* 60: 131–75.

Jayakar, Atmaram S. G. 1902. 'The Shahee Dialect of Arabic'. *Journal of the Bombay Branch of the Royal Asiatic Society* 21: 246–77.

Kogan, Leonid, and Maria Bulakh. 2019. 'Soqotri'. In *The Semitic Languages*, edited by John Huehnergard and Naʻama Pat-El, 280–320. London: Routledge.

Morris, Miranda J., with Ṭānuf Sālim Nuḥ Di-Kišin. 2021. *The Oral Art of Soqoṭra: A Collection of Island Voices*. 3 vols. Leiden: Brill.

Morris, Miranda, and Janet C. E. Watson, with Domenyk Eades et al. 2019. *A Comparative Cultural Glossary across the Modern South Arabian Language Family*. Journal of Semitic Studies Supplement 43. Oxford: Oxford University Press.

van der Wal Anonby, Christina. 2014a. 'A Grammar of Kumzari, a Mixed Language of Oman'. Ph.D. dissertation, Leiden University.

van der Wal Anonby, Christina. 2014b. 'Traces of Arabian in Kumzari'. *Proceedings of the Seminar for Arabian Studies* 44: 137–46.

Watson, Janet C. E., and Barry Heselwood. 2016. 'Phonation and Glottal States in Modern South Arabian and San'ani Arabic'. In *Perspectives on Arabic Linguistics XXVIII: Papers from the Annual Symposium on Arabic Linguistics, Gainesville, Florida, 2014*, edited by Youssef A. Haddad and Eric Potsdam, 3–37. Amsterdam and Philadelphia, Penn.: John Benjamins.

Watson, Janet C. E., Abdullah al-Mahri, Ali al-Mahri, Bxayta Musallam Khōr al-Mahri, and Ahmed al-Mahri. 2020. *Təghamk Āfyət: A Course in the Mehri of Dhofar*. Wiesbaden: Harrassowitz.

Watson, Janet C. E., and Miranda J. Morris. 2013–present. 'Modern South Arabian Languages (MSAL) Bibliography'. In *Arabian Peninsula Languages Dataverse*, edited by Erik Anonby and Janet C. E. Watson. Toronto: Borealis. Online at https://doi.org/10.5683/SP3/DKFOWU.

Williams, Cen. 1994. 'Arfarniad o Ddulliau Dysgu ac Addysgu yng Nghyd-destun Addysg Uwchradd Ddwyieithog' ['An Evaluation of Teaching and Learning Methods in the Context of Bilingual Secondary Education']. Ph.D. dissertation, University of Wales. [Welsh]

PART I
HARVESTING THE SEA ON THE MUSANDAM PENINSULA

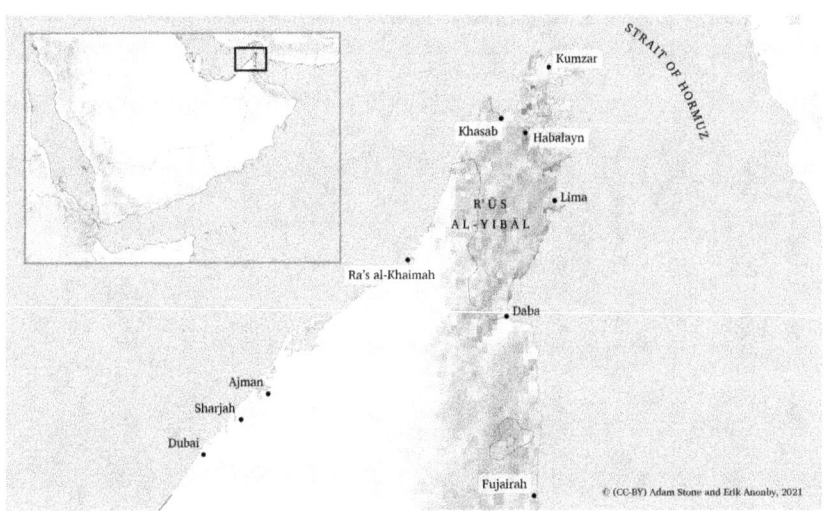

Map 2: Musandam Peninsula

A TYPOLOGY OF FISH NAMES IN KUMZARI

Erik Anonby and AbdulQader Qasim Ali Al Kamzari

Acknowledgments

We wish to express our gratitude to the many Kumzari fishermen, young and old, who shared their knowledge about fish species with us.[1] In particular, we honour the memory of the late Ēlikō Šōbubō, Ali Abdullah Shobubo al-Kumzari, who, in addition to his consummate skill as a teller of tales woven through with the language of nature, had a deep knowledge of the sea and all the species that live in it. In addition to the authors, several other people have made major contributions to this study, but in keeping with their request they remain anonymous.

---

[1] English fish names used in this study, which follow those in the Comparative Lexicon, are generally those found in FishBase (https://www.fishbase.org). Abbreviations used in this study are as follows: sp.: species; K.: Kumzari; Ar.: Arabic; B.: Btahret (Bathari); Bl.: Balochi of Jask, Hormozgan, Iran; Bn. Bandari; GAr: Gulf Arabic; H.: Hobyot; M.: Mehri; MSAL: Modern South Arabian languages; MusAr: Musandam Arabic; MP: Middle Persian; Mn.: Minowi (Minabi); P.: Persian; Sh.: Shehret; Sq.: Soqotri; SwIr: Southwestern Iranic (Iranian). Modern Standard Arabic data: Randall (1995) and AbdulQader Qasim Ali Al Kamzari, field notes 2020; Gulf Arabic and Musandam Arabic: Abdul-

1. Introduction

The Musandam Peninsula, located at the north-eastern tip of the wider Arabian Peninsula, is a rocky thumb of land jutting into the Strait of Hormuz (Figure 1). Here, shallow gulf waters open up into the Gulf of Oman, itself part of the wider Arabian Sea. The varying depths along the coast and the underwater coastal shelf provide a rich environment for sea life.

The Kumzari people, with a population of about 4000, live at the northern tip of Musandam in their mother village, the historical *wāliyit* (principality) of Kumzar. Each year, they migrate from the village to their summer quarters in the cities of Khasab and Daba (Dibba) (Zimmermann 1981), and many families have now permanently settled there. There are also smaller communities of Kumzari people living in the metropolises of Ajman, Abu Dhabi, and elsewhere (Anonby and Yousefian 2011, 30–31, 152).

Qader Qasim Ali Al Kamzari, field notes, 2020; Modern South Arabian languages (B., H., M., Sh., Sq.): Morris, Anonby and Watson (2024); Middle Persian: MacKenzie (1971); Balochi: Hassan Mohebbi Bahmani and Erik Anonby, field notes, 2020; Bandari: A'lam (1999); Keshmi (Qeshmi): Anonby (2015); and Minowi (Minabi): Mohebbi Bahmani (2006), Anonby (2015) and Hassan Mohebbi Bahmani, personal communication, 2014 and 2020. We especially thank Hassan for the additional fieldwork and checking carried out for the Minowi comparative data, and we acknowledge the contributions of a Balochi fisherman from Jask, Hormozgan, who chose to remain anonymous.

Figure 1: Musandam Peninsula.

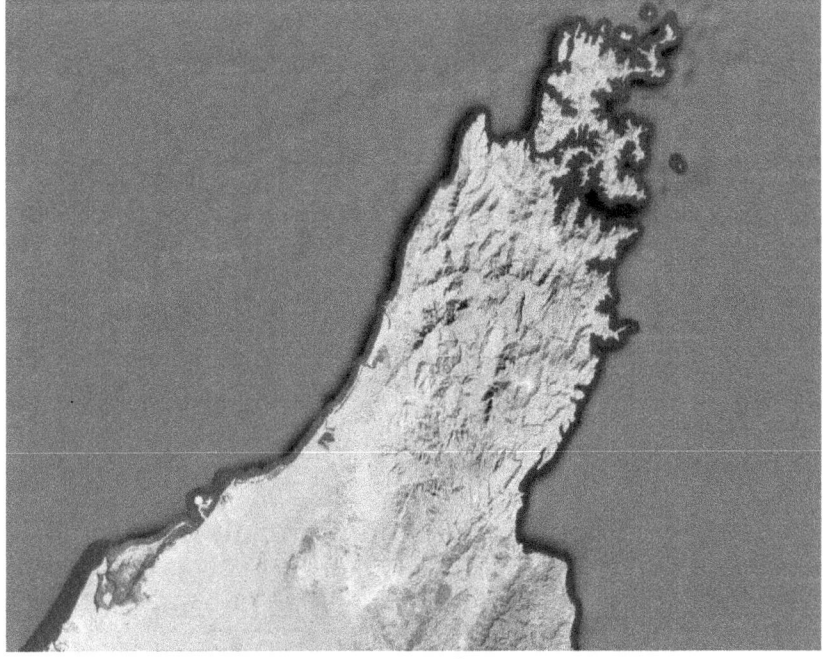

Source: www.google.ca/maps.

Part of the historical *šiḥūḥ* (Shihuh) Arab ethnic federation of the region (Lorimer 1908, II:1040; Thomas 1929, 75), Kumzari people speak their own language, which is unintelligible with Arabic and Persian but shares some elements of both languages (van der Wal Anonby 2014), in addition to a fully articulated grammatical system of its own (van der Wal Anonby 2015).

In this paper, we look at one of the richest domains of the Kumzari lexicon: fish names. The paper opens with an overview of the importance of fish among the Kumzari, and outlines the context and methodology of this study, along with a consideration of its contribution and limitations (1.1.). The analysis of this lexical domain opens with the question, "In Kumzari, what is a fish?" (2.1.). We then consider lexical variation among speakers, and the way that species are defined and labelled (2.2.–2.4.). The heart of the article proposes a typology of Kumzari fish names, with associative labels, descriptions of physical appearance, and other more complex ways in which fish are conceptualised (3.). The wider context of fish names is explored and situated through analysis of their linguistic characteristics, their use elsewhere in the lexicon, and their relevance for understanding the history of the Kumzari language (4.). The paper concludes with final reflections (5.). An explanatory lexicon of the 198 Kumzari fish labels in the data is presented as an appendix.

1.1. Research Context, Methodology and Contribution

This study offers an inventory and analysis of terminology in a single domain of vocabulary in the Kumzari language: fish types. As part of the wider sphere of a livelihood that revolves around fishing, fish names constitute the richest and most important lexical set relating to the natural world as it is conceptualised by Kumzari people.

There are several directions from which the study of the Kumzari fish lexicon could be approached, among others lexicography, oral literature, anthropology, ethnobiology, and biology as practiced in the dominant 'western' scientific framework. Although this study is fundamentally lexicographic in nature, given the background of the research team, we have aimed to draw insights from all of these fields to the greatest possible extent. Still, the study does not purport to be an exhaustive ethnobiological account of fish in Kumzari, or a full description of fish species in the region from a strictly biological perspective.

The data in this paper were collected during twelve months of fieldwork in the Musandam Governorate of Oman, divided into three periods between November 2006 and March 2009. Based during this time at Leiden University in the Netherlands, the first author of this article was welcomed, along with Christina van der Wal Anonby, as guest researcher by the International Centre of Sultan Qaboos University in Muscat, Oman, and by local governmental authorities in Khasab. Elders among the Kumzari language community, along with a large cohort of language consultants, made the research process both possible and rewarding. Publications proceeding from fieldwork include a grammar of the Kumzari language (van der Wal Anonby 2015) as well as several related publications (van der Wal Anonby 2014; Anonby 2011, 2012; Anonby, 2020; Anonby, A. Q. Al Kamzari and Y. A. Al Kamzari, 2023; van der Wal Anonby, 2023) and conference presentations (for example, Anonby, van der Wal Anonby, A. Q. Al Kamzari and Y. A. Al Kamzari, 2018). Two three-week periods of field research were subsequently carried out in 2010 and 2017. The current study, which focuses on fish, has recently been further developed and completed within the context of the *Symbiotic Relationship between Language and Nature in Southern and Eastern Arabia* research group, funded by the AHRC (Arts and Humanities Research Council) and hosted within CELCE (Centre for Endangered Languages, Cultures and Ecosystems) at the University of Leeds.

Despite an initial research interest in Kumzari phonology and the ethnobiology of birds, fish names quickly emerged as a topic where virtually every speaker of Kumzari is brimming over with knowledge and interest. The research began with a simple question: what are the names of fish types in Kumzari? Due to the overwhelming number of fish names, and the fact that our understanding of Kumzari phonology was not initially stable enough to transcribe these names consistently, it took several weeks to develop a somewhat complete lexical inventory. Research began with younger and middle-aged men (*šābaban*) in the regional centre of Khasab, who were familiar with better-known fish types. After this, the list was significantly supplemented through interviews with fishermen, especially older ones, in both Khasab and Kumzar.

In order to make sense of the many fish names, and the ways that these fish species are described, we used Randall's seminal study on *Coastal Fishes of Oman* (1995). There have been subsequent additions to the literature on fish species of the Gulf, and we have consulted these in preparation for the publication of the current study, but this was the most up-to-date and relevant resource accessible to us during the main period of fieldwork in 2008. While we did not have an English copy in the field, the book was at that time available in Arabic translation (كتاب الكائنات الجرية في سلطنة عمان), along with English and scientific labels, on the website of the Ministry of Agriculture and Fisheries of the Sultanate of Oman. Interestingly, this book, though remarkably comprehensive, could not address all of our questions for the identification of fish species. Younger speakers of the language engaged well with the book, but in many cases had insufficient knowledge of fish to relate the Kumzari fish names reliably to the illustrations in the book. While some of the fish identifications were reliable, there were also recurrent cases where speakers associated a particular Kumzari label with a fish species which was not (according to Randall, 1995) known to occur in the waters around Musandam. At other times, these speakers were certain that they had seen a particular fish species illustrated in the book, but they did not know which Kumzari label applied to it; and a number of Kumzari fish species could not be related to any of the species illustrated in the book. Older speakers, much more familiar with the fish themselves, were in contrast unable (or in some cases perhaps simply not inclined) to relate their knowledge of fish species to the two-dimensional visual representations of the printed page.

A further, indispensable phase in the data collection process, then, was to join fishermen at the pier and, as able, to accompany them out to sea (Figures 2 and 3). In this way, it was possible to relate experiences of fish directly to the literature and to confirm or revise hypotheses for fish identification that we had developed beforehand. By the end of the third research period, our understanding of Kumzari phonology was sufficiently advanced so that the transcriptions of all fish names could be refined and confirmed with multiple speakers as part of a more general check of the draft dictionary.

As mentioned above, this study does not attempt to offer a comprehensive description of the region's fish species according to a strictly biological approach within the 'western' scientific framework. The starting point for description and analysis in this study is the Kumzari fish labels rather than technical English labels or Latin-based scientific names. As recounted in this section above, we have attempted to relate the Kumzari labels to the species described and illustrated in Randall (1995), but encountered methodological difficulties during this process. Further, during his own fieldwork for the 1995 volume, Randall himself encountered 52 species unknown to western science, so it is likely that some of the Kumzari species have not yet been documented or labelled by biologists. For these reasons, we view our hypotheses of correlations between the two inventories as an indexing tool rather than a definitive identification. For this reason, in order to avoid the impression of conclusive species identification, we also limit ourselves English species names rather than the stricter Latin-based binomial nomenclature used by biologists.

In addition, and also touched upon above, this study is not intended as a comprehensive ethnobiological account of fish in the complex and integrated cultural context of fishing, along with livelihood and broader cultural themes.[2] It is based on an analysis of the fish names themselves. This said, it is informed by an ethnobiological approach and—without having this explicit intention—takes a first step in the direction of Kumzari

---

[2] As a point of comparison, an example of an integrated ethnobiological study of birds conducted by the first author is found in Anonby (2006). An example of a lexical study on Arabic fish names in a fish market on the Red Sea Coast was authored by Provençal and Skaarup (2016).

ethnobiology, since the fish names themselves contain a wealth of cultural information and open a window into realities of Kumzari life, history, and traditional scientific knowledge.

Figure 2: *Li kūkū* 'gillnet' fishing
with Hakim, Yusuf and Hassan al-Kumzari.

Photo: Erik Anonby, 2008 (CC BY 4.0).

One related, and important additional aspect, of the study of fish which is outside the scope of this study is the place of fish in Kumzari oral tradition. This topic has been treated more completely in van der Wal Anonby (2015; 2023; 2024), and Anonby, van der Wal Anonby, A. Q. Al Kamzari and Y. A. Al Kamzari (2018).

To return to the scope and contribution of this study as expressed above: this study provides a first inventory, description and analysis of fish names in Kumzari. Lexicological in nature, it provides a systematic picture of the structures and the nature of this profoundly rich domain of Kumzari vocabulary, itself inspired by the wealth of biological diversity in the seas of the region and the importance of fish for the lives of Kumzari people.

Figure 3: Fish catch from *li kūkū* 'gillnet' fishing.

Photo: Erik Anonby, 2008 (CC BY 4.0).

2. Fish and Fish Species

Before proceeding to a typology of fish names in Kumzari and a description of their linguistic characteristics, we examine the basic idea of what 'fish' means to speakers of the language (2.1.). We then look at how fish species are defined (2.2.) and labelled in the language (2.3.). Variation among speakers, which is important but limited in the context of the small language community, is briefly considered (2.4.).

2.1. In Kumzari, What Is a Fish?

Cross-linguistically, ethnobiological categories vary significantly, from high-level groupings down to the level of species. In Kumzari, animals are brought together in the top-level category of ḥīwan (Ar. ḥayawān). Humans (maxluq or ādamī) are outside of this category. Terrestrial mammals are prototypical ḥīwan, and there is no other categorical label to refer to them. There are, however, three substantial primary subgroups among ḥīwan: birds (ṭēr; Ar. ṭayr, GAr ṭēr), fish (mīʔī; P. māhi), and 'creeping things' (dwabb; Ar. dābba). The latter category englobes reptiles (snakes and lizards), amphibians, arachnids (scorpions and spiders) and centipedes. True insects (mosquitos, fleas, flies, bees, beetles, ants, lice, etc.), like mammals, do not fall into any primary subgroup. Instead, insects exist as small families and individual species at the periphery of ḥīwan. The category of fish (mīʔī) is the focus of this study.

The ethnobiological definition of 'fish' is often ambiguous and fluid in the world's languages and cultures, with species of varying degrees of 'fishiness' included in the category. In English, for example, there are organism types with the term 'fish' in their names, such as the insect 'silverfish', which is clearly not a fish in the minds of English speakers, let alone western scientific classifications. However, its label suggests that it has been and can be perceived as acting or looking like a fish. There are further organisms such as cuttlefish, crayfish, and even starfish which—although not conceptualised as 'fish' by most present-day English speakers,[3] due to the imposition of western scientific taxonomies in educational discourse—were widely thought of as fish, or at least associated with them, through much of the language's history.

This same categorisational flexibility and fuzziness is true of fish (mīʔī) in Kumzari. When responding to the question, "What is a fish?", speakers first identify 'prototypical' fish, but also refer to sea cucumbers, jellyfish, shrimp, crabs, lobsters, dolphins, whales and even sea turtles, and possibly shellfish. However, when asked if these species are indeed types of mīʔī, speakers will hesitate, and then acknowledge that (at a lower place on the animacy hierarchy) shellfish, jellyfish, sea cucumbers and crabs are not mīʔī, nor are sea turtles (at a higher place on the animacy hierarchy). Shrimp, lobsters, cephalopods (squid and cuttlefish), dolphins and whales, on the other hand, are comfortably within the category of mīʔī, certainly for Kumzari people who have not been subjected to formal education, and to varying degrees among those who have.

The Kumzari term for 'fish' is unusual within the language in that it is found both as a collective noun mīʔī ('fish in general'), and an etymologically related but distinct count form

---

[3] Some scientists prefer to call starfish 'sea star' in English, to reflect the 'modern' western idea of 'fish', but of course this group of organisms is no more truly 'star' than 'fish'.

may (pl. *mēyan*).[4] To our knowledge, there are no other nouns in the language with this three-way formal distinction.

Within the category of *mīʔī*, some species fall into intermediate-level families. The families with the diversity of species are *kūlī* 'shark', with at least twenty members, and *paw* 'ray', with about half as many. The latter category, which takes its name from the prototype species *paw* 'bluespotted ribbontail' includes rays, guitarfishes and skates. More often, smaller families are grouped together with a shared genus-type label that is part of the fish's name (see 2.3. below).

2.2. Defining Kumzari Fish Species

In some cases, there is an exact correspondence between fish species in Kumzari and those defined in the 'western' scientific taxonomy, but in other cases one or the other of the taxonomies is more finely differentiated than the other.

One-to-one correspondences with the western scientific taxonomy. Many of the species in the Kumzari list correspond to individual species in the western scientific taxonomy, to list a few: *čum sāʔit* 'paeony bullseye', *fōringī* 'common bannerfish', *ḥama ẓmāmō* 'Oman anenomefish' and *qurfē* 'yellowtail scad'.

Underdifferentiation vis-à-vis the western scientific taxonomy. In Kumzari, one prominent departure from the strict 'one label

---

[4] This term exhibits unusual behaviour in English as well, but there the noun form 'fish'—unlike most other nouns—can be used as a collective noun as well as a singular noun, and a true plural 'fishes' is also used, at least by some speakers.

per species' set up as an ideal in binomial nomenclature,[5] as practiced in western science, is the grouping of fish types that share a set of characteristics. Groups such as 'poor-tasting colourful fish of a certain size' are referred to with a single species label in Kumzari, even when differences between them are visible to speakers. Some examples of such species in the Kumzari taxonomy are as follows:

būt murwan	'red sweeper, obliquebanded cardinalfish'
gmō	'redspot emperor'
rubbaṭ	'whipray, electric ray'
sabu kan'ad	'McCosker's wrasse, yellowstriped cardinalfish'
saptik	'anthias, rosy dwarf monocle bream'

This tendency could be attributable to the fact that practical considerations, such as desirability (or avoidance) of a species as food, or the use of the same net type to catch these similar fish types, can be more important in the differentiation of species than simple appearance. Such underdifferentiation of species types in Kumzari compared to conventionalised western scientific classifications occurs in most languages.[6]

Defining species by life stage. The opposite situation, whereby Kumzari species are more finely differentiated than their counterparts in the western scientific taxonomy, also occurs—

---

[5] But not adhered to in all cases, such as for canines and felines.

[6] Including folk classifications among speakers of English and other European languages.

frequently, in fact—in relation to life stages of fish. In particular, Kumzari often applies more than one label to a single organism type at various stages of its life cycle, with no general term that brings together these names. This suggests that in the Kumzari ethnolinguistic taxonomy, the organism is being treated as a distinct 'species' at each stage of its life cycle. Kumzari speakers are aware that the labels refer to a single organism type at various stages of development, so this type of classification has nothing to do with lack of scientific knowledge. Rather, Kumzari scientific knowledge is structured in a way that reflects the fact that species change appearance over the course of their development; the desirability of a particular fish type as food during a given stage of development; and factors such as sustainable fishery, since spawning fish—especially lobsters and shrimp—are left alone to assure the sustainability of fish stocks.

A number of fish organism types have distinct names for two life stages (small / large):

fish sp.	čūk pārawē / pārawē
rabbitfish sp.	gawgaw / čāwuẓ
blueline snapper	purġar / āqadī
large needlefish sp.	qrambiṣ / qunwaḥ
smalltooth emperor	rāmišt / rōbāyō
milk shark	tirxēnit / īfē
longtail tuna	wīr / wīr barḥ
kawakawa	xlēsī / jārid

There are five organism types with distinct names for three life stages (small / medium / large):

potato grouper	*bahlul / āmur / lākō*
bull shark	*burqēb / qrādī / rējimī*
shark sp.	*čūk jmēs / jmēs / jubbē*
king soldier bream	*ḥallūma / sanksar / kōfar*
grouper sp.	*lašt / lēdam / lāḥafī*

Finally, two organism types have distinct names for four life stages, from small to large:

spangled emperor	*tarbō / nīm gdīr / gdīr / mkindī*
kingfish, etc.	*xubbaṭ / maẓāraq / kanʔad / maysānī*

2.3. Labelling Kumzari Fish Species

As is likely the case across the world's languages, the two most common ways of referring to species in Kumzari—in particular fish species—is through use of unique labels, and through accompaniment of a generic label with a specific label. There are also a few cases where a single identical label is used for two unrelated fish species.

Unique labels. The frequency of unique labels, which account for a majority of the Kumzari fish species names, is evident from the comprehensive list in the Appendix.

Generic labels accompanied by descriptors. The following are straightforward examples of generic family labels compounded with a descriptor to designate species types (discussions of these descriptors are found in the following section [3.]):

būt	'small fish sp. (family)'
būt murwan	'red sweeper, obliquebanded cardinalfish'
būt dām	'Arabian bluestripe dottyback'

ēraraġ	'bream sp. (family)'
ēraraġ čāf	'red-filament threadfish bream'
ēraraġ dašt	'Japanese threadfish bream'
qātal	'venomous fish'
qātal čaf	'false stonefish'
qātal dašt	'draco waspfish'
šupṣ	'lobster'
šupṣ jayšan	'heavily armoured lobster sp. with antennae'
šupṣ šufrāqō	'lobster sp. with no antennae'

Just as frequently, however, a single label can be used in Kumzari for a fish family as well for the prototype species for which that family is named.

ḥampōlaṣ	'ḥampōlaṣ (family)'; 'fish sp. which includes emperor angelfish, semicircle angelfish and yellowbar angelfish'
ḥampōlaṣ ārabī	'Jayakar's butterflyfish'
ḥampōlaṣ šāʔin	'common dolphinfish'
qambab	'qambab (family)'; 'Picasso triggerfish, goldenfinned triggerfish'
qambab garagumba	'starry triggerfish'
sēḥak	'guitarfish (family)'; 'bowmouth guitarfish'
sēḥak ārabī	'granulate guitarfish'
sēḥak fārsī	'spotted guitarfish'
sēḥak šāʔin	'giant guitarfish'

šuqqar	'*šuqqar* (family)'; 'Malabar blood snapper'
šuqqar čāf	'golden cardinalfish'

In order to avoid confusion between identical generic and specific labels, exemplified by the first item in each of the three sets here, the English-language scientific tradition has over the past century imitated the principles of Latin-based binomial nomenclature by affixing the term 'common' to unitary species labels that also appear in compounded names for other species. However, dual use of a single label for a family and for the prototypical member of that family was prevalent in the original English-language taxonomies.

In the data, almost all fish family labels in Kumzari are also used in compounded species names. However, the family labels *kūlī* 'shark' and *dābit* 'shark subfamily' are not.[7]

Use of a single label for more than one species. There are three labels which are used for two separate species:

ḥallūma	'king soldier bream (small stage)'; 'red fish sp. similar to king soldier bream (small stage)'
kōr	'whale shark'; 'Gulf blenny'
tirxēnit	'milk shark (small stage)'; 'milkfish'

In the case of *ḥallūma*, speakers confirm an impression of overall similarity, even though the colour of the two species is dif-

---

[7] An example of this situation in English is the term 'poultry', which refers to a grouping of bird types but is not used as a species label, or as part of any bird species label.

ferent; whale sharks, as well as the Gulf blenny, are likened to a *kōr* 'blind person'; and (as suggested by the English names), milk sharks and milkfish exhibit in common a white secretion when slit.

Synonymy. For ten types of fish in the data, two or more names are used for a single species. Setting aside the case of *ab dēnō / abu dēnō* 'silky shark' and *laḥlaḥ / šayn* 'needlescaled queenfish', whose variants are socially defined (see 2.4.), members of other sets appear to be synonymous.

ālaq tarḥin / ālaq tarḥētin	'needlefish (etc.)'
biyyaṭ / biyyaḍ	'sandbar shark'
ʔmēd / mēd	'round flat yellowish fish sp.'
garagumba / qambab garagumba	'starry triggerfish'
qāpṭ / qāṭ	'white fish sp.'
saptik / saftik / siftik	'anthias, rosy dwarf monocle bream'
taḥadī / kūku taḥādī	'rainbow runner'
umbē / imbē	'dark fish sp. similar to *āmur*'

Still, even where social considerations do not intervene, synonymy can be gradient: in the case of *mayg* and *rubyan*, either term can be used as a generic label for 'shrimp and prawns', but where *mayg* is more often used as a species label for small shrimp, *rubyan* is associated with large shrimp and prawns.

2.4. Variation among Speakers

The Kumzari language community is small and closely knit, and in the fish lexicon—as elsewhere in the language—there is relatively little variation among speakers. The greatest point of variability is in the types of fish that people know, and how many, rather than differences in the labels that they give to these types. Some fish types are known to all speakers of the language, whether because of size (for example, *kārabō* 'white dolphin', *kūlī* 'shark'), value as food (*kanʔad* 'kingfish [etc.]', *ūmat* 'sardines', *wīr* 'longtail tuna [small stage]'), distinctive appearance and behaviour (*faql* 'porcupine fish', *fār* 'flying fish') or commonness (*šōbubō* 'Indo-Pacific sergeant'), among other characteristics. However, older community members, and those for whom fishing is a way of life, have a much richer and more extensive knowledge of fish. And even among fishermen, there are complementary areas of expertise in fish lexicon which are related to the type of boats or nets that a particular person uses.

There are two instances in the data where usage of a particular fish name is correlated to ethnic lineage: reportedly, among some clans and families, the silky shark is typically referred to as *ab dēnō*, and among others as *abu dēnō*; similarly, *laḥlaḥ* is used by some groups for the needlescaled queenfish, whereas other groups call it *šayn*. Other cases where two equivalents are available do not show a clear pattern of usage, and can consequently be considered synonyms (2.3.).

3. A Typology of Kumzari Fish Names

A high proportion of Kumzari fish names—roughly half—are descriptive, either making use of a semantically transparent descriptor added to a generic label (see 2.3. above) or being directly named for another concept. Descriptive labels can be organised into several (partially overlapping) categories:

- o association with—and usually also perceived resemblance to—other fish species (3.1.);
- o resemblance to other animal species and other appearance-related traits (3.2.); and
- o a set of more complex descriptors which are not based on physical appearance, including use of personal proper names, human interaction with and conceptions of fish species, and references to habitat (3.3.).

3.1. Association with Other Fish Species

Several fish species are named for their association with other fish. The species *qambab garagumba* 'starry triggerfish' is a *qambab* 'triggerfish' that resembles *garagumba* 'fish sp.'; *sabu kanʔad* 'fish sp.' (lit. 'kingfish *sabu*') that looks like *kanʔad* 'kingfish (etc.)'. In contrast, the *angiẓ kanʔēdin* 'cuttlefish' (lit. 'kingfish cephalopod') is associated with *kanʔad* 'kingfish (etc.)' because they both get caught in the same *kanadyō* 'fishnet tunnel for catching kingfish'; luckily, both are a desirable catch. In the case of *mām šāwan* 'redmouth grouper' (lit. 'mother of *šāwan* [orange rockcod]'), the connection is also likely based on the cohabitation of the two species rather than their resemblance to each other. The flounder, which is known as *nān paw* (lit. 'ray bread'), presents an evocative scenario in which both species participate.

When different fish species share a single label (see 2.3. above), for example *tirxēnit* 'milk shark (small stage)' and 'milkfish', one species label is likely derived from the other, but the direction of the naming process is synchronically ambiguous.

3.2. Descriptions of Physical Appearance

Physical appearance is central source from which fish labels are derived. This includes resemblance to other animals, colour, and other appearance-related traits.

Resemblance to other animals. A number of fish are named for resemblances to other animals as well—all of which are non-marine vertebrates—including mammals, birds, reptiles, amphibians and insects:

mouse:	*dnān mišk* 'sohal' (lit. 'mouse tooth')
leopard:	*sēlik numr* 'dragon moray' (lit. 'leopard moray'); *namarāni* 'spotted shark sp.' (cf. K. *numr* 'leopard', Ar. *namir* 'leopard, tiger')
horse:	*asp* 'seahorse; yellow seahorse' (lit. 'horse'); *asp sirx* 'thorny seahorse' (lit. 'red horse')
bull:	*ġā ġalġul* 'dark fish sp.' (lit. '*ġalġul* bull'; *ġalġul* is an opaque term)
cat:	*gēlō* 'sea catfish' (cf. Mn. *galu* 'sea catfish', points to now-opaque link to sporadic SwIr *gelu, gulu* 'cat'; Anonby, Taheri-Ardali, and Stone 2021, 122, 133)
chicken:	*būt murwan* 'red sweeper, obliquebanded cardinalfish' (lit. 'chickens' *būt*, with *būt* referring to a small fish sp.)

	dgēgō 'torpedo scad' (cf. MusAr of Khasab *dgēg* 'chicken'[8])
rooster:	*xrō diryīʔin* 'turkeyfish' (lit. 'sea rooster')
hawk:	*sēḥak šāʔin* 'giant guitarfish' (lit. 'hawk guitarfish')
snake:	*mār diryīʔin* 'snake-eel; snake-eel sp.' (lit. 'sea snake')
	mār paqqatīnin 'spotted snake-eel' (lit. 'spotted snake')
frog:	*šupš šufrāqō* 'lobster sp.' (lit. 'frog lobster')
palm weevil:	*dipsī* 'blacktip trevally' (lit. 'palm weevil')

For snake-eels, resemblance to snakes is clear. In other cases, further knowledge of the fish illuminates the comparison. The *ġā ġalġul* (lit. 'ġalġul bull') has frontal horns, and the *xrō diryīʔin* 'turkeyfish' (lit. 'sea rooster') exhibits fins that resemble the comb and wattle of a rooster. The imposing teeth of the dragon moray have inspired the name *sēlik numr* (lit. 'leopard moray'), and *šupš šufrāqō* (lit. 'frog lobster'), with a round head and no long antennae, is likened to a frog. The *namarāni* 'shark sp.' (cf. K. *numr* 'leopard', Ar. *namir* 'leopard, tiger') has spots like a leopard. Since fish are integral to the livelihood of Kumzari people, it is interesting to note that fish are named after land animals, rather than the other way around.

---

[8] In some Modern South Arabian languages, the terms for 'torpedo scad' are similar: *dəjējo* (Sh.) and *dəgāgóh* (M.). This suggests either a direct relation between Kumzari and these languages or, more likely, that 'chicken' as a base term for this fish type came to be used in Arabic and has subsequently been borrowed into other languages (the Kumzari term for chicken is unrelated: *mrū*).

Colour. Perhaps surprisingly, only a handful of Kumzari fish names refer directly to colour: *ġbar* 'shark sp. with ruddy dorsal fin tip', which literally means simply 'dusty brown' (cf. Ar. *ġubār* 'dust'); *biyyaṭ/biyyaḍ* 'sandbar shark' (cf. Ar. *abyaḍ*, MusAr *byaḍ* 'white'); *laqmit sūd* 'brown shark sp. with black dorsal fin tip' (lit. 'black morsel'; cf. Ar. *aswad* 'black'); and *samarānī* 'shark sp.' (cf. K. *sāmar* 'charcoal', Ar. *asmar* 'charcoal colour'), which is marked with charcoal-coloured spots. Interestingly, as demonstrated by the Arabic cognates here, all four of the colour terms are of Arabic origin, even where inherited basic colour terms (*spēr* 'white'; *sīya* 'black') are available in Kumzari. This suggests that the fish names have been influenced by or even borrowed from regional Arabic varieties (see also 4.1. and 4.3. below). Finally, although less directly lexicalised, the colour of *sitraġ* 'wrasse-like fish sp.' (lit. 'razor') is likened to the green boxes of 'Lord' brand razors that were sold in the past.

Other descriptors based on physical appearance. Other appearance-related descriptive labels range from references to size, body features, body parts, and other more spectacular comparisons.

The term *čūk*, which does not occur on its own but which speakers say is related to *čikk* 'small; child' is found as a compounding element in the species names *čūk jmēs* 'shark sp. (small stage)' and *čūk pārawē* 'brown fish sp. (small stage)'.[9] The

---

[9] For a discussion of the role of life stages in defining species, see 2.2. above, and for discussion of 'father' and 'mother' as compounding elements, see 4.1. below.

Kumzari term *nīm* 'half' is added to *gdīr* 'spangled emperor' to describe the medium-small stage of that species.

The *manqab*, a shark species with a pointed snout, derives its label from the Kumzari term for 'beak', while the name *pēčak* 'Arabian hound shark' signals its resemblance to a wooden mallet. The goatfish *rīšō* (cf. *rīš* 'beard') is named for its chin barbels (whisker-like appendages), and *mār paqqitīnan* 'spotted snake-eel' is known for its spots (*paqqitan*). While *may xārin* 'squirrel fish, sixline soapfish' has a spiny body (cf. *xār* 'bone, thorn, spine'), the *qambab čap* 'blackedged puffer' is compared to a *čap* 'paddle', and a round, flat yellowish fish sp. *ʔmēd* is named after a pillar (Ar. *ʕimād*). Secondly, some speakers maintain an unusual word-initial *ʔm* cluster (Anonby 2011, 377) in the fish name *ʔmēd* 'round, flat, yellowish fish sp.' (cf. Ar. *ʕimād* 'pillar'). The paeony bullseye *čum sāʔit* (lit. 'clock eye') is named for its enormous eyes, and the near-extinct sawfish (Moore 2017) *šamšīrī* (cf. *šamšir* 'sword') for its flat, elongated snout. A heavily armoured lobster species *šupš jayšan* is likened to the army (*jayš*), and the term *kraḥ dēw* 'toothless fish sp. similar to *qrambuṣ*' literally means 'ogre's sandal'.

The white face of the common bannerfish *fōringī* (lit. 'Portuguese person, European') brings to mind the Portuguese merchants that shaped the history of the region in past centuries, but the *xālaq* (lit. 'countenance, good looks') is the handsome one. Whale sharks as well as the Gulf blenny (both *kōr*) are likened to a blind person (also *kōr*). The label *marya ryānī* (cf. *marya* 'Maryam' [short form], *aryāni* 'naked'; cf. Ar. *ʕār, ʕuryān* 'naked'), which the late fisherman Aliko Shobubo himself used to refer to a small, transparent fish species, continues to amuse people.

For many of the fish names above, the English equivalent is equally descriptive (and sometimes almost identical in substance!), hinting at the cross-linguistic primacy of assigning appearance-related names to unusual-looking fish.

3.3. Descriptive Labels beyond Appearance

Appearance constitutes the most prevalent basis for the terms used to name of fish species, but it is not the only one. There are a few fish names based on personal proper names and salient aspects of human interaction with fish. In addition, some refer to the habitat and geographic distribution of a given species.

Personal proper names. Fish species with labels that appear to be derived from personal proper names include the Oman anemonefish *ḥama ẓmāmō* 'Muhammad Zmamo', and the family of angelfish and similar fish known as *ḥampōlaṣ*, itself likely borrowed from Arabic *ʿanfalūṣ* but recast through folk etymology as a compound, with the initial segments structured like *ḥam*, the short/prefix form of 'Muhammad', and the remainder of the word (*pōlaṣ*) opaque but bearing a distant resemblance to a name. The playful fish name *marya ryānī* (lit. 'naked Mary') similarly shows the short/prefix form of *maryam* (see also the end of 3.2. immediately above). Further, the terms *ḥālamō* 'seabream' and *ḥallūma* 'king soldier bream' share a triconsonantal root *ḥlm with the woman's proper name Halima, which in Kumzari is usually rendered *ḥalūmō* or *ḥēlumē*. Finally, the species *bahlul* 'potato grouper, small stage', borrowed from Gulf

Arabic *bahlūl* (also a fish species), has its origins in the Arabic proper name *bahlūl*.

Human interaction with species. A family of venomous fish *qātal*, along with its component species *qātal čāf* 'false stonefish' and *qātal čāf* 'draco waspfish' are aptly named as killers (cf. Ar. *qātil* 'killer'). The fishing group *rōra mōturō* 'children of Matar' have named slender groupers *kam rubʔ* (lit. 'quarter to [the hour]'), the time when by chance they would catch them. In addition to their species name, cobia *sikl* bear the honorific title *šēxa mēyin* ('sheikhs of fish'), itself perhaps calqued on Musandam Arabic *šēx issamak* (similarly, 'sheikh of the fish').

Habitat and geographic distribution. Two bream species, *ēraraġ čāf* 'red-filament threadfin bream' and *ēraraġ dašt* 'Japanese threadfin bream', are distinguished by references to habitat along the shore (*čāf*) or in the open sea (*dašt*). The same distinction is made for a pair of venomous *qātal* (lit. poison) fish species: *qātal čāf* 'false stonefish' and *qātal dašt* 'draco waspfish'. The term *čāf* is further applied, without an explicit corresponding *dašt* species, to distinguish *šuqqar čāf* 'golden cardinalfish' from the prototypical *šuqqar* 'Malabar blood snapper'. Conversely, *dašt* appears in the names *ālaq dašt* 'Chinese trumpetfish' and *šāwan dašt* 'yellowfin hind' in distinction to the simply labelled *ālaq* 'needlefish (etc.); hound trumpetfish' and *šāwan* 'orange rockcod'.

A second labelling dichotomy is set up between fish found along the coast of Arabia (*ārabī*), and those more typical of the Iranian coast (*fārsī* 'Persian'). In a couple of cases, these labels come in a pair: *sēḥak ārabī* 'granulate guitarfish' vs. *sēḥak fārsī*

'Arabian(!)/spotted guitarfish'; *rubyan ārabī* 'small prawn sp.' vs. *rubyan fārsī* 'large prawn sp.'. Other species are only represented by *ārabī* or *fārsī* in opposition to a simple label: *angiẓ ārabī* 'cuttlefish' vs. *angiẓ* 'cephalopod (family); angelfish sp.'; *ḥampōlaṣ ārabī* 'Jayakar's butterflyfish' vs. *ḥampōlaṣ* 'angelfish (family); angelfish sp.'; *xarkuk ārabī* 'Red Sea parrotfish' vs. *xarkuk* 'parrotfish (family); parrotfish sp.'; *xēnō fārsī* 'Indian Ocean oriental sweetlips (etc.)' vs. *xēnō* 'sweetlips (family); sweetlips (sp.).'; *jārid fārsī* 'striped bonito' vs. *jārid* 'kawakawa, large stage'.

Three further species are named in reference to their habitat: *būt dām* 'Arabian bluestriped dottyback' (cf. *būt* 'coral'), *may gawdin* 'fish sp.' (lit. 'cave fish') and *sēḥak jīrī* 'giant guitarfish' (lit. 'sand guitarfish').

4. Fish Names in Wider Linguistic Context

The importance of the study of fish names in Kumzari extends beyond an understanding of how fish types are conceptualised (2.) and a typology of the labels used for these species (3.). Here, we highlight linguistic structures that appear in fish names (4.1.), the use of fish names elsewhere in the lexicon (4.2.), and the contribution of fish names to an understanding of the language's history (4.3.).

4.1. Structural Characteristics of Fish Names

Sound symbolism. There are three cases of exact reduplication in the fish names, something which might be due to sound symbolism: *gawgaw* 'rabbitfish sp.', *kūkū* 'small blue and yellow fish sp.', and *laḥlaḥ* 'needlescaled queenfish'. In addition, names of three other species display structural repetition that may also be semantically expressive: *gā ġalġul* 'fish sp. similar to yellow trunkfish', *garagumba* 'fish sp.' and *gurgurō* 'small white and black fish sp.'. For the latter two species, the expressive function of the names seems already to be presented in similar associated terms found in regional Arabic (*garagumba*, Anonby, field notes 2008; *jurjūr*, Randall, 1995).

Taxonomic similarity and phonological similarity. There are several sets of fish species where taxonomic similarity is accompanied by phonological similarity. The seabream *ḥālamō* and king soldier bream *ḥallūma* share the same consonantal content, which can often be traced back to a single etymological source in Kumzari (as in Arabic). The two life stages of *qrambiṣ-qunwaḥ* 'large needlefish sp.' both start with *q*, and the three life stages of *lašt-lēdam-lāḥafī* 'dark fish sp. similar to *xālaq*' all start with *l*. These similarities could be due to chance, but semantic associations with certain sounds, or at least some kind of phonological analogy, might also play a role.

Unusual phonological structures. Two unusual phonological structures show up in fish names. First, the phoneme *h*, which elsewhere has almost always shifted to glottal stop (e.g., Ar. *šahīd*, K. *šēʔid* 'witness'; MP *kahwan*, P. *kohne*, K. *kaʔnaġ* 'old [thing]'), is retained in the term *bahlul* 'potato grouper, small stage'—perhaps as a result of recent borrowing or reinforcement from regional Arabic which shares this term. Secondly, some speakers maintain an unusual word-initial ʔ*m* cluster (Anonby 2011, 377) in the fish name ʔ*mēd* 'round, flat, yellowish fish sp.' (cf. MusAr of Khasab, also ʔ*mēd*; Ar. ʕ*imād* 'pillar'), which is nonetheless a systematic output exhibiting a pervasive shift of pharyngeal ˤ [ʕ] to glottal stop ʔ [ʔ] in Kumzari borrowings from Arabic and internally in some Arabic varieties of Musandam Peninsula.

The historical noun suffix -it. In Kumzari, the historical feminine/individuation noun suffix *-it* is associated with Semitic-type vocabulary of considerable time depth (contrasting with recent borrowings from Arabic, which use the modern Arabic suffix *-a* in its place). The suffix *-it* is found in the names of a number of fish types: *dābit* 'shark', *čum sāʔit* 'paeony bullseye', *ḥilbit* 'broomtail wrasse', *laqmit sūd* 'shark sp.', *mār paqqitīnan* 'spotted snake-eel', *rāxamit* 'long, thin and round silvery-coloured fish sp.', *tirxēnit* 'milk shark (small stage); milkfish' and likely *ālaq ṭarḥētin* 'barred needlefish' (where *-it* becomes *-ēt* due to suffix-induced vowel lengthening and umlaut, as explained in Anonby 2012; also cf. this species' alternate name *ālaq ṭarḥin;*). While some of these names may be derived (*rāxamit* resembles the MusAr term *rāxamī* 'slow-moving person') or innovated vocabulary that uses existing terms with *-it* (cf. *sāʔit* 'clock', *laqmit* 'morsel', *paqqit* 'spot'), the other names, which are semantically opaque, may be older (*ḥilbit, tirxēnit*).

Fish names and the proper/definite suffix -ō. In Kumzari, personal proper names are often accompanied by a fossilised definite suffix *-ō* (cf. Anonby 2012; van der Wal Anonby 2015), for example, *ḥalūmō* 'Halima', *bešīrō* 'Bashir'. This pattern is sometimes extended to generate proper-type nouns in other lexical domains including species names. For fish, it appears with moderate frequency, on 21 of the 198 fish labels in the lexicon.

In some cases, it is possible to identify the stem to which the suffix is attached through comparison with other lexical items, especially when the semantic connection is clear, for example, *rīšō* 'sulphur goatfish' (cf. *rīš* 'beard'). The fossilised quality of the suffix is evident in that (unlike personal proper names) it can be further marked for definiteness—both definite and indefinite: *rīšōʔō* 'the sulphur goatfish', *rīšōʔē* 'a sulphur goatfish'.

In addition, the suffix -*ō* is applied to terms borrowed from or held in common with other languages:

ab(u) dēnō 'silky shark', cf. Ar. *ab* 'father', MusAr *dēn* 'ear'
ambarō 'banded monocle bream', cf. K. *ambar*, Ar. *ambār* 'ambergris'
dgēgō 'torpedo scad', cf. MusAr (Khasab, urban varieties) *dgēg* 'chicken'
gurgurō 'striped white fish sp.', cf. Ar. *jarjūr*, GAr *gargūr* 'needlefish'
nagrō 'silver fish sp.', cf. GAr *nagrōr* 'silver fish sp.', P. *noqre* 'silver'
šōbubō 'Indo-Pacific sergeant', cf. K. *šōbub*, MusAr *šōbib* 'heavy rain'
xēnō 'rubberlips', cf. Ar. *xanāy* 'rubberlips'

In still other cases (e.g., *gmō* 'emperor sp.', *lākō* 'potato grouper, large stage') the stem is opaque and the presence of *ō* as the word ending may be coincidental.

'Mother' and 'father' constructions. Mother- and father-type descriptive/associative compounding constructions, well-known from Arabic, show up in Kumzari fish names. One of these names is, in fact, directly borrowed from Arabic: *ab(u) dēnō*

'silky shark', lit. 'father of ears' (see 3.2. for discussion of labels referring to physical appearance). Other names historically constructed in this way might include *ambarō* 'banded monocle bream' and *imbē/umbē* 'fish sp. similar to *āmur*', but the etymology and internal structure of the latter terms are unclear. Another fish name, *mām šāwan* 'redmouth grouper', contains the Kumzari word for mother, and it could likewise be a historical element in the opaque construction *māmadī* 'yellow fish sp. similar to *xālaq*'.

The morpheme may *'fish' as a compounding element.* A small number of fish names contain the word *may* 'fish' as a compounding element: *may gawdin* 'fish sp.' (lit. 'cave fish') and *may xārin* 'squirrel fish, sixline soapfish' (lit. 'thorn fish'). The label *maysānī* 'kingfish (etc.) (large stage)', for which the segment *sānī* is opaque, may also have developed its structure in this way. The relative scarcity of this construction in Kumzari stands in opposition to scientific English labels for the same set of fish, where (as evident from the complete list below), the compounding element '-fish' is found with dozens of fish types: angelfish, bannerfish, butterflyfish, dolphinfish, kingfish, parrotfish, porcupinefish, etc.

4.2. Use of Fish Names Elsewhere in the Lexicon

While it is more often the case that fish names are derived from qualities found elsewhere in the lexicon, a few fish names are themselves applied to other domains.

One small type of net anchor, *sinna paw* (cf. *sinn* 'net anchor'), is likened to a flounder (*paw*), and sometimes simply called *paw*.

A ropeful of strung fish is a *čikkit*, and the constellation Pleiades is called *čikkit byāḥō*, where *byāḥ* is a white fish species.

Fish names can be used as a *lāqab* 'nickname', as in the case of the late *ēlikō šōbubō* (Aliko Shobubo; cf. *šōbubō* 'Indo-Pacific sergeant') and *ḥas qābabō* (Hasan Qababo; cf. MusAr *qabāb* 'tuna sp.', = K. *wīr*). Both of these men loved to catch and eat these fish types. There is also a family known as *gmōʔō* (cf. K. *gmō* 'redspot emperor', *-ō* 'the'), and one person with the informal last name *ḥalūmō*, which is a proper name that sounds like a fish name (see 'Personal proper names' in 3.3. above).

Fish labels are also applied to types of people generally: the term *lāẓuq* 'remora' is applied to children who follow someone around, and *rāxamit*, which is a 'long, thin and round silvery-coloured fish sp.' that moves slowly in the water, is also used to describe 'slowpokes'—people who move or work slowly.

4.3. Fish Names and the History of the Kumzari Language

While the provenance of the Kumzari language is complex (see 1.), a study of any aspect of the language, including the lexicon of fish names, provides insight into its history.

Many Kumzari fish names are likely innovations—terms that originated within the language and which are not found in other languages. The presence of such terms underlines the unique and relatively insular (or, more precisely, peninsular) nature of the language community: one which has drawn on its own linguistic resources. Some of the many possible innovated terms include *angiẓ* 'squid, cuttlefish', *burqēb* 'bull shark (small stage)', *čāwuẓ* 'rabbitfish sp.', *ēraraġ* 'bream sp.', *jurbaḥ* 'silver bream-like sp.', *saptik* 'anthias' and *xarkuk* 'parrotfish (etc.)'.

From a wider comparative perspective, though, the lexicon of fish names is firmly grounded in the Arabian linguistic sphere. While the categorical term *may* is likely descended from MP *māhīg* (cf. also P. *māhi*, Keshmi *moy*; Anonby 2015, 179), a high proportion of the fish names are shared with Arabic, whether through borrowing from Arabic or through common inheritance. A number of examples have been given in various sections above, but a representative set of such words which are clearly related to common Arabic vocabulary is collected here as well:

Kumzari	Arabic (Modern Standard)	
ālaq	*ʕālaq*	'needlefish'
faql	*faql*	'porcupine fish'
īfē	*ʕīfā*	'milk shark'
kanʔad	*kanʕad*	'kingfish (etc.)'
qāpṭ	*qābṭ*	'seabream sp.'
rubbaṭ	*rābaḍ*	'ray sp.'
šāxur	*šāxūr*	'Indian snapper'
šayn	*šayn*	'needlescaled queenfish'
sikl	*sikl*	'cobia'
ūmat	*ʕūma*	'sardine'

Many further species names shared with Arabic have not been conventionalised in Modern Standard Arabic, but Kumzari speakers confirm that they are in use among regional varieties of Arabic: *abu dēnō* (=MusAr), *bahlul* (MusAr *bahlūl*), *dgēgō* (MusAr *dgēgō, dyēyō*), *dipsī* (GAr *dibsī*), *laḥlaḥ* (=GAr), *qambab* (MusAr *qrambab*), and *šupṣ* (MusAr *šibṣ*) (for glosses, see the full species list in the Appendix). Still other species have names that clearly appear to be related to Arabic words, but neither Modern Standard Arabic resources on fish names nor our consultation with MusAr speakers of the region attest to use of these names in Arabic: *biyyaḍ* 'sandbar shark' (cf. Ar. *abyaḍ* 'white'), *qātal* 'venomous fish' (cf. Ar. *qātil* 'killer'), *laqmit sūd* 'shark sp.' (cf. Ar. *laqma* 'morsel', Ar. *aswad*, pl. *sūd* 'black').

Yet other fish names are found in common with Balochi (Bl.) and SwIr languages to the north, in particular Bandari (Bn.) varieties including Minowi (Minabi) (Mn.); and, less commonly, Persian.[10]

Kumzari	Balochi	SwIr (Mn. unless marked otherwise)	
gēlō	*gelū*	*galu*	'sea catfish'
kārabō	*karābū*	*karrābu*	'dolphin'
kūlī	*kūlī*	*kuli*	'shark'
mayg	*meyg*	*mayg, maygu* (P.)	'shrimp'
pārawē	*parāwū*	*parāwu*	'fish sp.'
paw	*paw*	*pow*	'ray'
pēčak	*pīčak*	—	'shark sp.'

[10] Sources for the Balochi and SwIr data here are summarised in footnote 1. Since species identifications sometimes differ between the sources, consult the explanatory lexicon at the end of the article for the most precise possible identification in each language.

šang	šangū	šeng	'butterflyfish'
sanksar	sangsar	sangsar	'grunter/seabream sp.'
ṣārm	sārm	sārm	'queenfish sp.'

A long history of mutual interaction among all languages of the region is confirmed by fish names common to Arabic, Kumzari, Balochi and SwIr languages of Iran—whatever the ultimate origin of any of these names.[11]

Arabic	Kumzari	Balochi	SwIr[12]	
ʿanfalūṣ	ḥampōlaṣ	—	āmfolos	'dolphinfish sp.'
byāḫ (GAr)	byāḫ	bīyā	biyāh, biyā	'mullet sp.'
gargūr (GAr)	gurgurō	gorgorū	gargaru	'fish sp.'
hāmūr	āmur	hāmur	hāmur (Mn., P.)	'grouper'
jayḍar	jaydar	gīdar	gidar	'yellowfin tuna'
qarfa	qurfē	karfe	karfa	'scad sp.'
ṣāl	ṣāl	ṣāl	—	'trevally sp.'
xanāy	xēnō	xannū	xennu, xannu	'sweetlips sp.'
xlēsī (MusAr)	xlēsī	xeleysī	xalāsi	'tuna sp.'
zbēdī (GAr)	ẓbēdī	zobeydī	zobādi	'pomfret sp.'

---

[11] Sources for the Balochi and SwIr data here are summarised in footnote 1. As mentioned with the previous table, since species identifications sometimes differ between the sources, consult the explanatory lexicon at the end of the article for most precise possible identification in each language.

[12] Mn. unless marked otherwise.

Further, many fish terms are shared between Kumzari and the Modern South Arabian languages (MSAL), at least sometimes with Arabic as an intermediary, and at times with a shift in which species it applies to. For example, there is a type of pufferfish in Shehret, *fuḵl~fugl*, whose name is obviously related to both K. and Ar. *faql* 'porcupinefish'. The Musandam Arabic label *qrambab* 'triggerfish' clarifies the link between cognates in Kumzari on the one hand, and MSAL on the other: K. *qambab* vs. Sq. *ḵarbōbə*, Sh. *ḵerbót*, H. *ḵerbót*, *ḵerbōbət*, M. *ḵərbōbət*, B. *ḵerbābət*. Conversely, the Kumzari word for whale, *šawḥaṭ*, is more similar to MSAL (Sq. *śīḥāṭə*, Sh. *śəbḥáṭet*, H. *śōḥáṭet*, M. *śaḥṭət*, B. *śḥáṭət*) than it is to Ar. *ḥūṭ*; as Bayshak (2002) has pointed out, this particular item is evidence for a direct link apart from Arabic. The Kumzari term *dībē* 'shortfin mako shark' is equivalent to the term used for the same species in MSAL: Sq. *dībə*, Sh., Ho., M., B. *ḍībə*. The same situation is found with K. *kōr* 'whale shark' and *fār* 'flying fish', with recurrent but varied correspondences in the MSAL: Sq. *fériher~férifer*, Sh. *ferr~ferér*, H. *ferfír*, M. *fərār*, B. *férri* 'flying fish'; Sq., Sh., B. *kɛr*, M. *karr* 'whale shark'. Coming full circle, the latter term extends to Iranic languages of the wider region: in both Minabi (Bandari) and Balochi, the equivalent terms for the latter species are *kuli kar* (Mn.) and *kūlī kar* (Bl.).

To return to the idea of innovation within Kumzari: still other Kumzari fish names make use of Arabic as well as non-Arabic sources from existing vocabulary, but their application to fish species is novel. The shared Kumzari and Musandam Arabic term *manqab* means 'beak' in both languages, but in

Kumzari it is used as a name for a type of shark. Conversely, the inherited word *sitraġ* 'razor' (cf. MP *awestarag*, P. *ostore*) is applied to a fish species in Kumzari. The Kumzari terms *nān* 'bread' and *paw* 'ray sp.', known from elsewhere in SwIr (Mohebbi Bahmani 2006), come together in Kumzari as *nān paw* (lit. 'ray bread'), the name for flounder. There are even species which have ostensibly coupled an Arabic term with an inherited SwIr term to produce a new Kumzari term: *kam rub^ʔ* (lit. 'quarter to [the hour]', cf. P. *kam* 'less', Ar. *rub^ʕ* 'quarter') refers to the slender grouper, and the paeony bullseye has been labelled *čum sāʔit* (lit. 'clock eye', cf. P. *češm*, Keshmi and Minowi *čehm* 'eye'; Ar. *sāʕa* 'hour, watch').

5. Conclusion

This article provides an inventory, description and analysis of fish names in Kumzari, an endangered language spoken at the tip of the Musandam Peninsula in eastern Arabia. The ecological richness of the waters around this peninsula are encoded and brought to life in the elaborate typology of fish names in this language. As with any language, Kumzari exhibits a unique system for conceptualising fish and expressing distinctions between various types of fish. The 198 labels for fish types in the language draw on a range of lexical resources: association with other types of fish; physical appearance, including resemblance to other types of animals, colour, and a collection of other more complex referential associations; and a strong representation of descriptive labels beyond physical appearance, drawing on personal proper names, human interaction with species, and delineation of habitat. Several interesting linguistic features, including sound symbolism, definiteness, and 'mother' and 'father' constructions, recur in the labels used for fish types. While some fish names are held in common with languages of the region, showing linguistic relationships that date back to previous millennia, other labels appear to be language-internal innovations, known only from Kumzari.

Appendix: Explanatory Lexicon of Kumzari Fish Types

The following table lists each of the 198 fish labels in the Kumzari lexicon, including species names as well as family groupings. Kumzari labels are listed in English-based alphabetical order. Each Kumzari fish name is accompanied, as much as possible, by an English equivalent as found in FishBase (https://www.fishbase.org); see the methodology in 1.1. above for explanation and caveats. Species for which we were not able to provide a substantive identification are described in the terms used by Kumzari speakers, including description of physical appearance, size, habitat, and similarity to other fish species. Sociolinguistic variation in the labels used is discussed in 2.4. above.

Etymologically related words in Kumzari, Arabic and other languages of the region are also proposed where known.

	Kumzari name	English equivalent	related terms in regional languages
1.	ʔmēd = mēd	round, flat, yellowish fish sp.	MusAr (Khasab) ʔmēd 'fish sp.', Ar. ʕimād 'pillar'

2.	ab dēnō = abu dēnō	silky shark	Ar. ab(u) 'father'; Ar. uđun, MusAr dēn 'ear'; cf. also Sh. đəmēwi, M. đinf
3.	abu dēnō (see ab dēnō)		
4.	ambarō	banded monocle bream	Bl. ambarū 'fish sp.'; ? K. ambar, Ar. ʕambār 'ambergris'; ? K. ambar, P., ambār 'storehouse', GAr, Ar. ʕambār 'storehouse, ward'; ? Ar. umm, MusAr imm 'mother'
5.	anfuẓ	fish sp. (description and identification uncertain; may be a synonym for ḥampōlaṣ 'fish sp.')	Ar. ʕanfalūṣ 'common dolphinfish', Mn. ānfolos, āmfolos 'fish sp.'; ? K. ḥampōlaṣ 'fish sp.'; ? Ar. ʕanfaṣ 'bad-mannered person'
6.	angiẓ	cephalopod (squid and cuttlefish) (family)	
7.	angiẓ ārabī	cuttlefish	K. angiẓ 'cephalopod'; K. ārabī, Ar. ʕarabī 'Arab (adj.)'
8.	angiẓ kanʔēdin	squid	K. angiẓ 'cephalopod'; K. kanʔad, Ar. kanʕad 'fish sp.'
9.	asp	seahorse (family); yellow seahorse	K. asp, P. asb 'horse'; Bl. asp 'fish sp.'; Mn., Bl., aspak 'fish sp.'
10.	asp sirx	thorny seahorse	K. asp 'seahorse'; K. sirx, P. sorx 'red'
11.	ālaq	any of several types of fish with a narrow snout; specifically, refers to hound needlefish	Ar. ʕalāq 'fish sp.'
12.	ālaq dašt	Chinese trumpetfish	K. ālaq 'fish sp.'; K. dašt 'open space, open sea'; P. dašt 'field, plain'

13.	ālaq ṭarḥētin = ālaq ṭarḥin	barred needlefish	K. ālaq 'fish sp.'
14.	ālaq ṭarḥin (see ālaq ṭarḥētin)		K. ālaq 'fish sp.'
15.	āmur	potato grouper (bahlul-āmur-lākō), medium stage	Ar. hāmūr, P., Mn., Bl. hāmūr 'fish sp.'
16.	āqadī	blueline snapper (purġar-āqadī), large stage	
17.	bahlul	potato grouper (bahlul-āmur-lākō), small stage	GAr, MusAr bahlūl 'fish sp.', Ar. personal name
18.	billō	greater amberjack	? K. billa 'slobber'
19.	biyyaḍ (see biyyaṭ)		
20.	biyyaṭ = biyyaḍ	sandbar shark	Ar. abyaḍ, MusAr byaḍ 'white'
21.	burqēb	bull shark (burqēb-qrādī-rējimī), small stage	
22.	būt	small fish (general term); small fish sp. (family)	MusAr būt 'small fish'
23.	būt murwan	red sweeper, five-lined cardinalfish (Randall: obliquebanded cardinalfish)	K. būt 'fish sp.'; K. murwan 'chickens'
24.	būt dām	Arabian bluestriped dottyback	K. būt 'fish sp.'; dām 'coral'
25.	byāḥ	mullet (general term)	GAr byāḥ 'mullet', Mn. biyāh, biyā, Bl. bīyā 'fish sp.'
26.	čāwuẓ	rabbitfish sp. (gawgaw-čāwuẓ), large stage; possibly squaretail rabbitfish and white-spotted rabbitfish	? Bl. čaġūk 'fish sp.'

27.	čum sāʔit	paeony bulleye	K. čum, Keshmi čehm, P. česm 'eye'; K. sāʔit, Ar. sāʕa, P. sāʔat 'clock, hour'
28.	čūk jmēs	bigeye hound shark, scalloped hammerhead shark and smooth hammerhead shark (čūk jmēs-jmēs-jubbē), small stage	K. čikk 'small, child'; Bl. čūk 'child'; K. jmēs 'shark sp.'
29.	čūk pārawē	large dark brown fish sp. (čūk pārawē-pārawē), small stage	K. čikk 'small, child'; Bl. čūk 'child'; K. pārawē, Mn. parāwu 'fish sp.'
30.	čūm	medium-large red fish sp.	
31.	dābit	shark (family of large sharks within kūlī 'shark')	
32.	dgēgō	torpedo scad	MusAr (Khasab, urban varieties) dgēg 'chicken'; cf. also Sh. dəjējo, M. dəgāgóh, 'torpedo scad'
33.	dipsī	blacktip trevally	K. dipsī, MusAr dibsī 'palm weevil', itself from Ar. dibs 'date syrup'; GAr dibsī, Bl. depsī 'fish sp.'
34.	dībē	shortfin mako shark	Sh., H., M., B. dībə, Sq. dībə 'shortfin mako shark'
35.	dnān mišk	Sohal surgeonfish	K. dnān, MP, P. dandān 'tooth'; K. mišk, MP mušk 'mouse'; Mn. muš dandon, Bl. moškū 'fish sp.'
36.	ēraraġ	bream sp. (family)	
37.	ēraraġ čāf	red-filament threadfin bream	K. ēraraġ 'fish sp.'; K. čāf 'shore, beach'
38.	ēraraġ dašt	Japanese threadfin bream	K. ēraraġ 'fish sp.'; K. dašt 'open space, open sea', P. dašt 'field, plain'
39.	faql	porcupinefish	Ar. faql 'porcupinefish', Sh. fuḵl~fugl 'pufferfish sp.'

40.	*fār*	flying fish	Sq. *fériher~férifer*, Sh. *ferr~ferér*, H. *ferfír*, M. *fərār*, B. *férri*
41.	*fijmē*	short-beaked common dolphin	B. *fēmi* 'common dolphin', *fīdīm* 'shark sp.'
42.	*fōringī*	pennant coralfish (Randall, 1995: common bannerfish)	K. *fōringī*, Ar. *faranja*, *ifranjī*, P. *farangī* 'foreigner, European'
43.	*garagumba = qambab garagumba*	starry triggerfish	MusAr *qrambab* 'fish sp.'; Sq. *ḵarbōbə*, Sh. *ḵerbót*, H. *ḵerbót*, *ḵerbōbət*, M. *ḵərbōbət*, B. *ḵerbābət* 'triggerfish'
44.	*gawgaw*	rabbitfish sp. (*gawgaw-čāwuẓ*), small stage; possibly squaretail rabbitfish and white-spotted rabbitfish	? Bl. *gāmgām* 'fish sp.'
45.	*gā ġalġul*	fish sp. similar to yellow trunkfish but darker and with a smaller tail	K. *gā* 'bull'; Lori *gā*, P. *gāv* 'bull'; Bl. *ġarġūl* 'fish sp.
46.	*ġbar*	shark sp. similar to hardnose shark but which has a ruddy yellow-brown dorsal fin tip	K., GAr *ġbar* 'dust, dust colour'
47.	*gdīr*	spangled emperor (*tarbōnīm gdīr-gdīr-mkindī*), medium-large stage	Mn., Bl. *gedīr* 'fish sp.'; ? Ar. of Sharqiyah *xuwayḍar* 'emperor sp.'; cf. also Ar. *jayḍar*, Sh. *jēḍər*, *gēḍər*, H., B. *gēder*, M. *gēḍəb*, *gēḍər* 'yellowfin tuna'; Bn., Bl. *gīdar* 'tuna sp.'
48.	*gēlō*	sea catfish	Mn. *galu*, Bl. *gelū* 'sea catfish'; SwIr (e.g., Bakhtiari of Chilteh Dudera) *gelu* 'cat' (Anonby, Taheri-Ardali and Stone, 2021, 122, 133)

49.	gmō	redspot emperor (Randall, 1995: saburbir emperor)	? Ar. *naqīmawwa* 'fish sp.' (Randall, 1995)
50.	gurgurō	small, fast-swimming white fish sp. with black stripes	Mn. *gargaru*, Bl. *gorgorū* 'fish sp.'; ? Ar. *jarjūr*, GAr *gargūr* 'barred needlefish; spinner shark'
51.	ḥallūma₁	king soldier bream, small stage	K. *ḥallūma₂* 'fish sp.'; ? K. *ḥālamō* 'fish sp.'
52.	ḥallūma₂	fish sp. similar to *ḥallūma₁* but which is red	K. *ḥallūma₂* 'fish sp.'; ? K. *ḥālamō* 'fish sp.'
53.	ḥama ẓmāmō	Oman anemonefish	K. *ḥam, ḥama* 'Muhammad'; Sq. *zaʿmōmə ~ zaʿmāmə* 'pufferfish'
54.	ḥampōlaṣ	grouping of several types of fish, including angelfish, butterflyfish and dolphinfish; specifically, refers to emperor angelfish, semicircle angelfish and yellowbar angelfish	Ar. *ʿanfalūṣ*, B. *ʿanfəlūs*, Sh. *ʿamfəlūs*, M. *amfəlūs* 'common dolphinfish'; cf. also Mn. *ānfolos, āmfolos* 'fish sp.'
55.	ḥampōlaṣ ārabī	Jayakar's butterflyfish	K. *ḥampōlaṣ* 'fish sp.'; K. *ārabī*, Ar. *ʿarabī* 'Arab (adj.)'
56.	ḥampōlaṣ šāʔin	common dolphinfish	K. *ḥampōlaṣ* 'fish sp.'; K. *šāʔin* 'hawk, eagle, vulture'; P. *šāhīn* 'falcon'
57.	ḥālamō	seabream	Bl. *halīmū* 'fish sp.'; ? K. *ḥallūma* 'fish sp.'
58.	ḥilbit	broomtail wrasse	
59.	ḥillē	shrimp scad	
60.	imbē = umbē	fish sp. similar to *āmur*, but which is darker and lives in shallow water	? Ar. *umm*, MusAr *imm* 'mother'
61.	innānē	honeycomb stingray	
62.	ifē	milk shark (*tirxēnit-ifē*), large stage	GAr *ʿifō*, Ar. *ʿifā, ʿifa*

63.	jaġbib	fish sp. similar in colour to āmur, but which is smaller, has a large head, eyes and mouth, and is of poor quality for eating	? Sh. jaʿbobít 'skipjack tuna'
64.	jaydar	yellowfin tuna	Ar. jayḍar, Sh. jēḏər, gēḏər, H., B. gēder, M. gēḏəb, gēḏər 'yellowfin tuna'; Bn., Bl. gīdar 'tuna sp.'
65.	jārid	kawakawa (tuna sp.) (xlēsī-jārid), large stage	Bl. jarhād 'fish sp.'
66.	jārid fārsī	striped bonito	K. jārid 'fish sp.', Bl. jarhād 'fish sp.'; K., Ar. fārsī, P. fārsi 'Persian'
67.	jmēs	bigeye hound shark, scalloped hammerhead shark and smooth hammerhead shark (čūk jmēs-jmēs-jubbē), medium stage	
68.	jubbē	bigeye hound shark, scalloped hammerhead shark and smooth hammerhead shark (čūk jmēs-jmēs-jubbē), large stage	
69.	jurbaḥ	fish sp. similar in shape to saptik but silver in colour	
70.	kam rubʔ	slender grouper	K., P. kam 'less', K. also 'time remaining to the hour'; K. rubʔ, Ar. rubʕ, P. robʔ 'quarter'
71.	kanʔad	medium-large stage of fish sp. (xubbaṭ-mazāraq-kanʔad-maysānī) which includes wahoo, kingfish and Spanish mackerel	Ar. kanʕad 'fish sp.'
72.	kārabō	white dolphin	Mn. karrābu, Bl. karābū 'dolphin sp.'

73.	kāraraġ	fish sp. similar to *qurfē* and *wīr*, but blue on top	
74.	kāsal	minnow; sardine	
75.	kāsal xālalin	large minnow or sardine sp.	K. *kāsal* 'minnow, sardine'
76.	kmā	frigate tuna	
77.	kōfar	king soldier bream, large stage	Ar. *kawfar*, Bl. *kūfar* 'fish sp.'
78.	kōr₁	whale shark	Sq., Sh., B. *kɛr*, M. *karr*, cf. also Mn., Bl. *kūlī kar* 'whale shark' (lit. 'deaf shark'); K. *kōr* 'blind person', MP *kōr* 'blind'; K. *kōr₂* 'fish sp.'
79.	kōr₂	Gulf blenny	K. *kōr* 'blind person', MP *kōr* 'blind'; K. *kōr₁* 'whale shark'
80.	krāḥ dēw	fish sp. similar to *qrambiṣ-qunwaḥ* but without teeth	K. *krāḥ* 'sandal'; K., MP *dēw* 'ogre, demon'
81.	kūkū	small blue and yellow fish species with white underside and a small mouth	
82.	kūku taḥādī = taḥādī	rainbow runner	K. *kūkū* 'fish sp.'; K. *taḥādī* 'fish sp.'
83.	kūlī	shark	Mn., Bl. *kūlī* 'shark'
84.	laḥlaḥ = šayn	needlescaled queenfish	GAr *laḥlaḥ* 'fish sp.'
85.	laqmit sūd	shark sp. similar to hardnose shark but which is brown with a black dorsal fin tip	K. *laqmit*, Ar. *laqma* 'morsel'; Ar. *aswad* 'black'
86.	lašt	small stage of *lašt-lēdam-lāḥafī*, a fish sp. similar to *xālaq*, but dark	

87.	*lāḥafī*	large stage of *lašt-lēdam-lāḥafī*, a fish sp. similar to *xālaq*, but dark	
88.	*lākō*	potato grouper (*bahlul-āmur-lākō*), large stage	
89.	*lāẓuq*	remora (suckerfish)	K. *lāẓuq* 'child who follows people around'; Sh. *ləzāk̲*, B. *ləṣāk̲*, Mn., Bl. *lāzūk* 'fish sp.'; ? Ar. *lāṣaq* 'glue'
90.	*lēdam*	medium stage of *lašt-lēdam-lāḥafī*, a fish sp. similar to *xālaq*, but dark	
91.	*manqab*	any of several shark sp. including blacktip shark, hardnose shark, sliteye shark, whitecheek shark	K., MusAr *manqab* 'beak'
92.	*marya ryānī*	large minnow sp. with transparent flesh	K., Ar., P. *maryam* 'Maryam' (proper name); K. *aryānī*, cf. also Ar. ʕ*ār, maʕrī, ʕuryān* 'naked'
93.	*manṭa*	sailfish, marlin	Mn., Bl. *mantūl* 'sailfish, marlin'
94.	*may gawdin*	fish sp. similar to *kam rubʔ* but whose mouth and head are larger	K. *may*, P. *māhi* 'fish'; K. *gawd* 'cave, hole'; cf. also Lori *gawd*, P. *gawdāl* 'hole'
95.	*may xārin*	fish spp. including squirrelfish and goldenstriped soapfish (Randall, 1995: sixlined soapfish)	K. *may*, P. *māhi* 'fish'; K., P. *xār* 'thorn, spine'; also K. 'bone'; ? Bl. *xarak* 'fish sp.'
96.	*maysānī*	large stage of fish sp. (*xubbaṭ-maẓāraq-kanʔad-maysānī*) which includes wahoo, kingfish and Spanish mackerel	? K. *may*, P. *māhi* 'fish'
97.	*mayg*	shrimp; small shrimp	Mn. *mayg*, Bl. *meyg*, P. *maygu* 'shrimp'

98. *maẓāraq*	medium-small stage of fish sp. (*xubbaṭ-maẓāraq-kanʔad-maysānī*) which includes wahoo, kingfish and Spanish mackerel	
99. *mām šāwan*	redmouth grouper	K. *mām* 'mother'; K. *šāwan* 'fish sp.'; ? Bl. *šammām* 'fish sp.'
100. *māmadī*	fish sp. similar to *xālaq*, but yellower	
101. *mār diryīʔin*	snake-eel (family); possibly, sea snake; specifically, refers to ringed snake-eel	K., Mn., P. *mār* 'snake'; K. *diryīʔin* 'of the sea; fisherman'; cf. also K. *dirya*, P. *daryā* 'sea'; Mn. *mār deriyāi* 'snake-eel'
102. *mār paqqitīnan*	spotted snake-eel	K., P. *mār* 'snake'; K. *paqqit* 'spot'
103. *mārānī*	snake-eel sp.	? K., P. *mār* 'snake'
104. *mēd* (see *ʔmēd*)		
105. *mkindī*	spangled emperor (*tarbō-nīm gdīr-gdīr-mkindī*), large stage	
106. *nagrō*	fish sp. which resembles Bengal snapper, but is silver	GAr *nagrōr*; Sh. *nəgrḗr*, H. *nəgrúr*, M. *nəgrūr* 'small-spotted grunter'; cf. also P. *noqre* 'silver (n.)'
107. *namarāni*	shark sp. with light spots	K. *numr*, MusAr *nimr* 'leopard', Ar. *namir* 'leopard, tiger'; cf. also Sq. *nimérihun, nímerhun, nimrāni*, Sh. *nimrāni*, M., *nəmrāni, nimrāni, nibrāni* 'tiger shark'

108. nān paw	flatfish: flounder, and possibly sole	K., P. nān 'bread'; K. paw, Mn. pow (Mohebbi Bahmani 2006), Bl. pav 'ray', Bl. nān paw 'fish sp.'
109. nāwukō	zebra shark	
110. nīm gdīr	spangled emperor (tarbōnīm gdīr-gdīr-mkindī), medium-small stage	K., P. nīm 'half'; K. gdīr 'fish sp.'; Bl. gdīrak 'fish sp.'
111. paw	ray and guitarfish (family); bluespotted ribbontail	Mn. pow (Mohebbi Bahmani 2006), Bl. pav 'ray'
112. pārawē	large dark brown fish sp. (čūk pārawē-pārawē), large stage	Mn., Bl. parāwū 'fish sp.'
113. pēčak	Arabian smoothhound (Randall: Arabian hound shark)	K. pēčak 'wooden mallet', Bl. pīčak 'shark sp.'
114. purġar	blueline snapper (purġar-āqadī), small stage	Bl. pūlūġār 'fish sp.'
115. qambab	triggerfish; triggerfish sp. which includes Picasso triggerfish and golden-finned triggerfish	MusAr qrambab 'fish sp.'
116. qambab garagumba (see garagumba)		K. qambab 'fish sp.'; K. garagumba 'fish sp.'
117. qambab čap	blackedged puffer	K. qambab 'fish sp.'; K., Bl. čap 'paddle (n.)'
118. qarṭabō	fish sp. similar to šōbubō but green, blue and red	
119. qāpṭ = qāṭ	goldlined seabream	Ar. qābṭ 'fish sp.'
120. qāṭ (see qāpṭ)		
121. qātal	venomous fish (family)	K. qātal 'poison', Ar. qātil 'killer'; Bl. kātel 'venomous fish sp.'

122. *qātal čāf*	false stonefish	K. *qātal* 'fish sp.'; K. *čāf* 'shore, beach'
123. *qātal dašt*	draco waspfish	K. *qātal* 'fish sp.'; K. *dašt* 'open space, open sea', P. *dašt* 'field, plain'
124. *qāẓum*	blacktip reef shark	
125. *qrādī*	bull shark (*burqēb-qrādī-rējimī*), medium stage	Ar. *qurādī, qarāzī*, GAr *qurādī*, Bl. *qarādī* 'shark sp.'
126. *qrambiṣ*	small stage of *qrambiṣ-qunwaḥ*, a needlefish sp. which is larger than other needlefish sp.	
127. *qunwaḥ*	large stage of *qrambiṣ-qunwaḥ*, a needlefish sp. which is larger than other needlefish sp.	
128. *qurfē*	yellowtail scad	Ar. *qarfa*, Mn. *karfa*, Bl. *karfe* 'fish sp.'
129. *rāmak*	ray sp. similar to *rubbaṭ*	Bn. *rāmak* 'eagle ray'
130. *rāmišt*	smalltooth emperor (*rāmišt-rōbāyō*), small stage	
131. *rāxamit* = *ṣōman*	long, thin and round silvery-coloured fish sp.	K. *rāxamit*, MusAr *rāxamī* 'slow-moving person'
132. *rējimī*	bull shark (*burqēb-qrādī-rējimī*), large stage	
133. *rišō*	sulphur goatfish	K., P. *rīš* 'beard'; Bl. *rīšū* 'fish sp.'
134. *rōbāyō*	smalltooth emperor (*rāmišt-rōbāyō*), large stage	Bl. *rubāhū* 'fish sp.', cf. P. *rubāh* 'fox'
135. *rubbaṭ*	whipray sp., electric ray (possibly marbled torpedo, among others)	Ar. *rābaḍ* 'fish sp.', Sq. *rōbaṣ, rōbəḏ* 'ray', M. *rābəḏ* 'whipray sp., ray sp.'
136. *rubyan*	prawn; shrimp	Ar. *rubyān*, H., M. *rəbyān* 'prawn'

137. *rubyan ārabī*	small, dark prawn spp.	K. *rubyan* 'prawn'; K. *ārabī*, Ar. *ʿarabī* 'Arab (adj.)'
138. *rubyan fārsī*	large, light-coloured prawn spp.	K. *rubyan* 'prawn'; K., Ar. *fārsī*, P. *fārsi* 'Persian'
139. *sabu kanʔad*	McCosker's wrasse, yellowstriped cardinalfish	K. *kanʔad* 'fish sp.'
140. *sāfin*	tiny white fish sp. with a black tail	Mn., Bl. *sāfī* 'fish sp.'
141. *samarānī*	shark sp. with dark spots	K. *sāmar* 'charcoal', Ar. *asmar* 'charcoal colour'
142. *sanksar*	king soldier bream, medium stage	Bn., Mn., Bl. *sangsar* 'javelin grunter'; ? P. *sang* 'stone'; ? K., P. *sar* 'head'
143. *saftik* (see *saptik*)		
144. *saptik* = *saftik* = *siftik*	anthias, rosy dwarf monocle bream	
145. *sēḥak*	guitarfish (family); specifically, refers to bowmouth guitarfish	Mn. *sihak* 'fish sp.'
146. *sēḥak ārabī*	granulate guitarfish	K. *sēḥak* 'guitarfish sp.'; K. *ārabī*, Ar. *ʿarabī* 'Arab (adj.)'
147. *sēḥak fārsī*	spotted guitarfish (Alec Moore, pers. comm. 2021: Oman/Bengal/spotted guitarfish; Randall, 1995: Arabian guitarfish)	K. *sēḥak* 'guitarfish sp.'; K., Ar. *fārsī*, P. *fārsi* 'Persian'
148. *sēḥak jīrī*	giant guitarfish	K. *sēḥak*, M. *ābádyət sāḥūk əl-knēnaḥ* 'guitarfish sp.'; K. *jīrī* 'sand'
149. *sēlik*	moray (family); specifically, refers to a sp. that includes honeycomb moray and palenose moray	Bl. *sālak* 'moray'

150. *sēlik numr*	dragon moray	K. *sēlik* 'fish sp.'; K. *numr*, MusAr *nimr* 'leopard', Ar. *namir* 'tiger'; cf. also Sq. *némiro, nímiher*, Sh. *nəbrít, inmirít* 'moray'
151. *siftik* (see *saptik*)		
152. *sikl*	cobia	Ar. *sikl* 'fish sp.', Sq. *sāḵel*, M. *sxalát*, B. *sxalét* 'cobia'
153. *sitraġ*	fish sp. similar to cleaner wrasse, but which is green or yellow	MP *awestarag*, P. *ostore* 'razor' (MacKenzie 1971, 14)
154. *siflindō*	silver snake-eel sp.	Ar. *sif rāndō* 'fish sp.'
155. *skindan*	snapper sp. which resembles other snappers but is multicoloured and has larger teeth	
156. *ṣāl*	silver-white trevally sp.	Ar. *ṣāl*, Bl. *sāl* 'fish sp.'
157. *ṣāqatan*	skipjack tuna	
158. *ṣārm*	Talang queenfish	Mn., Bl. *sārm* 'fish sp.'
159. *ṣāwawē*	skate	
160. *ṣnāfē*	streaked rabbitfish	Ar. *ṣanāfay* 'fish sp.'
161. *ṣōman* (see *rāxamit*)		Bl. *sommān* 'fish sp.'
162. *šamšīrī*	sawfish	Bn., Bl. *kūlī šamšīrī* 'sawfish'; K. *šamšir*, P. *šamšīr* 'sword'
163. *šang*	butterflyfish (family); specifically, refers to a species which includes dark butterflyfish, exquisite butterflyfish, masked butterflyfish, threadfin butterflyfish and vagabond butterflyfish	K. *šang* 'comb', P. *čang* 'harp'; Bn. *šing, šengu*, Mn. *šeng*, Bl. *šangu* 'fish sp.'; cf. Sh. *mīšəṭ* 'butterflyfish sp. (lit. 'comb')

164. šawḥaṭ	whale		Sq. síḥāṭə, Sh. śəbḥáṭet, H. śōḥáṭet, M. śahṭət, B. śḥáṭət; cf. also ? K., Lori šaw 'night'; ? Ar. ḥūt 'whale'
165. šayn (see laḥlaḥ)			Ar. šayn 'fish sp.'
166. šāwan	strawberry hind (Randall, 1995: orange rockcod)		? K. šaw 'night', šāwan 'nights'
167. šāwan dašt	yellowfin hind		K. šāwan 'fish sp.'; K. dašt 'open space, open sea', P. dašt 'field, plain'
168. šāxur	Indian snapper		Ar. šāxūr 'fish sp.'
169. šōban	fish sp. similar to ṣāwawē		
170. šōbubō	Indo-Pacific sergeant		K. šōbub, MusAr šōbib 'heavy rain'
171. šupṣ	lobster (general term); spiny lobster		MusAr šibṣ 'lobster'
172. šupṣ jayšan	heavily armoured lobster sp. with long antennae		K. šupṣ 'lobster'; K., Ar. jayš 'army'
173. šupṣ šufrāqō	lobster sp. without antennae		K. šupṣ 'lobster'; K. šufrāqō 'frog'
174. šuqqar	Malabar blood snapper		GAr šuqqar 'fish sp.'
175. šuqqar čāf	golden cardinalfish		K. šuqqar 'fish sp.'; K. čāf 'shore, beach'
176. šūma šuqqar	humphead snapper		K. šuqqar 'fish sp.'
177. taḥādī (see kūkū taḥādī)			? Ar. itaḥād 'union'
178. tarbō	spangled emperor (tarbō-nīm gdīr-gdīr-mkindī), small stage		
179. tirxēnit$_1$	milk shark (tirxēnit-īfē), small stage		K. tirxēnit$_2$ 'fish sp.'
180. tirxēnit$_2$	milkfish		K. tirxēnit$_1$ 'fish sp.'

181.	*umbē* (see *imbē*)		
182.	*ūmat*	minnow or sardine	Ar. ʕ*ūma*
183.	*wīr*	long-tailed tuna, small stage	Bl. *havūr* 'tuna sp.'
184.	*wīr barḥ*	long-tailed tuna, large stage	K. *wīr* 'longtail tuna'; K. *barḥ* 'huge'; Mn., Bl. *havūr* 'tuna sp.'
185.	*xarkuk*	parrotfish; specifically, refers to a species which includes bluebarred parrotfish and falcate-fin parrotfish	
186.	*xarkuk ārabī*	Red Sea parrotfish	K. *xarkuk* 'fish sp.'; K. *ārabī*, Ar. ʕ*arabī* 'Arab (adj.)'
187.	*xāġur*	twobar seabream	
188.	*xālaq*	brownspotted grouper	K. *xālaq* 'countenance, good looks'; Ar. *xāliq*, P. *xāleq* 'creator'; cf. also Sq. *ḥálḥal*, *xálxal*, Sh. *ġalfūk*, H. *xalxál*, *xolxól*, B. *xalxāl* 'brownspotted grouper; other grouper sp.'
189.	*xēnō*	sweetlips and rubberlips (family); specifically, refers to a species which includes minstrel sweetlips, painted sweetlips and whitebarred rubberlip	Ar. *xanāy*, Mn., Bl. *xannū*, Mn. also *xennu* 'fish sp.'; ? K. *xan* 'compartment', *xēnō* 'the compartment'
190.	*xēnō fārsī*	fish sp. which includes Indian Ocean oriental sweetlips and blackspotted rubberlip	K. *xēnō*, Ar. *xanāy*, Mn., Bl. *xannū*, Mn. also *xennu* 'fish sp.'; K., Ar. *fārsī*, P. *fārsi* 'Persian'
191.	*xiṣwānī*	spottail shark	
192.	*xlēsī*	kawakawa (tuna sp.) (*xlēsī-jārid*), small stage	MusAr *xlēsī*, Mn. *xalāsi*, Bl. *xeleysī* 'fish sp.'

193. *xrō diryīʔin*	lionfish (Randall, 1995: turkeyfish), including clearfin lionfish and largetail lionfish	Mn. *korus deryāi*, Bl. *korūs* 'turkeyfish'; K. *xrō*, MP *xrōs* 'rooster'; K. *diryīʔin* 'of the sea; fisherman'; cf. also K. *dirya*, P. *daryā* 'sea'
194. *xubbaṭ*	small stage of fish sp. (*xubbaṭ-maẓāraq-kanʔad-maysānī*) which includes wahoo, kingfish and Spanish mackerel	GAr *xabbaṭ*, Sh. *xabbāṭ*, Bl. *xobāt* 'fish sp.'
195. *xubr*	fish sp. similar to *āmur*, but much larger	
196. *xwaykar*	bigeye trevally	
197. *ẓbayšō*	small fish sp. with black speckles	
198. *ẓbēdī*	fish sp. (description and identification uncertain; possibly pomfret)	GAr *zbēdī* 'fish sp.', Sh. *zəbēdi* 'fusilier sp.', Bn. *zobayda* 'pomfret', Mn. *zobādi*, Bl. *zobeydī* 'black pomfret'; cf. also K. *ẓubd* 'butter', Ar. *zubd* 'foam, froth'

References

A'lam, Hušang. 1999. 'Fish, ii. Salt Water Fishes'. *Encyclopaedia Iranica* IX: 668–71. New York: Center for Iranian Studies, Columbia University. https://www.iranicaonline.org/articles/fish-ii, accessed 1 September 2021.

Anonby, Erik. 2006. 'Bāhendayal: Bird Classification in Luri'. *Journal of Ethnobiology* 26 (1): 1–35.

———. 2011. 'Illustrations of the IPA: Kumzari'. *Journal of the International Phonetic Association* 41 (3): 375–80. https://doi.org/10.1017/S0025100311000314, accessed 1 September 2021.

———. 2012. 'Stress-Induced Vowel Lengthening and Harmonization in Kumzari'. *Orientalia Suecana* 61: 54–58. https://uu.diva-portal.org/smash/record.jsf?pid=diva2:657333, accessed 1 September 2021.

———. 2015. 'The Keshmi (Qeshmi) Dialect of Hormozgan Province, Iran: A First Account'. *Studia Iranica* 44 (2): 165–206. https://doi.org/10.2143/SI.44.2.3144299, accessed 1 September 2021.

———. 2020. 'Emphatic Consonants Beyond Arabic: The Emergence and Proliferation of Uvular-Pharyngeal Emphasis in Kumzari'. *Linguistics* 58 (1): 275–328.

Anonby, Erik, AbdulQader Qasim Ali Al Kamzari, and Yousuf Ali Mohammed Al Kamzari. 2023. 'When Water Shapes Words: The Kumzari People of Musandam Peninsula and the Language of the Sea'. In *Language and Ecology in Southern and Eastern Arabia*, edited by Janet C. E. Watson, Jon C. Lovett, and Roberta Morano, 81–104. London: Bloomsbury.

Anonby, Erik, Mortaza Taheri-Ardali, and Adam Stone. 2021. 'Toward a Picture of Chahar Mahal va Bakhtiari Province, Iran, as a Linguistic Area'. *Journal of Linguistic Geography* 9: 106–41. https://doi.org/10.1017/jlg.2021.8, accessed 1 September 2021.

Anonby, Erik, Christina van der Wal Anonby, AbdulQader Qasim Ali Al Kamzari, and Yusuf Ahmed Ali Al Kamzari. 2018. 'The Language of Nature in Kumzari and the Arabic Dialects of Musandam'. Paper presented at the *Symposium on Language and Nature in Southern and Eastern Arabia*, University of Qatar, Doha, 18–20 February 2018.

Anonby, Erik, and Pakzad Yousefian. 2011. *Adaptive Multilinguals: A Survey of Language on Larak Island*. Uppsala: Acta Universitatis Upsaliensis. https://urn.kb.se/resolve?urn=urn:nbn:se:uu:diva-162008, accessed 1 September 2021.

Bayshak, Maryam Salam. 2002. 'Are There Traces of Sassanian in the Language of the Shihuh, and Is Kumzari among the Affected Varieties? The Shihhi Dialect in the Light of Linguistic Science'. *Al-Khaleej* 8541: 12. 17 October 2002. [Arabic]

Lorimer, John G. 1908–15. *Gazetteer of the Persian Gulf, Oman, and Central Arabia*. Calcutta and Bombay: Superintendent Government Printing.

MacKenzie, David N. 1971. *A Concise Pahlavi Dictionary*. Oxford: Oxford University Press.

Mohebbi Bahmani, Hassan. 2006. *A Linguistic Study and Description of the Minabi Dialect*. Tehran: Sabzān. [Persian]

Moore, Alec B. M. 2017. 'Are Guitarfishes the Next Sawfishes? Extinction Risk and an Urgent Call for Conservation Action'. *Endangered Species Research* 34: 75–88. https://doi.org/10.3354/esr00830, accessed 1 September 2021.

Morris, Miranda J., Erik Anonby, and Janet C. E. Watson. Forthcoming. 'Comparative Lexicon of Fish and Other Marine Species in Languages of Southern and Eastern Arabia'. In *Harvesting the Sea in Arabia*, vol. 2, edited by Erik

Anonby. Cambridge Semitic Languages and Cultures. Cambridge: Open Book.

Provençal, Philippe, and Birgit Skaarup. 2016. 'Arabic Fish Names Gathered at the Fish Market in Hurghada (al-Ġardaqah), May 2011'. *Journal of Semitic Studies* 61 (1): 231–46. https://doi.org/10.1093/jss/fgv038, accessed 1 September 2021.

Randall, John E. 1995. *Coastal Fishes of Oman*. Honolulu: University of Hawaii Press.

Thomas, Bertram. 1929. 'The Musandam Peninsula and Its People the Shihuh'. *Journal of the Royal Central Asian Society* 16 (1): 71–86.

van der Wal Anonby, Christina. 2014. 'Traces of Arabian in Kumzari'. In *Proceedings of the Seminar for Arabian Studies* 44: 137–46. https://www.jstor.org/stable/43782857, accessed 1 September 2021.

———. 2015. 'A Grammar of Kumzari, a Mixed Perso-Arabian Language of Oman'. PhD dissertation, Leiden University. https://openaccess.leidenuniv.nl/handle/1887/32793, accessed 1 September 2021.

———. 2023. 'The Language of Kumzari Folklore'. In *Language and Ecology in Southern and Eastern Arabia*, edited by Janet C. E. Watson, Jon C. Lovett, and Roberta Morano, 189–98. London: Bloomsbury.

———. 2024. 'Mṣaww wa Maḥḥar: The Sea in Kumzari Poetry'. In *Harvesting the Sea in Southeastern Arabia*, vol. 1, edited by Janet C. E. Watson, Miranda J. Morris, and Erik Anonby, 89–103. Cambridge Semitic Languages and Cultures. Cambridge: Open Book.

Zimmermann, Wolfgang. 1981. 'Tradition und Integration mobile Lebensformgruppen: Eine empirische Studie über Beduinen und Fischer in Musandam, Sultanat Oman'. PhD dissertation, Georg-August-Universität, Göttingen.

MṢAWW WA MAḤḤAR: THE SEA IN KUMZARI POETRY[1]

Christina van der Wal Anonby

1. Introduction

Facing the Strait of Hormuz and the Gulf of Oman, and voyaging inward to the Gulf on their seasonal migration to the oasis city of Khasab, the people who inhabit Musandam are never far from the sea. It is integral to Kumzari culture; an intimate knowledge of the marine geography, tides, sea creatures and plants that surround their remote peninsula is vital to their existence as fishers.

Like the flooding seas that created their coastal villages, values inseparable from their environment shape Kumzari society. Folktales and narrative poems bring to mind an indigenous perspective of nature as it flows through their daily interactions. Surrounded and sometimes inundated by the sea, literature and livelihood join to echo the reality that their decisions are ultimately overruled by the capriciousness of the sea.

---

[1] The author wishes to gratefully acknowledge the kindness and expertise of the storyteller, the late Mr Aliko Abdullah Shobubo al-Kumzari, and the language consultant, Mr Noufal Mohammad Ahmed al-Kumzari.

In the traditional folktale *Sōntyō* (=S), a sheikh's daughter refuses the offers of many suitors, and instead asks for a boat to be built so that she can travel the seas to meet her fate. The poem embedded in the tale follows a description of carpenters building the dhow to her specifications, which include making it impermeable to the sea (S47–61):

> *dgō ba yē kin ba mē sōntī-ē.*
> *sōntī-ē gap byār,*
> *lōḥī gap-ē na,*
> *wa kin ba mē inda yē xānaǧ-ē.*
> *xānaǧ-ē kin ba mē inda yē,*
> *qafala pi wā = indur,*
> *āw byāt na,*
> *inda yē na,*
> *āw sōr-ō na.*

> She said to him, "Make me a raft.
> A big raft bring,
> that is a big wooden one,
> and make for me inside it a house.
> A house make for me inside it,
> [that] locks from the inside,
> so that water cannot go,
> inside it cannot go,
> [so that] seawater [cannot go]."

Even in this preamble to the poem, there are instances of poetic anadiplosis and epiphora bolstering the girl's efforts to withstand the sea. Anadiplosis links the 'tail' and 'head' of successive clauses by repeating the words *sōntī* 'raft' and *xānaǧ* 'house' at the end of one line and the beginning of the next: *kin ba mē* **sōntī**-*ē. sōntī-ē gap byār* 'Make me a **raft**. A big **raft** bring' and *kin ba mē inda yē* **xānaǧ**-*ē. xānaǧ-ē kin ba mē inda yē* 'make for me inside it a **house**. A **house** make for me inside it'. Epiphora repeats the last word of successive lines. In this case the negative *na* harnesses Kumzari grammar, which obliges each verbal complement to be negated: *āw byāt **na**, inda yē **na**, āw sōr-ō **na**,* literally: 'that water comes **not**, inside it **not**, sea water **not**'. In both forms of poetic repetition, the girl is refusing to allow the whims of the sea to diminish her construction.

The poem begins by introducing a direct quote from the sheikh's daughter, who gives her father instructions for where to launch the dhow. The poem continues to the end in a narrative of her travels. In reciting place names and sea conditions, her poem is reminiscent of the poems Gulf Arab sea navigators used to memorise sea routes, citing departure dates and ports, currents, seasons, winds, reefs, whirlpools, and tides (Lancaster and Lancaster 2011, 47).

In parallel to the change of plans in the girl's marriage, the fine details of her boat are lost to the sea as it becomes covered in barnacles, oysters, and green algae over the course of her journey. Her destination also reflects this break with an expected fate: in the distant land where her boat washes ashore, the girl meets the sheikh's son but hides in her boat. The prince follows her to the boat and then symbolically marries the boat before all is set to right and they voyage back together to her country.

2. Sea Poem from *Sōntyō*

(from S82–237)

xālaṣ tō'at = ā	82	When it is finished,
bō kard mē dirya-ō	83	go and plunge me into the sea.

kard-ī mē dirya-ō = ā	85	Plunging me into the sea,
bar mē ba mōmur wākiš mē	87	carry me to Mōmur Island, [there] release me.
ar jāga br-um	90	I shall go anywhere.
bard-in yē āw-an	172	They carried [the dhow] to the water.
wa dār-iš yē ba lenj-ō	173	And [the sheikh] gave [his daughter] to the dhow,
bard-in yē ba mōmur	174	They carried it to Mōmur Island.
wākid-in yē	177	[There] they released it.
abāra... āw-ō ōğar-ē = ā	179	Like... the ebbing tide goes out,
duġ-a yē ba quxayg	183	it took her to Quxayg Rock and
wa āw-ō čōt bāla purya = ā	185	the flowing tide comes in,
tēbur-a yē ba sar mistō	187	it carries her to Cape Mistō.
wa lenj-an tēmuš-in yē	190	When dhows see it [the boat],
č-in ba yē	191	they go to it,
rāy-in na abaša yē tk-in na	192	they cannot catch it.
rāy-in na sī-in yē nēxan na	193	They cannot bring it aboard,
gap-ē na = ā?	195	it being such a big one! you know?
xall gid-iš	197	It was covered with green algae,
mṣaww gid-iš	199	It was covered with barnacles,
maḥḥar gid-iš	200	It was covered with oysters,
wa ğaẓara gid-iš inda āw-an	203	It was covered with water,
yē wa āw-an sātē tā-ē = in	204	sinking until it was one [level] with the water.
inča xall ba yē	207	Like this, there was green algae on it
wa maḥḥar ba yē wa	208	and oysters on it and...
mād laba si-mā-an	212	time went by, about three months,
čār mā-an dirya-ō	213	four months, she was at sea,
čār panj mā-an	214	four or five months.
ammū ādamī jīr-in yē	215	All the people saw it.

ar čōt ba yē = ā	217	[but] of anyone who went to it [to look at it],
kas tāt-a yē na	218	no one wanted it.
ka byō nāšī būr	220	Then it came about that there was a storm wind. A nor'easter.
nāšī nāšī-ō āmad		
ḥamya wābur inda walēyit-ē	222	The storm wind blew up, [the boat] became beached in a country,
inda rāṣ xaymē inda lēmē	228	in Ras al-Khaimah, in Limah,
inda jāgē'ē ya'nī	230	in somewhere, that is to say.
ḥamya wābur ba čāf-ō	231	[The boat] became beached on the shore,
nāšī-ō wād-iš yē	232	the storm wind brought it,
ḥamya gid-iš bāla ba āw-ō gābanō-ō	233	beached it high on the spring tide.
araṭa yē gid-iš	235	It [the storm] stuck it [the boat].
āw-ō čōt pi yē ẓēran	237	Water flowed down from it.

3. Geography

The sea poem in *Sōntyō* begins with the certainty of known geography near to the girl's home, and ends with her uncertain fate in an unknown land. The sheikh's daughter gives very specific commands for where her newly built dhow should be put in the water. Her instructions rely on both the teller's and listeners' extensive knowledge of regional maritime geography. They know not only the places that would be obscure to outsiders, but also the weather and tidal conditions near those landmarks and their potential effects on her outbound voyage. The girl mentions *Mōmur*, a small island in the Gulf. The poem then situates her journey as the waves carry her out to a rock, named *Quxayg*, to where the tides are known to ebb at that time, and further on to flow into Cape *Mistō*, where other boats are passing by. Her boat finally becomes beached (*ḥamya*) on a shore (*čāf*). The faraway land where the storm washes her is characterised as being 'somewhere like' the distant cities of *rāṣ xaymē* (Ras al-Khaimah) on the inner coast and *lēmē* (Limah) on the outer coast of Musandam Peninsula. Both cities are destinations for Kumzari commerce and social relations, and represent the outer extent of Kumzari traditional territory, beyond which is classified as foreign.

At the point in the poem where the storyteller is reciting regional maritime geographical marks and place names familiar to listeners, the verb form used changes from the usual narrative verb form in realis aspect, to the imperfect (S179–95): **bard-in** *yē āw-an* 'They **carried** it to the water'... *purya=ā* **tēbur-a** *yē ba sar mistō* 'The flowing tide **carries** her to Cape Mistō'. The imperfect is used in Kumzari for ongoing or habitual actions, and appeals to the audience's commonly held detailed knowledge of the local tides and seascape.

An intricate acquaintance with coastal geography is necessary to navigate daily life in Kumzar. The lay of land and sea ties into every aspect of their lives. Knowing the exact location of small islands and jutting rocks in the Gulf saves them from shipwreck when there is a storm or fraught passage of sea-going vessels of all sizes. Each bit of rock is given a name, imbued with meaning pointing to its place in Kumzari history and culture. Some islands are used as pasture for itinerant herds of goats, but only in certain seasons, depending on rainfall. Others are landmarks for nearby whirlpools, fishing grounds, or distance from shore. Long inlets (*xōr*), whose locations were sometimes hidden behind limestone cliffs but known locally, in the past were used by ships to shelter from pirates and storms. The proceeds of storms, by depositing boats for repair, bolstered economies in villages along the fjords (Lancaster and Lancaster 2011, 56). Now as in the past, the distant harbours of Ras al-Khaimah and Limah are visited for their markets, to sell fish, goats, and dates, and to buy cloth and metal goods (Thomas 1929; Lancaster and Lancaster 2011, 52–53).

4. Tides and Weather

Kumzari livelihood relies on deep understanding of the tides and weather around Musandam. Various types of wind are named, moon phases are tracked, and seasonal rhythms are followed. Close attention to the tides and weather is both a means of survival as essential to fishing and twice-yearly travel to date plantations, and a central determinant of timing for visits to coastal markets and weddings. The sea poem in *Sōntyō* describes how the *ōğar* 'ebbing tide' carries the princess's boat out to Quxayg rock, and the *purya* 'flowing tide' takes her toward the coast. The wiles of the *nāšī* 'nor'easter storm wind' are a familiar force in the Gulf, whipping up large waves that cause both fish and fishers to retreat to their abodes.

Accurately reading the waves keeps people from traversing potentially deadly seas. In the past, sailors from beyond Musandam avoided the peninsula due to its choppy seas, strong currents, whirlpools, and fickle winds (Lancaster and Lancaster 2011, 55), instead trading their cargoes at ports on the outer coast (e.g., Dibba) or having a Kumzari guide them through the Strait. In *Sōntyō*, listeners recognise both the recklessness and bravery demonstrated by the princess as she embarked on the dangerous voyage; she prepared well but then yielded her fate to the sea.

In the *Sōntyō* poem, the princess makes it clear that her voyage is a matter of life and death, dependent on her fate at sea:

5. Excerpt from *Sōntyō*

(S92–103)

murd-um inda sōnty-ō y' = ā,	92	If I should die on that boat,
inda ḥamya būr-um, wa	93	If I should become beached, and
ra-m wa = bāla,	94	If I should go up,
ra-m maġrāb,	95	If I should go west,
ra-m mašrāq,	96	If I should go east,
ana yā tkī ba mē	97	If these things befall me,
balkē mān-um zindaġ.	99	Perhaps I will stay alive.
wa ana tēl-ī mē jāga mē	100	And if you make me stay where I am,
inda walēyit-ō = ā, tumr-um.	102	In this country, I shall die.

The tides and wind carry her boat east or west, out to sea or beached on the shore, and her eventual route determines the consequences in her future.

An intuitive orientation to the tides and weather preserves the Kumzari way of life. Visibility conditions, ocean depths, and the strength and duration of winds govern when people travel and when they take shelter in the village. Depending on these factors, they will subsist on dried fish or venture out to sea for a fresh catch. They may visit their regular fishing grounds or choose to avoid the parade of tankers, military boats, and smugglers in the waters of the Strait. Regularities of climate provide for scheduling of celebrations and memorials as well as seasonal migration between the oasis town and the fishing village. Conversely, many times important cultural events are lost to a sudden storm.

In the *Sōntyō* story a storm is magnified by a *gābanō* 'spring tide', causing the princess's boat to be deposited extremely high on the shore. Repetition of key words in the embedded poem, such as *nāšī* 'storm wind' and *ḥamya* 'beached', reiterates the sea's control over the wanderings of the girl's boat (S220–33).

> *ka byō*
> > *nāšī būr*
> > *nāšī*
> > *nāšī-ō āmad*
>
> *ḥamya wābur*
> > *inda walēyit-ē*
> > *inda rāṣ xaymē*
> > *inda lēmē*
> > *inda jāgē'ē ya'nī*
>
> *ḥamya wābur ba čāf-ō*
> > *nāšī-ō wād-iš yē*
>
> *ḥamya gid-iš bāla ba āw-ō gābanō-ō.*

Then it came about that there was
> A **storm wind**.
> A **storm wind**.
> A **storm wind** blew up, [the boat] became

beached
> in a country,
> in Ras al-Khaimah,
> in Limah,

in somewhere, that is to say.
[The boat] became
beached on the shore,
the **storm wind** brought it,
beached it high on the spring tide.

In the end it is this storm wind and spring tide, and not the resolutions of the girl or her father the sheikh, that carry her to her fate on a foreign shore.

Figure 1: Kumzari *lenj* (dhow), Strait of Hormuz

Photo © Christina van der Wal Anonby, March 2006

6. Sea Creatures and Plants

Recitation of the various living things that entangled her boat is in itself a repeated pattern in the sea poem's list section: all the creatures and plants the boat had *gidiš* 'taken on' prevented it from being *nēxan* 'boarded' by passing ships, because 'no one wanted it' (S218; S190–204):

> *wa lenj-an tēmuš-in yē*
> *č-in ba yē*
>   *rāy-in **na***
>   *abaša yē tk-in **na***
>   *rāy-in **na***
>   *sī-in yē nēxan **na***
> *gap-ē na = ā?*
>   *xall **gid-iš***
>   *mṣaww **gid-iš***
>   *maḥḥar **gid-iš***
>   *wa ğaẓara **gid-iš***
>   *inda **āw-an***
>   *yē wa **āw-an***
> *sātē tā-ē = in*

When dhows see it [the boat],
they go to it,
    they **cannot**
   catch it **cannot**
    They **cannot**
  bring it aboard **cannot**,
it being such a big one! you know?
   It was covered with green algae,
   It was covered with barnacles,
   It was covered with oysters, and
   It was covered
        with **water**,
sinking until it was one [level] with the **water**.

The girl's carefully constructed boat was overwhelmed by the stuff of the sea. Despite the distinctions of boatbuilding the carpenters took to ensure, the craft was exactly what she wanted (*hã, bābā! či tātī?* 'well, child, what do you want?' [S45]), when her boat became overtaken by algae and barnacles, *ammū ādimī jīr-in yē=ā, ar čōt ba yē=ā, kas tāt-a yē na.* 'All the people who saw it, anyone who went to it, no one wanted it.' (S215). Being covered in the detritus of the sea, her boat was presumed by onlookers to have been abandoned. The *xall* 'green algae', *mṣaww* 'barnacles', and *maḥḥar* 'oysters' that blight the boat are associated with a lack of maintenance on a sea vessel. The untameability of nature, symbolised in *Sōntyō* by the boat's becoming one with the sea and being taken over by sea creatures and plants, is the very characteristic that causes people to reject it. Its newfound wildness draws a sharp contrast to the care the princess took in originally constructing the boat, and foreshadows the futility of human sovereignty over nature.

7. Natural and Supernatural

Nature mentions in Kumzari folk tales are closely tied to magic, so that as the belief in magic fades, so too does knowledge of the natural and supernatural world. Reliance on nature for livelihood becomes tenuous as people take up other forms of work, in domains where the need for indigenous knowledge is lessened. Knowledge of business and government begins to encroach in precedence over knowledge of the sea and coastline as local economies change. This change is no better encapsulated than in the declining use of goatskin-and-cowrie-shell belts that traditionally adorned the bow and stern of Kumzari boats to protect against malevolent spirits.

A common saying among people of the Gulf is "The sea belongs to God, the land belongs to us" (Nadjmabadi 1992).

While the landscape is manipulable to humans, the sea is much more difficult to appease. The diminishing centrality of nature as an economic resource distances people from the sense of mystery and otherness that is the supernatural. Abandonment of seafaring likewise brings about the disappearance of oral traditions that uphold maritime life, such as poems used to memorise sea routes and songs for navigating the complex waterways of the Gulf (Lancaster and Lancaster 2011, 47). Economic and spiritual livelihoods are intertwined, thus dependence on the natural and supernatural wanes concurrently.

In the *Sōntyō* tale, as the princess in her boat journeys farther from the Kumzari experience and beaches on the shores of a distant land, new characters fall into downplaying the connection with nature. The foreign sheikh voices their communal disgust with the algae-covered boat: *sāl-ē di-sāl kaft-ē durya-ō!* 'For a year or two, it has been in the sea!' (S524). In the new country, the boat takes on a supernatural cast when the sheikh's son decides to marry it instead of marrying his uncle's daughter. The boat "squeaks" its oath as the marriage ceremony proceeds with the princess hidden inside (S588). Later in the tale, perhaps foreshadowing the lessening importance of the boat and of the natural world it represents, the sheikh's men threaten to break the boat to pieces, literally: to 'smash it into firewood'. They do not have the last word, however.

When the princess finally emerges from the boat, she breaks the spell of the mystery of the boat whom the prince has married, by exclaiming of the people: *sā bā rū mē jīr-in* 'Now they have seen my face!' (S829). In revealing her true character and separating herself from the boat, she breaks with her identity as an agent of the sea.

8. *Sōntyō*'s Destination

Throughout the poem narrating the princess's voyage, the action moves from the ordinary ebb and flow of tides close to home, to unpredictability in the capriciousness of a *nāšī* storm combined with an unusually high spring tide. The beaching places her boat in a new place beyond her control.

The sheikh's daughter goes from turning away marriage offers to marrying herself off posing as a boat, in a surprising twist of events for listeners. Reflecting the action linguistically, in lines 192–93 in *Sōntyō* the repeated negation *na* inherent in the grammar takes a poetic role, and reflects the girl's refusal to marry except on her own terms, after her boat is inundated with the detritus of the sea. Passing ships want to capture her boat, but the forces of nature prevent them, and they give it up to the sea. The girl declines marriage offers, but after her struggle against the confines of her country and being tossed on the waves, gives in and marries the boy to whom the sea has brought her.

A common cultural theme conveyed in Kumzari literature and life is reflected here: humans can decide things for themselves, but in reality, life is decided by the whims of nature. Similarly, Kumzaris have a traditional calendar that notes the best times for fishing based on tides and regular weather conditions, but this has become much less reliable in recent years, with out-of-season storms, catastrophes like the red tide algal bloom, and pollution of the sea by tankers.

References

Dostal, Walter. 1972. 'The Shihuh of Northern Oman: A Contribution to Cultural Ecology'. *The Geographical Journal* 138: 1–7.

Lancaster, William, and Fidelity Lancaster. 2011. *Honour Is in Contentment: Life Before Oil in Ras al-Khaimah (UAE) and Some Neighbouring Regions*. Berlin: de Gruyter.

Miles, Samuel B. 1994. *The Countries and Tribes of the Persian Gulf*. Reading: Garnet.

Nadjmabadi, Shahnaz. 1992. '"The Sea Belongs to God, the Land Belongs to Us": Resource Management in a Multi-Resource Community in the Persian Gulf'. In *Mobility and Territoriality: Social and Spatial Boundaries among Foragers, Fishers, Pastoralists, and Peripatetics*, edited by Michael J. Casimir and Aparnu Rao, 329–42. Oxford: Berg.

Thomas, Bertram. 1929. 'The Musandam Peninsula and Its People the Shihuh'. *Journal of the Royal Central Asian Society* 16: 71–86.

THREE ARABIC FISHING SONGS FROM THE MUSANDAM PENINSULA[1]

Erik Anonby and Simone Bettega

1. Introduction

The coasts of the Arabian Peninsula are home to fishing communities with rich and diverse oral traditions. While various other types of texts have been recorded, fishing songs of the Gulf have received little attention. The present study seeks to fill this gap through documentation of three Arabic fishing songs from the Musandam Peninsula of eastern Arabia, at the border between the main body of the Gulf and the Batinah coast of northern Oman. Although these are short texts—when repeti-

---

[1] The contributions of each author are as follows: Anonby—data collection and archiving, linguistic analysis, article drafting and revision; Bettega—linguistic analysis, article drafting and revision. We wish to thank the consultant for this study, Muḥammad Salūm al-Ḍhuhūrī, for sharing his knowledge and time with us. We are deeply grateful to Dr Maryam Bayshak for assistance with the initial transcription and translation, and for input on a number of challenging questions in the analysis; and to Dr Wolfgang Zimmermann for generously supporting the field research through planning, sharing of his contacts with community members, and logistical support. Partial support for the publication of this study has been granted through the Carleton University Research Impact Endeavour (CURIE) Fund.

tion is set aside, the longest is only ten lines—through them we are welcomed into the vanishing musical and literary treasury that has long been integral to the harvesting of the sea in Arabia. The songs also provide a window into the interplay among linguistic structures reflecting varied geographical provenance, social registers, and musical and literary style.

This study opens with a description of the Musandam Peninsula and the languages spoken there (1.1.). We set the stage for our study through a brief introduction to oral traditions of the Gulf, reviewing existing literature on this topic and reflecting on the enduring importance of these oral traditions, with a focus on fishing songs (1.2.). We then introduce the research context, the consultant, and the corpus of three songs that we will analyse: *ayāllā* 'O God', *xəbbāṭ* 'little kingfish', and *lā ramētə* 'I will not give it up' (1.3.). The body of the study consists of the presentation and analysis of these songs (2.–4.). We conclude with reflections on the purpose, musical and literary structure, and dialectal patterning of the Arabic in these songs within the wider regional language situation (5.).

1.1. The Musandam Peninsula and Its Languages

At the northern extremity of eastern Arabia, the Musandam Peninsula extends like a jagged finger into the Strait of Hormuz, between the waters of the Gulf and those of the Arabian Sea (Figure 1). Echoing the peninsula's geography, the languages spoken here are linguistically idiosyncratic and peripheral. The main language of the region is a collection of distinctive Arabic dialects with historical and linguistic connections to southwestern Arabia (van der Wal Anonby 2014a, 2014b; Anonby, Bettega, and Procházka 2022). Musandam is also home to Kumzari, an endangered language with fewer than 5000 speakers, that exhibits a deep mixture of Iranic and Semitic components at all levels of the language. Kumzari speakers likewise trace their origins to southwestern Arabia (van der Wal Anonby 2014a; Anonby and Yousefian 2011).

Figure 1: The Musandam Peninsula in the context of Arabia. The location of Habalayn, where the field research was carried out, is indicated with a white star.

© Erik Anonby, 2021 (CC BY 4.0). Background imagery © Google, Landsat, Terrametrics, 2021, used in accordance with Fair Use policies for the purposes of education.

This study focuses on the Arabic of the Musandam Peninsula. Musandam Arabic (hereafter MusAr) was first described cursorily by Jayakar (1904), followed up by a sketch of one particular variety by Bernabela (2011) more than a century later. Anonby, Bettega, and Procházka (2022) have also provided a historical and cross-dialectal comparison of singular demonstrative in

MusAr, while Bettega and Gasparini (2022) present a short text in the dialect of Lima. Often referred to in the literature as Shihhi (*šəḥḥī*) Arabic, in reference to the dominant Shihuh (*šəḥūḥ*) clans of the region, MusAr varieties are also spoken by Dhohuri (*ḍəhūrī*) people and by longstanding city dwellers (*ḥāḍarī*). The most distinctive varieties are those spoken in the fishing villages of the north coast, and the Bedouin dialects of the peninsula's central heights: both the mountains, and the dialects spoken there, are referred to as *rʔūs əl-yəbāl*, lit. 'heads of the mountains'. In contrast, the urban dialects spoken in the peninsula's two largest cities, Khasab and Daba (Dibba) are close to Arabic dialects of the wider Gulf region, and the other dialects spoken along the coast toward the main mass of Arabia are also transitional to Gulf Arabic (Anonby, Bettega, and Procházka 2022; see also the 'Map of Musandam' found at the beginning of this section).

1.2. Oral Literature and Fishing Songs in the Gulf

It is well-known that a rich corpus of oral literature exists in the traditions of the people who inhabit the southern shores of the Gulf. This corpus is largely, though not exclusively, connected to the main historical livelihoods along these coasts: maritime trade, fishing and the *ġōṣ* (pearl diving).

Although over the course of the last century the socio-economic reality of the Gulf coast has undergone dramatic changes, and very little of the traditional customs of life at sea in the region has survived, these oral arts are still commonly reenacted on specific occasions, such as weddings, festivals, or even private reunions among friends and relatives.

In spite of the fact that these oral traditions are still widely popular among Gulf nationals, they have to this day received little attention from scholars of Arabic in the West. Around the turn of the last century, a number of Omani folktales were collected and transcribed by a group of German dialectologists residing in the region (Sachau 1898; Rössler 1898, 1900; Brode 1902; and most notably Reinhardt 1894). In the same period, Jayakar published a collection of Omani proverbs (Jayakar 1900–1903, later amended and re-published posthumously as Jayakar 1987). Still, to the best of our knowledge, no analysis exists of the linguistic features that characterise the traditional Arabic fishing songs of the Gulf, along with Oman.[2]

In the following pages, we will present and analyse three such songs, collected in 2018 by Erik Anonby in Habalayn, on the north-eastern coast of the Musandam Peninsula. These songs are sung by Muḥammad Salūm al-Ḍhuhūrī, a retired fisherman.

These songs are exponents of a particularly popular genre in Gulf culture referred to as *nihmāt* (sg. *nihma*). They were heard aboard vessels all over the Gulf, from Kuwait to the northern shores of Oman, and beyond;[3] as we will see, the lin-

---

[2] An interesting, non-academic account of the subject, found in a recent article from the online magazine *Newlines* (available at: https://newlinesmag.com/reportage/the-forgotten-sea-shanties-of-the-gulf), testifies to the uninterrupted vitality of these traditions.

[3] Agius (2019, 119–21) provides several examples of sea shanties from the Red Sea and discusses general characteristics of this genre.

guistic elements they contain testify to this transregional distribution. As is the case with traditional sea shanties and fishing songs from other parts of the world, the main purpose of these melodies was to encourage the crew and boost their morale during the long hours of wearisome and often dangerous work. They also helped sailors keep the rhythm of their labour aboard the ship: this was the case for a specific subtype of *nihma*, called *yāmāl*, which was also used as a measure of time. In the Gulf, it was customary for the crew of each ship to include an individual specifically tasked with the singing of these tunes (the so-called *nahhām*; on all these topics, see Holes 2005, 6).

The Introduction to this compendium highlights the importance of 'translanguaging', where multilingual people interact with one another in multiple languages, among the communities that subsist through harvesting the sea around the coasts of Arabia. As Anonby and Al Kamzari (2024) have illustrated, this sociolinguistic phenomenon is operational in the context of the Kumzari language community on Musandam Peninsula, and many Kumzari fish names are shared with other languages in the wider region. The present study provides an intricate picture of the ways in which different varieties of Arabic—Gulf Arabic, Modern Standard Arabic, and the speaker's particular dialect of MusAr—coexist and oscillate in the context of such fishing songs.

1.3. Research Context, Consultant, and Corpus

The research for this study was carried out as part of the activities inspired by Janet C. E. Watson's workshops on *The Symbi-*

otic Relationship between Language and Nature in Southern and Eastern Arabia, funded by the Arts and Humanities Research Council (AHRC) and hosted at the Centre for Endangered Languages, Cultures and Ecosystems (CELCE) at the University of Leeds since 2017.

Alongside fieldwork for a separate project on the linguistic geography of Musandam Peninsula in 2018 (see Anonby, Bettega, and Procházka 2022), Erik Anonby collected oral texts featuring aspects of the peninsula's natural features, with a double focus on mountains and the sea.

Figure 2: Habalayn in late afternoon,
in the shadow of the mountain to the west

Photo © Erik Anonby, 2018 (CC BY 4.0).

The texts described in this study were collected in Habalayn (*ḥabalēn*), a fishing village on the north-eastern coast of Musandam Peninsula. Habalayn is nestled in the innermost reaches of the Habalayn *xōr* ('inlet', often locally translated into English as 'fjord'). It is backed by a steep ridge and protected from the winds of the open Indian Ocean by the encircling walls of the inlet. The settlement itself is accessible from the cities of the region only by sea (Figures 2 and 3).

Figure 3: Xōr Ḥabalēn (Habalayn Inlet). This photo shows the approach, by road, to a cove from which Habalayn can be reached by boat. Habalayn itself is located to the north, beyond the headlands visible on the left.

Photo © Erik Anonby, 2018 (CC BY 4.0).

There, Anonby worked with Muḥammad Salūm al-Ḍhuhūrī (Figure 4), a retired fisherman, 62 years old at the time, who now lives in Sharjah but returns to Habalayn on the weekends. When asked about oral texts relating to nature, al-Ḍhuhūrī sang the three fishing songs that we present in this study: *ayāllā* 'O God' (2.), *xəbbāṭ* 'little kingfish' (3.), and *lā ramētə* 'I will not give it up' (4.). Video and audio recordings of these songs have been archived in the *Arabian Peninsula Languages Dataverse* (Anonby, Bettega, and Procházka 2022) and are accessible at the following DOI: 10.5683/SP3/T7OIXY. In the following sections, which constitute the core of this study, we analyze and discuss each of the songs, considering lexicon, phonological features, and salient aspects of morphosyntax.

Figure 4: Muḥammad Salūm al-Ḍhuhūrī, consultant for this study.

Photo © Erik Anonby, 2018 (CC BY 4.0).

2. *Ayāllā* 'O God'

In the first song, *ayāllā* 'O God', the fisherman exhorts himself to brave the waves and continue working at sea, without resting. The consultant recounts that, in addition to being sung at sea, this song is sung at the mosque to the beating of the great *ṭabəl* 'drums' during the celebration of weddings.

> 1 ṣədag mən gāl wa-tkalla[m]⁴
> 2 ayāllā mā bə-kəlmət əmzāḥa
> 3 ayāllā mōyə baḥar b-aʿlī ba
> 4 ayāllā lā səmēt bə-r-rāḥa

> 1 He was telling the truth, who said and spoke:
> 2 O God, without a word of jest
> 3 O God, waves, sea, I will ride it
> 4 O God, I don't hear of rest

The song is constructed around these four lines. The lines are repeated in an ordered fashion, so that the whole text consists of 14 lines structured as follows: 1 2 3 4 / 1 2 3 4 / 3 4 3 4 / 1 2.

Each line starts with a melody in the major mode, but ends with a finely modulated minor melody employing quarter tones.

2.1. Wording

There are several minor variations in the wording of the lines as they are repeated. The second time that line 1 is sung, it starts with the invocation *ayāllā* 'O God', as invariably found in lines 2 to 4, but this word is omitted in the other two occurrences of

---

[4] Because some phonemic distinctions, especially vowel length and quality, are neutralised as part of the singing styles of these songs, we have transcribed segments based on the phonology of the spoken language rather than strict phonetic values. We describe the relationship between the spoken and sung phonology in the discussion of each song. In cases where segments are dropped completely as an effect of the song's structure, they are indicated using square brackets ([ ]).

line 1. In the latter two repetitions of line 3, the order of the words *mōyə* 'wave' and *baḥar* 'sea' is reversed, a fitting symbolic echo of the changeable waters. Finally, in the third repetition of verse 4, negation is expressed with the morpheme *mā* rather than *lā*.

2.2. Phonology

This song presents several notable phonological traits, helping to situate it with respect to geographically and socially defined registers. We look first at features of historical phonology (2.2.1.) and then bring together several interconnected discourse-related phonological features (2.2.2.). Brief observations on the consultant's own phonological traits are also included (2.2.3.).

2.2.1. Historical Phonology

As a first feature of historical segmental phonology, etymological **q* systematically surfaces as *g* (cf. *ṣədag* 'right' and *gāl* 'he said', line 1). This contrasts with the usual value (*q*) of this historical phoneme in the consultant's spoken language and in all other documented dialects throughout the Musandam Peninsula (Jayakar 1904; Bernabela 2011; Bettega, field notes 2014, 2016; Anonby, field notes 2018), instead aligning itself with the *g* reflex typical of the Gulf coast.[5]

---

[5] The *g* reflex is found in most varieties along the entire Gulf coast of Arabia, extending from southern Iraq all the way to the Batinah coast of northern Oman. Among some linguistic minorities in this area, however, *q* is the normal reflex of this sound. This is most notably the

Similarly, the phonetic value of *r*, which is realised as an alveolar flap [ɾ] in *baḥar* 'sea' (line 3) and *rāḥa* 'rest (n.)' (line 4) does not conform to the retroflex realisations typical of MusAr (approximant [ɻ] and a flap [ɽ]) (Bernabela 2011, 24–25; Jayakar 1904, 249–50; Bettega and Gasparini 2022, 210). Therefore, this second trait also situates the song outside the structural norms of the Peninsula's dialects.

In the repeated invocation *ayāllā* 'O God', the emphatic *ḷ* typically used in the word 'God' in Standard Arabic and as well as Arabic vernaculars (Ferguson 1956) is pronounced light, as *l*. The reasons for the choice of this form, whether dialectal or stylistic, are unclear to us.

The behaviour of the voiced pharyngeal *ˤ in this song is also less clearly diagnostic, but in this case because of its variability in the song. This historical phoneme is stable across almost all of the Arabic-speaking world. In the dialects of Musandam, however, it has been described as shifted to glottal stop ʔ or entirely lost (this second option is common in word-medial codas; see Bernabela 2011, 26). Anonby (field notes, 2018) has documented the occurrence of ˤ as a stable phoneme in the *ḥāḍarī* (urban) dialects of Khasab and Daba, but the spoken dialect of the consultant follows the more typical dialects of

---

case of the Baḥārna communities of Bahrain (Holes 2016) and certain villages in eastern Saudi Arabia such as Abu Thor and al-Qatif (Prochazka 1988 and 1990). In Oman, the situation is more complex, because while coastal settlements tend to have *g* or a mixture of *q* and *g*, in the interior one normally hears *q*—though even here it is also possible to find communities of Bedouin descent that systematically use *g*.

Musandam in relation to this feature. In the song here, we find two patterns attested: historical ʕ is retained in aʕlī 'I mount, I ride' (line 3), but is dropped altogether in səmēt 'I heard' (line 4).

The patterning of *ǧ is similarly ambivalent, not because it is variable—in this song it occurs only once, reflected as y in mōyə 'wave' (line 3)—but because the geographic distribution of the reflexes of *ǧ are uneven, both within and outside of Musandam Peninsula. With the exception of Khasab's ḥāḍarī dialects, where g is found, the dominant reflex of *ǧ across Musandam is y (Anonby, field notes, 2018). Interestingly, in the spoken language of the consultant, a palatal fricative allophone [j̵] (still acting as a contrastive phoneme j) dominates in word-initial position, but is more commonly merged with approximant y [j] intervocalically.[6] The pronunciation of y in mōyə matches its usual form in the wider Gulf region, where one normally encounters y (except in Oman, where g is the most common reflex; j [d͡ʒ] can also be heard sporadically across the Gulf, both because some minority dialects actually have this sound in their consonantal inventories, and because of the influence of Standard Arabic).[7] The y form appearing in this song is therefore not geographically diagnostic, since it fits in well with prevalent patterns locally and regionally.

---

[6] Anonby, field notes, 2018. This is similar to the 'free variation' that Bernabela identifies between j [d͡ʒ] and y [j] in the Jadi (əl-Ǧēdih) dialect of MusAr.

[7] For *ǧ > y in Gulf Arabic, see Johnstone (1965) and Holes (2018, 141). For *ǧ > g in Oman, see Holes (1989) and Davey (2016, 45–46).

While many dialects of MusAr exhibit *ō* (whether consistently or variably) in place of historical **ā*, in the spoken dialect of the consultant *ā* persists in all such cases (Anonby, field notes 2018) and this is the case in the song as well (for example, *rāḥa* 'rest' in line 4). Therefore, the patterning of this potentially diagnostic vowel is not pertinent for identifying the dialectal alignment of the song.

Two additional features in the phonology relate to the patterning of vowels. First, the so-called '*gahawa* syndrome', where in an *a* + guttural + C sequence the vowel *a* has been copied and inserted between the guttural and the following consonant, appears to operate in the item (*baḥr >) *baḥar* 'sea' (line 3). The *gahawa* syndrome is a common phenomenon in Gulf Arabic, though it is less clear how widespread it is in MusAr. While Bernabela (2011) makes no specific comment as to this point, Anonby (field notes, 2018) views it as a more generalised, predictable insertion of a short vowel between the final consonant cluster in most CVCC sequences in this speaker's dialect (e.g., *šəmaš* 'sun', *əšəb* 'grass') as well as other dialects of MusAr. Whatever the phonological basis for this patterning here, the two-syllable expression of this word is convenient from the point of view of the song's rhythm and metre.

A second vowel-related feature in this song is the occurence of so-called *ʾimāla*,[8] where final *a in non-guttural, non-emphatic environments is raised, whether to [ə] in the final syl-

---

[8] Literally, 'inclination' or 'leaning', the term *ʾimāla* is used in Arabic linguistics to refer to the raising and fronting of *a* and *ā* (Levin 2007; see Holes (2016, 67) for the patterning of this sound in Bahrain).

lable of *kəlmət* 'word' (line 2), or to [ɛ] at the end of *mōyə* 'wave' (line 3). (In both cases, the final vowel is phonologically neutralised, filling the place of both *a* and *ə* in these positions; we have chosen the symbol *ə* to make clear the raised value of the segment.) This differs from the non-raised realisation of *a* as [a] following the guttural *ḥ* in *əmzāḥa* 'joking' (line 2) and *rāḥa* 'rest (n.)' (line 4).[9]

2.2.2. Discourse-Level Phonology

In addition to segmental features shaped by dialectal sources and influences on the song, there are several discourse-level features that seem to be related to the genre of the text itself as a fishing song.

First, as for all of the songs examined here, the voicing style is like that of the muezzin—the prayer caller—both 'throaty' and somewhat sharp, sung in a manner that could carry over long distances, for extended intervals, and pierce the bluster of waves and wind. For this song in particular as well as the third song (where it will be examined in more detail), there is a pervasive pharyngeal overlay through the lines of the song, even in contexts where there is no reason to assume any underlying pharyngeal consonant or secondary dorsal articulation. This quality shows up recurrently in places such as the phonetically sustained second vowel of *ayāllā* 'O God' (even though, in

---

[9] Conversely, to achieve rhyme with these lowered vowels, etymological *ə is lowered to *a* in the word *ba* 'with it' at the end of line 3. This is one of many examples of discourse-level phonological phenomena which are treated in the following section.

contrast to its expected pronunciation in most Arabic varieties, the following consonant is not emphatic), and as an abrupt pharyngeal stop[10] following the vowel *a* that occurs at the end of each line.

This musical genre also affects the phonological quantity of segments. Contrastive vowel length known from the spoken language is overridden by the song's timing, with some presumably underlying short vowels pronounced with salient length (e.g., *tk*[aː]*llam* 'he spoke', line 1), and some underlying historically long vowels pronounced briefly (*ayāll*[a] 'O God', lines 2–4). As the examples show, this neutralisation affects the vowel pair *a/ā* in particular since, at least in the context of this song, there is no significant difference in phonetic quality between the two vowels. For consonants, gemination is likewise affected in the song, with additional phonetic length or constriction both weakly and variably perceptible to us even where it occurs clearly in the spoken language. This is evident from the pronunciation of these same words: *tka*[lˑ]*am* 'he spoke', and *ayā*[lˑ~l]*ā* 'O God'.

One further phonological phenomenon of a different type, being related to the edges of the phonological phrase, is the elision of final consonants in pre-pausal position. In this specific text, this happens once, in the word *tkalla*[m] at the end of line 1; the consonant *m* is consistently elided in the four iterations of

---

[10] The phonological overlay is generally pharyngeal, but in technical terms, this phrase-final phonetic segment is likely an aryepiglotto-epiglottal stop [ʔ], similar to what has been described by Heselwood (2007) and summarised in Anonby (2020, 6).

this line. A similar phenomenon has been noted by Bernabela (2011, 28) for the MusAr dialect of Jadi (əl-Ǧēdih), and by Bettega and Gasparini (2022, 213) in the dialect of Lima. Bettega's own fieldwork notes (2014, 2016) show this process is common across the Gulf region, at least in the speech of older informants, but to the best of our knowledge it has not been reported in published descriptions of dialects elsewhere in the Gulf (notably Johnstone 1976; Holes 1990 and 2016). Bellem and Watson (2014, 173–74), however, describe pre-pausal consonant elision in detail for the Arabic of Sanaa in south-western Arabia. There, it is the end-state of a synchronic process of consonantal weakening which is often signalled by 'compensatory' glottalisation. In the case of this specific MusAr song, speakers seem to be well aware of this aspect of their language and have exploited it to create rhymes that would otherwise be impossible: by removing the final *m* sound from line 1, all lines of the song now end with *a* (*tkalla* 'he spoke'; *əmzāḥa* 'joking'; *b-aʿlī ba*[11] 'I will mount/ride on it'; *rāḥa* 'rest').

In fact, enabled by the combination of rhythm overriding vowel length, as described above, and this loss of phrase-final consonants, all four of the song's lines end with the same CCV:C*a* structure.

---

[11] Due to the 'throaty' style in which the songs are performed, it is difficult to determine whether *h* is actually retained for the third person masculine singular suffix pronoun. We think it is not, in which case the entire pronoun would be segmentally unmarked on vowel-final stems such as the preposition *bə* 'to' (here lowered to *ba* for the purpose of rhyme). Our transcriptions reflect this assessment.

2.2.3. Idiosyncratic Phonological Traits

A close examination of the recordings shows that historical sibilants *s and *z are variably lisped as interdentals (example words: ṣədag 'right', line 1; and the second repetition of əmzāḥa 'joking', line 2), or at least are not grooved as one would expect for these fricatives. Further, in the first repetition of əmzāḥa, this same z is realised more like a dental stop, ostensibly due to progressive assimilation of occlusion from the preceding m. We consider all of these pronunciations as expressions of the consultant's individual speech style.

2.3. Morphosyntax

Moving on to morphosyntactic particularities of this first text, one salient feature is the preverbal b- element in line 3 (b-aʕlī 'I will mount/go up'). In both Gulf and Omani Arabic, this prefix has been described as a non-obligatory irrealis marker (Persson 2008; Eades 2012; Bettega 2019) that can appear in different contexts with very different functions: for example, it can introduce both protasis (antecedent) and apodosis (consequent) in conditional structures; it can be used as a temporal marker to codify future time reference, or as a modal encoding intention and volition; and it can even be employed on verbs that express the habitual past.

The line in which b- appears in the song (line 3) is hard to translate clearly without making use of a long paraphrase. As a point of context, it has to be kept in mind that in numerous Gulf dialects the word mōyə (< *mawǧa) can mean either 'waves' or 'high tide' (Holes 2001, 507–10), so the situational meaning here is inherently ambiguous. Be that as it may, the *b*-prefixed verb in this verse carries an implicit concessive meaning, so that a free translation of the whole sentence could read, 'O God, [even if there are] waves/high tides [and rough] sea, I will [nonetheless] ride it'. The phrase *b-aʕlī ba* literally means, 'I *will* go up with it' or 'I *will* go up by means of it', like a person who is pushed upwards by a wave. Here, the modal connotations of the *b-* prefix play a crucial role in that the whole line can be regarded as a highly compressed conditional structure, using a verbless protasis (*mōyə, baḥar*) with no explicit conditional marker and followed by a concessive apodosis introduced by *b-*; the volitional implications of this element are evident in this expression. Bettega (2019, 215–20) discusses several types of unmarked conditional sentences in Omani Arabic. Though none of the examples he presents attain the same degree of structural compression as line 3 of this song, it should be clear that the use of unmarked conditionals is entrenched in the dialects of the area, available to speakers for achieving specific rhetorical goals. The poetic nature of the text in question probably allows speakers to push this tendency even further than would be possible in everyday conversation.

One last grammatical element worth mentioning is the preverbal use of the negator *lā* with the suffix stem (i.e., 'perfective'), *lā səmēt* 'I did not hear' (line 4). While Arabic dialects are remarkably homogeneous in their default preverbal use of *mā* to negate finite verbs (sometimes accompanied by further, postverbal elements), the morpheme *lā* can be employed for coordinated negations (of the type 'neither... nor...') or, as in this case, to enhance the performative force of a threat or an oath (see Diem 2014, 1; Caubet 1996, 89).[12] Here the truthfulness of this statement is further reinforced by the use of a verb in the perfect, so that the whole line literally translates as 'I have not heard of rest', but which does in fact carry an imperfective reading: 'I don't hear of any rest', that is, 'I never have a chance to rest'.

3. *Xəbbāṭ* 'Little Kingfish'

The second song, *xəbbāṭ* 'little kingfish', provides a window into the cultural resources that are nourished through the harvesting of the sea. In this song, the fisherman takes the listener through the stages of the fishing cycle, from seeking out fish, and welcoming the fish that come to the nets, to looking forward to the windfall of profits from selling the fish. It is a lively, audacious shanty in which a fishing crew challenges the sultan with their skill and wealth.

At 10 basic lines, extended to 24 lines through repetition in the performance of the song, *xəbbāṭ* is the longest of the three songs described here—yet still fairly short and simple. Careful examination reveals a rich variety of noteworthy structures at all levels of the language.

1 *yā xəbbāṭ wēn-kam*
2 *kāməl šallat-u l-məḥām[əl]*

---

[12] It is worth noting that in MusAr a suffixed element *-lā/-laʔ/-la* is commonly employed to negate both verbal and non-verbal predicates (Bernabela 2011, 53, 86–87; Bettega and Gasparini 2022, 217–18; Anonby, field notes, 2018).

1	*yā xəbbāṭ wēn-kam*
2	*kāməl šallat-u l-məḥām[əl]*
1	*yā xəbbāṭ wēn-kam*
2	*kāməl šallat-u l-məḥām[əl]*
1	*yā xəbbāṭ wēn-kam*
2	*kāməl šallat-u l-məḥām[əl]*
3	*awwal zābə[n] bə-lʾ-ġābə*
4	*wə-l-yōm maraḥ bə-rʾ[kāb-ə]*
5	*ḥayyāllā ġērad ḥay*
6	*ḥayyāllā ġērad ḥayyā bə*
3	*yā awwal zāmba bə-lʾ-ġābə*
4	*wə-l-yōm maraḥ bə[-rʾkāb-ə]*
6	*ḥayyāllā ġērad ḥayyā bə*
6	*yāllā l-ġērad ḥayyā bə*
7	*ō zēd sawwa ḍaġᵃwəyyə*
8	*zamaṭ bē-hə s-səlṭān*
9	*ʿənd-um əd-dahab makᵃnūz*
10	*wə-l-warča fōg ən-nēṭān*
7	*zēd sawwa ḍaġᵃwəyyə*
8	*wə zamaṭ bē-hə s-səlṭān*
9	*ənd-um əd-dahab makᵃnūz*
10	*wə-l-warča fōg ən-nēṭān*

1	O little kingfish, where are you?
2	Did the boats take them all?
3	(Hey!) Before, [you were] taking refuge in the depths
4	But today [the camel] sat with a [loaded] back
5	Welcome, *ġērad*, welcome!
6	Welcome, *ġērad*! Welcome them!
7	(Oh!) Zayd brought together a fishing crew
8	(And) He defied the sultan with it

9   They have gold stored away
10   And coins on top of the banknotes

As can be seen from the transcriptions above, the song comprises ten lines, distributed as three verses of eight stanzas, each as follows: 1 2 1 2 1 2 1 2 / 3 4 5 6 3 4 6 6 / 7 8 9 10 7 8 9 10.

Although this is the longest of the three songs, musically it has the simplest feel. It is sung with a clear, lively voice, in a heptatonic major scale. Over the three verses, it spans a range of a full octave. In most cases, lines fall into musical pairs (1+2, 3+4, 7+8) with similar or identical melodies. While lines 5 and 6 differ significantly from one another, lines 9 and 10 are distinguished by the falling of the melody over the last half of line 10. The pace of the song increases with each verse. Pauses disappear between members of couplets in the final verse, and the song climaxes—both thematically and musically—in line 10.

In the following discussion, we examine variation in the song's wording (3.1.), and analyse salient structures in lexicon, phonology and morphosyntax (3.2.–3.4.). We then discuss phenomena related to 'versioning' of the song, for which a partial supplementary recording is available (3.5.).

3.1. Wording

As in the song *ayāllā* 'O God', there are a number of minor variations in the wording of the lines as they are repeated. These instances of variation underline the flexible and spontaneous nature of the song's exact rendering.

The word *yā* is added to the second repetition of line 3 (*yā awwal zāmba bə-lʾ-ġābə* 'Hey! Before, you were taking refuge in the depths'). While *yā* is typically a vocative particle, and is used as such elsewhere in the song, here it must be serving as a more general interjection 'hey!' since no one is addressed by name or other identity marker this line.

In the middle of the same line, a masculine singular participle *zābə[n]* 'taking refuge' alternates, in the second repetition, with a metathesised feminine form *zāmba* used as a collective (this is discussed further in 3.3.2. and 3.4.).

Lines 5 and 6 are almost the same; while line 6 ends with *ḥayyā bə* 'welcome them (lit. it)!', line 5 ends with a simple *ḥay* 'welcome!' It is unclear whether this difference is due to lexical alternation between two similar terms (both discussed in 3.2.), or if the shorter wording in line 5 is in fact the same term, but reduced as part of the discourse-related elision of final segments that takes place in many of the lines in this song (3.3.2.).

In the third repetition of line 6, *ḥayyāllā* 'welcome!' is replaced with *yāllā* 'come on! let's go!' (lit. 'O God!').

In the second repetition of line 7, the initial *ō* 'oh!' interjection is dropped from before the name *zēd* 'Zayd', which is itself lengthened significantly to absorb the extra syllable. For line 8, which is a continuation of line 7, the pattern is the opposite: *wə* 'and' appears only in the second repetition of the line.

Finally, as mentioned in relation to lines 5 and 6 just above, there are varying degrees of elision of the final segments in each line, which adds to the freshness and unpredictability of the song's composition each time it is sung.

3.2. Lexicon

As simple as this song may initially appear, a rich assortment of regional and local vocabulary is woven throughout.

Two notable lexical items in this song are names of fish, neither of which appears in Beech (2004), Holes (2001) or Al Salimi and Staples (2019). For the second fish in particular, the status and identification has proven challenging.

The song is named for the *xəbbāṭ* fish, which appears in the opening line. This word has also been transcribed in MusAr as *xabbāṭ* (Anonby and Al Kamzari 2024). Both of these word-forms are obviously similar to Kumzari *xubbaṭ*, used for the young stage of a group of fish species (likely *Scomberomorus guttatus* 'Indo-Pacific king mackerel', *Acanthocybium solandri* 'wahoo', and *Scomberomorus commerson* 'narrowbarred Spanish mackerel') most commonly referred to as 'kingfish' in English of the Gulf (ibid.). Related terms recorded from other languages but which lack precise species identification are *xobāt* (Balochi; Anonby and al Kamzari 2024) and *qobād* (coastal Persian; Bettina Leitner, pers. comm. 2021).

A second type of fish is referred to in lines 5 and 6 of the song. The name of this fish seems to be *ġērad*, but its phonological composition is difficult to establish on the basis of the recording. The voiced uvular fricative *ġ* is constant, but as there is a secondary 'lateral' or even 'palatal' feel to this initial consonant, it possibly appears with a coalesced or even lexically incorporated definite article *l-* in at least some of the repetitions (especially the second time), or perhaps contains a palatal *y*. Maryam Bayshak (pers. comm. 2020, 2022), who has reviewed this recording, proposes the transcription الأُيرد or لُييرد, pointing to possible phonemic forms *al-ʔērad* or *lyērad*,[13] and translates this term as 'anchovies'. While the obvious etymological source for this explanation, **ǧarād*, generally refers to 'locusts' in Arabic (Gulf Arabic: *yarād*, cf. Qafisheh et al. 1997, 657), its meaning has clearly been extended to fish species: a consultant from Masira Island, Oman, uses the term *al-yarād* for *Hirundichthys rondeletii* 'blackwing flying fish' (Bettega, field notes 2023), and *Euthynnus affinis* 'kawakawa', which is in the same family as the kingfish (*Scombridae* 'mackerels'), is known as *jārid* in the neighbouring Kumzari language (Anonby and Al Kamzari 2024, 45, 57, 74).[14] While these explanations are convenient, they do not account for the appearance of a uvular *ġ*—an otherwise unattested sound correspondence—that we hear each time this word is repeated in the song. The identification of this fish thus remains problematic.

Returning to the second line of the song, the verb *šallat* is found. This is a third person feminine singular form, used collectively (see 3.4.), of a verb meaning 'take', and with extended

---

[13] The first transcription is unexpected, since in Arabic the definite article is not used with vocative nouns. However, for both proposed forms, it is possible that the definite article has been reinterpreted as part of the noun stem. Regarding possible variation between (historical) stem-initial (**ǧ >*) *y* and *ʔ* in the proposed transcriptions, a similar phenomenon has been documented in Khuzestani Arabic, especially word-initially and before *ī* (Leitner 2022, 50).

[14] Interestingly, this term has also been extended and applied to *ǧarād al-baḥr* 'spiny lobster' in Standard Arabic (Wehr 1979, 142; note that Wehr glosses the term as 'langouste, sea crayfish').

meanings of 'remove, carry away, lift'. In much of the Arabic-speaking world, including some of the Gulf, the form *šāl* is found (Holes 2001, 287), but the *Wortatlas* (Behnstedt and Woidich 2014, Map 379a) shows that a cognate form *šall* is common in eastern and southern Arabia, and this extends to the Musandam Peninsula (Bernabela 2011, 78–80).

In the same line, we observe the word *maḥāməl* (sg. *maḥməl*), which is commonly used in all Arabic dialects of the Gulf as a general term for boats and ships of all kinds (see Holes 2001, 130), here serving as the agent noun for the verb *šall*.

In line 3 the verbal form *zābən*, which is an active participle of the verb *zaban*, is attested. A range of meanings is associated with this root in different dialects. In the Hajar Mountains of northern Oman, it translates as 'to auction', with special reference to cattle auctions that take place weekly in the towns of the area (Bettega, field notes, 2014, 2016). The same verb, however, is found in Sowayan's (1992, 272) study of the dialect of the Shammari tribe of Central Arabia, with the meaning of 'to seek refuge, to find shelter', and this is clearly the meaning intended here. This connection is hardly surprising, considering that most dialects spoken on the Gulf littoral today are descended from the Bedouin dialects of Najd (Holes 2007). The variable pronunciations of this word in the song, actually found as *zābə* and *zāmbə*, are addressed in the discussions of discourse-level phonology (3.3.2.) and morphosyntax (3.4.) below.

In the second half of the same line, the rhyming word *ġābə* appears. In almost every variety of Arabic, the root from which this word derives is connected to the idea of being absent or hidden (this is true of Gulf Arabic, cf. Holes 2001, 385; see also Wehr 1979, 806 for Standard Arabic). Maryam Bayshak (pers. comm. 2020) suggests that this word should be transcribed here as *ġabba*, and translated as 'deep sea'. This proposal is consistent with Holes (2001, 374), who records the noun *ġibba* or *ġubba* as 'ocean, deep sea' (though this meaning appears to be restricted to poetic registers of the language). We have already discussed how, in these texts, geminated consonants are weakly articulated, and contrasts based on vowel quantity are often neutralised (2.2.2.); as a consequence, a clear disambiguation between the two alternative transcriptions given above is not possible. It appears, however, that some overlap between these two roots exists in Gulf Arabic itself. For the verb *ġabb*, Holes also reports the meaning 'to disappear, be absent'. It would seem that a certain degree of ambivalence between $C^1\bar{V}C^2$ and $C^1VC^2C^2$ roots is common in the dialects of the area (see, for instance, the discussion about *šall/šāl* above). All in all, it seems clear to us that this word refers to the deep, open waters of the ocean, where the fish 'hide' and where it is difficult or impossible to catch them.[15]

The highly specific vocabulary item *maraḥ*, which is used in line 4, refers to the action of a camel sitting (cf. Brockett 1985, 195, who provides the corresponding causative *marraḥ* 'to

---

[15] We have also observed that two inlet names on the west side of the Musandam Peninsula—*ġubb* and *ġōban* (as listed in Anonby, Al Kamzari and Al Kamzari 2022)—are similar to this word, further supporting the idea that this root may refer to marine geography within the regional context of Musandam.

make [camels] lie down' and Sowayan 1992, 296, who gives the form *amraḥ* 'to spend the night; to go to sleep at night').[16] We interpret the full line *wə-l-yōm maraḥ bə[-rᵊkāb-ə]* as meaning 'But today [the camel] sat with its [loaded] back', with the camel being understood from the verb's internal semantics, and the camel's back being understood, from the topical context of the song, as loaded down with fish. As for the curtailed word *rᵊkāb-ə*, which only emerges in its full form in a separate recording,[17] this item has been documented as a plural noun *rčāb* with the meaning of 'mounted camels' (Sowayan 1992, 270; Holes 2001, 221; see also Wehr 1979, 413 for Standard Arabic). However, Maryam Bayshak (pers. comm. 2022), gives a richer understanding of the extended application of this term as it is used in this song:

> This [line 4] is an idiomatic statement used in Gulf Arabic to mean the abundance of things. Ironically, it describes the act of a camel sitting down while its back is loaded. As for *rkāb*, here it means 'what is put on the back of the camel'. The whole expression was called out

---

[16] Miranda J. Morris (pers. comm. 2023) has pointed out that the root *mrḥ* is also found in the Modern South Arabian languages (MSAL) Shehret, Hobyot, Mehri, and Btahret (Bathari). There, its meaning is connected to sores that can appear on the back of a pack animal due to a heavy load or a load inexpertly placed. In the MSAL, this root gives rise to both nouns and verbs with related semantics; see, for example, Johnstone (1981, 173) for Shehret and Johnstone (1987, 269) for Mehri.

[17] The full form of this line was observed during later research; see the discussion in 3.3.2., including fn. 25, for further context.

to the caravans when they had to stop for rest, and the animals were to sit down on the ground.

It is interesting that camels, which are not raised or employed on the Musandam Peninsula,[18] are mentioned in this traditional song, sung long before the days of refrigerated fish transport; this provides a historical link between the fishing crews and the fish markets of the cities beyond the area, and suggests that the song itself does not originate on the Musandam Peninsula.

In lines 5 and 6, the *gērad* fish (see in this section above for discussion of this fish name) are addressed with the expression *ḥayyāllā* 'welcome!'. This term, which is a fusion of the components *ḥayy*, from the verb 'to live', and *aḷḷā* 'God',[19] is more commonly found with a grammatically singular addressee—even when addressing a plural audience—in the spoken language of the Gulf: *ḥayyakuḷḷā* 'your (sg.) life', fused with *aḷḷā* 'God'. Line 5 also ends with the shorter form *ḥay*, which could either be a reduction of *ḥayyāllā* due to pervasive discourse-related shortening (3.3.2.), or a straightforward use of *ḥay* for the same purpose: an equivalent expression *yā ḥay* 'welcome!' is known from elsewhere in Arabic, for example, among older speakers in some areas of Oman (Bettega, field notes 2022).

The verb *zamaṭ* appears in line 8. In Hanzal (1978, 275) and Woodhead and Beane (1967, 206), both cited in Holes (2001, 224), it is given in the form *zamuṭ* and glossed with the

---

[18] Camels are nonetheless featured in the pictographs at Qada, near Khasab on the north-western coast of Musandam Peninsula.

[19] As signalled in 2.2.1., the resulting terms appear here with no perceptible phonological emphasis on *ll*.

intransitive verbs 'to boast, brag'. However, since in this song the sultan is the direct object of the verb, we translate *zamaṭ* here as 'defied': *zamaṭ bē-hə s-səlṭān* 'he defied the sultan with it'.

Two final items of interest, both found in line 10, refer to money. While *warča*[20] is a type of coin formerly used in the Gulf region (Maryam Bayshak, pers. comm. 2020), *nēṭān* 'banknote' is the broken plural of the Gulf Arabic word *nōṭ*, itself a loan from the informal English term '(bank)note' (Holes 2001, 534; Holes documents the form *nīṭān*).

3.3. Phonology

As for *āyāllā* (2.2.), we explore historical and discourse-related phonological characteristics of the song *xəbbāṭ* as a way of situating its geographically and socially defined registers.

3.3.1. Historical Phonology

Many of the phonological observations made for the song *āyāllā* (2.2.1.) also apply here, for example: historical *q is reflected as *g* (*fōg* 'on top of', line 10); rhotic *r* is consistently alveolar [ɾ] rather than retroflex (*maraḥ* 'it [camel] was made to sit', line 4,

---

[20] One cannot help but notice semantic and formal similarity with Ar. *warqa* 'leaf, piece of paper, banknote, thin piece of metal' (cf. Wehr 1979, 1245). This would point to a complete *q > *k > *č* sound path which, however, is not to our knowledge attested in any Arabic variety. (Similar sound changes in Arabic varieties which match only partially include: *q > *k and *k > *č* in the Baḥārna dialects of Bahrain, and *q > *j* [d͡ʒ] in Gulf Arabic; cf. Holes 2016, 50–55 and 59–63.)

and *warča* 'coin', line 10); *l* is not distinctively emphatic in *ḥayyāllā* or *yāllā* (lines 5 and 6); and the realisation of historical voiced pharyngeal **ʕ* is unstable, clearly audible in the first repetition of (ʕ)*ənd-hum* 'they have' but absent in the second.

In the word *ḍaġʷəyyə* 'fishing crew', historical **ḍ* is retained as a conservative emphatic alveolar stop *ḍ*. From a dialectological perspective, this is interesting because a fricative reflex *ḏ̣* is more common in much of the Gulf, and because in many dialects of MusAr, including that of the speaker, *w* and *ġ* are the usual reflexes of **ḍ*. Therefore, in this case, there seems to be a 'supra-regional' or perhaps 'classical' framing of the phonology.

The fact that this song is longer than *āyāllā* provides a more sustained opportunity to observe the patterning of *ʔimāla*—raising of historical **a* to *ə* (also discussed in 2.2.1. above). Parallel to its behaviour in the song *āyāllā*, word-final *ʔimāla* shows up in *ġābə* 'deeps' (line 3) and *ḍaġʷəyyə* 'fishing crew' (line 7). In the latter item in particular, for stylistic reasons that are not clear to us, and in contrast to other feminine/singulative endings in the songs, it is realised as a striking long and slightly diphthongised vowel [eːʲ] (see 3.3.2.). Word-final *ʔimāla* does not apply in *sawwa* 'he made' (earlier in line 7), perhaps because the final vowel is underlyingly long, or perhaps simply because *w* is patterning as a guttural consonant, as happens in the neighbouring Kumzari language (Anonby 2020, 295–98). Non-application of *ʔimāla* in *zāmba* 'taking refuge' (line 3) and *warča* 'coins' (line 10) is harder to explain. It could be due to unidentified emphatic elements associated with prior segments; or, in the case of *zāmba*, the fact that phrase-final deletion or metathesis is interfering with the raising process (see 3.3.2.); or simply an artifact of the stylistic variation that seems to be generally encouraged in this genre, as we allude to throughout the present study. In a couple of word-initial syllables, *ʔimāla* seems to apply in guttural contexts where we do not expect it: *xəbbāṭ* 'kingfish' (line 1) and *məḥām[əl]* 'boat' (line 2) (Holes [2001, 130] gives the latter word as *maḥāmil*). Admittedly, the centralised realisation of the short vowels in these initial syllables makes it difficult to be certain about their underlying identity.

One additional phonemic shift is attested in this song. As is typical in MusAr (Bernabela 2011, 26; Bettega and Gasparini 2022, 211–12) but uncommon elsewhere in the Gulf (Johnstone 1967, *passim*), historical interdental *ḏ has been replaced by its dental counterpart d in the word *dahab* 'gold' (line 9).

As a final element of historical segmental phonology, short u [ʊ] appears a couple of times in this song: once as a 3sg. masculine pronominal suffix in the line, *kāməl šallat-u l-məḥām[əl]* 'Did the boats take them all?', and once in a 3pl. pronominal suffix in the word *(ʕ)ənd-hum* 'they have'. (Depending on one's interpretation of ō in the first instance of line 7, it may also occur there; see 'Neutralisation of vowel length distinctions' in 3.3.2. for discussion). This is interesting because in most MusAr dialects, short u has been characterised as phonemic but heavily restricted (see, for example, Jayakar 1904, 254, as well as insufficient proof of contrast in Bernabela 2011, 29); in others, possibly including the dialect of the singer, it is not phonemic, occurring only as an allophone of ə in the context of labials and emphatics—or entirely absent, even in such contexts (Anonby, field notes 2018). In contrast, in Gulf Arabic as a whole it is almost always treated as phonemic (but see Leitner, Anonby, Taheri, and El Zarka 2021, 241–42 for an example of a Gulf dialect where it has been analysed as patterning as an allophone of ə). Regarding (ˤ)ənd-hum, we acknowledge that u [ʊ] could in fact be a rounded ə in the context of m.[21] In the case of kāməl šallat-u l-məḥām[əl], however, there is no obvious segmental conditioning context for the appearance of u; as Bernabela concludes for one dialect of MusAr (2011, 29), and Bettega (field notes 2014, 2016) has observed for others, the u in this morpheme (which is -hu in Standard Arabic) needs to be regarded as phonemic. (Yet, intriguingly, this vowel is not rounded in the same 3sg. masculine pronominal suffix in rᵊkāb-ə 'its loaded back' [line 4, supplementary recording],[22] or in lā ramēt-ə 'I will not give it up' in the following song—perhaps with a view to sustaining the rhyming schemes in these verses.)

Finally, and similarly at the convergence of historical phonology lexicon, and morphology, we observe the deletion of historical *h from the 3pl. pronominal suffix *hum in (ˤ)ənd-um

---

[21] Note, however, that in the song āyāllā, the vowel ə is not rounded in əmzāḥa 'joking' or səmēt 'I heard'. Still, the appearance of ə in these two latter items could be attributed to CV template-defined insertion rather than an underlying vowel, and may therefore pattern differently.

[22] In the discussion of this song's morphosyntax (2.3.), we will return to the question of why a singular pronoun is used for plural objects.

'they have' (line 9). This deletion may be the result of a pronoun-specific process (as described in Yoda 2017, 85, and especially common in 'sedentary' dialects) or a broader, productive morphophonemic alternation that avoids a sequence of three consonants (which are normally not tolerated in the vast majority of Arabic varieties; see Farwaneh 2007). However, in the small corpus treated here there is no possibility of comparing its patterning when attached to vowel-final stems, so the mechanisms of this process remain an open question.

To summarise the patterning of this song's historical phonology in its dialectological context, this text also shows ambivalence between retention of local features and adoption of regional Arabic features.

3.3.2. Discourse-Level Phonology

As is the case for historical phonology, phonological phenomena related to the discourse structure of this song, *xəbbāṭ*, mirror those encountered in the first song. An important case of metathesis and an additional pattern of vowel insertion also emerge here. The voice quality of this song also differs from the pharyngeal style of the first song.

Gemination. The length and constriction associated with consonant gemination, which appears exactly ten times over the ten different lines of the song, tends to be weak but still variably perceptible: *xə[bˑ]āṭ* 'little kingfish' (line 1), *ša[lˑ]at-u* 'they took' (2), *a[wˑ]al* 'first, before' (3), *ha[jˑ]ā[lˑ]ā* 'welcome!' (5, 6), *ha[jˑ]ā* 'welcome!' (6), *sa[wˑ]a* 'he made, put together' (7). Clear gemination on *y* in *ḍaġᵃwə[jː]ə* 'fishing crew' (also line 7) is perhaps surprising, since in many spoken dialects a geminate *y* is not typically pronounced in the ambiguous *īy*[iːj]~*ǝyy*[ijː] segment[23] except in context of discourse-related emphasis.

In the final three lines of the song, the presence of the definite article is signalled by phonetically variable gemination, differing even from one repetition to another, in *s-sǝlṭān* 'the sultan' ([sː]~[sˑ]; line 8), *ǝd-dahab* 'the gold' ([dˑ]~[d]; 9), *ǝn-nēṭān* 'the banknotes' ([n]; 10). The faint or absent gemination in the final lines may reflect weak phonetic signalling associated with the definite article, or it may simply be the case that the singer has preserved some phonological distinctions less rigorously toward the end of the song as its phonetic intensity tapers off.

Neutralisation of vowel length distinctions. Vowel length distinctions, in contrast, are frequently neutralised.

Most prominently, as occurs in the first song, underlying long *ā* and short *a* (as established from our independent knowledge of the spoken language) are equivalent in length and vowel quality in the context of this second song. To give a few examples: the vocative *yā* in line 1 is phonetically short; the first vowels in the consecutive words *kāmǝl* 'all' and *šallat-u* 'they (coll.) took them', which differ in spoken language, are pronounced the same in line 2; and the first vowels of *zābǝ*[n] 'taking refuge' (line 3) and *maraḥ* 'it (camel) was made to sit' (line 4), which are found in the same position of a musically

---

[23] Neutralisation between these two interpretations of this segment in Arabic has been confirmed in discussion with colleagues (Janet C. E. Watson, Bettina Leitner and Stefan Procházka, pers. comm. 2022).

echoed line, are also pronounced the same—phonetically long. In the second repetition of line 3, the initial vocative *yā* and *awwal* 'before' coalesce smoothly into two syllables—*yāwwal*—with a single long *ā* as the first vowel. The first vowel of the verb *zamaṭ* 'he defied' is pronounced long, even though it is short in the spoken language (see the discussion of this lexeme in 3.2. above), for no other identifiable reason than to fit well into the rhythm of the song.

Further, there are several possible instances of lengthening of underlying *ə*. At the end of the word *ḍaġʷwəyyə* 'fishing crew', itself at the end of line 7, it is pronounced like *ē*, even slightly diphthongised to [eːʲ]—even though there is no morphosyntactic basis to assume that the underlying form could be anything other than the historical feminine ending (most often realised as [ə] in the songs here); and without any clear conditioning factors from the phonology, even considering rhythmic structure of the song and comparing it to other lines to this one. In the second repetition (only) of line 8, the form [wiː] appears. 'We' interpret this form as a sung pronunciation of *wə* 'and' which, although we have not observed this in MusAr, is known from other dialects (for example in Egyptian and Bahraini Arabic, cf. respectively Woidich 2006, 159 and Holes 2016, 114). A more segmentally grounded alternative interpretation of this form as the Gulf Arabic word *wīya* 'with' makes no sense in this syntactic context ([__] *zamaṭ bē-hə s-səlṭān* '[__] he defied the sultan with it'). Later in the same line, in both repetitions, the vowel *ē* in *bēhə* 'with it' (line 8), which is composed of the preposition *bə-* 'with' and the feminine singular pronominal suffix -hə, may have been lengthened for the purposes of the song. Otherwise, it may simply be the product of a natural lengthening process associated with bə- in this context, as occurs in many Arabic dialects; Bernabela (2011, 55) gives clear examples of this alternation in MusAr.

Elision of final segments, and metathesis. As in the first song, final segments are frequently elided in the song xəbbāṭ for the prosodic purposes of timing and rhyme. In the four repetitions of line 2, məḥāməl 'boats' is consistently reduced to məḥām, thus fitting into the rhythm of that line; and because, as already discussed, the distinction between long ā and short a is neutralised in many parts of the song including the final sung syllable of the first two lines, this segmental reduction results in a perfect rhyme between wēn-kam 'where are you?' and məḥām. (It is difficult to determine whether the neutralised final vowels in these two words are pronounced more like short or long vowels— given the song's timing, we are inclined to view them as phonetically short; but in any case, these two vowels have equivalent vowel quality and length.)

In line 3, where the musical structure of the two halves is similar, an even closer parallelism is achieved by dropping *n* from zābən 'taking refuge' in the middle of this line's first iteration, thereby rhyming with ġābə 'depths' at the end of the line. When this line is repeated, a near-rhyming metathesised feminine/collective form zāmba is used (see 3.4. for a discussion of the grammatical basis of this second form).[24] Interestingly, clip-

---

[24] While it may be tempting to view the metathesised form as an error in articulation, the form zāmba was repeated three more times in an

ping and metathesis facilitate the same conformity to constraints of rhythm and rhyme, but metathesis allows for retention of an additional piece of segmental content.

All of the lines of the second verse (lines 3–6) have the potential to rhyme (ending with *ġābə* 'depths' / *rkāb-ə* 'its back' / *ḥayyā bə* 'welcome it!'), but in a reversal of the pattern described so far, where segments are suppressed in order to achieve a rhyme, the latent final rhyming syllables of *rkāb-ə* are not uttered in this recording. They are, however, fully pronounced in another version of the song, underlying the variability and dynamic potential of the song.

In the final verse (lines 7–10), the rhyming lines (8 and 10) are separated, and the final-syllable rhyme is achieved without any reduction of the words *sulṭān* 'sultan' and *nēṭān* '(bank)notes'.

While pre-pausal weakening occurs in natural speech in any language, the intricacy of its patterning in this song confirms that it is used as a rhetorical device that helps match the content of the song to its constraints of metre and rhyme.

Insertion of echo vowels. A curious phenomenon that turns up in the song *xəbbāṭ*, not found in the first song, is the insertion of echo vowels in the final words of four lines: in the musically parallel lines 3 and 4, *bə-lʔ-ġābə* 'in the depths' and *bə-*

---

additional, spontaneous rendering of part of the song, following the initial recording (see 3.5.).

rᵊ[kāb-ə]²⁵ 'with its [loaded] back'; and in the parallel lines 7 and 9, ḍaǧʷwəyya 'fishing crew' and makᵃnūz 'stored'. Unlike 'true' epenthetic vowels, there are no constraints in the CV templates, well-known from spoken Arabic (Farwaneh 2007), that would necessitate their appearance. There does not appear to be a clear 'rule' to which one can attribute the appearance of the echo vowels here but not in contexts which are at least somewhat equivalent, such as wēn-kam 'where are you?' (line 1). However, we suggest that a general preference for open syllables when singing, as well as moderate resistance to lengthening underlying short vowels in a long musical syllable (admittedly violated elsewhere—see 'Neutralisation of vowel length distinctions' earlier in this section), may factor in the emergence of the echo vowels. Alternatively, this may simply be artistic flair.

Voice quality. Finally, in contrast to the first song, there is no pervasive pharyngeal overlay in the singing style of this song.

3.4. Morphosyntax

Although xəbbāṭ is the longest of the three songs treated in this study, there is little to comment on in relation to morphosyntax. Here, we will look at one interesting case of constituent word order, and the patterning of grammatical agreement in the song.

Arabic poetry—both Classical and vernacular—is often caricatured as syntactically repetitive (Zwettler 1978, 71), alt-

---

²⁵ In the second repetition of this line, this word is reduced simply to bə[-rᵊkāb-ə]. However, in a separate recording of this song, the same speaker sings out the fuller form bə-rᵊkāb-ə in one instance (see 3.5.).

hough "irregularities of syntax and word-order can be conditioned by the requirements of meter and rhyme" (Zwettler 1978, 103). This song offers an intricate case of such syntactic flexibility in line 2:

> kāməl šallat-u l-məḥām[əl]
> all she_took-it the-boats
> 'the boats have taken it all'

In most present-day varieties of Arabic, including Gulf Arabic, subject-verb-object (SVO) is often identified as the dominant constituent order, with verb-subject-object (VSO) represented as a relatively common alternative. Here, if we consider *kāməl* 'all [of the kingfish]' as a determiner used in a nominal function, this would make it the primary object of the sentence (and the pronominal suffix *-u*, also referring to the kingfish, would be acting in a resumptive role). The boats, *məḥām[əl]*, are unequivocally the subject of the clause. Such an object-verb-subject (OVS) constituent order is therefore doubly unusual in Arabic—even by the standards of Arabic poetry—both because of the initial position of the object, and the final position of the subject. In the free translation above, we have interpreted this line as a question, 'Did the boats take them all?', but our optional interrogative interpretation is based on the structure of the discourse and has no bearing on word order. Rather, this reversal makes the object *kāməl* pragmatically prominent: 'all'. Equally importantly, it allows the text to fit into the rhythmic structure of the song and, with further poetic gymnastics—the combined clipping of the final syllable in *məḥām[əl]* and neutralisation of the vowel length distinction with *a* in *wēn-kam* 'where are you (pl.)?' at the end of the preceding line (3.3.2.)—facilitates a rhyme between the song's first two lines.

Finally, certain phenomena related to gender and agreement can be commented upon in passing. In the second verse of the song, the collective noun *xəbbāṭ* (which appeared in the preceding line) is referred to with the masculine singular suffix pronoun -*u*.[26] The active participle *zābə*[*n*], in line 3, and whose subject is also *xəbbāṭ*, also appears in the masculine singular. Interestingly enough, in the second iteration of this verse, the participle appears in the feminine singular instead.[27] Variation in the type of agreement that collective controllers trigger is extremely common in spoken Arabic, resulting from the fact that these nouns are morphologically akin to masculine singular nouns, but are interpreted semantically as non-individuated

---

[26] This is the only occurrence, across all three songs, of a masculine singular suffix pronoun in the form -*u*. This is considered a typical 'sedentary' form in eastern Arabia, and can be found in northern Oman (Holes 1989, 454), among the rural Shiite communities of Bahrain (Holes 2016, 83) and most notably in all Musandam varieties for which we have documentation (Bernabela 2011, 48; Bettega and Gasparini 2022, 207–8). The other occurrences of this pronoun either appear in the form -*a* (∼-*ə*), a so-called 'Bedouin' feature which is the standard realisation in 'mainstream' Gulf Arabic, or, following the preposition *bə* 'with', are not segmentally realised. It is not clear why it is only in this specific context that the consultant opted for the form -*u*, but this occurrence constitutes yet another example of the 'mixed' nature of the dialect in which these songs were recited.

[27] In the form *zāmba*, as opposed to the expected *zābna*. As discussed above, this word seems to have undergone first metathesis and then assimilation.

plurals (which have a dedicated agreement type in Arabic, that is, feminine singular agreement; on these topics see Bettega and D'Anna 2022, 87–90). Line 2 contains a further example of a non-singular controller triggering feminine singular agreement, in this case a true plural (*məḥām[əl]* 'boats') with its verbal target *šallat* ('they took away', literally 'it [f.] took away'). Masculine singular agreement with a collective appears again in line 6, where the singer salutes the *ġērad* fish with the expression *ḥayyā bə* ('welcome to them', but literally 'welcome to it').

3.5. An Unexpected Supplement

Unlike the other songs, which were only sung once, for *xəbbāṭ* the consultant broke into song after the initial recording session had wrapped up. We were unable to gather a recording of the whole second event; the consultant made it clear that songs come in their own time, and on their own (or his own!) terms. Still, although only a portion of the singing was recorded this time around, and with a hastily placed microphone so that the quality of the recording was not what we would have hoped for, it provides a useful point of comparison for analysis of the first production of the song.

First, the pace and feel of the song are different in this second session. It is faster and increasingly disjointed as it progresses. Perhaps it captures the consultant's memories of the excitement and frenetic action that attend any great haul of fish!; followed by dénouement and recuperation as the jubilant reality of the catch sets in. It certainly resolves the abruptness of the first recorded portion, which ends with a boast, but not yet any fish.

Structurally, there is a fair bit of lyrical variation in this additional session as well. The consultant repeats the lines of the middle verse (numbered as in the transcription above), interspersed with shorter lines as follows: *ḥayyā bə* / 6 3 4 6 / *ḥayyāllā* / 6 3 4 6 / *ḥayyāllā ḥayyā bə* / *ḥayyā bə* / 6 3 4 6. The generous intrusion of *ḥayyāllā* and *ḥayyā bə* gives the feel that the singer is both the initiator and the respondent in an antiphonous climax of call-and-response. Words such as *awwal* 'first' and *wə-l-yōm* 'and today' are sprinkled liberally in places where they were not used in the initial recording, suggesting that their function is as much rhythmic as it is linguistic. The song finally trails off into further snippets from these same lines. This supplementary text is therefore serendipitous in that it not only completes the discourse, but also reveals flexibility in the potential combinations of lines and words in a way that would not have been known from the more controlled context of the initial recording.

The supplement further allows for verification of specific, perplexing elements in the original text: the metathesised form *zāmba* 'taking refuge', observed once already in line 3 (3.3.2.), is repeated three times here, confirming that it is not a simple 'slip of the tongue'; and an unabridged utterance of *maraḥ bə-rᵉkāb-ə* 'it [a camel] sat with its [loaded] back', which is significantly shortened in all other repetitions of line 4 in the texts (also discussed in 3.3.2.), surfaces once here.

4. *Lā Ramētə* 'I Will Not Give It Up'

The third song, *lā ramētə* 'I will not give it up', is the shortest of the three pieces studied here. The consultant describes it as a song that is sung to bring luck for catching large fish. Here, the singer brings together the unwavering determination of the first song, *ayāllā*, and the defiance of the second song, *xəbbāṭ*, with an oath that he will never let go of the prized fish that he is hauling in. One can imagine a crew of fishermen using the song's slow, pulsating rhythm to coordinate the collective drawing in of a heavy fish hooked at the end of the *ḥabəl* 'rope, line'. As *ayāllā*, this song is expressed in the first person.

	1	ā wallā yā šaffī lā ramēt-ə
	2	ā la[w] təngəlū-nī lə-l-məʕāšə[r]
	1	ā wallā yā šaffī lā ramēt-ə
	2	ā la[w] təngəlū-nī lə-l-məʕāšə[r]
	1	Oh, I swear to God, O my tribe, I won't throw it away
	2	Oh, not even if you (pl.) carried me to the grave!

The song consists of two verses, each repeated twice, in a 1-2-1-2 structure.

Lyrically, this is the simplest of the three songs studied here, but its musical effect is both subtle and powerful. Although we have not conducted a systematic analysis of this song's musical properties, it seems to be composed of only 4 half-pitches, all adjacent to one another as on a rising and falling staircase; and, in contrast to the heptatonic (7 whole note) scale of the song *ayāllā*, which is more familiar to a western audience, it is seemingly tuned to a pentatonic (5 note) scale.

4.1. Lexicon

In line 1, the term *šaffī* appears. To our ears, the vowel is long, and gemination on *f* is hard to distinguish, perhaps even phonetically absent (?*šāfī*). Maryam Bayshak (pers. comm. 2020) views *šaffī* as the underlying form of this word, and this is the only form that we have been able to find in the literature: Brockett's (1985) dictionary of Arabic from Khābūra on the Batinah Coast of northern Oman.[28] In any case, as we observed with the terms *šall* and *ġābə* in the previous song, between dialects there is often structural ambivalence for words originating in the same historical root, so either form is possible. Regarding its meaning, Bayshak translates *šaff* as 'relatives'; Brockett translates it as 'tribal federation' (1985, 134). In our glossing of the song, we employ the intermediate term 'tribe'.

Beyond the word *šaffī*, along with the interjection *ā*, which is repeated at the beginning of each line for stylistic purposes, no lexical items stand out; but a number of phonological and morphosyntactic structures deserve further discussion.

4.2. Phonology

Despite its brevity, the song *lā ramētə* exhibits several points of phonological interest.

---

[28] Technically, Brockett transcribes this term as *šeff*, which is phonologically equivalent to *šaff* in conventional Arabist transcription.

4.2.1. Historical Phonology

As with the previous songs, historical phonology broadly situates the song *lā ramētə* within the larger regional context of the Gulf. Etymological **q* continues to be consistently realised as *g* in *təngəlū-nī* 'you (pl.) carried me'. Historical **ˤ* is retained as ˤ in *məˤāšə[r]* 'grave (n.)', but given the pharyngeal insertions in the vocal style of the song (4.2.2.), this interpretation of its phonemic identity is not definitive. Finally, *r* is again pronounced as a simple alveolar flap [ɾ] in *ramēt-ə* 'I gave it up'. This same phoneme is clearly elided at the end of the second repetition of *məˤāšə[r]*, but at the end of the first repetition it may persist as a weak retroflex approximant after a stylistically inserted pharyngeal; the acoustics of this segment are unclear in the latter context. Gemination, but no emphatic secondary articulation, is maintained in *l* in *wallā* 'I swear'.

4.2.2. Discourse-Level Phonology

Discourse-level patterning of the phonology is in some ways similar that of the previous songs. For example, the final segment of *məˤāšə[r]* 'grave (n.)' is elided, most clearly in the second repetition of this word, to facilitate a simple coda rhyme with *ramēt-ə* 'I gave it up' at the end of the prior line. Voice quality and vowel realisations are also remarkable, but they pattern distinctively here.

Voice quality. The voice quality of this song has a strong pharyngeal overlay, as is the case in the first song, *ayāllā*. In addition to a phonemic voiced pharyngeal ˤ, consistently retained in *məˤāšər* 'grave (n.)', a prominent stylistic (rather than phonemic) consonantal or secondary [ʕ]~[ˁ] breaks through at evenly synchronised intervals:

ā wallā[ʕ] yā ša[ʕ]fī[ˁ] lā[ˁ] ramē[ʕ]t-ə[ʕ]
ā la[w] tə[ʕ]ngəlū[ʕ]-nī[ˁ] lə[ˁ]-l-məʕāšə[ʕ]

Vowel length and quality. Vowels are prominent in this song. They are sung loudly and slowly; consonants are brief intervals in between.

As in the previous songs, vowel length distinctions are neutralised, and consonant gemination is compromised, to accommodate the rhythmic specifications of the song. The song's two lines follow identical timing (shown below, where '˘' is short, '‾' is long, and '___' is extra long), and the length of each vowel is entirely dependent on its place in the metre.

```
 ‾ ˘ ‾    ‾ ˘ ‾      ‾ ˘ ‾ ___
ā wallā   yā šaffī   lā ramēt-ə

 ‾ ˘   ‾       ‾ ˘ ‾    ‾ ˘ ‾ ___
ā la[w] tən_   gəlūnī   lə-l-məʕāšə[r]
```

Thus, long ā in the vocative particle yā is phonetically short, but the etymologically short a in šaffī is phonetically long. Further, in the latter word, the presumed gemination on f is difficult to distinguish.

In addition, with the 'wide-open' singing style, articulatory distinctions among all the vowels are reduced: all vowels gravitate toward an unrounded, open [a]. Thus, the following realisations are found:

ī > [ə] in šaffī 'tribe' and təngəlūnī 'you (pl.) carried me'
ē > [æː] in ramēt-ə 'I gave it up'
ū > [ʌː] in təngəlū-nī

ə > [ɐ] in *ramēt-ə*, twice in *təngəlū-nī*, and twice in *l-məʕāšə[r]* 'grave'

The diphthong in *law* 'not even if' is also levelled, to a monophthong [a]. This 'recalibration' of articulatory targets makes it hard to recognise the words in the song, and their underlying forms can only be confidently established by referring to context and to what is already know from the lexicon.

4.3. Morphosyntax

Although this song is only two lines in length, it exhibits some noteworthy grammatical constructions.

As was the case with line 4 in the first song (2.3.), in the first line of this song we find the emphatic negator *lā* combined with a verb in the suffix stem to enhance the validity of the oath being expressed—*lā ramēt-ə* 'I will not give it up'. The suffix stem normally encodes past temporal reference and perfective aspect, but here again it is employed for its modal properties: presenting a certain future event as certain, as if it were already accomplished.

In addition, the two verses of the song form a global conditional structure in which the apodosis (consequent) *lā ramēt-ə* 'I will not give it up' precedes the protasis (antecedent) *la[w] təngəlū-ni lə-l-məʕāšə[r]* 'not even if you (pl.) carried me to the grave'. As in the first line, the chosen verb form in the second line (*təngəlū-nī* 'you [pl.] carried me') is a suffix stem, not because of its intrinsic temporal or aspectual properties, but because of its modal connotations. Verb forms associated with 'pastness' are commonly employed in conditional structures in virtually all varieties of Arabic, as well as many other unrelated languages (including the strong counterfactual form in English, 'even if you carried me to the grave...'). This is particularly true in the case of counterfactual conditionals, which in the dialects of the Arabian Peninsula are often introduced by the particle *law*, itself typically translated into English as 'even if' (see Ingham 1994, 140 for Najdi Arabic; Brustad 2000, 259 for Kuwaiti Arabic; and Bettega 2019, 206–7 for Omani Arabic).

5. Conclusion and Reflections

In this study, we have joined Muḥammad Salūm al-Ḍhuhūrī on a voyage of discovery, at once literary, musical, and linguistic, through the inlets of the Musandam Peninsula and into the open ocean.

The three songs described in this study—*ayāllā* 'O God', *xəbbāṭ* 'little kingfish', and *lā ramētə* 'I will not give it up'—are a simple selection from the production of a single retired fisherman, in just one among some dozens of declining settlements along the coast of the peninsula. Even so, they are a rich and varied testament to the resilient, yet waning, livelihood and cultural heritage that have arisen through centuries of harvesting of the sea.

The three songs are born out of diverse undertakings, from the cooperative net-based harvesting of smaller fish to the hauling in of some of the sea's greater offerings at the end of a single line held by many arms. Musically, different scales and modes are represented. The length of the songs varies from two to ten lines, yet with the stanzas of the shortest song drawn out almost tortuously, and contrasting with the lively tempo and many repetitions of the lines in the longest song. Voice quality alternates between an even pharyngeal overlay in the first song, to a clear voice in the second song, to recurrent, non-contrastive pharyngeal intrusions in the third.

In terms of syntax, there is little variation from structures of the spoken language, although frequent and fluctuating interjections bring colour to the performance of the songs. One specific line in the second song, *kāməl šallat-u l-məḥām[əl]* 'Did the boats take them all?', which stands out as syntactically unusual, is motivated by a complex rhyming mechanism.

In the second song in particular, the lexicon is rich and almost every line contains an item of interest; many of these words are illustrative of Gulf Arabic as a wider dialect group.

As is often case in Arabic dialectology, historical segmental phonology provides many of the keys for understanding the geographic provenance and sociolinguistic status of the text. Interestingly, the phonological structures in the songs are ambivalent, cutting across geographical distinctions. For example, the retention of historical *ḍ in *ḍaġ*ʷəyyə* 'fishing crew', typical neither of the Gulf (where ḏ̣ is expected) nor of Musandam Peninsula (where reflexes such as w and ġ dominate), is likely an emblem of the influence that Standard Arabic exerts in vernacular varieties of the language. Local MusAr features, such as replacement of pharyngeal fricative ʕ with glottal stop ʔ—albeit sporadically—are also attested. In contrast, the characteristic Gulf Arabic realisation of *q as g, which is not known from any Musandam dialect, appears in two of the songs; and the realisations of r in all of the songs conform to the flap allophone typical of Gulf Arabic (along with most other Arabic dialects) rather than the retroflex allophone known from MusAr. The third person masculine singular suffix pronoun is also found as -ə in two of three cases, as expected in Gulf Arabic, with a single exception (the -u found in the second song; see fn. 26 for discussion). Idiosyncratic traits, like the lisping of sibilants, add further complexity to the analysis.

It is not only the historical segmental phonology which turns out to be of great linguistic interest. To return to the structure of the songs themselves, discourse-related processes are pervasive. There is a widespread tendency to neutralise phonemic distinctions of vowel length within the songs' cadence; and in the last song all vowels are phonetically levelled toward an open, central [a]. Perhaps most intriguingly, in tandem with the neutralisation of vowel length, each of the songs strategically eliminates final segments—as many as five!—to facilitate adherence to a rhyme scheme. Metathesis is also introduced as a mechanism for respecting rhyme. In other cases, the omitted segments themselves contain the unspoken key to the rhyming pairs.

Taken together, these features reveal a rich and unique text that leans toward structural norms of the Gulf generally, but embraces both local and geographically agnostic features. Historically, fishing crews in Musandam, as well as rights to fishing grounds, have been constituted according to specific places of origin and local social groupings hierarchies (Zimmermann 1981, 138–51; Zimmermann and Goldfuß 2023). Therefore, it is noteworthy that the song is regionally situated in addition to being locally defined. Still, even without frequent mixing of people of diverse origins within fishing crews, it seems to be the case that occasional intermarriage between communities, contact in shared spaces such as fish markets and—probably most importantly—sporadic intra-Gulf migrant labour, including fishing, have been sufficient to diffuse fishing songs along the coast. The mixture of linguistic varieties in this song is therefore a well-defined case of the 'translanguaging' found along other parts of the Arabian coast, and as described in the Introduction to this volume. (Considering that the varieties being mixed in the songs studied here are all dialects of Arabic, we light-heartedly submit that in this context the phenomenon might be aptly referred to as 'transdialecting'.)

Habalayn was once a bustling hub of fishing activity, complemented by a modest subsistence from the mountain behind. Now, like most of the villages around the peninsula, it has been all but abandoned, living on—at least for the moment—as a memory. The mosque has been rebuilt; while some houses are newly restored, others have fallen into disrepair. Few people still fish, and even fewer remember the fishing songs. Like Muḥam-mad Salūm al-Ḍhuhūrī, many of the original inhabitants now live in the Emirates, and only some of them still make the three-hour drive to gather in the village for weekends and holidays. More often, the alleys of Habalayn are deserted, inhabited by only the wind. Over the water, where the sounds of fishing songs were once heard, there is only silence.

References

Agius, Dionisius A. 2019. *The Life of the Red Sea Dhow: A Cultural History of Seaborne Exploration in the Islamic World.* London: I. B. Tauris.

Al Salimi, Abdulrahman, and Eric Staples. 2019. *A Maritime Lexicon: Nautical Terminology in the Indian Ocean.* Hildesheim: Georg Olms Verlag.

Anonby, Erik. 2020. 'Emphatic Consonants Beyond Arabic: The Emergence and Proliferation of Uvular-Pharyngeal Emphasis in Kumzari'. *Linguistics* 58 (1): 275–328.

Anonby, Erik, et al. 2022. 'Arabic Fishing Songs from the Musandam Peninsula'. *Arabian Peninsula Languages Dataverse*, edited by Erik Anonby. Toronto: Borealis Dataverse. DOI: 10.5683/SP3/T7OIXY.

Anonby, Erik, and AbdulQader Qasim Ali Al Kamzari. 2024. 'A Typology of Fish Names in Kumzari'. In *Harvesting the Sea in Southeastern Arabia*, vol. I, edited by Janet C. E. Watson, Miranda J. Morris, and Erik Anonby, 31–88. Cambridge Semitic Languages and Cultures. Cambridge: Open Book.

Anonby, Erik, Simone Bettega, and Stephan Procházka. 2022. 'Demonstratives in Musandam Arabic: Distinctive Archaisms and Innovations'. *Arabica* 69: 675–702.

Anonby, Erik, and Pakzad Yousefian. 2011. *Adaptive Multilinguals: A Survey of Language on Larak Island.* Uppsala: Acta Universitatis Upsaliensis. https://urn.kb.se/resolve?urn=urn:nbn:se:uu:diva-162008, accessed 1 September 2021.

Beech, Mark. 2004. 'The Fish Fauna of Abu Dhabi Emirate'. *Marine Atlas of Abu Dhabi*, edited by Cecilia Signorelli, Bruno

Nicolis, and Nādī Turāth al-Imārāt, 159–82. Abu Dhabi: Emirates Heritage Club.

Behnstedt, Peter, and Manfred Woidich. 2014. *Wortatlas der arabischen Dialekte, Band III: Verben, Adjektive, Zeit und Zahlen*. Leiden/Boston: Brill.

Bellem, Alex, and Janet C. E. Watson. 2014. 'Backing and Glottalization in Three SWAP Language Varieties'. *Arab and Arabic Linguistics: Traditional and New Theoretical Approaches*, edited by Manuela E. B. Giolfo, 169–207. Oxford: Oxford University Press.

Bettega, Simone. 2019. *Tense, Modality and Aspect in Omani Arabic*. Napoli: Università degli Studi di Napoli "L'Orientale".

Bettega, Simone, and Luca D'Anna. 2022. *Gender and Number Agreement in Arabic*. Leiden: Brill.

Bettega, Simone, and Fabio Gasparini. 2022. 'A Musandam Arabic Text from Lima (Oman)'. *Kervan: International Journal of Afro-Asiatic Studies* 26: 201–25.

Bernabela, Roy S. 2011. 'A Phonology and Morphology Sketch of the Šiḥḥi Arabic Dialect of əlǦēdih, Musandam (Oman)'. Master's thesis, Leiden University.

Brockett, Adrian A. 1985. *The Spoken Arabic of Khābūra on the Bātina of Oman*. Manchester: University of Manchester.

Brode, Heinrich. 1902. 'Der Mord Sejid Thueni's und seine Sühne: Erzählung im Omandialekt'. *Mitteilungen des Seminars für orientalische Sprachen an der Friedrich Wilhelms-Universisität zu Berlin* 2 (5): 1–24.

Davey, Richard. 2016. *Coastal Dhofārī Arabic: A Sketch Grammar*. Leiden: Brill.

Farwaneh, Samira. 2007. 'Epenthesis'. In *Encyclopaedia of Arabic Language and Linguistics*, vol. 2, edited by Kees Versteegh, Manfred Woidich, and Andrzej Zaborski, 35–39. Leiden: Brill.

Ferguson, Charles. 1956. 'The Emphatic *l* in Arabic'. *Language* 32: 486–52.

Heselwood, Barry. 2007. 'The "Tight Approximant" Variant of the Arabic "Ayn"'. *Journal of the International Phonetic Association* 37 (1): 1–32.

Holes, Clive. 1989. 'Towards a Dialect Geography of Oman'. *Bulletin of the School of Oriental and African Studies* 52: 446–62.

———. 1990. *Gulf Arabic*. London: Routledge.

———. 2001. *Dialect, Culture and Society in Eastern Arabia, vol. I: Glossary*. Leiden: Brill.

———. 2005. *Dialect, Culture and Society in Eastern Arabia, vol. II: Ethnographic Texts*. Leiden: Brill.

———. 2007. 'Gulf Arabic'. In *Encyclopaedia of Arabic language and Linguistics*, vol. 2, edited by Kees Versteegh, Manfred Woidich, and Andrzej Zaborski, 210–16. Leiden: Brill.

———. 2016. *Dialect, Culture and Society in Eastern Arabia, vol. III: Phonology, Morphology, Syntax, Style*. Leiden: Brill.

———. 2018. 'The Arabic Dialects of the Gulf: Aspects of Their Historical and Sociolinguistic Development'. In *Arabic Historical Dialectology: Linguistic and Sociolinguistic Approaches*, edited by Clive Holes, 112–47. Oxford: Oxford University Press.

Jayakar, Atmaram S. G. 1904. 'The Shahee Dialect of Arabic'. *Journal of the Bombay Branch of the Royal Asiatic Society* 21: 246–77.

———. 1987. *Omani Proverbs*. Cambridge/New York: Oleander.

Johnstone, Thomas M. 1965. 'The Sound Change *j* > *y* in the Arabic Dialects of Peninsular Arabia'. *Bulletin of the School of Oriental and African Studies* 28 (2): 233–41.

———. 1967. *Eastern Arabian Dialect Studies*. Oxford: Oxford University Press.

———. 1981. *Jibbāli Lexicon*. Oxford: Oxford University Press.

———. 1987. *Mehri Lexicon and English-Mehri Word-List*. London: School of Oriental and African Studies, University of London.

Leitner, Bettina. 2022. *Grammar of Khuzestani Arabic, a Spoken Variety of South-West Iran*. Leiden: Brill.

Leitner, Bettina, Erik Anonby, Mortaza Taheri, and Dina El Zarka. 2021. 'A First Description of Arabic on the South Coast of Iran: The Arabic Dialect of Bandar Moqām, Hormozgan'. *Journal of Semitic Studies* 66 (1): 215–61.

Levin, Aryeh. 2007. 'ʔImāla'. In *Encyclopaedia of Arabic Language and Linguistics,* vol. 2, edited by Kees Versteegh, Manfred Woidich, and Andrzej Zaborski, 311–15. Leiden: Brill.

Mejdell, Gunvor. 2006. *Mixed Styles in Spoken Arabic in Egypt: Somewhere between Order and Chaos*. Leiden/Boston: Brill.

Prochazka, Theodore. 1988. 'The Spoken Arabic of Abū Thōr in al-Ḥasa'. *Zeitschrift für Arabische Linguistik* 18: 59–76.

———. 1990. 'The Spoken Arabic of alQaṭīf'. *Zeitschrift für arabische Linguistik* 21: 63–70.

Qafisheh, Hamdi A., Tim Buckwater, and Ernest N. McCarus. 1997. *Gulf Arabic–English Dictionary*. Chicago: NTC.

Reinhardt, Carl. 1984. *Ein Arabischer Dialekt gesprochen in 'Omān und Zanzibar*. Stuttgart/Berlin: Spemann.

Rössler, Walter. 1898. 'Nachal und Wād il Maʿāwil'. *Mitteilungen des Seminars für Orientalische Sprachen an der Friedrich Wilhelms-Universisität zu Berlin* 2 (1): 56–90.

———. 1899. 'Die Geschichte von der Pockenkrankheit: Eine Erzählung im Omandialekt'. *Mitteilungen des Seminars für Orientalische Sprachen an der Friedrich Wilhelms-Universistät zu Berlin* 2 (3): 1–42.

Sachau, Eduard. 1898. 'Über eine Arabische Chronik aus Zanzibar'. *Mitteilungen des Seminars für Orientalische Sprachen an der Friedrich Wilhelms-Universität zu Berlin* 2 (1): 1–19.

Sowayan, Saad Abdullah. 1992. *The Arabian Oral Historical Narrative*. Wiesbaden: Harrassowitz.

van der Wal Anonby, Christina. 2014a. 'A Grammar of Kumzari, a Mixed Language of Oman'. Ph.D. dissertation, Leiden University.

———. 2014b. 'Traces of Arabian in Kumzari'. In *Supplement to the Proceedings of the Seminar for Arabian Studies 44: Languages of Southern Arabia*, edited by Orhan Elmaz and Janet C. E. Watson, 137–46. Oxford: Archaeopress.

Watson, Janet C. E., Erik Anonby, and Miranda J. Morris. 2024. 'Introduction'. In *Harvesting the Sea in Southeastern Arabia*, vol. I, edited by Janet C. E. Watson, Miranda J. Morris, and Erik Anonby, 1–26. Cambridge Semitic Languages and Cultures. Cambridge: Open Book.

Wehr, Hans. 1979. *A Dictionary of Modern Written Arabic*. Wiesbaden: Harrassowitz Verlag.

Woidich, Manfred. 2006. *Das Kairenisch-Arabische: Eine Grammatik*. Wiesbaden: Harrassowitz Verlag.

Yoda, Sumikazu. 2017. 'The Historical *h* in Some Eastern Maghribi Dialects Revisited'. In *Tunisian and Libyan Arabic Dialects: Common Trends, Recent Developments, Diachronic Aspects*, edited by Veronika Ritt-Benmimoun, 85–100. Zaragoza: Prensas de la Universidad de Zaragoza.

Zimmermann, Wolfgang. 1981. 'Tradition und Integration mobiler Lebensformgruppen: Eine empirische Studie über Beduinen und Fischer in Musandam, Sultanat Oman'. PhD dissertation, Georg-August Universität, Göttingen.

Zimmermann, Wolfgang, and Gabriele Goldfuß. 2023. *Magisches Musandam: Omans ferner Norden*. Hildesheim: Olms Verlag.

Zwettler, Michael. 1978. *The Oral Tradition of Classical Arabic Poetry: Its Character and Implications*. Columbus: Ohio State University Press.

PART II
HARVESTING THE SEA AMONG THE BAṬĀḤIRA

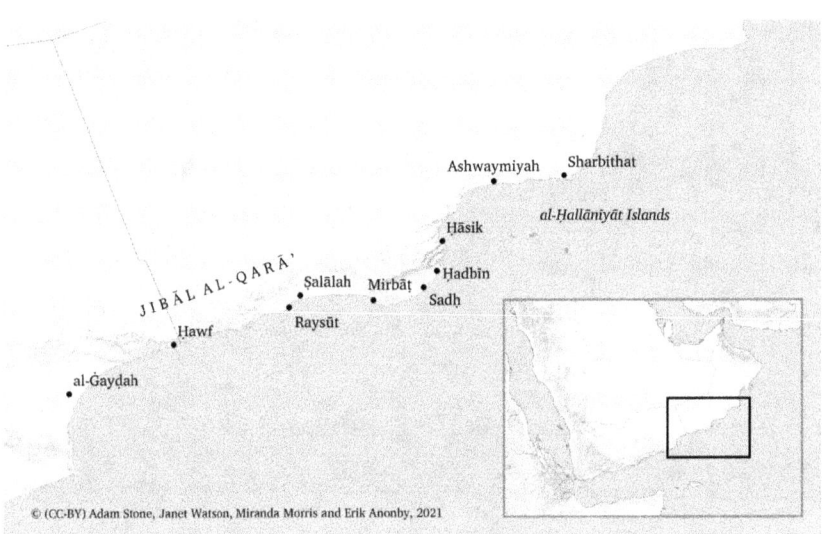

Map 3: Dhofar and adjacent areas of al-Mahrah

HARVESTING THE SEA AMONG THE BƏṬĀḤIRA[1]

Miranda J. Morris

Acknowledgments

I would like to acknowledge here my immense debt to all the men and women who have, over so many years, invited me into their homes, offered me hospitality and given so generously of their time. They displayed impressive patience and forbearance in allowing me to pursue them with pen and notebook and endless questions.

I lived in Dhofar from 1976 to 1980, first working for the Civil Aid Department, Office of the Minister of Dhofar, and then helping to establish the Dhofar Rural Health Service for the Ministry of Health. Thereafter (1981–1989), at the request of the late Sultan Qaboos and sponsored by the Diwan of Royal

---

[1] The abbreviations and printing conventions used in this chapter are : extended vowel (as a:), ... pause, √ root, lit. literally, [H] Ḥarsūsi, [M] Mehri, [E] English, KH Khalīfa Ḥamūd. Terms preceded with B are Bəṭaḥrēt. JA and [JA] refer to Janaba Arabic, the dialect of Arabic spoken by the immediate neighbours of the Bəṭāḥira and by the crews of the trade ships that called in along the coast. Terms preceded by Ś are Śḥerēt. After Arabic, Śḥerēt is the most widely spoken language of Dhofar.

Court, I made two fieldtrips a year to Dhofar, each for two months, when I lived with families from different language communities and worked on the non-Arabic languages of the region, and the culture and traditions of their speakers. I would like to gratefully acknowledge here the support of the Diwan of Royal Court, Sultanate of Oman, for sponsoring my research in this way.

For the earliest work on Baṭaḥrēt, I would like to thank especially Khalīfa Ḥamūd Sālim and his late brother, Elḥəbāb Ḥamūd Sālim. When they visited Salalah in the 1970s, and when Elḥəbāb was an inpatient in the hospital where I lived (and where, sadly and all too soon, Elḥəbāb died), they spent time working with me in my home. I would also like to acknowledge the help given by other members of Khalīfa's family in the 1980s: his other brother, Fāyil; his late mother, Shaikha Mubārak Ḥamad; his late father-in-law, Zifena Musallim Daġash and late mother-in-law, ʿAyīla Subaʿ Msabbaʿ, and their daughter, Zeyūn Zifena, who became Khalīfa's wife. I am grateful to them for their kindness, hospitality and patient instruction over so many years.

In the 1980s, Khalīfa and his family were a constant support during my fieldtrips to the Baṭhari area, opening their home to me on the escarpment above the coast for weeks on end. Here, Zifena was generous with his time, recording material for me and explaining various customs and traditions. The late Saʿd Qāsim Aṭali was often with us and proved to be another kind and patient teacher. When living down on the coast in Sharbithat, I would like especially to thank the late Mehri

Muḥammad Sālim for his patient instruction. Sālim Muḥammad Saḳr and his late mother, Shīḥa Ḥamad Saˤd, were also particularly helpful. Another key teacher of these years, but mainly in Salalah, was the late Musallam Mṭawwaˤ ˤĀmir: he spent many hours with me, listening to recordings and patiently helping me to transcribe and interpret them. He was also of the greatest assistance in starting to build a lexicon of Bəṭaḥrēt.

For the latest period, January 2013 to December 2016, I would like to acknowledge the Leverhulme Trust for funding the project 'Documentation and Ethnolinguistic Analysis of the Modern South Arabian Languages: RPG-2012–599', led by Janet C. E. Watson. This involved some four months of fieldwork a year in Dhofar, some of it with the Bəṭāḥira, when I was able to develop and expand my earlier research. Khalīfa played a major role again in these years: he was a data collector for Bəṭaḥrēt, as well as a key interpreter of the recordings, both in the field and in Salalah. In 2015, he even came to stay with me in Scotland for a month to work on material we had collected.

Although their work does not appear in this but another volume (see footnote 2), for particular assistance in these later years, I would like to thank other members of the late Zifena's family: his daughter, Sowma Zifena, in Ashwaymiyah, and his son, Muḥammad Zifena, in Fāṣa. I would also like to pay tribute to the indefatigable assistance of the late ˤĀmir Māgid Suleyyim and his wife, Nasra Sālim Shemlān, in Ashwaymiyah; Maḥmūd Mšaˤfi Musallim, Sālim Muḥammad Saḳr and the late Rubeyyaˤ Adahaba Suleyyim, also in Ashwaymiyah, and Bakhayyit Saˤad Saḳr in Sharbithat.

1. Introduction

I first started to use the phrase 'harvesting the sea' in the 1980s, after spending time living with the Bəṭāḥira on the Dhofar mainland and with the islanders of al-Ḥallānīyah opposite (the only island of the group inhabited today). This made it clear that 'fishing' alone was not an adequate description of the efforts these two groups made to wrest a living from the sea. They had little else. Cultivation was not an option for either; on al-Ḥallānīyah island the only livestock were a few feral goats, while the Bəṭāḥira owned a small number of goats, even fewer sheep, and the odd camel or donkey as a pack animal.

Figure 1: Camel pack saddle

Photo © Miranda Morris, 1980s

2. The Bəṭāḥira[2]

Today, the Bəṭāḥira are a small tribe in the central area of the Sultanate of Oman (Muḥāfaẓat al-Wusṭā, The Central Governorate). Their area runs along the coast from modern Ḥāsik eastwards to Ashwaymiyah, extending inland to the escarpment and to areas of the desert plateau above. This region is described by those living in Dhofar (B *ṣəfūr*) simply as Ś *śerók̠*, 'the east(ern area)'. Moving westward from Ṣawk̠ərə, their main settlements were Śerbiṯōt (modern Sharbithat); Mingíy (the former settlement of those now living in Sharbithat, accessed today by a rough track); Warx (the former settlement of those now living in Ashwaymiyah, only accessible on foot or by sea); Ashwaymiyah (formerly called Gizərēt[3] and later Šwēmyət or Šwēmīyət); Ḥaṣbərəm~Ḥaṣbərə and Ḥāsik. Apart from Mingíy and Warx, all these coastal settlements are today connected to Ṣalālah (B *ṣəlōlət* ~ *ṣəlólt*) by tarmac roads. Offshore lie the al-Ḥallāniyāt islands (formerly the Kuria Muria islands). The Bəṭāḥira knew little of the islanders: until recently neither they nor the al-Ḥallāniyāt islanders owned boats with engines powerful enough to cross the seas that lay between them. Nor did they share a

---

[2] A fuller description of the Bəṭāḥira, their language and their history, can be found in the introduction to a collection of some 400 transcribed and translated Baṭḥari texts in: Miranda Morris (2024). *Ethnographic texts in the Baṭḥari language of Oman*. Wiesbaden: Harrassowitz.

[3] Not to be confused with the al-Ḥallāniyāt islands which are called in Bəṭaḥrēt *gəzírət*, pl. *gəzēyir*.

common language: the al-Ḥallāniyāt islanders spoke Śḥerēt[4] which the Bəṭāḥira did not understand while the Bəṭāḥira spoke Bəṭaḥrēt, another of the six MSAL (Modern South Arabian Languages), today called Báthari by most younger Bəṭāḥira and non-Bəṭāḥira.

From the little that we can discover, it seems likely that the Bəṭāḥira originated as one of a group of indigenous inhabitants of the drier areas of the wider Dhofar region. Later, progressively squeezed out of the more fertile watercourse systems and desert plateaus by more powerful and numerous incomers, they were finally left with little but the infertile strip of coast which they inhabit today. They believe that there was a time when their numbers were very much greater, when they controlled territory '*mən Ġadōn ɛ-Ġadōn*', that is from Wadi Ġadōn in the west, by the Yemeni border, up to Wadi Ġadōn at the eastern limits of their present area. Oral tradition relates their name, 'Bait Baṭḫā' or 'Bait Baṭḫār', to B *baṭḫ*, 'fine gravel, sand', illustrating their great number in times past.

The Bəṭāḥira offer two conflicting myths to explain their downfall. One is the story of *nāḳat Ṣāliḥ*, 'the she-camel of the Prophet Ṣāliḥ', from whose four teats flowed four miraculous liquids. In their version of the myth (there are other versions with different protagonists all over southern Arabia), this prodigious she-camel was slaughtered by squabbling Bəṭāḥira. As punishment, God sent them a plague of ants (B *nōmīl*) which ate

---

[4] These islands were settled by Śḥerēt-speaking people of the Śḥaró tribal confederation, fleeing disturbances on the mainland.

up and destroyed everything, causing the death of the majority of the Bəṭāḥira.

The other version attributes their decline to a long and disastrous period of war with the B *burtuġāliyīn*, 'the Portuguese'. Even today, the Bəṭāḥira tell the story of the battle in which the *burtuġāliyīn* slaughtered 700 pregnant Baṭhari women, and point to extensive burial sites they believe to be a consequence of these conflicts. There are mounds said to be mass graves, and blocked-up ledges in cliff faces in which the corpses of Bəṭāḥira and their Portuguese enemies are said to have been laid. In this version, the few Bəṭāḥira who survived the wars were reduced to trying to eke a living from their present marginal area.

Today the dead are buried in graveyard areas special to each clan: *aˤabú yəśléluw əgənāzət bə-ḍarāb té mədínət, k-akābər. áwkaˤuw teh əté zəhébuw. mġārə áwkaˤuw teh berk akābər wə-áwkaˤuw leh mədēkif wə-áwkaˤuw leh mən əṭáyn. u-mġārə ḥōśśuw leh bəṭḥā*, "People take the bier of long staves to the graveyard, right to the grave. They lay it down (on the ground) until they are ready. Then they lower (the corpse) into the grave and block the body into the grave niche with large rocks to keep the earth from it. Finally they fill in (the whole grave) with sand."

Turning to more modern times, that the Bəṭāḥira once had greater authority is suggested by the fact that older men and women still recall the days when they were able to extract a fee from any non-Bəṭāḥira harvesting the frankincense trees in areas around Ḥāsik, or who landed fish and shark[5] at certain beaches and bays that the Bəṭāḥira controlled.

When I first spent time in their area, in 1978, carrying out a survey for a polio eradication programme, the Bəṭāḥira were a small tribe. At this time, their population along the coast comprised fewer than 300 people. By other tribespeople of the area, they were regarded as *ḍaʿīf*, or 'non-tribal, inferior', not of course a description the Bəṭāḥira would use of themselves.

Figure 2: Gāt watering place with cave shelter

Photo © Miranda Morris, 2014

---

[5] Although shark are fish, both terms are used because it was shark hunting that dominated the commercial activities of Baṭḥari fishermen. Also because the Bəṭāḥira themselves differentiate between *ṣayd* 'fish', *ḥūt* 'large fish', and *ləxām* 'shark'.

Their lives were relentlessly hard. Sweet water was always in short supply. Rare rains filled a few rock pools in the mountains behind, but mostly their water was obtained from lagoons or water-scrapes dug in seasonal riverbeds and was more or less saline. There was a small permanent water source at Mingíy and

Figure 3: Women fetching water in goatskins, Al Jazir

Photo © Miranda Morris, 1970s

brackish water in the Warx lagoons (the two main centres of population), but otherwise this lack of water meant that women spent much of their time, when not searching for firewood, gathering shellfish or looking for fodder for their few goats, walking considerable distances to fetch water and then carrying the heavy waterskins back to their families.

Like their bedouin neighbours on the plateau above, most Bəṭāḥira were rarely stationary, but moved around according to weather, rare flushes of rains grazing, and, of course, the availability of fish and other marine foods. They gave everything in the natural world its own name, dividing living organisms into 'tribes' and 'families': *həmōtən l-ərawnə? maġrēbtən. wə-ləxām fxāyəḏ, kel ḳəbîlət bə-həms. wə-hermīt. kúlə śay wə-heh maġrēb bə-hə́məh,* "The names (of creatures) in the sea? They're well known. And shark are divided up into clans, each tribe with its own name. Likewise, the vegetation. Every single thing has its own name."

Figure 4: Unloading goods from dhow to dugout

Photo © Miranda Morris, 1980s

Before slavery was abolished in the 1970s, traders in the wider region owned slaves, including a small number of minor traders among the Bəṭāḥira. However, these were always few in number, and were concentrated mainly in the small permanent settlements of Ṣawkərə, Ḥāsik or Ḥaṣbərəm~Ḥaṣbərə.

Before 1970, when Sultan Qaboos began his rule and everything in Oman started to change, there were no road communications in the Baṭhari area and only a handful of Bəṭāḥira owned a camel for transporting goods or a dugout canoe for fishing. A small number travelled along the coast in the boats of others, and one or two even went as far as East Africa as passengers on the wooden trade boats that seasonally plied the Gulf and the south Arabian coast. Otherwise, they were very cut off from communication with others:

> hem nəkəˤēn xabīr məhímm[JA] u-bēn ˤagəlét h-əxabīr, hem heh nēkaˤ semḥ yəsīruw ḍar rəkōb il seh axayēr l-ərəkōb. wə-hem gəbəlīl tsyūrən bēs ərəkōb la, nəntəkāl ṭad il heh yəsyūr axáyr, el yəḵāṭaˤ la bə-xabīr wə-yənāka ˤ bə-xabīr h-aˤabú. wə-hem nōkaˤ fisáˤ la, ber el yəkérəb l-aˤabú mən ḥān aḥás ḥad yəhāmaˤ la hem heh yəṣˤāḵ, yəlíbəd búnduḵ bə-térti wə-l-shəlēṭ té aˤabú yəbtəhéṣ́uw wə-yənākaˤuw teh wə-yexēbərən tého.

If the news was really important for us and we were in a hurry to learn all about it, if it was a flat area, they'd go off on riding camels, the best of the riding camels. And if it was a mountainous area that the camels couldn't cross, we'd choose someone really fit who wouldn't tire easily and give up, and he'd go to fetch the news for people. If he couldn't come back quickly (enough), once he was close to people but out of earshot were he to shout, he'd let off a shot from a gun two or three times to alert them, and the people would come to him and he'd give them the news.

Some Bəṭáḥira went to fish along the al-Jāzir coast to the east, the home area of their traditional allies, the Arabic-speaking Janaba. Many of those who arrived by sea to trade were also Janaba, from Ṣūr and Jaʕlān in northern Oman. Over the years, a number of Janaba settled in the Baṭhari area and there was considerable intermarriage between the two groups.

After the 1970s the situation of the Bəṭáḥira began to improve, and the way of life I am describing here came to an end.

3. Harvesting the Sea

The Bəṭáḥira depended for their survival on harvesting the sea, and over time they devised complex procedures and rules for managing the marine environment, some examples of which are given below in 'Community Self-Regulation' (section 3.19.). Although it was the men who went out to sea and who processed the larger fish and shark, women too helped catch fish on occasion:

> wakt hēn... aṣáyd el ḥātwi berk ʕayák. wə-mən nəksēh ḥātwi berk ʕayák, aʔáynəṭ tślōlən aṣṭārsən wə-neffərād beh, ḥad mən šérgi wə-ḥad mən ġárbi. ḏih el bərəkāt ḥelōk? tənākaʕ ḏih mən aġáwf wə-təzhá berk aṣāṭər twat ərbīʕsa. wə-mən yəfərēd mən aṣāṭər? ḍik bəgədāt mən ḥelōk wə-ḍik bəgədāt mən ḥelōk eté fōr wə-hégər abárr. hēmʕak wəlá? ḏah ḥālət aḥawlá.

> Sometimes... the fish would become stranded in pools (i.e., left by the receding tide). And when we find them stranded in pools, the women would take their baskets and we'd drive them (into a corner), some (lit. 'one') from the seaward side and some from the landward side. This one would crouch down (holding open the mouth of her

basket) there? And this one would approach from higher up and drive the fish forward into the basket, towards her companion. And if they were to escape from the basket? That one would chase them from there and that one would chase them from there until they flew up and landed on dry land, do you hear or not? This was how it was for people long ago.

However, mainly women harvested the sea by gathering a wide variety of shellfish and crabs. It was the women who managed the few goats which provided occasional milk, male kids for food, and skins to make the vital leather bags used for transporting liquids and for the men to use in fishing. When nylon gillnets became available, the shark catch rose dramatically, and women began to be involved in processing these too.

Figure 5: Cutting and shaping leather

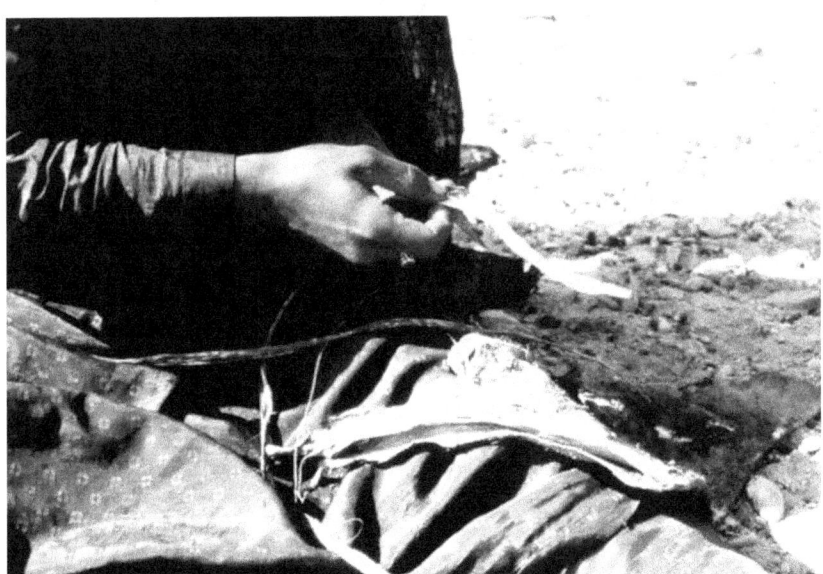

Photo © Miranda Morris, 1990s

There was a close relationship between the Bəṭāḥira of the coast and the bedouin of the desert plateau above. The Bəṭāḥira would give the bedouin fish and other sea products when times were hard in the desert, setting a prominent marker to indicate to those above that there was a surplus of fish, or handing part of the catch to hungry bedouin who came down to the coast in search of food. In their turn, when the sea was unproductive or too stormy to fish, the bedouin would reciprocate with milk products, palm leaflets and fresh or dried meat.

Figure 6: Early morning among the goats, upper plateau

Photo © Miranda Morris, 1980s

3.1. The Sea

The Bəṭāḥira say that the sea, *rawnə*, is a *kēfərət* 'a non-believer', that is, without mercy. *el fēzˤan mən ərawnələkan mətˤátən ˤar mins. nəbˤār hēs bə-ḥalléy mən aḳál lə-mətəˤát w-əmətˤát šēn śa la,*

We'd go off at night to it because there was so little (else) to eat. We had no (other) food."

Some said that the sea was male one year and female the next. In the male year the seas were stormy and fishing poor, while in the female year fishing was usually good. It was also said that: ʿemōruw ərawnə? ədə́ni mabnōt ḏar ḵarān ṭawr. wə-nəhāḵ əṭawr tənāka<ʿ> kuwwét. yəʿēməruw aḥawlá, "They used to say of the sea? (That) the world was built on the horns of a bull. When it bellowed, the sea would rise up and there would be storms. That's what they used to say, the ancestors." Another tradition was that the sea was controlled by an iron chain. As the seasons progressed, the chain would lengthen, and in the monsoon months, the seas would grow wild. When, after the monsoon, it started to wind itself back in and shorten, the seas would once more grow calm. I was also told by some Bəṭāḥira that the 'stone seashells' (i.e., fossil shells) sometimes seen in their area were the result of a terrible occasion when, one monsoon, the chain snapped and the seas swept over the land, sweeping up and over the caves where people were living. Then God, moved by their plight, fixed the chain more firmly so that the seas could never again cover the land.

The sea was full of dangerous creatures: all kinds of shark prowled, there were stingrays, stonefish, sea snakes and harmful jellyfish:

aṣammā́ṭət təkaʿ b-ərawnə u-kel li təlyūfh txádəm beh hes ḥəmāwəḵ lə-śeyāṭ yaġáyr yənāfʿas ṭfēr l-aʿrān tənādxan beh. u-seh tənākaʿ kə-śéte. het thām xayr mən ərawnə wə-seh təltágak bə-ḵəḏáʿl! had—ḥašā́š—yəlébs xatḵān lə-ʾaynəṭ mins.

The ṣammáṭət jellyfish is to be found in the sea. If it touches anyone, it leaves marks like burns from a fire, though these can be treated successfully if you fumigate yourself with goat dung. They arrive in winter. You want nothing but good things from the sea, but these can kill you with the savage pain (they cause)! Some people—forgive me—wear women's clothes as protection against them.

The hammerhead shark, while extremely desirable as a catch due to its value as a trade item, was greatly feared and its behaviour closely observed: *hes təḳáʿ gīʿānət—hoh śink tēs la b-aʿáyni, ʿar əġeré l-aʿabú—hes gīʿēt, hes xaṭəfēt, yəʿēmeruw ttoh əbínsa ssēhem. w-əbínsa mən yənkáʿuw mən hēfələs berk ərawnə, yəsīruw ḫānāfho. hes ələxām ḏen yəsīruw*, "When it's hungry—I've not seen it with my own eyes, but people say it is so—when it gets hungry as it goes along, they say that it eats its own young, the hammerhead. And its young, when they emerge from her belly into the sea, can go along under their own steam. They make their own way just like this (other) shark."

The sea year had its own seasons when certain types of fish would reach the Baṭḥari shores. For example, the season of *ḥeyšūf* occurred around March: *nəḥísəb əwárx ḏénəmə, əwarx ḏénəmə nəʿāmer heh ḥeyšūf. heh yəʿēmeruw bə-ʿarabīyət 'šahr ṭəlāṯa', w-enḥa nəʿāmer heh ḥeyšūf, bə-bəṭaḥrīyit nəʿāmer heh ḥeyšūf*, "We'd calculate the arrival of this month. This month we call *ḥeyšūf*. In Arabic they call it 'the third month', but we call it *ḥeyšūf*. In Bəṭaḥrīyit we call it *ḥeyšūf*."

Ḥeyšūf was followed by *rəkféf* (*sirīh yənāka° warx l-erkəféf* 'after it comes the month of *erkəféf*'), marked by the arrival of the queenfish, a very valuable fish. *nəkəʿēs 'əwárx lə-rəkféf*:

yənākaʿ mən boh, śə́tə wə-ḳayṣ́. ʿād ərawnə hādəʾ, bēs riyáḥ la. heh dek šəṣ́yōḵ əbəṭáhari aḥāwəlí, ləbōduw əramēd əmbáʿdəh, "Then there comes the 'month of the rəkféf': it comes from here, winter and summer, when the sea is still calm, and there is no wind. That was the hardest time for the Bəṭāḥira in earlier times: they became weak and useless (lit. 'ash') after that."

Rəkféf is followed by warx lə-ṭāḵā sīrīt, 'the month of the bluefish on the move', another highly valued fish. After warx lə-ṭāḵā sīrīt comes ríffə ~ riffēt, a period when small fish arrive in shoals, fish which could be caught in cast nets to be used as bait: əmbáʿdəh tənākaʿ aʿáyd, əríffə; tənākaʿ aʿáyd ədelafēt, wə-sirīs tənākaʿ əmeḥwērrāt, wə-sirīs tənākaʿ əgerrāt, "After it the shoals of sardine-type fish arrive, the ríffə. The ḏəlafēt type arrives, followed by the meḥwērrāt, followed by the gerrāt."

After ríffə ~ riffēt comes the season of the śeṭráx, the great amberjack, another very valuable fish: sirīs tənākaʿ śəṭráx. śəṭráx nəʿāmer hēs. tənākaʿ ḳayḏ, nāśaʿ, nəʿāmer hēs nāśaʿ, ḳayṣ́āt. wə-nḥíseb lēs w-aʿabú yəḥēsəbuw lēs mən ráḥaḳ wə-ḳarīb, "After it the great amberjack arrive. We call it śəṭráx. It comes in the summer, at nāśaʿ. We call it nāśaʿ, a summer season. And we'd calculate the time of its arrival. People from far and near would calculate the time of its arrival."

Nāśaʿ is a period at the end of the summer, a time when the Bəṭāḥira say the ḥazāzi, bəkšīt and a few yəbāba shark start to arrive. (Most of the other shark came with the shoals of sardine-type fish.) As well as nāśaʿ, there are other more general terms that describe the time of year. For example, tərmá is at the end of the monsoon, when the sea is just beginning to calm down but is still too wild to go out to fish. (mən bēn) ərabʿayāt is the period when the ṣɛrb season comes in after the monsoon recedes, and the ḥwētəm star rises, bringing storms: ḥwētəm baʿl kuwwét mən bēn ərabʿayāt, "The ḥwētəm star brings storms and comes between the end of the monsoon and the beginning of ṣɛrb."

Another way of dividing up the sea year was by the rising and setting of certain stars, the 'star seasons', each influencing the sea and the weather in its own way. For example, the Pleiades, ṭəréyyət, rising at the onset of the monsoon, bring gales:

> ərəggét lə-ṭəreyyət? ərəggét? o:h kuwwét! ərəggét beh śa la!
> ᴶᴬmā tfīdək!ᴶᴬ beh śa la ḥūt. ḍarbə tkūn beh. tənākaʿ bə-šīlli. wə-təġēyib ʿabú wə-ttībər ədənāwəg.
>
> The gales of the Pleiades? The rəggét winds? Oh, but they're fierce! The rəggét bring nothing (good)! They're of no use to you! They don't bring any big fish with them, just violent storms. They arrive with the šīlli star at the very end of the summer. And they bring death to people, and they smash the wooden sailing boats.

Different 'stars' brought a different kind of low cloud and mistiness: tərīd lə-ṭámmə, 'the mist of the ṭámmə star', a thick fog; tərīd lə-rəggét, 'the mist of rəggét', a thick mist; tərīd lə-šaʿrān, 'the mist of the šaʿrān star' and tərīd lə-shēl, 'the mist of the shēl star', both light mists. These are differentiated from other kinds of mistiness: tərīd lə-mwēdaʿ, 'the mist that greets', a mist said to leave the al-Ḥallāniyāt islands to cross the seas to the Baṭhari coast 'to greet it' (yəwáddaʿahᴶᴬ), or tərīd lə-rəbšīš, 'rəbšīš mist', patches of mist that move from place to place.

Stars were indicators in other ways. For example, when a camel with bound udders returned to the settlement in the evening, no milk was taken from her, either by her calf or by her owners, until such time as the *kəbkēb ḏ-eḥfō*, 'the star of unbinding the udder' rose. Stars also foretold the future: if someone saw the evening star, *mə́štəri*, and the dawn star, *záhra*, close together—something said to occur only once a year—this foretold either the viewer's death or their future wealth.

3.2. The Monsoon

Life changed during the monsoon months: fishing was severely curtailed, and the winds, mists and drizzle made life by the sea uncomfortable as well as unprofitable. Most Bəṭāḥira moved inland to the more sheltered areas at the foot of the escarpment at this season. This was when they harvested the tiny dates produced by the few wild date-palms that grew at the head of small watercourses there.

> əxérəf nawb wəla ḵennōn? ḵennōn wə-heh aḥā́yə ˤabú. yətēwyuw mə́nəh. yəśtəléluw ləh mən bəṭāḥərət wə-mən məharē wə-mən ḥāgénbət, kel yəśtəléluw ləh, yətēwyuw mə́nəh.

> Were the wild dates large or small? Small, but they kept people alive. They would eat them. They'd transhume to wherever they grew, the Bəṭāḥira, the Mahra, the Janaba. They'd all transhume to them to feed on them.

This was a very hungry time of year. Old men vividly recall swimming out to sea as soon as the seas began to calm down and the trade boats began to sail past their shores.

Figure 7: Plaiting wild date-palm fibre

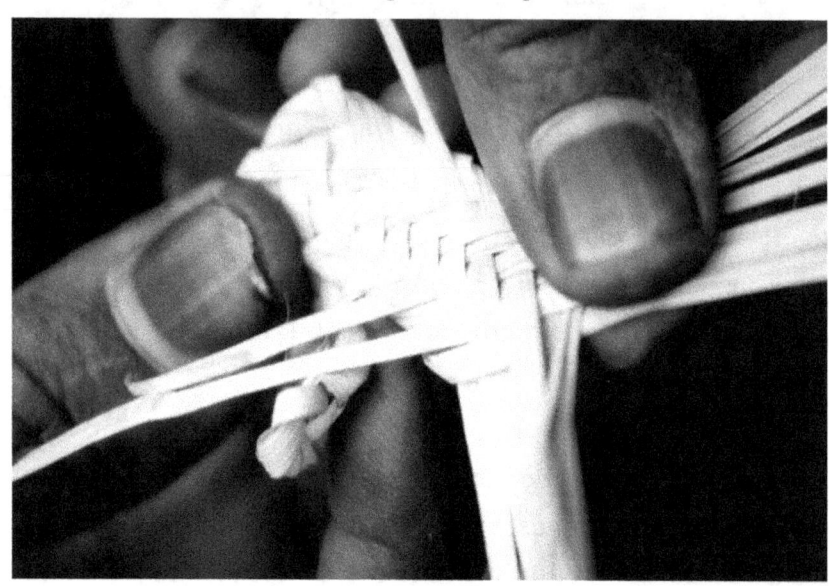

Photo © Miranda Morris, 1980s

mən ənśényəh dánəg? ṣɛrbí? nōfxan ənídən. śa la hwēri. nəwəṣáls ḏar nīd, nərābaḥ ḏar ənīd. u-mən nəšḵədéms ḥad yəsyūr šēn wə-ḥad yəffəlāt mínēn. wə-zōmuw tēn... dəblét tāmər wələ ḥāmsət ḏə-bən. tāmər? ənṭɛ́rḥah berk ənīd. ənfə́kkəh mən əməśráʿa, nəbə́lḵ əməśráʿa, hām heh tāmər mékən? w-ənbə́lḵəh berkíh. wə-məġārə nənífxah. wə-nənāfxah wə-nərābaṭ leh wə-nərābaḥ beh. ərawnə təlyūfh la.

As soon as we saw a wooden trade boat, in the post-monsoon season? We'd blow up our goatskin—there weren't any dugout canoes! We'd reach it on an inflated goatskin, we'd swim out to it on the goatskin. And when we got right up close to it, some would go along with us (i.e., give us something), and some would run away from us (i.e., give us nothing). And they would give us... a handful of dates or a roasting of coffee-beans. Dates? We'd put them inside the goatskin. We'd open it up, at the neck-end. We'd open up the *məśráʿa* end, if there were a lot of dates? And we'd open it up (and put) them inside. And then we'd inflate it. We'd inflate it, tie it tightly and swim off with it. The sea didn't get anywhere near it (i.e., the dates).

3.3. Glimpses of a Way of Life

In the late 1970s, an elderly man reminisced:

> ḥayātho ʿar seh, aʿabú ḥawlā, aʿabú yəśxōlōl bə-ḳaʿ həlákəmə, el šáho ḥab w-əl šáho tāmər w-əl šáho bənn. ḥayātho ʿar ḥayāt əbēli w-aṣáyd ḏékəmə. wə-yənētxuw. aḥád mánho yəṭáʿam məṭəʿát la ġayr aṣáyd lə-mġadéft. mət ʿānāt ʿašfōr, śīdəfāt, ḥawēn, ṣəfəlḥāt, zikt, yingēn… yəlák kel, əntóhsən mən ərawnə. wə-śēnəḥāt. hām enkaʿāt gə́ni, ənḳə́rs. śēṭə əntōh məns śa la, əntōh berk əmətəwé, berk aṣáyd. w-ənḳə́rs. wə-neḳēḏen lēs wə-naxarēfən lēs tá ṣɛrbí tkūn šēn, əgə́ni.

That was their life, the earlier generations: they stayed in that area there, without grain, without dates, without coffee beans—all they had was what the Lord gave them and that fish. Some people never tasted anything but the fish caught in the castnet. When the tide was out (there were) shellfish, sea lemons, moray eels, abalone, rock oysters, sea slugs… all those we used to eat. From the sea. And chitons. If a sack (of cereal) came, we'd hide it. We wouldn't eat any of it (i.e., on its own) in the winter months. We'd just put a little of it into (other) food, add a little to the fish. And we'd hide it. We'd make it last the summer and the months of the monsoon: it would be with us, the sack, right until the ṣɛrb season (with the trade boats) came round again.

There were rare dates from the wild date palms, or the fruit of the desert palm, *Nannorrhops ritchiana*:

syērən fənānə h-aˁárf, u-bēsən məġḳāḳ u-tēwən mən əməġḳāḳ. u-bēsən maˁnīn, gērm, əntōh mən əgáˁ. gərmānētən, axárf. ḥāwīl ləḳāṭwəs wə-hes bers mekən ṭérḥwəs bərk maˁūn u-ṭōḳwəs. hes bers kels rəḳáḳət, ḥelōbuw ḏars śxáf u-xedōmuw məġámsə u-mən ˁāṭərīt skōbuw bərkēs.

We used to set off for the wild desert palms. They have tender inner stems that we'd eat. And they'd have fruiting stalks, fruit which we'd eat. Out of hunger. Tiny fruit, seasonal fruit. First, they'd pick them, and when they had enough, they'd put them in a dish and grind them up. When they were ground up, they'd milk some milk on top of them and make a hollow in the middle (i.e., of the fruit porridge) into which they'd pour some buttermilk.

Figure 8: The *Nannorrhops* desert palm, with edible fruit

Photo © Miranda Morris, 1980s

The wild palm was also the principal source of fibre for making milking bowls, baskets and containers of all sorts, as well as for fishing equipment.

aꜥárf? awḵāt ḵōlḥan tēsən, ftə́kkən mə́nsən aꜥárf. ḥad yəślōl mən ꜥĀrah ꜥárf. wə-nəxádəmsən ḵeyād wə-nəxádəmsən əṣṭār nəślōl bēsən ṣayd wə-nəślōl bēsən tāmər.

The wild palm? At times we'd pull (the branches) off, strip the fronds from them. People would go and collect *Nannorrhops ritchiana* leaflets from wadi ꜥĀrah. And we'd make cordage from them and we'd make them into baskets. We'd carry fish and dates in them.

The ꜥ*arf* also provided medicine: to treat pain and general malaise, a powder of dried leaflets was mixed with water, and the greenish liquid (*saḵr aꜥárf*) used to wash the entire body.

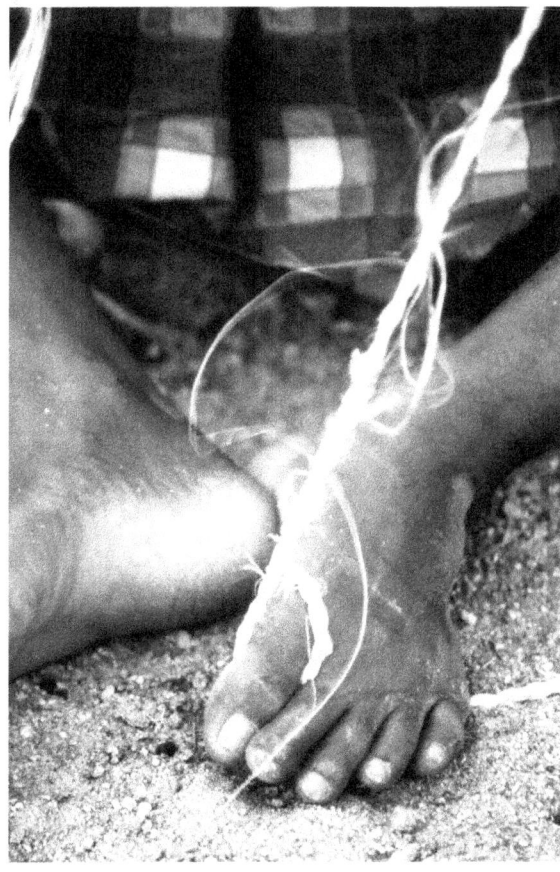

Figure 9: Twisting fibre into cordage

Photo © Miranda Morris, 1980s

Figure 10: Working *Nannorrhops* fibre with a bodkin

Photo © Miranda Morris, 1980s

Once emptied of their grain, the sacks were important material goods and were carefully differentiated. The basic term for sack was *gə́ni~gə́nyət*, pl. *gəwēni*, a small sack being *gunāyḗt*, the diminutive form. The biggest of all was the *mərḥəlḗt*, made by sewing together a number of sacks or lengths of sacking. Then there was the *kə́ndiy*, the sack in which the sorghum (*ḏirrḗt*) from Swāḥil (East Africa) was imported. It held six *ferēsil*-worth. There was the *məsárfə* which held four *ferēsil*-worth. The *furúsult* (pl. *ferēsil*) was a measurement learned from the peripatetic traders, in this area equivalent to some 28 lbs. How much a sack still contained was important to know, whether it was *fókaḥ*, 'half full', *śəlḗṭ*, 'a third full', *ribəʕḗt*, 'a quarter full', *xāmḥət*, 'a fifth full', and so on. One or two Baṭḥari traders owned a *seds*, a measure made from half a coconut, used especially for measuring out sorghum, rice or other cereal: *seds mən* ḵahf, ḵahf l-erśabét. əmakyōl bə-seds. wə-seds kel ḥad yaślōl hēmənəh. ənḥízəf la. hem ḥazōfk, ṭad təzémha xáybət wə-ḥad təzémha mékən, "A seds is made from an outer shell, the (half) shell of a coconut. The measuring is done (by scooping) with a seds measure. And (with a) seds measure, each one goes off with his (fair) share. We don't scoop it out any old how. If you were to measure out like that, you'd give one person too little and another too much." Others used a scoop made from bark (ḵalifōt), preferably from an acacia.

Otherwise, most measurements were determined by the human body. Thus, the smallest amount was miślol ḥaṣ̌ābaˤ 'amount that can be pinched between fingers and thumb'. Then there was ḵabṣ 'amount that can be grasped in one fist'; ṣ́áġaf, 'amount that can be held in a clenched fist'; kef, 'amount that can be held in a cupped hand'; and ḥafən, 'amount that can be held in two cupped hands'. To measure length and breadth, a féṭər was the span of thumb to forefinger; a śebr the span of the outspread fingers, thumb to little finger; a gəmṣ the span from the little finger of the clenched fist to the point of the elbow; a ḏəráˤ the distance from the elbow to the tip of the extended middle finger; and a bāˤ the distance from fingertip to fingertip of outstretched arms.

For counting and recordkeeping physical objects were used:

ḥāwīl hes yəḵáˤ šen śay mékən, yēkaˤ ṣayd əw ləxām, yəḥsébuw teh ˤabú. kel yəġārəb ḥsāb la, yaślōl ṣəwéyr wələ yəˤáḵəd bə-ḵayd, ṭīt ser ṭīṭ wələ ˤāśər ser ˤāśər. wə-yēkaˤ yəġērəb tēsən ḥsābəh mən yáġwə, mən yəġálaṭ.

Earlier, when we had a lot of something, fish or shark, people would have to count how many there were. Anyone who didn't know how to calculate (i.e., in his head) would use stones (to do it), or would tie knots in a length of rope, one after the other, or ten followed by another ten. Then he would know how many he had, so that he wouldn't be cheating or making a mistake.

Accessing the high plateau above meant finding a way up the steep cliffs of the escarpment.

> ḥāwīl ḥērémtən xáybət wa-məkān el heh śúri la yaġáyr kel li yədlōləh. syērən ənḥá wa-naślōl əmətəˁátən w-əmōhən ḍar əgəmōl wa-śōbbən śigərēt. hes bérən ba-ˁamḵ la-śigərēt kōsən məḵəfād wa-śébbeh la əgəmōl. wa-mġārə śōllən ṣəwéyr mən əraṣ́ḫ la-gəbəlīl wa-xədōmən tēsən əl-ḥārəm, rəṣ́ādən tēsən əté ərtəfəˁāt. wa-xərēgən mən ḍárha əgəmōl əmətəˁátən w-əmóh wa-ṭōrḥan teh xəfīf. śēnən teh ḥāwīl yəháyuw. wa-ġērən teh b-əməḥtām wa-śébbéh. rəkāt əl-ṣəwéyr il naxál əməḵəfād əté ṭáwlaˁ. hes ṭáwlaˁ elḥāḵən leh əzáməlah əḥáwlí, əmətəˁát w-əmóh wa-zəmōlən tēsən ḍárha wa-ġērən teh.

In the early days there were few tracks and the area was very difficult except to one who knew it well. We went (once), taking our food and water on (our) camel. We set off up the pass. When we were halfway up, we came across a steep drop which the camel couldn't get up. So we gathered bits of rock broken off from the escarpment and placed them on the track, stacking them one on top of the other to make a slope. We unloaded the food and water from the camel's back to lighten it—we thought otherwise it might topple over and fall. We then led it up by the halter rope. It climbed up it, stepping on the rocks piled up under the steep drop until it got to the top (of the built-up track). When it had reached the top, we fetched the load of food and water, loaded it up and led it off.

3.4. Living Quarters

It was only within living memory that the Bəṭāḥira started to build single-room huts from stone rubble, though sometimes these were little more than windbreaks.

> əmšaʿέr? ya hām šaʿārən! ənšaʿūr bə-zerb. nəxádəm zerb, zəwērīb. mən ʾəbōn. ʾəbōn? wə-nəzérəbsən ḍar əṭītsən. ḍeh ənzírbəh... hām mədēt? ənzírbəh mən aṭaráf šérgi. wə-hām bəlōt? ənzírbəh mən aṭaráf aʿálawi.

> A place to spend the night? That's if we had a place to spend the night! We'd spend the night in a *zerb* semicircle of stones. We'd make a semicircle of stones, a small semicircle of stones. From stones. Rocks? We'd stack them one on top of the other. We'd build this semicircle of stones... if the (prevailing) wind was the *mədēt* wind from the south-west? We'd build it with its back to the sea. And if (the prevailing wind) was the cold *bəlōt* wind from the north-east? We'd build it with its back to the north-east.

But the shelter offered by the *zerb* was usually minimal:

> wə-kədōt ʿar ʾəbōn wə-xədāwər. u-mən ġəsəráww nəḳṭōṭ beh mən ḥəbūr. yəḳáʿ ṭad šeh rádiy wəla dišdášt wə-seh hwínət. w-axayār mə́nho ḍárho gə́ni yəšáf bēs.

> And the 'home' was nothing but rocks or caves. In the evening we would shiver away in them from the cold. One person here or there might have a piece of cloth to throw over himself, or a full-length cotton gown, but it would be very thin and worn. The luckiest of them might have a sack to sleep under.

The stone huts provided more permanent dwellings than the caves, overhangs and hollows scooped among bushes that the Bəṭāḥira had used before: *hem yəḳáʿ ḥəbūb lého, bəlōt wə́la yəḳáʿ*

lého mūsé, yēḳaʕuw bə-xadāwər. w-el kéddə, xadərdār, xadūr, "If there was a lot of wind, the cold winter wind from the northeast, or rain, they would be in caves. Not (proper) living quarters, just tiny caves. Caves."

Sometimes a temporary shelter was set up beneath an acacia: *w-ənšūf māġáyr bə-ḥarāṣ̌? ənḥífər. hām enḥá b-abárr, ḥfōrən ḥarāṣ̌ etá xadəmāt daxšīr,* "And we used to settle to sleep under nothing but an *Acacia tortilis*. We'd dig a hole (beneath it). If we were inland (i.e., where the larger acacias grow), we'd dig under an acacia to make a hole as a shelter." Any rubbish was kept well away from the sleeping quarters: *kənést ḍar ḥarāṣ̌, bə-ḏābəl lə-ḥaraṣ̌, nərūd ḍársa bə-ʕaṣ̌āṣ̌ lə-ṣayd wə-rəhōtən wə-ḥáḳaḳ wə-ġabbān l-embərwātən, wə-kel ṯāmh la, tərdē bēs, w-aḥád yəḳarābs la mən əguwwét l-aḏāyəs,* "(We'd make) a rubbish dump on (another) acacia (or) to one side of (another) acacia, and throw fish bones, fish heads, tins and children's excreta on it: anything you didn't want you'd throw on it. No one would go near it because of its foul smell."

Closer to the sea, they would dig themselves in among the saltbush vegetation that grows along the shore:

wə-hām enḥá b-ərawnə, əl-ʕəfirīt, yəʕēməruw hēs 'ʕəfirīt'. ṭīt ṭaʕb wə-ṭīt ʕəfirīt wə-ṭad ʕarʕéyr. ṣ̌ōṯēt yəlánəmə? kélho nəḥífər báho. tá xadōmən kə́nnəs… ḏ-ergəmōt əl-kədōt. u-lāttədən bēs enḥá w-aġayāg. enḥá w-aġyāgən w-əbúnyən. kə́llən faxərə.

And if we were beside the sea, the *'ʕəfirīt' Atriplex* bushes. They call them *'ʕəfirīt'*. There's one kind called *'ṭaʕb'*, *Suaeda*, and one called *'ʕəfirīt'*, *Atriplex*, and one called *'ʕarʕéyr'*, tamarisk. Those three? Any one of them, we'd dig around and under them until we'd made, as it were…

as it were, a 'lid' for a home (i.e., an overhang to shelter beneath). And we'd all squeeze into it together, we and the men. Us and our men and our children. All of us together.

The *Atriplex* bushes provided the best shelter. They were taller than the *Suaeda* and more common than tamarisk bushes.

> aʿafīr, ənšūf ʿar bēsən bə-mədēt, ənšūf bēsən mən ġárbi. wə-bə-xerēb wə-balōt ənśētə bēsən mən šárgi. tēli ḏə-xerifīt wə-ṣerbí té təhbēb lēn əbəlōt. mən təhbēb əbəlōt šuwgēśən.

> The *Atriplex* plants? We'd have only these to sleep amongst at the time of an onshore *mədēt* wind. We'd sleep amongst them on the landward side. And when a hot offshore *xerēb* wind blew from inland or a cold *bəlōt* wind from the north-east, we'd spend the winter amongst them on the seaward side: at the end of the monsoon and the post-monsoon season. Until the cold *bəlōt* north-east wind started to blow. When the *bəlōt* wind started to blow in winter, we'd move off elsewhere.

The verb *dáḥdaḥ* describes this making of a hollow among saltbush: it is glossed as 'to scrape out a hollow among the roots of saltbush to make a sleeping place with some shelter from the prevailing wind'. Sand could be spread inside to make a softer bed, and taller stems of *Atriplex* cut and spread over the living *Atriplex* bushes to provide a rough sort or roofing. This practice produced a mocking saying among the Bəṭāḥira: ṣenḥ lə-ʿəfīrīt wəla ṣenḥ lə-ġayyít, "A shelter in an *ʿifīrīt* hollow or the shelter of a young girl?"

When staying in the foothills or in the plateau above, other types of temporary shelter were made, such as the *hzēr*, a

Figure 11a: Former living quarters at Mingiy

Figure 11b: Former living quarters at Mingiy, with Maḥmūd Mšaʿfi Al-Baṭhari (used with permission)

Photos © Miranda Morris, 2014

Figure 12a: Former living quarters at Warx, with graves

Figure 12b: Former living quarters at Warx, with cave shelters behind

Photos © Miranda Morris, 2014

semicircular shelter of lopped acacia branches: *ġaseráww? nəślōl hə-hzēr w-ənṣānaḥ beh*, "In the late afternoon? We'd carry (some branches) to make a brushwood semicircle and we'd shelter in it (from the cold and wind)." When an acacia grew too low to shelter beneath, two or three branches from a dead acacia were used to prop up one side of the crown to make room for people or goats below. This was called *mēśḵef (mən aḍarāb lə-ḥarāṣ)* 'a shelter (of acacia branches)'. If available, a length of sacking or old clothing was spread over the crown and wooden props to increase the area of shade.

A length of cloth could be spread over any structure to provide temporary shade: *wə-xadōmən xadīr ḍar ḥarāṣ. wə-nəxdárs... ʿar seh b-axaṭḵāyɛ́nyən*, "And we'd make a canopy (for shade) over an acacia tree. We'd make shade... just with bits and pieces of our clothing." On the coast, temporary shade was made by digging four driftwood posts into the pebbles and stones of the foreshore and stretching a length of material across the top. This was called *ʿə́nnə*.

It was important to protect the few precious goats of the coast from cold and wet. A small, semicircular shelter (*zirī́bət*) of acacia branches was made for them: *wə-xadōmən zirī́bət h-aʿrān. nəxádəm hēsən ṣenḥ tərbāṣan beh mən ḥəbūr*, "And we'd make a small, curved windbreak for the goats. We'd make a shelter for them to couch behind out of the cold." Sometimes a circular stone pen was built, roofed with seaweed or saltbush branches: *nəxádəm ḥarrát hə-hēṭār mən təlġámən ḥāmōtsən*, "We'd make a dry-stone pen for the female kids so that they couldn't

Figure 13: Goat drinking dewdrops

Photo © Hugh Morris, 1970s

(go off with their dams) and suckle them." The term *ḥarrát* turns up in a poem in which a poetess said, cursing witches: *wēzəmə tēsən əmōbəḥāt / wə-məṣáwbəx wə-ḥarrát*, "I'll give them (i.e., the witches, as a place to live) the empty stone foreshore / Or the dusty plains, or the pens of heaped stones!" Mature female goats were separated from their kids at night. If there were no *ḥarrát* shelter, the kids would be roped together by means of a length of rope with a series of nooses through which the heads of the kids were fed.

> *hēṭār təḱá‘an ḏābəl w-a‘rān əniyāb təḱá‘an ḏābəl. nəxádəm ḱayd lə-‘arf wə-heh yənḱə́ṭa‘, šə́ḵṭá‘. u-mġārə nəxádməh mən əlyūx, əlyūx lə-ḱáṭan, wə-den yəḥtərēkən la bə-hēṭār, bəhaw! wə-nəhēmyən tēs 'rigəlēt'.*

The female kid goats would go on one side (of the acacia), and the mature goats on the other. We'd make a

> rope out of *ˁarf Nannorrhops ritchiana* fibre, but that would break, it was friable and brittle. So then we made it from (pieces of) the gillnets, the cotton gillnets, and that would hold the kids fast. It wouldn't budge, indeed not! We call it *rigəlēt*.

Along the coast the goats found little natural graze or browse. So pairs of women took it in turn to lead their community's goats inland in search of fodder. They would spend the day with them, gathering firewood and fodder, and return home in the late afternoon. Unfortunately, goats were reluctant to feed on marine products. In times of desperation their owners would force them to eat such foods by holding their noses firmly shut and then poking small fish, fish skins and other fish debris into their mouths. While they might eat fresh shark that had been boiled and squeezed dry, they could not be persuaded to eat salt shark. Sometimes, driven by hunger, the goats would eat discarded spiny lobster shells (but not crab shells), fish washed ashore and dried to a crisp, or dried fishbones. They readily consumed any items of clothing or leather and plant fibre containers, so such possessions had to be hung up well out of their reach.

Some families owned a wooden box (*bə́ndis*, pl. *bənáwdis*) in which they could store precious possessions, but *bənēdis ḏen heh ˁar skik. el heh əlwāḥ*[JA] *la*, "These boxes were made from odds and ends of driftwood. They weren't (properly made) from planking." Nor was such a box thief-proof: a man recalled how he had buried his box of food beneath a mound of rocks and covered the whole mound with an old cotton gillnet, pegged down all around. Nevertheless, a hyena still managed to chew through the net, knock the rocks aside and get at the food. Later, aluminium boxes with a hasp that could be padlocked shut (sənduk͟~sandík͟, pl. sənáwdək͟) became available, and these were hugely popular.

3.5. Fishing

Men fished from the beach with homemade cast nets (mġadéft) of differing circumference and mesh size, each with its own name, as śógəd, ġall, ṣównəwāt~ṣōn, śáġar. They fished with hook and line from rocks and cliff ledges, or out at sea from inflated goatskins. On the shore, they would make a shallow pit into which they would throw anything they caught: w-əməktōl beh mənk͟ēl. hes yənāka ͑ bə-ṣayd yərūd bəh berk əmənk͟ēl, "The sites for line-fishing have a hollowed-out area: when he catches a fish, he throws it into the hollow (to keep it safe and mark it as his property)." They would set lines at dusk from clifftops to catch the shark and other large fish which came inshore to feed at night. Much fishing had to be done in the dark, and sometimes fishermen had to let themselves down on a rope to reach a good place from which to fish: the risk of accidents on the precipitous cliff ledges was high. Families or groups of bachelor fishermen would move along the shore, setting up home beneath rocks there or in shallow caves above the beach, any place from which they could keep a close eye on the sea.

The Bəṭāḥira had many terms to describe different methods of fishing and the hooks that were used: forms from the root √ ͑dn described fishing for the more valuable large fish such as kingfish, greater amberjack, cobia or blacktip trevally, with a strong line, a large hook called *maʿdīn*, and bait of a tempting fish such as a mullet. Forms from the root √*ndġ* described fishing for larger fish with the big *məndīġ* hook, fashioned locally from a large nail. Forms from the root √*ṣrb* described fishing from rocks revealed by the receding tide for medium-sized fish such as snappers and smaller groupers, emperor and sea bream, using a finer line with a smaller (imported) *gəndēwi* hook. Forms from the root √*šwm* described fishing with a fine line and a small homemade *ráfəḳət~rəfáḳət* hook beaten from a small nail, with a bait of crab, to catch fish such as small sea bream, snapper or wrasse. Forms from the root √*ḥbl* described fishing from a cliff for shark and turtle, using a multi-plied, strong line and the largest hook of all, the *ḥadīd*.

Figure 14: Night quarters for fishermen near Mingiy

Photos © Miranda Morris, 2014

After shark, the main prize was a ḥūt, 'a large fish', a fish that would feed many, or that could be used as barter or processed to sell to the trade boats: yənākaˤ tēn əgīr, berk aˤáyd, 'the gīr fish (i.e., the large ḥūt fish and shark that follow the migrating shoals of small sardine-type fish) come to us, amongst the sardines'. Among the ḥūt, the ṭōnik 'kingfish' (Indo-Pacific king mackerel or narrowbarred spanish mackerel) was particularly prized.

> əṭōnīk aḥawlá, aḥawlá yəḥísəbwəs ṣādti ṭəréh. hes təḳáṣ̌bis fákhi, təgzérs, təḳáˤ mən ṭérti. w-aḥawlá yəṭráḥuw tēs mən térti. təkṣáṣən mə́nəh nxal ədərwēt mən sərānə, náḥfi ṭəréh, ḏeh naḥf u-ḏeh naḥf. hem ber gəzōrək tēs fákhi, tənḥāfh, ṣ̌əkkát. afákh təhēdyən teh fákhi ṭərti u-tənḥāf mə́nəh té sə́rəf sə́rəf.

> The kingfish, the first people, our ancestors, considered it to be equivalent to two fish. For when you'd divided it into two halves, (when) you'd cut it in half, it became two fish. Our ancestors reckoned it to be equivalent to two (fish). You'd cut beneath the dorsal hump, from behind, to make two sections, this section and this section (i.e., one half with the head, the other with the tail). When you'd cut it (i.e., each half-fish) in two, you'd open (each half) out flat, split down the middle. You'd divide this half into two (further) halves and then you'd slice (each bit) across until it was all slices.

Hungry fisher families encouraged one another with songs, mocking those lacking in skill and praising those who were successful.

> hām ber ḳadəmə́ / ˤĀmer wə-Hzáˤ
> yənkáˤo bə-ṣayd / tá yəxás bə-ḳaˤ

> *t-aṣaʕé yəṣʕáy / w-əgīʕān yəsbáʕ*
>
> If they got there first / ʕĀmer and Həzáʕ.
>
> The two of them would catch so many fish / That (some) would be left to rot on the ground.
>
> So that those coming down from the desert above in search of fish would go back up happy / And the hungry would be sated!

Or they would criticise a man having a lie-in during the monsoon instead of getting up before sunrise to set off to catch the precious *terʕān* pompano, one of the few fish which could be caught during these wild months:

> *kul yəḥām nəwṣárs / wə-yəmśēś 'bʕéli śabḥ'*
>
> *el yəšūf tá kə-saḥḥ / tá yəfégig leh aṣábḥ*
>
> He who wants half its head / And to savour 'the fat-filled ones'.
>
> Does not lie sleeping until the sun is well up / Until dawn breaks on him![6]

3.6. Shark for Trade and Barter

For the Bəṭāḥira to be able to barter for or buy the necessities they were unable to produce themselves—cotton fibre to make fishing equipment, dates, cereals, cloth and knife blades—they had to have something to trade. There was a steady demand throughout the wider region for dried fish and dried shark meat (and later, shark fins).

---

[6] *mśēś*, lit. 'to chew on something soft'; *nāṣer* 'half of the head, split down the middle'.

Shark were trapped in homemade gillnets or caught on the lines set from the clifftops. The gillnets were tied together in a line of ten, set perpendicular to the shore. Each fisherman would swim out on his inflated goatskin with his net and stone 'anchor(s)'. He would tie his net firmly to his neighbour's and set his anchor(s). Because some positions in the line were considered to be better than others, for fairness, lots (herwáʿ) were cast to determine which position each net was to occupy. The position closest to the shore (məráwwas) was disliked: it caught few shark, except in high summer when certain types of shark came close inshore to feed. The position furthest out to sea, the tenth (ʿā́serət or məwáxxar), was equally undesirable: laborious to set and check, and a great distance to tow any shark caught to the shore. The positions further out to sea were always less liked, the sixth (hḗtət), seventh (hḗbaʿt), eighth (ṭḗmənət) and ninth (tḗsaʿt). The best of all were the second in line (rəkít), the third (šéltət), fourth (rḗbaʿt) and fifth (xā́mhət).

A shark trapped in a gillnet was towed ashore, its weight lessened by strapping inflated goatskins onto it. It was then carried to the məxṭáʿ, lit. 'cutting area', a level place cleared of stones and debris, for processing. The head, tail and fins were removed, the trunk split open along its length, the guts removed, the flesh scored in parallel lines and salt rubbed in. The trunk was then folded shut and left for the night. At sunrise the next morning, it was opened out flat, more salt was rubbed in and then it was left out in the sun. In the late afternoon it was turned over and placed flesh-side down, and at dusk it was once more folded shut. This was done daily for at least a week, until the trunk had hardened and completely dried out. Pits (*maléffa*, pl. *malēfəf*) for storing the dried shark were dug high on the foreshore, and the dried trunks were laid in them between layers of pebbles and dried seaweed: *ḏar ələxām áwḳaʕ śaʕr, u-mən ḏar śaʕr áwḳaʕ ḥawbōn u-mən ḏar ḥawbōn, rāṣəl. ḥawbōn ḳánnətən, rāṣəl*, "Put seaweed above the (layer of) shark, and above the seaweed put (a layer of) stones, and above the stones put (a layer of) pebbles: small stones, *rāṣəl*." Once filled, the pit was closed and left until the autumn when the wooden trade boats, the *máwsim*, arrived. *tənākaʕ də́nəg wə-nəśtēm mins. ḥad ḏə-šeh śay yəśtēm mins wə-ḥad ḏə-šeh śa la…* "Trade boats would arrive and we'd buy things from them. The one who had something (to sell) would buy from them, and the one who had nothing…"

Figure 15: Warx and lagoon with former shark pits in foreground

Photo © Miranda Morris, 2014

Sometimes they could order items from the boats trading along the coast.

> baʿéli mkálla kel ḏə-šeh śay yəxəṣāb šého, yəxəṣāb... nə́rmi məxáwrig mən twot aḳáyḏ wə-nəxəṣāb šého. ḏə-heh šeh śay yəxəṣāb. wə-yənāka'ho əməxṣāb wə-śay zyūd. wə-ḏə-heh śa la yəśtēm mən dōlho. akṭīr nəśtēm mən dōl eZífənə wə-Bəxéyyit nḥá, lə-láḥak ənḥá.
>
> The people of Mukalla, anyone who had something (to sell) could order things from them. He'd order... We'd set the (shark) nets at *məxáwrig*, as soon as summer came in, and we'd make our order with them (then), the man who had (goods to trade). The order would come, usually with some extra. The person who had nothing (to sell) had to buy (directly) from them. Most of us would buy (what we needed) from Zífənə or Bxéyyit (two local Baṭhari traders), we ourselves, in our day.

In bad weather, the fishermen had to put the shark into the shark pit before they were quite dry. These shark were called *xaserḗt* and were prone to spoilage and grub infestation, so never got as good a price as the properly dried shark. In the winter months when the trade boats were active along the coast, any shark caught were just salted and left for two days to partially dry out. After being washed in the sea, this kind of shark, called *gínnə*, was ready for sale. It never went into the *məléffə* pit. Traders would buy such shark still damp (*ġamṭīṭ*), and then either dry them on board or sell them as they were at their final destination, and the buyer would complete the drying process. Like the *xaserḗt* shark above, these never got as good a price as the fully dried shark. The *gínnə* method of dealing with shark was not possible in the summer months: it was too hot, and anyway, at this time, the trade boats were few and far between. Instead, in summer, the shark would be spread out on the pebbles of the upper beach, skin-side down, and turned every second day until the trade boats arrived.

Large fish other than shark were also salted and dried for sale or barter. The Spanish mackerel or kingfish (*ṭōnīk*) was a particularly valuable fish. There was always a demand for its salted and dried flesh, and fresh it was excellent eating, feeding many people. Indeed, pieces of its raw flesh were given as a tonic to the debilitated or sick, in the same way as pieces of raw goat liver. To process the *ṭōnīk* for sale, the fish were gutted, split open butterfly fashion, salted and then folded shut and set out to dry, but in the shade, never in the sun. In the hot summer months, they had to be processed as quickly as possible and sometimes had to be stored while still damp, preserved under an extra layer of salt. In the cooler months they could be left out until completely dry, when they were stacked in a cave or small stone pen to wait for the traders.

The Bəṭāḥira had little else to sell. They could sometimes trade some of the salt they'd harvested to passing boats. If they had any to spare, they might trade shark liver oil to visiting crews who had beached their boat to scrub it clean of barnacles and weed, or to carry out repairs. Some years there was a demand for cuttlebone. There was plenty of this along their coast, but the demand was unpredictable.

3.7. The Lack of Boats

Until recently the Bəṭāḥira owned no boats, not even dugout canoes. The dugout only arrived in the days of older fishermen still alive today. Even then, only a small number from the community could afford one. (Illustrating this, one day I was with a group of old men and women as they enjoyed recalling exactly which man first managed to get hold of a dugout, where it had come from, its size, and what name had been given to it by its proud owner.) However, the fishermen recognised the different types of craft that sailed past them, or stopped off to trade or to beach their boats. The most widely used term among the Bəṭāḥira for a wooden sailing boat (*beden* in Omani Arabic) was *dánəg* (pl. *dənāwəg ~ dənōgər*). The *zəʕúmət* (pl. *zəʕéyəm*), was another wooden boat they often saw (*səmbūk̲* in Omani Arabic, and some Bəṭāḥira also called this type of boat a *sə́mbək̲*): *zəʕúmət el heh dánəg la*, "A *zəʕúmət* boat is not the same as a *dánəg* boat." From travelling with trade boats or talking with others, they learned the names of other craft: the *zəwáfi* boats of date palm ribs bound with coir fibre (*līf*), whose stern was the same shape as its prow; the *ʕarṣát*, a wooden craft with a single sail, and the *ʕabərí* or *bū xášəm* (lit. 'with a long nose or beak')', a boat of wooden planks stitched together.

3.8. Use of Inflated Goatskins or Shark Stomachs to Go Out to Sea

In place of sea-going craft, Baṭhari fishermen used inflated goatskins. They swam out on one to set their gillnets, returning later to see if they had caught anything. They would bring one or more extra goatskins with them, rolled up and tucked beneath one arm. These were for tying to the gillnet to lessen the weight as they hauled it up to examine it for fish. If there was a shark, a goatskin float was tied to it to make it easier to tow ashore.[7] This was something I witnessed myself in Mingíy in the 1980s.

This need for goatskins to use at sea as well as in the home meant that it was essential for a fishing family to rear at least a few goats. That some fishermen were forced to make use of a dried shark's stomach instead of a goatskin for sea work only goes to show how severe the shortage of goats was: *hem tḥām tərābaḥ ləh, əgəšēr lə-ləxām, táxərgəh wə-təwāḳaˤ beh milḥāt wə-təḳāšˤah té ḳéšaˤ wə-yəṣmōm lə-nəfxát nəfāxən teh,* "If you want to use it to swim on, the shark stomach, remove it, salt it and then set it to dry. Once it's quite dry and strong enough to take being inflated, we'd inflate it." A shark stomach was not as strong as a goatskin and was said to be more susceptible to tearing on the barnacled rocks. I have recorded stories in which an imperfectly cured shark stomach gave out a smell that attracted shark, with terrible consequences. When a family only owned a single goatskin, the men and women would have to share it: the women using it to fetch water in the morning and handing it over to the men to take out to sea in the afternoon.

Even line fishing could be done from an inflated goatskin. A fisherman would tie his equipment onto the skin, wrap his

---

[7] At the British Museum (Room B, panel 11, bottom) you can see a panel entitled 'Crossing a river. Assyrian c. 845-860 BC. Assyrian officials supervise as the army crosses a river, probably the Euphrates. Some soldiers are to cross on inflated skins'.

bait and knife-blade into a scrap of cloth and wind this around his head, then paddle out to sea. He would manoeuvre the skin to make a seat—like a saddle on a horse—and would sit astride it, his legs tucked tightly around the skin, leaving both hands free. When he had finished fishing, he would tie his fish to one end of the extra length of line he had brought with him and reel this out to float far behind the skin. This was so that any shark in the vicinity would go for the fish rather than for the fisherman. One fisherman told me of a time when a shark went for the fish on his line, and by the time he reached shore there were no fish left.

Figure 16: Tanning a goatskin

Photo © Miranda Morris, 1980s

3.9. Bait

For the larger more valuable migratory fish, the best bait (*ṣamdēt*) was a sardine, but shoals of sardine and other small migratory fish were not plentiful inshore. All too often the shoals swam past too far out to sea for the Bəṭāḥira to be able to catch them. So instead, before setting off, they first had to catch fish by line or net to use as bait. Or they would go at low tide to hunt among the rocks and pools for crabs, spiny lobster or octopus.

> syērk wə-kōsk tēs bə-dəxšīr, wə-śōllək hēs məsmēr wə-dəġāṣ̌k tēs əréhs beh əté xarōgənə fˁēmsa. mēnˁak tēs bə-fˁēmsa wə-labōdək bēs ḏar ḥawbōn əté mātāt. ḳašābək tēs w-akātələk bēs bə-śwēr. wə-tówə liy ṣayd bēs.

> I went off and found it (an octopus) in a hole. I took a pointed rod of iron and stabbed away at its head with it until its tentacles (lit. 'legs') emerged. I grabbed it out by the tentacles and beat it on a rock until it was dead. I cut it up and used it as bait on my line. And I got a bite with it.

The octopus, squid, cuttlefish and spiny lobster were not much liked as food; the Bəṭāḥira say disapprovingly: 'They have no blood, no fat'. tərəbáḥt wə-ġatráwwət wə-śīrəx wə-ˁašfēr hēsən ṭáˁam la. yətēwyuw tēsən aˁabú lekín hēsən ṭáˁam la w-el tənāfˁan tōk ˁar ṣayd. śabḥ śa la bərkēsən, yəlán kélsən, "An octopus, a cuttlefish or a squid, a spiny lobster and a sea snail have no flavour. People do eat them, but they have no taste. Nothing does you any good except fish. They have no fat, those others."

But when really hungry people did eat octopus:

> tərəbáḥt yakātəluw bēs wə-yətēbəxwəs. yōm yḥémuw tēs yətēwyəs. yegēldwəs əgəlādət mən aġáwf w-akśáˁwəs. hem keśəˁāt ləffēs wə-awkaˁēs bərk əgwēni wálə awkaˁēs bərk... ḥayállah śay.

An octopus, they'd use it to linefish with, or they'd cook it. When they wanted to, they'd eat it. They'd remove the outer skin and they'd dry (the rest of) it. When it's dry, roll it up and put it into sacks, or put it into… into anything!

Crabs also provided bait: *ḥayśyōt? ḥayśyōt ḥawərēt? ḏih hwinət, hwinət wə-seh ṣamdēt. ṣamdēt hə-kētəb wə-ṣamdēt hə-ḳalāwət wə-ṣamdēt hə-bənāwət wə-ṣamdēt hə-mēryət wə-ʿanəḳāb wə-hə-ʿaṣāb, wə-hə-ṣayd ḏeh ḳennōn*, "The *ḥayśyōt* crab? The dark-coloured crab? This is a miserable creature. It's a poor thing but it's (useful as) bait. Bait for the *kētəb* sea bream, for the *ḳalāwət* snapper, for the *bənāwət* drum and for the *mēryət* sea bream. Also for the *ʿanəḳāb* bream, the *ʿaṣāb* emperor, and (other) small fish like these."

Once caught, the crabs could be kept alive for several days. Their legs were broken off to disable them and they were placed in the shade, watered and fed with bits and pieces of marine material: *el ʿād təmyōt la. nəwāḳaʿ hēs ṭirūr. wəla ṭirūr aṭáḥḥ, wəla śaʿr*, "It won't die yet. We give it bits and pieces to nibble at. Either bits and pieces from the shore, or seaweed."

Some fish could only be tempted by a very specific bait. The *terʿān* pompano was a key resource throughout the wild monsoon months: *eterʿān naśámdən tēs bə-ṣāfə. aṣṣāfə entəkūkah mən kermām. yaʿśōś bə-kermām. wə-kermām hes herēm ḏih yaʿśōś beh. heh máwsim, ṣāfə. wə-ʿādəh ḳennōn nəʿāmer hēs 'ṣāfə' wə-mən yaʿḳār nəʿāmer hēh 'fēḏeḳ'*, "For the *terʿān* pompano we use a bait of an immature mussel. We knock them off the rock—they 'grow' on the rocks (in the sea). They grow on the rocks like this vegetation here. They have their own season, the *ṣāfə* mussels. When they're still immature we call them *ṣāfə* and once they are full sized we call them *fēdek̬*."

If no bait were available, the fishermen would use a lure (*ʿāwər*) instead. They were skilled at making these from the stems of certain plants, whittling a section to make it look like a tiny fish or a sardine. If they had caught a firm-fleshed fish, such as a *skfīt* emperor, *ṭeráḥa* seabream, *ṭāk̬a* bluefish or *terʿān* pompano, they could make a *məṣṭāṭ* bait by taking a finger-length slice of its white flesh, laying it on a piece of thickly twisted cotton (*ftilət*), tying the two together and then binding them to the line above the hook. With the cotton frayed out to look like a tail, once in the water it looked like a fine fat sardine.

3.10. Equipment and Care of Equipment

The equipment used to harvest the sea was minimal and mostly made *in situ*. Nets of differing mesh size were made from cotton fibre brought down from northern Oman. All kinds of lines were twisted and plied from the same material. Hooks were hammered from nails extracted from debris that floated ashore—ships' timbers, planking, old crates and so on—from the larger marine nails, large hooks to hook turtle or shark, right down to small fine hooks made from tacks. Strong threads were twisted and oiled to make a twine used to bind the hooks to the lines, and sinkers were made from holed stones or rare fragments of lead.

All fishing equipment was precious and had to be properly cared for. The cotton equipment was treated at intervals with plant extracts to toughen it and to stain it a darker colour to make it less visible: *habġ śōllən teh mən hərmīt wə-hes təḳáˤ śōk moh wə́lə rawnə təblōləh té yəḳáˤ ṭéri. wə́lə hem śōk moh la, təbíṣəḳ ləh, (tə)tífəl ləh. wə-təmārax śwēr beh əté taḥwīrōr. mən yəśāns aṣáyd wə-təférəd. təḳáˤ hes ərawnə, el ḥawərrāt śwēr,* "The 'habġ' *Heliotropium longiflora* plant: we'd take (leaves) from the plant. If you had water or sea water, you'd wet it until it was all damp. Or if you didn't have any water, you'd spit on it, wet it with your saliva. And then you'd smear the line with it to darken it. So that the fish wouldn't see the line and swim off. It would become like (the colour of) the sea, the line would turn a darker colour."

Certain seashells were gathered and burned to make a lime preservative (*ḥek*). Cotton lines and nets were soaked in it to stop them rotting. In the shark-fishing season this had to be done every three to four days. If not, it was said that "the shark would smell the nets and avoid them."

> *ḥāwīl ənḥá rēdən b-ərа́wnə śhəlét yōm. wə-mġārə əlyūx ləbōduw ˤáfər. wə-mġārə śōllən táho mən ərа́wnə wə-ˤesōfən báho bə-ṭirīt wə-śōllən táho əté der əməḥkākə wə-śēlbən táho. wə-xōśṣən ḥek b-əməḥkākə wə-ṭórhan bēs rawnə. w-ezyēdən tēs ḥek əté ġadóh ḥek mékən wə-ġadóh ləbōn. mġārə ḥōkkən beh əlyūx kel waḳt ṭad. wə-kədōsən táho hawb əl-sāˤa. ṭórhan táho wə-ḳśáˤən táho wə-ġasərа́ww rēdən báho b-ərаẃnə.*

First, we'd set the (gillnets) out at sea. Three days running. And then the nets would change colour and become reddish-coloured (i.e., from algal growth). So then we'd take them out of the sea and beat them in the shallows. Then we'd carry them to the liming pit and hang them up

> to drip, shaking (the water from) them. We'd add *ḥek* lime to the liming pit and then add salt water. We'd add more lime until it was full of lime and (the water) had turned white. Then we'd bleach the nets, one at a time. We'd stack them in a heap and leave them there for about an hour. We'd leave them there and then we'd spread them out to dry. And that afternoon we'd set them out at sea again.

Hooks were re-sharpened, and the vital goatskin floats oiled, any defects repaired, and any holes patched. Once a fisherman owned a *hūri* dugout canoe, it was treated with the greatest care. During the monsoon months it was drawn up high on the shore and turned upside down on props to keep it from direct contact with the ground. Hermit crabs could damage dugouts which were not raised on props: *waḵt ḏeh li yerśōś, ḥaykēk? yətoh aḵalfāt*, "At this time those crawlers, the hermit crabs? They'd eat away at the caulking (i.e., cotton waste mixed with shark liver oil and hammered into any cracks in the wood)." The dugouts were soaked in shark liver oil to stop the wood drying out and cracking. When the seas grew calm once more, the dugouts were made ready for going out to sea by filling them with seawater for a few days and then rubbing them down to rid them of the strong smell of shark liver oil; otherwise the smell would frighten the shark away. The green algal growth and the barnacles that build up over time on the base of a dugout were carefully scraped off: *hes tənākaˤ mən ərawnə, ədə́nəg təḵáˤ bēs śaˤr wə-xáras wə-yəghēbuw tēs b-abárr wə-yaˤrémwəs wə-yəṣáluw tēs bə-ṣift wə-təḵáˤ šərár* "When it (the dugout) comes up from the sea, it is (covered) with seaweed and encrusted with barnacles. They would drag it up the shore and scrape this off and then oil it with shark liver oil until it was clean and smooth."

3.11. Salt

Salt (*milḥāt*) was essential for processing and preserving fish, and especially the commercially valuable shark. The best for this (and for cooking) was sea salt, either that extracted from the bodies of brackish water such as the lagoons and estuaries of the coast, or, after the high monsoon tides or after a storm, from saltwater pools and caves close to the shore.

The Bəṭāḥira differentiated between many types of salt: *séfi*, fine grains of salt gathered from around a body of saline water or rock pool; *ḏársi*, lumps of discoloured salt collected from the banks of an estuary; *enṭēri~enṭiri* were fragments of salt-impregnated matter scraped from around a lagoon (*wə-milḥēt enṭiri, ḥanít lə-xār? təmláḥ bēs la*, 'but the *enṭiri* kind of salt, the whatsit of the lagoon? Don't use that to salt it [i.e., food]'); *ságat~sġat*, the crisp, salty crust found in the vicinity of a lagoon, and in certain caves and overhangs in the mountains above, where it makes reddish streaks. Salt could be extracted from the saltiest water (*zaʿāḵ*) of a lagoon by boiling it down, and this was called *milḥāt lə-xār*, 'lagoon salt'. Water could be made salty for cooking by soaking salt-laden plants such as *Dyerophytum indicum* (*émlaḥ~məlaḥláḥ*) in water and then straining it.

Enṭēri~enṭiri is soft and looks like earth, and was mainly used medicinally: put on the fire with a little water, boiled, and the paste smeared over a major wound or sore. If bound with a bandage, the cloth would set hard like a plaster cast. This property was useful when treating a fracture: the limb was tightly bound in strips of cloth soaked in the paste, applied as hot as the patient could stand.

The various kinds of rock salt collected in the mountains were not usually used for cooking or preserving. *Milḥāt lə-gəbəlīl*, 'mountain salt', was used in the manufacture of gunpowder; *miláḥt~milḥāt əl-gənōt*, a kind of rock salt found at Gənōt, was powdered and used to strengthen leather and dye it dark brown. A kind of carbonaceous mudstone[8] called *samd* was collected and used in the same way to produce a black dye. *milḥāt lə-ʕarēśi* was a rock salt found in the interior desert: the white chunks were reduced to a fine powder and used to treat a variety of eye conditions (*təkáʕ ləbənēt wə-nawb wə-seh dáwi lə-ʕayéntən*, "it's pale-coloured and comes in large chunks and is medicine for eyes").

3.12. Non-Fish Marine Food

There was plenty of food to be had from the sea apart from fish. The sea slugs, sea lemons, sea cucumbers, spiny lobsters, squid, octopus and cuttlefish were mainly caught by men, while shellfish were mainly gathered by women. Sea urchins could be broken open for their edible gonads. A wide variety of shellfish were eaten: all kinds of sea snails, mussels, rock oysters, chitons, limpets, clams and cockles. Shellfish were at their fattest in the autumn and winter months, and at these times groups of

---

[8] I am indebted to Alan Werritty for this identification.

women would set off for the best shellfish sites, armed with a metal spike for prising shells from rocks or for spearing cephalopods and other marine invertebrates.

ˁagərēz lə-gəmōl? yəkūn ṭawīl. wə-yəkūn ˁar nātfax. el ḥāṭṭat. yəkūn ṭawīl w-el ḥāṭṭat. wə-mən fənānə boh? beh nəkfīf ḳennōn, ḍafīr. wə-yətóh beh, wə-yəˁayš beh.

An ˁagerēz lə-gəmōl 'camel testicle' sea slug? It's long. And it just inflates itself. It's plump (lit. 'ripe'). It's long and fat. And at the front, here? It has something like a small scab. (Something like) a fingernail. And it eats with it, it keeps itself alive with it.

wə-ḥawīl mən nhām nəġāṣ ha-śīdəfāt? yəskōk lēn əxádər. māt thām ənxárəg śīdəfāt yəkūn bə-xádər lə-śīdəfāt. nəṭābxah. nəḳālaˁ bə-wəˁā moh w-əmóh nəḳālaˁ beh milḥāt w-əntābxah. (tə)ṭābxah bə-śeyāṭ. tfhēś beh etá yəbhēl. mən yəbhēl? tśḳōḳah bə-skīn. təḳáśbəh tá (tə)tālaˁ əgəlādət ḥāwərēt l-aˁámris wə-yəṭālaˁ ttih əṣāfi əl-ḥilw l-aˁámrih. ənkáśbəh wəḏīr wəḏīr, wəḏīr wəḏīr, wəḏīr wəḏīr? naxərāgəh w-əntóh.

And before, when we wanted to dive for śīdəfāt sea lemon? It would block the entrance to its niche (lit. 'cave') against us. When you wanted to get the sea-lemon out, there it would be in its śīdəfāt 'cave'. We'd cook it. We'd put water in a cooking pot and salt the water, and we'd cook it. You'd cook it on the fire, boiling it until it was ready to eat. When it was ready to eat, you'd split it open with a knife. You'd cut the black outer skin away and put it to one side, and the pure good flesh you'd put to another side. We'd cut it up slice by slice, slice by slice, slice by slice? We'd take it (a slice) and we'd eat it.

yingīr? ədəffēth mən əmṣáˁ līnət wə-mən aġáwf bēs ḳaśərīt, ḍárəh ḳaśərīt. wə-ḍar əḳaśərīt śay yəṭəmōr beh, hes śef. beh śēf, hēmˁak? yēḳaˁ b-ərawnə k-aˁánət, wə-ḥāwīl yətēwyuw teh. yəṭēbxuw teh bə-ṣifēri, yəfḥāś sāʿat əté yəbəhél u-mēt el bēhəl, yətēwyuw mánəh, w-əmətəwéh śūri.

A *yingīr* sea cucumber? Its body below is soft, but on top it has an outer skin. It has a sort of outer skin on top. And there on top of the outer skin grow something like hair. It has (something like) hair, do you hear? It can be found at low tide and people used to eat it. They'd cook it in pots, let it boil for a while until it was ready and then eat it. And its flesh is good.

Diving for foods such as these was only possible when the sea was calm and clear. The frothing, churned up seas of the four to five months of the monsoon made most diving impracticable. The occasional 'red tide' or algal bloom brought by onshore winds from the east in the hotter months also made the sea too murky for diving: ərawnə ḥūr dəmkərát. hes ərawnə dəmkərát wa-təġyōṣ bēs təbṣār śa la, "There's a red tide today. If there's a red tide and you're diving, you can't see anything."

3.13. Hunting Turtle

The Bəṭāḥira, like the Janaba fishermen to the east of them, were renowned above all for their skill in hunting turtle. Their preferred turtle was the green turtle. They would climb to a high point to look for one coming up for air, or they would see one far below, feeding. They caught them either by casting for them with a strong line and large iron hook, or, if a fisherman was down on the shore or out at sea, he would swim silently up behind the turtle and try to place a hook in its neck, by hand. Helped by others, he would play it on the line until it was exhausted, when it would be towed ashore, turned upside down and butchered. The meat and fat of a turtle used to be regarded as the best of all eating. An old man told me in the 1980s: *aḥāmis axáyr mən ḥūt l-əráwnə kéləh. ḥāwīl. wə-nāṣerə aʿabū yətēwyuw tēs la yaġáyr hem aḥád axáybət mən aḥawlā*, "Turtle is better than all the fish in the sea, (at least) we used (to think so). Nowadays people don't eat it, except one or two of the older people." They knew what their preferred turtles liked to feed on: *(tə)tōh śaʿr kéləh, lekín baʿlít ʿaləfēt tkūn śūrōt*, "they (turtles) eat all kinds of seaweed, but the kind that feeds on *ʿaləfēt* seaweed is very good."

A great celebration would be held when a turtle or a dolphin was caught, or if there was a good haul of prime fish such as bluefish. Women would dress in their best, and after everyone had eaten their fill, there would be singing and dancing.

> *aġabīr? nənáḥag leh. əbēhər? nənáḥag lēs. terʿān ḏih sīrēt wə-tənáḳaʿ b-əlyūx, mən kōriyə*[JA]*? ənḳáhəb nənáḥag lēs. aḥāmis? nənáḥag leh, l-ʿaʿamméy l-aʿabú', l-ʿaʿamméy lə-ḥaytām'.*

> The dolphin? We used to dance for it. The large mullet? We used to dance for it. The migrating *terʿān* pompano fish when caught in the gillnets? When some twenty (were caught) at once? At midday we'd dance for them. The turtle? We'd dance for it: the 'mother of the people'? The 'mother of the fatherless'? (i.e., even the fatherless would get plenty to eat if there was turtle.)

3.14. Nothing Went to Waste

The main priority for people so often hungry and with so few material possessions was to waste nothing. To give a few examples:

The swim bladders of larger fish (ġōṣ~ġawṣ) were inflated, rubbed with salt and hung up to dry for two or three days, and then used as containers for the purest shark or fish liver oil.

Even when eating something as everyday as a chiton, as well as the fleshy foot, the hard muscular girdle of the shell was also pared off and eaten.

Tobacco (təmbēkə~tənbēk) and snuff (nəšḱét) were rare treats, and the Bəṭāḥira had various ways of stretching the little tobacco they could get hold of. They would take a piece of cloth and char it at the fire. Then they would take a small amount of tobacco leaf and hold it over the fire until it changed colour. The tobacco and the charred cloth were crushed together, and the powder used as snuff. Smokers would also scrape away around the mouth and stem of their soapstone or wooden pipes to remove fragments of nicotine and other deposits, and carefully add these to the little tobacco they had.

Eye-black, koḥl, was appreciated as a cosmetic but was also believed to sharpen the sight. Imported antimony was rare and substitutes had to be found. One alternative was to use lamp-black made by collecting soot from burning oil. The best was that made from shark liver oil cooked in a little pot with another inverted on top. The greasy soot was scraped off into a shell, and a scrap of cotton dipped into it repeatedly until all the grease had been absorbed. This oily cotton was stored in another shell and used as eye-black. If the cotton was soaked in butter or melted marrow fat before being dipped into the 'soot', the preparation lasted well. Cephalopod ink too was collected and used to stretch a small amount of eye-black.

On the rare occasion that a camel was slaughtered, the fat of the hump would be carefully shared out. Small pieces would be salted and dried and kept in a shell to use for oiling and waterproofing leather.

The slaughter of one of the few goats was a major event and the meat was made to last: *əlēlət aḥāwəlēt naʿtēśyən məśáwbisa w-əlēlət əmtélyət naʿtēśyən ḥadgdēlsa*, "On the first evening we'd eat the bits of it which are roasted (i.e., the internal organs that do not keep well), and the second evening we'd eat the back legs." The most precious parts, the *kəndōl*, namely the sternum (*kḥó*), head (*rih*) and heart (*ḥalbīb*)—all the parts with most fat and most savour—would be offered to the elders or to any visitor(s) present. *éxərguw əkəndōl fənānə h-aʿabú xēhār, yəśuwhālə̄h*, "Take out the *kəndōl* parts first and give them to the old men: they deserve it." The other prime parts of the carcass, the larger marrow bones (*enṣifót*), the liver (*šəbdīt*), and the intestines (*məʿuwyān*) would be carefully shared out among all those present. Some of the meat of the carcass was cut into long thin strips and hung up to dry in the sun. These were stored to be eaten as a future treat or, when the sea had not provided anything, to flavour a plain cereal dish.

Even in the 1980s older people were grumbling about what they saw as the extravagance of the younger generation:

> *hes nəxádəm mətəʿát, īrēz, wə-thərāk ṣifərēyət, náxərgəh məns w-əntōh, nəkhārəh. hes nāṣərə la, nāṣerə hes thərāk ṣifərēyət, ḥad yəkḥārs la. ʿar yáwkaʿ bēs moh wə-yəkəhāb. wálə yəšʿār bēs wə-kə-saḥḥ áxərgəh.*

> When we used to cook food, rice, and it would burn onto the pot (lit. 'the pot would burn'), we'd take (the burned

bits) out and eat them. We'd scrape out the pot (i.e., and eat the scrapings). Not like nowadays. Today if food gets burned onto the cooking pot, no one scrapes out the burned bits. They (just) put water in it and keep on chatting. Or they leave (the pot) overnight and in the morning remove it (i.e., any burned-on food).

The Bəṭāḥira devised ways of making the best of shark which were too small to be worth processing, or of the pieces cut off before the shark was processed, such as the head. *nasālˤan ərı́ḥ*, "We remove all the flesh and skin from the head." Making a meal from this was a somewhat laborious process: first the layer of skin, subcutaneous fat and flesh was sliced all the way round from the base of neck to the snout (as you might peel an orange from top to bottom). This was then peeled away from the cartilage below, leaving only the eyes, producing a series of strips held together by the snout. The whole thing was boiled, and once cooked, was put into cold water to soak. When cold, the outer hard skin could be rubbed off and discarded, and the part underneath was cut into slices and eaten. It was said to be very soft and quite delicious and was called *səlāwaˤ*, lit. 'cheeks'. Even the the coiled sperm ducts[9] of the mature male shark, *ˤōmid*, were cooked and eaten with relish.

Not everyone owned a knife blade. Flints could be knapped and used instead.

> *hām el šey skīn la? əsyūr hə-ˤabēyil. ˤabēyil tkūn bə-Gənōt. wə-yəkūn heh məkənīn. maġrīb. bə-Gənōt ənbīl. nəˤāmər hēsən ənbīl. wə-yənēkədwəsən. yənēkədwəs wə-yənēbəlwəs tá tkūn hes skīn. thēmˤi? wə-hām hēt bəráḥ bə-barr? aˤabīl ḏeh*

---

[9] I am indebted to Alec Moore for the identification of *ˤōmid*.

aḥāwər ḏeh, yəkūn ḍar ḥadīyib. ḍar aḳarān? tsyūr wə-təníḳdəh. tkūn seh skin. aˁabú yəsḗḥeṭuw beh ˁarān. wə-yəkūn ləbōn, bˁéli Gənōṯ, ḏeh b-ərawnə yəkūn ləbōn. nəbrét. ənəbrét tkūn b-ərawnə. tkūn bə-giḥāb, mən dōl ḥawbōn bə-giḥāb? tkūn bēsən.

If I had no knife(blade)? I'd go for flints. There are flints at Gənōt. And there is a special place where they can be found (lit. 'a safe refuge'). A known place. In Gənōt there are flint beds. We call them *ənbīl*, 'flint beds'. And they knap them and chip away at them, whittle away at them until they're (as sharp) as a knife, do you hear? And if you're outside, inland? Flints of this dark-coloured type are to be found on top of little mounds of rock. On top of (little) rocky protrusions (lit. 'horns')? You go and chip away at it until it becomes (like) a knife. People used to cut the throats of goats with it. Those found at Gənōt are pale-coloured. The ones found by the sea are white (and called) *nəbrét*.[10] The *nəbrét* ones are found by the sea, on the dry foreshore (i.e., beyond the reach of the sea). Where it's stony, up on the high dry foreshore? They're to be found there, amongst them (i.e., among the stones).

Or the teeth of shark could be used:

ələxām yəkḗrhuw beh. wə-yəḳéśəbuw bēsən ərəhōtho wə-yəshéṭuw bēsən. yəślōl ḏābəl mən xah. axáyr amṣáˁi. fidīm? beh məṯēni niyāb wə-šēn hes əmwās. minḗdəm ḏiríf? wə-bəṣīr? yəxádəm... yəḳérḥ aˁámrəh b-əmṯēni fidīm. ˁar hām ber māt wə-ber heh əriḥ ḳāśaˁ, wə-ber enṣalṣōl əmṯēniha. wəla ˁādha ṯéri, yəxáreg hōk la.

---

[10] Glossed as: 'flint stones found by the sea, one side black and one side white'.

They used to shave their hair with shark (teeth). They'd cut their hair with them and they'd cut the throats (of animals) with them. He'd take a section from a jaw: the lower row of teeth is best. A *fidīm* shark?[11] It has teeth. It was like a razor blade for us. A skilled person? With good eyesight? He'd use… he'd shave himself with the teeth of a *fidīm* shark. But only once it was dead and its head has completely dried out and its teeth become loose. If it was still fresh, you couldn't get them out.

Or shards of glass:

aw bə-ḳirzān. bə-ḳarāz. naḳṣōṣ ləḥāyit wə-naḳṣāṣ(s)ən? bédəli̍ᴬ məkāyin? məkāyin śa la. ṭəbōren ḳarāz, hēmʿak? ḥašāk… w-aḳṣēṣan beh wə-ṭhārən beh.

Or with small glass bottles. With a small glass bottle? We'd cut the hair of the beard, trim the hair? Instead of razor blades? There weren't any razor blades. We'd break a small glass bottle, do you hear? Forgive me… we'd use (shards of) it to cut hair and to make ourselves ritually clean (i.e., by removing pubic and axillary hair).

3.15. Cooking

One of the problems faced by the Bəṭāḥira was the lack of firewood in their area. Alternative fuels such as dried seaweed or old pieces of net had to be used instead. This lack of fuel, combined with a shortage of water and scarcity of cooking pots, meant that a number of ways of preparing or preserving food without the use of water were devised. All sorts of sea creatures and cuts of fish were preserved in salt, smoke, sun or wind.

---

[11] Pigeye shark, whitecheek shark or dusky whaler.

Any fuel was used sparingly: either the catch was put directly onto a small fire, or tucked into the embers, or cooked on fire-heated stones. Turtle and other large sea creatures were cooked slowly in pits underground. Fish were cut up in a variety of ways, usually to ensure that they needed as little time on the fire as possible. All fish had to be cooked right through: *aġalīl əntóha la, hem yəxérəg mən śeyāṭ wə-yəḳáˁ beh ḏēr*, "We don't eat insufficiently cooked fish, if it comes off the fire and there is still blood in it." Some of the terms for preparing and cooking fish are described below.

maxmīd~mxamdōt~xamīd is fish baked in hot ash:

> ḥāwīl nawśáˁ śeyāṭ u-met el həmədāt śay mən aṣáyd ənxámdəh wə-śay mən aṣáyd ənséraf wə-ṣḗbən teh lə-śeyāṭ. śay yəḳáˁ mekən wə-śay yəḳáˁ xaybət. hem heh mekən, aṣáyd yaˁgāb śeyāṭ təḳáˁ ḳewīyət, wə-hem heh xaybət yaˁgāb śeyāṭ ḳewīyət la; nekérfədən teh té yəbhēl. məġārə hem bəhēl naxrāg əḳəśyār il ḍárha w-aˁśayś w-ərīh w-əntóh. ḥad minēn yətóh mən maxmīd wə-ḥad minēn yətóh mən məsərīf.

> First we'd light a fire. When it had died down, some of the fish we'd cook in the hot ash and some we'd cut into pieces and roast directly on the fire. Sometimes there'd be many (fish) and sometimes only a few. If there were a lot it had to be a hot fire, but if there were only a few only a gentle fire was needed. We'd turn it over and over until it was fully cooked. When it was ready to eat, we'd take it off the fire, remove its skin, bones and head and then eat it. Some of us would eat it cooked in one piece in hot ash and some of us would eat it cut across in sections.

mawšīḵ (JA *māšōka*) was a method of cooking fish (and especially *duˁéyr* mullet) directly on the fire. Some removed the entrails, others left them in, depending on the type of fish and what it has been feeding on: əmawšĩḳ? txerāg əli berk hēfələh. hām yətōwə śay, wəla tōh əwarš wəla tōh śay? "(To do) the mawšīk? You'd remove everything from its stomach, if it had been eating anything or had been feeding on warš weed,[12] or had eaten something (undesirable)?"

nġal~nəġāl were small pieces or large flakes of flesh removed from any leftover fish. They were picked clean of skin and bones and dried in the sun and stored in cloth or sacking. It was usually eaten just as it was, dry.

məṣalmút~məṣlámət (pl. mṣālim~məṣalēm), also called śéryiḥ, were pieces of fish larger than the nġal above, and fresh rather than cooked. This way of preserving fish was used when there had been a good catch. After everyone had eaten what they wanted, any raw fish remaining were prepared for drying by gutting, cutting off the head and removing the backbone. The fish was then laid out flat and cut at an angle into very thin slices, taking care not to cut through the skin below. The fish were then spread out on a flat, dry surface and left out in the sun. Some rinsed the sliced fish in salt water before drying it. This kind of dried fish kept well (əmṣalmút txayūs la, "the mṣal-

---

[12] warš is an algal growth that appears on rocks and in the sea in the monsoon months. The Bəṭāḥira say: əwarš ərəbəṭōt l-ərawnə, ʿafərēt wə-ḥṣərēt, yəḳáʿ bēs ṣayd yətóh mánəh. wə-hes yətōh əduʿéyr əḍáy bēs əwərš, wə-təṭʿām b-axáhk, mən ənəġəlōt l-aṣáyd, "The warš weed is the foam and froth of the sea. It's reddish and greenish and fish swim amongst it, eating it. When the duʿéyr mullet eat it, they smell of the warš, and you can taste it in your mouth, the taste of the 'sweat of the fish'."

mút dried fish don't go off") and could also be sold or used in barter.

A preparation similar to *məṣalmút* was *ṣfēyif*, but this was done with larger fish. The raw flesh was cut across thinly on the horizontal before being salted and sun-dried. This was similar to the way the meat and fat of camels, goats, ibex and gazelle was preserved, in which it was cut into long ropes (*məkədēd* or *kədīd*), salted and dried in the sun. In a turtle, the ropes of meat and fat had their own name, *kasyēr*. The meat of large shellfish too could be preserved by cooking it and then threading it on a string and drying it in the sun and wind. Preserved *ṣfēyif* flesh was generally chewed without further preparation.

For special occasions, a dish called ʿ*ársi* was made, said to be a speciality of the Jaʿlān area in the north. Whatever cereal was available was cooked and then pounded to a paste with any flesh the fishermen had to hand, dried or fresh. The mixture was stirred hard and long until it formed a coherent paste, when it was poured out onto a serving dish or flat rock to be eaten.

Another special dish was *ləkīš*. For this, a fine whole fish of a type known to have a lot of fat, such as a *ṭāka* bluefish or large *duʿéyr* mullet, was cooked in as little water as possible, and left to cool. Once cold, it was pounded to a paste, sometimes with added cereal, sometimes not. The liver of a small shark was then mixed in. If there were no bluefish or mullet, the fresh meat of a small shark could be used instead. In hard times, an inferior type of *ləkīš* was made using the livers of a small and otherwise valueless shark: *wakt akáyḍ hem el yəkūn* šēn śa la, el šēn maḥḥ wələ ṣə́laṭ wələ tāmer wələ śay, nexerāg šəbīd əl-bə́ni bəkšīt wə-nəwāḵˤas berk ḥab w-əntóh. nəˤāmər heh ləkīš, "In the summer, if we had nothing, no butter oil and no vegetable oil and no dates, we'd remove the livers from a young bəkšīt shark and put them with the cereal and eat them together. We call it ləkīš."

3.16. Preparing Shark as Food

Fresh shark meat was not much liked by the Bəṭāḥira, the dried flesh was preferred: wə-ləxām hem el gēˤak gēˤak, toh mə́nəh xáybet. wə-heh el śūri la wə-yəˤáləz bōk. ˤar mən akál lə-śay, "Shark meat, if you're really hungry, eat a little of it. It's not good food and makes you feel sick. It's only (eaten) when there is nothing else." Also, a shark of any useful (i.e., commercial) size was too valuable as a barter or trade item to be used just as food. However, there were some dishes were made with shark:

ḥalūb was a dish made with fresh shark. Pieces of flesh were boiled and then put into cold water with some salt. When cold, the flesh was squeezed and wrung out until as dry as possible. If any fresh shark liver were available, this would be melted down over a slow fire and its oil added to the shark flesh. A line in a poem says: nəḥalīb mən ələxām / u-məxaṣīrə šəbdīt, "We'll make ḥalūb of fresh shark meat / And add a relish of freshly melted shark liver."

Another way of making fresh shark meat more palatable was to make mədmə́lōt. The flesh was cooked in water; a bed of stones was heated and the liver placed on top. Then a further layer of hot stones was placed on top of the liver and the liver turned frequently to stop it burning. When liver and flesh were ready, pieces of sacking were put on the ground and the cooked shark flesh was broken up into small pieces. The cooked liver was placed on top of the shark flesh and the sacking folded over on top. The whole bundle was squeezed and wrung until the liver and its oil had melted into the shark flesh.

Once dried, shark flesh was for trading, not for eating. Nevertheless, pieces had sometimes to be trimmed off the trunk to improve the appearance before it was buried in the *məléffə*, or there were shark which hadn't dried well enough to sell but should be eaten before they spoiled. Small pieces of dried shark (*ḳóśaˤ*) were usually chewed and eaten without further preparation, or they might be soaked in water and then squeezed and rubbed hard to make them softer to eat. This was called *ˤarīḳ*, from the verb *ˤarōḳ* 'to rub hard, as between the fingers'.

> ələxām əl-ḥōli, hām šēn mətəwé la, ənḳáśəb mə́nhe mātən. ənḳáśbəh bə-skīn. hémə̣h mātən. ənḳáśəb mə́nhe mātən, mən dōl xōgən beh h-əmilḥāt. wə-nəślōləh té berk əmóh. wə-hām berk əmóh əntəḳōkah bə-ˤābən. əntə́rḥ hābən nxálha wə-hābən ḍárha, wə-nətḳōkah w-ənrūd beh berk əmóh w-ənráḥśah. wə-nəˤāmər heh 'ˤárik'. əntóh.

> The year-old (dried) shark: if we had nothing to eat, we'd cut a *mātən*[13] strip from it. We'd cut it off with a knife. It's called *mātən*. We'd cut a *mātən* strip off it, from where we had slashed it for the salt. And we'd take it to where we could put it in water. And once it was in the water we'd beat it with a stone. We'd put a stone beneath it and a

---

[13] The strip of flesh between the slashes into which salt was rubbed: if a strip is given a hard yank, it peels off.

stone on top of it and we'd beat it, and (then) we'd throw it into the water to wash it. We call it ˤárik̰. We'd eat it.

3.17. Fats and Oils from Fish and Turtle

In all creatures the Bəṭāḥira prized the fat above all else. They have a different name for every kind of fat, in fish, shark and turtle, as well as in livestock. As fat from livestock was a rare treat, mostly the Bəṭāḥira had to get their fat from sea creatures. The fatty parts of a fish were considered to be the best parts: the belly fat, the intestines, the head, the tail and any subcutaneous fat (*ḏek məfāləḵ el beh gawd la əmətəwéh axáss, axáyr sərfét*[14] *il bēs gawd*, "That section with no skin, it's inferior eating. The side with the skin is best.") The flesh itself was the least important bit.

The very best fat was to be found in the larger groupers, the cobia, the greater amberjack and certain mullet and emperors. Fish fat was cut up and melted down to be used as a dipping sauce for the cooked flesh, or for a few dates or cereal. The Bəṭāḥira differentiated between the fats in fish. For example: *ḵerṣāb~ḵarṣēb* is the belly fat; *məḱérṣáˤ~məḱérṣíˤ* is the fat and stomach of larger fish, especially large groupers; *ṣarmāt* is the fat beside and above the liver, while *kərōś* is fat from any fish when it has been stuffed into the swim-bladder or stomach of a large fish, such as a tuna. *Kərōś* was cooked over a slow fire and eaten just like that, or its contents were poured over other food as a rich treat.

---

[14] *sərfét* (pl. *serf*) is a fish halved along its length and then each half cut across in sections.

The plentiful fat extracted from the carcass of a healthy turtle was regarded as especially valuable. The ġallét (əmʿuwiyān) was the middle stretch of the intestine and/or the layer of fat that lay around it.[15]

> əġallét bēs śabḥ, ərəbṣát. txádəmən tēs aʾáynəṭ wə-ḥad mən aġayāġ. txárəg məns ferṭ wə-təḳáʿ rəbṣát lə-śabḥ. rəbṣát baʿlēt əmʿuwiyān. ḥad yətoh la nīt, ʿar behəlét. wələ ʿemōrən txédəm tuʿāl berk enxarīr.
>
> The middle stretch of the large intestine has fat, the rəbṣát fat. Women and some men would work it. She'd remove the partially digested material from it and what remained was the rəbṣát. rəbṣát is the fat of the turtle belly, found around the intestines. No-one would eat it raw, only cooked, because we used to say that otherwise it would give you worms in the nose.

The orange-coloured rəbṣát fat is particularly rich, and is found in the upper belly, while the ġallét fat in the lower belly. Both kinds were preserved by salting and stuffing the large bowel (yəḵḏālət) of a green turtle with them. Fishermen prepared the yəḵḏālət as a container by salting it heavily and hanging it up in the wind and sun to dry. No cooking was necessary. The yəḵḏālət could also be stuffed with turtle meat and fat which had been cut into ropes and hung up to dry. After chopping these into tiny pieces, they were stuffed into the yəḵḏālət with a little salt. This fat 'sausage' was rubbed all over with salt and hung up in the wind and sun. Once quite dry, the top was tied

---

[15] The upper part of the intestine is called maʿgīg əl-ʿīd, the part called bəgēlyət in a goat carcass, and which children inflate and play with like a balloon.

down, and now the family was the proud possessor of a source of meat and fat which was said to keep almost indefinitely.

For fish oil, the best livers to melt down were those of groupers, triggerfish and leatherjackets. The livers were cut up and put in a shell or other container over a slow fire until the oil had finished oozing out. This oil was fine enough to be taken directly as a food (but a very impoverished Baṭḥari woman I knew had thirteen live births and, with no goats and little breast milk, tried to rear her children on fish oil. Tragically, not one of her babies survived beyond two years.)

Among shark, the best oil was *ṣift lə-biˤl*, the oil extracted from the livers of the sawfish. The next best was *ṣift lə-śāṣət* made from the livers of the lemon shark, sicklefin lemon shark or whitetip reef shark. Third best was the oil made from the livers of the *bəkšīt* pigeye, spinner or bull shark. The livers of these shark also made the best medicinal oil, and especially for the condition known as *fekk*, 'wound inside the chest',[16] which caused persistent chest pain and a cough often accompanied by blood. One small shellful was drunk every morning to 'close the wound'. Otherwise the most widespread treatment for any illness was cauterisation: *hes təḱáˤ bōk waˤk u-berk axáyr wə-śōllək śay w-aṣbáḥk axáss, bōk əmwēhən wə-ṭaˤbét. ḍek šəgnōb. w-əgánb heh mēṣḥar: ṭad l-ərī́ḥ wə-ṭad lə-ketf wə-ṭad boh l-aṣāla^ˤ ḱennōn*, "If

---

[16] Most probably tuberculosis: during a 1980s survey we found that the majority of Baṭāḥira were suffering from this disease, though they were marginally better off than the inhabitants of al-Ḥallāniyah island opposite, where during the same survey only a single newborn baby was found not to have the condition.

you got a head cold, recovered but then carried something (heavy) and took a turn for the worse, you'd develop *məwēhən*, 'a pain on one side of the upper chest', and a cough. This was called *šəgnōb*. *Ganb* was treated by cauterisation: one on the head, one on the tip of a shoulder, and one here, on the smallest rib."

By pouring a little fish liver oil into a shell and inserting a cotton wick, a light could be made if urgently needed:

> ṣaft nəxádəm mə́nəh, naṣāryən beh té nəbəṣār. nəwāḳaʿ aṣáft bə-ḥakḳát wə-nəxádəm heh ftílət lə-ḳaṭn wə-naṣāryən beh. hes aṣáft ṣāfyət, nəślōl ġāzəl, aġāzəl nəxádəm mə́nəh ləyūx, ḳaṭn, nəxádəm mə́nəh atáh ləṭə́ṭ, txádəms ftílət. wə-təwāḵʿas berk aṣáft.

> We'd use fish liver oil. We'd make lighting from it so that we could see (in the dark). We'd put the oil in an old tin and make a cotton wick for it and set it alight. If the oil was pure, we'd take some cotton—the same cotton we use to make the gillnets—and make a twist of it like that. You'd make a wick out of it, and you'd put it inside the oil.

A coarser oil made from shark livers was used as a dip for other drier foods and was also taken in very small quantities as a tonic. However, it is said that not all shark liver oil was edible: that of the blacktip or the hammerhead could produce an allergic reaction with severe itching. This thicker, less pure oil was smeared over a camel once it had been treated for mange, or, when the Bəṭāḥira started to own wooden dugout canoes, this or the scrapings from the bottom of the shark liver drum was the preferred material for oiling the wood. This kind of oil was made by placing the huge livers in a container, usually an old oil drum saved for the purpose, and then boiling them down, stirring continuously. As the livers began to break up and produce an oily liquid, they had to be pounded with a heavy club in between stirrings. When a layer of pure oil finally separated out, the mixture was left to cool and the oil sieved through a piece of cloth.

3.18. Useful Non-Food Items from the Sea

The sea provided many useful things apart from food. For example, the toothed rostrum of a sawfish could be used as a weapon, or in dancing, could be flourished instead of a sword:

> əbiˁl, ḥāwīl yəstəlébuw səlīb, yəlēbəduw beh. ḏeh ḵennōn yəkín xafīf wə-ḏeh nawb yəkín ṭkīl. wə-śay yəḵṣéṣuw beh wə-śay yərēdyuw beh.

> The sawfish: in earlier times people used to use them (i.e., the rostra) as weapons, they would hit people with them. The smaller ones are light and the bigger ones heavy. Some were used to cut with, and some were thrown away.

The spear-like bill of the sailfish or marlin made a skewer around which strips of meat and fat were wrapped, and shark-skin was useful as a file:

> yəhínənuw ḥaskināt ḏār hayṣāt. hayfīt ələxām? mən təṭráḥs bə-śeyāṭ wə-téfhśis? xarāg ḥámərət əli ḏárha. hayṣāt? nəhá nəˁāmər hēs hayṣāt.

> They'd sharpen knives on the rough sandpapery skin of shark. The skin of the shark? If you put it on the fire and bring it to the boil? Remove the tough layer of skin on top. The hayṣāt? We call it hayṣāt.

The long, flexible tail of certain stingrays could be used as a whip, and the stomach contents of dark rock crabs made a medicine for chest complaints or whooping cough:

> ḥayśyōt ləbənēt tənāfaˤ la, axáyr aḥāwərēt il təḳáˤ bə-ḳəśēr. bēs dáwi. hes təḳśɛ́rs, ḏeh bə-hēfələs, aḥāwər, ənḥá nəˤāmər heh aġābs, ˤamōruw heh dáwi. yətēwyən teh. mən təḳáˤ bōk ṭaˤbét. ḏik ḳeśəˤīt nəˤāmər heh ṭaˤbét wə-ḏik məšaġərōt nəˤāmər heh śḥāḳ.

> A white (ghost) crab is no good, the black one found among the rocks is better. It contains medicine. When you remove its shell, this black stuff in its stomach—we call it its excrement—they say that this makes a good medicine. They'd eat it. When you had a cough. That dry kind of cough we call ṭaˤbét, and that other we call śḥāḳ, 'whooping cough'.

Shells provided a variety of containers: small cooking pots; scoops to measure the precious grain; serving dishes for melted fat; receptacles for precious materials such as snuff or eye-black; feeding bottles to drip milk or fish oil into the mouths of babies. A shell could serve even as a container to hold the last breath of the dying:

> əmēyət hes yəmét ḥāwīl agˤārən teh lə-ḳabəlét, awḳáˤan b-əréh boh. wə-maˤtēdən awḳāfən heh ḥawm šəklālən heh bə-ḥawm ənismɛ́th nəxál axáh. u-maġāṭən heh ḥādōtha wə-fˤēmha té yəḳáˤuw tuww. wə-ṣatōmən heh aˤyāntha mən yəḳáˤ tuww la.

> When a person dies, first we lay him down on the ground facing west, placing his head right here. And then we hold up a shell under his mouth to catch his last breath. And then we stretch out his hands and legs so that they

lie nicely, and we close his eyes so that he doesn't look bad.

Many useful materials drifted ashore, from woods of all kinds (some with useful nails) to cuttlebone to valuable ambergris. Beachcombing was a serious activity practised by people of all ages.

3.19. Community Self-Regulation

The Bəṭāḥira devised a complex system for regulating the harvesting of the sea so that the weak and disabled were given some protection, a system to ensure that no member of the tribe was left out. To give a few examples:

During the hard and hungry monsoon months there were clear rules about who could fish what, where, and when, and, importantly, how the catch should be shared out—at times of widespread hunger the distribution of fish was strictly controlled. At such times, people would gather wherever the men were fishing. All the fish they caught were cut up and piled in small heaps, each heap being equal to one 'share', each share to be divided among five people. Then lots were cast to determine which group of five would receive which heap of fish. The casting of lots was a device commonly used by the Bəṭāḥira to make decisions that all would accept were fair.

> *hes nakātələn atxōf ṣayd. atxāfuw bə-ṣayd, ˤamōruw: "hēdyuw! hēdyuw herbá ˤtko." ḥātsəbən. "hīt bə-kədōtš kam?" ˤamórš: "enḥá xammáh. hoh w-əribá ˤi w-əbínyən śōṯēt: xammáh." het šōk əríḥ. dek ezīmə teh śabḥ. wəla hām hoh l-aḳātələk wə-nōk ˤak b-aṣáyd? wə-ta ˤábk? het hōk əríḥ wə-hoh kīrəś.*

> When we'd been line-fishing, by the late afternoon there would be fish. The (fishers) would come back in the early evening with the fish and they'd say: "Share them out! Share them out among your people!" We'd make our calculations. "You in your home, how many are you?" You'd say: "We are five people. Myself, my husband, and our three children, so five." You have the head, then we'll give the fat to that other one. Or if it was I who had caught the fish on my line and had gone to the trouble of catching it? You'd get the head and I'd get the stomach.

What fishing was possible during the months of monsoon wild seas was firmly regulated. Rabbitfish were one of the few fish that could be caught at this time. Customary law said that these fish may only be fished for at night, not during daylight hours, and even then not just anywhere. In the Mingíy area, for instance, fishermen were only allowed to fish for rabbitfish at seven named coves, and even then they were allowed only to catch enough to feed their families, not to take any extra to dry for later consumption or for barter or trade.

When fishing at night, and especially for the valuable *duʿéyr* mullet, another key fish of the monsoon period, a fisherman would draw a line, *məgárrat*, on the beach before he left to indicate that this section of the shore had already been fished. A fisher who arrived later would see this and go to another area to try his luck. This was not done when fishing for *duʿéyr* in the daytime. During the monsoon in the Xīmīt area, the rules for fishing the *duʿéyr* mullet were different again. By the end of the summer, sailing ships were no longer passing by on their way back from East Africa, or on their way to Oman and the Gulf. From this time on, no private, individual fishing for *duʿéyr* mullet was permitted. In addition, when fishing in the Xīmīt fishing area, everyone had to be careful to make no noise: there was to be no playing of games, no scuffing of sand or throwing of stones. This risked frightening this vital but timid species away, driving the fish out into deeper and inaccessible waters. For the whole duration of the monsoon, any *duʿéyr* mullet caught were seen as belonging to the whole tribe. None but Bəṭāḥira were allowed to fish the Xīmīt area, and moreover, only at night and only when there was no moon or when the moon had set. In addition, every fisherman had to cover his head and conceal his cast nets 'so that the moon couldn't see them.' Nor could any fishing begin until all the fishermen were assembled. Only then would the person elected as foreman give the call to say that the casting of nets could begin. Non-fishermen would come from all over the area to sit and wait above the shore for the fishing to come to an end. All *duʿéyr* caught were carefully divided up according to the number of adults in each household. Again there was a casting of lots to ensure fair distribution. (A child counted as an adult once he or she 'could eat a whole mullet at one sitting').

As a final example, the traditional rules about the third vital fish of the monsoon months, the *terʿān* pompano, were even more complicated. People used to flock to the Gənōt area where these fish congregated at this time of year. Fishermen were allowed to try and catch a pompano, but not with a bait of its favourite food, the tiny *ṣāfə* mussel that grew among the monsoon algae. A fisherman could try and gaff the fish, or bait his hook with another bait, or even make a cast with an empty hook, but he may not use a ṣāfə. If he were to catch a pompano at this time of year with ṣāfə bait, his fish became ʿawf, 'taboo', and no-one should eat it. It was an additional rule that this particular fish could be eaten only by Baṭḥari men and in the hours of daylight. When a man brought terʿān pompano back to where his family was waiting at nightfall, he had to conceal them in a basket held behind his back, and, as he drew near, make a low continuous whistle to warn any women of his approach. The women then had to take the fish from the basket with their eyes closed, and look away while they put them on the fire to cook. Even then, only a Baṭḥari woman could take it in her hand to cook. If she were pregnant by a non-Baṭḥari man, she temporarily forfeited her Baṭḥari status and could only eat these fish when cooked by someone else. She recovered this status once she had given birth. In the 1980s I was told that terʿān and turtle were the 'principal food of the very first ancestors'. Because of this, many still say today that any terʿān pompano should be rubbed with dirt after being caught to make them look unappetising. Otherwise the 'spirits of the ancestors' would be drawn irresistibly from their graves towards it, and would 'take over' the person who had the terʿān, so great had been their lust for its flesh when they were alive.

The Bəṭāḥira allowed non-Bəṭāḥira to fish their beaches, but they extracted a fee, ʿārib, from them if they brought anything valuable ashore, such as a turtle, a good-sized shark, or even ambergris. In Ḥāsik, those using fish traps (kerkār) had to pay a one-off fee to the first Baṭḥari who came to claim it. Of course, such fees were rarely paid in cash, but in more useful items, such as cotton fibre, cereal or cloth.

There were rules too for determining ownership of any find of value washed up on the shore or found floating in the shallows after a storm. Customary law controlled the ownership of ambergris, ships' timbers, planks, crates, nails—anything of consequence. This law laid down how far above the tideline an item had to be placed to establish ownership; it determined how its value should be calculated and shared if it had been seen by more than one person; it specified what share was due a non-Baṭḥari if he or she had found something in Baṭḥari territory and handed it over to a Baṭḥari.

3.20. Passing on Expertise to the Next Generation

Adults taught children about harvesting the sea, sometimes by encouraging them to watch or help them as they worked, sometimes by passing on factual information, such as where the *keṣʿáyr* trevally was to be found: *ḏeh keṣʿáyr kennōn? yəlībəd ḥawīr wə-yəšaʿūr bə-kāṭer*, "This small kind of *keṣʿáyr* trevally? They come in shoals and they spend the night in the current." Or they would show them how, with a rabbitfish, the first thing to do was to remove the gallbladder (*mirr*), and only then could the intestines be taken out and squeezed slowly from top to bottom to remove the partially digested contents (*ferṭ*). The fat-rich intestines could now be enjoyed, either eaten raw, or cooked. They would explain to them that this process was not necessary for rabbitfish caught at night: as they only feed by day, at night their intestines are empty of *ferṭ* and can be eaten straight away.

These 'clean' rabbitfish intestines were called *máklaṭ: l-akalṭāt, bēs ferṭ la*, "clean rabbitfish intestines: they contain no partially digested matter." Children were taught when fish would be fat and when lean, for example, the *ṭāka* bluefish. *mən kátər l-əməsīr ḥāwīl təkádər la tsyōr la mən śábhəs, u-məġārə hes tkānah el ḥad yətóhs la mən axátəm*, "Because of all their travelling: they start off being hardly able to move they are so fat, and then when they come back (i.e., to the Baṭhari seas), they are so thin that no one eats them." Or they were taught how to recognise a fish: *terˤān bēs 'xah' la, ˤar ḥarkīk*, "A tərˤān pompano has no 'mouth' (i.e., no teeth), it's nothing but gums." They would be taught that this kind of pompano spawns in winter: it grows very thin at this time and is hardly worth catching. It starts to fatten up again in the post-monsoon *ṣɛrb* season at the the time of the rising of the *ləḥēmər* star.

Sometimes adults would recite practical little ditties to children, such as:

> *śwēr tfyūd əla bəġáyr gəndēwi / w-əgəndēwi tfyūd əla bəġáyr ṣamdēt.*
>
> *əgəndēwi tfyūd əla bəġáyr kədēt / wə-kélsən tfyūd əla bəġáyr ṣamdēt.*
>
> The fishing line is no good without a hook / And the hook is useless without bait.
>
> The hook is useless without a sinker weight / and they're all useless without bait.

Or:

> *akáyd yəfyūd la bəġáyr məḏərā*[17] */ w-əməġadéft ṭṭékəd la bəġáyr təkədí.*
>
> The (shark) line is no use without a big chunk of bait /
> And the cast net will not sink without (lead) weights.

Or a parent would repeat lines from short poems to help implant the information in a child's memory, as:

> *xerḗb xerḗbək əbēli / hes xerḗbək ewġadīt.*
>
> Oh *xerḗb* wind, may the good Lord destroy you / Just as you destroyed our chances of catching the small *ṭāḵa* bluefish! (Because when these winds start to blow, the bluefish swim out to deeper seas.)

Or:

> *ṣéri ber mədīt / əli yəlbōd ḥiyāb*
>
> *nebśḗrən beh / əmbaʿd əxerḗb.*
>
> The *ṣéri* wind from the north-west, child of the *mədīt* wind from the southwest / That blows away the sea mists lying low over land and sea.[18]
>
> We call down blessings when it arrives / After the searing hot winds from the interior!

Some mnemonic lines were clearly learned from their Janaba neighbours to the east, speaking their own dialect of Arabic, as:

> *səlḥūb / lā mí / wə-lā gəhūb*

---

[17] *məḏərā* (pl. *mḏawri*) '(when setting shark ropes from cliffs overnight) large chunks of fish used as shark bait'.

[18] Some say *əli yəlbōd ḥayēm* rather than *ḥiyāb*, 'which blows (the sea) right up to the pebbly ridge high above the tideline'.

The *səlhūb* wind? / Neither rain / nor black rainclouds (does it bring).

Or:

ḥəbbēt ḥəbūb əkōs / rīḥ syāḥīyə

ʔin sékkərət mən ṣabḥ / tyīk ʿasərīyə

wə-tyīk yōm bə-bérḵ / tənšāf lə-wāḏīyəh

I love the gentle *kōs* wind from the southwest / A gentle *syāḥīyə* wind that goes everywhere (i.e., across sea and land).

If it dies down in the morning / A dust storm will come to you.

And a day of lightning will come to you / Its flashing clearly visible.[19]

Children also learned about fishing through play: they would throw fragments of cereal on the surface of a lagoon and when the tiny lagoon fish rose to feed, they would practise casting miniature homemade cast nets over them. Any fish they caught were placed in a container with salt below and above and left until quite dried when they became toys to play with.

3.21. Beings from the 'Other World'

The spirits of the 'other world' were always present. Sometimes heard, they were never seen, only sensed. The most numerous were the spirits of their Bəṭāḥira forebears. They were known as *əmōwət~əmēyit*, 'the dead', or *(e)skún*, lit. 'inhabitants', here of the *mədínət* 'graveyard': *əmdínət l-əmōwət. kel li yəmét nəwākʿah*

---

[19] Janaba Arabic √n-šwf, 'to be visible'.

bərkēs, 'the place of the dead. Anyone who dies we place them in it'. These spirits were also called as bə́ni šūf,[20] as in parts of Dhofar. Such ancestral spirits caused little trouble as long as they were treated properly. They usually stayed in their underground world, emerging to go fishing, cormorant hunting or simply to see what was going on and how their descendants were faring. On the anniversary of their death, they would come up above ground to find the gifts left out for them by their descendants to mark the date: the spirits of the dead had to be placated with gifts. If they were treated with insufficient respect, they became dangerous and vengeful and were to be avoided. For example, a limb touched by one of the angry 'dead' became paralysed and lifeless. The spirits had an affinity with felines, leopards, certain birds of prey and hyenas: *wa-hes yərékəb ḏа́rsa mōwəṭ, eskūn yərékəbwəs? aˁárri yənā́ṣaˁ*, "And

---

[20] In eastern Dhofar the spirits of the dead were known as *bēt ɛ-šūf* (in central and western Dhofar more commonly as *il-xōfiyīn*). These ancestral spirits were believed to have a similar lifestyle to their living descendants, constantly on the move with their livestock. It is said that in the past the living and the dead were visible to one other, until the day a woman goatherd ran out of milk and a *bēt ɛ-šūf* camel herdswoman gave her some camel milk. The woman goatherd liked it so much she determined to try and get hold of a spirit she-camel. It was a time of good rains and the camels were well fed and frisky. She placed her old and crippled father in the path the spirit camels took as they came back home in the early evening. As she had planned, the camels trampled her father to death. When she demanded compensation, the spirits did indeed give her a single she-camel. However, they told her that from that day on no living person would ever see any member of the *bēt ɛ-šūf*.

when a spirit of the dead rides it, the ancestral spirits ride it (i.e., the female hyena)? The male hyena roars and moans."

Certain places in the Baṭhari area were particularly associated with the spirits of the dead. One of these was Məḥābāṭ, a deep hole near Ṣaʕīt cove. This bay was owned by Məḵāzaʕ Wahaibi, not the Bəṭāḥira, who had to pay a landing fee if they caught a valuable fish here. Sometimes a goat would find its way down the hole and then be unable to extricate itself. When this happened, only a Baṭhari man of the Məšérma clan was allowed by the spirits to climb down and rescue it. Even then, only under certain conditions: he must be naked—removing even the waist-string worn by all males from birth and any ring worn on hand or ear; he must wear no eye-black; and his head must be shaved bare and covered with a layer of dried or drying seaweed bound round with a length of cordage twisted from the fibres of the *Nannorrhops* desert palm.

Spirits were also associated with cairns (ʕasēm, pl. ʕasmīn), erected to mark clan or tribe boundaries, or to commemorate a specific death or conflict. If a Baṭhari passed by a cairn, s/he would pick up a stone, spit on it and throw it at the pile, saying something along the lines of: *rēdək ḍark śəddét*, "I cast any evil on top of you!" In the 1980s, an elderly man told me that he recalled women throwing stones at a person to curse them: they would spit on a stone, lay a curse on it and then throw it at their victim with further curses. The accursed would fall ill with a wasting sickness and within two months or so would be dead. Indeed, Bəṭāḥira women were often feared by people of other tribes as having alarming powers: able to conjure up winds, direct the creatures of the sea, cause water to disappear or to become undrinkable.

The jinn (*gənnéy*, fem. *gənnīt*, mpl. *gənnó*, fpl. *gənnéytən*) were also dangerous visitors from the other world, though they could be repelled by throwing water in their face (*ṣəbōl*). A jinn would always steal a child he had produced with a human, and it was believed that the human parent could only recover their child by cutting the jinn's forehead and flicking some of its blood over the child to force the jinn to release it. This potency of blood was further illustrated when listening to two old men reminiscing about the days of the slave boats. They said you could steal a young slave by rowing out to the boat and telling the captain you wanted to buy one of his cargo. When the boy or girl was lowered into your dugout, the trick was to suddenly push off from the ship, pushing the child into the bottom of the dugout. If, between boat and shore, you managed to bite a shred of flesh from the ear of your captive and make it bleed, the child then became your property.

As is common elsewhere in the wider region, the Evil Eye was to be avoided: it brought sickness or some other misfortune. Various strategies were employed to circumvent it: for example, if two breastfeeding or pregnant women met, they would give one another a small scrap of material from their clothing to avert the 'Eye', an exchange known as *məgrīr* (pl. *məgrōr*). An illness called *gerr* (from the same root as *məgrīr*) could be caused by a baby being given the breastmilk of an 'inappropriate' woman (a slave feeding the baby of a free woman and vice versa). This could only be cured by cauterisation: one brand on the *xamrét l-ərîh*, 'the soft spot, the fontanelle'; one on the *ḳəṣṣát*, 'the middle of the upper forehead', and one on the *ḳermá^ʕ*, 'the hollow at the base of the back of the head'.

Figure 17: Leather and wood cradle, back view

Photo © Miranda Morris, 1970s

4. In Conclusion

The Bəṭāḥira harvested the sea out of necessity, to survive. There were few alternative foods: some milk products from their few domestic animals or bartered with the bedouin of the plateau above in exchange for fish, and rare meat from male kids and lambs. They hunted certain birds, and in particular plump cormorant nestlings. At night, men lowered themselves down cliffs and crawled along ledges, listening for the cheeping of the nestlings. They then 'fished' for them with a special hooked gaff (*mawm*). The only other meat came from an occasional hare or rock hyrax, or an Agamid lizard trapped in its lair, its skin tanned to make a container for dates, fat or oil. For those few who had access to a gun of some kind, there might be a gazelle or an ibex to share. Any other food—dates and date syrup for sweetness; *kiśr* coffee-bean husks to be boiled up again and again, and of course sorghum—came with the trade boats. All of these had to be paid for with dried shark meat and other fish.

To catch enough to trade and to eat, the Bəṭāḥira had to have real expertise: it was only this that made survival possible. Bəṭaḥrēt is an unwritten language, so much of this huge body of knowledge could only be passed down the generations through stories and short poems encapsulating these hard-earned skills.

However, the sea can no longer be harvested as it used to be. The numbers and species of fish have decreased.

> əbəkśīt akaʿāt hes abáṯḫ ḏek mən kéṭəris. nāṣərə əl-ḫūt ḵēl lēn w-əl-ḫūt śa la wə-xáybət. w-əduʿéyr lə-ḥáləh yənōkaʿ la. wə-ʿabū gərēfwəh mən barr wə-rawnə.

> The *bəkśīt* shark used to be like that sand there, so many of them there were. Now the large fish have grown fewer. There are no large fish anymore, or very few. And the *duʿéyr* mullet no longer comes when it used to, and people have scooped them up (i.e., with seine nets) from the shore right out to sea.

The climate is changing:

> w-əmbōn əmilsē yəsádek, el hēs nāṣərə la. nāṣərə yənōkaʿ śa la. əmbōn heh yəsádek lə-ḥáləh. men nəśənēs, mən aʿabú yəśényuw abárḵ, nḥá nəḏēllən minəh, nəkənūn bə-xadōr ḏ-ikənúnən tēn.

Before, the rain could be relied on, not like now. Today nothing comes. In the old days it used to fall at its appointed time. As soon as we saw it, when people saw the lightning, we'd seek refuge from it, we'd shelter in caves that would keep us safe from it (the rain).

And the language? An elderly woman said:

> wə-nāṣərə ʕar... ḥāwīl məkān əl-ḥaskānyən wə-ġarɛ́ əl-ḥaskānyən... Bəṭaḥrēyət. enḥá šēn ʕar ḏénəmə: śōṭēt hēxār wə-ʕágizi ṭert li yəgtéryuw Bəṭaḥrēt. w-əbēḵi? yagáyr yəšḥáwəlwəs yagár yəgtéryuw bēs la. ᴶᴬraḥ bəhə́m əmdāris, wə-raḥáw bəhə́mᴶᴬ ʕarabīyət. hēmʕak? ġarɛ́... yəlónəmə šēn mən təráṭ.ᴶᴬ

> And now there is only... in earlier times our people had their own area, their own language... the Baṭhari language. We have only this (now, i.e., in the settlement here): three old men and two old women who speak Bəṭaḥrēt. And the rest? They might understand it, but they can't speak it. The schools have taken them (i.e., the younger people) away, and the Arabic language has taken them away, do you hear? The language... those (things) are all that remains to us of (our former) culture.

With the loss of the language and the disappearance of the small number of elderly men and women who still speak the language and remember the ways of the past, all this hard-won knowledge, with the cultural traditions and socio-economic practices of the speakers, will be lost too.

5. Baṭḥari Texts: Introduction

5.1. Collecting Audio Files

When I lived in Dhofar in the 1970s, I worked with the Bəṭāḥira and visited their area regularly as part of my job with the Civil Aid Department of the Office of the Minister for Dhofar, and later when working with the Rural Health Service for the Ministry of Health. I was able to carry out some preliminary work on their language with Bəṭāḥira who came to the regional capital of Salalah,[21] and to make some recordings. When I left Oman in 1980 to return to the UK, I was invited by the Diwan of Royal Court, Oman, to pursue my researches into the MSA (Modern South Arabian) languages and the way of life of the speakers. Subsequently I made two extended field trips a year, some of which were to the Baṭhari area. I stopped fieldwork in Oman in 1990 and began to work in Soḳoṭra.

From 2013 to 2016 I worked on a project headed by Janet C. E. Watson, funded by the Leverhulme Trust.[22] Janet Watson, Domenyk Eades and I worked on documenting five of the MSA languages, Śḥerēt, Mehri, Ḥarsūsī, Hobyōt and Bəṭaḥrēt. I concentrated mainly on Hobyōt and Bəṭaḥrēt, the most endangered

---

[21] Many came to be treated for tuberculosis, very widespread in their area, and had to stay in an isolation ward until such time as they were no longer in danger of infecting others. I was living in the hospital compound, so was close by for visits.

[22] Documentation and Ethnolinguistic Analysis of the Modern South Arabian Languages: RPG-2012-599.

of the MSAL languages, though I also made recordings of Śḥerēt and eastern Mehri.

All but one of the texts[23] presented here are from the earlier period, the late 1970s to 1990.

5.2. Subject Matter

For both the earlier and later recordings, my aim was to try and elicit ethnographic material that would illuminate the way of life of the Bəṭāḥira prior to the accession of Sultan Qaboos in 1970. I asked about specific skills, customs and management systems, and tried to encourage speakers to reminisce about their past lives, to recall stories they used to tell and poems they used to sing.

5.3. The Speakers

None of the speakers represented here are still living, and they were all elderly when they made the recordings. With no opportunity to attend any sort of school, they were all the product of a purely oral culture.

5.4. The Use of Arabic

Even in the 1970s when I started to work with the Bəṭāḥira, Bəṭaḥrēt was a dying language, and for the majority of the younger generation, Arabic was already the language of daily use. The Arabic they spoke was the dialect of the Janaba, their neighbours to the east, a large and powerful tribe found in

---

[23] 6.2. Memories of Hungry Times [20130404_B_B02_memories.wav (13.14)].

northern as well as in southern Oman. The principal traders who used to call in at the Baṭḥari anchorages to buy their fish were from the Ṣūr region, an area dominated by the Janaba tribe. In the south the Janaba and Bəṭāḥira shared a similar terrain and way of life. They had many traditions and customs in common, they often fished together and they intermarried. The children of such marriages were often bilingual in the Janaba dialect and Baṭḥari. In the transcriptions below, most of the Arabic terms used were borrowed from, or heavily influenced by, this dialect of Arabic.

5.5. Equipment

These early recordings were made either with a Uher Report 4000L portable reel-to-reel tape-recording machine, 1981 model, or with an ordinary inexpensive cassette recorder—I no longer remember which model.

5.6. The Editing of Sound Files

The transcribed texts presented here do not come with the metadata of the archived audio files of the later 2013–2016 period, but are referenced according to my own filing system of the time (e.g. [1980 BATTXT3]). Nor are the transcribed texts always direct transcriptions of the recordings themselves, but ones modified or corrected by subsequent work carried out in the 1980s in Oman. This involved listening to the recorded tapes with various Baṭḥari speakers and data interpreters, especially Zifena Musallim Daġaš, Musallim Muṭawwaʿ ʿĀmir, Mehri Muḥammad Sālim, Shaikha Mubārak Ḥamad, Shīḥa Ḥamad Saʿd and Khalīfa Ḥamūd Sālim (the last named the only one of this group still alive today). The transcriptions below represent their preferred version at that time. The texts have been further edited to remove repetitions, slips of the tongue, incomplete words, the odd *mm...*, *er...*, *ah...*, and so on.

6. Texts

6.1. The Terror of Life Before and Life Today

1. ḥāwīl hes nəġídəf bə-xarifīt, əlū šiš əbréš ṯḥémi tərīd[24] b-əbréš w-el təġídəf bə-xarifīt ḏikəmə. təˁāmər la ġayg yəḳáfəd bēs wə-yəxarāġ məns. w-aḳášiy tənākaˁ b-aġáwf mə́nəh wə-heh əmṣáˁ yəġyōṣ. yəfēġəzuw hə-šəbdítš.

Before, when we used to cast the nets during the monsoon, if you had your son with you, you would rather throw your son away than go and cast a net in that monsoon sea! You would say it would be impossible for a man to go into it and return from it (alive)! The waves come right up while he dives right down. They squeeze your liver (i.e., with terror), even to think about it!

2. əwáḳət el ḳəṣərāt... šāhid allāh ḥām l-əfdé... ˁar nāṣerə bōk nəsīm. nərūd bēsən mən ḏar ġərf wə-nəwāḳˁan əṭəwīl b-əmṣáˁ əġə́rf ḏek li nəṣār ḏárha. ḏárha aḳáṣiy wə-nəxálha mən ḥān nərūd bə-śwēr yēḳaˁ həbəˁēt abwáˁ l-əmṣáˁ. u-mən ḥānə nərūd b-əmġādəf ṭad yəˁēməruw heh śḗṣət, ləxām, yədə́rəġ əmbēnwəs ənḥá w-əmbēn əmġadéft.

---

[24] 2fs., addressing me, a woman.

The times were hard... may God be my witness, I would rather pay in compensation... but now you can breathe![25] We used to cast them from a ledge over the sea, and we'd put the long rope[26] below that ledge we were standing on. The waves would be breaking over it, and below it, where we'd cast the line, it might go down seven *bāʕ*![27] And where we'd cast the nets, a kind of shark which they call the *śāṣət*[28] would be swimming around between us and the net.

3. ᴶᴬ*yətāgi allāh səbḥānəh ʕazz wə-gill*ᴶᴬ*! yəʕēmǝruw aḥawlá il ho ebēli yəḥə́rəs bənēdəm mən śay yəṣrórəh, wəla ʕemōruw mən yəbʕār əbnēdəm b-ərawnə tədə́rəgən əmbēnwəh w-əmbēn əməġadə́ftəh hābaʕ hwēməś, el ʕād yəśānsən la wə-yəfāzaʕ mənsēn. ebēli ṣərəfēsən mə́nəh mən śān yəxádəm l-aʕámrəh w-əbínha lə-mətəʕát.*

May God keep us safe—to Him be all praise and honour! The early ones said that the good Lord protects people from harm. They used to say that when a person goes out to the sea at night, between him and his net lie *hābaʕ hwēməś*, 'seven monsters of the sea', but he neither sees them nor is paralysed by

---

[25] Literally and metaphorically: people are now healthy enough to be able to hold their breath when diving.

[26] *ətəwīl* 'the long one': the rope around the circumference of the net. I.e., he'd throw the net but hold onto the end of this rope. When he saw fish going into the net, he'd gently pull this rope in to trap them in the net.

[27] *bāʕ*: the distance from fingertip to fingertip of outstretched arms (equivalent to a fathom).

[28] *śāṣət*: whitetip reef shark, lemon shark or sicklefin lemon shark.

fear of them. The good Lord keeps him safe from them so that he can labour for himself and for his children to provide food.

4. u-nəkəˁāt aˁáyśə ḏíkəmə eté ṣɛrbí. nōkˁan swēfər u-nōkaˁ tāmər. u-mékən aʔáynəṯ aṣábərsən eté ṣɛrbí, ḥsābsən, hem rəbəˁīn wə-hem xamsīn. šēn enḥá śaft bə-ṣɛrbí nəsḥāṯ. u-tśíni əmēgaˁ ḏin? il təṯḳōḳi bēs əbín? árbaˁ bēs keyl ḏirrét ḏin. təˁēməruw aṭáh. aṭaˁām ənḥá nəˁāmər hēs 'ḏirrét'.

And that is how we lived until the post-monsoon season, ṣɛrb, arrived. (Then) the people on the trade boats would come and dates would come. And many were the women who had to wait for their marriage portion until the ṣɛrb season, be it 40 or 50 (silver Maria Theresa thalers). We'd hold the wedding feast in the ṣɛrb season. We'd slaughter something. And you see this mortar? The one you grind the coffee beans in? It holds four *keyl* scoops of this sorghum. You do like this (with it). Our food, we call it *ḏirrét*, 'sorghum'.

5. ḏek nōkaˁ bə-ṭīt wə-ḏek l-aġbōr ṭīt u-ṭad nōkaˁ bə-ṭīt. u-bérs ˁar ṭīt, erēbˁat, nōkaˁ bēs ṭad. ehtēdyuw tēsən bə-ḥawm, ḏek fəngān. u-fəngān ḏek wáḳtən ˁadīm, śa la fəngān, ˁar šého ḥawm ḏen l-agādaḥ mən ərawnə yəhtēdyuw beh. yəḳśábwəh nīʔ. ḏek waḳt xaṭāf.

That person would bring one (measure), another would add another measure, and another would bring another. And there would still be one lacking, the fourth. Another person would bring (that). They'd share it out with a seashell, that coffee cup. At that time there was no such thing as a 'coffee cup': they just had this shell washed ashore from the sea to use to share it out. They used to chew it (the grain) raw. That time has passed.

6. nāṣərə xāmməh ʔālāf^{JA} w-aṣáft śhanét əl-mōṭər^E ḥakáḳ wə-xaṭkān u-məta'át u-kel śay yəférəkuw teh l-a'abú: əməta'át yətēwyuw tēs u-xaṭkān wə-ḍay² wə-kel śay təhtēdyən teh a²áynəṭ. u-mən ḍars məshəṭāt əl-ʿalōg ḍárha śabḥ aháwb lə-ṭawl lə-hed.

Now five thousand (Omani riyals) as a marriage portion, and for the wedding feast a carload of tins and clothing and food. And they share out everything between people. They eat the food, and the clothes and perfume and everything the women share out (between the families). And over and above that, they slaughter a camel calf, which has fat on it the length of a hand!

[1980s BATTXT4. B17]

6.2. Memories of Hungry Times

1. yōḳʿan enḥá... zəmān, yōḳʿan enḥá zəmān, mən saʿt. yōḳʿan bə-Gənōt. yōḳʿan bə-Gənōt. śxōlālən, yēkaʿ aháwb əl-warx bə-Gənōt. w-əl-híni? məʿayśə śa la. ṣayd ʔin ḥāṣələn. lēlət e-nōkʿan bə-ṣayd, naʿtēśyən w-əntóh. wə-lēlət e-nōkʿan bə-śa la, ənšaʿūr lə-xalí.

We were once... a long time ago. We were once, a long time ago, a long time ago. We were at Gənōt. We were at Gənōt. We stayed there, at Gənōt, for what must have been about a month. And for what? There was no (other) livelihood. (For) fish, if we got any. On a night we caught fish, we'd prepare them and eat them for our evening meal. And on a night we caught nothing, we'd go to bed empty-bellied.

2. wə-śxōlālən warx. baʿd warx, syērən. xarēgən. wə-šaʿárən bə-Gənōt. enḥá yōḳʿan bə-... ḥāwél bə-Ləḳak. šaʿārən bə-Gənōt. b-ilēl

baʿárən. u-nōtxan. ḥárramnā yin eḏráyən teh (KH śa la) bhaw. śa la. śa la məʿayšə, ḥūt śa la. u-ṣēbaḥ lēn aṣabḥ.

And we stayed for a month. After a month we moved off. We left. And we spent the night at Gənōt. We'd been at… before that we'd been at Lə́kak. We spent the night at Gənōt. We set off to fish with cast nets in the dark. Damned if we got anything, if we made anything bleed![29] (KH Nothing?) Not a thing! Nothing. Nothing for us to live on. There were no large fish. And morning broke on us.

3. *kə-saḥḥ enhá ʿamōren: "gəhīmə Ḥaṣīfə". Ḥaṣīfə, naxl. zəmān, hawlí. Ḥaṣīfə naxl. abátn lə-Šweymīyə. abátn mən aġáwf. (KH mən aġáwf. təʿēməruw heh 'baṭn'?) nəʿāmər heh 'baṭn'.*

In the morning, we said: "We'll go to Ḥaṣīfə." At Ḥaṣīfə there are (wild) date palms. A long time ago, before. At Ḥaṣīfə there are (wild) date palms. (In) the wadi of Šweymīyə. At the top of the wadi. (KH The top of the wadi. You call it [i.e., a wadi] baṭn?). We call it *baṭn*.

4. *helōk məkāni ṭəréh. məkān yəʿēməruw heh Kəllét. məkān yəʿēməruw heh Kəllét wə-məkan nəʿāmər heh Adārit. məkān nəʿāmər heh Kəllét wə-məkān nəʿāmər heh Adārit. ənzēn? əlí śxōlōl b-Adārit,* [JA]*hām mərtāḥ. bə-ġayit əl-ḥazn*[JA]*, śay yənēkaʿuw xérifho ʿar xaybət.*

There are two places there. One place they call Kəllét, a place they call Kəllét. And (another) place they call Adārit. We call

---

[29] Lit. 'to cause to bleed', a stock phrase for being successful when fishing.

one place Kəllét and one place Adārit. Right? Those who stayed at Adārit weren't very happy. Sad to say, only a few of the dates had ripened.

5. əli śxōlōl bə-Kəllét, Kəllét ṭaybəh^JA. Kəllét tərās^JA Kəllét, ʾāxər šay. ʾāxər šay Kəllét. howm lə-Kəllét, híni Kəllét? howm lə-Kəllét "ʾāxər ʾāxər, ʾāxər lə-naxl. ʾāxər lə-naxl mən aġáwf, ʾāxər eh... l-abáṭn."

Those who stayed at Kəllét, Kəllét was good. Kəllét, don't you know Kəllét, at the very end (of the wadi)? Kəllét is right at the very end (of the wadi). The name 'Kəllét' means what? Kəllét (means) 'the very end'. The final, the final date palms. The final date palms at the head, at the end of eh... the wadi.

6. (KH təʿēməruw heh Kəllét) nəʿāmər hēs Kəllét, Kəllét ʾāxər. wə-seh naxl, naxl Kəllét. bēs moh u-bēs naxl wə-ʿabú zəmān ḥawlí yəśxōləluw bēs. əlí šeh əníśərə^JA wəla rān wəla baʿr (KH ʾáywa?) yəśxōləluw bēs. wə-nəśxōlō:l té yəktəmāl minēn šaʿrān.

(KH You call it Kəllét) We call it Kəllét. Kəllét, right at the end. And it's a place of (wild) date-palms, the Kəllét date palms. It has water and date-palms, and in the old days people used to stay there. Those who had livestock, either goats or camels. (KH Yes?) They would stay there. And we stayed right until the šaʿrān star-season came to an end.

7. mən ektəmōl minēn šaʿrān, śxarēgən. śxarēgən etá Šweymīyə. (KH Šwēmyət) Šweymīyə... Šwēmyət. śxōlālən bə-Šwēmyət, śxōlālən ʿādən warx. ʿer wəla l-axṭōr (nə)nātax b-ilēl. ʿer wəla lə-śwēr. ʿer wəla śay, etá: ektəmōl minēn šēl.

When the šaʿrān star-season came to an end, we left. We left and went to Šweymīyə. (KH Šwēmyət) Šweymīyə... Šwēmyət.

We stayed in Šwēmyət. We stayed (there) for a further month. Either we'd go down to the sea at night, to cast our nets, or we'd fish with hook and line. Or something (else), right until the *shēl* star-season came to an end.

8. *mən ektəmōl minēn shēl, warx lə-shēl ektəmōl? šuwgāśən (KH sir shēl, habó təʿēməruw: "hādəˀ...?") "k-əl-shēl..." "əshēl ahādəˀ / wə-ġafík śūrōtən." (KH śūrōtən) "wə-ġafík śūrōtən." ser əshēl, əshēl ahādəˀ. "wə-ġafík śūrōtən / ser əshēl ahādəˀ." ənšəxrāg. ənšəxrāg.*

When the *shēl* star-season had come to an end, when the month of *shēl* had finished? In the late afternoon we set off. (KH *shēl*, what is it you say about *shēl*: "Calm...?") "At the *shēl* star season..." "The seas of *shēl* are calm / And the time of calm seas[30] is lovely." (KH Lovely.) "And the time of calm sea is lovely." After *shēl*, the seas of *shēl* have calmed down. "And the time of calm sea is lovely / Once the seas of *shēl* have calmed down." We left. We set off.

9. *Warx. (KH tsīruw Warx?) áha. śxōlālən bə-Warx. ḥōlən beh. śxōlālən. śxōlālən... ṣerbāt, gifgīf. śxōlālən ṣerbí. śxōlālən śéta. u-dīkəmə ḥālətni*[JA]. *yənākaʿuw tēn ḥerbáʿtyən mən aġáwf, mən ġárbi, əbedw.*

(For) Warx. (KH You went to Warx?) Yes. We stayed at Warx. We made our home there. We stayed (there). We stayed... all through the *ṣɛrb* post-monsoon season. Through the *gifgīf*[31] peri-

---

[30] *ġafík* 'calm seas': as the *shēl* star-season comes to an end, periods of calm seas and wild seas alternate.

[31] *gifgīf* 'the state of the sea in between the monsoon and post-monsoon (*ṣɛrb*) seasons'.

od at the very end of the monsoon. We stayed there right through the ṣɛrb season. We stayed there throughout the winter. And that was how we lived. Our friends and neighbours used to come down to us from above, from inland, the bedouin.

10. yəwréduw lēn (KH yḥémuw ṣayd) yḥémuw ṣayd wəla ḥāmis wəla ġabīr wəla ḥūt. wəla ləxām (KH áha, śay mətəwé) ʔayy^JA məʕáyšə. əfəṭān? yawmət el nēthuw baʕṣ̌, ʕabú šáho həbáʕr. yawréduw baʕr. həbáʕr.

They'd bring their animals to water them in our area. (KH They wanted fish.) They wanted fish or a turtle or a dolphin or a large fish. Or shark. (KH Yes, something to eat.) Anything to keep them going. I remember? One day, some of them came down, people with camels. They were taking camels to water. The camels.

11. wə-lēlət, yawmət əl-mirād, ḥad əla yəḥélbsən həbáʕr eh... əl-ġarbiyīn, bʕél abárr (KH yəḥēlbsən la) yəḥēlbəsən la tá tərédən nəhōrə, tərédən ḍar əmóh lə-Warx. təwrédən.

And at night, on the day they watered them, no-one would milk the camels eh... the inland people, the people of the desert. (KH They wouldn't milk them.) They wouldn't milk them until (the camels) had been to water at midday, been to drink at the water at Warx. They would drink.

12. mən erādna... enḥá ber šēn xabīr, yínsən həbáʕr ḥūr aġáyg fəlān l-ewrōd, allāh yərḥámhəm, əfəṭānho heh bə-ḥāl Saʕd, Saʕd ber... ber Šərēgi. əfəṭānho, əfəṭānho wə-heh bə-ḥāl əNíftəh, allāh yərḥámhəm. wāyidīn^JA əfəṭānho, heh bə-ḥāl Ḥəwārīz. méken, méken, ʔabú méken, ʔabú ḥawlá.

Once they'd drunk... the news had reached us that on that day it was the camels of such-and-such a man which had come down to water. God have mercy on them! I remember them: the late Saʿd, Saʿd the son of... the son of Šərēgi! I remember them, I remember them. And the late Níftəh, God have mercy on them! I remember so many of them: the late Ḥəwārīz. Many, many. So many people, the people of before.

13. wə-yewréduw. ənzēn. enḥá mən əmbōnih erédən. enḥá w-əbúnyən w-əribīʿyən. tá ḍar əmóh (KH tsélabuw) nəsəlāb. w-aʿabú hēkuw, hēkuw həbáʿrho. hēkuw, hēkuw, hēkuw ta: rúwyən həbáʿr.

And they took them down to water. Right. We had already fetched (our) water before, we and our children and our people. (We were) right above the water. (KH You were waiting.) We were waiting. And the people came and watered, they watered their camels. They watered them and watered them and watered them until (all) the camels had drunk.

14. ebrēkuw həbáʿr w-enḥá śxōlālən. yēkaʿ ahāwb əl-fākh əl-sāʿa. sāʿa? məgārə ʿaśēśwəsən wə-helōbuw. wə-helōbuw. əfətān, allāh yərāḥməh wə-yaġfúr leh! heh bə-ḥāl Saʿd, Saʿd Msállim (KH yēkaʿ rəḥīm, dīkəmə waktəh).

They couched the camels and we all sat down (together). It might have been for about half an hour, an hour? Then they got them to their feet and they did the milking. And they milked (their camels). I remember, God have mercy on him and forgive him any sin! The late Saʿd, Saʿd Msállim. (KH He was a kind man, that one, at that time!)

15. ʔinnə heh rəḥīm ḏek, ḏékəmə. yədáwwər^JA ṭāsə, ṭāsə beh śxaf, yəḥéləb. Bāti Šīgə šeh, həbáʿrha, allāh yərāḥməh wə-yaġfúr leh. wə-šeh eh... Ḳarṣáym yəlá, Yáḥiy. (KH šíddənə ḥad.^JA) áha. (KH eh! ber əMsállim) ^JAəráb ʿa ʿādha ṣaḥḥ^JA? (KH ber māt) ber māt? (KH mm.) allāh yərāḥmah wə-yaġfúr leh! lā-illāh ʔil-allāh!

He was indeed kind, that one. That man. He looked around for a small bowl, a bowl with some milk in it—it was he who was doing the milking. He had camels of the Bāti Šīgə bloodline, God have mercy on him and forgive him any sin! And he had eh... those Ḳarṣáym camels, Yáḥiy.³² (KH What a one!) Yes. (KH Eh, the son of Msallim!) Is the man (i.e., Yáḥiy) still alive? (KH He died.) He's dead? (KH Mm.) God have mercy on him and forgive him any sin! There is no God but God!

16. (KH yā xayr bun!) yā xayr... yā xayr bun! yā xayr bun, bə́ni Msállim! yā xayr ʔawādim!^JA lā-illāh ʔil-allāh! məgārə yədáwwər láho bə-ṭāsə. yāt^JA Enṭáyfa, egīʿa, šeh sərbét. taʿbān.

(KH What excellent sons [he left behind]!) What excellent... what good sons! What good sons, the children of Msállim! What excellent people! There is no God but God! Then he looked around for a bowl for them. The late Enṭáyfa, he was really hungry. He had a lot of young children. He was in a poor way.

17. ^JAyədáwwer ləhé^JA bə-ṭāsə. yəʿāmər heh: "śxāf! agtəbíg!^JA śxāf!" (KH "śxāf") wə-yəśxāf. yəʿāmər heh: "śxāfk ʿād! śxāf! rəwí!" yəʿāmər heh: "^JAʿāzim náfsik^JA!" wallāh fēṭənik əbehəlít (KH "ʿāzim ʿar náfsik!") "^JAʿāzim náfsik^JA!"

---

³² The nickname of Yáḥiy. They were Janaba bedouin.

He looked around for a bowl for him. He said to him: "Drink milk! Take and drink! Drink milk!" (KH "Drink milk!") And he drank the milk. He said to him: "Drink more milk! Drink milk! Drink your fill!" He said to him: "Go on: as much as you want (i.e., there's plenty)!" By God, I remember his words! (lit. 'word') (KH "Go on: just as much as you want!") "Go on: take as much as you want (there is plenty)!"

18. "^JAtəbā zāyid? ʕāzim náfsik^JA!" (KH "thām zēyid?") "thām zēyid? ʕāzim náfsik!" ʕamōr: "la…" ʕādho śxāfuw. ʕamōr hēmʕak wəla? "mən śxáfən enhá w-ərəbīʕyən w-əbúnyən ʕād əlí šēn? enhá ṣədōrən warx." wə-yəlāk ewtəkīluw.

"Do you want more? Go on: take as much as you want!" (KH "Do you want more?") "Do you want more? Go on: take as much as you want!" He said: "No…" They had already drunk some more. He said, do you hear or not? "What we've drunk (now), ourselves, our people, our children and the others with us? That will last us for a month!" And those people went on their way.

19. w-enhá lə-hāləh dékəmə. u-nakātələn. u-nənātax. u-məʕayša (KH sīrāt) məʕayša māšiyə. seh məʕayša taʕbānə. yōm mən hayyām? yōm mən hayyām tšəghēm tēn ʕayd, tənākaʕ tēn aʕáyd. (əm)bōnis, hāwéls ʕabú.

And as for us, that was how we lived. We fished with hook and line. We fished with cast nets. And that was how we survived. (KH Life went on.) (This) way of life continued. It was a very hard way of life. One day? One day, in the morning, sardines arrived. The sardines reached our area. In the early days, the way people lived before.

20. hes tənākaˤ ˤayd wə-yəhōmaˤwəs yənākaˤuw ˤabú. yənēkaˤuw əl-ḥūt wə-yənēkaˤuw ələxām wə-yənēkaˤuw aṣáyd. yōm mən ḥayyām, yəˤēməruw hēs 'yōm mən ḥayyām lə-Maˤfédət'. tšəgəhēm bə-ˤayd wə-ləxām. ləxām wə-ˤayd wə-ṭāḳa.

When sardines arrive and they hear about it, people come. The large fish would come and the shark would come, and (all sorts of) fish would come. One day they named: 'one day at Maˤfédət'.[33] (On that day) sardines and shark arrived in the morning. Shark and sardines and ṭāḳa bluefish.

21. (KH wə-ṭāḳa) áha. ḥad yaḳātələn wə-ḥad yármī^JA hēmˤak? wə-ḥad, hēmˤak wəla, l-əmḳádərəh. šəghəmōt tēn aṭāḳa, díkəmə seh, w-aˤáyd? šowḳáˤan bēs. armēni^JA. əlyūx ləbədáho. (KH rēdko bə-lyūx b-ərawnə).

(KH And bluefish.) Yes. Some fished with hook and line and some set (gillnets), do you hear? And all (lit. 'someone'), do you hear or not, did whatever they could (i.e., to catch fish). In the morning ṭāḳa bluefish arrived, that was what happened. And sardines? We got going right in amongst them. We set the gillnets. The gillnets got them. (KH You set the gillnets in the sea?)

22. əlyūx rēdən báho berk ərawnə. w-abérḳˤan bə-ṭaḥḥ. ḥad yənātax, wə-ḥad, hēmˤak wəla? yaḳātələn. (KH h-aṣáyd) h-aṭāḳa. kels ṭāḳa. kállis ṭāḳa hēmˤak? wə-^JAxaḏēna hāẓẓəne^JA. ṣētən h-ərūḳətni, məˤáyšətni.

---

[33] The name of a shark-fishing site near Warx.

We set the gillnets in the sea. And we raced here and there along the shore. Some with cast nets, and some, do you hear or not, with hook and line. (KH For the fish.) For the bluefish. They were all bluefish. All of them were bluefish, do you hear? And we took whatever we could get. For something to eat, for survival.

23. *Khalīfa eh... šuġl*^{JA} *ṭad, šuġl taʕb. ḏar ənīd. ɛ-Khalīfa, ber xadōmək? Khalīfa, ber akātələk teh? (KH la.) ber xadōmək teh? ah? (KH la.) ʕādək el xadōmək teh la? (KH ʕādi la.) Khalīfa, ber xadōmək teh!*

Khalīfa eh... one way of working—exhausting work!—on the goatskin. Khalīfa, have you ever done it? Khalifa, have you fished from one with hook and line? (KH No.) Have you done it? Yes? (KH No.) You've never done it? (KH Not yet.) Khalīfa, I've done it!

24. *u-ber syɛ̄rk ḏar nīd. u-ber kātələk (KH la, hāḏa bers...) ah? (KH bers šēn) bers šíko, ahá? (KH mən dōlək, ʔáywa) ah, mən dōli hoh. bers šíko. áha. zēn. (KH áxlaf ġayris!) la, la, wāyid šiy.*

And I've gone out to sea on a goatskin. And I've fished with hook and line from it. (KH No, this is already...) What? (KH We've already done that.) You already have it, yes? (KH From you, yes.) Ah, from me. You've got it already. Yes. Right. (KH Turn to something else!) No, no. I've got lots (to say)!

25. *zēn. tēmmən b-əwáktni li enhá beh. w-ənʕayš. w-ənʕayš. enhá: eta:... bérən tēli. Khalīfa, b-ilēl, hām el šēn ḥad yəʕíśər tēn la? tšuwġār əlēl ṭəbəryān. (KH wə-tślōlən aṣáyd.) wə-tślōlən aṣáyd állah b-il-ʕafw! (KH tślōlən aṣātər.)*

Right. That time of ours came to an end, that time we were living in. And we survived. And we lived. We (went on like that) until... we were at the end (of these early days). Khalīfa, at night, if we had no one waiting on shore to take our fish from us? The hyenas would go for them in the night! (KH And would take the fish.) And would take the fish, God damn them! (KH They'd take the whole basket!)

26. tśĺōlən aṣāṭər... (KH w-aṣáyd) wəla... šēn gə́ni. wə-tśĺōlən lēn lə-ḥūtni. mən nəṭə́wi eh... aṣāṭər... (KH e:yh! nədəkōt béko bert ˤAli) tkəs aṣāṭər... aṣāṭər šowḳaˤāt beh bert ˤAli. hēmˤak? bert ˤAli. ṭəbərīn hēmˤak? ber nəgəfāt lēn... əzēn wə-šēn, kel ber ṣ́əllāt lēn!

They'd take the whole basket... (KH And the fish.) Or... we'd have a sack. And they'd steal our large fish from us. When we came back at night (after fishing) eh... the basket... (KH Eh! She'd come across your stuff, the daughter of ˤAli.[34]) She'd find the basket... the basket in which they'd been put, the daughter of ˤAli, do you hear? ˤAli's daughter! The hyena, do you hear? She'd shake and worry away at our basket (i.e., to get at the fish)... the good and the bad, she'd carry the lot off!

27. ṭerḥāt tēn ḥābīṭ. "habó?" "habó?" "twōth ṭəbərīn! twōth ṭəbərīn wə-ber twōt l-aṣāṭər wə-twōt... wə-ṣ̌abəṭāt... ʾin əməksōt b-aṣāṭər ḏíkəmə." kélha bəkōt la, hēmˤak? zēn. ṭēwən.

And she'd leave us with absolutely nothing. "What?" "How?" "The hyena's eaten them!" "The hyena's eaten them and it's eaten the basket! And it's eaten... and it's taken... everything

---

[34] ˤAli is ˤAli ber Ḥsayn, the popular nickname of the fox.

there was in that basket!" Not a thing was left of it, do you hear? Right. We'd come back at night.

28. *hes ṭēwən, hēmʕak wəla? kéddə. el fíḳiy. w-el ṣanḥ. w-el kéddə, xadərdār, xadūr! xádər. nəġtaṣ̌ōm beh. yəkūn šēn eh... wəla mənsūl... Khalīfa tġāribis əmənsūl? (KH aġārbis əmənsūl, ʔáywa) zēn. tkūn seh... (KH ḥāwərēt) ḥāwərēt. mən ʕAmān yəxēdəmwəs (KH áha) bʕéli ʕAmān yəxēdəmwəs (KH kínnis bišt) kínnis bišt.*

When we came back at night, do you hear or not? Living quarters: no covers; no shelter; no (proper) homes. (Just) tiny caves. Caves! A cave. We'd curl ourselves up in a tight ball inside them (lit. 'curl up knees to belly with the head tucked in'). We'd have with us eh... either a *mənsūl* thin woollen cloak... Khalifa, do you know the *mənsūl*? (KH I know it, the *mənsūl*, yes.) Right. It was... (KH Black.) Black. From Oman. They make them (there). (KH Yes.) The people of Oman make them. (KH It's like a *bišt* cloak.) It's like a *bišt* cloak.

[20130404_B_B02_memories.wav (13.14)]

6.3. Making Nets

1. *əlix ṣ́əlwēṯ, el heh bátti ṭérti la. wə-hem ṭəlāṭək teh, yaḥṣōṣ wə-yēkaʕ ḳawí. ṭə́laṯ yəḳáʕ dəwayl wə-ṯə́ləṯi ṭəréhi ʔidántən. hem el ʕafīrōr, hūnōṭəh ərawnə, w-ələxām yəffəlōt mə́nəh. hem el ʕafīrōr yəḳáʕ həwīn, ṣ́aʕf, wə-yəbṣ́áreh ələxām u-hūnōṭəh ərawnə. wə-hem ləbədéh ələxām wə-dōraʕ beh, yəḳáʕ ṣ́aʕf, yəbṣ́árəh wə-yəffəlōt mə́nəh. wə-hem dōraʕ beh, yəbáṣ́əreh.*

The yarn used for the gillnet was three-ply, of three strands twisted together, not just of two strands. Because if you twisted three strands together, it would be tight and strong. The third (strand) could be old (yarn) but the other two were newly made. If the twine became red-brown, if the sea had rotted it, then the sharks would avoid it. If it was red-brown it would be weak and friable, and the shark could (easily) break it—the sea had rotted it. And if a shark swum into it (i.e, the gillnet) and got stuck in it, it would be weak and (the shark) might break out of it and get away. And if it had become entangled in it, it would break it.

2. ᶜlyūx el heh waḵtən ḏénəmə la. ḥāwīl yənākaʿ ṣōṭəli u-berəh zāḥib w-akátṇ yēḵaʿ maġṣ́ēf. ḥāwīl əṣōṭəli bʿél ədənāwəg aġṣ́āfwəh. šého ʿar ṣōṭəli. aġāzəl mən ʿamān. aḵalābho xāməh ḥə́btuw. ḥāwīl maġṣ́ēf, məġārə xāməh ḥə́btuw. təṭwāh[35] u-bərāmək teh lə-fxaḏ. ḥāwīl aġāzəl nəṭwāh. ḥāwīl ṣ́arx u-məġārə ṭēwək teh mən ṭəréh, mən bə́ṭṭi ṭəréh wə-awḵáʿk teh.

The gillnets—not how it's done nowadays. In earlier times, ṣōṭəli jute twine would come, ready to use. And the cotton came already plyed. Before, the boat people would already have plied the ṣōṭəli jute twine. They only had ṣōṭəli twine—cotton had to come from (northern) Oman. Place them one on top of the other until you have five strands. Firstly it was plyed double, then five strands (were plyed together). You'd twist it and roll it to thread on the thigh. Before, we had to twist the cotton fibre (i.e., ourselves) to make thread. To begin with it came as a

---

[35] təṭwāh, √ṭwy, 'to coil the worked thread into a skein: by rolling two threads together at a time around the knees to make a length of twine'.

loose hank of fibre and then you'd twist it double, you'd make a doubled strand and set it aside.

3. u-məġārə xadōmək tēsən mən xāməh. məġārə ṭēwək tēsən fáxərə, mən xāməh, kélsən ʿaśirīt. məġārə yēḳaʿ ḳabbət. məġārə bərāmək teh. wə hem ber beh ḥays, ḳəsōrək teh té yəḳáʿ məṭṭəlēṭ. u-məġārə xadōmək teh līx. ərīh mən aḏābəl bə-faʿmək w-ərīh mə́nəh bə-hédək. məġārə təġáṣ́fəh lə-ṭəréh u-məġārə məṭṭəlēṭ.

And then you'd work it to make five strands. Then you'd twist them together, five at a time, making ten strands in all. Then it was (rolled into) a ball. Then you'd roll the thread on the thigh (to make a tight twist). When it had a good twist in it, you'd ply it again, doubled over on itself, until it became triple-stranded. And then you'd work a gillnet with it. One end (of the twisted thread) would go on one side of your big toe (lit. 'foot'), and the other end you'd work with your hands. Then you'd redo it double, around your big toe, and then you'd treble it.

4. ḏik mən bə́ṭṭi ṭəréh nəʿāmər 'fərkéti' bə-bṭahrīt. yənākaʿ ṭad u-yēḳaʿ məṭṭəlēṭ, ṭəlātək teh tūliyīt. hem béreh məṭṭəlēṭ, métən teh l-aṭáwləh, yəxérəg mə́nəh ḥays. mən ġəsráwwən eté gēhəmə mən śān yəmṭōṭ. təġíḏəb beh bə-ḥays: tərábṭəh bə-ḥābən wəla bə-ḥarāṣ́.

The double-stranded thread we call fərkéti in the Baṭhari language. It would come as a single strand but it would be made triple-stranded: you'd twist it to make a triple-plyed rope next. Once it was triple-plyed, we'd stretch it out along its full length to get the kinks out of it. (We'd leave it) stretched taut from the late afternoon until the next day. You'd stretch it out really hard, tying it to a rock or an acacia tree.

5. kə-saḥḥ yəṣābaḥ lēyən w-ewēšken teh wə-ḳaṣābən teh u-wəśáʿan. w-entəḳāl: ṯḥām ṣōn wəla ṯḥām śaġr? hem ṯḥām ṣōn xadémih ḏərēʿ wəla śebr. wə-hem ṯḥām śaġr, ənkáʿ bēs ser əṣəfféy. əlaxām yōkəb berkīh té yəxánḳah, yəlátġah. w-aṣamdēt nəwāḳʿas la berk əlyūx, nəfāzaʿ mən əlaxām yətōh teh.

In the morning it would have become softer and more malleable. We'd wind it around the big toe and cut it and do the knotting. Then choose: do you want a ṣōn mesh-size net, or do you want a śaġr mesh-size net? If you want a ṣōn net, make it a ḏərēʿ[36] or a śebr length.[37] And if you want a śaġr net, bring it from behind the elbow. The shark swim right into it (i.e., the mesh) and it chokes the breath out of them. It kills them. And as for bait, we didn't put any in the gillnets for fear that the shark would just eat it (and go off).

6. əṣōn aṭáwləs həbəʿēt wə-həbəʿēt, ḳaṭʿáti ṯérti, yəxádəm ṭənʿášər bāʿ. śaġr təlāṯṯʿášər wə-təlāṯṯʿášər, ḳaṭʿáti ṯérti, yəxádəm het wə-ʿāṣari. ḳəṭáṭah ḳəṭáṭah, mən abárr, mən aġáwf eté aḳáṣiy. hem berəh berk ərawnə, yəltəwōṭ, yḥām yərēd beh b-ərawnə.

The ṣōn net is seven by seven in length, two sections, making twelve bāʿ spans[38] in all. The śaġr net is thirteen by thirteen, two sections, making twenty-six bāʿ spans in all. Roll it up, roll it up: from the shore, from the top of the shore right down to

---

[36] I.e., from the tip of the elbow to the tip of the extended middle finger.

[37] I.e., the span of the outspread fingers from the thumb to the little finger.

[38] I.e., the distance from fingertip to fingertip of the outstretched arms.

the waves. If he (the fisherman) was already in the sea, it would be already rolled up ready to set out at sea.

7. əkəṭáṭ ḳfēd beh b-ərawnə. wə-šōk ḥābən bēs ḳayd. het tərābaḥ ḏar nīd yəślōlk ʿar təġrāḳ. nōkʿak het berk ərawnə ḏar ənīd. hem bérek šərgí, awḳáʿk ḥābən, ḥābən ḏik śōllək tēs ḥawílk, ḥābən ṭáḳələṭ, nawb, rəbāṭək teh beh b-əlīx. nōkʿak het baʿl ənídək ḏar ḳerbīṭək^JA, wə-tsyōr beh aṭáh.

Take the rolled up (net) down to the sea, with a stone with a length of rope tied round it. You'd swim along on a goatskin which would keep you afloat and stop you sinking. You'd arrive out at sea, on top of the goatskin. Once out at sea, you'd put the stone, the one you'd brought with you, a heavy stone, a big one, you'd tie it onto the gillnet. You'd be out at sea with your goatskin, on your (inflated) skin, and you'd go along with it like that.

8. w-ərawnə ṭəwálət, eté gizírət. té tə́ḳṣa śə́ġəlik. w-əntérəh əlīx berk ərawnə. u-mən awḳáʿk yingīr məśáġər helōk, təwāḳaʿ ḏarsən ḏarāb. aḏarāb tərábaṭs bə-ḳayd té tśānəh əyingīr. w-aḏarāb mən aġáyṣat ḥádərə.

And the sea extends far, far out: right to the island![39] (And so you'd proceed) until you'd finished the job. And you'd set it, the gillnet, in the sea. And once you'd placed another stone anchor there, you'd place stick (markers) on them. You'd tie the stick markers onto a rope so that you could see where the anchor lay. And the sticks were from al-Ġaydah, to the west.

---

[39] I.e., the closest of the al-Ḥallānīyāt islands.

9. nəʿāmər hēs 'kəreb'. nḥām aʿlēm aḏarāb. wə-hem śēnən tēsən la, nəšáxbər ṭadīdēn: "śínko teh yingīr il heh ḏárha ʿalēm?" hem beh kəreb la, yəṯíḳəd, wə-hem beh kəreb yəṯfōf. hes yənākaʿ ləxām, yəmnáʿah mən əmbóh. yəxánḳah.

We call them kəreb, 'floats'. We need the sticks as (anchor) markers. If we couldn't see them, we'd ask one another: "Have you seen a stone anchor with markers on it?" If it (the gillnet) had no floats on it, it would sink right down, but if it had floats on it, it would float on the surface. When a shark comes along, it catches hold of it right here, it chokes it to death.

[1980s BATTXT2. B17]

6.4. The Homemade Fishhook and Using It

1. əmismēr: hem hə-ləxām, əmismēr nəṯḳōḳah lə-ḥābən, nəṯḳōḳ ḥadīd, ḥadīdət u-bēs mənṣāb. ḥābən əmṣáʿ u-ḥadīd mən aġáwf. u-ṭōkkən teh té yəḳáʿ ḳaṯán wə-nḥām heh zēyid la. wə-mən ṭōkkən teh mən fənānə eté yəḳáʿ ʿaráś, nōkʿan bə-fōrə u-ḳašābən teh ḏek ʿaráś wə-xadōmən heh śadáx.

The large mismēr hook: if for shark, we'd beat it out on a stone. We'd beat some iron, a piece of iron, with something to hold it by (lit. 'a handle'). We'd put the stone beneath and the piece of iron on top, and we'd beat away at it until it grew thin and flat and we didn't need it to be any thinner or flatter. When we'd beaten the front part out to make it broad and flat, we'd get a file and file that broad flat bit down, and (then) we'd make a śadáx flange or barb for it.

2. aṣadáx yəmānaʕ aṣáyd mən yəntífəġ wə-yaḥtərēk, məḥal lə-gəndēwi. áwkaʕ ḍarāb bə-śwēr w-əgəndēwi. əgəndēwi ḥə́dəd fənānə wə-ḍarāb w-əmbēnho ṣāfər. w-aṣáyd hes yəśān lə-ḍarāb, hes yəlbīnōn aḍarāb, yəkābəh ʕayd.

The flange or barb holds the fish tight onto the hook, so that it can't escape, so that it can't move, just like an (imported) gəndēwi hook. Put pieces of wood (i.e., lures) on the line near the hook. After the iron hook comes the lures, and between them there would be (a small piece of) brass. When the fish sees the lures, when the lures appear pale (and moving through the water), the fish think it's a sardine.

3. ṭōnīk bēs śwēr ráhak, u-mən ḥelōk gəḏōbək bēs xaráw xaráw eté śənāts əṭōnīk. təwōts wə-aġṭāk bēs əḥə́dəd. əḥə́dəd b-ərawnə yəśānəh la, ḥāwer. yəśān ʕar ḏek elbīnōn, aḍárb. əmáʕdis ʕayd. wə-yaġṭāk bēs əḥə́dəd. wakt mən awkāt təwōt əṭōnīk eté ḥə́dəd wə-aġṭāk bēs.

(I cast) the line far out for a ṭōnīk kingfish, and would then draw it in slowly, slowly, until the ṭōnīk caught sight of it. It would go for it, and the iron (hook) would stick in its (mouth). It would never notice the iron part in the sea: it was dark-coloured. It would only see that pale thing, the wooden lure, and it would think it was a sardine. And then the iron hook would stick into it. Sometimes the kingfish would even swallow the iron part, and it would hook right into it (i.e., into its gullet).

[1980s BATTXT2. B17]

6.5. Liming Nets

1. ḥāwīl lōmmən, nəláḳaṭ əməḥār: ʿašfēr wə-ḥanāwəḵ, ámma təḳádər t́śléləh. nəślōləh berk aṣāṭer u-məġārə nəsyōr té ḥarṣ́ wə-ṭəbōrən ḏarāb wə-xadōmən ś́eyāṭ nawbət wə-awḳáʿan əməḥār berkēs wə-awgādən tēs eté bəhēl. ṭeráḥan teh té yəḳṣām. wə-ś́ōllən teh wə-awḳáʿan ḏarāb ṭəwyāltən. xadōmən teh hes aṭáh.

First we'd collect, we'd pick up seashells: sea-snail shells and conch shells, as many as you could carry. We'd put them in the large ṣāṭer fibre two-handled basket. Then we'd go off to an acacia shrub and break off some sticks and make a large fire. We'd put the shells in it and leave them until they were ready. We'd leave them to cool. Then we'd take them out and we'd put down long sticks. We'd do it like this with it.

2. wə-awḳáʿan ḏarsən ḥanāwəḵ wə-ḏar ḥanāwəḵ mən aġáwf awḳáʿan ʿādən ḏarāb. wə-mən ḥān əriyáḥ xadōmən hes wəś́áʿt wə-awḳáʿan bēs ś́eyāṭ. u-hes dəfərāt, ʿamərāt "rurururu". hem heh bəhēl yilbīnōn, yəḳáʿ elbīnōn mékən, yəlbīnōn. u-hem el heh bəhēl la, yəḳáʿ ḥāwər, nīʾ, yəḳáʿ ḥāwər. heh ləbədōk ḥāwər hes ḏeh.

And we'd put conch shells on top of them (the sticks), and then on top of the shells more sticks. And then we'd make a channel in the direction the wind was blowing, and we'd make a little heap of kindling and we'd light the fire there. When it was going, it would make a noise: rurururu. When they were ready they'd turn white. They'd be really white. They'd turn white. And if they were not ready, they'd be dark-coloured, still raw. They'd be dark-coloured. They'd look as if they were black, like this.

3. *məġārə lōmmək teh berk ṣāṭer. ləḳāṭək teh u-śōllək teh b-aṣāṭər wə-ḍik lēltēn ṭórḥak teh. u-gēhəmə ṭōkkək teh eté yəḳáˤ hes ərəmīd, eté ləbōd hes ərəmīd. məġārə ṯērək teh bə-moh, moh ḥark̠, u-kəmāṭək leh. áwḳaˤ aṣāṭer bə-xabbét il məknēn mən əriyáḥ lə-śān 'yəfhēś'. awḳáˤk tēsən berkíh ḥaṣṣ mən śān 'yəfhēś'.*

Then I'd gather them up into a *ṣāṭer* basket. I'd pick them up and take them off in the basket. I'd leave them for those two nights, and then the next day I'd crush them until they were like fine ash, until they looked like fine ash. Then I'd soak them in water, hot water, and I'd cover them over.[40] Put the *ṣāṭer* basket (of soaked powdered shells) into a hole in the ground, protected from the wind so that they can 'boil'. I'd put (red-hot) stones among them so that they 'boiled'.

4. *u-məġārə hes heh bəhēl, śōllək əlīx, əlīx ḍah li yəmēnaˤ əlaxām berk ərawnə. wə-hes əxarāg teh... ḥōkkək teh eté yəlbīnōn. wə-hem awḳáˤak teh la, yaˤfīrōr, yəlébəd ˤáfer wə-yəḍāyəh əlaxām wə-yənākaˤ bə-śa la hem əlīx el ˤafīrōr. wə-hem ḥōkkək teh yəlbīnōn wə-yənākaˤ bə-ləxām.*

Then, when it was ready, I'd take the gillnet, that gillnet that traps the shark in the sea. And when I'd taken them out... I'd soak them to bleach them. And if I didn't put them in that, they'd become red-brown, they'd turn brownish-coloured. If the nets turned red-brown, the shark would be able to smell them and the nets would catch nothing. But if I limed them, they'd become pale-coloured and they'd catch shark.

[1980s BATTXT2. B17]

---

[40] √kmt, 'to cover over with st.', here, so that the water stayed hot and no wind would get in to cool the contents.

6.6. The ṭōnik Kingfish

1. əṭōnīk yəxádəm hes mismēr, śēnyə den əmismēr? hes teh. ḥāwīl ṭōḵḵuw teh. məġārə ʿōṣəl leh, ʿōṣəl wə-ʿōṣəl wə-ʿōṣəl leh té šəwṭōḵ, u-nōkaʿ bə-śwēr. wə-śwēr ʿōṣək tēs beh əmbóh bə-ḥadīd, u-məġārə mēnʿak tēs śwēr bə-hádək u-ḥadīd bə-hádək u-rēdək beh u-šáwkaʿ ráḥak.

(For) the ṭōnik kingfish he'd work a nail (i.e., to make a hook). See this nail? One like this. First they'd beat it out. Then he'd tie it round and round and round and round (the stem of the iron hook) until it had become absolutely rigid. Then he'd fetch the fishing line. And the line, you'd tie it on here, with the ḥadīd fishhook (lit. 'piece of iron'). And then you'd take the line in your hand and the iron fishhook in the (other) hand, and you'd cast it so that it landed far out to sea.

2. wə-hem lēs səkərət u-śay riyáḥ la, yəwāḵaʿ arḥāḵ. u-məġārə gəḏōbək teh lə-xarāw xarāw té nəkəʿāt əṭōnīk wə-təwōt w-aġṭāḵ bēs. nəkəʿāt əṭōnīk wə-mənəʿāt bə-ḏarāb, wə-ḥádəd ləbədēs ərīhs. wə-ḥádədəs yəhēmiyuw teh 'gəndēwi', yəhēmiyuw teh 'məndaġ', yənídəġis əmbóh, yəlátġas.

If the sea was calm and there was no wind, it would go further out. Then you'd pull it in, slowly, gently, until the ṭōnik kingfish came and took the bait and it would be hooked. The ṭōnik kingfish would come and grab the pieces of wood (i.e., the lure), and the iron fishhook would catch it on the head. And the piece of iron they call a gəndēwi. Or they call it a məndaġ, because it yənídəġ 'it hooks into' it (i.e., the fish) right here and kills it.

3. mən ḍar rih lə-ḥābən tərūd lēs śwēr wə-tənākaˁ bēs. śay mínsən yəlíbdis əríhs wə-tənākaˁ el mātāt, u-śay mínsən təgíḍəb wə-təˁāmər "rururururu", bəṣərāt ərawnə, mən ḍar ərawnə mən aġáwf. eté tə́kṣa śwēr. wə-mən tə́kṣa śwēr ḥōddək bēs. hem heh ḳarīb bə-ləxā nəsāfk tēs, wə-hem heh ráḥaḳ, aġṭāḳ bēs, kəlābək bēs bə-kəllōb.

Standing on top of a rock, you'd make a cast for it and you'd bring it in. Some of them would have been struck on the head and would arrive dead, while some you'd have to pull in, and it (the kingfish) would go *"rurururu"* as it ploughed through the water (i.e., fleeing out to sea), right on the surface of the water, until it ran out of line. And when the line ran out, you'd pull it in. If it were close by, right there beneath you, you'd jerk the line hard (to bring it out). But if it were further out, and had been hooked, you'd have to pull it in with the gaff.

4. aḥawlá, aḥawlá yəhísəbwəs ṣādti ṭəréh. u-hes təḳášbis fákḥi, təgzérs, təḳáˁ mən ṭérti. w-aḥawlá yəṭráḥuw tēs mən ṭérti. tikṣáṣən mən nxal əḏərwít mən sərānə, náḥfi ṭəréh, ḏeh naḥf u-ḏeh naḥf. hem ber gəzōrək tēs fákḥi, tənḥāfh, śəḳḳát. fakḥ təhēdyən teh fákḥi ṭə́rti u-tənḥāf mə́nəh té sə́rəf sə́rəf.

The first people, our ancestors, considered it to be equivalent to two fish. For when you divide it into two halves, you cut it in half, it becomes (like) two fish. Our ancestors reckoned it to be equivalent to two (fish). It would be cut beneath the dorsal hump, from behind, to make two sections, this section here and this section there (i.e., one half with the head, the other with the tail). When you'd cut it in two, you'd open (each half-fish) out flat, split down the middle. You'd divide this half into two (further) halves and then you'd slice (each bit) up, until it was all slices, slice by slice.

5. ḏeh fāliḵ el beh gawd la əmətəwéh axáṣ, axáyr sə́rfət il bēs gawd. əríh lə-ṭōnīk śūri, w-əḏənōb hēn ənḥá, béreh maġrēb. hes ərātib lə-məʕāšāt il mən dōl ḥkawmət. aʕaḵáf li-ʕāmmən ənḥá. u-ḥāwīl aġáyg ḥad hes teh la, u-məġārə ʕayōnuw teh aʕabú. šawḵaʕāt beh ʕayn, el seh śūrōt la. u-maʕtēd enkuwrōd.

This section that has no skin makes inferior eating, the section with the skin is the better. The head of the kingfish makes excellent eating and its tailpiece belongs to us.[41] That's a fact known to everyone, like a salary paid by the Government. The tailpiece is an inheritance from our (famous) ancestor. In the times before there was no-one like him, but then people grew envious of him and put the Evil Eye on him. He had the Evil Eye put on him. It was a bad thing that happened to him. And then (as a result), he became quite mad.

[1980s BATTXT2. B17]

6.7. 'Stars' and Fish

1. mən kān ərəbʕiyāt,[42] ṭad ḥwētəm, 'baʕl ḵuwwét'. ṭad kēḏəb, əmbēn əxarifīt w-əmbēn əṣɛrbí. ʕād elḥāḵ la ḥwētəm, ḥwētəm ʕar mən səréh. ərə́ffə w-ərəkféf ʕar ṭad: mēt nōkʕanə yətēwyuw mánsən wə-yəḥāsəbuw lēsən. wə-rəkətáho awárx lə-ṭāka: ṭad warx lə-rəkféf wə-ṭad warx lə-ṭāka. kel aʕabú yəkēdəmuw hēsən lə-rūgə^JA, yəḥāsəbuw hēsən, mətəʕát.

---

[41] I.e., The Məšérma clan, the clan of the speaker.

[42] I.e., September, October, etc.

In between the end of the monsoon and the beginning of the post-monsoon autumn ṣɛrb season, there is a star-season called ḥwētəm, 'The one that brings storms'. There is one called kēḏəb, between the monsoon and the ṣɛrb post-monsoon season, before the ḥwētəm star arrives: ḥwētəm comes after it. The season of ráffə[43] and rəkfēf[44] fish is one and the same: when they arrive, they (i.e., the Bəṭāḥira) eat them. They work out when they're due to arrive. And after them comes the month of the ṭāka bluefish: one month for the rəkfēf and one month for the ṭāka. Everyone sets off for wherever they're to be found, to get something to eat. They calculate the time of their arrival: (they're vital) food.

2. ʿamōr 'awárx lə-ṭāka'. ʿemōruw tsyōr əl-Yemən ḳəbált lə-ḥagg. w-awárxəs el tsyōr beh ʿādəs tsyōr b-awárxəs tkənáḥ beh. u-mən kétər lə-məsīr ḥāwīl təḳádər la təsyōr la mən śábḥas, u-məġārə hes tkānəḥ el ḥad yətóhs la mən axáṭəm.

It's called 'The month of the ṭāka bluefish'. They say that (the fish) travel towards the Yemen. In the direction of the Ḥajj. And in the same month they go (there), on that same month they come back. And from all their travelling... to begin with, they can hardly move, they're so fat, and then when they come back, no one can eat them, they're so thin!

3. ʿāds tsyōr lə-dīrət əl-ġatámm. tsyōr lə-hind, dīrət əl-ġatámm, herbáʿtən ḥāwīl 'ġatámm'. nəkəʿēš awárx lə-rəkfēf: yənākaʿ mən

---

[43] Small shoaling fish.
[44] Queenfish sp. (a carangid).

boh, śə́tə wə-ḳayṣ́, ʿad ərawnə hādəʾ, bēs riyā́ḥ la. heh ḏek šəṣ́yōḳ əbṭā́hira aḥawlá, ləbōduw ərəmēd əmbáʿdəh.

They still have to go to the land of the Ġatámm.[45] They go to India, the land of the Ġatámm. Our friends there used to be 'ġatámm' (i.e., no-one could understand them). Then comes the month of *rəkfēf*: they come from here, winter and summer, while the sea is still calm and there is no wind. That was the hardest time for the Bəṭā́ḥira in earlier times: they became weak and enfeebled after that (lit. 'they became like ash').

[1980s BATTXT4 B.17]

6.8. The Moray Eel

1. ḥəwēn? hes təwōkəb ḥedək mən śān lə-ṣəfilḥēt, t̠ām táxərgis, heh yətúhk, ḥəwēn, yəḳáśab ḥādōtka, yəḳáśab ḥed bhaw! yaġáyr… heh yəġúraḥ u-bēs samm.

The moray eel? When you put your hand down into (a crevice) for an abalone, to get it out, it bites you, the moray eel. It cuts your hands, it cuts right into your hand, my goodness! But… it makes a wound and it's poisonous.

2. u-bʿéli gizərīt ʿamōruw yətēwyuw teh. hoh śink tā́ho bə-ʿáyni. ʿamōruw beh ʿarāwək wə-yəxárguw tēsən u-məġā́rə yətēwyuw teh. əmā́tən beh ʿarḳ: ṭad lə-syōr b-əmā́tən əmbóh u-ṭad b-əmā́tən mən əmbóh.

---

[45] ġatámm, a term used by the Bəṭā́ḥira to describe people who 'live at a distance, who are not "Arab", and whose language is incomprehensible'.

The people of the Jāzir plain eat it, they say. I've seen them doing so with my own eyes! They say it has two (poison) channels which they remove, and then (they can) eat it. The fillet of flesh each side of the spine has a (poison) channel, one along here and one along here.

3. enḥá nəxádəm mínəh ṣamdēt wə-nəwāḵˁas bə-ḥadīd wə-nərūd beh b-ərawnə. wə-hoh ber śink teh kə-kfōr, ˁáləwi, yəṣōduw beh. ˁamōruw ḥāwīl edlōluw aḵáˁ, ˁar nāṣərə fēṭənək tēs la. śə́fho yəxádəmuw b-ərawnə, yaḵāṭəluw wə-yəġayē̂ṣuw lə-śūrēn.

We ourselves use them as bait. We put (the bait) onto a big iron hook and we cast it into the sea. And I've seen the unbelievers with them (i.e., moray eels), to the east: they use them to fish with. They say that long ago they (i.e., the unbelievers) knew (this) land, but now I forget how (that story) goes. But they do indeed know how to work the sea: they fish with hook and line and they dive with lines.

[1980s BATTXT 2. B14]

6.9. Living from the Sea Before (a)

1. əwakət lə-xarifīt naˁtām bə-xədāwər il xadəmēsən əbēli bə-Mingíy ḏénəmə. ənhōrən nəślōl śūrēn wə-nərūd bēsən berk aḵáṣiy. w-aḵáṣiy elbinōn hes ḏeh wə-nərūd seris. śwēr təwāka ˁ bēs ṣamdēt, ḵaṣ̌əbāt lə-duˁéyr wəla mən śisənāt wə-təwyōts ṣādə.

During the monsoon season we'd spend the nights in caves, caves that the Lord made, in this place of Mingíy. By day we'd take our lines and cast them in the waves, and the (breaking) waves would be white like this, and we'd cast beyond them.

You'd put bait on the line, a piece of *duˁéyr* mullet or *śīsənāt* rabbitfish, and a fish would go for it.

2. mən təwyōts aṣādə ˁamórk bēs aṭáh: gəḏōbək tēs, ˁadōlək tēs abárr. mən ˁamōlək bēs aṭáh, ˁādək rēdək tēs. təmmút saˁt təwyōts ṣādə, hem kūn əbēli yḥām hōk. áwḵˁak ṣamdēt h-əgəndēwi lə-śwēr wə-rēdək teh wə-seh nəkəˁāt aṣādə hem əbēli yḥāms hōk. wə-gəḏōbək tēs wə-rēdək tēs k-əribáˁts.

When the fish had taken the bait, you'd do like this: you'd pull it in, you'd bring it up ashore. Once you'd done like that with it, you'd make another cast. After an hour or so, (another) fish would bite, if the Lord so willed it for you. You'd put bait on the hook of the line and you'd cast it, and it would approach it, the fish, if the Lord so willed. And you'd pull it in and throw it (into the hollow dug to hold caught fish) to join the other (lit. 'its companion').

3. w-əmətəˁát l-aˁabú ˁar heh, aṣáyd. hes rēdyuw teh abárr ˁādəh bə-śwēr, ləbōduw teh bə-ṣōwər, tətḵōḵs l-ərī́hs wəla bə-skīn wəla bə-yənbīt, škíyy, l-ərī́hs eté təmét. wə-təzém ḥerbáˁtka li yəḥáṣer. təxrāg mánəh əgəndēwi wə-śōllək teh.

And people had nothing but this as food, fish. Once they'd thrown it on the ground, while it was still on the line, they'd hit it with a stone. You'd knock it on the head, or (use) a knife or a dagger, a sword-blade, on its head until it was dead. And you'd give (some of) them to any close friends or family there with you. You'd take the hook out of it and take the fish off with you.

[1980s BATTXT 2. B14]

6.10. Living from the Sea Before (b)

1. ḥāwīl b-əgīˤ, hes aˤabú el gīˤuw wə-mətəwé ˤar mən aṣáyd w-axayār lə-ṣayd ṭōnīk wə-terˤān wə-śīsənāt wə-ˤaṣāb wə-sxalét wə-nəṭēyə wə-ˤanəkāb wə-mékən mən əkennōn.

In earlier times, in the hungry times, when people were very hungry and there was nothing to eat but fish, the best fish were *ṭōnīk* kingfish, *terˤān* pompano, *śīsənāt* rabbitfish, *ˤaṣāb* emperor, *sxalét* cobia, *nəṭēyə*[46] and *ˤanəkāb* king soldier bream. And many of the smaller fish.

2. terəbáḥt wə-ġatráwwət wə-śīrax wə-ˤašfēr hēsən ṭaˤm la. yətēwyuw tēsən aˤabú. hēsən ṭaˤm la, w-el tənāfˤan tōk ˤar aṣáyd. ədə́nīs^JA śa la berkēsən, yəlán kélsən. aḥāmis axáyr mən ḥūt l-ərawnə kéləh. wə-nāṣərə aˤabú yətēwyuw tēs la yaġáyr hem aḥád xaybət mən aḥawlá.

Octopus, cuttlefish, spiny lobster, and sea snails have no flavour. People used to eat them, but they have no taste. Only fish does you any good. They have no fat in them, all those others. The turtle is better than all the fish in the sea, but nowadays people don't eat them, except one or two of the older people.

3. əġəbēr ḥāwīl aˤabú yəbtəśéruw beh wə-nāṣərə yətēwyuw teh la. ḥāwīl yəˤāməruw ˤād heh b-ərawnə, yəṣˤākuw bˤél abárr wə-yəˤāmeruw hého: "wə-ġəbē:r, ġəbēr! ġəbēr wə-ˤar xəbīr?!" yəˤāməruw bˤél abárr əġəbēr el heh śáwi la: śay mə́nəh el ḥad yətóh(əh) la mən ˤasāwət, yəkdōdəh la. wə-śay mə́nəh śūri wə-yətēwyuw teh aˤabú. lēyən.

---

[46] Not identified.

As for dolphins, people used to be delighted to see them, but nowadays they don't eat them. Before, the people of the coast used to call out to them while they were still out at sea; they'd call out: "Oh dolphin, dolphin! Are you a dolphin or (only) news of one?!" The people who live by the sea say that dolphins are not all the same: some of them are inedible, their flesh is rubbery and dry, and can't be cut into strips and dried. But some have good flesh and people eat it: it's soft and tender.

4. śídəfāt wə-śēnaḥt yətēwyuw tēsən nīt wə-ḥád yətábəxsən. lékən fēḏək ḥad yətóh(əh) la nī². yingēn yēḳaʿ b-ərawnə k-aʿánnət wə-ḥāwīl yətēwyuw teh. yəṭēbəxuw teh bə-ṣifēri, yəfhāś sāʿat eté yəbhēl. wə-meyt el bəhēl yətēwyuw mə́nəh. wə-ṣəfēlaḥ yətēwyuw tēsən, yefhāśuw tēsən wə-yətēwyuw tēsən. wə-hem śēmək tēsən tənākʿan bə-dərēhəm kə-bʿéli śafūr.

The śídəfāt sea lemon and the śēnaḥt chiton can be eaten raw, but some people cook them in water. But mussels are never eaten raw. The sea slug can be found at low tide and people used to eat it. They'd cook it in pots, let it boil for a long time until it was ready and then they'd eat it. Abalone were eaten: they'd cook them in water and then eat them. And if you sold them, they would bring money from those who live in Dhofar.

5. əbiʿl, ḥāwīl yəstəlébuw silīb, yəlēbəduw beh. ḏeh ḳennōn ykun xəfīf wə-ḏeh nawb ykun ṯḳīl. wə-śay yəḳṣéṣuw beh wə-śay yərēdyuw beh. yəwə́kəb berk aʿyéntən lə-lyūx wə-h-əməkəḏáyr w-aʿyéntən ʿamərēt aṭáh. yəwə́kəb əmbóh wə-yəmānʿas.

The sawfish: people used to use them (i.e., the rostrum) as weapons in earlier days, they would fight one another with them. This smaller kind (of rostrum) is light, but this bigger one is heavy. They used some of them to cut things up with, and some they would just throw away. (The sawfish) goes into the mesh of the gillnets, right into the knots, and (then) the mesh (lit. 'eyes') would go like this. It (i.e., the sawfish) would go in here, and (the mesh) would hold it fast.

6. terəbáḥt: terəbáḥt yōm tksēs ḏar gəbəlīl, txərēgs wə-təlībəd bēs. txərēgs wə-təmānʿas b-əríhs. u-bēs ḥādōtən təmānaʿ bōk. təlábdis ḏar gəbəlīl té təmét. yaḳáṭəluw bēs wə-yəṭēbəxwəs yōm yḥémuw yətēwyəwəs. yəgēldwəs əgəlādət mən aġáwf w-akāśaʿwəs. hem ḳeśəʿēt, awḳaʿēs berk... ləffēs wə-awḳaʿēs berk gáni, wələ awḳaʿēs berk... ḥayállah śay.

Octopus: when you find an octopus on rocks, you pull it out and you hit it. You pull it out, holding it by its head. It has (many) tentacles (lit. 'arms') with which it clings onto you. You beat it against a rock until it's dead. They use it (as bait) to line-fish with, and they cook it in water when they want to eat it. They remove the outer skin and they dry (the rest). When it's quite dry, put it into... roll it up and put it into a sack, or put it into... into anything.

7. ġatəráwwət: əġatəráwwət hes terəbáḥt nōbəh[JA] yəṭēbəxwəs. təgādaḥ, śay məns təgādaḥ mən ərawnə. w-aḳánnət li tkūn aháwb l-aṭáh yənētxuw bēs əmġādəf. wə-śay yaḳātələn bēs u-śay yəṭēbəxwəs wə-yətēwyəwəs. aġābəs yəxēsən əməġadéft. ġatəráwwət wə-terəbáḥt: aktír ġatəráwwət təxádəm ḥāwər, aġāb. yōm təgʿār ḏárha məġadéft, xeyās, ḥāwər.

Cuttlefish: the cuttlefish is like the octopus, the same: they cook it in water. It drifts ashore, some of them drift ashore from the sea. And the small one of about this (size), they use cast nets to catch it. Some they use for line fishing and some they cook and eat. Its faeces foul the cast net. Cuttlefish and octopus: the cuttlefish produces most of the black stuff, the faeces. When a cast net lands on it, it fouls it and turns it black.

[1980s BATTXT1. B17]

6.11. Life Before for Bəṭāḥira Spending Time on the Plateau Above

1. *ḥāwīl nəḳáˁ... nəśxōlōl bə-gizərīt. u-waḳt śēyən, əmətəˁát xaybət, w-əmóh maṭk śa la u-heh ˁādha xaybət. nəślōl bə-nəyād moh ḍar əgəmōl wə-nəsxōwəl leh mən xāməh ḥayyām. waḳt təḳáˁan ṭérti wə-sēn niyāb, wə-śay mən awḳāt yəślōl mən árbaˁ təḳáˁan ḳənyāntən wəla dəwyōl, tślōlən moh la, təṣġālən teh.*

In the early days we were to be found... we'd stay in Gizərīt, the Ashwaymiyah area. They were hard times: there was little food and no sweet water, and moreover there was very little (of any water). We used to go to fetch it in leather skins on camel(back) and would sometimes take up to five days to do it. Sometimes it (i.e., the camel) could carry two skins, if they were large ones, and sometimes four skins, if they were small or old and weren't good for carrying water because they leaked.

2. *w-ənhá nəḳáˁ ˁala^{JA} ṣayd wə-ḥāməs w-əlxām, əmətəwē. wə-śxāf xaybət yəḳáˁ śēn. hes yəḳáˁ moh ḳarīb, nəġə́rəf mínəh bə-shāltən mən əmáˁdən. wə-hes təḳáˁ məḥsāt ġazírət, nəślōləh ˁar bə-ḳeyād,*

nədɔ́ləh, əngídəb beh bə-ḳeyād. w-ədɔ́ləw yəḳɔ́ˤ mən nayd il nəślōl beh mən əmṣɔ́ˤ.

And for food, we lived off fish, turtle and shark. We had very little milk. If water were close by, we would scoop it up in metal bowls. And if it were a deep water-scrape (i.e., a hole dug in a sandy flowbed), we could only get at it by using ropes: we'd bring it up (in a skin bucket) on ropes. The bucket was made of a leather bag and we'd get (the water) up from below in it.

3. ədɔ́ləw lə-nayd nəwāḳaˤ beh ḳeyād rəbəˤāt, aṭád mən dābəl mən yəḳˤāl əmóh, wə-nərūd beh l-əmṣɔ́ˤ. fənānə nəhāḳa əgəmōl, nəwāḳaˤ heh mərḳī wə-nəwāḳˤah wə-nəkbōb beh moh eté yəṣúdər. əmərḳī təḳɔ́ˤa mən ṣifərīt nawb wə-mən śay nawb yəmānaˤ moh mékən.

We'd attach four ropes to the (mouth of the) leather bag, one to each side, to stop the water spilling out, and we'd pour it out. First we'd water the baggage camel: we'd put down a large dish for it and we'd pour water into it until it had drunk its fill. The large dish was a metal cooking pot or any large container that held a lot of water.

4. (nə)nāḳaˤ b-əgəmōl wə-nəbɔ́rkəh wə-nəzíməl leh. hem šōk zɔ́məl mékən, təxfōf l-əgəmōl mən əmóh, wə-hem šōk ˤar śay xaybət, təmɔ́l ənayd. nəghām kə-saḥḥ hes yēḳaˤ əmoh ráhaḳ, wə-nəkhāb ḍárha eté ġasráwwən. hem əmḥási bēs ˤar xaybət, ḥad yəślōl fənānə wə-ḥad mənēn sərānə. hes yəḳɔ́ˤ əmóh ˤar xaybət, tśxōlōl eté yəgēmˤan.

We'd bring up the camel and couch it and then load it up. If you had a heavy load (of other things), you'd lessen the amount of water. But if you had only a little baggage, you'd fill the water-skin right up. If the water were distant, we'd set off at first light and and stay by the water from noon until the afternoon. If the water-scrape had only a little water in it, one person would take it first and the others of us had (to wait and) take it after him. If there were only a little water, you had to wait while it (i.e., the waterhole) filled up again.

5. *yihərēk bə-kermām lə-ḳarb l-əmóh wə-nəślōl bə-ḥādōtyən mən yihərēk wə-nəwāḳaˤ bə-gəwēni, wə-ḍar əmóh mən aġáwf nəwāḳˤah, ˤəśí l-əgəmōl. hem nḥām məswāk lə-xah, ḍarb mən yihərēk, nəḳáśbəh, ḥāwīl ˤar bə-ḥādōtya, wə-məġārə nəślōləh wə-nemēṭələn teh bə-skayn. yaġáyr ənḥá ḥāwīl ənxádəməh la. ˤabú báho maˤd la ḥāwīl, yēdaˤuw la el heh yənāfaˤ.*

Salvadora persica 'yihərēk' bushes grew in the mountains beside the water. We'd gather *Salvadora* material by hand and put it in sacks and then load it up, putting it on top of the load of water we were carrying: this was for the evening feed for the baggage camel. If we wanted a tooth-stick from the *Salvadora* bush, a stick of *Salvadora*, we'd cut it: first just with my hands and then we'd take it and whittle it to shape with a knife blade. But we didn't use tooth-sticks before: the early people were fools, they didn't know how useful the *Salvadora* bush was (for this).

6. *əgəmōl yəślōl əmóh h-əbáˤləh wə-yəślōl ḥerbáˤtha hem ḥad l-eḳérəbho mən śān aˤabú. hes təḳáˤ ˤārān kə-ʔaynaṯ tənˤāḳan bēsən. aˤrān tənˤāḳan bēsən aʔáynaṯ mən hān tədlōlən hēsən əráˤi eté ġasráwwən té ewēgəhən bēsən hə-kéddə. yəḥélabuw mənsēn wə-yelġámuw hēṯārisən.*

The baggage camel carried water for its owner, who would also take it (i.e., water) to other members of his family and close associates if they were nearby. If women had goats, they would take them out to graze. The women would herd the goats to any place where they knew there was grazing. Then in the afternoon they'd bring them back home. (Then) they'd milk them and put the goats' kids to suckle.

7. wə-təwrédən tēsən ḥānāfsən wə-təkhābən šēsən ḍar əmóh eté ġasráwwən, té ewēgəhən lə-kédda. kul ḥad mánho yədlōl kədōtəh. hes ewēghək lə-kədōt mən ḍar əmóh el wərādək, u-wēṣələk e-kədōt, təhábrək^H əgəmōl wə-təḥṭōṭ mánəh əzémal li ḍárha.

And they (i.e., the women) would take them to water separately, staying with them beside the water for the hours of the noonday heat, and then in the afternoon they would take them back home. Each one (i.e., of the goats) knew its way home. When you got back home from the water, from where you'd gone to fetch water, when you reached home, you'd couch the camel and unload whatever it had on its back.

8. əniyād nəʕálkan tēsən bə-ḥarś, wə-yihərēk nəkbōbəh mən əgawēni h-əgəmōl yaʕtēśian teh. hem nḥām nəbʕār, nəwḥāf əgəmōl, wə-hem l-aʕtēmən té kə-saḥḥ, nəśárəh bə-ḳayd.

We'd hang the water-skins in acacias, and we'd tip the *Salvadora* fodder out of the sacks for the camel to have its evening feed. If we were going to set off again at night, we'd tether the camel in the couched position, but if we were going to stay there for the night, we'd (just) hobble it with a rope around its forelegs.

9. hes əgəmōl gēhəmə šeh śa la mən əkanām w-el ġōbbuw lə-moh, əbáʕləh yaśbōb śay mən kermām mən ḥān yədlōl bēsən əkanām wə-

yəḵúnəm. hem ʿar xaybət, yəślōləh. wə-hem mékən, yəzíməhl ḏar əgəmōləh wəla śay mən ərəkōb eté yənākaʿ beh e-kədōt.

If by morning there were no fodder left for the camel, or if they were not taking it to water every day, its owner would go up one or other of the mountains to where he knew fodder plants grew and would gather fodder. If there were only a little, he'd carry it (back) himself. And if there was plenty, he'd load it on his baggage camel or on some other riding camel to bring it back home.

10. *hem śa la bə-kermām, el kōsə śa la mən əḵanām, yəxábəṭ heh berk səmmét hem šeh səmmét. wə-hem šeh səmmét la, yəxábəṭ berk saḥt wəla śay mən axaṭḵān, yaġáyr sen təḵáʿan ḏek wáḵtən axaṭḵān xaybət.*

If there were nothing to be found in the mountains, if he found no fodder at all, he'd knock down twigs and foliage (from an acacia) onto a fibre mat, if he had a mat. If he had no mat, he'd knock the twigs and foliage down onto a length of woollen cloth[47] or onto any piece of clothing. But in those days, there was very little clothing.

11. *wə-təxábəṭ ʿəśí. hem heh mékən wə-hfaḥk mínəh té kə-saḥḥ, heh śūri té kə-saḥḥ. wə-hem heh xaybət wə-fərāġən teh ərəkōb, təxábəṭ hēsən gēhəmə fśí, wə-ġasráwwən təxábəṭ hēsən ʿəśí.*

You'd knock down foliage for the evening feed (for the camel). If there was plenty and some was left over for the morning, it would still be good the next day (as fodder). But if there was

---

[47] A length of woolen cloth woven in northern Oman.

only a little and the riding camels had finished it all, you'd have to go in the morning and knock down more for their midday feed, and in the afternoon you'd have to go (again) and knock down more for their evening feed.

12. śay mən awḳāt təḳáˤ hebəlēt: hem seh ḳánnət nəˤāmər hēs seyr, wə-hem bers nawb, nəˤāmər hēs ˤanəśáyt, təḳáˤ bēs ḥaṭṭāt. wə-hem seh ber ḳeśəˤāt, nəˤāmər hēs nəḳəśīt. yəlán həmōtən aḥawlá (hə-)ḥebəlēt.

At certain times of the year, the acacia would have pods. When they're tiny, we call them *seyr*, and when they're larger we call them *ˤanəśáyt*: these have seeds inside. When they've dried out we call them *nəḳəśīt*.[48] Those are the names our forefathers gave to the fruit of the acacia.

13. šāho ˤar... yəḳúnəm mən kermām, mən alásaf w-əyihərēk. wə-hem śa la lásaf wə-yihərēk, yəxábəṭ mən ḥarāś. wə-hem ḥarāś bēs śa la wə-ḳanām śa la wə-ráˤi śa la, el ˤād śay ḥélət la yaġáyr ḥélət l-əbēli.

They only had... he'd gather fodder from the mountains, from the *Capparis cartilaginea* 'lásaf' and the *Salvadora persica* 'yihərēk' plants. And if there were no *Capparis* or *Salvadora* plants, he'd beat down twigs and foliage from an acacia. And if the acacia had nothing, and there were no fodder plants and no grazing, then there was nothing further you could do, and only God could provide a solution!

---

[48] Dried acacia fruit lying on the ground.

14. baʕl ərawnə hem šeh rəkōb wə-təḳáʕnə xaybət, aḥawlā šáho axáybət hbḗʕar yaġáyr aḥád tə́ḳaʕ šeh ṭīt wə-ḥad tə́ḳaʕ šeh ṯə́rti. baʕl ərawnə hem el ʕād šeh xabāṭ la, yəwúzəmsən ṣayd. mən kul ṣayd li yənākaʕ beh yəwúzəmsən mínəh.

The man who lived beside the sea, if he possessed camels—but these were few in number: people had very few camels in the old days, except for one or other who might own a single she-camel or might have two. The man who lived by the sea, when there was no longer any foliage to be gathered as fodder, would feed them (i.e., the camels) on fish. He'd feed them on any kind of fish he could catch.

15. wə-hem el ʕād šeh ṣayd la, u-šeh ləxām ḳennōn, yəsérfəh, yəwúzəmsən mínəh. wə-ḥāwīl hes nāṣərə la, mətʕát śa la mən baʕd əṣɛrbí. wə-śéte el ʕād yəṭʕámuw la mətʕát l-abárr yaġáyr ḥad šeh axáybət wə-ḥad šeh śa la ʕar ṣayd wə-śxāf.

And if he had no more fish, but had only a small shark, he'd slice it up and give them some of that. The early days were not as it is today: after the ṣɛrb post-monsoon season there was nothing to eat. And in the winter months, people had not a taste of food from the land, unless one or other had a very little (i.e., still some grain left over, or wild game). Some had nothing but fish and milk.

[1980s BATTXT1. B17]

6.12. Which Fish Make the Best Eating

1. ṭōnīk wə-terʿān axáyr mən aṣáyd. terʿān əməkənéts b-akáʿan axáyr Warx mə́nho kel təḳáʿ bēs aṣā́fə. wə-bʿéli Warx yənēkaʿuw bə-terʿān. ḥāwīl ḥayāt l-aʿabú ḥawlā ʿar mən ḥādōtho.

ṭōnīk kingfish and terʿān pompano are the best fish of all. In our region the best place for terʿān pompano is at Warx where the ṣā́fə baby mussels are to be found. The people of Warx catch terʿān pompano. In the early days people had to live on what they could get with their own hands.

2. əduʿéyr śūri ləkān əduʿéyr yaʿzōz la, kel yətóh mən əduʿéyr yēḳaʿ beh həmmét la, yaʿgāb ʿar yəšīf. mən baʿd əduʿéyr axáyr śīsənāt, bə-śīsənāt axáyr həmméts mən aṣáyd kéllah, əbáʿlis yəḳáʿ ḳəwí.

The duʿéyr mullet is a good one, but is no respecter of persons: if you eat duʿéyr you have no energy, you just want to sleep all the time. After the duʿéyr mullet, the next best is the śīsənāt rabbitfish. The śīsənāt gives more vigour than any other fish: the man who eats it is very strong.

3. u-mən báʿdis ṣayd lə-śwēr: ʿaṣāb wə-xalxāl wə-rēdeḳ wə-ṭəráht wə-ḳəsáʿt. w-əḳənyān axayār mə́nho ʿaṣāb w-axáss mə́nho ṭəráht. u-mən báʿdis əlxādi, w-axáss əmbáʿdis aṣállət w-ərəǵá wə-śərwī. yəw-télyəh śərwī wə-zēnəb, ʿar seh axáyr əzēnəb mən śərwī.

After that, of the line fish, come the ʿaṣāb emperor and the xalxāl and rēdeḳ groupers, the ṭəráht sea bream and the ḳəsáʿt grouper. Of the small fish, the best is the ʿaṣāb emperor, and the worst is the ṭəráht sea bream. And after that the əlxādi.[49] And

---

[49] Not identified.

the worst after that is the ṣállət ponyfish, the rəġá trevally and the śərwī mackerel tuna. And following that is the zēnəb tuna, but the zēnəb tuna is better than the śərwī mackerel tuna.

4. axáyr əṭōnīk mə́nho. aʿśə́ṣ́as hēš̃ʲᴬ mən śān təmṣōṣ mə́nəh. w-ərī́hs śūri w-aṭáʿməs śūri. wə-seh nawb wə-təbdōd l-aʿabú yətēwyuw mins hes aʿabú mékən w-el gēʿuw. mən ərī́hs l-əd̠ənōbs seh kéllis śūrōt. təbdōd l-aʿabú.

The ṭōnīk kingfish is the best of them all: what bones for sucking! And its head is excellent, with a very good flavour. Also, it's very large and can be divided up among (many) people. When there are a lot of people and they are very hungry, they can all get something to eat from it. From its head to its tail, it is all excellent eating and it can be shared out among (many) people.

5. sirīs axáyr sxalét wə-sir sxalét əbēhər. əbēhər d̠ēr bēs xaybət. ʿamōruw əbēher lə-ḳawl l-aʿabú ḥawlá, əbēhər ṣayd l-ənəbī. axáyr mə́nho aʿaṣāb h-aṣ́aft. w-axáyr śīsənāt.

After that, the best is the sxalét cobia, and after that the bēhər mullet or milkfish. The bēhər has little blood, and the early people used to say that the bēhər was the Prophet's fish. For a wedding feast the best is the ʿaṣāb emperor or the śīsənāt rabbitfish.

6. aṣáyd el heh də́wi hə-máraṣ́ yaġáyr aṭábaʿ lə-nafsét: śay təḳádər (tə)tóh mə́nəh wə-śay təḳádər (tə)tóh mə́nəh la mən aʿalzét. hem heh tāmər wə-hem heh śxāf wə-hem heh ṣayd, kul təḳádər (tə)tōh mə́nəh. hem teṯ bīrót axáyr mən aṣáyd (tə)tóh mən ʿaṣāb wə-xōd̠éyr wə-ṣaḳfēt: d̠ek e-nəkəʿēn əlláwh. hes yəḳáʿ max yəḳáʿ śūri.

Fish have no medicinal virtues, it's just a matter of personal taste. Some you can eat and some you can't because they nauseate you. Whether it is dates or whether it is milk or whether it is fish, you can eat any and all of it. If a woman has recently given birth, the best fish for her to eat are ʿaṣāb, xōḏéyr or ṣakfēt emperors—that fish we had last night. Anything that's fat and in good condition does you good.

7. *būn əlaxām naʿāmər hēsən hes təḳáʿan ḳənyān, hem seh bə-hēfəl l-aʿámmíh wəla gaʿrāt mən ḳerīb, ʿādəh beh agarrát, naʿāmər heh ʿulṣ. wə-hem heh ber aṣáyd naʿāmer heh əbḳāl. ber aṣáyd bə-hēfəl l-aʿámmíh nəhāmyən teh bəḳāl. wə-hes béreh... gaʿrōtəh aʿámmíh naʿāmər heh əber lə-ṣayd ḳənnōn. ḥad yətōh(əh) la.*

Shark young when still in their mother's belly or just born, still with the navel chord, we call ʿulṣ. If it's the young of fish, we call them əbḳāl 'eggs': the young of fish still inside their mother are called bəḳāl 'eggs'. When they've... when their mother has given birth to them, we call them 'the tiny young of fish'. Noone eats them.

8. *aṣáyd xanōf hes ʿaṣāb wə-gāmmōtən: yəwēṣyuw mánho aʿabú. el sen śūrōtən la hə-ġayg mən ʾaynəṯ. el ʿād yaʿśōś hə-ʾaynəṯ əbaʿlsən.*

The fish xanōf, a sea bream, is like an ʿaṣāb emperor or the various gēm catfish: people advise against eating them. They're not good for a man as regards intercourse with women: the man who eats one can't get an erection and go with women.

9. *hem embēre ḳənnōn axáyr śīsənāt mən aṣáyd kéllah nawb wə-ḳənnōn. u-mən báʿdis axáyr ədu ʿéyr. ʿar seh śīsənāt bēs ḏay el heh*

śúri la. ʿamōr ṭad ġayg mən nəkəʿāt beh aʿámmíh saʿṭāt teh aṣál lə-śīsənāt wə-yəṣrōrəh la.

For a young child, big or small, the best of all is the *śīsənāt* rabbitfish. After that the best is the *duʿéyr* mullet. But the *śīsənāt* has a smell which is not very pleasant. One man told me that his mother, after giving birth to him, fed him on oil extracted from *śīsənāt* rabbitfish, and it did him no harm.

10. fə-yínnis[JA] śīsənāt śūrōt bə-hēfəl lə-nawb wə-ḳənnōn. ənhá ḥānāfyən kel embərwātən yətóh mən aṣáyd nəmnáʿah la. wə-bə-ḥəlléy hes dəfərāt śeyáṭ máwkʿah ḍársa wə-nəbəṣār la w-əl zéhəd il bēn!.

This is because *śīsənāt* is good for the stomach of old or young. Ourselves, we let the children eat any sort of fish, we don't stop them. At nighttime, when the fire was burning, we'd put (whatever fish we'd caught) on top of it, even though we couldn't see a thing and had nothing but our own wit and skill (to guide us)!

[1980s BATTXT2. B 17]

6.13. Mussels

1. fēḏek? yəlāk fēḏek yəṭēlaʿwəh bə-ḥadīd, məsáwmər. wə-nōkaʿuw w-erbēśwəh w-ebrēkwəh kih[JA]. ebrēkwəh, ṣáffwəh, u-nōkaʿuw bə-ṭad boh, ṭad boh, u-ṭad boh, ṭad boh tá xedōmuw méken mənəh məsṭáḥ,[50] məbṭáḥ nawb.

---

[50] *məsṭáḥ* usually refers to an oblong area on which sardines are laid to dry in a single layer.

Mussels? Those mussels, they'd get them off (the rocks) with a length of iron, with pointed rods of iron. And they'd come and lay them in rows. They'd lay them down (lit. 'couch them')[51] like this. They'd lay them down, place them in rows: they'd bring one and put it here, one here and one here and one here until they'd laid down lots of them, (making) an oblong, a large flat area.

2. edfōruw leh śeyāṭ mən əmbóh mən dōl ərhōtho mən əmbóh... mən dōl aḳáṣiy mən əmbóh. nōkaʿuw bə-ḍarāb xaybət wə-edfōruw śeyāṭ. wə-nōkaʿuw bə-śaʿr, śaʿr ḳāśaʿ, ḏar fēḏek kéləh. difirōt beh śeyāṭ mən əmbóh wə-mən əmbóh, aḍarāb tēwuw, (tə)ṭōlaʿ berík śaʿr wə-dēfer śaʿr kéləh.

They'd light a fire for them here, at the top (of the rows) here... at the outer edge here. They'd bring a little firewood and light a fire and they'd bring seaweed, dried seaweed, and lay it over the mussels. When the fire had caught here and here and the firewood had burned down (lit. 'been eaten'), it (the fire) would move up into the seaweed until all the seaweed was alight.

3. mən dōl tśényəh nakaʿéh śeyāṭ la, tegēləl leh śeyāṭ, théref leh śeyāṭ aṭáh w-aṭáh w-aṭáh w-əl-bóh w-əl-bóh. nəxálsa fēḏek. mən béhəl, mātāt śeyāṭ u-béhəl ffēḏek, ʿemórk beh aṭáh bə-ḍarb, lōmmək teh fáxərə mən əmbóh mən əmbóh té ləbōd fáxərə kiwéz. enkáʿ wə-fḳékah wə-té mínəh. ṣud bə-ʿašfōr ʿar bə-ḍarāb. ʿar fēḏek.

Wherever you'd see (an area) not reached by the fire, you'd bring some burning material on top of them (i.e., the mussels)

---

[51] The mussels are laid in a single layer on the ground and then a fire is lit on top of them.

to cook them. You'd move burning material over them like this and like this and like this, to here and to here. The mussels would be underneath. When they were ready, when the fire had died right down and the mussels were cooked and ready to eat, you'd do like this with a stick: you'd gather them together in a heap, bringing them in from here and here until they were all piled together in mounds. Come and open them up and eat! Fish and shellfish (were cooked) with wood: only mussels (were cooked like this beneath seaweed).

[Tape Sharbithat 6 1982 SIDE A. B14]

6.14. Using Fish and Shark-Livers for Illumination

1. aṣál^{JA} nəxádəm mínəh, ənṣāryən beh té nəbəṣār. nəwāḵaʿ ṣal bə-ḥakkát wə-nəxádəm heh ftílət lə-ḳaṭn wə-naṣāryən beh. hes aṣál ṣāfyət, nəślōl ġāzəl, aġāzəl nəxádəm mə́nəh əlyūx, ḳaṭn, nəxádəm mə́nəh aṭáh ləṭə́ṭ, txádəms ftílət wə-təwāḵʿas berk aṣál.

We'd use fish oil for it. We'd make lighting from it so that we could see (in the dark). We'd put oil in a tin and make a cotton wick for it and we'd see by it. If the oil was pure (i.e., strained), we'd take some cotton—the same cotton we use to make the gillnets from, cotton—and we'd make a twist of it like that. You'd make a wick out of it and you'd put it into the oil.

2. aṣáft lə-ləxām ġayr. aṣáft l-esféyk tēs u-məġārə tədṣōṣ bə-gōdīl lə-śeyāṭ telbāks té tədəfār. wə-tədəfār eté kə-saḥḥ. u-məġārə hem śa la mins, təxádəm ṭīt wə-təḳáʿan hes tēs. naʿmōləh bə-ḳerráʿt wə-ʿəbīl.

Shark liver oil is different. You'd purify the shark liver oil and then you'd poke it with a burning stick until it caught fire, until it flamed up. And it would stay burning until morning. And then if there was none of it left, you'd make another one just like the first. We'd use a metal striker and a piece of flint on it (i.e., to light it).

[1980s BATTXT2]

6.15. Shark-Fishing

1. ḥāwīl əmətˤát (nə)nākaˤ bēs ˤar bə-dənāwəg wə-seh ġālyət. nəślōl mən bāmə ləxām wə-nassāfərən beh. ḥad minēn yassāfərən əmkélli wə-ḥad minēn lə-swāḥil. wə-yənēkaˤuw wə-yəśyōmuw teh. ṭīt ḵawzərət bə-ṭəmənēt wə-təḵáˤan bə-zēyid mən ˤaśirēt. ho bˤéli tāmər wə-ḏirrét yəśēmyuw tēsən.

In earlier times we could only get food by boat and it was expensive. We would take (dried) shark meat from here and set off to sea with it. One of us would go to Mukalla and another to East Africa. They'd get there and they'd sell it: a single ḵawzərət of dates cost eight (Maria Theresa silver thalers), and it could be more than ten. Those who had dates and sorghum would sell them.

2. əḏirrét gə́nyət ṭeyt təwúṣəl eté arbaˤīn wə-zēyid. ḵarš fiśśét. ṭeyt, ləxām, yəśēmyuw tēs aḥawlā bə-śolṭēt wə-seh təḵáˤ nawb. wə-ṣɛrbí yəśēmyuw tēs seh wə-ʔaḏāntsa bə-rəbˤāt wə-xāməh. wə-seh kə-ḵaḏ ˤar bə-śolṭēt. enḥá hes nəṣəbāṭ mən dōl ḥerbáˤtyən il šáho śay, əttəgūr, yəśēbəruw lēn eté ḵayḏ, té tənākaˤ aˤáyd kə-ḵayḏ, yēkaˤ bēsən ləxām.

Sorghum, one sackful, cost up to forty (Maria Theresa thalers) or more. A silver thaler. The people before would sell one, a single shark, for three (silver thalers), if it was a large one. In the ṣɛrb post-monsoon autumn season they could sell it and its fins for four or five (silver thalers). But in the summer they only got three (silver thalers) for it. As for us, when we took (foodstuffs) from those of our people who had them, the traders, they would give us until the summer to pay, until the the summer shoals of sardine arrived, and with them, the shark.

3. tənākaʕ el xaṭəfāt. wə-nərābaḥ lēs bə-niyād wə-təḳáʕan šēn əlyūx mən ġāzəl. ḥāwīl nəbírməh wə-nəkísrəh wə-nəwāśʕah u-məġārə yəḳáʕ līx wə-yənākaʕ bə-ləxām. wə-ḥad minēn yənākaʕ bə-ləxām bə-ḳeyūd mən ḏār ərəhōtən. nəxádəm heh ḥalḳát mən ḥadīd wə-nəwāḳaʕ bēs məḏərā mən ṣayd wə-yəḍāyəh ələxām wə-yənākaʕ ləh.

They (i.e., the sardine) would arrive and then go on past. And we'd swim out to them on (inflated) goatskins, taking our cotton gillnets with us. First we'd twist (the cotton fibre) to thread, then we'd ply it, then we'd knot it, and then that would be a gillnet for trapping shark. And some of us fished for shark with ropes let down from the headlands. We'd make an iron ring for it and bait it with large chunks of fish. The shark would smell it and come to it.

4. yənākaʕuw bə-mətəʔát wə-xaṭkān wə-tāmər. ḥāwīl (nə)nākaʕ beh mən ərawnə wə-śōllən teh eté əmḳáwṭaʕ wə-nəḳášbəh. naʕwēlən teh, aʔaydāntən məkān w-əláxəm məkān. wə-məġārə (nə)nākaʕ bə-milḥāt wə-nəmālḥah wə-dəfōnən teh bə-ḳáʕ eté jéhemə. rəhāśan teh mən ərawnə wə-aḳśáʕan teh b-aġáwf eté ḳéśaʕ. u-ṣōmmən teh ṭad ḏar ṭad. aḥád minēn yəśyōm lə-ttəgūr w-aḥád minēn yəṭráḥ lə-ṣɛrbí.

(These shark) would bring us food and clothing and dates. First we'd bring the shark up out of the sea and carry it to the cutting ground. We'd cut it open and gut it, putting the fins in one place and the (rest of the) shark in another. Then we'd fetch salt and we'd salt it and bury it in the ground until the next day. Then we'd wash it in seawater and set it to dry, high above the tideline, until it had dried out. Then we'd pile (the dried shark trunks) up, one on top of another. Some of us would sell to the traders and others would leave it (i.e., selling their shark) until the ṣɛrb post-monsoon season.

5. əmilḥāt[52] nəmēśələn teh mən axār wə-nəślōləh bə-ḏābəl lə-xār mən ḫān əḵeśəʕāt wə-nəṭráḥah té yəḵśáʕ. u-meyt el ḵēśaʕ śōllən teh. milḥāt mən xádər hem heh lēyən śōllən mínəh, nəḥízəf mínəh bə-gáni. kel ḥad amá yəḵádər yəślōləh hem heh ġayg wə-hem teṯ.

As for salt, we'd scrape it up from around the brackish lagoon and pile it up on a side of the lagoon where it was dry, and leave it to dry out. When it had dried out, we'd take it away. As for rock salt (lit. 'salt from a cave'), if it was soft enough, we'd take it just like that, scooping it into a sack. Each would take as much as they could carry, man or woman.

6. wə-hem heh lēyən la, nəślōl ḥābən wə-nəlíbəd bēs wə-nəślōləh. wə-hes yəḵáʕ šēn milḥāt lə-xār la, hem nōkaʕ ḏəhēb, əmūsé, w-axār el beh milḥāt la, nərdōd lə-xədāwər wə-nəślōl mínəh, lə-mətəʕát wəla lə-ləxām wə-ṣayd.

---

[52] Although milḥāt has the feminine marker (-āt), it seems to be regarded as grammatically masculine here.

And if it were not soft enough, we'd take a stone and knock it off (in chunks), and then carry it off. And when there was no salt to be had from the lagoons—if there had been a flood, rain, and the lagoon no longer provided salt—then we'd go back to the caves (for rock salt) and take that: for food or for shark and fish.

[1980s BATTXT1. B14]

6.16. Shark Fishing, Processing and Selling

1. *syērən wə-rēdən wə-nōtxan hə-ṣayd bə-Mingíy u-bə-Śerbiṯōt u-bə-Gizərēt. wə-yəbˤáruw aˤabú wə-Zifənə ˤar ber ˤamōr hého mən təḳáˤ ˤánnət yəbˤáruw hēs, yəslébuw aˤánnət, mən təˤēn ərawnə yəbˤáruw hēs wə-yənātxuw k-aˤánnət l-ərawnə. wə-yewēgəhuw lə-xədāwər wə-yəšáˤaruw ḥalákəmə.*

We used to go and set the gillnets and cast (our) nets for fish in Mingíy and in Sharbithat and in Ashwaymiyah. People would go off in the night. And Zifena had said to them that once the tide was out they should go in the dark for them (i.e., fish). (He said) that they should wait for low tide: when the tide had gone right out, they should go off in the night and cast their nets at low tide. And they went back to their cave dwellings and spent the night there.

2. *wə-kə-saḥḥ yəghə́muw wə-yəsdōluw əlyūxho mən ələxām. wə-fənānə bərk ərawnə ḍar nayd. ənayd yənēfxwəh u-ber nēfəxwəh yərēbəhuw leh nəxál hfēlho. wə-təftōkuw mən dōl rēdko əlīx. ˤátḳəs aṣáyd w-ələxām bərk aˤyántən l-əlīx: śay mēyət wə-śay ṣaḥḥ. yəfēzaˤuw ˤar yəḳtáṭuw leh əlyūx. yaˤtəwēnuw.*

And in the morning they'd go off to remove the sharks one at a time from their gillnets. And before that they had gone out to sea on a goatskin. They would inflate the goatskin, and once inflated, they would swim out on it, placing it beneath their bellies. And you'd all go out to wherever you'd set the gillnet. The fish and the shark would be all mixed together in the mesh of the nets: some dead and some alive. They would be afraid of wrapping the nets round it (i.e., a large shark). They would help one another.

3. mēluw ḏárha əlyūx mən yəntékho. wə-yəġfōḳuw beh boh wə-yəġéśyuw ḏárha əlyūx. wə-yəmēnaʿuw b-əḏənōbəh boh, bə-ʿaḳáf. wə-yərēbəḥuw beh, yḥémuw abárr. ṭəréh wəla śōṯēt. wə-hem heh nawb, yəśléluw teh rəbʿāt. wə-hem heh ʿamḳí, yəśléluw teh ṭəréh. wə-hem heh ḵennōn, yəśléləh ʿar ṭad hem heh ġayg ḳawí. hem heh mēyət yəḥdéduw, yəḥdéduw. śōṯēt wəla rəbʿāt, el yəmḥānho aʿabú la.

They'd spread the nets over the top of it to keep it from biting them, and they'd bind it around tightly and cover it completely with nets.[53] And they'd hold onto it tightly by the tail—here, at the tail end.[54] Then they'd swim off with it, aiming for the beach. Two or three men. And if it was a very big shark, four people would tow it. And if it was a medium-sized shark, two. And if it was a small one, one man alone, if he was a strong man. If the shark was already dead, they'd pull it in, pull it in.

---

[53] Gloss: 'especially over its mouth'.

[54] ʿaḳáf 'tail; tail end', only of fish or shark.

Three or four men. That one (i.e., a small one) caused people no trouble.

4. wə-hem heh ṣaḥḥ, yəmḥānho aˤabú. aˤabú yəfēzaˤuw mə́nəh yətého. yərábəṭwəh b-aˤyāntən b-əḏənōb əmbóh b-aˤámkah. b-əríh ḍar aˤarwét l-ənayd. hes əl-hūri, ġaláki, hes yəsyōr aṭáh. u-tərábəṭ lēs hes hūri ḏárha əríh lə-ləxām. yərēbəhuw beh wə-yədēfərwəh ənayd hes ḏárha ələxām.

But if it were still alive, it caused them trouble alright! They were terrified that it would bite them. They would tie it up in the mesh of the nets, around its tail here and around its middle. And its head was placed on top of the ropes that join the legs of the goatskin together. As if it (i.e., the inflated goatskin) were a dugout canoe. Look! Like when it (i.e., a dugout) goes along like this. And you'd tie the shark's head onto it (i.e., the goatskin) just as (you'd tie it onto) a dugout canoe, a dugout with the head of a shark on top of it. They'd swim off with it and they'd push along in front of them the goatskin bearing the weight of the shark.

5. heh b-əlyūx yəkṭáṭuw leh ələxām. fəˤēmka, tərābaḥ, tərífs bēsən mən sərānə eté tədíkəm abárr. mən tədíkəm abárr təgḏāb b-aˤyāntən l-əlyūx tá ṭaḥḥ, l-aġáwf b-abárr. wə-dəfōnwəh té ġasəráww. dəfōnwəh bə-ṭə́rət, mən əyōm ḥfōruw heh. ḥfōruw heh wə-áwkaˤuw ələxām bərk xabbét il ḥfōrwəs wə-dəfōnuw leh abáṭḥ. əyōm yəxyōsh.

They'd have wrapped the shark up in the gillnets. Your feet, you'd swim, you'd kick out with them behind you until you reached the shore. When you reached the shore, you'd drag the nets by their mesh up onto the beach, onto dry land. They would bury it (the shark) and leave it there until the afternoon. They'd bury it in the wet sand. They'd dig a hole for it to keep it out of the sun. They'd dig a hole for it and put the shark in the hole they'd dug and they'd cover it with sand. The sun would spoil it.

6. wə-ġasəráww ftēkwəh wə-ftēkwəh skīn wə-ftēkwəh ḥaśərīm, wə-bérho hōnnuw sskin. wə-kaṣ̌ābuw ḥāwīl ərı́ḥ u-məġārə kaṣ̌ābuw a²aydéntən. u-məġārə naxāt aḵām u-śərəxéh wə-məlḥēs hem šeh milḥāt lə-gəbəlīl u-šeh milḥāt lə-xar. wə-šeh axáyr əmilḥāt lə-xar, təwṭāḵ ətə́wi, təḱá'an beh təw'āl la. yəxayōr il milḥāt mékən beh, l-awṭāḵ teh. u-ṣ́átəməh wə-ṭárḥah té kə-saḥḥ.

And in the evening they'd take it out and they'd take a knife or a flint (and they would have sharpened the knife already). First they'd cut off the head and then they'd cut off the fins. Then he'd cut out the *aḵām*[55] material and then he'd score (the flesh) in lines and salt it. Either with rock salt, if he had it, or with salt from the lagoon. And the best is salt from the lagoon: it makes the flesh strong and hard, and it won't become maggoty. It's better if there's plenty of salt on to really toughen it and make it hard. And (then) he'd fold it over on itself and leave it until the next morning.

---

[55] *aḵām* (root uncertain): in a shark, blackish matter beneath the cartilage. Described as 'like old blood', it runs from the chest to the tail. It is cut into pieces, cooked and eaten and is said to be very good. Possibly *aḵām* is another term for *'ōmid* (see footnote 8), 'the coiled sperm ducts of the mature male shark'.

7. mən kə-saḥḥ ḵəlēb leh bə-milḥāt u-mən ḥelōk áḵśaʿah, ṭəráḥah b-əyōm. mən yəḵśáʿ yəṣmōm, yəzbōr. ḥfōr xabbét ḏársa ṣəwēr wə-śaʿr. ḥāwīl ḏar ələxām śaʿr mən yəlḥáḵah nədéʾ, wə-ḏar śaʿr ṣəwēr mən śān el yətōh teh la kəlōb. śaʿr l-ərawnə ḥāwər. wə-ṭəráḥ axabbét ġazírət. áwḵaʿ śaʿr nəxálsən.

In the morning put (more) salt on it and then set it to dry. Leave it out in the sun. As it dries, it becomes hard and stiff. Dig a (big) hole with stones and seaweed (on the bottom). First seaweed on top of the shark to protect it from dew; then, on top of the seaweed, stones to keep the wolves from eating it. Black seaweed from the sea. And make the hole good and deep. Put a layer of seaweed beneath them (i.e., the stones).

8. u-məġārə áwḵaʿ ələxām. eté bers məlyōt. u-ḏar ələxām śaʿr u-mən ḏar śaʿr áwḵaʿ ḥawbōn u-mən ḏar ḥawbōn rāṣəl, ḥawbōn ḵánnətən, rāṣəl. ḥawbōn niyāb u-nəxálsən arāṣəl u-ḏeh śābkənə. aʿabú ḏek wáḵtən yəḵáʿ lého ḵayṣ hes aṭánəmə, u-mən baʿdəh xarifīt. yətērḥwəh xarf[56] wə-yəśxəléluw xarf w-əté ṣɛrbí. hes yəḵáʿ ṣɛrbí w-ədənāwəg ber xaṭáfnə.

And then put in the shark, until it (i.e., the hole) is filled up. And on top of the shark, seaweed, and on top of the seaweed, stones, and on top of the stones, (a layer of) pebbles: tiny stones, pebbles and gravel. Large stones and beneath them pebbles and gravel: these together would make a close-packed layer with no gaps. It would be summer for people at that time, just as it is now. And after that comes the monsoon. They'd leave them there throughout the monsoon. They (i.e., the shark

---

[56] More commonly *xarifīt*.

trunks) would stay there for the whole of the monsoon until the post-monsoon ṣɛrb season arrived; when it was the ṣɛrb season and the trade boats would be sailing past.

9. ḏek waktən nōkaʕuw aʕabú yəśtémuw ləxām. nōkaʕuw bə-tāmər, bə-kiswét, b-iriz. laxm ṭad bə-ḳírši ṭəréh. ḥāwīl ənawb mən ḳírši wə-fakẖ, ələxām ənawb yənākaʕ... ələxām el heh síwe la: baʕṣ́ nawb wə-baʕṣ́ mə́nho ʕamḳí wə-heh kel ṭad bə-ṭə́mənəh, ənawb bə-mékən w-əḵennōn bə-xaybət w-aʕamḳí b-aʕámḵ. ʕōdwəh kērəgət ʕāśəri, yəʕēməruw hēs kērəgət. ṭawr b-arbaʕīn, ṭawr bə-sittīn.

At that time people would arrive to buy shark. They'd bring dates, clothing, rice. One shark would fetch two silver thalers. In the old days a big one used to fetch two and a half silver thalers, a large shark would fetch... shark are not all the same: some are big, some medium-sized, and each one has its own price. The big one would fetch a lot, the small one a little, and the medium-sized one a medium price. They reckoned a *kērəgət* at twenty dried shark: they used to call that a *kērəgət*. Sometimes that would fetch forty silver thalers, sometimes sixty.

10. ḳarš ḥāwīl fəṣ́ṣ́át. el heh riyālko la, ḏeh. ḏeh nōkaʕuw beh ʕar nāṣərə. mən nōkaʕ riyāl ḏek, ḏek heh šíko... ḥāwīl ʕar fəṣ́ṣ́át. əriyāl ḏeh biš axáyr mə́nho kel. nōkaʕuw fṣ́āl k-aʕabú w-aʕabú kélho tēgəruw, eté ʔaynəṭ. ʕēməlnə e-ṭīt mágəfaṣ́ u-kel ṭīt buk ʕamələāt. ḥāwīl ġayg šeh ʕāśəri, axayār šeh miyōti ṭə́rti wəla miyōt. wə-ḥad yəwāfə ədaynəh w-əmətəwé. wə-ḏékəmə il ʕatēśyuw teh wəla fēśyuw beh.

The thaler before was a silver coin, not this *riyāl* of yours, this one here. They've only introduced this one recently. Once that (kind of) *riyāl* arrived, that kind which you have... before there was only silver coinage. This (new) *riyāl* is the best of all (the currencies). It's brought people plenty: everyone has become rich—even women! Each woman has a bundle of money, and each woman has a wallet (for her money). In earlier times a man might have twenty silver thalers, and the very best of them might have two hundred or a hundred. And some only enough to cover his debts and (the cost of) his food. And that is what they had (to manage on) for their midday and evening meal.

11. aḥád mə́nho yəṭáˤam məṭəˤát la ġayr aṣáyd lə-mġadéft. mət ˤānāt, ˤašfēr, śídəfāt, ḥawēn, ṣəfəlḥāt, zikt, yingēn, yəlák kel əntóhsən mən ərawnə. wə-śīnəhāt. ḥədḥēd hes nḥām náxərgəh əntáˤam teh. heh ḥāwər w-yəṭēbək b-əgəbəlīl. nəníkfh w-əntēwyən teh. wə-ṭad mən yətóh mə́nəh yəḳáˤ axáh mən ləbənēt hes ḏeh məġārə yəḳáˤ ˤāfər. ˤāfər.

Some people never tasted anything but the fish caught in a cast net. When the tide was out (there were) sea snails, sea lemons, Moray eels, abalone, rock oysters, sea slugs—all those we used to eat, from the sea. And chitons. The *ḥədḥēd* sea urchin: when we wanted to, we'd get it out (of cracks and crevices) and eat it. It's black and it sticks onto the rocks. We'd hook it out and eat it. And when some eat it, their mouth, from being white like this? Then turns red. Really red.

12. wə-nəkəˤāts ḏek, aˤállət, təkrīz. təkrīz hes əribáˤah, ˤar yəlán beh məṭōˤan la, bēs śkaˤ la. aˤašfēr hes təḳáˤ ərawnə ˤánnət əntóh mən ˤašfēr. wə-śinš yəlán bedw? el ˤād šého məṭəˤát la ḥāwīl. yətēwyuw ˤar mən dōl ənḥá, mən məṭəˤát l-ərawnə. šého śa la ˤar aˤránho wə-xaṭm. bə-ḥelléy hes tənātax b-əməġadéft, yəlíbdək

əgibalīl boh. u-mən tšə́bdi tēn, ġaláḳi! u-mən šəḵwēyuw, syēruw mənēn.

And then we come to the—what's its name?—the *təkərīz* sea urchin. The *təkərīz* sea urchin is like the other (urchin), but it has no spines, no thorns. The shellfish: when the tide was right out, we'd eat shellfish. And see these bedouin? Well, in the days before, they had no food. They'd eat from what we had managed to get, from the food the sea provided. They had nothing but their goats, and they were very thin. At night, when you cast your net, the rocks would get you here. And if you think we're lying, just take a look! And when they (i.e., the bedouin) had got their strength back, they would leave us.

[1980s BATTXT4. B17]

6.17. The *līx* Gillnet

1. *əlīx yəwēśaʿwəh aʿabú minnāk*[JA] *mən ədəbáy. taḵāsərwənəh wə-təḥyōswənəh wə-təwēśaʿwənəh kərāxīn. yənōkaʿ mən ḥelōk zāhib*[JA]*. lōk ʿar təwāḵaʿ beh ḳayd wə-təwāḵaʿ beh kerīb. yəwāḵaʿuw ʿar ʾəbōn. ʾəbōn mən ədəśámmət. wə-yallāh, berk ərawnə.*

The gillnet was knotted by people over there, in Dubai. The factories[57] would ply the thread, twist and knot it. The (net) would reach us from over there, all ready to use: all you had to do was to add rope and floats. They'd put on stones (i.e., as weights), stones from the limestone pavement. And then, by God, into the sea with it!

---

[57] *kərāxīn* 'factories' seems to be treated here as a sort of feminine plural.

2. *ṯēbəruw ədəśámmət heh aˤabú wə-yəwēkaˤwəs beh mən śān yəṭəḳād b-ərawnə. ʾəbōn ləbōd aḳáˤ u-mən aġáwf tətfōfən bə-kerīb. yənākaˤ ələxām mən əmbóh wə-yəwōkəb beh. yəwēkaˤuw beh yingīr lə-ḥadīd, yəmānaˤ aḳáˤ. u-mən ḏirs yəˤēməluw gərāyə.*

People would break up the limestone for it and attach (pieces) to (one edge) of it (i.e., the net) so that it would sink right down in the sea. The stones would fall to the bottom, and (the other edge) would float on the surface, (suspended) by the floats. The shark would come from here (i.e., the open sea) and swim into it (i.e., the net). They'd put an iron anchor on it that would keep it held down at the bottom. And on top they'd put markers (of ownership).

3. *yənākaˤ ələxām wə-fənṭāwət wə-biˤl wə-… ḥūt kel. ṭad mən śān əṭōnīk wə-ṭad mən śān ələxām, ˤayéntən nawb mən śān ələxām, wə-ˤayéntən ḵenyántən mən śān əṭōnīk. ṭad 'līx' wə-ṭad 'milšáġət' mən śān ələxām.*

The shark would come, and the *fənṭāwət* ray and the sawfish and… all sorts of big fish! (There was) one (gillnet) for the *ṭōnīk* kingfish, and one for the shark: of large mesh size for the shark and of smaller mesh size for the kingfish. One was called *līx*, and one was called *milšáġət*, for the shark.

4. *nəḵṯōṯ əlyūx. ərīh yəsyūr aṭáh b-ɛmíh[58] w-ənhá nərābaḥ ḏar nid, ˤar heh mənfáx, ənīd yəštíḵuw mánəh. nərábṭah bə-rigəlét lə-fənānə, nərábəṭ ənīd bóh wə-bóh té yaˤzīz ələxām mən ərawnə. w-ənhá nədyúr^JA mən sérīh wə-nərābaḥ.*

---

[58] This is more Śḥerēt than Bəṭaḥrēt.

We'd roll the nets up. The top end would go like this, in the water, and we'd swim out on a skin, but it would be inflated. The (same) skin they used to drink from. We'd tie it (i.e., the goat skin) to a loop at the front: we'd tie the goatskin here and here so that it would keep the shark up on the surface of the sea (i.e., keep it afloat). And we'd go round behind it (i.e., the shark), and we'd swim off (with it).

5. əlġáyə^{JA} ənḥá nərābaḥ eté yəṣáḥḥ abárr. ber b-abárr, gōrruw tēn ḥerbáʿtyən té barr. ber b-abárr enēkṭən əlīx wə-bəlākən teh mánəh. wa-nəsīrən[59] beh l-ərawnə wə-rəḥáṣən teh. u-məġárə gōrrən teh yəkṣáʿ.

Anyway, we'd keep swimming until we were close to the shore. Once we were close to the shore, our companions would pull us in to the beach. When we'd reached the beach, we'd clear the net and untangle it (i.e., the shark) from it. Then we'd take it to the sea and wash it clean. Then we'd drag it up (the beach) to dry out.

6. ḥfōrən heh xabbét, məġárə dəfōnən teh mən əyōm, mən əyōm təlḥákah. té ġasəráww. ġasəráww rēdən b-əlyūx ərawnə, awgāśən tého b-ərawnə w-atxāfən. mən əntáxf ʿawēlən ələxām bə-skīn u-mōlḥan teh bə-milḥāt.

We'd dig a hole for it and then we'd bury it to protect it from the heat of the sun, so that the sun couldn't reach it. Until the afternoon. In the afternoon we'd set the nets (again) out at sea. We'd set them in the afternoon and we'd come back (to shore)

---

[59] Unusual form.

in the early evening. Once we were back, we'd gut and cut up the shark with a knife, and we'd salt it.

7. wə-nəˤāmər heh 'ərī́h', il heh šérgi nəˤāmər heh 'ərī́h'. wə-kel heh məwássəṭ[JA] nəˤāmər heh 'aˤámḳ', wə-kel heh sərānə nəˤāmər heh 'əmdéyyəl'[JA]. əḳənyān nəˤāmər hēsən ṣownāt, w-əniyāb nəˤāmər hēsən śġūr, əlyūx lə-ḳaṭn. den həmōtsən əlyūx lə-ḳaṭn il hēmyuw tēsən aḥawlá.

And we called it 'the head': that (part of the) gillnet furthest out to sea we called 'the head'. And the part in the middle we called 'the middle', and then everything behind (i.e, getting ever closer to the shore) we called 'the tailpiece'. The smaller nets we called ṣownāt, and the larger nets we called śġūr, the gillnets made of cotton. These are the names of the cotton gillnets given by the people who came before us.

[1980s BATTXT 1. B14]

6.18. Shark Attacks

1. ε-ġíti, enḥá nəkdūd berk ərawnə w-ərawnə kēfərət ʔasləh, w-el yēdˤan la el heh ḥalāl wəla ḥarām. enḥá nəkdūd w-ələxām yəˤāmər aṭáh berk aˤáyd. əmūsé gōrr əbəṯhá den əlbóh u-gərréh berk ərawnə w-ərawnə ləbədāt taˤrīt márra, təbəṣār śa la. u-rōbḥan ḍar anād naġəlét.

My sister, we used to labour hard in the sea. And the sea is a godless unbeliever in origin, and we don't know whether it is ḥarām or ḥalāl. We used to work away while the shark were like that among the sardines! The rains had washed the sand and soil right down to here, had washed it right into the sea, and the sea had become really cloudy from all the silt, and you could see nothing. And we swam out on the skins and they were new and still exuding moisture.

2. w-əmbēra hes allāh ḳáddər leh, əmbērə la, ber śeb. rōbaḥ ḍar hēfəl lə-ləxām, nəʕāmər heh 'gəśēr'. wə-heh guwwét wə-śef ləxām ᴶᴬḏāləm mərsūl lehᴶᴬ. ḏāyə əgəśēr ḏik əguwwét. ḏāyəh ələxām, ḏāyəh ələxām, u-nōkaʕ mərsūl leh. w-əmbērə ḳarīb, ḳarīb liy hoh, arḥāḵ mən ḏeh la. yēdʕak la eté nəkəʕāt wə-ʕamərēt beh sərmāx b-ərawnə w-əmbērə yəḳáʕ ᴶᴬgāmtēn hābaṭᴶᴬ. wə-heh l-ebṭóh la.

And there was a boy, as God decreed—no, not a boy, he was already a young man. He swam out on the (inflated) stomach of a shark. We call it gəśēr. And it smelled bad. And what should happen but a terrible shark was sent (i.e., decreed by God) to him. It smelled the bad smell of that inflated shark stomach. The shark smelled it. The shark smelled it and came, sent (by God) to him. And the boy was nearby, close to me, no further away than this. I knew nothing at all until it (i.e., the shark) had arrived and there were splashings and thrashings as it dragged the boy down into the sea (to a depth) the height of two men! It didn't take long.

3. w-ələxām śəriyéh w-əlḥakéh káʕ u-fəkkéh əmṣáʕ u-ṭōlaʕ liy əmbērə. erōṭaḥ hēfələh ḏeh kéləh wə-herəkīt ḏin kéləs. u-fəṣəléh faʕm u-hēfəl u-ḳaṣāb aʕárḵ əl-śḵhəl. u-mən təḵəṣāb aʕárḵ əl-śḵhəl təmét. rōṭaḥ ḏen aṭáh u-rōṭaḥ ḏen aṭáh. hərəkīt ʕāds śay məśébəh. amá táwi lə-fʕēm eróṭḥah la.

The shark took him by the skin and dragged him down to the bottom. It let go of him down there and the boy came to the surface, right beside me. All this stomach of his was gashed, and this hip too. It had severed his leg from his stomach and had cut through the ʿarḵ əl-ə́ḵḥəl (lit. 'the root of the eggs'), the main blood vessel. Once the ʿarḵ əl-ə́ḵḥəl is severed, you die. It had slashed this like that and slashed this like that. The hip was still something like (a hip), and as for the flesh of the legs, it hadn't slashed that.

4. el ṭōlaʿuw mə́nəh əmʿuwiyān mən əmbóh, ṭōlaʿuw mən əmbóh aʿánət. enḥá bʿél ədērtən enḥá ġatámm, el ḥad syēr la k-aʿabú ḥarrāmīyə^JA, b-el śínən la əlátəġ lə-yənēbi^JA wəla əmnēdək. aʿabú bədōd, fxídət, erkūn mən bəddét ṭīt. el heh mən bəddétən ənḥá. xāṭək teh bə-hābaʿ ʾəbāri.

His intestines had extruded from here, they had come out a bit from here. We in our area knew nothing:[60] none of us had gone off with others to reive, nor had we witnessed any killing with daggers or guns. People were divided into subtribes, clans, family groups of a single clan. He (the young man attacked by the shark) was not of our subtribe. I sewed him up with seven stitches (lit. 'needles').

5. l-əḥáwləs nəkəʿāt aʿáyd w-aġáyg ḏek yədlōl aḵáʿ. śtəllāt əlyūx u-bérəh xarifīt, u-məkān el heh məkān śūri. śaḵ. xāṭəmən əlyūx, kel yəxáṭəm əlyūxah. baʿṣ́ mə́nho ġaṣəbátho ərawnə əlyūxho u-baʿṣ́ gərāfuw məns. eté ġamədāt əyōm. mékən.

At the same time the next year, the sardines arrived as usual, and that man (i.e., another man sitting with the speaker) knows

---

[60] ġatámm: see footnote 44 above.

the place. The gillnets had been lifted out (i.e., for the last time), for the monsoon season was already starting. And it wasn't a good place: it was constricted (i.e., with no room for manoeuvre). We had tied the gillnets together in a long line, each person had tied on his own nets. The (wild) seas had washed away the nets of some of them, and others were (already) dragging their nets out of the sea. Until the sun set. (There were) lots (of shark).

6. *hēb l-aġáyg ḏen tǝwōth ǝlbóh bǝġáyr ḏen mǝkān. yǝḳáʕ ḥašbáʕ lǝ-fǝʕēm ḳerfǝdātsǝn mǝn ḥānǝ tǝwōtsǝn ǝlǝxām, b-aʕárḳ. u-baʕṣ́ mánho mǝrǝṭātho ǝlyūx il yǝʕáyšuw*[JA] *bého. baʕṣ́ mánho tǝwōtho ǝmbóh, ʕar ǝtíh el ḳaṣ́ǝbāth la. aġáyg edēwiyǝn teh w-ǝlyūx txērgǝn mǝn ǝrawnǝ. wǝ-nǝkǝʕāt lǝxámi ṭǝréh, b-ǝbēḳi aṭláʕuw teh la. kélǝh ġāb. u-gǝḏōbǝn mǝns ḏih.*

The father of this man (i.e., another man sitting with the speaker) was bitten here, as well as in this place. (His) toes were left curling the wrong way up from where the shark bit them, biting right through the tendon. They (i.e., shark) had gone right through and out the other side of some of their gillnets, the nets that were their livelihood. They (i.e., shark) had attacked some of them here, but the flesh was not sheared off. We treated the man and the nets were taken out of the sea. Two shark were got out (i.e., out of the gillnets) but they didn't manage to get the rest up (out of the nets): they were all lost. Out of (all of) them we only managed to drag this one out.

7. *ġasráwwǝn yǝḳáʕ beh ǝbēʕat lǝ-ʔalf. ġasráwwǝn. wǝ-ḏik ǝl-ʕasǝrīyǝ*[JA] *nǝgḏēb hawb ǝl-ḳaymǝt ʔalf. wǝ-xarifīt ʕatǝmyōt lēn, w-el ʕād exrēgǝn mǝns la. ṭōlʕan ǝlyūx wǝ-kel ṣ́ay wǝ-axxǝrēfǝn. bʕél*

aʿrān ṭōlaʿuw əl-ḥerbáʿtho u-bʿél ərawnə axxərēfuw lə-ṣayd. yənātxuw heh hēn amá šého mən mətəʿát.

In the afternoon there could have been a sale worth a thousand in it (i.e., in this cove). In the afternoon. And that night we could have pulled out about a thousand's worth (of shark). But the monsoon was making it impossible for us to go out to sea and we could no longer take anything out of it. We brought the nets and everything up (i.e., to the shore) and moved off to our monsoon quarters. Those who had goats went up to their people (in the desert plateau above), and the sea people went to their monsoon quarters for (monsoon season) fishing. They worked with their cast nets to get anything edible for us.

[1980s BATTXT4. B17]

6.19. When Sālim Yəḥēš Was Attacked by a Shark

1. *ḥāwīl ʿabú fīḳōr. el ʿād šáho śa la yaġáyr ʿarān, u-bʿél ərawnə mətwého mə́nəh: ʿašfór wə-ṣəfəlḥāt wə-śədəhāt wə-zikt. w-əl-waḳt māhūb. wə-tənkáʿan ʿayd yəfréruw berkēs wə-yətēwyuw məns ələxām. yəġléḳuw ləxām w-ələxām yəśōmwəh mətəʿát, yəġléḳuw mətəʿát bə-ṭəmōn ələxām: aʔayḏāntsa wə-ttíḥs.*

Earlier, people were very poor. They owned nothing but a (few) goats, and those who lived by the sea ate from it: shellfish and abalone and chitons and rock oysters. And they were hard times. The sardines might come, and, flying among them and feeding on them, the shark. People used to look for a shark to sell in exchange for food. They'd buy something to eat with the money they got for the shark: their fins and their (dried, salted) flesh.

2. *hes śényuw aˁáyd šəghəmōtho u-berkēs ələxām, ˁamōruw: "enhá ənśēm ḥānāfyən mən śān lə-mətəˀát!" gəhēmən, fōrrən kélən. ṭad dərāg šey, Yəḥēš, Sālim Yəḥēš. ənhá bˁél əgawd, bˁél ənīd, den yəštíkuw mánəh. Yəḥēš yədərāg*[JA] *šiy hoh. yəkūn nawb wə-nərābaḥ ḏárha məḥál ˁabərét əl-hūri wálə sáṭṭərə ḏih.*

When they saw the sardines had arrived in the morning, and amongst them the shark, they said: "We'd sell our very selves for something to eat!" We all set off, we hurried down (to the shore), all of us. One man went with me, Yəḥēš, Sālim Yəḥēš. We were people who used a skin (to swim on), people who used a goatskin, the one that people used to drink from. Yəḥēš came out with me. It (the goatskin) was a big one and we swam out on it (together), in place of a dugout canoe or this boat with an engine (i.e., of today).

3. *rōbḥan. hes wēṣalən aˁáyd, ənkós teh ələxām yəˁāmər aṭáh ḏar aˁáyd mən agáwf. mān yḥām yərūd b-aˁámrəh bárkih? wə-ho ələxām yōb*[JA] *abˁáyr əl-ḥay*[JA]*, yḥām yətóh aˁabú, beh ḏehən la. əlīx ləbīd. rōdən b-əlīx b-ərawnə. wə-hes yēkaˁ béhəl ələxām, yətíkəd, yətfōf la. wə-hes yēka béhəl ələxām la, yətfōf.*

We swam out. When we reached the sardines, we found them (i.e., the shark) going about amongst them like this, above the shoal of sardines. Who would (willingly) fling himself in amongst that lot? And they were shark as huge and terrifying as a camel stallion in rut that goes for people, out of its mind! The gillnet had been struck (i.e., by shark). We had set the gillnet in the sea. When shark are ready (i.e., have stopped breathing), they would sink down, they would no longer float. And when shark were not yet ready (i.e., were still alive), they would float on the surface.

4. śay ménəh ṯḳayl u-śay ménəh yəṭáwlaʕ aġáwf. hoh līx ṭad yəṭáwlaʕ aġáwf ḳarīb u-hoh nōkʕak yəʕállǝm allāh hoh nōkʕak mǝn ǝmbóh. hoh nōkʕak tǝwáthe wǝ-Yǝḥēš yǝnākaʕ mǝn ǝmbóh. ġātbǝrǝn ḥalákǝmǝ. ʕamōrǝn: "hə́ni śawr? wǝ-^JAhēš aná́ġr^JA?" nǝktǝlōṯ bǝ-ḥānāfyǝn. ǝmǝtǝlē heh b-ǝġīb⁶¹ w-ǝnḥá kǝnḥētǝn mǝn ǝrazḳ, mǝn nǝlḥāḳ ḥūt.

Some of them are heavy, and some rise up to the surface. One of my nets had been brought to the surface. It was nearby and I approached it, God alone knows whether I approached from here (or from elsewhere). I went towards it and Yǝḥēš was coming from over here. We met up out there and we said: "What should we do now? What's the plan?" We spoke to one another. Finally he said we should leave it: we should go back (to the shore), leaving what God had given us, not trying to catch the large creature.

5. "axáyr aḥśǝmét. axáyr ǝgimǝlét." axáyr šāmánk teh, ǝšāmānǝh mǝn ǝġaré l-aʕabú mǝġārǝ. gǝḏōbǝn, gǝḏōbǝn, gǝḏōbǝn, ṭabbēn ǝlyūx. gǝḏōbǝn teh eté aṭláʕan teh. hes el aṭláʕan teh, fˁēm mǝniʕāt leh ǝmbóh, mǝmnáʕt mǝn ǝmbóh. hínǝ śawr? tǝrā yin meyh b-ǝl-ḥūt mā śay ǝrḥámǝh. ḥūt ^JAmā yǝrḥām^JA. mēyit wǝ-yḥām yǝmét ʕar bǝ-ḥad, fālǝk xayr mǝn allāh!

(I said:) "Better we should respect (what God has sent us). Better we should complete (what we have started)." Better I had

---

⁶¹ Unusual form, possibly < Arabic verbal noun ġayb, 'withdrawal'.

done as he had advised, that I had listened to him, rather than worry about what people might say afterwards. We pulled and pulled and pulled, rolling up the nets as we went. We pulled away at it until we had brought it up to the surface. When we had got it up, (his) legs were seized (i.e., by the shark) here, they were grabbed right here. What to do? You see, huge fish have no compassion. Huge fish have no mercy: even though in the throes of death itself, it wants to take someone to their death with it, may God send you good fortune!

6. wə-hoh taʿbān mən əyéhəd^{JA}. aǵáyg ḏek beh tih. ʿamōrən: "habó naʿmāl?" ménaʿ tiy sāʿat. axárgən ḍarāb mən aḏarāb l-əlyūx w-ewēkəb tēsən b-axáh, axáh lə-ləxām, əmbēn ələxām w-əmbēnəh. hes eté áwḳaʿ bēs aḏárb aṭákəmə, mənəʿāt axáyr, aktīr. ʿamórk hoh: "axáyr nəmānʿas b-aʿyāntsa." wə-hes mēnʿan aʿyāntsa, ʿamərāt aṭáh: ḥāwīl el ʿeḳəṣ́āt tiy u-məǵārə fthāt axáhs.

And I was exhausted from all the exertion. That man with me was stout (lit. 'had flesh'). We said: "What shall we do?" He held on to me for a while. We took out some of the sticks from the gillnets and I put them inside the shark's mouth, between the shark and him (i.e, Yəḥēš). When the stick was placed like that, the shark just held on all the more, gripped even tighter. I said: "Better to grab it by its eyes!" When we grabbed it by the eyes, it went like this: first it threshed madly around me and then it opened its mouth.

7. seh el təwōth lə-faʿməh. hes fthāt axáhs, naxērgən tēs. nḥāmh yəmét b-abárr mən ərawnə. ʿamōlən la hes táho, ʿamələ́t l-ərábʿah. ^{JA}əlēn əndárr abárr.^{JA} ʿamōr: "sēddə aʿámri u-gəhām ḥānēf." mən

ṣaḥḥ l-abárr, mənəʕātha ṭād, mənəʕātha bāmə, fālək xayr. bə-faʕməh, wə-tfālxas aṭá wə-txádməs śəmráx.

It had got him by the leg. When it opened its jaws, we got it (i.e., the leg) out. We would rather he (i.e., Sālim Yəḥēš) died on land rather than out at sea. We didn't do as those others did with their companion.[62] (And so we swam along with him) until we reached the shore. He said: "I can manage by myself," and he went along on his own. When he had reached the shore safely, another shark grabbed him, it took hold of him here, may you meet with good fortune! By the leg. And it split his leg right open like that, and tore the flesh to tatters.

8. xadəmāt śəmráx ṭad aṭáh wə-seh śəmərxāt la. mən šərxáth, mən ṭaʕmēt əd̠ēr, bələkāt. aġáyg həb^JA ráxməh, aġáyg ^JAḥábbət ərīḫ^JA. agdáḥ aʕámrəh l-abárr. shébwəh aʕabú w-edēwyuw d̠ek.

It shred the flesh in one leg like that, but it (i.e., the other leg) was undamaged. Once it had split open his leg, once it had tasted blood, it let go. The man was no weakling (lit. 'he was no vulture'), the man was a hero! He got himself from the sea to land. People pulled him out and they treated that man.

[1980s BATTXT1. B17]

6.20. Turtle Fishing

1. ḥāməs: hes aġayāg yəxádəmuw hēs śwēr u-ḥadīd wə-raṣṣēn. ḥadīd aʕkār mən d̠eh. ənxarér ḳáṭən u-mən əmbóh beh ḥadīd hes

---

[62] Another story, in which the companions of a severely injured man were too appalled at the sight to do anything for him, but just sat and watched him die.

kəllāb mən yəbtɔ́ləḵ. el mənəʕéh. u-yəḳáʕuw hes ləbbōdi əbə́ndəḵ. yərūd beh śə́nyə lə-ʕayn mən ḥān lə-śānə ḥāməs. wə-hem śənóh ḥāməs la, yərūd beh la. wáḳət hes təḳáʕ ráḥaḵ u-wáḳət hes təḳáʕ nəxálka.

Turtle: when the men (wanted to catch) a turtle, they'd make a line for it with a large iron hook and sinker weights. The iron hook was bigger than this; the tip was fine and here there'd be a piece of iron, (hooked) like a gaff, to stop it (i.e., turtle) slipping off and getting away. It held it tightly on. They (the turtle fishermen) would be like a good shot with a gun. He'd make a cast for it, by eye, to wherever the turtle had been seen. And if he didn't see a turtle he wouldn't make a cast for it. Sometimes it would be far out, and sometimes it would be right there, beneath you.

2. mən ḍar əgəbəlīl bēs ḳayd mən sərānə u-yaġṭāḵ bə-ḥāməs u-yaḥāwələn bēs mən ḏār əgəbəlīl eté yáwṣələs barr. yəḳáʕ šeh ʕabú hes yəḳáśəbuw tēs bə-skīn wə-yəhtēdyuw tēs. u-kel ḥad mə́nho yəślēl hēmənəh bə-ṣāṭər wə-šuwgōś lə-kədōt.

On top of the cliff there'd be a(nother) length of rope behind, and he'd hook the turtle and then manoeuvre it along the clifftop (lit. 'mountain') until he got it close to shore. He would have (other) people with him to help him cut it up with a knife and share it out. Each one would take his share in a ṣāṭər basket and in the late afternoon would go off home.

3. bēs təkədí mékən ṯkeyāl u-nəḥāsəb hēs təwṣāl aḳáʕ. hem bēs təkədí ṯkeyāl wə-nəḥāsəb hēs təwṣāl aḳáʕ, hes yərūd bēs yəsyōr

ráḥaḵ. u-hem bēs təkədí ṭḵeyāl la, xafīf, tərəḥāḵ la. u-təzhérs mən təxtə́rəṭ u-mən təġēf mən aḥāməs.

It (the turtle line) had many heavy sinker weights, and we'd judge it (the cast) so that it would reach the bottom. If it had heavy sinker weights, and we'd judged correctly (i.e., that the weights would be heavy enough) to reach the bottom, when he made his cast it would go a great distance. But if it didn't have heavy sinker weights but was light in weight, then it wouldn't go far. And you'd try and judge it (i.e., the cast) just right so that it didn't slip off (i.e., so that the hook didn't just pass over the carapace but lodged directly in the flesh of the turtle), nor drift away from the turtle.

4. hes šuwḵaˤāt yəˤāmər bēs aṭáh eté ḥadīd yaġṭāḵ b-aḥāməs. hem gōrrək teh bə-ḥays heh yaġṭāḵ bēs, wə-hem gōrrək tēs bə-ḥays la, yaġṭāḵ bēs la, yəntífəġ məns wə-het tšˤār əl-xalī́. hem el ˤād šōk taww la, aḥāməs fərədāt. ḥad mə́nho yəgídəb məns mən shəlēṭ, ḥad mə́nho mən ṭə́rti...

Once it (i.e., the hook) had landed, he'd do like this with it (i.e., give it a hard tug) to lodge the hook firmly lodged in the turtle. If you jerked it hard when you hooked the turtle (that would be fine), but if you didn't give it a good jerk when you hooked it, it wouldn't get properly lodged (in the turtle) but would slip out, and you'd spend the night empty-bellied! If it didn't go well with you, the turtle would swim off and get away. Some of them would pull in three (turtles), some two…

5. u-šaxbérəh, her aġáh, ˤamōr: "habó hes təġyōṣ lēs?" hes nəġyōṣ lēs, ḥad mə́nho šého nād u-šého ḳayd mən sərānə. u-baˤṣ mə́nho

yəgyōṣuw tēs mən fənānə. ḥāwīl nəślōl ḳayd ṭawīl, śwēr ġaláṣ́ət. u-nəxádəm bēs ḥadīd hes gəndēwi ġálaś, wə-nəsyōr. wə-šēn nād u-nəsyōr nəxál kərmām mən ḥān nədlōl aḥāməs.

And he asked him, his brother, he said: "How did it go when you dived for it?" When we dived for it, some of them had goatskins and a length of rope behind. Some of them would dive down in front of it. First we'd take a good length of rope, a good stout line. And we'd use a large iron hook for it, like a thick gəndēwi fish hook, and we'd set off. We'd have goatskins with us, and we'd set off (i.e., swimming) beneath the cliffs to where we knew turtles were to be found.

6. u-hem ənśānəs təgyōṣ wə-tənfōf, enḥá nəktérə məns mən tśān tēn. nōfxan anād u-rəbāṭən bēsən arîh lə-śəwrēn. u-ġāṣ lēs ṭad minēn, kel il heh zə́rəf. u-nōkaʕ mən sərānə wə-seh el ġāṣāt. hem nōkaʕ mən fənēs tśānəh wə-tfə́rəd. u-hem nōkaʕ mən gamb, tśānəh wə-tfə́rəd. yaġáyr hem heh mən sərēs, mən ser əd̠nōbs eté yəwəṣāls.

And if we saw one diving down and coming up to breathe, we'd hide from it so it couldn't see us. We'd inflate the goatskins and tie one end of the line to them. One of us would dive down for it, whoever was the most expert. Once it had dived down, he'd come at it from behind. If he were to come at it from the front, it would see him and swim off. And if he were to come at it from one side or other, it would see him and swim off. (It only works) if he comes at it from behind, from behind its tail, until he's right up close to it.

7. el ġāṣ b-ərawnə eté yaġṭāk bēs. hem aġṭōk bēs mən sərānə, mən ḥāl fʕem, mən dōl fʕem, el ʕād tšmānaʕ la mən ḳəwwéts. wə-hem

aġtōḵ bēs b-aġāṯəs wə-ḵə́rəb lə-hed, seh tšmānaˤ taww, w-el ˤād bēs bār la. mən taġtāḵ bēs wə-tfə́rəd, mōnaˤuw ḵayd bˤél anād eté egdéḥuw tēs abárr w-aḵérfəduw tēs. sərbaḵāt ḥādōtsa. təntəsēmən hes bənēdəm.

He'd dive right down into the sea to put the hook in. If he hooked it from behind, by its back flippers, by the back flippers, it would be is impossible to control, it's too strong. But if he hooked it in the neck, or close to a front flipper, it could be managed, it would no longer have all its strength. Once you'd hooked it and it swam off, those on the inflated goatskins would hold the line tight (i.e., the one attached to the inflated skins) until they had managed to pull it up onto the beach and turn it upside down. It would kick out and thrash around with its flippers. It breathes in and out, just like a human being.

8. ḵašābən tēs, ḵāṭˤan tēs, ḵātˤan tēs xayr śarr. bēs ṯad fəlkát nəxál faˤm, u-nəšwét nəxál hed, u-ġarrát b-aġáwf mənsēn kélsən. u-maˤuwyān u-ṯə́wi u-śabḥ, ḥāṣəṣ lə-fəlkát, u-ṯad mərgēn bərk əmˤuwyān. her bəḵāl ḥfōrən, ḥfōrən hēs gāmət^JA. u-təḵáˤ məsálət la, yəḵáˤ ḥaṣṣ. məġamṣōt. təġmāṣ bənēdən mən aṭáwləs.

We'd cut it up. We'd cut away at it. We'd cut away at it, for better or worse. It has fat in the upper thighs and buttocks, beneath the back flippers, in the breast area beneath the front flippers, and in the belly above everything else (i.e., viewed from upside down: the turtle would be lying on its back). And intestines and meat and fat: the ḥāṣəṣ fat of the upper thighs and buttocks, and another kind of fat called mərgēn, in and around the intestines. For eggs, we'd dig down. We'd dig down a man's height for them. And it (the site of the eggs) wouldn't be in the soft floor of a flow bed, it would be in hard stony ground. Concealed. Deep enough down to conceal a person.

9. ʿalākən śeyāṭ u-áwḳaʿan bēs ḥaṣṣ. u-hem śeyāṭ dəfərāt la, lēs əriyáḥ la, nəślōl mən śábḥas u-nəlíbəd bes ḥaṣṣ bərk śeyāṭ. tədífər té təmə́rət. áwḳaʿan bēs śabḥ, áwḳaʿan bēs tih eté el mēləʾ baʿl əmaṣbít. tēwən mə́nəh wa-áwḳaʿan mə́nəh. wa-ḳəsyēr, ḏen il yəʿēməruw heh 'ḳəsyēr', akśáʿan mə́nəh. ḏen ḳəsyēr yəḳáʿan mən tə́wi, el heh śabḥ la. śay mən śábḥ nəmílḥah, yəḳśáʿ, məmláḥ, w-əntóh mə́nəh lə-ḳəsyēr.

We'd light a fire and we'd put stones in it. And if the fire didn't catch, if there wasn't enough wind for it, we'd take some of its fat and throw it on the stones that were in the fire, and then the fire would catch (and burn) until (the stones) were red hot. We'd put fat on top of them and we'd put meat on top of them until the stone bed of the roasting site was filled full. We'd eat some of it, and some of it we'd set aside (for later). And the ropes of meat cut up small, this they call ḳəsyēr, some of it we'd dry. This ḳəsyēr was of meat (only), there wasn't any fat. Some of the fat we'd salt: it would be dried and salted, and we'd eat bits of it with the ḳəsyēr meat.

10. məlḥāt əgəbəlīl, mən kərmām məḳáwṭaʿ beh. bə-kərmām yəḳáʿ xádər beh məlḥāt, śay mən xadāwər yədlóluw teh aʿabú. śábḥ l-ebhəlōth milḥāt. hem l-ebhəlōt la yəxyōs, yəḳáʿ bēs tuwʿāl wə-tərūd beh. mən ṭērən teh ḳašábən teh. xadōmən mə́nəh ṭəwyāl hes ḏeh, hes ḏeh, ḳəsyēr, ḳəsyēr, wə-akśáʿan teh.

(We'd use) rock salt from the mountains, cut out of the mountains. In the mountains there might be a cave with salt inside, certain caves that people know about. Salt preserves fat. If it's not preserved in this way, it goes off, becomes all maggots and grubs and you have to throw it away. Once we'd washed it (i.e., the meat, in sea water), we'd cut it up. We'd make it into long (strips) like this, like this: *ḳəsyēr* ropes of meat, *ḳəsyēr* ropes of meat. And we'd dry it.

11. *syōrən h-əbēdiyə u-mən nəgyáˤ tēwən mə́nəh ḏen ḳəsyēr fənānə. u-məġārə ḳašābən mən śabḥ u-tēwən mə́nəh məḳəṣāt məḳəṣāt. "əḳəsəyēr maṯk hem šeh aġáh!" ḥəbāt lə-hēfəl wə-ḳeśərāt lə-ṭádaˤ. ḥāwə təgə́rfəh bə-skīn. w-əntōh(əh). śūri.*

We'd go to the desert areas above and when we were hungry we'd eat some of it. This *ḳəsyēr* dried meat to start with, and then we'd cut some pieces of the (dried) fat and we'd eat it, chunk by chunk. "The ropes of meat are very sweet if they have their brother (i.e., fat) with them!" The *ḥəbāt* is the plastron shell of the belly and the *ḳeśərāt* is the carapace shell of the back. The *ḥāwə* tissue that joins the top to the bottom shell you'd scrape off with a knife. We used to eat it. It's very good.

[1980s BATTXT4. B17]

6.21. Turtle Fishing Equipment and the Turtle

1. *heh əlīx məstōt, ġálaṣ́, mən śān yəḳáˤ ḳəwí. het bəṭāwəṭ. u-beh ḥə́dəd u-təkədí. śay beh ḥə́dəd əmbóh u-śay beh əmbóh. wə-hes ənśān ḥāməs b-ərawnə nəfḥāt, nərūd beh lēs u-nəġṭāḳ bēs. baˤl ḥāmis il yəġṭāḳ bēs hes ələbbādi lə-búnduḳ: mən yəśān ahāmis yəġṭāḳ bēs.*

The gillnet was made of six-stranded (twine), thick, so that it was really strong. Six strands. And it had an iron hook and a sinker weight. Some put the hook here and some put it here. When we'd see a turtle in the sea coming up to breathe, we'd cast the line at it to hook it. The turtle fisherman who hooks a turtle is like the man who is a good shot with a gun: as soon as he sees the turtle, he gets the hook straight into it.

2. ḥāwīl heh yəśbōb ḏar kermām wə-yəġálak̚ hēs. hes śənyēs yəxádəm ḥas la, seh tfə́rəd mən thāmaʿ ḥas l-aʿabú. yəxítəlis té yagṭák̚ bēs. wə-ḥāmis hēs məhal il yagṭák̚uw beh. u-mən ḥān śənyēs bə-ḥalāl, rədóh lēs bə-śūrēn. wə-hes seh nəfḥāt, heh agṭák̚ bēs bə-ḥays, rədóh bə-ḥə́dəd bə-śūrēn hēs seh nəfḥāt wə-heh giḏəbíh aʿánət aʿánət eté śənyíh ber wēṣəl aġáṭyəs.

To begin with, he'd climb a cliff above the sea and look for one. When he saw it he'd make no sound—it swims off if it hears a human voice. He'd creep up on it until he was able to hook it—a turtle has a (certain) place where they'd (try to) hook it. When he saw one in clear water, he'd cast for it with the lines. When it came up to breathe, he'd cast with all his strength. He'd cast the hook and the lines when it came up to breathe and then he'd pull in the line bit by bit, bit by bit, until he saw that it (i.e., a hook) had reached its neck.

3. mən yagṭák̚ bēs yaḥāwələn bēs eté tṣál abárr. eṣəlāt abárr, ḥāwīl hes b-ərawnə, yənākaʿ bēs ṭad, u-hes awṣəlōt abárr, təkáʿ t̚kálət wə-tenēwəhan tōk bə-ḥādōtsa wə-fʿēmsa. ʿar ho yek̚erfédwəs: aṭádʿas yəkáʿ əmṣáʿ wə-hēfəlis b-aġáwf. tenēwəhan la, təkádər la. yəmnáʿuw tēs aʿabú bə-ḥādōtsa wə-yəgréruw tēs eté taʿtə́zz mən ərawnə. mən ḥān təlḥōk̚ ərawnə yəkáś̌əbuw tēs la, mən əḏēr yəxīsən ərawnə.

Once he'd hooked it, he'd move it along until it was close to the shore. Once it had reached the shore—to begin with, when it was in the sea, it would be light, and a single man could manage it. But once it was on the land, it was very heavy and it would struggle and go for you with its front and back flippers. But they would turn it upside down: its back to the ground and its belly uppermost. Then it wouldn't struggle any more—it couldn't. People would take hold of it by the front flippers and drag it up the beach until it was well clear of the sea. They'd never butcher it within reach of the sea because the blood would pollute the sea (i.e., and bring bad luck).

4. śabḥ lə-fˤēm yəhēmyuw teh 'fī́lək' wə-śabḥ lə-ḥādōtən yəhēmyuw teh 'əniš́wāt'. wə-śabḥ lə-ḥēfəl yəhēmyuw teh 'əġarrát'. w-əmˤuwyān ṭad mə́nho yəhēmyuw teh 'əġálaḏ̣', mən ḥān axayār. wə-ṭad mə́nho yəhēmyuw teh 'rə́ḳaḳ'. wə-śábḥ il bə-məˤuwyān yəhēmyuw teh 'ərə́bś'.

The fat around the back legs is called *fī́lək*, and that around the front flippers is called *niš́wāt*. The fat of the belly is *ġarrát*. And of the intestines, one kind is called *ġálaḏ̣*, 'the stout', and that's the best kind. And the other is called *rə́ḳaḳ*, 'the slender'. And the fat of the intestines is called *rəbś*.

5. əḏābəlis boh mən ḥān yəḳə́šəbuw teh bə-skin yəhēmyuw teh ḥāwə. wə-ḥādōtən wə-fˤēm yəhēmyuw tēsən 'əṭəlāfīġ lə-ḥāmis' w-'əṣəfāwər lə-ḥāmis'. əttə́wi il berk ərī́hs yəhēmyuw teh 'əṣəfēyər l-ərī́h'. əmaˤmáˤs yənāfaˤ la, wə-šəbdíts had yətōhs la, yərēdyuw bēs aˤabú. wə-kə́li yətēwyuw tēs wəla heh śūri la. ḳeśərə́ts ḥāwīl aˤabú yəślḗluw tēs hes təḳáˤ ḳəśəˤēt wə-awḳáˤwas ḏar əmóh wə-yəskēbuw

bēs ḥamóh^M l-aʿrān wə-hbēʿar. ḥəbāt lə-hēfəl yərēdyuw bēs, tənāfaʿ la.

The rim here, where they'd cut it open with a knife, they call the ḥāwə,[63] and the front and back flippers are called the ṭəlāfiġ of the turtle, or the ṣəfāwər, 'the claws' of the turtle. The meat of the head they call the ṣəfēyər l-əríh, 'the plaits of the head'.[64] Its brain is no good, and no-one eats the liver, people throw it away. The kidneys are eaten, but they aren't very good. People used to take the carapace once it had dried out and put it above a water(ing) place and pour water into it for the goats and the camels. The plastron bottom shell is no good for anything, people throw it away.

6. wə-hem bēs bəkāl yətbáxuw tēs bə-ṣifərīyit w-əṣifərīyit bēs moh. wə-yəwākaʿuw tēs ḍar śeyāṭ w-əṣifərīyit təfhēś eté bəhēl. yḥām sáʿti térti. hes bəhēl ehtēdyuw tēsən. wə-fkāśən. axrāgən əkəśyēr əlébən wə-tēwyən ḍek axayār. aḥád yəṣrórəh w-aḥád yəṣrórəh la.

And if it had eggs inside, they'd cook these in a pot of water. They'd put it on the fire and the pot would boil away until the eggs were cooked and ready to eat. They need about two hours. When they were ready, they'd share them out. We'd crack them open. We'd remove the white skins on top and eat the good bits (inside). They make some people ill, but others are fine.

[1980s BATTXT2. B17]

---

[63] The tissue that joins the upper to the lower shell.

[64] ṣəfēyər l-əríh, 'the plaits of the head' on both sides of the head, i.e., where plaiting of the hair would begin: close to the head, above, below and behind the ear area, ideal places for hooking a turtle.

6.22. The Story of the Arrogant Girl and the Turtle

1. ʿamōr: ṭīt bəṭaḥrēt mən bʿéli warx el ʿarsōt bə-ṭad məhərí mən bʿéli hbēʿar, bʿél əbādiyə, bədəwí. wə-gəhəmōt šeh hə-bʿéli hbēʿar. u-məġārə nēkaʿuw tēs aġwōtsa. u-baʿl abárr yəḳáʿ aḏāyəh nizḥ, el hes bʿél ərawnə la il beh aḏáy lə-ṣayd. nēkaʿuw tēs aġwōtsa u-báho ḏáy lə-ṣayd. ʿamərēt hého: "ftərékō máni. béko ḏáy lə-ṣayd."

He said: A Baṭhari woman from Warx married a Mahri man, from the camel people, from the people of the desert. A bedouin. And she went to live with him, with the camel people. And then her brothers came (to visit her). The man of the desert smells sweet, not like the fisher people who smell of fish. Her brothers came to her, smelling of fish. She said to them: "Move off from me a bit! You stink of fish!"

2. u-məġārə rēdyuw bēs aʿabú wə-ḳefədāt ḥerbáʿtsa. hes l-aḵbəlāt láho, ho šáho ṣayd. u-kel ṭad ḏárha msar. yəḳáʿuw la bəġáyr msar: ḥāwīl ʿamōruw kel heh beh msar la leh ʿawf. hes l-aḵbəlāt lého ʿamərēt: "taʿbéruw biy aġwōtya! wə-taʿbérən biy əmkəmənátko." wə-ho el ġərābuw.

And then the people (of her husband) rejected her, and she went back down to her own people. When she went forward to greet them, they had fish with them and each one was wearing a headcloth. They'd never go without some sort of head covering, because it used to be said that the man who wears no head covering is accursed. When she went to greet them, she said: "Greet me and make me welcome, my brothers! And may your little head coverings[65] greet me and make me welcome!" And they realised (i.e., how arrogant she had become).

3. u-məġārə nōkaʕuw bə-ḥamis wə-l-agʕāruw tēs. w-aḥāmis bēs bār, kəwwét, śay ʕaṣīm. yənākaʕ bēs la hwēn, ʕar kəwí. wə-ʕamēruw aġwōtsa: "teṯ il nəkəʕāt," aġátho, "təmānaʕ la hed ḥānēfs." hes təmānaʕ tēs aḥāmis, heds təlíbəd ḍar hēfəlis u-bēs ṣəfāwər: kel təlíbəd ḍars wə-təmúrḵ mɔ́nəh. hem lāfāt əgawd bəṣərāth. wə-hem lāfāt əríh fətxáth. wə-hem lāfāt aʕṣāś ṯəbərāth. yaġáyr kel yəġārəb hēs yəmnáʕs.

And then they caught a turtle and had got it down on the ground. Now the turtle is immensely strong, powerful, impossible to imagine how strong. A weak man can't manage it, only a strong man. And her brothers said (one to the other): "The woman who has just arrived"—their sister—"she won't be able to hold a front flipper by herself!" When you hold onto it, the turtle, its front flippers beat on its belly[66] and it has claws: anything it (i.e., a claw) strikes, it goes right through it and out the other side. If it touches skin, it tears it open, and if it touches the head, it splits it open, and if it touches a bone, it breaks it. Unless a person knows how hold on to it properly.

4. ʕamēruw hēs: "təmnáʕi la hed aḥāmis. máġdiyə tiš." ʕamərēt: "bert hɔ́bi. hoh əḥémər raʕéyf eté l-əḥémər hed əl-ḥāmis la?" hes mənəʕāts, gəḏəbāts aḥāmis u-rədōts ḍar hēfəlis wə-ʕasəfāts bə-hed

---

[65] Diminutive of kəmet, pl. kəmēm, a skullcap worn by men and boys; also, a close-fitting cap worn by young girls. Said by their sister disparagingly.

[66] The turtle is turned upside down to immobilise it.

əmbóh lə-k̠āns, wə-hed əmbóh əl-k̠ān məšáġər. wə-yēdʿak bēs la ḥayyāt wəla seh mātāt. wə-ḥāwīl hes nəkəʿāt ḥerbáʿtsa: "taʿbérən biy əmkəmənə́tko!"

They said to her: "Don't hold on to the turtle's front flipper: it would be the death of you!" But she replied: "(I am) the daughter of my father! I who can control a wild camel, how could I not control the front flipper of a turtle?" When she took hold of it, the turtle dragged her along and flung her down on her belly. It struck out at her with its front flipper, there on her hip, and again on the hip of the other side. I don't know whether she survived or whether she died. And to think that when she first came up to them she had said: "And may your little head coverings greet me and make me welcome!"

[1980s BATTXT2. B17]

PART III
HARVESTING THE SEA
IN CENTRAL MONSOON DHOFAR AND
AL-MAHRAH

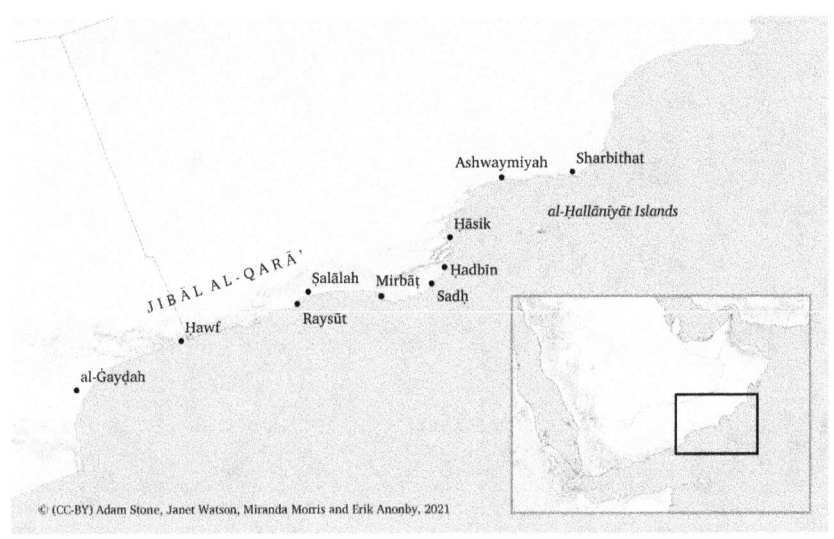

Map 3: Dhofar and adjacent areas of al-Mahrah

HARVESTING THE SEA IN CENTRAL MONSOON DHOFAR AND AL-MAHRAH

Janet C. E. Watson, with Miranda J. Morris,

Alec B. M. Moore and Said Baquir

Acknowledgments

We acknowledge with many thanks our funders, the Leverhulme Trust for project grant RPG-2012-599 (January 2013–December 2016), during which time the texts for this chapter were collected, annotated and archived; the Endangered Languages Archive (ELAR), and in particular Mandana Seyfeddinipur and Stephanie Petit for enabling us to produce archives of the four Modern South Arabian languages spoken in Dhofar; Carleton University, for enabling us to create a dataset associated with texts in this chapter through Borealis; and our local collaborators: our research administrator, Saeed al-Mahri, our data collectors, Abdullah al-Mahri, Ali al-Mahri and Khalid Ruweya, and all our many Mehri and Śḥerēt consultants who wish to remain anonymous.

1. Introduction

This chapter discusses aspects of harvesting the sea along the central coastline of monsoon Dhofar and to the east of this region, with some mention of al-Mahrah in eastern Yemen. Dhofar is home to four of the indigenous Modern South Arabian languages, Mehri, Śḥerēt, Hobyōt and Bəṭāḥrēt (Baṭhari), which are at various stages of endangerment (Watson and Morris 2015; Watson et al. 2019). The chapter is based on fieldwork with Śḥerēt and Mehri speakers. Fieldwork was conducted by Watson together with Alec B. M. Moore in 2014, and, on three separate occasions, by Watson alone in early 2014, late 2015 and late 2016. It is told through the voices of fishers and through Watson's diary and fieldnotes. Notes from Watson's fieldwork conducted in al-Ġayḍah, Yemen in 2013 are also referenced. The chapter is followed by transcribed, translated and annotated audio and audio-video texts, with titles of the original audio and audio-visual recordings as given in the Shehret and Mehri ELAR archives where available: The documentation and ethnolinguistic analysis of Modern South Arabian: Shehret | Endangered Languages Archive (elararchive.org) and The documentation and ethnolinguistic analysis of Modern South Arabian: Mehri | Endangered Languages Archive (elararchive.org). The media files are also available through Borealis, housed at Carleton University: Harvesting the Sea in Central Monsoon Dhofar and al-Mahrah media files | Arabian Peninsula Languages Dataverse (borealisdata.ca). The chapter is structured as follows: fieldwork methods; the climate of Dhofar and al-Mahrah; the cultural value of fishing; fish types and uses; names; fishing methods and tools.

Harvesting the Sea in Central Monsoon Dhofar and al-Mahrah 343

2. Fieldwork

Fishermen were audio and audio-visually recorded in Mirbāṭ and Ḥāsik over three days in 2014, and further recordings were collected by Watson in Sadḥ in late 2015 and 2016. Most of our consultants are Śḥerēt speakers. Speakers in the recordings included or referenced in this chapter were between their late seventies and early thirties. Some were born before 1947 or between the floods of 1947 (known as 'the year of the al-Ḥaymar star': ʿōnut əlḥīmər Śḥerēt, snēt əlḥaymər Mehri) and the floods of 1959 (known as 'the year of drowning': ʿōnut ɛ-ġarḳēt Śḥerēt, snēt ḏ-əġarḳāyət Mehri). Younger speakers include a male speaker in his early thirties from Sadḥ (text 8.1.1., 'Diving for Abalone') and a male speaker aged 40 from Jufa, now living in Mirbāṭ (text 8.1.4., 'Shellfish and Snails'). In late 2016, Watson also interviewed women about shellfish collection.

Audio recordings were recorded either on an Olympus LS-11 digital recorder or on a Marantz PMD661 solid-state recorder with external Audio-technica microphone, and saved in lossless WAV format at 44 kHZ, 14-bit. Audio-visual recordings were produced on a Canon HDXA20 video recorder with an external Audio-technica microphone and saved as either MOV or MTS files. During fieldwork with Alec B. M. Moore, a set of high-resolution photographs were presented to fishermen as slides on a laptop for fish identification. These photographs were used for the elicitation of fish names from Śḥerēt and Mehri fishermen. Fieldwork included talking to fishers about the sea, and eliciting the names of fish, fishing tools and description of fishing methods and fish preparation, with a focus on methods traditionally used in the past. We collected names of fish, shellfish, rays, turtles and shark from Moore's photographs and, where available, from identification at the harbour and on the rocks. For several fish types, our consultants failed to agree on the names. While regional and dialectal differences are to be expected, as well as fish 'nicknames' varying within communities, this lack of agreement was more intra-community, and particularly the case in the identification of fish from photographs: partly due to the fact that many of the older consultants suffered from poor eyesight, and partly the need to handle the fish to establish its identity. This lack of consistency must be taken into account in reading this contribution.

3. Climate

In contrast to Musandam and Soqotra, Dhofar and al-Mahrah are marked by exhibiting four distinct seasons: the monsoon period (*xorf* Śḥerēt, *xarf* Mehri) from early June to early September, the post-monsoon period (*ṣirb* Śḥerēt, *ṣayrəb* Mehri) from early September to early December, winter (*śéte* Śḥerēt, *śētu* Mehri) from early December to early March, and the hot season (*ḳuṭ* Śḥerēt, *ḳayṭ* Mehri) from early March to the end of May.

In contrast to Soqotra, which is subject to the south-west monsoon winds between April and October, and the north-east monsoon winds from November to March, the monsoon period in Dhofar and al-Mahrah is typically marked by strong winds, constant light rains and mist. This distinctive climate has a significant effect on fishing, as fishermen cannot go out to sea during the monsoon period. As the monsoon winds begin, the sea is said to be 'closed'. Once the winds of the monsoon period die down and the sea is said to be 'open', the fishermen prepare their nets and boats to go out to sea, described as a period when fishermen would go 'up' (i.e., out to sea) and *ígaḥ eṣēgi* (Śherēt) 'the large seine nets go in (to the sea)'. The sea is described as 'going up' in relation to the land, so that when fishers go out to sea they go up, and when they return to land they go down. On dry land, when someone moves away from the sea (*min erɛ́mnəm*, Śherēt) they are said to be going towards the land (*yol ɛʰr*, Śherēt). The monsoonal climate also resulted in a symbiotic relationship between the people of the coast and the people of the mountains, one consequence of which was considerable multilingualism across the communities: during the monsoon period, when the sea was 'closed' to fishing, coast dwellers would move up to the mountains to help mountain dwellers with seasonal agricultural work.

4. The Cultural Value of Fishing

Among the non-coastal Mahrah communities, fishing is not considered to be an honourable profession. Some Mahrah will say that their older relatives feel sick at the sight of the sea, and that they could never eat fish or tolerate its smell. The coastal Mahrah were, however, famous as sailors and shark fishermen (Miranda Morris, pers. comm.), and fish holds a cultural significance even for those who despise the occupation. During the hot season between March and end of May when the grazing becomes poor, dried sardine would be fed as a staple to livestock, as was and continues to be the case in Musandam (cf.

Anonby, this volume). People from the mountains would come down to the coast to barter cattle and goat products for dried sardine as well as imported goods such as sugar, tea and rice. Today dried sardine continues to supplement the diet of livestock, but is added in smaller amounts to imported hay to mitigate the taste of sardine in the milk. On longer journeys, the Mahrah would take strips of dried shark together with dates for sustenance.

Figure 1: Old fishing boat, eastern Dhofar

Photo © Miranda Morris, 1970s

Among coastal communities, fishing has always been tolerated as an essential profession. Diving for abalone (*Haliotis mariae*; Śḥerēt ṣifíźḥót, pl. ṣfúźaḥ, Mehri ṣəfəlḥāt, pl. ṣfōləḥ), which are to be found only in the east of Dhofar from Mirbāṭ to Ḥāsik, is prized, due to the price abalone can fetch, and is conducted by non-coastal divers, often non-local, as well as coastal dwellers.

Watson's principal consultant in al-Ġayḍah, M005, said he used to travel regularly to Ḥāsik to dive for abalone.

In Dhofar and al-Mahrah, fishing continues to be conducted in a subsistence manner, with men fishing with lines (śwīr, pl. śwōr Mehri, or ḵtēl) and hooks (ḵiźé, pl. aḵlēt Shḗrēt, ḵlīw Mehri, ḵīlē Mahriyōt[1]) from the shore and the rocks, casting cast nets, laying seine nets and setting fish traps. Even today, men can be seen throwing out lines along the beach in Salalah, and small boats going out to lay seine nets for sardine (Clupeidae; ʿad, sgv. ʿīdit Shḗrēt, ād, sgv. ʿīdit Mehri) and other small pelagic fish. The nets are then emptied into small motorised boats (traditionally dugout canoes, hūri, pl. hūrūn Mehri) and taken to shore. Once the sardines have been tipped onto the shore, people will come with their buckets to collect what they need for their families. The fish are considered a blessing from God, and to be shared, with the unspoken understanding that no one will take more than they need for themselves.

5. Fish Types and Uses

5.1. Drying and Preservation of Sardine and Other Fish

Sardine arguably has the greatest cultural significance in the region, due to the fact that sardines can be easily dried and stored, or used as supplementary fodder for livestock during the hot season when there is no or little good pasture available. They were also eaten and used as fertiliser (Dostal 2009). There

---

[1] The dialect of Mehri spoken in the eastern part of al-Mahrah, Yemen.

are two main types of sardine: Indian oil sardine (*Sardinella longiceps*; ʿad ʿiźól Śherēt, ād aylōl Mehri), which are harvested during the hot season towards the end of April and beginning of May, and the fatter post-monsoon sardine (ʿad ṣɛryót Śherēt).[2] Sardine catching used to be conducted at seasons determined by particular stars (Dostal 2009, 20). In the audio recording 20130216_ShehretCWJ_J006_sardinefishing in the Shehret archive at ELAR, the speaker says: *min her zaḥam ṣɛrb / min her ṣ́ēġi igaḥ* 'from when the post-monsoon period came, from when the seine nets went in'.

Figure 2: Drying sardines, Mḥayfīf, al-Mahrah

Photo © Janet C. E. Watson, 2013

---

[2] The sardines of the hot period are thin (spawning or having recently spawned), and the sardines of the post-monsoon period are fatter.

Today the drying of sardines continues all along the flatter coast in al-Mahrah and at fewer places in Dhofar. The sardines are lain out under large disused nets known as *məddēt* to protect them from gulls, and occasionally turned with a stick until they are dry. All of the dried sardine would be eaten apart from the head (*ḳəlyūf* 'eating dried sardines', Mehri). They used to be bought and stored by livestock owners in holes dug in the sand and covered with dry earth. They would then be mixed with the leaves of the shrub *Pteropyrum scoparium* (Dostal 2009, 18) to supplement the diets of camels, cows and goats during the hot season. The sardines affect the taste of the milk and meat, as noted in 20130216_ShehretCWJ_J006_sardinefishing, with the term *ṣift* (Śḥerēt) used to describe the sardine taste.[3] The latter part of text 8.2.3., 'Cast Nets, and Sardine Catching and Drying', describes the drying of sardines. Dried sardines continue to be fed as supplementary fodder to livestock, although with purchased hay and pelleted feed now available they are no longer as vital as they once were. Today sardines are mainly frozen and transported for sale.

Other fish that are typically dried and stored are rabbitfish (Siganidae; *śīẑób* Śḥerēt)[4] and shark (various taxa, with Carcharhinidae of major importance; *lxim*, sg. *lxyūt* Śḥerēt, *ūxaym* Mehri, *lxaym* Mahriyōt). The drying of both shark and rabbitfish is considerably more complicated than that of sardines. In the

---

[3] Thus, *ṣift* means both 'shark-liver oil' (see below) and 'taste of sardine in meat/milk'. Thanks to Mohammed al-Shahri for this information.

[4] *sīsín* around Raysūt, *sīsḗn* in the central Śḥerēt-speaking area.

case of rabbitfish, it is boiled for around 15 minutes, opened out flat, the bones and skin removed, and the flesh then dried for two to three days on a clean, flat surface. The resulting dried rabbitfish is known as *ḳóśaʿ*. Text 8.1.6. below, 'Making Fish Traps, and Rabbitfish', describes the process of drying rabbitfish.

Figure 3: Drying sardines, al-Muġsayl

Photo © Miranda Morris, 1970s

In the case of shark, the fins, the tail and the head are removed. The head would be thrown away. The primary and secondary dorsal fins, the pectoral fin, pelvic fin, anal fin and the bottom of the caudal fin (the tail) would be dried and sold with the salted flesh to traders moving between the Gulf, Oman and East Africa, etc. (Miranda Morris, pers. comm.). The liver (known as *ʿaylōḵ* in Mehri) would either be preserved to make shark-liver oil (*ṣift* Sherēt, *ṣəft* Mehri), which could then be used to oil wooden boats or to burn in oil lamps, or to make a dish called *ṣaynəṭ*.[5] The remaining meat would be cut up, salted and left for three or four days. It would then be placed on clean, stony ground and turned until completely dried. In the case of the small, slim pointed-head shark (milk shark *Rhizoprionodon acutus* and similar species; *síbəli*), the head and tail would be thrown away, and the shark cut in two. It would then be dried on a clean, flat surface, on nets known in Dhofari Arabic as *šrēbik*, or hung from a line. Speaker J042 in text 8.1.2. on shark drying compares the drying of milk shark to the air drying of meat strips practised elsewhere in Dhofar and al-Mahrah.

Larger fish, including emperor (*Lethrinidae*), king soldier bream (*Argyrops spinifer*), groupers (*Serranidae*, including small-scaled grouper *Epinephelus polylepis*), and shark would be dried, salted and tinned. The process involved boiling in oil drums, removing the head, bones, scales and skin, slashing the fillets and salting them, then turning and leaving them for 40 days, after which time it is ready to eat. It can be eaten like that or cooked in sauces. Such fish dried and placed in sacks is called *ḥanít*. The tinned fish is known as *málaḥ*, and frequently exported. It is described in an audio and audio-visual text in the Shehret ar-

---

[5] According to Miranda Morris (pers. comm.), this is traditionally cooked in a hole in the ground with the liver sandwiched between layers of shark flesh, and each layer overlain with red-hot stones. (20130414_MehriMo_M005_ZaynaTpreparation, an audio recording on modern *ṣaynəṭ* production recorded in al-Ġayḍah, is included in the Mehri archive at ELAR).

chive at ELAR on sea trade from Sadḥ to the west and east: 20141117_ShehretEJ_J046_seatradebetweenSudhtowestandeast.

Figure 4: Dried shark, al-Ġayḍah

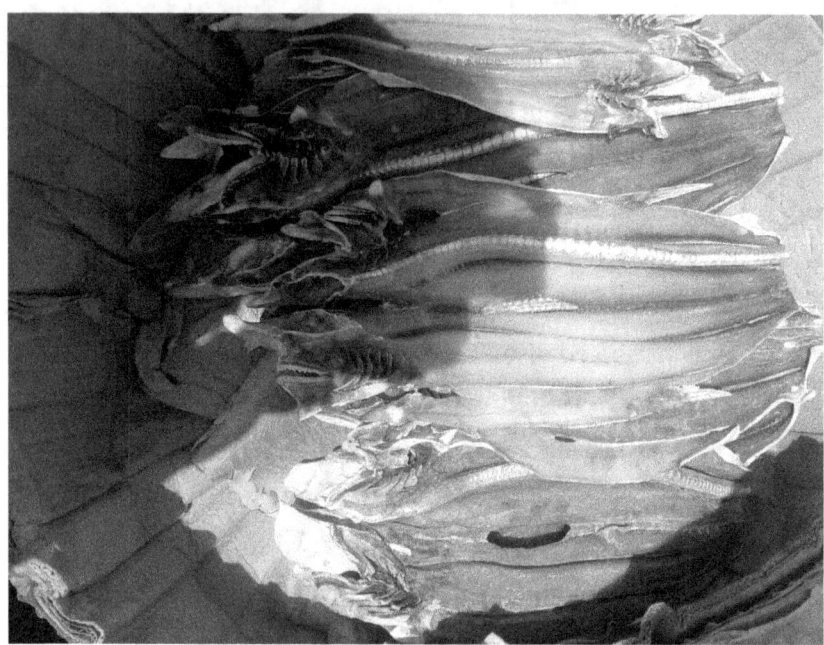

Photo © Janet C. E. Watson, 2013

5.2. Sadḥ and Abalone

Sadḥ, the area in which most of Watson's fieldwork was conducted, was considered by its inhabitants to be a jewel of plenty. Blessed by a natural harbour, people could make their living either by tapping frankincense in the hills to the north of the harbour or by catching fish from the sea. The inhabitants of Sadḥ originated from several different tribes, and current inhabitants are all speakers of Śḥerɛ̄t, though with significant variation in the language used. The fishing situation in all areas investigated differs markedly from that of ten and twenty years ago, with all fishers describing having to go further out to sea to catch fish and complaining that most fish they catch are far smaller than they were in the past.

Figure 5: Drying abalone, Ḥadbīn

Photo © Miranda Morris, 1970s

This is particularly the case with the prized abalone–that fetch huge prices today in East Asia. In the texts on sea trade between Sadḥ and the west and east, the speaker describes periods when up to 35 shipping vessels would be harboured at Sadḥ, and how one could walk from one side of the bay to the other by stepping across the boats. The government now attempts to preserve the abalone by imposing a ten-day diving season, which is announced in the later post-monsoon period, and requires a permit. The fishers complain that the season is not long enough, and in some years no diving season is announced. In mid-November 2014, when Watson was in Sadḥ, the diving season had not yet been opened, and fishers were concerned that the winds were increasing and that they would be worse by early December. Individuals do not always respect the restrictions of the diving season, and Watson notes in her fieldwork diary some young divers bringing in illegal abalone on 18 November 2014. Text 8.1.1. below describes diving today for abalone, the clothes divers would wear, and government efforts to conserve the abalone.

6. Names[6]

In the following, unless otherwise noted, names are provided in Śḥerēt. The English names were provided by Alec B. M. Moore in the field. In discussing the names of fish, it is essential to bear in mind that we did not elicit the same names for species across all consultants, even within a single community. This is due partially to differences in the relative experience of consultants, and partially to the fact that photographic slides made identification more difficult. Many of the Mahriyōt names provided by Geva-Kleinberger (2009) and elicited from Askari Hujayran Saad in Heidelberg through photograph identification, for example, differ from those Watson elicited from the same speaker at the fish market in al-Ġayḍah: Geva-Kleinberger provides ġäzbīt hibʿayd (sic = ġaṣbīt hibʿayt) tentatively for 'peacock grouper' (2009, 56) whereas in consultation with Miranda Morris it denotes 'parrotfish'. Some names were more consistent

---

[6] For illustrations and descriptions of the known 930 shore fishes (defined as occurring to a depth less than 200 metres), see Randall (1995).

across speakers than others, for example: *gə́da~gúdɛ́* for 'cobia', *feráḥt~firáḥt* for 'king soldier bream', *ṣarf* for *Sciaenidae* (either drums or croakers), *šīṣa* for 'lemon shark', *zerb* for 'queen fish',[7] and *sayfranda* for 'cutlass fish'.

The names of fish and shellfish tend to be in the local language, in our case Śḥerēt or Mehri, while many names of shark appear to be Arabic, as in *ḏəmāwi* (dusky whaler, *Carcharhinus obscurus*), *jibēba* (oceanic white tip, *C. longimanus*; bull, *C. leucas*), *ḏība* (mako, *Isurus* spp.), *maṭlūṭ* (large hammerhead, *Sphyrna* spp.)~blacktip' (*C. limbatus*),[8] *nimrāni~nibrāni* (tiger shark, *Galeorcerdo cuvieri*), *kɔ̄fi* (Mehri *kūfi*) (immature hammerhead) and *bū ḥnak* (Arabian smoothhound, *Mustelus mosis*). Indigenous shark names included *iṯˤayl ɛ-rɛ́mnəm* (zebra shark, *Stegostoma fasciatum*), *sennūrət* (bigeye thresher, *Alopias superciliosus*; pelagic thresher, *A. pelagicus*; bramble shark, *Echinorhinus brucus*), and *šīṣa* (white tip reef, *Trianeodon obesus*; black tip reef, *C. melanopterus*; lemon shark, *N. acutidens*).

Watson's consultants in Sadḥ suggested Arabic names were used there because few sharks were caught in the area. The use of Arabic names for sharks could also be due to the fact sharks are frequently exported. The commercial relevance of shark in Bəṭāḥrēt, Mehri and Śḥerēt is reflected in the naming of particular fins (Miranda Morris, pers. comm.): *ˤalaf* 'fins (in general)', *īḏɛ́n* Śḥerēt, *īḏēn* Mehri 'pectoral fin' (otherwise 'ear'), *ḏarbét* Śḥerēt, *ḏərwēt* Mehri 'dorsal fin' (otherwise 'hump [of

---

[7] The Old Arabic term for 'queen fish'.

[8] Also, immature hammerhead.

camel]'), *ḏanúb Šḥerēt*, *ḏnūb* Mehri 'tail', 'caudal fin' (otherwise 'tail'), and in the naming of sharks denoting not a particular species, but rather the age/size (Miranda Morris, pers. comm.), with each of the following terms referring to the number of shark pieces that can be extracted from that particular shark: *gerēnīyəh* 'one (piece)' > *mansūf(əh)* 'two (pieces)' > *maṭlūṭ(əh)* 'three (pieces)' > *marbūʿ(ah)* 'four (pieces)'.

Some names describe a range of fish within the same species, in a number of cases with additional attributes: from the photographic slides, we elicited *ḳaṣʿɛr* (Mehri *ḳəṣayr*, Mahriyōt *ḳəṣʿayr*) for the trevally species (Carangidae), including bigeye trevally (*Caranx sexfasciatus*), golden trevally (*Gnathanodon speciosus*), with the attributed *ḳaṣʿɛr ʿofər* (Mehri *ḳəṣayr ōfər*, Mahriyōt *ḳəṣʿayr ʿōfər*) for blacktip trevally (*Caranx heberi*); *jēḏər~gēḏər* (Mehri *gēḏər*) for the tuna species (Scombridae),[9] including: frigate tuna (*Auxis thazard*)', yellowfin tuna (*Thunnus albacares*), bigeye tuna (*T. obesus*), Indian mackerel (*Rastrelliger kanagurta*), skipjack tuna (*Katsuwonus pelamis*), striped bonito (*Sarda orientalis*), long-tailed tuna (*T. thonggol*) and kawakawa (*Euthynnus affinis*), with the terms *jēḏər bū ḥmad* for 'albacore tuna (*T. alalunga*)' and *jēḏər bu ġus* for 'yellowfin tuna'.

For the ray species, *ṭabbawḳət* (Mehri) denotes 'manta ray (*Mobula* spp.)', 'spotted eagle ray (*Aetobatus* cf. *ocellatus*)', 'leopard ray (*Himantura uarnak*)', 'cownose ray (*Rhinoptera* spp.)', 'cowtail stingray (*Pastinachus* spp.)', 'porcupine ray (*Urogymnus asperrimus*)', 'banded eagle ray (*Aetomylaeus nichofii*)' and 'blue-

---

[9] For types of the tuna species found on the Omani seaboard, see Randall (1995, 371–76).

spotted fantail ray (*Taeniura lymma*)', with *ṭabbawkət rībəṣ́* also for 'cowtail stingray', and *ṭabbawkət fanaṭṭi* for 'devil ray (*Mobula* spp.)'; *mīx* denotes the billfish species, including: black marlin (*Makaira indica*), blue marlin (*M. mazara*) and swordfish (*Xiphias gladius*); *ʿabédyət* (Mehri *abadyət*) denotes the guitarfish species, including: guitarfish (*Acroteriobatus* and *Rhinobatos* spp.), giant guitarfish (*Rhynchobatus* spp.), although *kɛrš̃eli* (Mehri *krayš̃əli*) was also given for Salalah guitarfish (*Acroteriobatus salalah*), bowmouth guitarfish (*Rhina ancylostoma*), and, by at least one of our consultants, for giant guitarfish (*Rhynchobatus*).

For some species, names vary according to the size and age of the fish: *kaṣʿér* (Mehri *kaṣayr*) (yellowtail scad, *Atule mate*) is known as *gəš̃rān* when small; *jēḏər~gēḏər* (Mahriyōt *jēḏər*) (tuna, albacore tuna) is known as *maʿdud* (Mehri *mādūd~maʿdūd*) when small; *sizób* (rabbitfish) is known as *hérran* when small; *ḥamš̃ék* (emperor, Lethrinidae) is known as *ʿaṣ̄ēt* when small; the hammerhead (Sphyrnidae) is often known as *kɔ̄fi* (Mehri *kūfi*) when small; and at least in eastern Yemen, according to M005, *kəṣʿayr*[10] (golden trevally, *Gnathanodon speciosus*) is known as *bā drēb* when small.

Alongside the names, we collected information about how particular fish would be caught, and their cultural value and significance: *bēher* (milkfish, *Chanos chanos*; also various mullet [Mugilidae]) would be caught in either gill, seine or cast nets; *nəgrɛr* (Mehri *nəgrūr*; small-spotted grunt, *Pomadasys commer-*

---

[10] This name appears with three different definitions: the trevally species in general, yellowtail scad, and golden trevally.

sonnii) by line; mīx 'marlin' would be caught by line or in gill nets; təbbā́nah (Mehri; frigate tuna) would be caught in all types of net, but not in fish traps; tərān (Mehri; pompano, *Trachinotus* spp.) would be caught in cast nets when small, and by line when larger. In terms of cultural information, ṭarnīk (Mehri ṭānīk~ṭərnīk; kingfish, *Scomberomorus commerson*) was said by many to be the most prized fish for eating; itˤayl ɛ-rɛ́mnəm (zebra shark, *Stegostoma fasciatum*) was useless and would be thrown away; ṣarf (Mehri ṣōrəf; drum, Scianidae) would arrive with sardines around Salalah, but not in the east; bāl əškay (Mehri; sawfish, Pristidae) had not been seen for thirty years; feráḥt~firáḥt (king soldier bream) develops a hump when it becomes large, leading to its popular name jəmál~gəmál 'camel' (interestingly given in Arabic, though among Watson's consultants in Sadḥ given as jū̃l with the Mehri form as bˤayr 'male camel'); ˤabédyət (Mehri ābádyət), a name elicited both for the giant guitarfish and for the smoothtooth blacktip shark (*Carcharhinus leiodon*) was described as valuable; dəgāgo (Mehri dəgāgóh; torpedo scad, *Megalaspis cordyla*) was not good to eat, but cheap; ɛ̄xanṭ lxim (carpet shark, *Chiloscyllium* sp.) was not eaten; the meat of bū ḥnak (Arabian smoothhound, *Mustelus mosis*), though said to be not very good, would be eaten; rībəṣ (cowtail stingray, *Pastinachus* spp.) stays low on the seabed, has three spikes and is slimy.

We also recorded anecdotes associated with fishing, such as that of three boats that caught the same shark. The problem in this case was resolved by awarding the shark to the boat that had come against the wind.

The names of some fish derive from the relationship of humans to the fish, or man's perception of the fish, such as the alternative name for billfish (*mīx*) (marlin, sailfish and swordfish), *zrōḳət* (Mehri) likening the speed of its movement to that of the swift black *zīrəḳ* snake. Below in text 8.2.4. we include a Mehri legend that explains the popular origin of *ġaṣbīt hibˤayt* 'the struggler with seven' for the parrotfish (Scaridae), so called because seven men were unable to corner it and catch it. Although not mentioned in the text, the parrotfish secretes a protective mucus cocoon, particularly at night, making it extremely slimy and thus not easily captured. The name of a pompano (*Trachinotus* spp., *raḥtót* Shərēt, *rəḥtōt* Mehri) is described in the text on how *raḥtōt* got its name below as being related to the popular belief that it ate from the shore, licking at sand in the same way as a cow would lick her calf or a tulchan equivalent.

In addition to names of fish and related marine creatures, the fishers of Dhofar also have specific terms for large amounts of particular fish. This is significant not just for the specific terms, which depend on the fish described, but also the lack of terms for large amounts of other marine creatures that have high cultural or commercial value. Thus, a large number of rabbitfish is described in Shərēt as *siźób termḗt*, a large number of fish in general as *múṭur ɛ-ṣud*, and a large pile of sardines as *ˤad gaˤrót* or *ˤad nēgár* (Khalid Ruweya, pers. comm.). However, on questioning consultants there appear to be no specific terms for large amounts of shark or of abalone, despite their obvious high cultural and commercial value.

7. Fishing Methods and Tools

Both men and women were and continue to be involved in harvesting the sea: men would catch fish, and women would collect shellfish, including abalone. Women would never fish with a line or net. Attempts to elicit the full paradigm of the verb *botór* (*btūr* in Mehri, *btōr* in Mahriyōt) 'to line-fish' from Watson's Śḥerēt consultant, Khalid Ruweya, always resulted in being told that women do not fish and therefore that feminine singular or plural forms would never be encountered. In Sadḥ, I was told that men would traditionally work livestock and fish, women would work livestock and collect shellfish, and both men and women would harvest frankincense. Several types of shellfish are collected, some of which are eaten raw, such as *zikt* (rock oysters, e.g., *Saccostrea* spp.), *śenḥót* (chiton, Polyplacophora) and *śidíf* (sea lemon, Onchidiidae) (see text 8.1.3. below), and others, such as *ʿaṣ̌fór* (winkles; shellfish in general), *ʿaṣ̌fór śirór* (winkles), *fédək* (mussels) and *śfúẑaḥ* (abalone, Haliotis) are boiled or baked in a clay oven. The shellfish function not only for food: the opercula of certain shellfish are ground and added to incense, another occupation of women, and the shell of the conch shell (*ḥank*) would be used as a feeder jug for small babies or old people, the feeder called *ḥanṣ̌ít*.

The main tools for collecting shellfish are *mefóg*, a tool with a flat end for removing *zikt* 'rock oysters' and *śfúẑaḥ* 'abalone'; *gəzərét*, pl. *gizér*, a type of matchet with a wooden handle and flat metal end for abalone; *gərídt*, pl. *giréd ḏə-ḥadíd* a steel bar used for removing rock oysters; and *gindet ḏə-ḥadíd*, which has a hook on one end and a flat section on the other end, where the hook is used to remove ḥedḥéd (ḥadḥayd Mehri) 'edible sea urchins' and the flat section to remove abalone.

Nets differ according to the fish to be caught, with seine nets (śġēt pl. śíġí Śḥerēt; śagyət, pl. śwāġi Mehri; grif, pl. agrift Śḥerēt, gərfēt, pl. grēf Mehri), gill nets (iźéx, pl. lxixt Śḥerēt, lyawx Mehri, halyaxt Mahriyōt) for shark and larger fish, and smaller-meshed cast nets (məġdift, pl. məġódof Śḥerēt, mġədfēt, pl. mġōdəf Mehri) for sardine and smaller fish. The landing page of the Shehret archive at ELAR features a video in which a speaker from Mirbāṭ describes different parts of the cast net; the collection also includes videos in which the same speaker demonstrates casting a cast net. Fish would be tipped from the large seine nets into collecting nets (śógəd, pl. śigád Śḥerēt, śōgəd, pl. śgáwwəd Mehri), tied round the hips. Collecting nets would also be used by divers to store abalone they collected. Fish traps capture several different types of fish. In Sadḥ, they were mainly used to catch rabbitfish, but they also trapped other fish, including small shark. Later the government provided subsidies for imported black metal fish traps to catch spiny or rock lobster (Palinuridae, śīróx Śḥerēt, śayrəx Mehri). The advantage of the new fish traps was that small or female lobsters could be easily identified and thrown back into the sea. When the government subsidies were removed, people returned to catching spiny lobsters with gill nets; using gill nets, small and female lobsters could not be so easily identified and returned to the sea, thus leading to a reduction in both the number and size of the lobsters. This is described in the Śḥerēt text on fish traps (8.1.5.) below.

Traditionally, fishnets, fish lines (śɔ́r Śḥerēt, śwīr, pl., śwōr Mehri) and fish traps (ḳarḳór, pl. ḳarábḳər Śḥerēt) were all produced from locally sourced natural materials. Fish traps were made with fibre produced from twigs gathered from *Acacia senegal* (ṭū́r Śḥerēt, ṭəmmūr Mehri) and *Indigofera oblongifolia* trees ([a]ḥśít Śḥerēt; cf. Miller, Morris, and Stuart-Smith 1988), and from the 1980s, according to Watson's consultant in Raysūt, with imported bamboo (described using the term for 'slim camel stick [usually of bamboo]' bəkū́rət, pl. bəkūrū́nta Śḥerēt). Text 8.1.5. below (cf. also Miller, Morris, and Stuart-Smith 1988, 318) describes the traditional production of fish traps. Small branches and twigs would be chopped down from the trees in the wadi, in the case of *Indigofera oblongifolia*, and higher up from the wadi sides, in the case of *Acacia senegal*. These would then be placed in brackish water from a month to a month and a half to ret down. The retted fibres would be separated into strands and woven to produce the fish traps.

Gill nets, seine nets and cast nets used to be made from cotton, or from the Arabian Dragon Tree, *Dracaena serrulata* (ʕirób Śḥerēt, ayrōb Mehri), or from coir (bənj~bəng Mehri). The natural fibre would be twisted and woven to produce the net material. Gill nets would be placed in the sea with a float and a flag to signal its position, and a stone (limestone, ḳaṣṣ in Mehri) anchor to hold it in place.

Nets, lines and traps made from natural materials could be mended when they perished, but they were easily subject to rotting from the sun and the sea water. In text 8.1.5., the speaker says that you would place the fish trap in the morning and return to it in the evening or vice versa, because if it was left longer than seven or eight hours the number of fish inside the trap would cause it to 'explode'. The new nylon nets and lines, by contrast, do not perish as easily, but they cannot be mended, because 'they were made in the factory'. Thus, the independence of fishers regarding their equipment and their control over it diminished markedly with the production of factory-made fishing tackle. Nylon was said by Watson's consultant in Raysūt to have been introduced in 1968, and by the Mehri consultant from Ḥadbīn around 1965. The aluminium fish traps were introduced in the early 1980s. The Mehri text 'Fish Traps' (8.2.1.) below is the transcribed and translated video of a Mehri fisherman describing the parts of an aluminium fish trap available in the Mehri archive at ELAR.

References

Dostal, Walter. 2009. 'Die Beduinen Südarabiens und das Meer: Sozialanthropologische Beobachtungen über den Sardinenfang'. In *Philologisches und Historisches zwischen Anatolien und Sokotra: Analecta Semitica In Memoriam Alexander Sima*, edited by Werner Arnold, Michael Jursa, Walter W. Müller, and Stephan Procházka, 17–25. Wiesbaden: Harrassowitz.

Geva-Kleinberger, Aharon. 2009. 'Maritime Terminology in the Mehri-Language of the East Coast of Yemen'. In *Philologisches und Historisches zwischen Anatolien und Sokotra: Analecta Semitica In Memoriam Alexander Sima*, edited by

Werner Arnold, Michael Jursa, Walter W. Müller, and Stephan Procházka, 51–62. Wiesbaden: Harrassowitz.

Miller, Anthony, Miranda J. Morris, and Susanna Stuart-Smith. 1988. *Plants of Dhofar, the Southern Region of Oman: Traditional, Economic, and Medicinal Uses*. Muscat: Office of the Adviser for Conservation of the Environment, Diwan of Royal Court, Sultanate of Oman.

Randall, John E. 1995. *Coastal Fishes of Oman*. Honolulu: University of Hawaii Press.

Sima, Alexander. 2009. *Mehri-Texte aus der Jemenitischen Šarqīyah*. Edited by Janet C. E. Watson and Werner Arnold, in collaboration with ʿAskari Hugayrān Saʿd. Wiesbaden: Harrassowitz.

Watson, Janet C. E. 2023. Harvesting the Sea in Central Monsoon Dhofar and al-Mahrah media files, https://doi.org/10.5683/SP3/ZC3IGS, Borealis, V1.

Watson, Janet C. E., and Miranda J. Morris. 2015. 'The Modern South Arabian Languages'. *The Middle East in London: Endangered Languages* 11 (5): 9–10.

Watson, Janet C. E., and Miranda J. Morris. 2016a. Documentation of the Modern South Arabian Languages: Mehri. ID: Mehri (0307). Berlin-Brandenburg Academy of Sciences and Humanities. Endangered Languages Archive (ELAR).

Watson, Janet C. E. and Miranda J. Morris. 2016b. Documentation of the Modern South Arabian Languages: Shehret. ID: Shehret (0308). Berlin-Brandenburg Academy of Sciences and Humanities. Endangered Languages Archive (ELAR).

Watson, Janet C. E., Miranda J. Morris, Abdullah al-Mahri, Saeed al-Mahri, Munira al-Azraqi, and Ali al-Mahri. 2019. 'Modern South Arabian: Conducting Fieldwork in Dhofar, Mahrah and Eastern Saudi Arabia'. In *Arabic Dialectology: Methodology and Field Research*, edited by Werner Arnold and Maciej Klimiuk, 91–107. Wiesbaden: Harrassowitz.

8. Texts

The texts in this section are divided into Ṣ̌herēt and Mehri texts. Where the same speaker provided more than one text, his texts are given together, with a short description of the speaker for the first text in the set. Note that a forward slash indicates intonation break in the transcription.

8.1. Ṣ̌herēt Texts

8.1.1. Diving for Abalone

This text was recorded by Janet Watson on 4 October 2015 in Leeds on a Marantz PMD661 solid state digital recorder with an external Audio-technica microphone. The speaker was in his early 30s at the time of recording. He comes from Sadḥ and is a member of the Bit Amir Gid subtribe of Bit Samōdah. The audio recording can be accessed from Borealis or the ELAR Shehret archive by entering in the search box 20151004_ShehetEJ_J108 _abalonediving.

1. nḥaʰn / ḥanūṭər leš nāṣənun be-ṣirb / nāṣənun min ʿōnut də-ʿōnut / yizḥom eṣirb / her zaḥám eṣírəb / eṣírəb yikin beš ġobṣ / yiġiṣ yɔ̄ erɛ́mnəm / gere ṣfúźaḥ

We are now going to tell you about the post-monsoon period. Now from one year to the next, the post-monsoon period comes. And when the post-monsoon period comes, it is time for diving people dive in the sea for abalone.

2. yɔ̄ / yibtilún / gere ġobṣ / yiśtīm ēlmɛ́thum / yiśtīm emlɛ̄bisɔ̄hum / šabāb^A yiśtōm (sic) yiśtīm ezˤānəf / yiśtīm emlabs ɛ-ġobṣ / b-iśtīm ɛkšɛ̄m

People prepare themselves for diving. They buy their equipment. They buy their clothes. Young men buy flippers. They buy clothes for diving. They buy goggles.

3. min munəhum yɔ̄ / iź eġēg ēta / ol ˤad yixodem / yilɔ̄s elebs^A lo / yilɔ̄s bass hīfót be-flāyīn / b-īkin šohum ^Ayistaxdimu^A ˤar jezɛ̄r[11] / yiġiṣ ˤar be-jezɛ̄r iź kol ˤōnut

Some people, older men, don't use, they don't wear specific clothes; they just wear shorts and vests. They have, they just use matchets; they just dive with the type of matchets that were used in the past.

4. b-īnɛ́ṯ zete ṭo^hn / īnɛ́ṯ zéte tebtəlún gere ġobṣ xaṭoḵɛ̄sən b-elibssən be-srilotɛ̄sən / īnɛ́ṯ / be-her zaḥám ġobṣ be-ġoṣ eyɔ̄

And women do likewise, women also prepare themselves for diving with their dresses and clothes and undertrousers, women. That is when the diving season comes and people dive.

5. eġēg yibġíd min k-ḥáṣaf / yibġid min k-ḥáṣaf / de yibġód śe be-minhúm yibġíd ˤak hūrún / minhúm yibġíd ˤak sayyārúnta iġiṣ min ḵeśór

---

[11] *jizɛ̄r* have a long broad blade with wooden handle.

Men go from the morning. They go from the morning, some of them go in boats, some of them go in cars and dive from the rocks.

6. šẽˁaš hit / nḥaʰn nsójel nah / ε: zeyn^A

Are you listening? We are recording now. Good.

7. min źahún d-īġiṣ ˁaḵ hūrún yikin yɔ̃hum atġĩd ˁaḵ šūm (ˁaḵ) hūrí / yibġíd min k-ḥáṣaf b-īġiṣ be-her ber ġoṣ u-ber šóhum ṣfúźaḥ / bə-ˁaḵ... ēġēṣɔ̄hum / ˁaḵ eśigód

Those who dive from boats will spend the whole day under the sun in the boat. They dive from the morning. They dive and when they have dived, they will have abalone in their collecting nets.

8. eśijód yikin inεh

What are collecting nets?

9. śójəd yikin lebre / ḥanit / śójəd śe d̠e-nēlūn be-śe d̠e-xīyét / lebre śójəd / lebre / aywah^A / lebrε eśójəd yiḥótələš ṭanuh min lḥaḵ ε-ḥaḵɔ̄hum¹² / tḥótələš be-ḥaḵḥaḵək / śójəd

A collecting net is for whatsitsname... such-and-such, some collecting nets are made of nylon and others of cord, for the collecting net for, yes, for the collecting net. The collecting net they tie like that from around their waist string. You tie it round your hips, the waist-net.

---

¹² ḥóḵə 'thong worn by men from boyhood below the waist'. (The Bəṭāhira believe that 'if you do not give a boy a ḥóḵə he will never grow to be a real man'; Miranda Morris, pers. comm.).

10. *ah*

Yes.

11. *be-thī̃l ʕamḳəš esfúźaḥ / her ber šek ṣfúźaḥ / tɔ̄ḳaʕ ʕaḳ śójəd / teṣmím / bə-haṣɛr miźi śójəd / ber miźi śijədɔ̄hum yidíri / minhum ɛ-koll ɛ-d-īġiṣ ʕaḳ hūrí / yinújəf ʕaḳ hūrí / b-īšúnax s̃ĩn / mġora tidūrən yiġiṣ / koll ɛ-šɛh d-īġiṣ min ɛʰr / yidúrɛ ʔɛʰr*

And you carry the abalone in it. When you have abalone, you put them in the net to collect (them) together. And when the collect-ing net is full, when their nets are full, they come back up; those who dive from boats tip them into the boat and rest a little. Then they go back to dive, those who dive from the land come back to the land.

12. *b-īšúnax elohún ṭɛr ḳiśór / be-śe be-xalɛ́l ṭɛr / ʕaḳ ḥaṣ̌ / b-īšírek s̃ḗhīhum b-īšúnax / mġor yidūrən yiġiṣ / be-šum ṭahu:n ed kɔ̄lʕayni / ber īġiṣ śaʰliṭ ġēṣ / ber īġiṣ ġobṣɛ́t ṭrut / ber īġiṣ orbaʕ ġēṣ / fhimš̃ hit*

And rest a little on the rocks, and some in bays on the beach, and they make their tea and rest. Then they dive again, and they keep doing like that to the early evening. Some dive three times, some twice, and some four times. Do you understand?

13. *b-īźanuh šuʰm / yɔ̄ kal se lo / de yiġiṣ ġózər / ġabbēṣún / yihōrət eġózər / be-de yiġiṣ ʕaḳ ɛ̃sir be-de yiġiṣ s̃habɛ́t be-de yiġiṣ s̃habɛ́(t) ṭrut / de śeliṭ s̃hāb*

And that is them. People aren't all the same, some dive in deep waters, divers, they go down deep, and some dive to the depth of a man, and some to the depth of one stroke, and some to the depth of two strokes, some three strokes.

14. *s̃hāb ínɛh*

What are strokes?

15. *eshabét yˤū̃r / eshabét ġabṣét / her nāṣanu he ˤū̃k ṭanuh / dinūn eshabét / eshabét / eshabét hes bɔ̄ˤ / be-flo bɔ̄ˤ ṭruh / śaʰṭít bīˤíta / b-eġēg yɔ̄ kall ġabbēṣún kall ᴬnafs aš-šīᴬ lo / de yġiṣ ġózər / de yġiṣ ˤak ˤamk / eshabét ṭrut be-śeliṭ s̃hāb / be-de yġiṣ b-ɔ̄ṭih ˤak ē̃ṣír*

A stroke, they say a stroke is a dive. If now if you do like that (makes to swim one stroke), that is a stroke, a stroke. A stroke is like from fingertip to outstretched fingertip,[13] or two or three fathoms. And men, all divers don't do the same thing. Some dive deep, some dive a middle depth, two fathoms or three fathoms, and some dive down from above the surface within their depth.

16. *s̃ē̃ˤaš hit*

Do you understand?

17. *bē-ṭohun / her s̃ahkót erémnəm axɛr / yistaġallūᴬ eyɔ̄ yifórah eyɔ̄ axɛr be-s̃ahak yihōrət aġaʰl / yilhik edəlɔ̄f źə-b-āġáʰl / b-īnḗṭ kadālikᴬ / b-īnḗṭ her ˤágab tġáṣən / thójərən s̃ahak / haṣɛr s̃ahkót lesen erémnəm rhim yˤū̃r yɔ̄ s̃ahak nśḗk / nśḗk / thōrtn īnḗṭ kśóšən ˤak edlɔ̄f / tkśóšən / tġólkən ˤak edəlɔ̄f gere ṣfúźah / ˤak... ē̃ṣir lo / aġal min ē̃ṣir / ˤak eskfótsən bē-ṭaʰn*

And like that, and when the tide has gone right out, people exploit it. They prefer the tide to be out and they can go further down. They can reach the bigger rocks that are further down,[14]

---

[13] I.e., a fathom.

[14] And revealed by the low tide.

and women do the same thing. Women, if they want to dive, wait for the tide to go out. When the tide has gone out properly, people say *šaḥak nṣēk*[15] *nṣēk*, women go down and collect shellfish from the bigger rocks. They look among the rocks for abalone, not at a standing depth, less than a standing depth, while sitting like that.

18. *šē̃ʕaš hit / be-kɔ̄layni yinufṣ́ / yinufṣ́ koll ɛ-šɛh be-ḥallɛ́t yinufṣ́ də-ḥallɛ́t yibġód ḥallɛ́t b-īḥifṣ́ ṣfúźaḥɔ̄hum / b-īśīm ṣfúźaḥɔ̄hum / b-ɛ-šɛh be-gyɛl be-flo ʕak ɛ̃rábkɛz / yibġíd ɛ̃rábkɛz b-īkin šóhum ɛ̃rábkɛz yɔ̄ tigɔ̄r / yikin šeš merkɛ́z / merkɛ́zə / ḏahun (= lahun) / b-īšírek ḳit gere ṣfúźaḥ* (sic) *ġabbɛ̄ṣún*

Are you listening? And in the early evening they leave. They leave, and everyone from the town goes to the town. They go to the town, and they gather up their abalone and sell their abalone. And those who are from the mountains or the centres go to the centres. Traders have centres. They have a centre, a centre. Here they make food for the abalone (sic)—for the divers.

19. *šē̃ʕaš hit / b-īzhím də-lahín b-īśīm ṣfúźaḥɔ̄hum / de yišimdɛd ḳarošēš / kɛš*[16] */ yiḥíl drēham mdīd* (sic) *mdɛd / be-de yisójələn / ʕādatan*[A] *yikin nḥaʰn tasgīl*[A] *tōlēn axɛr /* [A]*ettasgīl ʕabārah*[A] */ yizídək / maṭalan*[A] *her kun saʕr*[A] */* [A]*xamsīn*[A] *ḳerōš / ettasgīl*[A] *yikin* [A]*xams we-xamsīn*[A] */ xamsīn be-xū̃š*

Are you listening? And they come here and sell their abalone and receive their money as cash—they take their payment as

---

[15] √*nṣk* 'to dry out'.

[16] English 'cash'.

cash and some register. Usually it is better for us to register, and regis-tering means you receive more. For example, if the price is 50 OMR, by registering it would be 55 OMR, 55 OMR.

20. b-ɛ-šamdéd yḥī̃l xamsīn kḗš / b-ɛ-sógel yisógələn ɛd mid̠ túẑar ˁabārah^A túẑar śḗm / mit d̠ə-śḗm / yixtarígən mən ^{A}xams wa-xamsīn^A / xamsīn be-xū̃š / b-ɛ-šamdéd yišamdéd be-xamsīnḗš kḗš ḥaṣɛr d̠i^{h}n

While those who sell for cash would receive 50 cash, those who register until the trader sells, when they sell, it will work out at 55, 55, while those who take cash would get their 50 at that time.

21. šḗˁaš hit / be-d̠anun šɛh ġobṣ / nāṣənū / nāṣənún / ˁak ḥakī̃t / ˁū̃rót ṣfúźaḥ ḳel / be-ˁédem / be-ˁōnut tū̃naˁ / be-ˁōnut fotḥ mūsəm^A / ˁōnut yikin ġobṣ be-ˁōnut yū̃naˁ / eyɔ̄ yiḳófəl / yˁū̃r gere l-ˁod ṣfúźaḥ źanuh tanġard̠an^A flo ˁod at-tamū̃n be-flo ṭa^{h}n

Do you understand? And that is diving. Now, now in the time of the government, it says that the abalone have become less, and they will die out, so one year they forbid (diving) and one year the season is open. One year there will be a diving season, and one year it will be prohibited. People close (the sea), they say so that those abalone won't die out, won't come to an end or suchlike.

22. šḗˁaš hit / b-īkin tawˁīyah^A / gere yɔ̄ / yaˁni^A baˁl ^{A}asmāk^A / b-eyɔ̄ iẑanū baˁl ^{A}senen al-baḥr^A / yihorg kə-ġabbḗṣún / b-ol ḳorfəd be-dəlɔ̄f / b-o-t̠hamūl^A kəśḗfót / yistaxdamū^A kśḗfot ˁak erémnəm / b-ol tḳorfəd be-dəlɔ̄f / b-ol xorb egidirít / ġɔ̄ṣ / ġobṣ / nṭif / gere

tḥāfaḍu[A] *l-eṣfúźahɔ̄kum / be-gere ṣfúźaḥ tkinən ol ˤod tənġarḍan*[A] *lo maṭalan*[A] *aw innū ol ˤod temū̃n lo*

Do you understand? That is raising awareness for people, I mean fishermen and those people who work by the sea tell the divers not to overturn the rocks or take (underwater) torches, or use torches in the sea, or overturn the rocks or wreck the envi-ron-ment, diving (should be) clean in order to preserve your abalone, so that the abalone don't become extinct and don't die out.

23. *be-tkinən eṣfúźaḥ təktóren be-tsnúdən gīl*[A] *ḏanuh b-egīl*[A] *ɛ-sireš b-egīl*[A] *ḏak ayɛ́nka*ˤ */ fhimš̃ hit /* [A]*hāḏa be-nisbah*[A] *l-ɛġobṣ / her də-ˤod śe suwēl*[A] *śe ṭānī*[A] *be-flo śe ḏ-ol foṭank toš lo* [A]*allāhu l-ˤālim*[A]

So that the abalone increase and are sufficient for this genera-tion and the next generation and the generation after that. Do you understand? This is about diving, and if there are any more ques-tions or anything I haven't remembered, God alone knows.

8.1.2. Shark Drying

This text was recorded by Janet Watson on 10 November 2014 in the fisherman's house in Ḥāsik together with Alec B. M. Moore. The speaker is from Bayt Kamd and was in his mid-40s at the time of recording. He also provided text 8.1.3. The re-cording was produced on an Olympus LS-11 digital recorder. The audio recording can be accessed from Borealis or the ELAR Shehret archive by entering in the search box 20141110_ShehretEJ_J042_sharkdrying.

1. *aywah*[A] / *lxim ēb yiḳośaʕəš yɔ̄* / *kīźúm* / *nāṣən lo* / *kīźúm* / *zamān*[A] *ɛ-kīźúm ʕad o śe heš saʕr*[A] *lo* / *lxim ēb yiḳóśaʕəš yɔ̄* / *yiśḳiḳəš yizḥam beš mi r-rémnən yirudəš b-īźex* / *be-flo be-šakəh* / *šakəh yʕūr̃ heš*

Yes, large shark would be dried in the past. Not now, in the past. In the past, when it wasn't yet worth much, large shark were dried: they would cut it open along its length, gut it and then open the trunk out flat. They would bring it from the sea and put it in gill nets or with a long line with many side lines called *šakəh*.[17]

2. *inɛh iźex inɛh*

What are gill nets?

3. *iźéx de yʕūr̃ heš* / *iźéx ɛ-lxim* / *yʕūr̃ heš mlɛ́šaġ* / *mlɛ́šaġ* / *yikin iti* / *yʕūr̃ heš malšġah*

Some people call them *iźéx*, gill nets for shark, they call them *mlɛ́šaġ*. *mlɛ́šaġ* are large. They call them *malšġah* (in the singular).

4. *lxim ēb* / *yɔ̄ yiḳóśaʕ*

Large shark, people dry (it)?

5. *aywah*[A] / *elxim ēb yiḳóśaʕəš yɔ̄* / *li-məddət* / *xĩš ēm šɛt ēm ṭanuh* / *šɛh b-īźḥotš* / *b-iśḳiḳəš* / *kīźúm yiśḳiḳəš* / *yixanúṭ* / *ʕalaf*[18] / *zaʕānɛ̃š k-ēnúf* / *yišerək iźéx* / *b-iźex šabkah*[A] *yʕūr̃ heš mlɛ́šaġ* /

---

[17] 'Longline fishing' in *Wikipedia* (accessed 26 March 2024): Longlining used a long line, called the main line, with baited hooks attached at intervals by means of branch lines called snoods.

[18] Dhofari Arabic.

mġor yiškikəš / ˤalaf k-ēnuf īḏɛn k-ēnufs / b-eḏarbét / b-eḏanúb ḏaʰn kall yiḥū̃š k-ēnfóf / yəkun yaˤṭuf k-ēnfóf

Yes, large shark used to be dried for around five or six days, like that, together with salt, and they would cut it up. In the past, they would cut it up and remove the fins. The fins would be on their own. They would make gill nets, and the gill nets they would (also) call them *mlḗšaġ*. Then they would cut it up. The fins would be on their own, the pectoral fin on its own, the dorsal fin and the caudal fin, they would be all taken. They would be all gathered together.

6. *b-ette ḏahun ɛ-biḳi / yišerek heš mižḥót / erɛš yirudḗš / erɛš o yḥī̃š de lo / erɛš ɛ-lxim / yirúdi beš / erɛš / b-aˤṣ́ḗṣ́ yikin beš* (sic) *də-losk b-ette / yiḥū̃š / ɛm erɛš yirudḗš / be-šebdét ɛ-lxim / šebdét / yiḥū̃s / yiḳolaˤəs ˤaḳ tinkét / flo ˤaḳ deram / h-ēṣiftəs / yišerek ṣift / ᴬnafs aš-šī / aywahᴬ / yˤū̃r hes ṣift*

And the remaining flesh, they would add salt to it. The head would be thrown away. No one would take the head. The head of the shark would be thrown away. The head and the bones, they would be attached to the meat. They would take it, the head they would throw away and the shark liver, the liver, they would take it and put it in a tin container or in an iron drum, for its oil. They would make shark-liver oil. The same thing, yes, they call it *ṣift*.

7. *šebdét ɛ-lxim yiḥū̃s / yišerk hes ṣift / yiḳólaˤ ˤaḳ dirēmēt / kižúm yɔ̄ / yū̃šaḥ bes yɔ̄ ezˤām her ijḥabsən / her ijḥab bə-zaˤī̃t / yū̃šaḥ bes ezaˤī̃t ezaˤī̃t / yišórək ṣift ḏoʰn*

They would take the shark liver. They would make shark-liver oil from it. They would put it in drums, and in the past people used to oil their wooden boats with it when they brought them to dry land. If they brought a boat in, they would oil the boats with that oil, they would use that shark-liver oil.

Figure 6: Shark liver, al-Ġayḍah

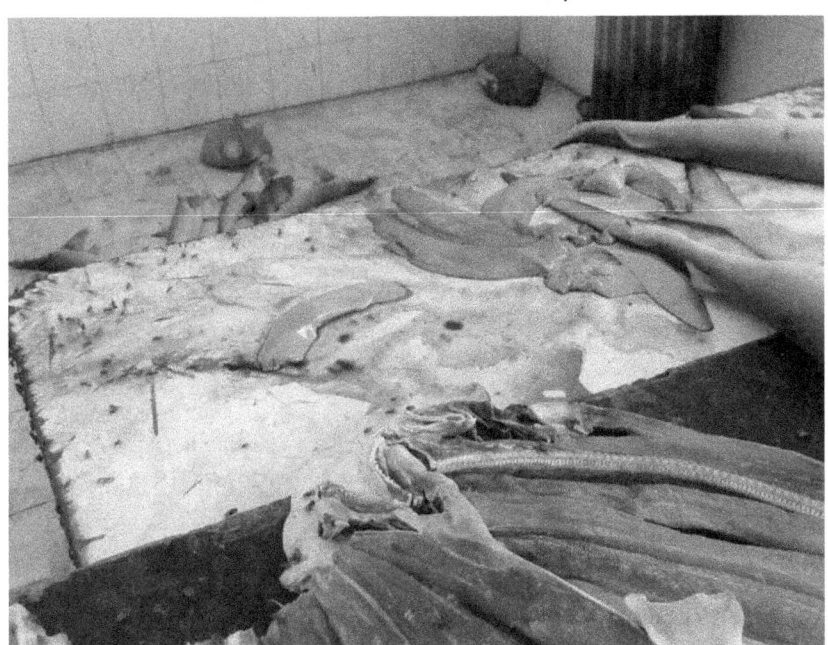

Photo © Janet C. E. Watson, 2013

8. be-lxim ḏahun yɔ̃ləḥəš b-īḵolˤaš fiṭrah[A] / lxan (sic)… [A]yōmēn ṭalāṭah[A] / de rīˤ ēm / ˤaḵ ĩẓaḥót ḏohun / mən ṭɛr rīˤ ēm yinúteb beš / yiḵośaˤəš / b-egdirít / ṭɛr ḥasəlil[19] nṭif / yiḵólaˤš ḏahun b-īḵerfédəš / ay / lxim / ber śḵiḵ / lxim / b-ījumaˤš b-ījumˤū / toʰn

---

[19] Bəṭāḥrēt ḥaṣəlṣīl, pl. ḥaṣəlṣāl or ḥaṣəlīl, pl. ḥaṣəlāl, small smooth pebbles, stones; Hobyōt ḥaṣalīt (s. and pl.), small, smooth stones, pebble(s) (Miranda Morris, pers. comm.).

And that shark they would salt it and leave it for a while beneath (sic)... for two or three days, some (would leave it) four days in that salt. After four days, they would take it out and they would dry it on the ground, on clean stone. They would leave it there and turn it over, yes, shark, it would be already cut up, the shark, and they would gather it all up, like that.

9. ^{A}ba^{ʕ}d fiṭrah^A / ber šóhum mɛ́kən / yiśīməś / tijjór iźan ba^{ʕ}l lanjɛ̄t yiśīm lxim / ḏa^{h}n kiźum lxim ēb / amma^A lxim niṣán / ḏa^{h}n i^{ʕ}ūr heš nḥa^{h}n síbəli / lxim niṣán n^{ʕ}ūr ḏa^{h}n ykīn l-ɛ^{h}r / n^{ʕ}ūr heš síbəli

After a while, when they had a lot, they would sell it. Traders on the large ships would buy shark, in the past large shark. As for small shark, that we call *síbəli* (milk shark and other small shark spp.), the small shark would be near to the shore, we call that *síbəli*.

10. *síbəli*

síbəli shark.

11. aywah^A / kaś^{ʕ}ún / síbəli ḏahun / ḏahun síbəli / yišerekš / seréf / fokḥ ṭroh / erɛš yerudi beš / b-eḏanúb irudēš yikin niṣán / yišerekš / seref ṭanuh / yikośa^{ʕ}əš / aywah^A / y^{ʕ}ūr heš ^{ʕ}awal^A / don šɛh

Yes, it is dry, that milk shark (or sliteye shark or smoothhound shark),[20] that *síbəli* kind, they would split it in two. They would throw away the head, and the tail they would throw away, it is

---

[20] Milk shark, sliteye shark and smoothhound shark are all known as *sibəli* in Śḥerēt. Bəṭāḥrēt distinguishes between different types of *sibəli* (Miranda Morris, pers. comm.).

small. They would fillet it like that and dry it. Yes, they call it ˤawalᴬ (when it is dry). That's it.

12. ˤawalᴬ

ˤawalᴬ.

13. ˤawalᴬ ahaʰn / ykin ber ḳaśáˤ / fīh būʰn yɔ̄ yišerekš nawˤaynᴬ šɛh

Yes, ˤawalᴬ. That is when it is dried. Here people do two types of it.

14. be-śḥerēt yˤū̃r heš inɛ́h

What do they call it in Śḥerēt?

15. be-śḥerēt yˤū̃r heš / lxim ḳeśˤún bassᴬ / nīṣán

In Śḥerēt, they just call it dried shark. (It is) small.

16. yikin síbəli

It is síbəli shark (or sliteye shark or smoothhound shark).

17. yikín síbəli / aywahᴬ / síbəli / síbəli ḍahun / nḥaʰn nˤū̃r heš síbəli / be-šeh nīṣán / m-elxim ēb yˤū̃r heš elxim ēb bassᴬ / ḍon nīṣán síbəli / nˤū̃r heš lxim nīṣán síbəli / ykin lxim / aywahᴬ

It is milk shark, yes. That milk shark, we call it síbəli (milk shark and other small shark spp.), and it is small; and large shark they just call large shark. The small one is síbəli. We call small shark síbəli (milk shark, sliteye shark or smoothhound shark). It is shark, yes.

18. be-yiḳośaˤ yiḳośaˤ síbəli ˤaḳ / ˤaḳ ūt / flo ˤaḳ soṭaḥ

And they dry, they dry small shark in the house or on the roof?

19. ˤaḵ ūt / ṭɛr soṭḥ flo ˤaḵ ūt flo ˤaḵ śīnš šrēbik / ḏ-ol śe yilḥaḵo-hum lo ˤar iṭˤol b-iźa^Hn ḥayawanāt^A lo / yiḵóśaˤəš / yikin aywah^A yiḵolbəš ˤaḵ / de yiḵoləb ˤaḵ tinkét ˤaḵ emih / be-de yũlaḥš ˤādi^A / be-de yišorek miźḥot ˤamḵeš / lɛkin axɛr her ḵolaˤk ˤaḵ emih miźḥót / mih ɛ-rɛ́mnəm / yiṭólaˤ ˤófər rḥim / yiṭólaˤ nṭef axɛr / d-iśūm / de riyālayn^A / de riyāl^A / ḥaḵ ɛr ḵiśaˤ / ḵeśˤún maḥtāj^A / ḏa^hn síbəli

In the house or on the roof or in the house or in, have you seen those nets, so that foxes and such animals can't reach them. They dry it. They put it in, some put it in a tin container with water, and they salt it, and some people put salt in it. But it is best if you put it in salt water, sea water, it turns out nicely red and turns out cleaner. They sell, some for two riyals, some for one riyal, when it is dry, and it is properly dry. That is *síbəli*.

20. yiḵośaˤ b-egdirít

Do they dry it on the ground?

21. ɛ̄ b-egdirít / yallāh^A b-egdirít / yiḵóśaˤ b-egdirít be-śe ṭɛr ḵud her šek ménzel rḥim / ṭɛr sóṭaḥ / yišérek heš ḵud / b-īḵólaˤəš ṭɛr ḵud ḏa^hn / flo de b-egdirít / ˤaḵ šarābīk^A21

Yes, on the ground, on the ground. They dry it on the ground or on a line if you have a suitable place, on the roof. They put up a line for it, and they put it on that line, or on the ground on nets.

22. ṭɛr ḵud

On a line.

---

[21] Dhofari Arabic.

23. yikin / aywah^A / ṭɛr ḳud yikin ṭaʰn gans ette her ikbeb ette lo / yikin ṭɛr ḳud / šɛh ṭaʰn yśerek ḳud ṭaʰn / yśerek ḳud ṭaʰn sīda^A / ōḳa^ʕ ṭērəś ṭaʰn / ol ʕad yimī gdirit lo / ykin mertafa^ʕA / mən ḥaši / mən ḥayawānāt^A / ol ʕad itīś lo / ykin nṭef axɛr / ṭɛr ḳud / y^ʕalḳənəś ^Aaywah ʕalayś nūr^A / y^ʕalḳənəś

Yes, that is okay, on a line, like they do with strips of meat. It will be on a line, like that. They make the line straight, and you put it on it like that; it won't be too close to the ground. It should be high up away from the dust so that animals don't eat it; and it is cleaner on a line. They hang it, yes, you are right, they hang it.

24. bə-flo b-egdirít her nṭift b-o śe ḥaši lo / ṭɛr ḥasəlíl rḥim nṭif / yikśa^ʕ b-egdirít ʕādi^A / yiṣolḥ axɛr / ḏaʰn mən nāḥiyat^A esíbəli / amma^A lxim ēb yiśūm ʕar bə-jumalēt^A ṭoʰn faxra / kiźúm / nāṣan yiḥū́ś kallaś ber kumblit[22] nāṣan ber iśīmś ^Akāmil bass^A / l-ēreś be-l-ez^ʕān be-śebdét kāmil^A yiśīmś ṭoʰn / šarikāt^A / kiźúm kol śe ʕar kiś^ʕayn be-miźḥót be-ṭanuh

Or on the ground if it is clean and there is no dirt. On pebbles that are clean, it can be dried just like that on the ground. It will turn out better, that is in terms of the *síbəli* shark. In terms of large shark, they used to all get together to sell it wholesale in the past. Now they buy and sell (the shark) whole with the head and the fins and the liver. They sell it like that to the companies. In the past, everything was dried with salt, etc.

---

[22] From English 'complete'. The whole shark.

8.1.3. Sea Lemon

This text was recorded on 10 November 2014 by Janet Watson in the fisherman's house in Ḥāsik, on an Olympus LS-11 digital recorder. The audio recording can be accessed from Borealis or the ELAR Shehret archive by entering in the search box 20141110_ShehretEJ_J042_sealemon.

1. *eśidíf / yikin ɛxxóḳeš inɛh*

The sea lemon, what does it look like?

2. *śidífə / xoḳeš jins eśenḥót / lākin ēb*

It looks like a chiton, but big.

3. *yikin ʿaḳ erɛmnəm*

Is it in the sea?

4. *yikin ʿaḳ erémnəm / yikin ʿaḳ ḳəśɔ̄r ʿaḳ šáḥəḳ erémnəm / ʿaḳ šáḥəḳ ɛ-rémnəm / yikin ʿaḳ ekəśór / gins ɛ-śenḥót yikin / yʿūr heš śidóf*

It is in the sea. It is on the rocks when the sea is out, when the sea is out. It is found on the rocks, like a chiton. They call them *śidóf* 'sea lemons'.

5. *ay ahaʰn / bə-xoḳeš inɛ́h*

Yes, and what does it look like?

6. *xoḳeš / šakleš^A jins ɛ-danuh / jins ɛ-śenḥót / śənáḥ / lākin ēb / yikin / akbar^A mes / b-īkin də-ləsk bə-fədənín / ʿaḳ erémnəm aḥyānan^A yikin / ʿaḳ erémnəm / yikin ʿaḳ erémnəm / o yiṣ̌hor be lo šɛh / yikin ʿaḳ erémnəm*

It looks like, it looks like that, like a chiton, chitons, but large. It is bigger than that, and it sticks to the rocks in the sea, sometimes it is, in the sea. It is in the sea. It doesn't appear much. It is found in the sea.

7. *śīdíf ay / beš kaḥf*

The sea lemon, does it have a shell?

8. *beš kaḥf / lā^A kaḥf gins έ-taˤmέr egins έ-ṣfuẑḥót lo / b-egins έ-ḥalekimma^{23} lo / kaḥfš yaxtalif^A / ṭan twābiq^A / ṭa^{h}n / daragāt^A šerok ṭa^{h}n gins ṭa^{h}n daragāt^A / lebre*

It has a shell, but not a shell like the abalone, and not like the grapsid crab; its shell is different. It comes in layers like that, it has steps it makes like that steps, like...

10. *lebre gɔ̄d*

Like leather?

11. *aywah^A lebre jɔ̄d / jɔ̄dəš ḥārád / yiŝxənúṭ ˤar bə-ḥadīd^A*

Yes, like leather. Its skin is hard, and only comes off with a metal implement.

12. *aha^{h}n*

Yes.

13. ... *bə-skīn flo bə-ḥadīd^A o yiŝxənúṭ lo ṭabέˤï^A / txanuṭ ˤaš mġorέ ḥak-έr širokk iẑó^{h}n śīdíf / txanṭəš bə-txanúṭ / beš te / bə-də-ḥāḳál laḥm jins jins šakl^A jins έ:- / ḏanuh / eśənáḥ / lέkin yikin ēb xέrɛn*

---

[23] The audio gives *ḥalέḳ*, but most probably should be *ḥalekimma~ḥarkimma*, a type of swimming crab.

xanuṭs̃ ḏahun te ʿamḵeš də-ḥāḳál / yɔ̄ḵaʿ ḏahun ekaḥf aʿāli trúdi beš

Figure 7: Sea lemon, Ḥāsik

Photo © Janet C. E. Watson, 2011

With a knife or with a piece of metal, it doesn't come off easily. You remove from it (the tough skin) and then when you have done those sea lemons, you remove it and you remove, it has meat, inside is meat like, like, like (that of) a chiton, but it is a bit bigger. You take out that meat in it from inside. You take the upper shell and throw it away.

14. tḥı̃l tīš də-ḥāḳál / ʿak lhafheś leš / ʿādi / b-id ʿak tīš nū ṭabéʿi[A] / śīdíf / mā məškilah[A] b-o b-iṣ̄or lo / yaʿni[A] te mən ġér ḏoʰr / o šɛ́h beš ḏoʰr lo gens śenḥót / yʿoḏer lo / yitīš yɔ̄ ʿādi[A]

You take the meat that's inside. If you want to boil it, that's okay, the sea lemon. And if you want to eat it raw, that's okay. There's no problem, and it doesn't harm, I mean, the meat is without blood. It doesn't have any blood, like the chiton, it doesn't harm, and people eat it normally.

8.1.4. Shellfish and Snails

This text was recorded in Mirbāṭ by Janet Watson in February 2014. The speaker, from the Bit Amir Gid subtribe of Bit Samōdah, was around 40 at the time of recording. He was brought up in Jufa and married into a family in Mirbāṭ. The recording was produced indoors on a Marantz PMD661 solid state digital recorder with an external Audio-technica micro-phone. The audio recording can be accessed from Borealis or the ELAR Shehret archive by entering in the search box: 20140226_ShehretEJ_J008_shellfishandshells.

1. ˤankólot hókum be-ˤaŝfór[24] / be-fheré / mintok mən ˤaŝfór yikín be-ḳaśiríta īźáʰn be-ḳeśór / ḍahún ˤaŝfór / ˤaŝfór yikín ˤaŝfór / b-īkín zikt / b-īkín śənáḥ / ḍanū yɔ̄ / kiźúm her ḥa-yfūt mən hērət də-ˤod kiźúm zamān^A ḳaṭˤát / be-d-ˤod eḳeḥáṭ be-ṭaʰn ḳeḥaṭ / yiḥofś yɔ̄ ˤaŝfór / yitī ˤaŝfór

I'm going to tell you about shellfish and snails. Shellfish are found on the rocks, on the rocks by the sea, that is for shellfish.

---

[24] ˤaŝfór refers both to generic edible shellfish and to turban shell winkles specifically. With attributes, ˤaŝfór denotes different subspecies: ˤaŝfór ḥɔ̄r 'small black winkle', ˤaŝfór hōśún 'large black winkle', ˤaŝfór eśīror 'topshell'.

Shellfish include turban shells and rock oysters and chitons. Those people in the past, if they were dying of hunger... in the past there was a lack of food, there was a dearth of food, and people would collect shellfish. They would eat shellfish.

2. *yɔ̄ ḳíźźún eníṣún / yindírhum yɔ̄ zikt / ezikt / yiḥanítəs / yixɔ́lṭəs ṭaʰn yiṯḥīnəs / ʕaḳ emih be-ṭanuh be-ḥaḳ-ērɔ́t nafs emih / yɔ̄zəməs ḳallɛ́n ʕaḳ ḥanš̃ít / ezikt / nafs^A enúśəb š̃īn / kīźúm lā zamān^A / yɔ̄zəməs ḳíźźún / yinúdərs ḳíźźún / ezikt / be-ʕaš̃fɔ́r / yitīhum yɔ̄ / yitīhum eskún be-d-ʕod nāṣáh / yiḥū̃hum ɛ̄t*

In the past, people would feed small children rock oysters. Rock oysters, they would do such-and-such, they would mash them up, they would liquidise them in water like that and when they became like water, they would feed them to small children in a clay (or shell) feeding jug, just like we do (now) with milk. In the past, you see, in the past, they would feed them to small children. They would feed babies with them, rock oysters, and (older) people would eat shellfish. Families would eat them and still do now. They take them home.

3. *b-ezikt də-ʕod nāṣáh ī́nɛ́ṭ / txodəməs / be-siḳ / be-ṭɔ̄ḳət / ṭɔ̄ḳət o-dʕak lo / be-siḳ ahaʰn / be-siḳ be-sedḥ be-ḥosk / īźanuh də-ʕod yɔ̄ d-ixɔ̄dəms / eḳɔ̄ti be-ʕaśīrít ḳarɔ́š̃ / ḳɔ̄ti ɛ-zikt ēb / be-ḳɔ̄ti nīṣán be-xū̃š̃ / ahaʰn*

And rock oysters, women still work them in Mirbāṭ and Ṭāqah. Ṭāqah, I'm not sure about, but definitely Mirbāṭ, and Mirbāṭ and Sadḥ and Ḥāsik. There people still make a living from them: one tin sells for 10 OMR, a large tin of rock oysters, and a small tin for 5 OMR. Yes.

4. *be-fḥeré / də-ʕod īźoʰn b-efḥeré / efḥeré yikín her kunut múse mɛ́kən / elḥamurún wəla doṭó / yikín yiśóni erdɛ́m efḥeré ṭɛr ṣīróftən / bə-de yiśúni ṭaʰn feḥrɛ̃t / yiʕū̃r heš yō feḥrɛ̃t / yinḥaj her bɛr kíśaʕ bɛr fɛ̄t / zamān^A yinḥój besen ḳiźźún / yinḥój besen ḳiźźún yiśórəksen / ḳiźźún yinḥój besen ṭoʰn gere yóġfol besen / b-īźáʰn ʕaśfór / be-fḥeré*

And snails. There are still those, and snails, snails are found if there is a lot of rain: *elḥīmər* or *doṭo* rains, then people see snails on areas of flat bedrock, and they see, people call it *feḥrɛ̃t*. When they are dry and have died they (the children) play, in the past people used to play with them. Children would play with them and do such-and-such with them; children would play with them so they could amuse themselves with them. And that is about shellfish and snails.

5. *mintok mən zikt / ezikt ḏinuh tkin nafs^A / lhis fudún / tiṭḳíḳenəs īnɛ̃t / tkin šesen / jiréd ḏe-ḥadīd^A / tiṭḳíḳenəs be-tənútəben / mḳoṣot ṭaʰn ette / ōḳənəs ʕaḳ inɛ šū̃əš hɛ / ʕaḳ ṣáḥan tōlísen / be-thũlensen / ttoljən ʕaḳ ṭallājah be-śe tōzəmenəš ɛ / hudūy / be-śe tīš sɛʰn*

And rock oysters. Rock oysters are like, like stones. Women knock them off the rocks. They have iron rods with them. They would bash at them and pull them off. The flesh is like a small bit of meat. They put them in, what's it called, in a bowl they have with them and take them and freeze them in the freezer. And some they give as presents and some they eat themselves.

6. *be-kol inɛh šū̃əš šɛh / kol in ʕagəb bisen tōzəmensen aktar śe ʕar hudūy / be-ttīsen / hudūy hadīt tōzəm yō ʕayśerɛ̄sen / be-ṣənáḥ / l-his / l-his / l-his ezikt / śənáḥ zete tśmĩnəs / be-her bɛr šisen ḳaḥf*

ḏə-… / ḏə-zikát / ɔ́ḵaˤ ṯēɾəsen his ˤāŝərī ŝənáḥ / ˤaŝírít iẑóʰn / ŝənáḥ / be-ḏan eŝənáḥa / be-ˤaŝfór / be-zikt / be-fḥeré /

Figure 8: Shellfish meal, Sadḥ

Photo © Janet C. E. Watson, 2016

And everything, what's it called, everything they want they give mainly as presents or eat them. Presents, a present, they give to their friends. And chitons are like rock oysters, chitons. Chitons they also collect, and if they have a clay pot of rock oysters, they will put on top of them around 20 chitons, or 10 of those chitons. And that is about chitons, and turban shells, and rock oysters and snails.

8.1.5. Fish Traps

The speaker of this text is a fisherman from Mirbāṭ in his late forties. The recording was produced on 3 August 2014 in Mirbāṭ on an Olympus LS-11 digital recorder by one of our data collectors from the Bit Amir Gid subtribe of Bit Samōdah, who also provided text 7.1.4. The data collector conducted the interview and appears in the text as interviewer, indicated by his questions. The audio recording can be accessed from Borealis or the ELAR Shehret archive by entering in the search box: 20140803_ShehretEJ_J040_fishpots.

1. ^{A}b-ism illāh ar-raḥmān ar-raḥīm / bə-nisbah^A li-xadəmɛ́t ɛ-ḳarábḳər ɛ-sīźób

In the name of God the merciful, the compassionate, in relation to making fish traps for rabbitfish,

2. yixódəm yɔ̄ ḳarábḳər iźanuh yilɔ́d yɔ̄ / yibǵíd mən bū^{h}n be-śḥɛ^{h}r / b-īlɔ́d ṭũr / bə-ṭũr ḏanuh yiṯḥinš ʿaḳ ḥarítī / orx / orx u-fóḳaḥ

To make fish traps people would cut down, they go from here to the mountains and cut down *Acacia senegal*, and this *Acacia senegal* they would crush it in brackish lagoons for a month or a month and a half.

3. mġor yinuśsš / ḥasɛr nśoss yiḥṹš b-īḳófʿaš / be-yiśérek ḳarábḳər eḳarábḳər źanuh irṣ̌ef / b-īrémnəm / ṭɛr šwāṭī^A ṭɛr iźanuh xalɛ́l iźanúh / ʿaḳ xalɛ́l mən tɛl yikin sīźób mən tɛl eyɔ̄ d-ġórob waḍaʿ^A sīźób ḏanuh

Then they separate the strands of the retted down fibre. When they have separated out the strands, they take these and weave them, and they would make fish traps. These fish traps are weighed down with stones in the sea, on the shore, or in small inlets, in places where there are rabbitfish, where people know there will be rabbitfish.

4. bə-kol in kisi ʕamḳóhum ṭabʕanᴬ yiṭifhum mən ṭɛr / ʕɛśar ṭrut ēm ʕɛśar ṭrut ʕɛśar ṭrut sāʕúnti bə-flo m-ṭer šɛt sāʕúnti / yiṭif yiṭif iẓanuh ḳarábḳər ḳarábḳər ɛ-sīźób

And they would find everything in them. Of course, they go and inspect them after 12 days (sic), 22 hours or 27 hours, they inspect the fish traps for rabbitfish.

5. lākinᴬ xadəmɛ́thum inɛ yśírek beš yɔ̄ / ḏaʰn ḳarḳór ɛ-ṭūr yol iśérek beš yɔ̄ / xadəmɛ́tš inɛ́h?

But how do people make them, rabbitfish fish traps made from *Acacia senegal*. What does it involve?

6. eḳarḳór ɛ-ṭūr / yizḥím bə-ṭūr / mən šḥɛʰr / be-ḥaṣɛr zaḥam be-ṭūr / enfēt yirhínš / yirhínš gére yirġóṣ lohum / ʕaḳ emih yirhín / ʕaḳ emíh / yirhínš ʕaḳ xāríti bə-flo b-irémnəm

For fish traps made from *Acacia senegal*, they bring *Acacia senegal* from the mountains. And when they have brought the *Acacia senegal* wood, first they put it in water to ret down. They ret it so that it softens and becomes flexible. They ret it down in water, in water. They ret it down in brackish inlets or in the sea.

7. aywahᴬ

Yes.

8. gere yirġoṣ lohum bə-ḥaṣɛr rhinaš ʕɛśer ēm / zēd núḳaṣ / yinuśsš / yinuśsš yaʕniᴬ yilɔ̄dəš / yilɔ̄dəš bə-yinuśsš nīṣún nīṣún

So that it becomes flexible, and when they have retted it for ten days, more or less, then they separate the threads. They separate the threads, they beat it, they beat it and separate it out into small strands.

9. *aywah*[A]

Yes.

10. *mġor yikófʿaš / yikófʿa... ḏanu kífaʿ ḏanuh / ykin heš xadəmέt / yišérek enfḗt rī̃t / rī̃t ḏinuh lo / tkin ʿamḵḗt / mġora yišérek śiḵát ṭit bɔ̄ṭih / bə-ṭit b-āġaʰl / b-īśírek heš xoh*

Then they weave it. They weave it. That weaving is an art. First, they make a long strip. That long strip is in the middle, then they do a section for the top, and a section for the base, and they make a mouth for it.

11. *ḏaʰn kalš mī̃ ṭ-ṭū̃r kīžúm / yixódəm yɔ̄ ḏaʰn kalš mī̃ ṭū̃r / mġorɛ ḥasɛr d-gáhaz / yiḵolbəš erémnəm / be-yaʿniʰ yišxadī̃š gere sīžób / gere sīžób*

In the past, that was all from *Acacia senegal*, people made it using *Acacia senegal*. And then, when it is finished, they put it in the sea and they use it to catch rabbitfish, for rabbitfish.

12. *leḵaláʿ mś ēm / ʿaḵ erémnəm?*

How many days do they leave it in the sea?

13. *her ḵlobk toš k-ḥáṣaf / ṭifš kɔ̄lʿayni be-ḵólobk toš kɔ̄lʿayni ṭifš k-ḥáṣaf / be-sīžób kīžúm mabjéd be-ṣud mabjéd yaʿniʰ b-īġárig lóhum lo / mən ʿóśər sāʿúnti tā ʿóśər ṭrut sāʿúnti / o yzḗd ol ṭanuh lo*

If you placed it in the morning, you inspect it in the late afternoon, and if you placed it in the later afternoon, you inspect it in the morning. And in the past, there was lots of rabbitfish, and lots of fish, so they wouldn't have to wait long, between ten and twelve hours, no longer than that.

14. yaʕni[A] be-her kísɛ her zēd l-ṭanuh yifójiš yifójərəš eṣud / linū[A] / gere ṭarób īźanu ərġaśíti / b-išxnúṭ meš eṣud / li-ḏālik[A] ḳolʕaš mən šɛt ɛd šūʕ sāʕúntī ṭūni sāʕúnti / b-īṭifš

But if they find, if they are left any longer than that the fish would burst it, burst it, because those sticks would be soft, and the fish would come out of it. For that reason, they would leave it for seven hours, eight hours and then inspect it.

15. ɛ: salēm hɛt / be-ḏa[h]n xadəmét ɛ-sīźób

Thank you, and that is about dealing with rabbitfish.

16. ḏi[h]n xadəmét ɛ-sīźób / be-nisbah[A] l-xadəmét ɛ-śīróx / kīźúm o śe ḳarábḳər gere śīróx lo / kīźúm śīróx yixódəmš yɔ̄ ʕar be-śēkíti / mġóra yišxədím heš yɔ̄ ḳarábḳər ɛ-sīźób / ḥaṣɛr zhūt šarika[A] ʕagyót be-sīźob (sic) be-śīróx ṣaḥḥi[A] / yišxədím yɔ̄ ḳarábḳər ɛ-sīźób gere śīrox / be-[A]ʕalā ṭūl[A] ḥaṣɛr / b-istamirr[A] yɔ̄ li-waḍa[ʕA] ḏahun miṭ mśēn ʕayún

That is about rabbitfish. With regard to catching spiny lobsters, in the past there were no lobster pots. In the past, people used to catch spiny lobster with nets, then they began to use fish traps designed for rabbitfish. When a company came that wanted a live lobster, people would use fish traps designed for rabbitfish for lobsters, and that was the case for several years.

17. axarēt zhūt ḥakīt / be-zhūt be-ḳarábḳər / ḳarábḳər ṭa[h]n ḥāríti / yʕūr ḳarábḳər aḥ-ḥakīt / źanuh ol mabgód b-ɛrṣ lo / ḥakīt sɛh zhūt bohum mən xārij[A] / be-zūthum ṣayyādīn[A] iź ixódem śīróx

And then the government came, and brought fish traps, black fish traps. They were known as government fish traps. They weren't to be found in the country before then. The government imported them. They gave them to fishermen who fished for lobster.

18. ʿūrót hohum śóxdam źanuh gere śīróx / līnu^A eḳarḳór ḏa^{h}n ɛ-zḥam beš / her ʿamḳəš śe niṣán be-flo ʿamḳeš śe ūnṭa^A iḳelob d-erémnəm / be-ḏahun śīróx ēb / yiḥū̃š / b-iśī̃š

(The government) said to them, use these for lobsters, because the fish traps they brought, if there was something small in it or a female, they would throw it back into the sea, and the large lobsters they would take and sell.

19. axarēt ^{A}yaʿni stamirr ewaḏa^{ʿA} ḏanuh / miṭ mśēn ʿayún / ^{A}min ṭummah^A / ḥakī̃t ol ʿad zḥū̃t be-daʿm^A lo / eḳarábḳər lo / aywah^A kēl eḳarábḳər yixorg eḳarábḳər b-iṣ̌ēʿ mən šūm / be-ṯḥ̃ihum erémnəm / eḳarábḳər / b-ol ḥakī̃t ol ʿot zū̃t yɔ̄ ḳarábḳər lo ḳolob yɔ̄ fene l-elxixt

Then the situation continued like that for a while, for several years. Then the government no longer gave any subsidy, no more fish traps, yes and the fish traps corroded and became unusable because of the sun or because they were taken by the sea, the fish traps. And the government gave people no more fish traps and people went back to using gill nets.

20. xodúm be-xodúm śīróx b-elxixt / ^{A}ṭabʿan ntījɛt^A ɛ-śīróx ɛ-xidim b-elxixət / boh erémnəm o bes ^{A}kammīyāt kabīrah^A mən eśīróx lo / ʿayún iźahun enfúti ed bísen ^{A}kammīyāt kabīrah^A ber yɔ̄ xulṣ̌š / b-ol ʿad śe ʿar ^{A}ḥājāt basīṭah^A

And they caught lobsters with gill nets. Of course, the result of catching lobsters using gill nets was that there are no longer a large number of lobsters in the sea. Those years where there were lots of lobsters, and now people had finished them off. You only see a few now.

23. nāṣənu her xdumk śiróx atizḫum ʕar be-^Aḥāgah basīṭah^A / o tinúfaʕ menfáʕ lo / bɛk zaḥamk be-ʕāśīrit kīlo bɛk ʕāśīrit ṭruh kīlo bɛk / yaʕni^A zēd be-núḳaṣ

Now if you try to catch lobsters you will only get a few, not enough to be of any use. You'll bring in around ten or twelve kilos, more or less.

24. lākin śiróx ḏanuh / íne šũəš śiróx da^hn ḫɔ̄r da^hn ḳarḳór ḫɔ̄r ɛ-śiróx / her ṭir / beš xadəmɛ́t yixódəmš yɔ̄

But that lobster, what's it called, for the lobster, that black fish trap for lobsters, if it got broken, is there anything that people could do to mend it?

25. lōb əl-xadum lo / ^Aʕalā ṭūl^A / ḏahun ^Aʕalā ṭūl^A yiṣ́yeʕ mən ḥaṣ ɛ̄ ṭir / ol xadum o beš śe lannu šɛh ʕar mn ẽṣnaʕ / ed-śīk ʕar be-xadəmɛ́t ẽṣnaʕ ol xadəmɛ́t ḏ-īd lo

No, nothing can be done at all. It's ruined from the moment it got broken. There is nothing one can do, because they just come from factories. They are made in the factory and not by hand.

26. zaḥám l-ēṭo^hn

They come like that (readymade).

27. zaḥám l-ēṭohun / be-her ṭēr / be-flo tētš šūm / be-flo xaróg / b-ol ʕod / yiṣ́yɛʕ be-yəʕboṣənš lo / abadan^A / yixalof ʕar ṭad ūdín

They come like that, and if they break, or the sun degrades them or they are finished, that's it, they can't be used anymore, at all. They have to be replaced with a new one.

28. *yixalof ʕar ṭad ūdín*

They have to be replaced with a new one.

Figure 9: Boys with broken fish trap, Mirbāṭ

Photo © Hugh Morris, 1970s

8.1.6. Making Fish Traps and Rabbitfish

This text was recorded by Janet Watson on 4 November 2015 in Sadḥ on an Olympus LS-11 digital recorder. The speaker is from the Bit al-Amri subtribe and was in his early 70s at the time of recording. He migrated to Kuwait for work from the 1960s, which shows in his occasional use of Arabic. The audio recording can be accessed from Borealis or the ELAR Shehret archive by entering in the search box 20151104_ShehretEJ_J046_makingfishpots_rabbitfish.

1. nḥaʰn kiźúm / ɛrṣ̌ ḏaʰn / ɛrṣ̌ ɛ-sədḥ / sədḥ / yɔ̄ išorek ḳarábḳər / ḳarábḳə(r) ɛ-ṭū̃r

We in the past, in this place, the place of Sadḥ, people used to make fish traps, fish traps from *Acacia senegal*.[25]

2. eṭṭū̃r inɛh

What is *Acacia senegal*?

3. ṭū̃r raġab ɛ: (...) šajarah^A

Acacia senegal is a branch, a tree.

4. hermi(ti) / herúm

Plants, a plant.

5. herúm / herúm / yilɔ̄d meš ṭarób / b-āxs̃t / axs̃t / ʕaḵ ṣ́ʕayb / be-ṭū̃r b-ɔ̄ṭíh

A tree, a tree, they chop the wood from it. And *Indigofera oblongifolia*, *Indigofera oblongifolia* in the wadis, and *Acacia senegal* from further up.

6. huṭuʰn

Where?

7. būʰn / ʕaḵ jiyɛl ḏan ɛ-s̃īn / ejyɛl kalləš / yikin beš ṭū̃r ṭū̃r / yilɔ̄d meš ṭarób ɛ-ṭū̃r / b-īlɔ̄d mən eṣ́ʕayb źanúh / yilɔ̄d axs̃it / yilɔ̄d / b-ijɔ̄rdəhum b-ijɔ̄rdəhum / erġēb niṣún / yinítəb bóhum / bə-šajarah^A (sic) / bə-ṭarób yiḳólaʕš / u-mġora yifóḳaḥš fóḳaḥ ṭroh ṭaʰn

---

[25] For flora descriptions, see Miller, Morris, and Stuart-Smith (1988).

Here in the mountains here by us. The whole mountain area has *Acacia senegal*. People chop wood from the *Acacia senegal*. And they cut down from the wadis, they cut down *Indigofera oblongifolia*. They chop (them) down and remove rough small twigs etc. They take the small branches and the tree, they leave the large ones. Then they split it in two like that.

8. *b-īḵóśaˤ / yiḵólaˤš / yũi ṭruṭ flo śileṭ ēm yiḵíśaˤ / be-ḥaṣɛr ḵiśáˤ / ḥaṣɛr ḵiśáˤ / yirhínəś ˤaḵ emíh / be-ḥaṣɛr / erġaś xērín / erġaś xērín / ḥaṣɛr erġaś xērín / yiḵófˤaš / yiḵófoˤ / b-īšírek ḵarábḵər / yišírek śiḵát ṭruṭ*

And they dry, they dry it for two or three days until it is dry. And when it is dry, when it is dry, they ret it down in water. And when it becomes softer and more supple, a bit suppler, when it is suppler, they weave it. They weave, and they make fish traps. They make two sections.

9. *b-īšírek erī̃š / b-īšírek xoh / ḏanuh yiḵólbəś ˤaḵ emih / ˤaḵ emih / aywah^A / b-āġá^hl / yišírek hes maḥbíṭ ṭa^hn / maḥbíṭ / beš fedənín / fedənín*

They make the long strip (that joins the top to the bottom), and they make the mouth. That they place in the water, in the water, yes, down. They make a wall for it, a low wall with stones, stones.

10. *emaḥbíṭ yikin*

What is the low wall like?

11. *maḥbiṭ ho^hr / lebre ḥo^hr / ḥɔ̄r ɛ-ḵarḵɔ̄r / yɔ̄ḵaˤ ˤamḵə(š) ḵarḵɔ̄r / yikin fədənín mi-bū^hn be-m-bū^hn be-m-bū^hn be-m-bū^hn / be-yɔ̄ḵaˤš bū^hn bə-yɔ̄ḵaˤ ṭīrəš / ṭit bū^hn / be-ṭit bū^hn / ṭit bū^hn / fedənín / be-*

xoh ber bū^hn xoh / ˤamḵəš / beš xoh / yɔ̄jaḥ ṣud ilahú^hn / b-īḥū̃š / eṣud ɛ-ṣaˤfót

The low wall is like a pen, a pen for the fish trap. They put the fish trap in it. There are stones here, here, here and here. And they put it there and place stones, one here and one there (to weigh it down), and the mouth is here in the middle, it has a mouth where the fish enter, and it captures them. The kind of fish with scales.

12. *be-xoh yikūn ɛmt ɛ:*

And the mouth faces?

13. *lā / yol jiyɛl yol jiyɛl / o ykin yol erɛ́mnəm lo / yikin ˤar ḥaṭíh / ṭa^hn / yol giyɛ́l / eṣud ɛ-ṣaˤfot / eṣud ɛ-ṣaˤfót / yitīš yɔ̄ / yitīš / yixoṣərən beš l-ḥit / bə-flo tū̃r*

No, towards the mountains, not towards the sea. It faces upwards (towards the land), like that, towards the mountains. (The kind of) fish with scales, fish with scales, that people eat. They eat it. They use it as a relish with rice or dates.

14. *be-sīźób / yiḵoṣ́ˤaš / b-īfhiśś / bə-mih ḏ-erɛ́mnəm / ˤaḵ dərḗm / dərḗm / dərḗm / ˤaḵ dərḗm / be-flo tinkét / be-flo ṣefərīt / ḥaṣɛr bíšɛ́l / yijúraḥš / yijuraḥ b-egdirít / b-īfolḵəš / yinútəb b-eṣaˤfót / b-inútəb serf ḏanuh be-serf ḏa^hn / b-inúteb ˤayśóś ˤaḵ ˤamḵ be-yɔ̄ḵaˤš o / yirúdi beš*

And rabbitfish, they dry it and boil it in sea water, in an oil drum, an oil drum, an oil drum, in an oil drum, straight-sided metal container with a screw-on lid, or in a pan. When it is cooked and ready, they spread it up. They spread it on the ground, then they split it into two. They remove the scales.

They remove the fillet on one side, and then the other side. They remove the bones from the middle. They don't leave them, they throw them away.

15. be-ḏanuh ṣud yɔ̄kaʕš ṭad ṭɛr ṭad ṭad ṭɛr ṭad ṭad ṭɛr ṭad / be-ḥaṣɛr tim / yiḥūš b-īkoṣʕaš ṭɛr / ṭəbjét rḥīt / ḥósəb ḥósəb

And that fish they place one on top of the other, and when they have finished, they take it and dry in on a good level place with pebbles.

16. ṭəbjét rḥīt

A good level place.

17. ṭɛr múkśaʕ rḥim / yɔ̄kaʕəš alʕayni / išḥayr / her o ṭof lo be-šóhum ṣud / yɔ̄kaʕəš ɛṭaʰn / ṭaʰn / ṭaʰn / ṭaʰn / lebre ṭaʰn nah / lebre ḏinuh

On a good drying place. They leave it in the evening today, and if they haven't inspected and they have fish, they leave it like that, like that, so that.

18. ey

Yes.

19. b-īkolʕaš ɛd kerére / lɛkin yikin yɔ̄ tōləš / ʕar ṭīrunta / b-ʕar iṯʕól / o ytīš / k-ḥáṣaf yikóṣaʕəš o ṭaʰn šɛh lo k-ḥáṣaf yišīrek beš ṭaʰn / yikólbəš / b-īkólʕaš [A]yōmēn / ṯelet iyyēm[A] / be-ḥaṣɛr kiśaʕ / kiśaʕ rḥim / yɔ̄kaʕ ʕak jūni / be-yɔ̄kaʕ yɔ̄kaʕ ṭahun be-xxalif [A]bə-l-maṯal[A] / ɛ-ṭaʰn b-ēṣud / ṣud eṯ-ṯāni[A]

They leave it until the next day, but there have to be people with it to keep off hyenas and to keep off foxes, so they don't eat it. In the morning they dry it. Not like that, in the morning they do like that. They turn it over, and they leave it for two or three days. And when it has dried properly, they put it in a sack, and they put, they put (it) like that and then do the same again, like that with the fish, the other fish.

Figure 10: Traditional fish traps, eastern Dhofar

Photo © Miranda Morris, 1970s

8.1.7. Shark-Liver Oil Lamps

This text was recorded by Miranda Morris in 1980 in Ḥadbīn on an Uher Report 4000L portable reel-to-reel tape recorder, 1981 model. The speaker, from the Shahri tribe, was an old man at the time of recording, from Ḥadbīn. The even-numbered sections are questions and interjections by Miranda Morris. The recording, 1980_J051_Tape4_Hedbeen_Side2_EJ_sharkliveroil lamps, can be accessed from Watson's Borealis dataset.

1. ṣift / yiśírək ṣift / be-yɔ̄kaˤ ˤamkəš ftilt / śṭərér

Shark-liver oil. They use shark-liver oil, and they put a wick in it, a strip of cloth.

2. ftilt mən śṭərér naˤ?

A wick from a strip of cloth, yes?

3. śṭərér / ftilt / be-yɔ̄kaˤs / erɛšs ˤak̮ eṣíft / b-erešs ˤalī d-enfíj b-śxōṭ ḏek ˤalī / wə-yəṣírid wə-yiśirók

A strip of cloth, a wick. And they dip one end of it in the shark-liver oil. The top end of it (the wick) sticks (out of the oil) and that end is set alight, and it makes a light and so it goes.

4. wə-ftilt ˤak̮ ínɛh?

And what is the wick in?

5. ˤak̮ ɛ-ṣift

In the shark-liver oil.

6. ṣift / miš^A śabḥ / ṣift?

Shark-liver oil, not fat, shark-liver oil?

7. lā her śe šīš śabḥ ˤamér šīš b-flo ˤak šīš ṣift

No, if you have fat, use that, or if you have shark-liver oil (use that).

8. ek̮aḥf ek̮aḥf? ṭaˤór?

A pot? A pot? Of clay?

9. ˤar k̮aḥf lā k̮aḥf ṭaˤór / k̮aḥf flo ṣafrayyət flo káˤab k̮erṭóṣ lo k̮aḥf lo / yiśirək ˤamkəš ṣifét / wə-yɔ̄kaˤ ṭers śṭərér lo

Just a pot, a clay pot, clay pot or a metal dish or some utensil or other or a carton—no! A clay pot. They put shark-liver oil in it, and they put the strip of cloth in it, don't they?

10. ᴬwa-hāḏa ftilt / yaʿni yaḥrak / wa-bə-l-layl lāzim tijurr šway-yah šwayyah miṯl hāḏaᴬ / tzīd ftilt

And this wick, I mean, it burns, and at night you have to keep pulling it out like this lengthening the wick?

11. ᴬlā lā tzīdᴬ lo / ssínud ṭit

No, no you don't lengthen it, once is enough.

12. ᴬṭūl il-layl?ᴬ

For the whole night?

13. ed túnjah

Until dawn.

14. kalʿayni kāl

The whole night?

18. ʿāṣər kalš / éwa

The whole night, yes.

8.2. Mehri Texts

8.2.1. Fish Traps

This text was recorded by video by Janet Watson in Ḥāsik on 11 November 2014 in the yard of the Governor's house. The speaker is a fisherman in his 50s from the Bit Thuwar subtribe, who lives in Ḥadbīn. He also provided the texts 8.2.2. and 8.2.3. The aluminium fish trap described here is made from meshed wire, concave hexagonal in shape, with flat top and bottom sections, a mouth in the centre of the inner concave, and a section on the side which can be opened to remove the trapped fish. The video recording can be accessed from Borealis or the ELAR Mehri archive by entering in the search box 20141111_MehriHask_M044_fishtrap. It should be viewed together with the transcription/translation.

1. ṣarōmah ḏōmah / xahh

Now that is the mouth.

2. xahh / xahh ḏ-əḳərḳōr

The mouth, the mouth of the fish trap.

3. wə-ḥābū mət yəḥaym yərṣāfəm tah yəṭarḥəm tah l-ūṭōmah

And people, when they want to weigh it down (with stones), they lay it like that.

4. wə-ḏ-īḳōbəl abarr / ḏ-īḳōbəl abarr / bərk ərawrəm ḏ-īḳōbəl abarr yəkūn

And it (the mouth) faces the shore. It faces the shore. In the sea, it should face the shore.

5. wə-ḏīmah śikkāt ālūt / śikkāt

And that is the top section, the (top) section.

6. wə-ḏīh ərīt / ərīt / ḏīmah

And that is the side wall. The side wall, that.

7. wə-ḏih śikkāt awxayt

And that is the base section.

8. *wə-ḏōmah ʔayōb / yəfətk mənh əṣayd / ʔayōb*

And that is the (door or) part from which the fish come out.

9. *ahā̃ / mət barh / mət barh bərkih əṣayd / ahā̃*

Yes, when it, when there are fish in it, okay,

10. *nnəgfih ūṭōmah grē yftēk mənh əṣayd mən ḥalahm*

we tip it like that so that the fish come out from there.

Figure 11: Modern fish trap, Sadḥ

Photo © Janet C. E. Watson, 2016

11. *wə-mət barh nḥōm nərṣ̌əfh / nāmōl xīṭayt bawmah wə-nrəṣnəh*

And when we want to weigh it down (again in the sea), we put a string here and bind it,

12. bass^A lagrē l-ād yəftēk mənh əṣayd lā / wə-hēh ḏōmah / ḏōmah / əḳərnēt yʔamrəm hīs

just so that the fish don't escape from it. And that there, that they call the corner.

13. wə-ḏīmah ākōt / ākōt

And that is the front rounded part, the rounded part.

8.2.2. Shark Nets

The speaker was interviewed by Janet Watson on 11 November 2014 in the Wali's house in Ḥāsik, recording on an Olympus LS-11 digital recorder and simultaneously on a Canon HDXA20 video recorder with external Audio-technica microphone. The speaker is the same as for text 8.2.1. The audio and video recordings can be accessed from Borealis or the ELAR Mehri archive by entering in the search box 20141111_MehriHask_M044_sharknets.

1. əlyawx hāśən

What are gill nets?

2. əlyawx k-ənhōr ḏə-ġōzəl wə-śī ḏə-bəng / bəng / bəng mən harmayt / bəng mən harmayt / yəḥaṭməm tah / yəḥaṭməm tah mət barh / xīṭayt ḳəwīyət / yəwaśam tah / yəwaśam tah yāmīləh śabk / śabk ṭwayl / śabk ṭwayl

Gill nets in the past (were made of) cotton and some from coir, coir. Coir comes from plants. Coir comes from plants. They would twist it. They would twist it until it became strong cord. Then they would knot it. They would knot it to make nets out of it, a long net, a long net.

3. *ahã̄*

Yes.

4. *wə-yāmīl bih ḳayd mən aġawf wə-ḳayd mən xōṭər mən aġawf bih krīb / krīb*[26]

And then they would make a cord above and a cord below. Above there would be floats, floats.

5. *aywah*[A]

Yes.

6. *ʔalāmah*[A] */ gərē yəṭfēf / wə-mən xōṭər ṣwayr*

A flag (as a marker) so that it would float, and beneath were stones.

7. *hāśən mən ṣwayr*

What type of stones?

8. *ṣwayr / ādi / ṣwayr ḳəṭ mən əḳā*

Normal stones, stones just from the ground.

9. *ḳəṣḳayṣ*

White pebbles?

10. *lā lā ṣwayr ḏə-ḳaṣṣ*

No, no, limestone stones.

11. *ḏə-ḳaṣṣ / ahã̄*

Limestone stones, okay.

---

[26] A line of floats attached at intervals along the top rope from which the gill net is suspended (Miranda Morris, pers. comm.).

12. yāmīl bih ṣwayr ḏə-ḳaṣṣ / wə-yəraṣnəm tēsən mən xōṭər grē yənṣāb / ykūn śabk his ūṭōməh aġawf / məmtadd / ḏə-mattəd w-ārayś / mən aġawf bih krīb / yətfūfən bih ṭār ḥmoh / ləgrē ūxaym mət ḏə-nūka / yāḳā bərk aʔamḵ / yəmanah / yəġnūḵ[27] bərkih ūxaym m-boh m-boh / lə-hān əbēlī hərzəḳawk / ərəzḵ^A m-hāl əbēlī wə-ḥābū ṭakməh sabab^A

They would use limestone stones and they would tie them beneath so that it (i.e., the gill net) would stay upright. The net would be above like that stretched out, stretched out and wide. Above there would be floats that would float above it on the surface of the water, so that when sharks came, they would land in the middle. It would catch them. Sharks would be throttled in it here and there, as much as God blessed you with. Blessings come from God and people rely on that.

13. wə-ṭād / ḏə-ġōzal / ṭawrən his tah ūṭakm / ḏə-ġōzal mən əkaṭan ṭawrən / yəwaśam tah / yəwaśam tah ḥābū / wə-yāmīl his əmġadfēt lākin aʔaynəh nōb his ūṭōməh / wə-... wə-hēh ṭwayl / ṭawrən / ṭwayl ūṭakm wə-yāmīl bih krīb

There would be one (net) from cotton, also like that one, of cotton, of cotton too. They would knot it (to make nets). People would knot it, and they would make nets like cast nets, but the eyes of the mesh would be large like that, and it would also be long, long like that, and they would make floats for it.

---

[27] This probably should be from √xnḳ 'to throttle'; however, the audio clearly has /ġ/ in place of /x/.

14. ṭwayl hīs ḥāśən

How long?

15. ṭwayl / hīs / m-bawmah tā ṭār agārᴬ ḏēk / ṭwayl / ʕəšrayn bāʕ / ʕəšrayn / wə-śī / śalāṯayn / wə-śī xamstāšər / ʕalā / ʕalā ḥisəb / kullᴬ aḥād l-əmḳədawrəh / kullᴬ aḥād l-əmḳədawrəh

As long as from here to the asphalted area over there, (that) long: 20 metres, 20 and some would be 30, and some 15. It all depends, each according to their ability, each according to their ability.

16. ṭād aḥād ših ḥābū yəkadrən yāmīl ṭwayl / ḥābū ār ṭād walā ṭroh yāmīl ḳsayrayn

Some people had others who were able to make a long one. If there were only one or two people they would make it shorter.

17. wə-yallah-yi / wə-hūwāri / ār ḏə-ṭarb / gərr / yəgrawr bə-ġādūf / yəgrawr / yəgrawr ahã̄ / bərk ərawrəm / yāmīl bih / ġādūf yāmīl bih lawḥ / wə-hēh ṭarb / ūṭōməh / wə-yəgrawr bih / śī lā məkāyinᴬ

Like that, and dugout canoes were made of wood, and (people) would row with paddles. They would row. They would row, yes, in the sea. They would fashion paddles from planking, and it was a wooden shaft like that, and they would row with it. There weren't any engines.

18. lā lā

No, no.

19. wə-yəradyəm bih bawməh / yənakam / b-ūxaym ḥazāzī

And they would set them (i.e., the gill net) here. They would bring in black tip (or bull or grey reef) shark.

20. yənakam bə-hā́śən mən ūxaym

What types of shark would they bring in?

21. ūxaym / aywah^A / yənakam bə-hazāzi / ḏəmāwi / wə-ynakam bə-għərat / wə-ynakam bə-šīṣa / wə-ynakam / bə-mənsūfəh / wə-ynakam bə-səbli / wə-ynakam bə-gerēnīyəh / əlyōməh ḏə-bawməh

Shark, yes: they would bring in blacktip (~bull~grey reef) sharks (also known as ḏəmāwi), blacktip reef (~bramble) sharks and lemon shark. And they would bring in mansūfəh shark, and small síbili-type (one-piece) shark and larger gerēnīyəh-type (one-piece) shark—those (shark types) that are to be found here.[28]

22. wə-mġōrən yəśīm əh-ḥābū / wə-šīṣa / w-aʔābadyət / ʔābadyət ahã̄ / hōh ṣarōməh mġōrən mət śīnək tēhəm / hām śink wə-hām śīkəm ṣūrəh^A / əkūlət̲ hīkəm bə-həmətīhəm

And then they would sell them to people, and lemon shark and guitarfish. Guitarfish, yes. Now if I could see them. If I saw and you had pictures, I could tell you their names.

23. ^A wə-hāḏa l-ḥayāh^A ḏə-k-ənhōr ḥābū ʔār ūṭōməh šīhəm śī nīlū lā / šīhəm śī kyūd kyūd yāmīl mən əʔarf / təkṭayl

And this was the way of life before. People didn't have nylon, and they didn't have thread, apart from what they made from the desert palm, Nannorrhops ritchiana, təkṭayl.

24. təkṭayl hāh

What's təkṭayl?

---

[28] Shark are often named according to their size/age.

25. ət-təktayl ḥədāgəh / ḏə-śwūr / yāmīləs ḏ-əġōzəl / yəḥaṭməm tēs / yəḥaṭməm tēs ḳəṭənīn / wə-mġōrən yāmīləs / yəṣabġəm tēs bə-hrūm hamməh xarṭərīt / xarṭərīt / hrūm / yəṭkawkəh / wə-yṭarḥəm tah bərk ṣəfərayyət / wə-yəṭarḥəm tēs śwūr bərkih / grē tāḳā ḥūrūt / grē aṣayd l-ād yəśnēs lā wə-tāḳā ḳəwayyət

təktayl is *Citrullus colocynthis* for the lines, they would make it from cotton. They would twist it to thread. They would twist it very fine, and then they would make it. They would dye it with a plant called xarṭərīt (*Hermannia* sp.) a plant called xarṭərīt. They would pound it, and leave it in a pot and put the lines in with it so that it becomes black, so that the fish wouldn't see it and it would be strong.

26. wə-yāmīl bīs əkəlīw / ḥədayd / wə-ykatlən bīs / aywah[A] ḥədayd ḥədayd

And they would make a hook out of metal and line-fish with it. Yes, iron, iron.

27. ahā̃ / inɛh šūəš

What is it called?

28. ḥədayd / ḳəlīw ḳəlīw

Metal, a hook, hook.

29. ḳəlīw

A hook.

30. ləgrē ykatlən bih āṣāb / āṣəbīt / wə-rīdək / wə-ḳəlawwat / wə-ṭarān / əlyōməh yəkatlən bih ḥābū mən əbarr

So that they could line-fish emperor, and rock cod, and snappers and pompano. People would line-fish these from the shore.

31. *ahã̄ / hēt / hēt tk̲ōtəl*

Yes. You, did you line-fish like this?

32. *lā / hōh / lā əl-hōh ād lḥakk l-əlyakməh lā / lāmalhəm / lākin lḥakk ḥābū šīhəm əlyōməh / lḥakk tēhəm šīhəm əlyōməh də-yāmīlhəm*

No, that was before my time, to do that. But I did know people who had those things. I did meet those who used to make them

33. *wə-mġōrən ḥābū mən əttōli / nakam bīhəm mən mən barrah / də-hēm d̲-əġōzəl / ət-tāmōlən tēhəm məkāyin^A / k-ənhōr ār bə-ḥāditīhəm / bū mən ^Aəl-xamsīnāt mən əs-sittīnāt^A ū-boh / nakam ḥābū bīhəm mən mən mən barrah / nakam bīhəm mən dəbay wadak mən ḥō̃h lā / mən ūk̲ōn mən kūrīya*

And then people brought them from abroad, those of cotton that machines make (now). In the past, they were just handmade. From the fifties and from the sixties on, people began bringing them in from abroad. They brought them from Dubai, and I don't know from where else, perhaps from Korea.

34. *yāmīlhəm wə-hēm d̲ə-k̲əṭən / wə-mtəlayh nūka naylū d̲ōməh mən hīs nḥah fəṭnan*

They made them and they were of cotton. And then nylon came, in the time we remember.

35. *mayt nūka naylūn*

When did nylon come in?

36. nūka naylū bə- / ᴬyimkin xamsah wə-sittīnᴬ / wəṭōmah / bərk ᴬxamsah wə-xamsīn aw / sittīn aw xamsəh wə-xam[sīn]ᴬ / hāk bərk tārīx ḏōməh nūka nīlū / nūka ṣ̌yūġ ḏə-nīlu / wə-nūka layx ḏə-naylu / lyawx / wə-nūka mġədfayt ḏə-naylu / kośśīyən kalləh naylū ḏōməh / l-ād nūka ḳəṭən lā / linna ḳəṭən / tmōna snēt / mġōrən təṣ̌yē'

Nylon may have come around (19)65, around then, around (19)55 or (19)60 or (19)55. Around that time nylon came in, broad-meshed seine nets of nylon and gill nets of nylon, gill nets, and cast nets of nylon. Everything was made of nylon. There wasn't any cotton anymore because cotton would last a year and then become useless.

37. wəlā snēti ṭrayt hām ġayg yəḥafləs w-əġayg ādəh yəhtamm bīs / wə-mākini nīlu ṣarōməh mən ōśar snay yəmōna / hām əl-bəṣrīh əṣayd wəlā wīḳa ṭār ḳəśōr lā / wə-hēt thaflih / yəmōna xaymah snay hitt snay / wə-ḏīməh sēh ṣarōməh ʿāšū ḥābū l-ḏīməh əhḥənīt

Or two years if a man took good care of it and paid attention to it, but as for nylon, it would last for ten years, if fish didn't tear it or it didn't end up (snagged) on the rocks. If you took good care of it, it would last five or six years. And that's it now, people lived that whatsit.

8.2.3. Cast Nets, and Sardine Catching and Drying

The speaker was interviewed by Janet Watson on 11 November 2014 in the Wali's house in Ḥāsik. This text was recorded audio-visually on a Canon HDXA20 camcorder with an external Audio-technica microphone and saved as an MTS file. Only significant interviewer interjections by Watson are reproduced in this transcription. The video recording can be accessed from the ELAR Mehri archive by entering in the search box 20141111_MehriHask_M044_castnets_sardinecatchinganddrying.

1. *taww / amġōdəf*

Okay, cast nets.

2. *amġōdəf / amġadfēt ḥābū yəġadfəm bīs ġōzəl / yəwaṣam tēs bə-ḥāditīhəm*

Cast nets, for a cast net that people use to cast is of cotton. They knot it [into nets] with their hands.

3. *w-əġōzəl hāh*

And what is *ġōzəl*?

4. *əġōzəl kaṭən / mən kaṭən / yāmīl ḥābū / yāmīl / yəġazləm tah / ta ykūn kṭayn / xīṭayt ṭanuh / wə-ywaṣam tah / yəwaṣam amġadfēt ḏ-əṣayd / wə-ywaṣam amġadfēt ḏ-əʔayd / wə-ywaṣam śōgəd / śōgəd ḏ-iślawl bih aʔayd / yəġadfəm b-əmġadfēt ʔayd / mġōrən yəhḵāʔəm tēs bərk śōgəd wə-yəślawl yəhḵaśam tēs aʔayd / 'sardīn' atēm tʔamrəm*

ġōzəl is cotton, of cotton people make it. They work [the thread] until it is fine, a thread like that, then they knot it; they knot cast nets for fish, and they knot cast nets for sardine. They also knot collecting nets, collecting nets that they carry the sardine in. They use cast nets to catch sardines, and then they put them into a collecting net, and they take them to dry, the sardines. You call them '*sardīn*'.

5. *w-amġadfēt tkīn (sic) / amġadfēt tkūn / nōb*

A cast net, a cast net is large?

6. *aywah*[A] / *tkūn sʾayt ḏirɛʾ* / *ṭamənīt ḏirɛʾ* / *ūṭōməh* / *əḏirāʾ ḏah* / *ḏōməh ūṭōməh* / *ṭamnīt* / *wə-sʾayt* / *bass ūṭōməh* / *wə-yġadfəm bīs mən abarr ḥābū* / *yəġadfəm bīs ʾayd* / *wə-yġadfəm bīs ṣayd ḏə-sīẓ́ōb*

Yes, it will be nine cubits (span from elbow to tip of extended middle finger), eight cubits, like that. That is a cubit, like that, eight or nine, just like that. And people cast them from the shore. They catch sardines in them and catch rabbitfish.

7. *wə-yġadfəm bīs əgišrān* / *wə-yġadfəm bīs ədwayr* / *ḏōməh ḏ-əṣayd* / *w-əmġadfēt ḏ-əʾayd yġadfəm bīs ār ʾayd* / *mət nkōt ʾayd* / *ṣayf šahr xamsah* / *tnōka ʾayd* / *ḥābū yġadfəm bīs ʾayd* / *wə-šīhəm śōgəd yəślawl ʾayd yəhkaśam tēs u-mġōrən yəśīməs lə-bʿili əbkār* / *bʿili amōl* / *ḥārawn* / *wə-hibēr w-əbkār* / *grē ʾayd bars kśayt*

And they catch yellowtail scad in them, and they catch mullet in them. That is for fish, and the sardine cast net is just for catching sardine. When sardines come, in the summer, in May, sardines come, and people cast for sardines. They also have a collecting net. They take the sardines and dry them and then they sell them to cattle owners, livestock owners, for goats, camels and cows, because the sardine is dry.

8. *wə-fark bayn*[A] *əmġadfēt ḏ-əʾayd w-əmġadfēt*

And what is the difference between a cast net for sardines and a cast net?

9. *ḏ-aṣayd*

For fish?

10. *ḏ-aṣayd ahã*

For fish, yes.

11. śī lā / ār aʔayn

Nothing, apart from (the size of) the eye (i.e., of the mesh).

12. ār aʔayn

Just (the size of) the eye.

13. aʔayn ḏ-aʔayd əkannitt / aʔaynəs / ḳannitt ūṭōməh / ʔayn / śabk / wə-mākən ḏ-əṣayd nōb tkūn grē tkūn xfīft / wə-ḏ-əʔayd ḏīməh ḳannitt / wə-yāmīləs ʔayn ḳannitt

The eye for sardines is small. Its eye is small like that, the eye of the net, but for fish it is large so that it is lighter. And the one for sardine, this one is small. They make it with small eyes.

14. wə-hīboh yəġadfəm

And how do they cast (the net)?

15. yəġadfəm tēs bə-ḥādītīhəm / yəmanam tēs ṭār ḥaydəh / ykūn bīs ərṣōṣ / yāmīl bīs xīṭayt mən əxxōṭər / wə-rəṣṣayn / wə-mġōrən yəġadfəm bīs / wə-mət bars b-əḳā / yəġawṣ aġayg wə-yəślēs / yəślūl rəṣṣayn rəṣṣayn rəṣṣayn attā yəmnɛʔ axxahh / tkūn bār bərkīs ayd / yənagfəm tēs bərk śōġəd wə-yəślawl / ḥābū

They cast it with their hands. They take hold of it on top with one of their hands. It has lead weights (around the circumference). They make a cord from beneath and lead weights, and then they cast it. And when it has reached the bottom, the fisherman dives down to get it. He gathers up the weights handful by handful until he takes hold of the mouth [of the net]. There will be sardine in it. They tip them into a collecting net and people carry (them) off.

16. *wə-śōgəd ykūn hīboh*

What is the collecting net like?

17. *śōgəd ykūn his amġadfēt / lākin mrabbaʔ / bih xahh / wə-mən xōṭər ānbīt / wa hēh ṭwayl / ykūn śāṭayt ḏirɛʔ / śāṭayt ḏirɛʔ ṭawləh ṭawrən / wə-xxahh ykūn ūṭōməh / yəmanah aġayg ūṭōməh / lannū ūṭōməh ṭanuh bərk ḥaydəh / yəmanah / wə-yəṣbūb lih ʔayd bərkīs wə-ymōna xahh wə-yəślaləh ṭār āṭəməth / wə-yəsyūr*

The collecting net is like a cast net, but square. It has a mouth and at the bottom it is wide. It is long, it will be around three cubits, its length will be three cubits, and its mouth is like that. The man will take it like that, he will hold it like that in his hands, and pour sardine into it and take hold of the mouth and carry it on his back. Then he will go.

18. *wə-yəsyūr*

And he will go.

19. *yallah-yi / wə-yəḳawśa b-əḳā / b-əḳā / yənagfəm tēs / ṭār ḥayḳ / ṭār əraml / baṯḥ lā / yəhḳaśam tēs wə-mġōrən yəḳarfidəs bə-ṭīrōb / mən txīs / aʔayd / wə-mġōrən wət bār ḳśōt / yəślawləs wə-ydafnəm tēs bərk abaṯḥ wə-ydafnəm tēs bə-baṯḥ / attā ḥawl*

He will go, and he will dry (them) on the ground. They tip them onto the beach onto the sand, not on dust(y) ground). They dry them and then turn them over with sticks to stop them from spoiling, the sardines. Then when they are dry, they take them and bury them in dry earth and bury them with dry earth, until the same time a year later.

20. *tā ḥawl*

For a year.

21. *tā ṣayrəb / yəślawləs bərk əzōhi / bərk əxśīb / əxśīb ḏə-ṭīrōb / ḥanyōb / bāti śīrɛʔ / wə-yśīməs / bə-ṣəfōr wə-bə-sawk / wə-bə-sadḥ / bʕili hibēr wə-bʕili abḳār wə-bʕili ḥārawn yəsiġ hīsən h-amōl mət śī rḥəmēt lā*

Until the post-monsoon period. They take them in boats, in boats, in large wooden boats, sailing boats, and sell them, in Dhofar and in Mirbāṭ and in Sadḥ, to camel and cattle and goat owners. They scatter them (in fodder) for livestock when there is no good pasture.

22. *wə-ṣarōməh / ḥāyōm əlyōməh / ād aḥāḏ yəśtōm ād aḥād yəśtōm ʔayd*

And now, nowadays, does anyone still buy (them)?

23. *aʔayd*

Sardines?

24. *aʔayd mən bʕili mōl*

Sardines (do any) of the livestock owners (still buy them)?

25. *ṣarōməh / ḥābū / yəġadfəm ʔayd wə-yśīməs ār ṭiryīt / bərk ṭallājāt^A / wə-yśīməs / yəśīməs lə-ssawk / yəśīməs bərk swāg^A / məskūt / wə-dubay / wə-ṣəfūr / wə-ytawyəm tēs ḥābū ṣarōməh / yətawyəm tēs ḥābū / wə-l-ād aḥād yəhkaśas lā / yallah^A yəśtīməs / yallah^A*

Now people cast for sardines, but they sell them fresh, to cold storage vans, and they sell them. They sell them in markets, in

Muscat, Dubai and Dhofar, and people eat them now. People eat them. No one dries them anymore. They sell them. Yes indeed!

26. *l-ād aḥād yəhḳaśas lā*

No one dries them anymore.

27. *lā / ṣarōməh ād aḥād... wət ṭawr / wət sēh mēkən / yəhḳaśam tēs bʿili ḥārawn wəlā bʿili hibēr / w-abōḳi ṣarōməh bʿili sayyārāt[A] ār bərk əṭṭalg[A]*

No, now no one, only occasionally, if there are a lot (of them), goat owners or camel owners will dry them, and the rest now (are sold to) cold storage vans.

Figure 12: Hauling in sardines, Salalah

Photo © Janet C. E. Watson, 2011

8.2.4. How the ġaṣbīt hibˤayt Fish Got Its Name

This text was recorded in the speaker's house in the town of al-Ġayḏah, Yemen, on 14 April 2013. The Mehri dialect spoken here is known as Mahriyōt (Sima 2009). The speaker, from the subtribe of Bit Bakrayt, was in his mid-50s at the time of recording, and was brought up in the mountains above Ḥawf. He also provided text 8.2.5. The audio recording can be accessed from Borealis or the ELAR Mehri archive by entering in the search box 20130414_MehriMo_M005_howGhaSbiitHibaytGotItsName.

1. hīt ḥāwēl šxbərš tō min ɛh / ˤamərš hīni hāśən axah ġaṣəbīt hibˤayt wkoh / ᴬayš maˤnā / yaˤniᴬ ġaṣəbīt hibˤayt / ˤamūrən zamānᴬ / yəkaltəm ḳuṣṣāt / ˤamūrən ḏīmah / ġaṣəbīt hibˤayt / ṣayd ḏōmah ḏə-hummǝh ġaṣəbīt hibˤayt / ˤamūrəm / ḥōjəm tīs / hibˤayt ġyūj / yəḥaym yəġdafəms aw yəlḳafməs / mġōr ˤamūrəm / ḥōjəm tōs / hībˤayt ġyūj / wə-filtōt minhām

You asked me earlier about what. You said to me, 'What is ġaṣəbīt hibˤayt, why, what is the meaning of ġaṣəbīt hibˤayt?' We said in the past they told a story: we said this ġaṣəbīt hibˤayt, 'it escaped from seven', this fish called ġaṣəbīt hibˤayt. They said seven men cornered it. They wanted to catch it in a net or catch it. Then they said seven men cornered it and it escaped from them.

2. śīnəš / yaˤnī hibˤayt minhām ḳdūrəm ilḳifəm / ṣayd ḏōmah lā / sēh ġaṣəbīt hibˤayt / min būmah / nūkaˤ humməs / axah ḏə-ġaṣəbūt / hibˤayt ġyūj / ḳdūrəm yəlḳifməs lā / wa:-hamīmən tōs min ṭawr ḏakmah / ġaṣəbōt hibˤayt / wə-humməs nṣarōmah / ġaṣəbīt hibˤayt

Do you see? I mean seven of them (weren't) able to catch that fish, which is ġaṣəbīt hibˤayt. From that incident it got its name. I mean it escaped and seven men weren't able to catch it. And we call it (that) from that time on. It escaped from seven, and now its name is ġaṣəbīt hibˤayt.

8.2.5. How the raḫṭōt Fish Got Its Name

This text was recorded on 14 April 2013 by Janet Watson in al-Ġayḍah, Yemen, in the house of the speaker. It was recorded on an Olympus LS-11 digital recorder. The audio can be accessed from Borealis or the ELAR Mehri archive by entering in the search box 20130414_MehriMo_M005_howRaHthootFishGotIts Name_jfoonCows.

1. tārīx^A īmoh ^arbaˤtašar arbaˤah / alfayn wa-ṯalāt^ˤašar^A / wə-hōh ˤaskari ḥujayrān frēj saˤd

The date today is 14 April 2013, and I am Askari Hujayran Frej Saad.

2. kūṭōt ḏīmah / šxəbəríti jānīt ˤan / hōh ˤamərk hīs widˤaš wkoh hummǝs / raḫṭōt / ˤamərūt lā / ˤamərk līna yˤamrǝm zamān^A / zamān^A lā wə-ta nṣarōmah / yˤamrǝm hīs tǝrḫōṭ / əḥḥayk / yˤamrǝm / yaˤni təktəwītən ˤar lə-ḥayk

This story Janet asked me about. I told her, 'Do you know why it is called raḫṭōt (it licked)?' She said, 'No.' I said, 'Because in the past they used to say, not in the past... until now, they said she would lick the beach. They would say, I mean, she would only eat from the beach.'

3. widʿak hēh ḏōmah yaʿni kə-ṣudḳ aw lā lākin ḏōmah ġrōy min min zamān^A ḥābū yʿamrəm / lə-həmiməs rḥaṯōt / ʿar la-… / ləgrē ḏə-sēh / linna sēh ʿamolt / tərḥōṯ l-ḥayḳ / ttayw ḥayḳ ḳawts ʿar / ḥayḳ / wə-raḥṯōt ḏimah yaʿni^A min mi(r) raḥyūṯ / raḥyūṯ ḏōmah / yəkūnə / bə-lšēn / aw śī yətawyəh bə-xxoh wə-hēh / wə-hēh yaʿni / yəkūn / bə-maʿnā^A ḏə-ṣudḳ yaʿni^A / bihlīt ḏimah / raḥyūṯ yəkūn bə-rḥəyūṯ / bə-xoh / wə-bə-lšēnəh / ^Abə-ḏāt yaʿni^A

I don't know whether this was true or not, but this is what people would say in the past. They called her *raḥṯōt* just so that, so that she, because she did, she licks the beach, she just eats from the beach, her food is just the beach. And (the term) *raḥṯōt* comes from licking. That licking is with the tongue or something that you eat with your mouth and it is, and it is, I mean, it is. In the true sense, I mean, that word, *raḥyūṯ* is 'licking' with the mouth, and with the tongue in particular.

4. wə-raḥyūṯ ḏōmah / yaʿni^A his / his lē wət ḥābū ʿamləm his jfōn / wə-mġōrən / tərḥaṯ / tərḥōṯ / jfōn aw tərḥāyəh / bə-lšānəs / ^Alinnū / zamān^A ḥābū ykūn šīhəm / ḳawt xawr ykūn šīhəm ḥəbūn / wə-ykīn ḏə-ḥatūjəm lə-śxōf

And that licking, I mean it is like a cow when people make a tulchan for it, and then she licks it. She licks the tulchan or she licks it, with her tongue, because in the past people used to have little food, and they had children and they were in need of milk.

5. *wət lē / ya⁽ni^A / həgəjūt / wə-xāṣṣatən^A wət nk⁽ōt bə-fə⁽ōr / yəkīn šīhəm ḥəbūn / maḥtājayn^A lə-ndərēt*²⁹ *^Aḥatta l-yawm^A / yəshaytəm ḏakmah / fə⁽ōr / mġōrən lē / wət l-⁽ād śinūt ḥabrays lā / lā təb⁽ā lā / wə-lā thədrūr lā / wə-tkūn hədīt lā / wə-trōkəś*

When a cow, I mean, calved, and in particular when she gave birth to a bull calf; when they have children, they need milk for the children—still today. They slaughter that bull calf. Then the cow, when she can't see her calf anymore, doesn't give milk and doesn't give a lot of milk and she won't be calm, and she'll kick.

5. *aywah / l-ūṭōmah / ḥābū zamān^A bīhəm fkayr / ⁽amūrəm hīboh nə⁽mōl ⁽amūrəm nə⁽mōl his / jfōn / ya⁽mīləm his jfōn yəśadhəm əṭ-ṭār ṭīrōb / lə-his jfōn / kall snīnən / mġōrən wət yəhaym yəḥləmməs / yəḥagzəməs ū-mġōrən / yəhftīkəm his ⁽aynət / śxōf min / aśar⁽as / aṭ-ṭār jfōn ḏakmah / bass wə-sēh təṭyū bə-ḏakmah jfōn ṭād ḥabrays / wə-tərḥāṯ ḏakmah / śxōf*

Yes, because of that, people in the past had good ideas. They would say, 'What can we do?' They would say, 'We'll make her a tulchan.' They would make her a tulchan (stuffed calf-skin) and stretch it over sticks like a tulchan in the past. Then when they wanted to milk, they would take a little milk from the udder onto that tulchan, just that, and she would smell that tulchan as if it was her calf, and she would lick that milk.

6. *^Ayā subḥān allāh ya⁽ni^A / axasēh ḥabrays ya⁽ni / lxanīs / bass wə-thayd wə-tsōkən / wə-təb⁽ā / wə-thədrūr śxōf / l-ḏakm jfōn / də-bēh ṭāy / də-ḥabrays / wə:- / raḥyūṯ aw ərḥyīn / hīsə / ġəṣəbīt*

---

²⁹ *ndərēt* is milk especially set aside for young children, usually in its own little pot.

(sic) / hīs raḥtōt / wət tərḥā / baṯẖ / lākin^A ḳəṭ raḥtōt / ˤar ṣayd / wə-lākin^A ḏīh axah / bəḳrēt / yəkirn ḏakmah jfōn / wə-tərḥāyuh / wə-hīs ˤamərk təbˤā / wə-thayd

Praise be to God, I mean, as if it was her calf, I mean, beneath her, just like that, and she would become quiet and stand still and give milk, and give lots of milk for that tulchan that had the smell of her calf. And *raḥyūṯ* or *ərḥyīn* is like (the fish) *raḥtōt* when it licks the ground. But *raḥtōt* is just a fish but this is a cow. She caresses that tulchan and licks it and, as I said, she gives milk and becomes calm.

PART IV
HARVESTING THE SEA
IN SOQOṬRA

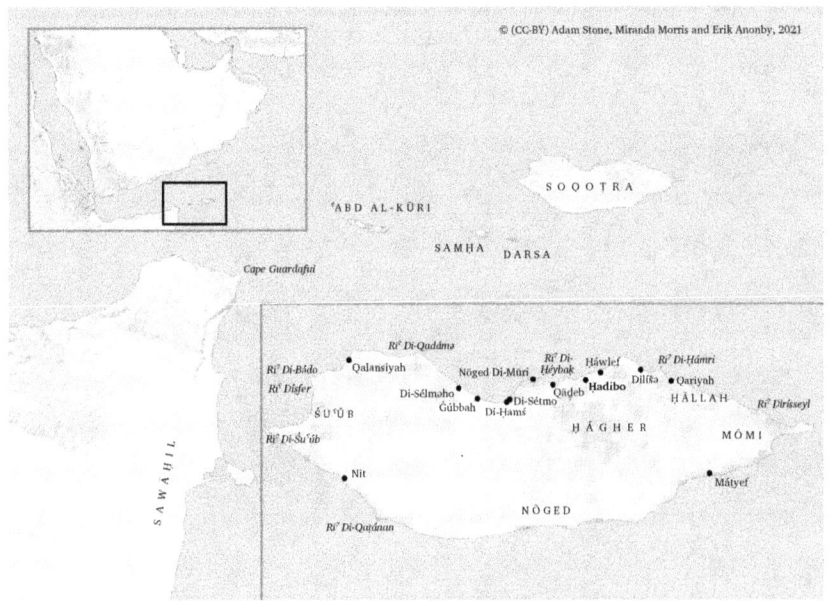

Map 4: Soqoṭra and neighbouring islands

HARVESTING THE SEA IN SOQOṬRA

Miranda J. Morris, Mubārak ʿĪsa Walīd al-Soqoṭri

and Aḥmad Saʿd Taḥkí al-Soqoṭri

Acknowledgments

My thanks go especially to my two coauthors, Mubārak ʿĪsa Walīd al-Soqoṭri and Aḥmad Saʿd Taḥkí al-Soqoṭri. Sadly, neither of them is still with us: Aḥmad Saʿd died in 2011 and Mubārak ʿĪsa two years later.

Mubārak's grandfather, Walīd, unusually for a Soqoṭri, started out as crew (*báhari*, pl. *baḥḥār*) on an Omani-owned trade boat. He finally rose to become a captain (*nōxədə*) on sailing boats owned by Muscat traders. Except for him, all the other crew members were Omani. In this way he travelled to the Gulf states as well as to Africa and Zanzibar, calling in at Soqoṭra on the way to Africa and again on the way back. Here he would take on a load of his own goods for onwards sale. He was well known on the island for refusing to take other peoples' goods on board unless they were prepared to come on board themselves and travel with their goods, at their own risk, and be entirely responsible for them. Mubārak's father, ʿĪsa, also worked for a time—reluctantly according to Mubārak—as a captain for two Soqoṭri boat-owning merchants, nicknamed locally the *hunūd*, the 'Indians', who lived on the north coast in the town of Qāḏeb

~Qāṣeb. However, unlike his father Walīd, he disliked the work and resigned. He married into a family from eastern Soqoṭra, and thereafter earned his living as a fisherman, pearl diver, date palm farmer and livestock breeder. Mubārak himself grew up working the sea, tending the date palms and helping with his father's livestock, transhuming across the island with the animals every year to Mōmi, the home area of his father-in-law in the east. Mubārak's fishing expertise relates especially to the principal fishing region of the island, the area running from Di-Ḥámri to Di-ʿAféro at Raʾs Mūri on the north coast (see the map of Soqoṭra in this volume).

Aḥmad Saʿd Taḥkí and his brother Ḥsan were both generous with their time, teaching me how the seas along the eastern coast of Soqoṭra were harvested. I spent a lot of time with their family on the island, but Aḥmad also came to work with me in Scotland on several occasions. Although the focus of our work was the Soqoṭri language and culture in general, rather than specifically marine matters, the fact that Aḥmad's extended family, unusually for the island, were as involved in working the sea as they were in date palm cultivation and animal husbandry meant that fishing formed part of our study. The transcribed texts that accompany this Soqoṭra section are all from Aḥmad.

I am very grateful for the help generously given by the ichthyologist Friedhelm Krupp, formerly of the Senckenberg Research Institute but currently working for the Arab Regional Center for World Heritage in Bahrain. I am equally grateful for the help given by Uwe Zajonz, marine conservationist and ichthyologist of the Senckenberg Research Institute. Both were very patient with the many questions I sent them and did their best to answer them in terms that might be comprehensible to a non-expert such as myself. Needless to say, the many errors that doubtless remain are my responsibility alone.

In 2020, I worked with Uwe Zajonz and many others on the *Atlas to the Commercial Fish of Socotra*, and as a result was able to send some queries about Soqoṭri marine terminology to Fouad Naseeb Saeed, Marine Expert, E. P. A. Soqotra. I would like to thank him for carrying out these checks for me. I would also like to thank Dr Abdul Karim Nasher, Professor of Zoology (retired), Sanaʿa University, for his time and expertise in checking the Arabic and listing the responses to my questions. I was interested to note that a number of the terms sent to Fouad for checking, terms used by the older fishermen I had consulted in the 1980s and 1990s, were apparently no longer recognised in the capital area, Ḥadibo, where Fouad lives and works. This loss of specialist vocabulary in the MSAL and its replacement by terms influenced by Arabic has been observed by other researchers in the field.

1. Introduction

The intention in this work is to try and provide a snapshot of how islanders harvested the surrounding seas in the days before the fisheries developed into a modern commercial enterprise in the 1990s. In the period recalled by my Soqoṭri informants, fishing was primarily a subsistence activity: people were working the sea to eat. Others hoped to catch something to trade with the boats that sailed to the island on their way to and from the Gulf, Oman and East Africa.

Full-time fishermen were almost entirely dependent on the sea for their survival.[1] Most were not indigenous Soqotri and many were bound to others—sultanic, Sayyid[2] and merchant families—at a time when such bondage or slavery was still practised. They were mostly landless and, with no rights to pasture or water, the majority were unable to manage more than a handful of goats or sheep to provide them with limited milk, meat, wool and leather from the poor grazings along the coast. While some escaped these confines through their own determination, for example, developing skills as blacksmiths, masons or experts in cultivation, full-time fishermen always had a hard life.

However, this was also true of nearly all islanders in the interior, people who depended on livestock for their survival. A number of these would not eat fish and regarded those who did so with some contempt or at least pity, though they might take part in the work of the sea by providing material for making fishing equipment, such as wood for fish traps, wool for parts of

---

[1] Indeed, the term *ṭáḥḥi ~ ṭéyḥi*, pl. *ṭáḥḥo ~ ṭéyḥo* used to mean just this, 'person of the coast, lacking or poor in livestock, dependent on fishing for a livelihood.' Today it only refers to people who live on the coast.

[2] *sayyid*, pl. *sādāt* or *sharīf*, pl. *ashrāf* (Soqotri *šerīf* pl. *ešróf*) are honorific titles given to descendants of the Prophet Muḥammad's family. The Mahri Sultan Sālim Ḥamad Saʿd moved to Soqotra in the 1880s. The sultans of Soqotra married islanders and usually had extensive families.

nets, locally grown cotton and other fibres. Some of them took to fishing at hard times of year, but with very basic equipment: a hook and line and sometimes a cast net, usually begged or borrowed from a fisherman. Also, it was not unusual for people from the interior to move down to the coast to live with a fishing family in the dry season when their animals were unproductive, or during a period of extended drought. They would offer their hosts reciprocal hospitality up in the mountains at times when their animals were in milk and the sea was unproductive. A few Soqoṭri families, like that of Aḥmad Saʿd, were as much at home in the sea as they were in the date palm gardens and finger millet terraces or managing their livestock.

Since most of my information came from fishermen of the northern or eastern coasts, the Soqoṭri terminology here is from those areas. Most full-time fishermen lived along the north coast: fishing was less important on the south coast (though it plays a major role today).[3] Along the south coast, although there were productive date palm gardens and a small number of hamlets, most people of the area were Soqoṭri tribesmen who had rights to areas of rangeland on the plateau above where they lived with their animals, coming down to fish only when

---

[3] Brown (1966, 5) wrote: "The relatively dense population of the Hadibu Enclave (bounded by Shuuk [i.e., Šiḳ, MJM], the slopes of the Haggier and Ras Hebak), which is what most visitors see, is quite misleading for the whole Island; and the townships of the North coast are not repeated in the South of the Island."

they needed to, and owning some share in the date palm gardens down below.⁴

However, it is a limitation of this work that it contains little information from the very active fishing port of Qalansiyah on the western tip of Soqoṭra. The fishermen here were mostly full-time and, like so many of the full-time fishermen of the north coast, originated from areas beyond the island itself. We are lucky that Serjeant wrote about Qalansiyah as he found it in 1967 (Serjeant, writing in 1967, cited in Doe 1992, 133–80). For a discussion of more modern fishing practices around the island, see Jansen van Rensburg (2016), where he also places the Soqoṭri marine culture within a broader historic and regional context.

---

⁴ See Brown (1966, 28) on the situation along the south coast, of owning a share in a dugout: he says of people there that "only a minority do so on the south coast.... This is partly due to the difficulty of working off the ocean coast; although when I was in the island it was the coast sheltered from the prevailing wind, the swell made it far more difficult to get a boat on or off the beach or shingle than anywhere on the north even with the trades blowing steadily. And partly, also, because these coastwise communities are seasonal shielings only and not permanently inhabited. That is, when the bedu are down in them, some of them go fishing." And "The passing dhows never touch on this coast.... The catches on the south coast, fresh or dried, must be almost entirely for local consumption there."

2. Soqoṭra, Trade and Island Fishermen

2.1. Soqoṭra

Soqoṭra is the largest of the inhabited islands of the Soqoṭra Archipelago. There are four islands and two sea stacks, lying some 400 km south of Ras Fartak on the Arabian mainland, the westernmost island, ʿAbd al-Kūri, lying only some 80 km east of Cape Guardafui on the Horn of Africa. The seas are rich in fish and coral communities, and are described as "biogeographic crossroads in the Arabian Sea" lying "in a transitional zone between the typical tropical fauna of eastern Africa and the unique fauna of the Red Sea, Gulf of Aden, Gulf of Oman and Arabian Gulf" (Krupp and Hariri 1999), and with species (Cheung and DeVantier 2006, 174–217)

> representative of three major bio-geographic realms; Arabia, East Africa—western Indian ocean and the broader Indo-Pacific. Located at the northwest corner of the Indian ocean, well east of the entrance to the Red Sea, the Islands stand in the way of several major ocean currents each carrying marine organisms and their larvae from different regions, all seeking a new home. The resulting species diversity of fish, corals and other invertebrates is exceptionally high and far exceeds previous speculations. In addition to species widespread across the entire tropical Indian and Pacific oceans, corals and fish previously thought to be restricted to particular areas, such as the Red Sea, Oman or the Arabian-Persian Gulf, or further afield in South Africa and even Japan, have now been found around the Islands. Socotra forms a kind of oceanic 'crossroads' where the bio-geographic realms of the Red Sea, Arabian Sea, east Africa, Indian ocean and the wider

Indo-Pacific all meet. Feeding on the plankton in these highly productive waters are whales and whale sharks, manta rays and huge schools of sardines and other fishes. The small fishes in turn fall prey to dolphins and other formidable ocean hunters such as tuna and mackerel, giant marlin, tiger, whaler and hammer-head sharks.

The gale-force winds of the southwest monsoon which blow from June to September bring most fishing to a halt, and during this period, until very recently, the island was cut off from the rest of the world.[5]

Figure 1: Wild monsoon seas and fishing settlement, east coast

Photo © Miranda Morris, 1990s

---

[5] The 'sea is closed' (ḵāful rínhem), for some four months, from dʸōti at the end of summer to the beginning of ṣerébhən at the end of the monsoon, when the monsoon winds fall and the sea calms down.

2.2. Lack of Seagoing Boats

Isolated by bad weather for four to five months of the year and with no natural harbour, the island never developed a major port. It had a bad reputation as a place of hazardous sailing, not only because of the monsoon gales of the summer, but also the winter storms of the northeast monsoon (November to January) and the strong currents that carried shipping onto hidden rocks and shoals and caused anchors to drag. Although good timber was available on the island,[6] the necessary boatbuilding skills and tools were lacking.[7]

Oral history reports that in the rule of Sultan Ḥamad bin ʿAbd Allah (reigned 1938–1952) an 'iron ship' laden with wood came to grief on the rocks of Mōmi at the eastern end of

---

[6] In the last days of the rule of Sultan ʿĪsa bin ʿAli (reigned 1952–1967) and in the early years of the PDRY (People's Democratic Republic of Yemen) which followed, Soqoṭra exported timber to Hadhramaut and Qishn: ḥímiher 'Zygocarpum', míṭəhān 'Buxus' and mítrur 'Croton', all of which grew to a good size in the central Ḥagher mountains. When imported beams and planks became available in the mainland markets the demand for Soqoṭri timber dropped away.

[7] See Brown (1966, 27): "No islander owns any kind of *sambuk* or larger craft. Those, some motorised, and some not, which are often to be seen working out of Kallansiya, do not belong to Socotrans but to Qsuris who come there regularly every year as a seasonal base. Some of these men have a wife and household in Kallansiya, as well as one in Qsur [MJM Qusayʿir]; but Qsur is their home port, and Qsur is where their profits go. They are of economic value to the island only in so far as they provide a free market for island dried fish in and around Kallansiya, spend some money there in the season, and occasionally employ some local people."

Soqotra. The sultan ordered the wood to be brought by pack animal, dugout and human back to his capital on the north coast. At that time (in the lifetime of Mubārak's father), there were two brothers of mainland origin in the town of Qāḍeb~Qāṣeb on the north coast who were ʾasātidə (s. ustād) or mʿālima (s. mʿállim), "men with boatbuilding expertise," who gained employment repairing visiting dhows.[8] Near Di-Išhəlítin, at Rēm (where until recently traces of these activities were still visible), and with the help of local carpenters and blacksmiths, they built the first Soqotri dhow (sɔ́dak) for the sultan, who named it al-ʿIzz.[9] They also built further boats for their own use. At around the same time other seagoing boats were purchased, one by a Baḥārith man of Ḥadibo, one by the three al-Hindi brothers of Qāḍeb. Neither of these survived al-ʿIzz: one "died of old age" in Qāḍeb and the other, possibly for the same reason, sank at sea (all aboard survived). Al-ʿIzz, captained by Khamīs

---

[8] There were a few other ʾasātidə~mʿālima: at Šiḵ, Ġalib Ḥamad (married to Mubārak's mother-in-law); in Ḥadibo, ʿĪsa Sayāqa and his brother ʾAnīna; and in Qāṣeb, ʿAmr Sālim from the Hadhramaut, a man skilled at carrying out repairs on wooden boats.

[9] Serjeant (writing in 1967, cited in Doe 1992, 163–64): "...[I]n the 1954 report... the only dhow on the island, which is owned jointly by the Sultan, is sailed round to Ḥadībūh from its anchorage at Stīmū and the tribesmen from the eastern area from the star Ṭarfah (which I calculate would be 12–14 February) bring in their ghee, mats, skins and Dragon's Blood. These and pearl shell are loaded and the dhow goes to Qaḍb (Haybaq) and Qalansiyyah where the same arrangements stand. The dhow then goes on to Mombasa."

Mḥāmid, did not survive into the reign of Sultan ʿĪsa bin ʿAli: dropping anchor in a storm it ran aground in the Di-Ḥamṣ area.

The availability of Soqoṭri-owned dhows on the island led to great improvements in trade, and regular trips to the local markets on the mainland.

Figure 2: Fishing dhow nearing Soqotra, *talbīs* raised

Photo © Miranda Morris, 1990s

It was now that the trade in ready-made goods began to flourish: for the first time Soqoṭrans were able to meet other traders and study the markets for themselves, discover what was available and learn which island products might be traded. Even so, as late as 1967 it was reported that the total contents of the shop belonging to the father of a ship's captain (someone one who might be expected to have a good variety of merchandise for sale) consisted of[10]

> waistcloths from Malaysia and from India (at three times the price), perfume, strong orange wine,[11] blue cotton cloth for girls dresses,[12] shirts, sugar, ginger root, *qishr* coffee-husk, biscuits in packets, Lifebuoy soap, detergent in packets, silver earrings in tins, belts (woollen webbing or plastic), tins of pineapples, small onions, tins of tomato puree, aspirin.

2.3. Visiting Boats and Seasonal Trade

2.3.1. Traders (*ṭawwāš*, pl. *ṭawāwīš*) and the Trading Season (*mōsəm*)

Before the island had its own seagoing boats, there were no major island merchants (for whom the Arabic term *tājir*, pl. *tujjār* was used). The traders that did exist on the island were a handful of men who could afford to buy up butteroil and trade it to

---

[10] Serjeant, writing in 1967, cited in Doe 1992, 179–80.

[11] Mubārak thought this might have been Vimto, which was still a popular celebratory drink when I first went to the island in the 1980s.

[12] Mubārak *kinēki*: the material and the name for the type of black overblouse made from it. This was worn by older girls and women over a length of locally woven black sheepswool which was wrapped around the waist, called *məzdērə*. The *kinēki* imported as cloth was stitched by the women on the island. It was square in shape, reaching down to the thigh, with a wide, square neck and loose, short sleeves. The material was usually *mərēkān~bərēkān* unbleached coarse calico from which most island clothing was made, dyed black. It fades and develops pale patches with age.

visiting boats for one or more sacks of grain or for cloth and other necessities. Such men were mainly to be found in the Ḥadibo area, Qāḍeb~Qāṣeb and Qalansiyah, though one or two came from the Di-Sétmo area and from Ḥallah on the east coast. Such people were all of mainland origin and were regarded as 'Arab' (ʿárab) rather than 'Soqoṭri' (skāṭərə).

2.3.2. Trade Boats and the Broker (dallāl)

Most of the boats calling in at the island[13] were from Oman[14] and the Gulf. They brought essential goods for the islanders as

---

[13] Serjeant (writing in 1967, cited in Doe 1992, 174) writes of the *fawlah* ceremony performed when a boat finally reached Soqoṭra, and notes Ibn al-Mujāwir's thirteenth-century account of this ceremony: an earthen pot had a sail, rudder and boat gear set upon it, some food placed in it (a little coconut, salt and ashes) and was then cast into the sea. Mubārak said that a *fawlah* ceremony was still performed as soon as a boat set anchor on arrival. Everyone did it: he knew of no boats from any country that did not. He described it as follows: as the boat came in to anchor, the sailors sang and drummed. A half-coconut filled with ash was turned upside down and placed on the bottom of the bowl, a particularly large gəmīmi (a hemi-spherical clay serving bowl with no lip and no foot); then more ash was piled all around and over it. A piece of cloth was stretched over this and tied down firmly to keep the coconut in place. To represent a mast, a length of date-leaf petiole (mízərid) was poked through the cloth right to the bottom of the bowl; then some mərēkān~bərēkān unbleached calico cloth was folded, rather as a parachute is, unfurled over the 'mast' to spread out to cover the bowl, forming a sort of tent. Then the whole contraption was hurled as hard as possible into the sea, where it 'exploded', a cloud of ash rising from it "so that it looked like a boat firing gunpowder," leaving the cloth floating on the surface. Once at anchor, a

well as any items that had been commissioned and stayed until they had loaded up with island products to sell in the overseas markets.[15] The sultan controlled all trade, and all taxes (ʿušūr) on imported goods were paid to him. In Mubārak's father's

---

goat, paid for either by the passengers or the captain, was brought out to the boat and slaughtered to celebrate their safe arrival.

[14] Schweinfurth 1897, 6–7: "I remarked in the roadstead of Tamarid (Ḥadibo) six Arab vessels… which had lain to here, on the voyage from Zanzibar to Muskat, in order to exchange rice and maize for the usual exports of the island, namely aloes, dragon's blood, a kind of inferior incense (Lege-ban) [lékəhəm, a commiphora sp. MJM], coloured woven stuffs, and, chiefly, melted butter and a kind of coarse sackcloth made of sheep's wool. These ships usually make the return journey at the time of the north-east monsoons, when Socotra serves as a half-way station from time to time. On the other hand, the intercourse with Makalla and other places on the South Arabian coast is slight, and no relations of any kind appear to exist with the Somali coast. Whenever the mountaineer catches sight of these Muskat and Zanzibar ships which have come for barter, he lays hands on all the provisions he has laid by and hastens down to the coast. A mart and exchange then takes place in Tamarid, which gives rise to all manners of rejoicings and lasts for several days."

[15] It is remembered that overseas traders sometimes married Soqoṭri women, some settling down on the island, others taking their wives back home with them for the duration of the monsoon season. Hulton (2003, 88) writes about a Soqoṭri wife of a trader from Maṣīra, Oman, in 1834: "The Naguedar [nōxaḏah, 'captain' MJM] brought his Socotrine wife with him, and as she cleaves to her native country rather than her husband, she has scraped twenty-five dollars together, and purchased her freedom."

time[16] there was one agent or broker (*dallāl*) for the whole of the Ḥadibo area and another for the Qalansiyah area.

A *dallāl* was known to, and used by, all visiting boats. His main job was to auction the trade goods they had brought. Initially the *dallāl* system operated only on incoming trade goods, not on the outgoing goods of butteroil, aloes, skins and hides, sheep wool rugs and so on. The *dallāl* "sat, slept and ate on" the goods entrusted to him until they were sold, his family bringing his meals to him. He could either buy up all the goods himself to sell on or come to an agreement with the captain or visiting trader on how to share any profit. Some traders left goods behind with the *dallāl* to sell[17] as and when he could, the money to be collected from him the following season. In the Ḥadibo area, one of the *dallāl*'s duties was to welcome a visiting captain or trader with a good meal (*karāmə*), but it was not part of his job to find passengers for him: this was arranged directly be-

---

[16] As a rough estimate, Mubārak was probably born in the 1940s, when his father was in his thirties. Mubārak's father was probably born in the 1910s and his grandfather in the 1880s. 'Mubārak's father's time' is perhaps best understood as stretching from the 1920s to the 1940s, and 'Mubārak's grandfather's time' as the late nineteenth and early twentieth century, on the assumption that they were likely to describe their memories of earning a livelihood in relatively early adulthood that predated their son's or grandson's memories.

[17] Mubārak said that the slowest items to sell were the dugouts, timber and mangrove poles (*kándələ*). These last, from seven to ten *durūʿ* in length, came from East Africa and were used in the construction of ceilings of mosques and the stone houses of wealthy island families. The length of the poles determined the dimensions of a ceiling.

tween the captain and the passenger. Mubārak remembers that the *dallāl* of the Ḥadibo area was a clerk (*kātib*) to the sultan, but that when he died, he was replaced by a man who was illiterate. The whole brokerage operation operated on trust—it was not necessary to be able to write.

Incoming trade was greater at Qalansiyah where boats could more safely anchor, and Serjeant, in 1967 describing the more tightly organised *dallāl* system in operation there, reports that:[18]

> By way of customs duties the Government takes ʿušūr, literally tithes, or ten per cent. In Qalansiyah these tithes used to be charged on what was imported or exported by foreigners, but now they are charged also on exports by locals who formerly were not taxed on what they exported.

He goes on to say that there the *dallāl* "acts as an intermediary and commission agent for the dhow captains in trading and finding cargoes and passengers," and that he "receives from the locals whose goods he sells to the outside world 1%; on goods imported he receives from the vendor 2.5%."

2.3.3. The Trading Seasons

The arrival of the trading boats was called *mōsəm*: first the *mōsəm əl~mən swāḥil* from the East African coast, and then later the *mōsəm əl~mən ʿāli*, from the Arabian seaboard, from Mus-

---

[18] Cited in Doe 1992, 170–72.

cat[19] and the Gulf (and later Aden).[20] Within living memory, the pattern of boats calling in at Soqotra was usually as follows:

(i) September (*ṣērǝb*, Ar. *futūḥ*)

As the monsoon seas calmed, boats arrived from Muscat and the Gulf. They primarily carried dates, but also cloth, and they brought with them any Soqotrans who had been working in Oman. They left the island practically empty for al-Mukallā and Aden, or, if they had taken on a cargo of dried fish, shark, sheep wool rugs and butteroil,[21] for East Africa.

(ii) From mid-winter to the early summer season (i.e., November to February/March)

Boats arrived from al-Mukallā and Aden to purchase island products, bringing tobacco from the Hadhramaut (called *tǝmbāk gǝbǝlīyǝ* on the island), cereals (especially finger millet) and dates.

---

[19] Some Soqotrans went to work the date harvest in Muscat, others in search of other seasonal labouring jobs or to fish when the monsoon made this impossible on Soqotra. Unlike Aden, no work permits were required for Oman. Mubārak's grandfather, one of his paternal uncles and a son of his maternal uncle all died while working in the Muscat area.

[20] In the years when the market at Aden was flourishing, the odd boat came from al-Mukallā and Aden in the period November–March to purchase butteroil, dried shark meat and sheep wool rugs. As well as goods from Aden, they brought tobacco, cereals (especially finger millet) and dates from the Hadhramaut.

[21] And when there was a demand for such items, also pearlshell oysters (*móṣǝliḥ*) and *di-ḥānǝ* lichens.

(iii) February and March (ḳéyaṭ 'early summer')

Boats arrived from Oman and the Gulf, largely empty, and mainly to take on salt and salt fish. If they had the space, i.e., if they had not loaded salt, they took any passengers who wanted to travel to East Africa.

(iv) April, May (dōtə 'late summer') to the beginning of the monsoon winds and the 'locking' (Ar. takfīl) of the sea in June.

Boats arrived from East Africa on their way to Oman and the Gulf. They mainly carried maize and loaded up with salt and salt fish. Such boats usually arrived in a group, and this was their only visit to the island. If they had space, they took on any Soqoṭri passengers who wanted to work in Oman (at this time of year, principally to work at the date harvest). If no mōsəm had arrived by the time summer had set in, many islanders faced starvation: their livestock, date palms and limited harvest of finger millet were never enough to allow the islanders to be self-sufficient through the long, stormy months of the monsoon.

2.3.4. Goods Purchased from Traders

Trade boats brought basic essentials which the islanders were unable to provide for themselves. The principal import was grain, mainly maize (məḳdḗrə) from Africa, and dates[22] from

---

[22] The date palms cultivated on the island were never able to supply enough fruit to satisfy the needs of the islanders. Soqoṭran dates were stored in goatskin bags, while the imported ones came in a variety of containers: round woven containers with an internal palm fibre cover

Muscat and Basra. Cloth was another essential, mainly lengths of unbleached calico (*mərēkān~bərēkān*), but also white muslin for turbans and black cotton for the tops worn by women over their sheep wool waistcloths. Iron for knife blades was another vital import, as was fishing equipment such as cotton yarn, hemp, coir, lead and fishhooks. In later years, needles and razor blades joined this list of basic needs.[23] *ʿušūr* 'taxes' had to be paid to the sultan by the islanders for any goods they wished to import, though the same was not true for traders and merchants from overseas.

(*kōṣərəh*) from Basra, a much smaller version from al-Qaṭīf in Saudi Arabia, and the oblong *gərāb* from Muscat.

[23] Aḥmad Saʿd and Mubārak ʿĪsa recalled the following items being imported in their lifetimes, some necessary 'tools of the trade', others 'luxury items' purchased by the small number of wealthier islanders of the permanent settlements of the north coast. *Trade Tools*: awls, iron rods, axe heads, basic carpentry and agricultural tools, saws, files, locks and bolts, basic smithing equipment. *Fishing Equipment*: lead weights, cork floats, fishhooks, the metal heads of harpoons (*mínzek*) and gaffs (*míṣḥaf~míšxaf*), cotton yarn, hemp and coir fibre for lines and nets, lengths of bamboo. *Clothing*: money belts, head shawls, ready-made clothing such as coloured waistcloths and shirts. *Household Items*: studded wooden chests, china coffee cups, paraffin and pressure lamps, wicks, spoons, scissors, coinage (usually silver rupees, *rəbābi*), paraffin and kerosene, matches, china butteroil storage pots. *Food*: cooking oil, coconuts, rice, spices. *Luxury Goods*: perfume oil, eye antimony, red, green and black cosmetic pastes, assorted silver jewellery, silver thread for embroidery, combs, dyes (for sheep wool rugs), indigo, myrrh, henna, hair oil (usually sesame), turmeric and other yellow powders used cosmetically as well as in cooking.

2.3.5. Goods Sold to Traders

These differed over time and according to demand, but butteroil was always the most important trade item.[24] Fresh milk was rarely drunk on the island; rather it was churned to make butter to be clarified to produce butteroil. Buttermilk was the basic food of the herding families (many even raising young stock on boiled buttermilk to save the fresh milk), and it was from this that they made their other milk products.

Of the island products, dried and salt fish were in demand in the Muscat and East Africa markets, butteroil in Muscat,

---

[24] Indeed, in the days of the last two sultans, Ḥamad bin ʿAbd Allah (reigned 1938–1952) and ʿĪsa bin ʿAli (reigned 1952–1967), there were still two merchants to whom butteroil and other island products were sold: ʿAbd Allah Baḥārith (of Ḥaḍrami origin, and said by Mubārak to have arrived on the island as an extremely poor man, but who built up his fortune by buying three lengths of aḥtīmi fishing twine for one measure of cereal [ḵurṣ ṭaʿm, ḳaḥf məḵdḗrə] and selling them on at two for one measure), and Saʿīd bin Ḥammād (of Gulf origin, said by Mubārak to have arrived with the pearlers as a rower). Soqoṭri control of the trade in butteroil only began once island traders owned their own boats; before this it was purchased by overseas traders. Ravenstein (1876, 124) writes that "Ghi constitutes the standard of value, but dollars and rupees are taken to be converted into earrings for their women," and Mabel Bent writes in 1897 (2010, 346) that "Butter is now the chief product and almost the sole export of the island, and Sokotra butter has quite a reputation in the markets along the shores of Arabia and Africa. The Sultan keeps a special dhow for the trade, and the Bedouin's life is given up to the production of butter. Nowhere, I think, have I seen so many flocks and herds in so limited a space as here."

Aden and al-Mukallā, sheep-wool cloth in Muscat and Aden, and pearlshell (and pearls) in Muscat and the Gulf. Other products, such as civet cat paste, cuttlefish bone, aloes juice, wild honey, *Dracaena* resin (both the processed 'cakes' and the droplets of pure resin), skins and hides, date pits[25] and lichens[26] were sold as and when there was a demand for them.

---

[25] Date pits were sold to visiting boats uncooked, but they were never an important item of trade. Islanders collected date pits, softened them by boiling and then fed them to their livestock. They also stored them in a hole dug for the purpose and watered them: as they sprouted, they were fed to livestock and were said to make a very nourishing fodder.

[26] The demand for *di-ḥānə* 'lichen' arose in the days when British were in Aden: a number of boats came to the island specifically to take on this cargo. Later, when sultans Ḥamad bin ʿAbd Allah and ʿĪsa bin ʿAli had their own trade boats, one or two trips were made at the end of the monsoon, as soon as the sea 'opened' for travel, and again just before it 'closed' at the approach of the monsoon. Sold by weight, the lichen was understood by islanders to have been used in the perfumery trade for which Aden was famous. See also Serjeant (writing in 1967, cited in Doe 1992, 197): "A strange export from the island is *shanā/shinā abyaḍ* (*Pettiger* sp.?). There appears to be a black (*sawdā*) variety as well as a white sort—as far as I know this word is not found in the Arabic dictionaries. It seems to be a sort of lichen collected by scraping it off the rocks after rain. In Socotri two types are distinguished *sʿanghir* and *dī ḥānah*. It is sold by the *gūniyah* but we purchased some in a plastic bag. My recollection is that it goes to Aden where it is used for a flavouring, but of this I am uncertain." A third kind of lichen called *ḥánnə* was used on the island for staining the skin and dyeing leather and cotton; *ḥánnə* is also the term for the imported *Lawsonia inermis* henna.

Figure 3: Old boats, north coast

Photo © Miranda Morris, 1990s

When the British were in Aden there was an upsurge in trade and many more boats began to visit the island from the Arabian mainland. There was renewed interest in butteroil, aloes juice, wool rugs, pearlshell and *Dracaena* products, as well as the more unusual items such as cuttlefish bone and the *di-ḥānə* lichens. This trade largely came to an end with the collapse of the Aden markets when the British left in 1967. With the arrival of the socialist People's Democratic Republic of Yemen that followed, the regular delivery of subsidised basic foodstuffs to the island meant that the islanders' year-round survival became more assured.

2.4. Fishermen: Seasonal and Full-Time

2.4.1. Full-Time Fishermen

These were considered to be among the poorest people of the island. They usually owned no land and had to seek permission from those who did to build even the most meagre hut. They rarely owned date palms, and, even where soil and water permitted, had no right to enclose land for cultivation. Many were of overseas origin, a mixed group of former slaves, immigrants from the African seaboard, settlers from the Arabian mainland and wrecked mariners. There was almost no market for fresh fish,[27] so whatever they caught went to feeding themselves, their families and their friends. Most fishing families tried to build up a small flock of livestock, handing them over to a herding family of the interior to look after when things were hard down on the coast[28] in exchange for fish and other produce of

---

[27] The opposite is true today: there is an excellent market for sea produce.

[28] Many terms concern seasons of poor fishing: (i) √ḥršm~√xršm: enḥáršim~enxáršim, '(sea) to not provide fish', as rínhem enḥáršimo ~rínhem ḥáršim, 'the sea gave nothing to eat'; or of a fisherman ḥáršim, 'he was empty-handed, got nothing to eat'; (ii) √ḥmšl~√xmšl: enḥámšil~enxámšil, 'to be a time of hardship, of a dearth of food (especially food from the sea)'; (iii) √hšr: ḥéšir yḥōšir l-eḥšér, '(sea) to be unproductive': ḥašéro rínhem, 'the sea gave nothing to eat'. The equivalent term for the herders of the interior was ḥázog, '(life) to be hard in the summer months when no summer rains fall', as ḥázog ʿíhin éʾefo, 'times were very hard for people', glossed as bíśi mése wə-bíśi rúʿd wə-bíśi ḳénhum di-ʿálf, 'no rain, no grazing, no foliage on the shrubs and trees to gather'.

the sea when times were hard in the interior. Like other islanders who owned no date palms, fishermen worked at the date harvest in exchange for dates, to supplement their otherwise rather monotonous fish diet.

Figure 4: A fisher home, east coast

Photo © Miranda Morris, 1990s

Women harvested shellfish, gathered and prepared bait, and spun sheep wool and local cotton for fishing gear. They helped drag the rafts and dugouts up and down the shore and went to meet the returning boats to receive the catch. They took it home and prepared and cooked whatever the men had caught, distributing any surplus among neighbours and friends. With a few exceptions,[29] they were not involved in actual fishing or

---

[29] Catching *məgrūməhem* porcupinefish by hand (see 3.6.) and trapping fish in rock pools.

diving (although I met a woman at Di-Ḥámri who was famous as a fisherwoman: she was an expert with the cast net and a skilled diver for pearlshell oysters).

On the small islands of ʿAbd al-Kūri and Samḥa, all men fished. On these smaller islands, there was little grazing for livestock,[30] water was scarce, and there was no ground suitable for cultivation. Here beachcombing was even more important than on Soqotra. Families on these remote islands remember collecting all sort of useful items that had floated ashore (*gidīḥa*): buoys (*bōya*), a variety of metal drums (*bərmīl*, pl. *brāmīl* or *drām*, pl. *drāmāt*), tins and metal cannisters, lengths of rope, sections of net, little glass vials (*krūz*) and larger glass bottles (*lōḳa*, pl. *ləwéḳ*), some with a screw top or stopper (*krūz máḥkem*)[31]—even edible items, such as coconuts (*nargīl*) or limes (*līm*). Most important was driftwood, and especially planks and sheets of plywood (*dērfə*). On ʿAbd al-Kūri, I visited huts constructed from driftwood—even some two-storey ones with ladders to give access to the upper floor—and a mosque was built with bricks recovered from a wreck.

---

[30] There had been so few animals here that butteroil had to be imported, mostly from the trade boats coming from East Africa. The islanders called it *ḥámʾi bənādiri*, 'butteroil from the big ports'.

[31] Even fragments of glass were useful. Islanders remember using them for cutting, for carving bone, incising clay pots, even for destroying vermin by grinding a fragment to powder, putting this inside a date and leaving it as bait for the hated feral cats and ravens.

2.4.2. Seasonal Fishermen

Most of the islanders were pastoralists, and many were also seasonal or part-time fishermen,[32] moving down to caves along the coast and setting up home there to find what food they could from the sea,[33] usually with only the most basic equipment.

---

[32] Capt. H. L. Flower, in his 'Report on Fisheries of April, 1944' in *Western Arabia and the Red Sea*, wrote that "over 1,840 people out of the 3,000 to 4,000 inhabiting the coastal settlements claimed to be dependent on fishing for a livelihood; 1,770 of these lived in eighteen settlements along the north coast; south-west of Kallansiya and along the whole south coast, the total population was reckoned to be less than 130 persons, of whom 73 were fishermen. The coastal community then owned 338 canoes and 6 row-boats." However, by 2000 there were 2,595 full- and part-time fishermen with a fleet of 40 sambouks: 36 wooden and four fibreglass (GRP) sambouks, 840 fibreglass (GRP) small fishing boats and 133 wooden canoes (Krupp and Hariri 1999, 3.3.1.).

[33] Most of the permanent fishing settlements that crowd the southern and eastern coasts today are a recent development. But Mubārak remembered a time when there were no seagoing craft at all along the southern coast. Only in the reign of the last sultan, when passports were issued and islanders were able to travel to the Gulf to seek work, did they begin to acquire the necessary funds to purchase dugout canoes. Mubārak's father told him that the people of the south coast fished with hand lines and cast nets only, and had no experience of boats of any kind. In the days of Sultan ʕĪsa bin ʕAli (reigned 1952–1967), his father and elder brother travelled in their dugout to the south coast in search of fish to make *kánda* (see 6.2.3.). On their return they reported extraordinary numbers of fish there and were amazed to find people there fishing only from the shore. They said they were hugely mocked by these islanders when they salted the fish

Some would seek work as unskilled labour with a fishing family in return for fish, while others spent a part of the long dry season—a time when their livestock were unproductive—down on the coast looking for fish (ˁɔ́gil əl~mən ṣódə, 'to go along the shore hoping to be given fish' or ištúʔub, 'to beg for fish'). They would wait for the dugouts to return and help drag the boats up in the hopes of being given a share of the catch.

Figure 5: Seasonal fishing settlement with stone-built boat shelters, a variety of fishing boats, shark-liver oil drums and gulls, east coast

Photo © Miranda Morris, 1990s

---

for the *kánda* and said to them: *yax! sínəhem kánda!* "Ugh! What a stink the *kánda* makes!"

The two hungriest times for the pastoralists were the end of the monsoon before the winter rains, and, in years when the unpredictable summer rains (*dōti*) had failed, the late summer months. At these times, less able members of a family would be sent down to the coast to try and find food there. In return, when summer or winter rains were good, members of any fishing families who had helped them would go up to the interior to enjoy the plentiful milk and meat. Some herders gathered suitable material for fish traps or made fish traps themselves and bartered them for the cast nets which only skilled fishermen knew how to knot.

3. Traditional Fishing: Fish

3.1. Introduction

'Traditional fishing' refers to methods prevalent at a time when Soqoṭra was still ruled by sultans. This was a time prior to the independence of South Yemen in 1967, and includes a considerable period afterwards, before new types of craft and fishing equipment reached the island and the fisheries were developed.

There is no specific term for 'going fishing'. Instead, we find such terms as *dúʔur*, 'to succeed in catching something, to be successful'; *búʔur*, 'to go fishing and catch something', and the more general *šáʿrik*, 'to go down to the sea to fish'.

It was a lack of modern fishing gear that limited the islanders' ability to harvest the sea as they do today.[34] As recently

---

[34] Serjeant (writing in 1967, cited in Doe 1992, 176) reports that "this was apparently the first year, 1967, that nylon (rather than cotton)

as the mid-1900s, it was still being reported that "the weakness of the fishing industry is its dependence on imports for the maintenance of craft and for tackle. Canoes and timber come from Malabar; cotton sheeting, cotton yarn, hemp fibre, wire traces, swivels and hooks are all imported from Aden or India. In 1943 and 1944 the fishing community suffered hardship through lack of such goods and the high prices of any available supplies."[35] Even in the late 1990s, it was reported that "longlines, handlines, ropes and floats[36] are available on the island (but at double the price of Aden or al-Mukallā); fishing nets, swivels, jig bones and hooks are purchased from al-Mukallā or Aden" (Hariri and Yusif 1999).

It is interesting to look at some fishing prices in 1990,[37] a time when the glass reinforced plastic (GRP) vessels powered by

---

ropes became available for use on Socotra." However, on the island it is remembered that modern lines and netting became available in the rule of Sultan Ḥamad bin ʿAbd Allah (reigned 1938–1952) from Aden, Muscat and Swāḥil (East African coast), and were present all through the reign of the last sultan, ʿĪsa bin ʿAli (reigned 1952–1967).

[35] Beckingham (1983). Mubārak remembers learning from his father that 1943 and 1944 were exceptionally hard years. The only fishing possible was with fish traps or cast nets and people were forced to rely on gathering shellfish (šáḥak) to survive. These were years of extensive cutting and pulping of living date palms (kídihir) to feed both people and their animals.

[36] Locally, floats were made from the thicker buoyant tips of date palm fronds.

[37] Information from Ḥsan Saʿd Khamīs of Rikǝlǝ on the east coast of Soqoṭra.

15hp outboard engines had begun to become available on the island.

Costs

A GRP boat cost 48,000–55,000 shillings (henceforth sh.): a down payment of 20,000–30,000sh., then an annual payment of 6,000–10,000sh. Loans were available for government employees.

One drum of diesel cost 1,700sh.

A 15hp outboard engine cost 35,000sh.

One set of good-quality shark nets cost 15,000–20,000sh.

One net for ḥaniṭ-fish (see 6.2.4.) cost 5,000sh.

One sack of Nōged salt cost 50–90sh. (more if the costs of transporting it by boat are included).

The necessary ropes (ḳeyūd) cost 500–700sh.

In addition, engine oil, floats, buoys and anchors had to be purchased (or alternatives manufactured on site).

Total fishing gear came to some 8,000sh.

Selling prices

One ṭarnīk kingfish fetched about 60sh.

One sack of ḥaniṭ dried fish fetched about 1,500 sh.

One medium-sized shark fetched about 1,700sh. (i.e., equivalent to the cost of one drum of diesel).

One small dried shark fetched about 200sh.

One drum of shark liver oil fetched about 4,000sh.

In the currency of South Yemen at the time, there were 20sh. to 1 dinar, and 1 dinar to 26 YR (Yemeni riyals, the currency of North Yemen). There were 12 YR to $1.00 (US Treasury figures for Dec. 1990),[38] making 1 dinar equivalent to $2.1. Using these figures, it is possible to gain some idea of the viability of fishing as a way of earning a living on Soqoṭra island at this time.

It could be said that it was this very lack of equipment that drove the islanders to devise ingenious ways of exploiting the little they had. Before the new types of gear became available, the island fishermen managed to make their own nets, fish traps, lures, hooks and lines to catch both smaller reef fish and shallow water demersal species such as snappers, groupers, sweetlips, emperors and trevally.[39]

The timing of the fishing seasons varies around the island. For example, the south coast does not suffer the same severe monsoon gales as other coastal areas of Soqoṭra, and on the north coast there are some sheltered spots where some fishing can still be done in these months: the ʿArírihon and Dilíšə beaches, for example, are used by fishermen from other areas at this time, because the seas remain relatively calm here and

---

[38] See '[US] Treasury Reporting Rates of Exchange as of December 31, 1990' (US Department of the Treasury, Financial Management Service, Credit Accounting Branch (202) 208–1832. March 15, 1991 (https://www.govinfo.gov/content/pkg/GOVPUB-T63_100-719640076e85ad2dbc3ce995fcb42b5f/pdf/GOVPUB-T63_100-719640076e85ad2dbc3ce995fcb42b5f.pdf, accessed 1 December 2020).

[39] Islanders remember that fish in the creeks and lagoons of both north and south coasts were so plentiful that at high tide men could walk into the water, make a bag of their waistcloth, and, beating the water and shouting to confuse the fish, drive them along so that they could scoop them into their waistcloth bags. Fish caught in this way were mostly ḥərə́bo 'mullet' and ʿábrəhem 'terapon'.

many fish come closer inshore in search of shelter from the storms.⁴⁰

It was the tradition that anyone could fish anywhere around the island. However, an exception was ʿArírihon at the very end of summer (*dōti*) before the monsoon arrived. This was because schools of the small goatfish known as *ḳanśáʿa di-ḳālis* would stop off here at this time. It was agreed among fishermen that anyone fishing then must do so very quietly, taking care not to frighten the fish back out to sea, and that each should take only enough for his own need, for bait or for food. At the end of the monsoon, when the sea calms down again, the same fish would come back to ʿArírihon and stay put for some time.

3.2. Fishing Terminology

The islanders have many different terms for different kinds of fish (often equivalent to those used by international fisheries experts: benthic, littoral, demersal, pelagic, and so on). Soqoṭri fishermen talk about *ṣodə di-ḳaʿ*, 'fish of the bottom', *ṣodə di-ḳéśʔor*, 'fish of the rocks, reef fish',⁴¹ *ṣodə di-šīmi*, 'fish of sandy

---

⁴⁰ For further detail, see Jansen van Rensburg (2016, 55–107).

⁴¹ Of coral: *dúrmə*, an extensive coral atoll, *məḳwāš*, a treelike branching stony coral, or *akwāx*, brain coral. Cheung and DeVantier (2006, 194) also mention a soft coral 'kabot', a stony coral 'herimhem' and a fire coral (the stinging hydroids *Millepora*), 'qasereh'. 'herimhem' means 'little tree or shrub', and 'qasereh' means 'stinger', but 'kabot' was not recognised by my informants (though it might be related to *kíbido*, 'small hillock'. The *ḳéśʔor*, often an hour or two rowing from the shore, are described by fishermen as having holes and crevices ('caves, houses and refuges') in which fish rested or concealed them-

areas', ṣodə di-ṭaḥḥ, 'inshore fish', ṣodə di-ġubbə, 'deep sea fish', ṣodə məḥāgir, 'migratory fish', ṣodə di-ḳāsir, 'stinging fish' (mostly Scorpaenidae), ṣodə di-mī́ḳlib, 'fish seen above the surface of the sea' (said to igáˤgaˤ wə-ī́ḳlib, 'thrash around and turn upside down'). These are mainly fish such as dolphinfish, tuna, kingfish, bonito, and the larger trevallies that leap out of the water in pursuit of smaller fish. A group of fish that includes ḳerbōbə 'triggerfish' (Balistidae), leatherjackets/filefish (Monacanthidae) and boxfish (Ostraciidae), di-ḥáyhul 'scorpionfish' (Scorpaenidae), ˤáskədo 'damselfishes and clownfishes' (Pomacentridae), fə́kərəš 'flatheads' (Platycephalidae), bətrā́rə 'sillago' (Silliginidae) is called ṣōdə ḥálḳek or ṣōdə ḥāliš~ḥálšiš. Various needlefish (Belonidae), cornetfish (Fistulariidae) and halfbeaks (Hemiramphidae) are all given the same name, ˤírho.

There are different terms for fish seen swimming together: ṣodə séyhur, 'fish moving around in small schools', ṣodə di-sōl, 'fish moving around in large shoals' (usually tuna, kingfish and other large predatory fish), mihlóˤo di-ṣodə, 'a shadow of fish', ṣodə di-ríkəbə, 'fish resting together close to the sea surface', and ḳérəmə di-ṣodə, 'a hill of fish' (usually referring to tuna or certain trevallies swimming together in a tight bunch, in greater numbers than a mihlóˤo di-ṣodə).

Fish processed for sale to the trade boats were described as beyáḍ, 'white' fish, an Arabic term borrowed from overseas traders, possibly referring to the pale colour of the dried and salted fish. These included 'kingfish' (ṭānīk~ṭərnāk), various

---

selves at certain times of the day, and on their upper surfaces coral 'trees' through which fish swam.

'trevallies' (*təmákerə, ráʔha, bɛ́kist, dāfin*) and 'bluefish' (*tāki*ʰ), fish regarded by the islanders as having a similar taste.[42] Another major fish grouping was *gʸaḥś* fish, mainly emperors (Lethrinidae) such as *fṣáʕhan, kteb, máʕsam, ḥídəher* and *bígəhel*, but also *nə́kak* 'grunts' (Haemulidae), *maʕrɛ̄mə* 'jobfish' (Lutjanidae), *di-nə́ktə* 'seabream' (Sparidae) and *sárḥīn* and *di-nə́ktə* 'threadfin bream' (Nemiteridae). Once processed for sale, these were called *kánda* (see 6.2.3.).[43]

A fisherman who caught a large number of fish at one go, be they of one kind or of different species, would recognise that he had found a *mírkiz* 'home base', *káʕar* 'dwelling place', *maṭʕīno* 'transhumant home' or *mə́kəher* 'evening refuge' of fish, and would take a careful sighting from a landmark so that he could return to the same place at a later date.

It was recognised that some fish were best caught at night: coral reef fish in general, shark and barracuda, while tuna, kingfish and the small fish they preyed on could only be taken in daylight. Fishermen said that the best times for most fishing were when the sun was low (at dawn and dusk) and at night (unless the moon was very bright and the fish would see

---

[42] Fishermen say that fish of different areas have a different taste: thus, the fish from Qadámə to Ḥáwlef have one flavour; from Ḥáwlef to Dilíśə another; from Dilíśə to Raʔs Mōmi another; those of the south coast as far as Rīʔ Díṣfer another, and from Rīʔ Díṣfer to Qadámə another.

[43] When the wind drops at the end of the monsoon (around October) and the sea grows warmer, the shallow demersal reef fish, such as groupers, emperors, snappers, sweetlips, trevallies come inshore to feed, and this is the peak season for catching them.

the fishing gear). In a dead calm (*ḥalóʔo*), the greediest groupers (Serranidae) such as the greenish, blotched *līhan* and *ḥáyhal*, or the reddish spotted/striped *ḥálḥal~xálxal* groupers were easily caught with a handline, coming to the bait even if both fisherman and his line were visible. At times of rain and thick cloud, when the lines were hard to see, fish (especially bottom-dwelling ones) were more readily caught; but if it had rained heavily and floodwaters had reached the sea, fish numbers would decline and fewer would come to fish traps.

In the hottest months of the short summer season too, fish numbers dwindled, sometimes disappearing altogether. Then, only the large trevallies (as *dāfin, ráʔha, ṭamákərə*) could sometimes be caught as they swam on their way past the island. These fish were called *ḳédəhum* ('the precursors'), and fishermen would climb up to any high point above the sea (*ḥalf ḳédəhum*) and drop a baited line or a lure, of bone (*ṣóḥəlo*), peeled *Cissus* stem (*ʕáṭerhe)* or *Adenium* twig (*ə́sfəd~tərīmo*) to try and catch one (see 3.10. below).

Anoxic red tides or algal blooms often occurred at the changeover of the seasons, that is, at the very end of the summer months, when the islanders were hoping for *dōti* rains to fall, and again at the very end of the monsoon in the *di-ṣérebhen* season, which ushers in the winter. Algal blooms make the sea dark-coloured and murky (*ində́mərik* or *mə́drək*, '*mə́drək*' also being the name of the 'star' in ascendance at these times). If the sea were calm, fish, usually smaller ones, would float ashore, initially living, later washing up dead. In a very hungry year, the freshest ones were eaten. Squid and cuttlefish also drifted ashore, usually dead. This *ində́mərik* 'murkiness' usually lasted for about a fortnight, the dying fish arriving towards the middle of the period, but the algal bloom has been known to persist through both the *mədōrik* 'stars', i.e., for 26 days, the fish beaching after the first week or ten days.

3.3. Nets

The ones most widely used were the circular cast nets (generically called *máʿdef~máġdef*, pl. *máʿduf~máġduf*), used by single fishermen. These were finely knotted nets with small weights[44] around the circumference and a draw thread which closed the net around the trapped fish when it was hauled in. The twine for the nets was spun from cotton bushes, *Gossypium barbadense* (*íʾiśirə*, pl. *ʾíśhur*), which were cultivated inside walled enclosures to protect them from livestock.[45] The harvested cotton was cleaned of seeds and then 'beaten' with the 'bow' (*méfəkt*), in the same way as sheep wool. It was then teased out to make a soft, loose rope of fibre (*ímdid*) which was spun (*yəʿə́wzal*) with a very tight twist to a fine yarn (*ḱáʾ*). This was wound into figure-of-eight twists (*máḥlil*), and these were then made up into

---

[44] Forbes (1903, xxv, xxvi) reports islanders in ʿAbd al-Kūri seeking to trade "lizards, fishes, turtle-shell and muscovite [mica MJM]" for lead sinkers for their nets.

[45] Sometimes other imported fibres were available: hanks of coir fibre (*benj*) imported from East Africa, and of cotton yarn (*kəllōn*). Another type of cotton yarn was called *ṣifárhən di-kerḥānə*, 'plaits of cotton yarn', *kerḥānə* being a type of cotton said to be less strong than the *kəllōn*. Cotton yarn was also called *ʿózəl~ġozəl*, from the verb 'to spin'.

balls (*kúbərə*). Threads were plied together (*yəḥāyis*) to produce twine of the desired thickness.[46]

The cast nets differed both in overall size and in the size of the mesh. The mesh was called ʿ*ayn*, 'eye', and its size was judged by the number of fingers that fitted into a single hole of mesh: from the smallest, "an eye of the size of a small child's finger," to "an eye that took four adult fingers." The knotting (*wáśaʿ, yúwśaʿ*) of the nets was skilled work, and many fishermen had to barter for a net from known craftsmen who had the necessary expertise.

The smallest net was made using the finest twine. The mesh was smallest at the centre, the mesh size increasing towards the circumference. The twine was made of three strands twisted together (*məṭállit*), and this kind of net took the most expert netmaker some nine months to make. The nets (*máʿdef* ~*máġdef*) *ṣīni*~*ṣōwnu*~*ṣínhən* and (*ṣīni*) *ś͑érə*~*śġéyrə* had a larger mesh size and were made from a twine of six strands twisted together (*sidḗsi*). These could be made by most full-time fishermen. The outer circumference rope (*ḥīrəho*) and draw thread[47] were twisted from handspun cotton (*ġázəl*~ʿ*ózəl*) or sheep wool

---

[46] On Samḥa, before imported cotton became available, *ṣínhən* and *ṣínhən ś͑érə*~*śġéyrə* cast nets were made from sheep wool yarn or the underbark of *Ficus salicifolia* (*íʾtib*). Sheep wool yarn was still used for the circumference rope even once cotton yarn reached the island.

[47] When casting from the shore, the net has a line which is used by the fisherman to draw the net shut.

(ṣaf di-tētin). Holed pebbles (mátḳel pl. mətāḳil)⁴⁸ or turban and topshell (ʿáfšer~ʿábšer) shells were tied as sinker weights at intervals around the circumference. Later on, tiny lead sinker-weights (rəsās) were used instead—these were already available in Mubārak's father's time.

A newly made net was treated by crushing the leaves and soft stems of *Ziziyphus spina-christi* to a paste and rubbing this hard into the net to lubricate the fibres and make them malleable. The net was then tied to something high up by the loop at the centre of the net (ʿalyémo), the rest of the net stretched downwards and weighted with rocks at the bottom. It was left like this for most of a day before it was used in the sea for the first time. Nets were also treated with the roots and stems of *Limonium* (ṣeṣíbə)⁴⁹ or *Periploca* (ftax) to strengthen the fibres.⁵⁰ If neither of these plants were available, various common wild *Indigofera* spp. (ḥəwīr~ḥəwīl) were used instead, the leaves

---

[48] See Beech (2003, 29) writing about 5500–3500 BCE stone sinkers: "Larger net sinkers may have been used in conjunction with gill nets or beach seines; small examples may have been used in conjunction with casting nets or small beach seine nets.... The first type of net sinkers are flat oval pebbles, notched roughly in the middle of their long sides."

[49] Crushed lightly and then rubbed between the fibres, or ground and added to water in which the fibres were left to soak overnight or longer.

[50] On Samḥa, the imported cotton yarn was dyed before being knotted: the whole *Limonium* plant was crushed and put into a pool of seawater and the cotton immersed and left to soak until it had absorbed the colour. The sheep wool used for nets was dyed in the same manner.

crushed to a paste and rubbed hard into the fibres.[51] These plant pastes also dyed the fibres a darker colour, making the net less visible to fish in rocky areas. For sandy areas, some fishermen, and especially on ʿAbd al-Kūri, would cook the fishing equipment in quicklime (*nūrə~nʸūrə*) to strengthen and bleach it. Homemade quicklime was added to boiling water and the nets dropped in and left to simmer. They were left to soak in the mixture overnight before being spread out in the sun to dry.

All nets were looked after carefully: it was said that with the right care a net could last for 10–12 years. Cast nets do not tolerate fresh water, so if a net became soaked in rainwater, the fisherman would quickly immerse it in saltwater. Like all other cotton fishing gear, nets were hung up in the shade in between fishing trips. During the long months of the monsoon, all fishing equipment not in use was stored in a place of shade, well out of the reach of the monsoon winds and rodents.

Each net was used for specific types of fish. The smallest, of 3–4 *durūʿ* (a *déraʿ*, pl. *durūʿ* is the distance from the elbow to the tip of the extended middle finger, a cubit) was cast by the fisherman standing in shallow water. The fish most commonly caught in this way were the small coastal pelagic fishes (anchovies, sardines, herrings, round herrings, sprats, mackerels,

---

[51] A paste of the crushed leaves was also used cosmetically to paint the face, starting off green but then turning blue. It was also used to dye unbleached calico or balls of newly-spun sheep wool: the material and the plant paste were added to water, and this was brought to the boil; the material was then spread out sopping wet—never wrung dry—in the sun to dry and change colour.

scads, fusiliers, flying fish, half beaks and silversides (Nichols 2001, 9.5.1). These small fish were usually grouped together as ʿídi, 'sardine-type fish', more properly the term for the Indian oil sardine.[52] Other smaller fish caught for food or bait with smaller cast nets were damselfish~clownfish (ʿəskə́do), goatfish (ḳanśáʿa), terapon (ʿábrəhem), fusiliers (səlmə́do), various flathead and sillago spp. (fə́ḳəreś), small sweetlips and seabream (both bōdiḥ).[53] If none of these fish could be caught, a fisherman in dire need of bait would cast his net into a large rock pool or lagoon and hope for the best. This kind of 'blind' casting was common when fishing at night.

The ṣíni~ṣōwnu~ṣínhən and (ṣíni) śʿérə~śġéyrə cast nets of 6–7 durūʿ were cast from the shore for medium-sized, inshore fish such as rabbitfish (śéysino), or from a dugout in waters of 2–3 bāʿ depth (a bāʿ pl. bəwáʿ is the distance between the extended tip of the middle finger of one hand to the extended fingertip of the other, arms stretched wide—around 6 feet or 1.8 metre, a fathom). The largest, 12-durūʿ net was cast from a dugout in deeper waters, often to catch small bait fish swimming in shoals out at sea.

Some full-time fishermen of the north coast also used a large circular net called máxwar, cast from a dugout in waters

---

[52] Shoals of these vital small fish arrive in great numbers as the sea calms down after the summer monsoon. During the rest of the year, they can be found here and there along the coast, but in the monsoon months they are largely absent.

[53] And in the Qadámə are in the west, flatfish, for which this area was renowned.

of some five bəwáʿ depth. A large rectangular cotton seine net of a smaller mesh than the ṣīni~ṣōwnu~ṣínhən was also used, laid in the sea at right angles to the shore. This was generally called míśgir~mśígəhir, a name also given to the net used to trap feral donkeys and goats.[54] In the Ġúbbah area, fishermen used a large circular cotton net called rígimi, a net with a slipknot (miśríṭo or śéraṭ). A type of beach seine with wings, called fēriʾ, was also used close inshore. These larger nets, referred to in general as kaṭəbə (an Arabic term), were only used by full-time fishermen working as a group.

In the rule of Sultan ʿĪsa bin ʿAli (reigned 1952–1967), an Emirati fisherman called Saʿīd Ḥammād, who had settled in Soqoṭra during the reign of the previous sultan, introduced the idea of fishing with the large girīf drag net, well-known on the mainland,[55] to catch small coastal pelagic fishes. These were dried and sold as géšaʿ~kóśaʿ (Ar. wazīf).[56] Later still, the large-meshed gill nets (lyūx) appeared and were used to trap shark and the largest fish.

---

[54] Palm-frond ribs were placed at intervals, vertically, to hold the net rigid. izīʿa dihé mśígəhur wə-lāṭ yímdid túyhin bə-rínhəm wə-yəʿāmer híyhin bārrūsi, ṭad bə-nʸaṣf wə-ṭad bə-nʸaṣf, "He would take his mśígəhur nets and stretch them out in the sea and set anchor-weights for them: one for one end of the net and another at the other end." (Aḥmad Saʿd Taḥkí)

[55] See Serjeant (writing in 1967, cited in Doe, 1992, 175): "The sardine seine net, the jarīf, operated by some forty men, which is so widely used on the coasts of Hadramaut, has no place in Socotra."

[56] In 2004, one sack of these sold for YR600.

3.4. Handlines (śúʔhur, pl. íʔiśhur)

Handlines were twisted from cotton fibre,[57] usually three strands (mətállit̠), and a careful fisherman re-twisted his cotton lines every day after fishing. Newly made lines were treated with *Periploca* (ftax), a plant that used to be common around Ḥéybak̟ on the north coast. The fisherman crushed the plant stems to a paste, smoothed this over his palms and then ran the lines through his hands again and again. This dyed the lines a red-brown colour as well as toughening them. When not in use, lines, like nets, were hung somewhere out of the sun in a place safe from rodents.

The term šikkə, for the more recent longlines, commonly of some nine bāʕ length, was borrowed from Arabic. Longlines attached to the dugout to catch larger fish such as shark and tuna were called šikkə ṣālil, and those tied to an anchor and left in situ for a period with a marker to indicate its position were called šikkə wāk̟aʕ. Longlines were used out at sea and from a dugout.

3.4.1. Hooks (ʕék̟əlhe, pl. ʕək̟ālihe)

Metal hooks could sometimes be purchased from the trade boats coming from Muscat[58] and the Gulf. Otherwise fishermen got hold of an old nail (mə́smar) or scrap of metal, and hammered

---

[57] On Samḥa, before cotton yarn became available, the underbark of *Ficus salicifolia* (íʔtib) was used to make twine for lines.

[58] Or purchased in Muscat: Soqot̠rans used to travel to Muscat to work, especially during the monsoon months.

and shaped them to a fishhook. If these were not available, fishermen had to make use of whatever was available: whittling a hook from the hard wood of a tree, such as *Zygocarpum coeruleum*. A hook could also be fashioned from the ulna (ḳówḥaf) of the front leg of a goat: there is a gap at the 'elbow' of the bone which can be carefully snapped to make a hook, though rather a fragile one.[59]

3.4.2. Trace or Leader (ʿamūd or ṭarb di-ʿékəlhe) and Swivels (mīdār)

The trace that protects the fishing line was usually made from the hollowed-out humerus of the lower back leg of a sheep or goat.[60] Later on, imported swivels (mīdār) were placed above the trace.

3.4.3. Weights or Sinkers *(rəsās)*

Although some ready-made lead sinkers were imported, more commonly fishermen used pebbles (óʔobən) or pieces of lead worked by the local blacksmith (ṣāyaʿ~ṣāyaġ). The use of dif-

---

[59] See Beech (2003, 291), writing about fishhooks from the fifth and fourth millennia BCE: "The earliest fish hooks in southeast Arabia are made of marine shell, usually from pearl oyster or large bivalves." He nowhere mentions finds of bone fishhooks.

[60] *rēḵuḵ yəʿúmər tus men ṣáḥəlo di-šfāniś; íno d-iʿāmər men miśneg di-óʔoz wə-íno d-iʿāmər men ṭálfə di-fólihi*, "The trace is made from animal bone; some make it from the narrow bone of the lower back leg of a goat, and some from the slender bone of the foreleg of a calf." (Aḥmad Saʿd Taḥkí)

ferent weights of sinkers was variously described as *šaʿrókən bə-rəsāsə*, 'we fished with a lead sinker to take the bait to the bottom'; *šaʿrókən bə-səlá*, 'we fished without a sinker so that the bait stayed floating on the surface'; or *šaʿrókən bə-rāḳab*, 'we fished with a very light sinker so that the bait remained suspended below the surface of the sea' (i.e., not sinking too far down').

3.4.4. Clubs, Gaffs and Spears

Among a fisherman's equipment was a short, heavy club (*məḳəláʿa* or *ṭárḳa*). As well as being used to stun larger fish, it was used to kill moray eels (*némiro*) which can grow to an alarming size. A fisher might also take a short spear (*múšʿiḵ*) or pointed stick (*šiyḵ*),[61] made by sharpening a shaft of hard wood to a point at one end and then fire-hardening it. This was used to stab (√šʿḵ, 'to pierce') moray eels or any other dangerous sea creature which had got into the fish trap. He might also use a hooked gaff (*mísḥaf*~*míšxaf* or *kəllāb*)[62] made by the local blacksmith: with a large hook at one end for shark and a smaller hook for large fish such as kingfish, tuna or bonito. The handle of the gaff was usually made from the widely available *Croton socotranus* shrub (*mítrer*).

---

[61] Used by pastoralists to dig up various edible corms and bulbs.

[62] *kəllāb*: *nəʿāmer ʿis kəllāb wə-náʿnən bis ʿaf išóʔki tan*, "we call it *kəllāb* and we used it to pull (a fish) in until it is right beside us."

3.5. Fishing with Handlines

Fishing with handlines was carried out in a variety of ways, the principal ones being:

3.5.1. Handlining from the Shore or from Rocks

One method was the fisherman whirling the line around his head before casting it, a method called *enṭílilun~inṭílilo*. In earlier years this was done using the bone lure (*rēḳuḳ*, see 3.10.), mainly to catch fish such as *ḳerbōbə* triggerfishes and leatherjackets, *di-ḥáyhul* scorpionfish, *ʿáyho ḳīhen* small jacks,[63] *ʿáskədo*, damselfish~clownfish and other small fish such as the *fə́ḳərəš* flatheads and sillago. Fish caught in this way were called *ṣə́də minṭílhil*.

3.5.2. Handlining from Cliffs and Overhangs or from a Dugout Canoe

This method was typically used to catch bottom-dwelling fish. The line had sidelines knotted (*mérkīn*) onto it, each one bearing one or two hooks (more when fishing in deeper seas), and a stone attached at the bottom as a weight. The hooks were baited with a 'sardine-type' fish into which the hook had been embedded until it was invisible. This method was called *inḵílilo* and the fisherman *náḳəlhel* pl. *náḳəlhul*.

Alternatively, a single line was used with a single, large hook and a trace above (if the fisherman owned one). Some dis-

---

[63] Many jacks are called *ʿáyho* when small, and *šáʔkid* or *ráʔḥa* when large.

tance below was a large stone, one with a natural or man-made hole or a square-shaped one with a projection around which twine of date palm fibre (aḥtīmi)[64] could be firmly tied. This method was used mainly to catch the gʸaḥš type of fish[65] found swimming around the sandy bottom of rock faces and coral atolls. In his dugout, the fisherman would study the current (ǝl-māyǝ): if moving away from the rock face out to sea, he would position himself right beside the rock face. If it were flowing from the sea towards the rock face, he would position himself at some distance from the rock face. He then lowered the line until it hit the sandy bottom, before drawing it up again to about two ḵāmǝ depth (ḵāmǝ, 'the height of a man'), and tying the other end of the line around his thigh. He would then sit in the dugout, letting the current do the work of moving the baited hook around in the water. This kind of fishing is called néḥǝbǝ (nǝnúḥub, 'we fish in the néḥǝbǝ way') and was used to catch fish such as fṣáʔḥan emperors, līhun and ḥáyhal groupers and the

---

[64] aḥtími, pl. aḥtóyhim were also used for the šēriyǝ rope for shark fishing (see 3.15.1.) or as anchor rope (ḵayd di-barrūsi). It was made from the smallest leaflets of the growing point (dilʕáyn) of a date palm, laid out in the sun to dry and then twisted into twine (taḥtīmǝn). That for fishing was three-ply (mǝṭállit̠), unlike the rope for the well bucket (miśiyo di-ʕúbǝhur) which was four-ply (mǝrábbaʕ).

[65] Fish such as the fṣáʔḥan, máʕsam, kteb, bígǝhel, ḥídǝher and ṣérʕe emperors; bū nǝ́ḵtǝ threadfin bream and sárḥīn and di-nǝ́ḵtǝ seabream; nǝ́ḵǝḵ sweetlips and maʕrēmǝ snappers. The term gʸaḥš is possibly related to jašš, used in the Gulf for trevallies (Carangidae) (see Al-Salimi and Staples 2019, 546).

ḳarbōbə triggerfish and leatherjackets so highly valued for their livers.

Another method was similar to the above, but was used in rocky terrain, and involved two hooks and two stone weights. The line was lowered until the stones hit the bottom. It was gently jiggled around to ensure that the hooks had not snagged on anything. Fishing with two hooks in this way this was called *šidlɛ́lə* or *inṭílilo di-šidlɛ́lə*.

During the monsoon, when the sea was too rough to venture out, fishermen used a similar method to fish from inshore rocks. The line was cast and the hook(s) allowed to sink to the bottom. A fish taking the bait would either swim off to an overhang to hide, or would swim out to sea, when it could be played until it tired. Fish caught in this way were commonly *bōdiḥ* sweetlips and *diʿan di-ʿārə* seabream, *rígaḥ* sweetlips and *mirāṭa* mojarra, all considered good eating.

3.6. Catching Fish by Hand

In times of hunger, even the less desirable fish were hunted, including by women. When groups of *məgrūməhem* porcupinefish came close inshore at low tide, women would wade into the sea up to their knees, carrying a container in one hand and a stem of the spiny *Lycium* shrub (*súʾhur*) in the other. They would poke a porcupinefish with the twig to startle it and make it inflate. It was then easy to pick up and put in the container, when it would deflate, water exuding from what islanders called its 'ears'.⁶⁶ When further porcupinefish were thrown in on top of it, it would struggle to reinflate, but in the absence of water, would die.

Smaller specimens were regarded as good eating: both flesh and cooking water were liked as being very 'sweet', the liver dissolving into the water. The preferred cooking method was to layer a number of the fish in a clay pot, add a little water, cover it, then leave the pot to simmer gently until the skin and spines had softened—a long time. After discarding the head, chunks of skin were picked off, given a good chew, and then discarded along with the spines. All the rest of the fish flesh was edible, including the softened bones. Although there are still plenty of these fish, Mubārak reports that no one bothers catching and eating them today.

3.7. Sea Birds as a Guide to Shoaling Fish

Out at sea, rafts of diving shearwaters (*bíšišt*) or circling cormorants (*sə́məno*)⁶⁷ were a good indicator of shoals of 'sardine-type' fish (see 3.9.1.) and the tuna and shark in pursuit of them.⁶⁸ Seeing a *naširīn*,⁶⁹ a large bird with a white front and multicol-

---

⁶⁶ People encountering a porcupinefish at sea, inflating itself defensively, would poke a stick into its 'ear' to make it deflate.

⁶⁷ The nestlings of both these birds were also hunted for food along the cliff ledges at night.

⁶⁸ See also Al-Saghier and Symens (2000, 1010), on the use by fishermen of large feeding flocks of birds to locate schools of smaller fish and tunas.

⁶⁹ *naširīn*, not yet identified.

oured back, diving into the water and bringing up fish in its beak, suggested the presence of larger types of fish. Closer inshore, the sight of the small white gull called kerrāˁ[70] diving at great speed was another indicator of 'sardine-type' and other small fish.

3.8. Attracting Fish

When the water was clear and still in rocky areas where fish were known to gather, fishermen would scatter small fragments of bait across the surface of the sea to attract them. This was called tíriher~téririn, 'temptation', or ḥābíbo, 'enticement'. If there were ripples or small wavelets, they crumbled the bait with coarse sand (šĭmi) to slow its descent to the bottom. The baited line was then gently let down, the current carrying it towards the rock face where the fish were feeding. It was hoped that, excited by the scattered bait, the fish would now go for the larger bait on the hook.

3.9. Bait (ṥámdə)

3.9.1. Small Coastal Pelagic Fishes

The preferred bait was one of the small coastal pelagic fishes, the 'sardine-type' shoaling fish. It was with this kind of bait that the valuable large fish such as ṭānĭk~ṭernāk 'Spanish mackerel' and zíhnin and ṥə́rwəhe 'tunas' were caught. Indeed, fishermen say that "no fish worth catching can ignore a bait of a 'sardine-type' fish." These include sardine, anchovy, herring, round her-

---

[70] kerrāˁ, not yet identified, but possibly a species of tern.

ring, chub and Indian mackerel, scad, sprats, fusiliers, flying fish and halfbeaks[71] (though the small ḳáššo 'Old World silversides' found close inshore were considered an inferior bait).[72] While having individual names, many of these small fish were collectively known as ʿídi, or 'sardine-type fish', though ʿídi properly refers to the Indian oil sardine. They were used as bait for catching medium to large fish, larger specimens being cut up as bait for even larger fish (mírgid di-ṣṓdə).

The hook was buried deep inside the fish and a length of line wound around its gills to keep the hook firmly in place. When line fishing, this bait was called mḗsīyo (vb. nəmḗsīyin, 'we fish with the mḗsīyo bait'). The best 'sardine-type fish' were considered to be the following (from largest to smallest): gḗdeb~gídeb~jḗdeb 'Indian scad', and 'blue or chub mackerel' > gərā́də 'delicate round herring' (similar in size to the former) > sḗli

---

[71] sḗli 'Gulf herring'; gərā́də 'delicate round herring'; ʿefirə́ro 'bluestripe herring'; rínnəb 'various anchovy spp.'; bíśaʿa 'various herring and shad spp.'; ḳáššo 'Old World silverside'; ʿírho 'halfbeaks', 'needlefish' and 'cornetfish'; fə́kəreš 'flathead and sillago spp.', as well as other fish such as ḳanṣáʿa 'goatfish'; ʿábrəhem 'terapon'; bṓdiḥ 'small sweetlips' and 'seabream'; səlmə́do 'fusiliers'; mírimaher 'lizardfish'; gḗdeb~gídeb~jḗdeb 'Indian scad', and 'blue and chub mackerel'; fériher~férifer 'flying fish'; and kə́libə 'sprats' (though kə́libə is also a general term for 'fry' and 'fingerlings').

[72] Described as "having heads big for their body, protruding eyes and very coarse-textured skin; migratory, arriving at the end of the monsoon and staying until the beginning of the next one; found in salt and brackish water, they are caught by net; not popular as food as they are all scales and bones and have a bitter-tasting head; can be used as bait if there is nothing else."

'Gulf herring' > ˁefiríro 'bluestripe herring' > biśaˁa 'various herring and shad spp.', as well as the biśáˁa di-ḥáṣlub 'herring and shad spp.' > ˁídi 'Indian oil sardine' > rínnəb 'anchovy spp.' > kə́libə 'sprats'.

The ˁídi Indian oil sardine and the kə́libə, sḗli, gərād and rínnəb were especially prized as bait. For the large fish of the deeper seas, the ˁídi and sḗli were regarded as the best bait; after them the gərādə, rínnəb[73] and kə́libə. These types of fish were usually seen in shoals further out at sea, while the other ˁídi 'sardine-type fish' ventured closer inshore. It was said that at times when the moon gave little light, the ˁídi ate very little and grew thin, but when it was full, they ate continuously and grew fat.

The ˁídi 'sardine-type fish' are all shoaling fish, their shoals differing in size and appearance, and experienced fisherman would know what kind of fish a shoal contained before he cast his net. These small but vital fish start to arrive at the beginning of winter as the seas calm down at the end of the summer monsoon, the rínnəb and sḗli leaving Soqotri seas at the end of winter. During the long months of the monsoon, the ˁídi fish tended to move out to sea, and in some years they failed to arrive at all. However, for much of the year they could be found in pockets here and there around the coast.

Many terms describe the ˁídi fish and their predators. For instance, on seeing the shoals moving towards the shore, people would say ˁídi gidóḥo bis, 'the sardine-type fish have been

---

[73] And in more recent years, fishermen have tried using dried rínnəb as bait.

brought (inshore)', i.e., by the larger fish pursuing them. Some other terms used to describe these fish and their predators are:

di-máḥsa refers to extensive shoals swimming towards the shore, fleeing the *kēr* whale shark, other shark and large predatory fish.

ʔirīfī refers to shoals seen in shallow waters, and especially those seen swimming into a sandy bay before sunrise or going back out to sea in the early afternoon. Fishermen spread the word that an *ʔirīfī* has arrived in such and such a bay and all hurry to take advantage of this opportunity. As long as the sea remains calm (*šwār*), this pattern of movement is repeated over a period of one to two weeks, but any wind sends the shoals straight back out to sea. The shoals come into the bays at dawn, seething on the surface of the sea and splashing as they try to escape the fish hunting them. When they go back out to sea in the early afternoon, they swim calmly, beneath the surface of the sea. Islanders say that by the end of their stay in a bay, the seabed has been turned dark by their excreta.

fogś refers to the thrashing and splashing of the fish pursuing a shoal, fish such as such as the *ráʔḥa*, *dāfin* and *ṭamákerə* trevallies, *ṭānīk~ṭə́rnāk* Spanish mackerel, *śərə́whin* skipjack and other tuna.

maʿrērə refers to a large shoal of *ʿīdi* corralled by circling predators, especially *zíhnin* and *śərə́whin* tunas, *ráʔḥa* trevallies and *śéʔḥer* barracuda.[74] A *maʿrērə di-léḥḥīm* ('a shark *maʿrērə*') refers to a school of fish being 'herded' by shark. The predators

---

[74] I have seen Soqoṭra cormorants (*sémənə*) do the same, circling a shoal of sardines to make a *maʿrērə*.

circle the shoal, force them up to the surface, and then dart in to pick off individual fish. A *maʿrḗrə* is usually broken up by the arrival of some huge predator rising from the depths, disturbed by the commotion. The *maʿrḗrə* then breaks up into many small *fogś* groups, each pursued by different predators.

ḥāber di-ʿídi refers to a shoal of *ʿídi* visible as a dark patch or shadow (*ḥāber*, 'streak') out at sea. *ḥāber di-ṣṓdə* refers to a school of larger fish seen out at sea.

3.9.2. Cephalopods

The next best bait after an *ʿídi* 'sardine-type fish' was one of the cephalopods: an *ʿáṭərhe* 'squid' or 'cuttlefish' or a *térəbaḥt* 'octopus'. Both were eaten by some of the islanders. The *Loligo* sp. squid, *ʿáṭərhe líbəhan*, 'pale-coloured squid' provided the best bait, while the *ʿáṭerhe ʿáfer*, 'reddish-coloured squid' (a term usually referring to cuttlefish [Sepiida]) was less desirable. Cephalopods were used especially as bait for *ṭə́rnāk* 'kingfish', *ráʾḥa* 'trevally' and the *śərə́whin* and *zíhnin* 'tunas', as these are not attracted to a bait of octopus. To prepare bait from an octopus, the outer skin was peeled from the tentacles and the white flesh beneath cut into sardine-length sections, each tentacle providing two pieces of bait. Squid and cuttlefish were treated in a similar way, but the flesh of the main body was also cut into strips.

3.9.3. Netting Lagoons

When none of the above baitfish were available, a net was cast in lagoons (*ḥor~xor*) to catch the kinds of fish which thrive in brackish or saline water (*rīho bíḳəbiḳ*), such as the ʿ*ábrəhem* 'terapon' and *ḥárəbo* 'mullet'. These fish are used whole as bait for larger fish, including rays and shark, or are cut into chunks to attract various bottom-dwelling fish.

3.9.4. Crabs (*ḥanśíʔo*, pl. *ḥánśe*) and Hermit Crabs (*ḥínkok~ḥínkuk~ḥáynkek*)

Crabs of all kinds provided bait: the pale ghost crabs (*ḥanśíʔo libíni*)[75] and all sorts of dark-coloured rock crabs (*ḥanśíʔo ḳśébeb*). They were caught by hand or were disabled by throwing a stone at them. The smaller legs (*śérəhān*), larger pincers (*məlḳez*, du. *məlḳázi*) and carapace were removed, leaving the innards and the thorax (*ḳɛrf*). This was split into sections to use as bait, the gap made by removing a leg providing a place to insert a hook. Fishing families would spend time collecting a number of crabs and would then remove their legs and put them in a container which they kept in a shady place. Given water, the crabs would survive for a day or more. Crab were used in particular to bait fish traps, where they attracted fish like the *samōmə, līhun, silīb* and ʿ*ílmə* 'groupers', and the *gʸaḥś* fish: principally emperors (*fṣáʿhan, máʿsam, kteb, ḥídəher, bígəhel, śérʿe* and *sárḥīn*), but also threadfin bream, seabream, grunters and certain snappers.

Hermit crabs were also used as bait. They were usually collected in the hours of darkness, but could also be found lurking in dark, shady places during the day. Like crabs, they could

---

[75] Ghost crabs were also used to treat whooping cough (*śkázə*, √š + kzy, 'to cough and cough to the point of choking or passing out'): they were boiled in water and the cooled and strained water drunk.

be kept alive for a few days in a container kept in a dark place. When needed, the shell was smashed and the soft body removed. After removing the head and pincers, the remaining flesh was ready to use as bait.

3.9.5. Bristle Worms / Polychaetes (ʿōmə)

A reddish worm called ʿōmə,[76] probably a species of bristle worm, made a bait as useful as a hermit crab, but was only available in sandy areas. Dug out of the sand, it had first to be laid in salt to dry it out and harden it: it would break up on the hook if used alive.

Bristle worm or hermit crab bait were used to catch ʿáržeb 'bonefish' (Albulidae), 'ladyfish' (Elopidae) and 'silversides' (Atherinidae), béhirə 'milkfish' (Chanidae) and 'tarpon' (Megalopidae), šōbiḥ, ḥínkəhon and ʿándaka 'snappers' and 'jobfish' (Lutjanidae), ktif 'sicklefish' (Drepanidae) and 'spadefish' (Ephippidae), érəhe 'pompano spp.' (Carangidae), ʿə́skədo 'damselfishes' and 'clownfishes' (Pomacentridae), mirāṭa 'mojarras' (Gerreidae) and 'ponyfish' (Leiognathidae), ḥáṭəhan 'threadfin breams' or 'false snappers' (Nemipteridae), rígaḥ, nə́kak and ḥádiyiḵ 'grunters' (Haemulidae), di-ʿan di-ʿārə and bōdiḥ 'sea bream' (Sparidae), ṣōrif 'drums' (Sciaenidae), ʾasīb and ʾasīb di-nəhárher 'unicornfish' (Acanthuridae) and bidbōdi or fə́kəreš 'flatheads' (Platycephalidae). Many of these were found in lagoons as well as in the sea. míśereḵ 'angelfish' (Pomacanthidae),

---

[76] Al-Salimi and Staples (2019, 553) give ʿūma, pl. ʿuwam, as 'sardine', but they also note that the classical Arab lexicographers refer to ʿūma as either an insect or a snake.

'batfish' (Ephippidae) and 'moonyfishes' (Monodactylidae) also came to this bait, but these fish were not usually wanted, either as food or as bait.

3.9.6. Other Bait

Mubārak said that there was always some sort of bait to be found, even if only the *ḳáššo* 'Old World silversides' swimming close inshore. Shellfish meat could be used to catch bottom-dwelling fish (*ṣódə di-ḳaʿ*), coral fish (*ṣódə di-ṣíʿəfə*) or rock fish (*ṣódə di-ḳéśʔor*), such as groupers and emperors. He himself never resorted to using mudskippers, blennies or gobies (*kibíʔhin*), but other fishermen around the island said that when desperate they did make use of these. Mubārak also spoke of a bait he had never used himself but had seen others using: a piece of white stone or smooth white shell around which a skilled fisherman would tie a line and use as a lure for very greedy fish such as the *ḥálḥal* 'grouper' (described as "a fierce and very fatty fish with a huge mouth that goes for anything—even a fisherman's toes"). If a fish took hold of this, a really clever fisherman might be able to land it, if he were able to jerk it from the sea hard and fast enough.[77]

---

[77] See Beech (2003, 291) writing about shellfish hooks from the fifth to the late fourth millennium BCE: "The earliest fish hooks in southeast Arabia are made of marine shell, usually from pearl oyster or large bivalves.... A further advantage of using shells with a shiny/glistening surface was that it served to entice fish to bite."

3.9.7. Transporting Bait

Bait was carried to the fishing site in a variety of containers made from plaited strips of date palm fibre. The ones most commonly used were a *mə́sfi*, a round, lidless basket with a carrying handle, a *kúffə* or *dáhanə* (both names were used), a squareish, lidless basket with no handles, or a *míllug*, an oblong container made from a length of woven date palm doubled back on itself, stitched at each side to make a pocket, and the remaining upper part folded over to close it, like an envelope.[78]

3.10. Lures (*rēḳuḳ*)

Lures were made from a variety of materials: from a twig of peeled *Adenium* shaped to look like a sardine, one end of the twig frayed out to look like a tail fin. Or from a piece of peeled *Cissus* vine (*əṣlíʿo di-ʿátərhe*) cut from between two joints of a stem, again with one end beaten to separate out the fibres to look like a tail fin. Alternatively, the slim bone of the lower hindleg of a sheep or goat (*mísneg di-teʾe* or *mísneg di-óʾoz*), or of the foreleg of a calf (*tálfə di-fólihi*) was hollowed out and roughly shaped to make a fish-shaped lure called *ṣóhəlo di-rēḳuḳ* ('bone lure'). A lure could even be made from lengths of white or yellow tape (*tel*), imported to decorate dresses, tied in a bunch and attached to the hook.

A lure had to be played (*šəmḗśi*): *korúmma šəmḗśiʾin tus, íkkən bə-rího mes kān tyóʾo ʿidi, w-ihālah ʿis hot wə-īti*, "If we wig-

---

[78] A *míllug* was also used to store pages of the Holy Qurʾān.

gle it around it looks like a sardine in the water and a large fish will leap to grab it and eat it." (Aḥmad Saʿd Taḥkí)

3.11. Fish Traps (ḳérḳor, pl. ḳerāḳir)

Though some seasonal fishermen made use of fish traps, they were mainly used by full-time fishermen. Many fishermen whose families relied on fish for the major part of their diet, worked more than one trap.[79] In rocky areas of the coast, fish traps were the main way of harvesting the sea during the long months of the monsoon when other fishing was only possible in a few sheltered areas, or along the south coast where the effects of the monsoon were milder.[80] At other times of the year they were used along the northern and southern coasts in sandy areas when the sea was calm: in the summer before the southwest monsoon, and at the end of the monsoon in the period of calm before the start of the northeast monsoon. When not in use, the traps were raised off the ground and left to dry in the sun.

In earlier times there was no 'closed season' (kítwə) for line and fish-trap fishing. This relatively new concept, imported from the mainland, was established later across the island for

---

[79] Mubārak used to work twelve ḳérḳor, each set at a different site. He prided himself on never using a marker buoy but instead judged a fish trap's position by lining it up with features on land. When working at the pearl fishing, he would set six traps one day and six the next.

[80] On Samḥa in the monsoon, fish traps could only be used in certain places on the southeastern side of the island, as the seas were too rough on the northwestern side where the main settlement lies. On ʿAbd al-Kūri too, the southern side of the island is very stormy in the monsoon months and fish traps could not be set there at this time.

the benefit of those full-time fishermen going after shark and the more valuable large fish.

There were two kinds of ḳérḳor:

The ḳérḳor maḥgílo was some three metres across and had eight to eleven ʕayn 'eye' (the same term used for the mesh in a net). This was the type of trap most widely used by seasonal fishermen, or by those who had no access to a dugout or who lacked the expertise to use the larger trap. The ḳérḳor maḥgílo was set at low tide, close to the shore. In bad weather[81] its position was marked by a float or buoy (mə́kfə) made from the thick stump of a palm rib (kérəbə, pl. kíreb), or a stick with a scrap of cloth tied to the top.

The large ḳérḳor was five metres or so across with 11, 12 or 14 'eyes'. This was rowed out to sea in a dugout, to a depth of some 12 bāʕ and let down over the side of the boat, its position again marked by a float or buoy.

3.11.1. Manufacture

Today, most traps are imported and consist of chicken wire stretched over a steel wire frame. In earlier times they were made by specialist craftsmen,[82] using local materials: the fruit-

---

[81] During the early winter and late summer months when the sea was often quite rough.

[82] Children watched adults weaving traps and copied them, making miniature ḳérḳor out of date palm material. They used them to practise catching small lagoon fish. They also made toy dhows from the same material, with a mast and a manoeuvrable triangular sail which they learned to set (taʕdílə) according to wind direction, before pushing the boat off into the shallower waters of the lagoon.

ing stalks (*fōtir*) of the date palm or strips of *Flueggea, Allophylus, Croton socotranus* or *Commiphora ornifolia* wood. Only live wood was used and only slim stems without a knot (*ənḳə́bo*) were cut. The selected stems were peeled, whittled to the correct length, and then torn between the teeth into flat strips. These were first laid in the sun to dry out, and were then taken to a lagoon and left to soften in the brackish water for three or four days. If there was no lagoon nearby, the strips were laid in seawater instead, for two or three days. The soaked pieces were then buried in sand and left for two days. They were now ready for weaving.

The strips were used in pairs to lend extra rigidity. First the base (*ṭábḳə di-g𝑦ḗmə*) was made, as this determined the size of the trap. Weaving began at one side of the base and worked across, ending at a corner (*ḥad̲ī́fo*). The completed base was braced with six sticks (*mə́nṣef~nī́ṣef*) made from a hard wood such as *Croton socotranus* or tamarix (*Tamarix nilotica*). Any excess was trimmed off, and then the top (*ṭábḳə di-ṣáʿnhən*) was woven. This was braced by three sticks (*mísgud*) leading outwards from the base of the V, one going vertically down the middle and the other two at an angle to each corner. Next, the long strip (*ḥáwiyah~ḥṓyə*) that goes right around the trap, joining the base to the top, was made, beginning at the 'mouth' (*ḥé~xá*). This strip was also strengthened with a number of bracing sticks (*rəkī́zi*, pl. *rekḗyiz* or *mántis*, pl. *mənā́tis*), which were used to manoeuvre the trap. Finally, the tunnel leading into the trap was made, wide at the mouth and growing narrower as it reached further inside the trap. Many craftsmen tied stout poles, usually of the ubiquitous *Croton socotranus*, to the base of the completed trap to lend added weight, so that when the trap landed on the seabed, it would be sure to settle on its heavier base. These poles extended beyond the trap at each side and served as carrying handles.[83] The newly made trap was left in the sea for anything up to ten days until it had lost its pale colour and become covered in the green algal growth that made it less visible to fish.

3.11.2. Selecting a Site

When selecting a site for the first time, a fisherman normally had to seek permission from the owner of the land. If this was given, he would construct a 'pen' for his trap (ḥor di-ḳérḳor, 'fish-trap pen') in any suitable (and unoccupied) site. He would not become the owner of the 'pen', able to pass it on to his children: rather, a 'pen' became part of the property of the landowner.[84] However, in practice, the fisherman could usually set his trap in the same 'pen' year after year and generation after

---

[83] See Jansen van Rensburg (2016, 125), where he was told by fishermen that the added weight of the poles prevented the trap being dragged by the current. He was also told that in rocky areas stones were placed on top of the tips of the poles to hold the trap down, while in sandy areas, the tips of the poles dug themselves into the sand and held the trap down in that way.

[84] On the island of ʿAbd al-Kūri this was not the case. Here, once a 'pen' had been constructed, it became the property of the fisherman who had built it. It was inheritable property, and others could use it only with permission. He was, however, not able to sell it to an outsider or to give anyone else permission to do so.

generation, as long as he acknowledged that it was not his private property (*mulk*).

3.11.3. Making a 'Pen' and Setting the Trap

The smaller *ḳérḳor maḥgílo*[85] was carried down to the beach at low tide, preferably in the late morning when the sea was warmer. The fisherman would then walk into the sea until the water reached his head, before diving down to clear an area for the trap. He would place rocks to form a roughly circular wall, the 'pen', and then return for the trap and set it inside the 'pen'. Once lodged on the seabed, he would place a heavy rock on top of each *mántis* bracing stick to weigh the trap down. He would then pile other rocks over and around the trap until it was barely visible, leaving only the 'mouth' of the trap uncovered. His next job was to clear a 'path' (*óʔorem*) through the rocks and weed to lead to the mouth of the trap. Finally, he would place bunches of soft green seaweed around the mouth to attract fish. If set not too far out, the trap was checked the next morning, the fisherman diving down to look inside. If set further out, it was only checked at the next low tide. If the fisherman saw that there were fish inside, he would attach ropes to each corner of the front of the trap and drag it ashore.

The larger *ḳérḳor* 'fish trap' was set further out to sea, lowered to the seabed from a dugout. It had to be weighted

---

[85] *maḥgílo*, lit. 'enclosed with stone walling'. It was called this because stones are built up around it to protect it from waves and strong currents which might wash it ashore. The walling also made the trap less visible, and the pile of rocks in itself attracted inquisitive fish.

down by three large rocks: one tied to the inside of the trap to lie just beneath the 'mouth' and one at each corner. The length of rope previously woven into the trap at one side of the mouth (but not tied to the trap), was used by the fisherman to lower the trap into the sea. Once on the bottom, the fisherman manoeuvred it into position, taking great care to ensure that the base rested on the seabed. (When pulling it up, the trap was manoeuvred to ensure that the base section of the trap with its six bracing sticks rested on the rim of the dugout, rather than the top section: this had only three bracing sticks and was not as strong). Once the trap was on the seabed in the correct position, the fisherman could jerk free the interwoven rope and pull it up into the dugout. Ideally this trap should be checked 24 hours later, but it could be left for up to three days. To raise it, the fisherman used a three- or four-pronged grappling hook (xaṭṭāf). He attached a heavy rock to it and then lowered the whole thing to land beside the trap. He then jiggled it around until one of its prongs had hooked into the trap, giving him some leverage as he pulled it up. If the sea was calm, the trap was perfectly visible from the dugout, and by judging current and tide, the fisherman could lower his grappling hook to the bottom and allow the current or tide to carry it to the trap.

Once the trap, large or small, was up, its contents were examined. If there were a lot of fish, the cords which hold the corners together were untied and the fish shaken out. If there were only a few fish, these were removed by hand through the 'mouth' of the trap. If there were no fish at all, the trap was reset in a different place. If a moray eel (*némiro*)[86] or any other dangerous sea creature were trapped inside, the short wooden spear with its fire-hardened point (*múšʕik̠* or *šiyk̠*) was used to dislodge it or stab it to death. On the north coast, a kind of marine eel called *bəkīli*, 'snake' sometimes turned up in a trap.[87] Mubārak used to eat these, though he was much mocked by others for doing so. He remarked that when it was hung up to dry, it dripped a reddish oil which had no fishy smell at all, though the flesh itself tasted like fish.

3.11.4. Fish Commonly Caught in Fish Traps

Of the fish caught in traps, mostly inshore demersal fish, the most highly valued were *šéysino* 'rabbitfish', *kanśáʕa* 'goatfish', *līhan* and *ḥáyhal* 'groupers', and various species of emperors and emperor breams. When a demand arose for the dried fillets of rabbitfish, these fish were processed for sale (see 6.2.5.). Otherwise *k̠érk̠or* fish were not usually sold but were for home con-

---

[86] Such as *Scuticaria tigrina*, a moray eel found in coral reefs in the Pacific and Indian Oceans (commonly known as the tiger reef-eel or tiger snake moray), or *Enchelycore schismatorhynchus*, another moray eel of coral reefs in the Pacific and Indian Oceans (commonly known as the white-margined moray, brown moray eel, or the funnel-nostril moray) (Uwe Zajonz, pers. comm.).

[87] Possibly the tiger snake eel (*Myrichthys maculosus*), a snake eel found in the Indo-Pacific which grows to a length of a metre (Uwe Zajonz, pers. comm.).

sumption. Today *ḱérḱor* fish are sold in the local markets like any other fish.[88]

3.11.5. Bait for the Fish Trap

The most common bait, especially on the outer islands, was seaweed (collectively called *śaʿr di-rínhem* 'sea hair' or *ṣáʿlef di-rínhem* 'sea leaves').[89] On the north coast of Soqoṭra, the one most used was *sílhil*, a yellow-green seaweed. Some was placed inside the trap, and some tied around the 'mouth'. Seaweed attracted herbivore fish, and especially rabbitfish, plentiful at certain times of the year and considered very good eating. However, removing rabbitfish from a trap had to be done with great care, as they have painful and venomous spines on the anal, pelvic and dorsal fins (hence one of another name for the fish, 'spinefoot'). Seagrass, also called 'turtle weed', gathered at low tide in areas where there were plentiful shellfish, was also good

---

[88] Mubārak commented that "almost anything can be offered for sale in the markets now, though usually traders specify the species they want to purchase from fishermen."

[89] Other seaweeds are *ḱárzaz*, which is very thick, fleshy and tough, and dries to a white colour and is not eaten by fish; *bū ḥanṣab* ('with tiny beads', i.e., air bladders); *sebtə* ('belt'), a strap-like weed; *ḱármaṭ*, another weed which is very soft and much liked by turtle, rabbitfish and other small herbivore fish; and *šmārix~šmāriḥ*, with very small air bladders. Both *šmārix~šmāriḥ* and *bū ḥanṣab* have air bladders (pneumatocysts) which dry to a light brown crisp. There is also a stout 'seaweed tree' known as *šagret yāsūr* from which small pieces were cut off and hung above the fire to dry in the smoke. A piece of this was sniffed to dispel evil.

as bait. The rather slimy green weed and the bright green 'lettuce-like' seaweed (Ulva; both called *eṣerī'o di-rínhem*, 'sea algal growth' or 'sea slime', or *ḳáʿṣaṣ*, a name for various *Enteromorpha* spp., also much liked by turtle and fish)[90] were collected from rocks at low tide and used as bait. On ʿAbd al-Kūri they also used a green-brown seaweed called *dáḥrer*.

To attract the larger, more valuable *gʸaḥš* fish—*samōmə, līhun, sīleb, ḥayḥal* and *ʿílmə* 'groupers', *fṣáʔhan, ṣérʿe* and *máʿsam* 'emperors', *bōdiḥ, rígaḥ* and *sárḥīn* 'seabream' (Sparidae) and 'threadfin bream' (Nemipteridae)—the best bait was always *ʿīdi* 'sardine-type fish'. In the absence of these, and if the trap were only to be left a short time (as overnight), a fisherman would either try and net some small non-*ʿīdi* fish to use instead or bait the trap with the flesh of *bílbil* 'oysters' or crab meat. The white ghost crabs (*ḥanšíʔo libīni*) were used either as *maʿtílihul*, i.e., crushed, tied into an old bit of netting and placed inside the trap, or crushed with coarse sand (*šími*) and crumbled to float around inside the trap. The sand mixture did not sink to the bottom, but 'flickered and gleamed just like tiny fish.' Crabs could also be prepared as *məʔáśnig*: the fisherman would spit 10–12 entire crabs on a handful of skewers (*məśékik*, s. *míśkek*) made from the flexible fruiting branches of a date palm and tie them to the inside of the top of the trap to sway in the current to attract fish. The ghost crab (*ḥanšíʔo libīni*) and all sorts of rock crab (*ḥanšíʔo kśébeb*) could be used as bait by just breaking them

---

[90] As observed by fishermen on ʿAbd al-Kūri, in early summer this weed "looks like a soft green moss, spreads by sending out 'threads'; if exposed to sun it dies back quickly, and stinks as it rots down."

open and attaching the meat of the larger legs and breast to the trap, leaving the smaller legs to fall to the bottom of the trap.

3.12. Stupefying Fish with Latex in Lagoons (šéber)[91]

This was primarily an activity of the monsoon months, when many islanders were down at the coast working at the date harvest and were "fed up with eating dates and longed for the taste of fish." Traditional ruling said that each lagoon (ḥor~xor) should only be exploited in this way once a year. This meant that all those in the vicinity of a lagoon about to be fished in this way had to be told well in advance so that as many as possible could share the result. Most of the lagoons of the island were fished in this way: Ḥadibo, Erhíno, Šiḵ, Díbini, Tów'aḵ (above Qáriyah—the lagoon at Qáriyah itself was too big), Máṭyef, Di-Kíbšib at Di-Sétmoh and Di-Núwtit near Qalansiyah.

The latex used was principally that of *Euphorbias* (*Euphorbia arbuscula* especially, but also *Euphorbia schimperi* or *Euphorbia spiralis*),[92] though *Adenium obesum* sap could also be used.

---

[91] On the north coast, a corvée, well remembered by Mubārak, imposed by the sultans on those people over whom they exercised most control, was the regular building up of the banks which kept the sea from flooding the lagoons. The purpose was to achieve just the right mix of salt and fresh water: good for marine life but also permitting the planting of date palms around the lagoon. If the water became too salty, the date palms died. Serjeant, writing in 1967, cited in Doe (1992, 167), briefly describes this custom.

[92] Bent (1897, 980) refers to this: "the tree euphorbias... the branches of which the natives throw into the lagoons so that the fish may be

Mostly it was the *Euphorbia* latex or *Adenium* sap alone which was used, but sometimes parts of the plant itself were crushed and used instead.

3.12.1. Method

It was on the heavily populated north coast that this method of lagoon fishing was the most organised. Three or four men would set off early in the morning to gather latex, taking several bowls with them and a goatskin of water. Before working the trees, they would first prepare a thick date and water mixture (*mēsi*) and rub this over their forearms and face, covering the rest of their body with sacking or their oldest clothing. When they reached the *Euphorbia* trees, they would each take a bowl, pour water into it to about a third of the way up and then go to the tree or shrub and strike the bark with a rock, collecting the exuding latex in a cloth held below. The cloth was then squeezed out into the bowl of water, and, as a bowl filled, its contents were transferred to the emptied goatskin.

By the time they got back to the lagoon, everyone from the area around would be waiting. One of them then walked out into the waters of the lagoon, towing the goatskin of latex behind him. Others carried bowls which they filled and refilled with latex from the goatskin. They poured the latex into the deeper waters of the lagoon where most fish tended to congregate, avoiding any shallower waters. Once the goatskin was considerably lightened, the remaining contents were poured di-

---

killed, and the poisonous milky juice of which they rub on the bottoms of their canoes to prevent leakage."

rectly into the middle of the lagoon. The toxic latex quickly brought gasping fish to the surface. The men who had gone to collect the latex and had carried it around the lagoon were rewarded by being allowed to take the first pick of the fish. After they had removed their share, it became a messy and splashy free-for-all, often lasting well into the evening. The water soon cleared and any taint of latex disappeared: it is said that the taste of the fish was not affected by the latex, nor were most livestock put off drinking the water (though some animals are said to have sniffed at it disapprovingly and been reluctant to drink for a day or so).

The fish most commonly caught in this way were *mīlax~ mīlaḥ* 'ladyfish', *ˁáržəb* 'bonefish', *béḥirə* 'milkfish' and 'tarpon', *ḥə́rəbo* 'mullet', *šōbiḥ* 'snappers', *ˁabrəhem* 'terapon', *feš* 'hawkfish', *rígaḥ* 'grunts', *di-ˁán di-ˁārə* 'seabream', *ṣōrif* 'drums', *ḥaglōlə* 'small pompano', and *míśərek* 'spadefish' and 'butterflyfish'. *mirāṭa* 'mojarras' and 'ponyfish' were also sometimes caught in lagoons, but they usually swam back out to sea at high tide.

3.13. Dangers of the Sea

Those working the sea had to be constantly on the lookout for a variety of harmful creatures. Greatly feared were the various kinds of moray eel (*némiro*)[93] and other kinds of eel which the

---

[93] Cheung and DeVantier (2006, 201) report that blackspotted moray, whitemouth moray, yellowmouth moray, and giant moray have all been seen on Soqoṭra. On ˁAbd al-Kūri, the treatment for a moray eel bite was to rub the site of the bite with the teeth of the eel itself.

fishermen called 'snakes':[94] bəkīli ʿabdəher 'blotched sea snake' and bəkīli ḥə́wro 'dark-coloured sea snake'. Possibly snake eels, they were eaten by hungrier fishing familes and were said to be full of fat. The entrails and what was seen as 'the poison sac' were removed and the rest cooked. After removing the skin, everything else was eaten. Mubārak once tried to make dried strips (mə́kədid) from one of these, but the flesh just deliquesced ("it melted away to nothing"), staining the ground beneath it black. These creatures are hated both for eating any fish they find in a trap, and because, once they settle in a trap, no fish will approach it. If a fisherman found one in his trap, he would spear it to death. There was another feared snake-like creature called di-ḥaṣáhan (also the name for the greatly feared giant centipede, Scolopendra sp.), described as "long, slender, and striped yellow and black."[95] This was only ever encountered out at sea, "floating on a mat of weed and debris." It was not seen inshore or found washed up on shore.

---

[94] But see Friedhelm Krupp (pers. comm.): "Even though they are common in the Gulf of Oman and the Arabian Gulf, no sea snakes have been recorded from the vicinity of Socotra. All sea snakes reported from the Red Sea turned out to be various species of marine eels. Perhaps the same holds true for sea snakes reported from Socotra (though it cannot be excluded that the pelagic sea snake, Hydrophis platurus, occasionally occurs in Socotran waters)." See also Uwe Zajonz (pers. comm.): "Possibly what the Soqotran fishermen describe is Myrichthys maculosus or Scuticaria tigrina, the tiger snake eel or moray eel, the tiger reef eel." See footnotes 86 and 87 above.

[95] Possibly the yellow-bellied sea snake, Hydrophis platurus.

Other feared sea creatures were stinging jellyfish: the ṣafáka of inshore waters and the ṣafáka di-ʿúbri encountered further out to sea. The small elongate puffer (gízəhel) and other poisonous puffers called zaʿmāmə~zaʿmōmə were also to be avoided. The inedible di-ḥóyhi ('of the ground'), a scorpionfish found among seashore rocks, with "venom in its spines"[96] caused acute pain and swelling if trodden on. Other Scorpaenidae were best left alone: the di-ḳáʿnhən di-rínhəm ('sea scorpion') or dəgāg ('cockerel'), "with spines on the head, puffed-out cheeks and wings like a locust,"[97] and the larger śkóʿ di-rínhem ('sea spine'), "with a spine on its head and a tail which exudes a pale venom." All these would sometimes come to a fish trap. There were harmful rays to avoid: electric and sting rays, as well as certain sea urchins, especially the úʔiriḥ~úʔiriʿ 'Diadema setosum' and gə́nəs 'Toxopneustes pileolus' (see 4.6.1.). The shoals of striped eel catfish (ḥāwər 'Plotosus lineatus') were another menace to be avoided: they have a highly venomous spine on the first dorsal and each of the pectoral fins.

---

[96] Freidhelm Krupp (pers. comm.): "This probably refers to the lionfish (Pterois spp.) or some other species of the scorpaenid family (Scorpaenidae)."

[97] Freidhelm Krupp (pers. comm.): "Species of Scorpaenidae usually have venomous spines on the head and the gill cover or operculum ('puffed-out cheeks')." Ref. 'wings like a locust', Freidhelm Krupp (pers. comm.) "This might refer to one of several species of Dendrochirus or related scorpaenid genera."

There were tales too of giant *gáḥban* clams which could trap a diver, pinning him on the seabed until he drowned,[98] but Mubārak said he had never heard of this actually happening. Ever pragmatic, he said that any experienced diver faced with what he suspected might be a giant clam would simply swirl water towards it. If it were alive it would emerge from its shell to test the water, when the gap between the two halves of the shell would become clearly visible and the clam could simply be given a wide berth. Much more to be feared, he said, were sharks[99] such as the shortfin mako (*dībə~dībé*), tiger (*nímərhan*) and hammerhead (*di-ḳérəhan*, 'horned'), all said to attack dug-out canoes. The *śáṣə~śḗṣé* 'blacktip reef shark',[100] when it comes close inshore to give birth, could also be dangerous if disturbed.

---

[98] Friedhelm Krupp (pers. comm.): "There are rumours in many parts of the world that the giant clam (*Tridacna* sp.) traps pearl divers if they happen to step between the shells. However, this has never been proven. Cousteau showed, with a gypsum leg, that it might actually be possible."

[99] *dībé wə-śíṣé tərá ləhīmi díki ná'ṣuṣ túyhi bɛ́nɛ. dībé tə'ārah hūri wə-tə'ōkib di-ḳānə; śíṣé korúmma káno bə-ṭahḥ wə́lə mibrəhe ber śíṣé wə-śíni mek mihló'o l-a'āmt di-gé'erə yhālah ṭhárək!* "The mako and the blacktip reef shark are two shark we are very scared of. A mako can reach a dugout and leap right inside it. A blacktip reef shark, if it is close inshore, or a young one, if it sees your shadow in the middle of a wave, it leaps on top of you." (Aḥmad Saʿd Taḥkí)

[100] Friedhelm Krupp (pers. comm.): "Although this species is usually harmless (certainly compared to the tiger shark) it sometimes bites the feet or legs of swimmers or fishermen wading in shallow water."

Full-time fishermen also had to cope with the everyday skin problems which result from constant exposure to salt water, and especially skin irritation (ḥarārə). Some relief from this could be obtained by washing thoroughly with hot sweet water, paying special attention to the private parts. Full-time divers suffering from red and inflamed eyes were treated by dripping warmed goat butteroil (ḥámʔi d-írəhān) into the corners of the eyes.

3.14. Fish That Cause Ciguatera Poisoning[101] and Other Illnesses

Puffer fish (Tetraodontidae) have viscera and skin which are highly poisonous.[102] The gízəhel 'elongate puffer' and other zaʕ-māmə~zaʕmōmə 'puffer fish' were understood by islanders to be

---

[101] Friedhelm Krupp (pers. comm.): "There are reports of ciguatera poisoning in parrotfish and many other species… this is caused by toxins produced by a marine microalgae, which are eaten by the fish."

[102] Friedhelm Krupp (pers. comm.): "The flesh and especially viscera (liver, ovaries) of Tetraodontidae contain tetrodotoxin, a powerful neurotoxin." See also: "Pufferfish tetrodotoxin deadens the tongue and lips, and induces dizziness and vomiting, followed by numbness and prickling over the body, rapid heart rate, decreased blood pressure and muscle paralysis. The toxin paralyzes the diaphragm muscle and stops the person who has ingested it from breathing. People who live longer than 24 hours typically survive, although possibly after a coma lasting several days. The source of tetrodotoxin in puffers has been a matter of debate, but it is increasingly accepted that bacteria in the fish's intestinal tract are the source." 'Tetraodontidae'. *Wikipedia, The Free Encyclopedia*. Wikimedia Foundation. 10 August 2024. https://en.wikipedia.org/wiki/Tetraodontidae.

potentially dangerous, and no one ate them without checking them first. To decide whether they were safe to eat, they were opened up and inspected: if they had no fat, they were discarded. If they had fat, the entrails were inspected. A "black spot between the liver and the heart" was an indication that these parts were poisonous and were discarded along with the liver and the head. Only then could the rest of the fish be eaten.[103]

In some areas around the island[104] certain fish were renowned for causing a condition known as ʿáṣṣob,[105] whose signs are dizziness and shivering, sometimes vomiting, hoarsening of the voice, cracking of the lips (di-íśfif), uncontrollable trembling, and the affected person mumbling nonsense and sometimes hallucinating.[106] The fish most commonly associated with

---

[103] In 1834 Hulton (2003, 158) writes of people on Kuria Muria islands (today al-Ḥallāniyāt MJM) rejecting certain fish (such as parrotfish and rock cod) when they consider them to be too lean, cutting them open to examine the mesentery.

[104] Especially fish caught from Di-Ḥámri eastwards, as far as Rīʾ di-Rísseyl at the eastern tip of the island and continuing around the point to halfway along the southern coast. Fish caught from Ḥáwlef westwards—to Qáṣeb and Qadámə—are said not to cause this problem. Friedhelm Krupp (pers. comm.): "Occurrence of ciguatera may be very localised depending on hydrographic conditions."

[105] Similar to the ʿáṣeb condition that eating certain plants causes in goats, or the more serious and persistent paralysis that afflicts camels eating Acridocarpus foliage at certain times of the year.

[106] Friedhelm Krupp (pers. comm.): "According to the symptoms described here, this obviously refers to ciguatera poisoning. Many species of reef fishes are involved in ciguatera. These include the herbivorous Acanthuridae (surgeonfish) and corallivorous Scaridae (parrot-

this condition were ṣáfrer 'butterflyfish', certain ḥárəbo 'mullet' and ʿáftəm 'sea chub' (Kyphosidae).[107] ṣáfrer and ʿáftəm fish are described as "having upturned snouts, humped backs and deep bellies," and Soqotrans who have travelled to the Gulf report that they are not usually seen there. The larger species of ʿáftəm which often come to the fish traps of the north coast are apparently called ʿaríyəḏ ('broad') in the Gulf. The ḥárəbo, 'various spp. of small mullet', are described as "extremely fat with little or no blood," and are said to be very common in the Gulf where they are a popular food. On Soqotra, ḥárəbo fish are seen as having an unpleasant smell which lingers on the skin long after handling—even after cooking.

It is the eating of the head, gills and stomach contents of these fish that produces the worst effects. Drinking water at the same time as eating the fish is said to exacerbate the condition. The initial taste of fish that cause this condition is said to be bitter "like tobacco," and the eater soon "develops pins and needles all over," grows weak, especially in the lower limbs, and is liable to become totally uninhibited: "revealing secrets and behaving improperly towards women in a way he would not nor-

---

fish), which are considered key vectors in the transfer of ciguatoxins to carnivorous fish. Many more species of carnivorous fish cause ciguatera poisoning. These include Muraenidae (moray eels), Lutjanidae (snappers), Serranidae (groupers) Scombridae (mackerels and tunas), Carrangidae (jacks) and Sphyraenidae (barracudas)."

[107] Uwe Zajonz (pers. comm.): "All three groups include species which feed a lot on microalgae: this might involve ciguatera poisoning."

mally," and generally behaving inappropriately.[108] It can take up to two days for the effects to wear off, weakness in the lower limbs being the most enduring symptom.

3.15. Shark (léḥḥīm, pl. ləḥāhum~láxīm, pl. ləxāhum)

All fishermen hoped to catch shark, principally for the oil made from their huge livers (see 5.2.5.), though trade boats were always happy to take dried salted shark meat (and much later, the fins). Given the lack of suitable equipment, the island fishermen could usually only catch immature shark or smaller species when they came close inshore. In the summer months some small shark were caught in large-meshed cast nets or with handlines from a dugout. There were no gill nets (lyūx) in earlier years: only towards the end of Mubārak's father's time did a few of these, made from coir fibre (benj), begin to reach the island from East Africa. Most shark fishing around the islands was carried out by boats visiting from the mainland, principally catching requiem and hammerhead shark. Some island fishermen worked on these boats and learned the necessary skills. Once suitable equipment for shark fishing became more readily available,[109] they put what they had learned into practice. The

---

[108] Always curious, Mubārak experimented with eating some of these fish to see how reliable such stories were but was careful to take himself far away from people to observe the effects, and staying away until he was completely recovered.

[109] The Soqoṭrans had no tradition of fishing with nightlines from clifftops for shark as did the Mahra of the mainland, nor did they rent out clifftops to visiting shark fishermen as did the people of the al-Ḥallāniyāt islands off the coast of Oman. The late ʿAbd al-ʿAzīz, shaikh

peak shark-fishing periods in Soqoṭri seas were after the monsoon (October to early December) and in the early summer (February to April), times when the sea was relatively calm. Today shark are caught with long lines (of 80–120 m with 20–40 hooks) and gill nets, as well as by hook and line.

3.15.1. Equipment for Shark Fishing

Sharks were most successfully hunted at night in the deeper seas (gúbbə).[110] The full set of equipment needed for these night-long trips consisted of the following:

> An old clay pot or the bottom half of a broken clay pot for cooking (serīdān 'onboard fireplace').
> Firewood, especially of Croton socotranus (mítrer), Zizyphus spina-christi (śóʔod) or Ficus cordata (ítʔib) wood.
> A live brand (məǵídihel) or embers (ḥōmo, pl. ḥémihum) with which to make a fire. These were kept in a clay pot lidded with clay, tin or wood. (The áṣ́ḥar fire sticks do not work out at sea.)

---

of these islands, told me that the Mahra used to come to the island during the monsoon season and pay a rent of between five and ten Maria Theresa silver thalers for the only suitable headland. He also reported that, if they had an exhausting passage from East Africa, Omani fishermen would call in at the islands for a rest on their way back home. Many of them had Soqoṭran wives and some took their Soqoṭran wives with them to Ṣūr to spend the months of the monsoon there.

[110] The area of the sea where sharks and the fish they feed on are to be found was called ruš, pl. riyéš, and one fisherman would ask another: al ská'akin h-arúš? "Aren't you going out to the deep area for shark?"

Fresh water in a lidded clay pot (*gísfə*). The pot was wrapped in damp sacking and the water used sparingly, drunk only when eating.

A basket containing bait. The best bait for shark[111] was chunks of *zíhnin* 'tuna', but other fish could also be used, as *śə́rwəhe* 'tunas', *ṣəṭíʕo* 'rays', *ráʔḥa* 'trevallies', *ḳarbōbə* 'triggerfish and leatherjackets', or two small *śéʔḥer* 'barracuda' tied together.

A thick sharkline. This consisted of a rope (*ḳayḏ*) some 10–30 *bāʕ* long, twisted from cotton fibre. At the top of the line was a loop called *šēri~šēriyə di-aḥtīmi*, 'cordage of date palm' (not as strong as the *ġozəl* 'cotton rope'); then came a sinker (*rəsās*), and a swivel (*dəwār*) with a length of hollow bone as a trace or leader (*ʕamūd*) at the bottom, and finally the large iron shark hook (*ʕéḳəlhe*) fashioned by island blacksmiths.

An anchor (*bárrūsi* or *íngəhər*). This was a rock (*óʔobən*) or a chunk of iron (*ḥádīd*). This was either square-shaped so it could be held firmly by the rope, or was bored to make a hole through which the rope could be threaded, or had a projection around which the rope could be tied.

Anchor rope. This was three-plyed (*məṭállit*) and usually made from date palm fibre (*aḥtīmi*, pl. *aḥtóyhim*), using the growing tips (*dilʕayn*) of the date palm.

---

[111] Bait for shark was called *laġzə* (Arabic and Soqotri) rather than *śámdə*.

A hooked gaff (mə́šxaf~mə́šḥaf or kəllāb) to hook through the cheek of the shark to give additional purchase as it was hauled in close enough to club.

Either a wooden club (məkəláʿa), a wooden pole with a metal tip (ṭárḳa), or a small axe (feʾs). Fishermen say that a shark has a thin skull: it is enough to hit it repeatedly around the head with a club or the metal end of a ṭárḳa. If an axe, this was used to hit the shark between the eyes to disable it before clubbing it.[112]

In the days of Sultan Ḥamad bin ʿAbd Allah (reigned 1938–1952), the mínzek 'harpoon' began to appear. This had a wooden shaft, usually of Ziziphus or Ormocarpum wood, and a metal head with a hollow base which was hammered over one end of the shaft and bound in position. It had a barb (śaʿl) at its sharp tip (rather like a large fishhook) and was attached by a length of chain to a rope of some 100–150 bāʿ made from date palm fibre and called dɛrg. This was kept coiled in a basket in the dugout. The loop of šēri~šēriyə 'cordage' on the shark line and the harpoon dɛrg 'rope' were both tied very firmly onto the dugout. When a shark had been harpooned, this length of rope was payed out behind the shark as it swam off, trying to escape.

---

[112] The exception to this is the nimrāni 'tiger shark' which on Soqotra is said "never to tire and never to die, however hard it is struck" (Mubārak). Indeed, fishermen report that it can cause such trouble that sometimes they have to cut the line and let it go.

3.15.2. Method

The fishermen would row around looking for signs of shark: a lot of flying fish (*fériher~férifer*), rafts of diving shearwater (*bíšišt*), a dark shadow on the surface of the sea indicating a large shoal of 'sardine-type fish' (*ḥáber di-ʿídi*) or school of other fish (*ḥáber di-ṣódə*), a *fogś* 'shoal of tiny fish' being pursued by larger fish such as tuna, Spanish mackerel or trevallies; a *máʿrērə di-léḥḥīm*, a shoal of fish being 'herded by shark'; or a shark coming up to the surface (*fonś*, 'coming up to breathe'). The fishermen would then lower a line baited with a chunk of fish (*náʿsə di-ḥōt*)—preferably a large piece of *zíḥnin* or *śə́rwəhe* 'tuna' or *ráʾḥa* 'trevally'—over the side. They would then tie another bait—the head and bones of a large fish (*mírgid di-ṣódə*)—onto a different rope and let this down some 10–30 *bāʿ* into the water. This was called *taʿlíḳə*, 'suspended' or *móḳənhīm*, 'taster' (from the verb √knm, 'to hand-feed'). This was to attract any shark in the vicinity. They also tied a fine piece of twine, *ḳátələ*, around the shark-line, leading back to the dugout: a twitch on this would tell the fishermen that a shark had taken the bait. If they had a harpoon, this was laid across the dugout at the ready. (The harpoon thrower was considered to be the real expert, the success or failure of the venture depending largely on his skill). Then the fishermen would sit and wait.

If a shark smelled the *taʿlíḳə* and began to circle the boat, the fisherman would slowly pull up the line with the 'taster' bait, at the same time bringing the baited shark hook close to it, to try and persuade the shark to take the baited hook at the same time as the *taʿlíḳə*. If it did, and they had a harpoon, this was when it was thrown. If it hit the shark, the harpoon rope had to be payed out quickly after the shark, the harpoonist spitting on his palms to cool the rope burn. Care had to be taken to prevent the shark doubling back and biting right through the line, and the fishermen continually jiggled the line around to distract it. If the shark seemed likely to exhaust this length of rope, another, the *mírkib* or *šēri*, a length of rope some 150 *bāʕ* long, kept coiled and ready in the dugout, was attached to the harpoon rope. If even the *mírkib* ran out, the last resort was to tie on the line that held the *taʕlīkə* 'taster'. The shark was played until it was exhausted enough for the fishermen to be able to begin to haul it towards the dugout. Once within reach, they would gaff it, ideally through the mouth or cheek. They would then drag its head up until it lay alongside the dugout, pull it clear of the water and and club it. Mubārak said that in most shark, the large liver lies just below the head, and a hard blow to this region, where the skin is very thin, severely disables the shark. A blow to the area at the root of the tail similarly incapacitates it.

If they caught a second shark, the smaller one was dragged inboard, while the other was towed behind the dugout. If they were in one of the larger dugouts and caught three sharks, again the smallest was brought inboard and the other two tied to each side of the canoe. The smaller dugouts were too small to take a shark of any size inboard.[113]

---

[113] Mubārak's brother had a dugout which could take four sharks, but it was an unusually large one.

3.15.3. Whale Sharks (kɛr)

Sightings of these are not rare, and Mubārak remembered a time when nine or ten were washed ashore on the east coast, in the area between Qáriyah and Raʔs Mōmi. He also recalled an occasion when the sultan learned of the beaching of a whale shark and, in the hope of finding great quantities of ambergris (see 4.7.2.), promptly sent a large group of his slaves to cut it open. Unlike the whale (śíḥāṭə), fishermen say that the whale shark is not at all afraid of people and makes no effort to avoid them, so when out at sea in a tiny dugout it is the fishermen who have to move out of the way. According to Aḥmad Saʿd Taḥkí,

> kɛr íno ʔēb wə-íno ḳíhen wə-íno kɛr di-śkef. wə-kɛr meyh kān ʿábdəher wə-di-ʔínḳaṭ wə-di-ḥáśiyuḳ. ṭī márra śə́rḳaḥ śīn kɛr w-inéḥeg biš təlāta ʿíyug bə-ṭādaʿ, tyóʔo korúmma inéḥeg bə-mídān miskído. w-iśébeṭ faḥərə.

There are larger whale sharks and there are smaller ones, and there is one we call kɛr di-śkef (i.e., with lines extending from the corners of its mouth, like the unweaned young of goats or sheep wearing the śkef weaning peg). The whale shark has blotches and spots and stripes and rings. One day a whale shark came ashore where we were, and three men danced on its back just as they would dance around the circumcision stone in the arena. And it was (large enough) to take them all (i.e., on its back).

On ʿAbd al-Kūri island the whale shark similarly aroused no fear, and islanders said that the headman of the island once walked across the back of a whale shark to remove some net tangled up around it.

4. Traditional Fishing: Non-Fish

4.1. Turtles

Turtles used to be caught and eaten.[114] Islanders readily distinguished between the sexes, and it was the female (*ḥōmis*) that was preferred as food, the male (*ʿábəhan*) rarely being pursued. The flesh, seen as 'meat' rather than as 'fish', was very popular, especially, it is said, with women and during the monsoon months, a time when livestock were largely unproductive, and most people were working at the date harvest and longed for the taste of meat. Islanders considered catching a turtle *ġanōmə*, 'booty', or *rizḳ*, 'a boon, a blessing'. This meant that it must be shared out equally with neighbours—those who concealed their catch and kept it to themselves would be pursued by bad luck.

The islanders distinguished turtles as follows. Most commonly occurring in Soqoṭri waters are the *beʿlə* 'green turtle' (*Chelonia mydas*), the *di-ʿabdérihon* 'loggerhead' (*Caretta caretta*) and the *ḳāraṭ* 'hawksbill' (*Eretmochelys imbricata*). The *nímələ* 'leatherback' was rarely caught but was sometimes seen out at sea. On the island of ʿAbd al-Kūri it was mainly the green turtle that was caught when it came ashore to lay its eggs in the early summer, though during the monsoon months that follow, the

---

[114] Forbes (1903, xxx) writes of ʿAbd al-Kūri: "The islanders must exist almost exclusively on fish, molluscs, and turtle—the latter so abundantly that they may truly be called *chelonophagi*."

hawksbill turtle too came ashore to nest.[115] The people of ʿAbd al-Kūri also talk about a turtle they call *dilwāšik* which they describe as similar to the loggerhead but smaller. Jansen van Rensburg suggests (2016, 146) that this might be the Olive Ridley turtle. Only small numbers of these come ashore to lay their eggs. On the north coast of Soqoṭra it was the loggerhead that arrived in the early summer to lay its eggs.[116] Islanders seem to have preferred the *beʿlə* 'green turtle' as food: its vegetarian diet perhaps making it more similar in taste to that of domesticated livestock.

4.1.1. Egg-Laying Females Caught Ashore

The female turtles crawl ashore and dig their nests between the high tide line (*ḥámǝhul*) and the dry sand (*šími*) at the top of the beach. The turtle was most easily caught when it was engrossed in laying its eggs, and people would sit out on the shore at night waiting for the turtles to arrive. There was no personal or direct ownership of the coves or areas of beach favoured by egg-laying turtles; it was a case of 'first there first served', though traditionally the turtle shell should be offered to those who were the owners of the area. A turtle was rendered helpless by being turned upside down and was then butchered. The turtle eggs were much liked, and islanders would walk the beaches and

---

[115] Forbes (1899, 634): "Numerous chelonian carapaces strewn about near their huts indicated that the hawk's-bill turtle was a common frequenter of their coasts."

[116] See Cheung and DeVantier (2006, 186).

coves looking for the telltale tracks and then dig in the sand for the eggs.

4.1.2. Turtle Caught at Sea

Although turtles were sometimes caught opportunistically out at sea, usually fishermen would row out to the turtle grazing grounds[117] to try and catch one. These feeding areas were given the same name as livestock pastures, *mírʿid*. These areas were well known, and it was recognised that such 'pastures' flourish and extend during the summer monsoon. Fishermen used a strong line and large iron hook to catch a turtle, baited with the liver of a *ḳerbōbə* triggerfish or leatherjacket. If a turtle were sighted, a fisherman would dive down, taking with him a hooked gaff (*máš́xaf~máš́ḥaf* or *kəllāb*), or a strong iron hook attached to a length of rope or stout fishing line which was kept in the dugout for such an occasion. According to Aḥmad Saʿd Taḥkí,

> If we see it emerging from the water, we get the gaff (*kəllāb*) into it and pull it in until it is close to the dugout. Then we decide what to do with it: tow it ashore or try and get it into the dugout? If the latter, we haul it in and lay it down on its back, and if the former, we tie a rope around one or more of its flippers (*ʾídbə*, du. *ʾidbíti*, pl. *ʾidbəhítən~ʾədāyib*) or around its neck (*fəḳəríro*), and then

---

[117] The islanders say that seagrass beds are to be found there on the north coast, at the eastward end of Ḥor Gírmə, at Di-Ḥamṣ and at Ġúbbah; on the west coast, at Díṭwaḥ lagoon, by Qalansiyah; and on the south coast, in a small, sheltered bay close to Maḥfírhin. But anywhere with a sandy bottom was worth trying.

row hard for the shore. We pull it up the shore and and turn it over on its back and then it is helpless. Then we whet our knives and cut its throat properly. Then we butcher it (*nəgāzəls*):[118] we cut the carapace (*kɛrf~kéśeribó ~ḳáśere di-ḥōmis*) from the plastron (*kɛrf di-kh̬ó*), and then we remove the meat and fat from the upper shell.

Sometimes a mating couple (*rátkəbo ḥōmis wə-ʿábəhan rəkɛ́bi*, 'they ride one another the female and the male turtle') were seen out at sea, and the distracted male could be caught by a fisherman swimming up behind it to hook it. Islanders say that when the female sees a fisherman coming, she casts off the male and dives down, but the male is slow to move off.

The people of ʿAbd al-Kūri owned very limited numbers of livestock and had few wild foods, so here turtle were a key food resource and fishermen expended a lot of time and effort hunting them. During the months of the monsoon many turtles came close inshore to graze the weed which flourishes at this time, in some areas spreading right up the shoreline. When fishermen in a dugout saw a turtle coming up to breathe, one of them would slip into the water, dive down with the line and large iron turtle hook, and quietly swim close enough to lodge the hook in its neck. It would swim off. The other end of the line was tied to the dugout, and the fishermen would hold hard onto it and wait for the turtle to exhaust itself. The smaller loggerhead turtle could also be caught out at sea: when one was seen resting on the bottom, one of the fishermen would slip into the sea as qui-

---

[118] The term *ṣálihib* is used for slaughtering and butchering sheep and goats (also birds), while *gízihil* is used for cows, camels or turtle.

etly as possible, hooked gaff or grappling hook in one hand, and swim behind the turtle. He would try to creep up on it and lodge the hook in its neck. If he succeeded, he would then drag it up, holding tightly onto the neck and a front flipper, until close enough to the dugout for the other fisherman to help. If the turtle were too large to be towed or hauled into the dugout, it was butchered there and then; if it was small enough to manoeuvre, it was towed ashore.

During the difficult months of the monsoon, when everyone was hungry, even dead turtles were put to use: the softer pieces of skin were scorched at the fire, ground fine, and water added to make an edible paste.

When cotton gill nets (*lyūx séʔher mən ġázəl*) became available, the ʿAbd al-Kūri islanders used these to trap turtle. These nets were some 60–70 *bāʿ* long and 3–4 *bāʿ* wide, with a mesh large enough to pass the forearm through. The fishermen set the net around the turtle grazing grounds at sunset, in this way sometimes catching more than one turtle at a time.

4.1.3. The Use of Remora (*lēmi*) to Catch Turtle

When a remora was caught,[119] it was sometimes kept alive and used for hunting turtle.[120] Fishermen would tie a fishing line

---

[119] Many islanders regarded these as good eating.

[120] Martin and Martin (1978, 120): "Before catching turtles was made illegal in Kenya in 1971, it was the Bajuns who went after them. They did so with the help of an eighteen-inch Remora sucker fish, to the tail of which they would attach a line. Then they would drop the Remora down into an area known for sea turtles. When the Remora found a

tightly around the tip of its tail or pass it through one side of its mouth and take it with them when they set off for the turtle feeding grounds. If they saw a turtle below, they would tie one end of the fishing line firmly around the bow of the dugout and then lower the remora into the sea. It would seek out the turtle and fasten itself to it (*ilásaḳ ʿis*). When the turtle swam away from the boat, it would tow the dugout behind it. The fishermen would play the turtle until it tired and came up to breathe more often and for longer. As long as the line and the remora held fast, the exhausted turtle could finally be approached and pulled in. If a *mə́nzek* 'harpoon' were available, this was used, or if the turtle were close enough, it was hooked in the neck or through a flipper with the *misḥaf~miśxaf* 'gaff'. Smaller shark were sometimes caught in the same way.

The fishermen from Raʾs Mōmi in eastern Soqoṭra were especially known for fishing in this way for turtle as a commercial enterprise. At the beginning of summer, a group of bachelor fishermen would travel from Mōmi to the north coast and set up camp beside the large lagoons. They would stay there for the

---

turtle it would attach itself to the shell and the fishermen would then pull in the line and, with the aid of an iron grapnel, they would pull the turtle up and into the boat." See also note 27 on p. 120: "The Bajuns are the only fishermen in East Africa to use a sucker fish, but this unusual method of catching turtles has been practiced in the past—in north-west Madagascar and the Comoro islands (Jack Frazier, pers. comm.)." See also Al-Salimi and Staples (2019, 570) about *lazzāq* or *lashāk* 'remora', where they refer to an "unusual and most likely fanciful account of their use in fishing in East Africa" mentioned in *The Book of Curiosities* written in eleventh-century Egypt.

whole summer season. The best place to set up camp was between Sírihin and Raʔs Dámar, because it was here that the main markets for turtle meat lay, the town of Ḥadibo and its satellite settlements.

First, they would go out to catch the remora, with triggerfish or leatherjacket livers (*šíbdə di-ḳarbōbə*) as bait. Alternatively, they would climb to a viewpoint to look out for the *kə́dəhe* 'rays' which arrive in great numbers in early summer when the sea is flat calm. Most of these would have two to five remoras lodged by the anus or just under the 'wings'. Fishermen say that when the ray excretes (the colour of its excreta varying according to its diet), it does so explosively, and this is what the remora feed on. Once the rays were sighted, the men would row out as quietly as possible to where they were resting and let down the baited lines. If they were lucky, the remoras on the ray would leave their ray host for the bait. They were then hauled in and tied to the dugout by the tip of the tail, the sucker disc on the head stuck to the side or bottom of the dugout. The men would then row for shore. They would leave the dugouts in shallow water with the remora still stuck on. Here they would quickly grow very hungry. When the men had collected enough remoras, they would get ready for the turtle hunt.

After sunset, the dugouts—usually nine men in three dugouts—would row out as quietly as possible to the inshore turtle feeding grounds. They would then sit and wait until they saw or heard a turtle coming up to breathe (at this time of year turtle movements can become visible at night because of the phosphorescence, *ḥāśim*). They would then loose the rope holding the famished remoras which would swim down and attach themselves to the shell of the turtle. When the turtle dived down, the rope was payed out and everyone had to row hard to keep up. When a dugout failed to keep up with a turtle it has been known for a remora to pull itself apart in its starved eagerness to hang on.[121] When the exhausted turtle was finally forced to come up to breathe, the dugouts would encircle it and try with gaff or grappling hook to bring it close enough so that they could grasp it by a back flipper: the back flippers are weak compared the strong front ones with their long, sharp claws. Once they had firm hold of it, they would tow it ashore, remove the remora(s) and turn the turtle upside down. Removing a remora had to be done correctly: it must be pulled forwards towards its mouth to make it loosen its grip, never tugged by the tail.

Turtle was valuable: shares (*tóbo*, pl. *tíyub*) of fresh meat and fat were sold by the *raṭl* weight, like dates and maize. One *raṭl* weight of turtle could be exchanged for one *ḵurṣ* weight of cereal (usually maize, *məḵdḗrə*)—a good price. The meat of the *beʿlə* 'green turtle' fetched more than that of the *ḵáraṭ* 'hawksbill' or the *di-ʿabdérihon* 'loggerhead'. Turtle meat was said to be particularly popular with women, and the long tail of the male, housing the penis, was sold as an aphrodisiac to men.

---

[121] This characteristic of the remora gave rise to the saying: *ya, kān ṭábək tyóʾo lḗmi!* 'Look, he would cling as tight as a remora!'

4.1.4. Turtle Consumption

A turtle had to be ritually slaughtered with a knife in the same way as a domesticated animal, the only sea creature to be killed in this way. The heart (*ílbib*), brain (*mīmaʿ*) and the head (*riʾ*) were discarded. Apart from the part called the *ḥāsid* (found near the head, and which causes severe diarrhoea if eaten), all the rest of a turtle is edible. The prized *mə́kšəd* 'meat and fat mixture' (pieces of meat cut up small, boiled in melted fat, then cooled and stored in a clay or tin container), could be made from turtle and dolphin in the same way as it was from domestic livestock.[122] It was kept tightly covered, and pieces were extracted only with a stick or the tip of knife: as long as no hand touches it, this preparation keeps indefinitely. It was saved for a treat or brought out for a special guest. The belly fat (called *ḥōbə* and equivalent to the *šéšiyo* 'mesentery fat' in livestock) was preserved by drying. This fat is said to be light-coloured in a healthy specimen, but of a darker colour in a sickly or thin one. Turtle eggs were usually eaten hard boiled.[123]

4.1.5. Use of Turtle Carapace and Plastron

The plastron was used as a dish on which to serve fish and shellfish, and the carapace made a trough for watering livestock or to wash in. A large carapace was used as a container and was

---

[122] This *mə́kšəd* mixture was never made from fish.

[123] However, I have had them scrambled in al-Ḥallāniyyah island in Oman.

kept at home, suspended from the roof beams or from a hook in the cave wall.[124]

4.2. Whales (śīḥāṭə, pl. śáḥaṭ)

It is not always clear when śīḥāṭə refers to a whale or to those members of the dolphin family known as 'whales': the killer whale, pygmy killer whale, false killer whale or pilot whale. However, śīḥāṭə are frequently seen out at sea, breaching or spouting from their blowholes. Although some islanders believe śīḥāṭə to be dangerous, it seems that they are not feared by experienced fishermen. Indeed, they report that the śīḥāṭə is a rather nervous, shy creature. I was told that if one was seen pursuing a maʿrērə, the fishermen would gather together and bang on their dugouts to frighten it away so that they could keep the fish for themselves. Mubārak recalled being out in his dugout with a companion and finding a dead whale floating upside down on the surface of the sea. They climbed onto it and cut open its stomach to look for ambergris. They found none, though he says they did find many decent-sized fish in its stomach.

4.3. Dolphins (ʿíləho)

Fishermen divide dolphins into roughly two types: those that swim far out to sea and approach boats inquisitively, and those

---

[124] See also the description by Mabel Bent from the late nineteenth century (Bent 2010, 291) of them being used as a chicken coop in Qalansiyah: "the little chicken houses made of a turtle shell with the earth scooped from under it."

that come close inshore but flee at the sight or sound of people.[125] It seems that these mammals were not deliberately hunted but were sometimes caught accidentally or found stranded on the shore.

Their meat (bəsáḳəhən or just teh di-ʿílǝho, 'dolphin meat') was considered good eating by many full-time fishermen, and, when left for a few days until rank and smelly, it also made excellent shark bait. Others avoided eating dolphin, saying that it brought on severe diarrhea (ṣúwraʿ), and would only eat it when there was no alternative.

The real value of dolphins lay in their fat, both that of the inner organs and the layer of blubber (ḥaṣifo di-ʿílǝho) beneath the skin, the latter considered to be of great medicinal value. To extract it, the skin and blubber were cut away in a single layer, softened by beating, and then cut into chunks and boiled in water. When all the fat had melted, the pot was taken off the fire. When it had cooled, the layer of fat that had set on the top was lifted off and stored in a clay pot. However, fresh dolphin fat was also called məṣaríṭo, 'causing loud farting', because eating too much upset the stomach. Melted fat (ṣífə di-ʿə́lǝho) was used medicinally to treat bad eyesight and was applied locally to treat fungal skin diseases. It was also drunk by those experiencing a deterioration in eyesight (ʿazkə). The meat and fat mixture called mə́ḳšəd (pieces of meat cut up small, boiled in melted fat,

---

[125] See Cheung and DeVantier (2006, 209), where they note that six species have been recorded so far in Soqoṭri waters: the long-beaked common dolphin, the humpback dolphin, the spotted dolphin, the spinner dolphin, the larger bottlenose dolphin and Risso's dolphin.

then cooled and stored in a clay or tin container) was made from dolphin, just as it was from sheep and goats. However, it was not as well-liked as the *mə́kṣəd* prepared from turtle (see 4.1.4.).

Once the *mínzek* 'harpoon' arrived, some people began to try and use it to catch dolphin: a dolphin seen swimming into a bay would be encircled by dugouts and harpooned. Today, it is said that some get entangled in the nylon fishing nets.

4.4. Rays and Guitarfish

Rays and guitarfish of many kinds were considered good eating, especially during the hungry months of the monsoon. They were also prepared for sale: after gutting, they were either slashed and salted, or left buried in hot sand for 24 hours to dry out. They were then washed in seawater and hung in the sun for three or four days before being stored in sacks to await the arrival of the trade boats. A fisherman could collect up to five sacksful if he worked hard. There was a great demand for this dried product, on the Arabian mainland as well as in the East African markets, where dried, salted ray fetched a good price.

Some stingrays and whiprays (as *ḳīrέʿe*, *kə́dəhe*, *rōbəṣ́*, and *ṣaṭíʿo*) were caught with hook and line. The fishermen would throw a piece of thick cloth or sacking over the tail area before taking hold of it, as the venom of the spines of some of these rays was believed to be very poisonous. If a fisherman saw a large ray while out in a dugout, he would dive down on top of it and try to gaff or hook it. Once back in the dugout he would let it tow him around until it exhausted itself. Fishermen say that when the ray felt its end drawing near it would lash out with its tail, trying to pierce the fishermen with its spines. As these are hooked in one direction only, they are very hard to extract.

Immature stingrays come close inshore to bask in the shallow waters. At this time a skilled fisherman could grasp it firmly around the tail, below the double spines, and whisk it out of the water. The liver of young stingrays was especially prized for its paleness and rich fattiness.

4.5. Shellfish and Shellfish Harvesting

As the many shell middens still visible in caves or beneath overhangs all around the island attest, the islanders were assiduous shellfish harvesters. At low tide, they would search along the rocks (*šáḥaḳ* '[tide] to go out' and 'to go to gather shellfish [at low tide]'): *wúddiki šēḥikin?* "Shall we two go and gather shellfish?" and *embūriye šáḥakən* "The children have gone to gather shellfish." Searching for shellfish was also done in the dark at night, by feel rather than by sight (in the period recalled here there were no torches). This was called *ṣáʿi*, and people would say: *wúddiki išmīriyun wə-ṣáʿiyun šáḥaḳ?* "Shall we two go and gather shellfish tonight?"

Some shellfish were eaten raw, others boiled in water, roasted on embers, or cooked by burying them in hot ash. In some parts of the island shellfish gathering was mainly the province of women and children, and it was considered shameful for a man to be seen doing this. Indeed, not everyone ate shellfish, and many were proud to boast that they had never done so. In the minds of some islanders—especially the tribesmen of the interior—eating sea snails was too close to eating land snails (*filə́mə*, pl. *fílihem*),[126] the gathering and eating of which was a rather furtive and discreditable affair, only done in desperation.

Shellfish harvesting was especially important during the long months of the monsoon.[127] At this time of year, wild seas made most other fishing impracticable, the majority of livestock were unproductive, and the islanders, busy with the date harvest, longed to relieve the monotony of eating dates. At this season too, the tides went further out and exposed more of the rocky foreshore. The tool for shellfish harvesting was simple: a short spear (*šiyk*) made from a length of hard wood, sharpened to a point at one end and fire-hardened. This was used to prise shellfish from the rocks, to spear fish in rock pools, or to extract octopus hiding in crevices.

The very popular *ḥamóyə* 'clams' and the *ʿábšer*~*ʿáfšer* 'turban shells' were most effectively gathered at night. The clams lay buried beneath stones and sand, and people would sit in the dark on rocks or damp sand and grope around, the sand

---

[126] The most popular being the large round ones (genus *Socotora*). However, the longer pointed ones (genus *Riebeckia*) and the much smaller pointed ones (*Achatinelloides*) were also gathered as food in times of great hunger.

[127] On ʿAbd al-Kūri, gathering shellfish in the long months of the monsoon was only possible along the northern shores of the island: on the southern side the seas were too wild. Life was at its hardest here at this season, and the islanders would usually transhume to the northern side of the island to fish from the rocks and feed on the shellfish there.

and grit blown around by the monsoon gales making them spit and cough. As well as cold and damp, those searching for shellfish at night faced other hazards, such as encounter with the ṣafāḳa 'jellyfish'.[128] If touched by hand and the hand then accidentally placed on the face, considerable pain and inflammation ensued. The ṣafāḳa di-móšḥiḳ 'stinging nettle of the low tide' was especially disliked. It was commonly found in the vicinity of the ḥamóyə 'clams', looked rather like the ʿōmə 'bristle worm' used as bait. If touched in error, hairs would break off its body and lodge in the flesh, causing the hand to swell very painfully.[129] People also feared coming into contact with the úʔiriḥ~ úʔiriˁ 'sea urchin' (see 4.6.1.) in the dark.

4.5.1. Shellfish Harvested

A wide variety of shellfish were gathered: *Ensis* razor shells, *Clanculus* topshells, *Euchelus* sea snails, *Monodonta* and *Trochus* top shells, *Lunella* turban shells, Arcidae ark clams, *Cardita* cockles, *Chama* saltwater clams, *Venus* clams, *Nerita* and *Murex* spp., various Tonnoidea,[130] *Polyplacophora* chitons and many more. Which shellfish were available differed from area to area, but the ones most commonly gathered were:

---

[128] ṣafāḳa is the name of a group of extremely irritant plants (as Tragia, Urtica and Waltheria) which have a sting like a stinging nettle.

[129] Possibly a species of fireworm (Amphinomidae). The only known treatment was to rub the sore part hard with your own hair.

[130] Mubārak commented that Tonnidae tun and fig shells taste like ḥimbōbə cowries.

The small white-fleshed clams (ḥamōyə pl. ḥamé'e, rated[131] 10/10);

Rock oysters, *Saccostrea* (zōkə~zə́ko, pl. ízku^h, rated 10/10). These were such a key food that they have their own verb: ízkik, 'to go and collect rock oysters': wúddiki ézkiko? "Shall we both go to gather rock oysters?";

Turban shells (ˤábšer~ˤáfšer, rated 10+);[132]

Various types of large limpet (ṣəwēlaḥ or ṣə́fəlḥo, rated 10/10);

Crepidula slipper limpets, and Fissurellidae keyhole limpets[133] (ʔidbīyə~ʔidbəhīyo, rated less highly than the ṣəwēlaḥ~ṣə́fəlḥo limpets);

The small hard-shelled nerites, such as *Nerita textilis* (called tə́bər ʔə́bəhān~tʸúbur ʔíbəhān 'stone breaker',[134] referring to the strength of blow needed to break the shell open to get at its meat; rated 10/10);

Hard-shelled bivalves such as cockles (məkhíro, pl. mkáhir) and scallops (məlbído) (both rated 10/10);

---

[131] Ratings obtained from a number of fishers.

[132] Also, a general term for edible shellfish.

[133] Forbes (1903, xxviii) reports seeing on ˤAbd al-Kūri "fields of dead mollusca—the most conspicuous and abundant being a large species of limpet with a perforated apex (*Fissurella*)."

[134] On Samḥa island also called ṣˤákəhan. The same root gives the verb ṣotˤak, a term used on the north coast to describe an area from which all useful shellfish have already been harvested: ṣotˤak dé ḥalf, 'This area has already been cleared of edible shellfish'.

Black and white knobbly cerith and frog shells (*kerá‛ad*, rated 3/10);

Topshells (*ḥílihin~di-ḥílihin*, rated 3/10);

Chitons (*śíḥānə~śíḥíno*,[135] whose flesh was eaten both raw and cooked. They are said to be liked by women especially; men only rated them at 3/10);[136]

Mussels (*fdīyiḳ~fodəḳ*, eaten by some islanders and not by others, and rated 6/10 by those who ate them);

The larger olive snails (*fá‛rher* pl. *f‛árher* or *f‛ar‛əher* pl. *f‛ar‛əhur*, rated 6/10);

Various winkles and periwinkles (*míririhin~mirəmíro~di-mérhen*, widely given a low rating because of the very bitter part that has to be extracted and discarded);

A type of black winkle called *ṭahəḳāno* (also given a low rating);

Cowries of various sizes (*ḥimbōbə* or *ḳaḥbōbə*: the larger ones *ílәhe*, 'cow', and the smaller *fólihi ber ílәhe*, 'calf', the best ones rated at 10/10);

Conches (Strombidae) and triton (Ranellidae). It was usually men who dived for these valuable shellfish (both generically called *ḥánṣə*, with smaller specimens being called *ḥináṣə gīm*, *ḥináṣə* being a diminutive form of *ḥánṣə*).

---

[135] The parts of the *śíḥíno* 'chiton' are: *śə́bə di-śíḥíno*, 'lip', the outer rim; *líśśin di-śíḥíno*, 'tongue', the flesh; *məḳáṣihi di-śíḥíno*, 'joints', the plates; *ka?*, 'thread', the girdle running around the interior. Eating 15–20 chiton raw was considered to be a remedy for jaundice (*bū ṣfar, ḥorf, ṣáfəra‛*).

[136] Unfortunately, I did not work with women when rating shellfish.

These were valued for their large opercula (*di-ḳówḥaf*, see 4.7.1.) as much as for their meat.[137] The spider conch (*ḥánṣ̌ǝ di-aṣābiˤ*, 'conch with fingers'), a very knobbly conch called *širīfǝ*, a smooth one called *ṭaḥāḳǝ*, and the large, ridged clams called *gáḥban* (*Tridacna* spp.) were all prized and rated at 10+.[138]

The highly prized abalone ([*di-*]*ʔidōnǝ*~[*di-*]*ʔidānǝ*) was a rare find. It was eaten both raw and cooked, and rated at 10+.[139]

The pearl oyster, *Pinctada radiata* (*bílbil*) held little meat and was hard work to gather. However, the meat of the more common black-lip pearlshell oyster, *Pinctada margaritifera* (*móṣǝliḥ*, rated at 10/10) was well liked, and in the days when there was a demand for pearlshell (see 4.10.), the flesh was widely eaten and also used to bait fish traps.

---

[137] Indeed, all big shellfish with large opercula were known generally as *ḥanṣ̌ǝ*. When I was staying in Ríḳǝlǝ on the east coast, my host and his brother went for an afternoon's diving session and came home with 13 large *ḥanṣ̌ǝ*. They were torn: should they eat their meat, or keep the shells to trade with a boat going to Aden where such shells were in demand? However, this meant letting the meat go to waste, as it can't be extracted without damaging the shell.

[138] The *ḥanṣ̌ǝ* was also used to treat dysuria in elderly men: the shell was heated to red hot at the fire and the patient crouched over it; the rising heat was believed to stimulate urination, initially only in drops, but then in a steady stream.

[139] One year, Mubārak dived for these, dried the flesh and sold it to a passing trader, but no further traders expressed an interest in these.

Figure 6: Conches freshly harvested, east coast

Photo © Miranda Morris, 1990s

4.5.2. Use of Shells

Melo shells of the family Volutidae were filled with milk and used to feed babies (when they were called *di-ḳáʿlə*).[140] Clam and scallop shells were used by potters to smooth the surface of their hand-coiled pottery before firing it (the name of the shell, *milbído*, comes from the verb √lbd, 'to tap, beat'), and the ridged shells of cockles were used to scrape away food burned onto the bottom of a cooking pot (the shell name, *məḵhíro*, comes from

---

[140] A *ḳaʿlə* is a small bowl fashioned from wood, clay or bark.

the verb √ḵḥr, 'to scrape, scratch away at st.'). Cerith and other pointed snails made temporary pipes for smoking homegrown tobacco.

Other shells made toys: cone shells were spun as tops; different sizes of cowrie shell used to represent 'livestock' to be 'herded': smaller ones representing sheep or goats, and larger ones cows or camels, with tusk, turret and auger shells (*šaʿárher* or *ṣóḥaṣaḥ*) representing their young. These last tiny, pointed shells were also strung together to make a rattle to entertain a baby in its hammock or to amuse a toddler. Girls would select the most beautifully coloured shells and make anklets and necklaces with them, using *keráʿad* 'shells' to imitate the beads of the *ḥaníšə~ḥaneyšə* 'necklace',[141] and *ʿábšer~ʿafšer* 'shells' to look like an amulet (*ḥarz*), worn around the neck. The shells were pierced for threading by placing them on the tip of a sharp flint (*ʿíbihel*) and tapping them repeatedly against this tip until the flint point broke through the shell.

4.6. Other Sea Creatures

4.6.1. Sea Urchins

Edible sea urchins were gathered at low tide and the gonads (sea urchin roe or coral) were scooped out and eaten immediately or were taken back home and cooked with butteroil. This last method is said to give off a particularly delicious smell, but to make the eater extremely thirsty. The gonads of both the black and white striped sea urchin ([*di-*]*ḵirīzi*~[*di-*]*ḵōriz*) and

---

[141] A small necklace of hollow silver or imitation gold beads.

the larger black sea urchin (ḥádhed) were eaten, those of the ḥádhed were generally eaten raw and were regarded as inferior to those of the (di)-ḳōriz 'sea urchin'. Some called the gonads ḥōmə di-ḳirīzi, 'sea urchin butteroil' (ḥōmə is the diminutive of ḥamʔī, 'butteroil'), while others just called them ḳaḥélǝhān or ə́bḳǝhal, 'eggs'. The úʔiriḥ~úʔiriˤ, pl. íʔiráḥān 'sea urchins' were carefully avoided. "They have barbed spines which penetrate deep into the flesh and continue to work their way ever deeper, even if the protruding part is broken off."[142] (Aḥmad Saˤd Taḥkí) The pretty flower urchin,[143] gə́nəs on Soqotra, was also given a wide berth, as it gives an extremely painful and toxic sting if touched. Areas where these two kinds of urchin occur in any number were avoided by the barefoot fisher people.

4.6.2. Crabs (ḥanśíʔo, pl. ḥanśə)

Some species of crab were eaten by some islanders, but in general, they were seen as a food of last resort. Those regarded as potentially edible were some of the ḥanśíʔo ḳśébeb 'rock crab', the ḥanśíʔo ḥə́wro di-rínhem 'black sea crab', and those crabs which grew to a good size in the safety of the many lagoons,

---

[142] Possibly *Diadema setosum*. (See Wranik 2003, 480: "[T]he spines are very thin, long, needle-like and have backward-facing barbs. They can form irritating wounds and inflict severe pain because they readily puncture human skin, penetrate deeply before they fracture and release a venom from their hollow shafts.")

[143] See Wranik (2003, 480) on *Toxopneustes pileolus*: "[I]ts small clasping organs are three-bladed and flower like… but they have poison sacs attached which contain a toxin that is potentially lethal to humans."

such as fiddler crabs (*ḥansĩʔo kśébeb di-mɔ́lḵaz*, 'rock crab with one large claw'), or the *Scylla serrata* mud crab, *ḥansĩʔo kśébeb ʕáfer* 'reddish rock crab'. Various swimming crabs (Portunidae), their final pair of legs flattened into broad paddles, were also eaten. These last, reddish in colour, used to arrive in great numbers at the very beginning of winter and at the very end of summer. Rafts would be seen swimming on the surface, often close inshore. Fishermen say that the *zíhnin* 'tuna' like them as much as the *ʕídi* 'sardine-type fish'. Many species of shark also love swimming crabs, and when a lot of these crabs were seen out at sea, the fishermen would know that shark would not be far off. Swimming crabs were variously called *zirígihan*, *bū mḵāsāt* ('with shears'), *bū mɔlāḵaz* ('with large pincers') and *ber mēyə~ber məʔɛ́yə* ('of the current').

4.6.3. Cephalopods: Squid (*ʕáterhe~ʕaṭeráyə*), Cuttlefish (*ʕáterhe~ʕaṭeráyə*) and Octopus (*térəbaḥt*)

Some fishermen ate octopus, squid and cuttlefish, and found their meat delicious (rating it 10/10), while others only used them as bait.

Octopus sometimes came to the fish trap, but usually they were hooked out of crevices at low tide, fished for with handlines or caught by diving.

A small reddish-coloured squid (possibly an immature cuttlefish), *ikídihən*, 'easily startled', was cooked and eaten, but was said to be very tough.

Cuttlefish were caught with handlines, usually with a bait of *ʕídi* 'sardine-type fish'; they never come to a fish trap. Cuttlefish reached Soqoṭri shores in great numbers in the early summer, some floating ashore dead. In the lifetime of Mubārak's father, when the British were in Aden, a short-lived demand arose for cuttlebone (ḥiléfə~ḥaléfo, pl. ḥəlfētin), and women and children would walk along the shoreline collecting them to sell to traders from al-Mukallā. As with the trade in the di-ḥānə lichen (the other ḥannə and sʿángəher lichens were not sold), the islanders had no idea what cuttlebone was used for—they themselves had no use for it. Some time round 1967, with independence and the establishment of the new Yemeni government of PDRY, the trade in cuttlebone and lichen came to an end.

Cephalopod ink (mədéd or dəwé)[144] was collected and given to others to use for writing, people such as the clerk (kātib) of the Qāḍi's court (máḥkama), teachers at the Qurʾānic schools, or the few who copied out sections (məshāft) of the Qurʾān. The ink was also sometimes used by the illiterate majority to mark their property.

---

[144] "We catch it by grabbing it around the head or neck. We milk the ink from its stomach (nəḥōləbs tsé men šériś walə tsé men ḳādəl). It passes its ink or its stomach contents as urine (ber tsáḥəm sé dəwé walə se əḳənīyo). You put the liquid in a container, cover it and wait for it to dry out and thicken. When you want to write with it, you add a little water and stir hard." (Ahmad Saʿd Taḥki)

4.6.4. Spiny Lobster (śīraḥ~śerīho, pl. śériyaḥ~śírxa, pl. śīrax)[145]

Spiny lobsters were caught with hook and line, hooked out of crevices at low tide, or, like octopus, were sometimes found in the fish trap. They were eaten by some islanders but were principally used as bait. By those that ate them, spiny lobsters were rated 10/10.

The islanders divided these creatures into different kinds: the most easily caught, śīraḥ 'spiny lobster', further differentiated according to appearance, as śīraḥ ʿábdəher 'blotched lobster', śīraḥ ʿáfer 'reddish lobster' and so on; the slipper lobster, variously ḱáfḱaft ('crackling, rustling lobster'), śīraḥ gírməhem ('lopped lobster') or śīraḥ ʿárabi ('Arab lobster'): it has a short, squat body and smaller and shorter legs than the śīraḥ; and the biggest of all, the deep-sea lobster (Puerulus sewelli), śīraḥ di-ḥaṣáhan, 'giant Scolopendra centipede lobster'.

4.6.5. Sea Cucumbers and Sea Slugs

Sea cucumbers:[146] ḥfoš 'rapacious, greedy',[147] mə́ḳəliz di-rínhem, 'glans penis of the sea', 'tiny sea penis', and the larger fáhal di-

---

[145] Nichols (2002, 9.8.1.): "The main target species is the scalloped spiny lobster (Panulirus homarus). Other species fished are: painted spiny lobster (P. versicolor), ornate spiny lobster (P. ornatus), long-legged spiny lobster (P. longipes) and pronghorn spiny lobster (P. penicillatus)."

[146] Krupp and Hariri (1999, 9.6.1.): "Sea cucumbers (currently only elephant's trunk fish Holothuria fuscopunctata and the white teat fish H. fuscogilva are exploited, though correct identification needs to be con-

rínhem, 'sea penis', were caught by diving, especially at night. At times, when the tide was really far out, they could also be caught by spearing. The ḥfoš 'sea slugs' were eaten locally, while the mə́kəliz di-rínhem and fáḥal di-rínhem apparently were not.[148] ḥfoš have to be cooked twice to render them palatable. The intestines are removed and then they are boiled in water (though some prefer to cook them in fresh milk instead). At the first boiling, the water turns greenish and is discarded; at the second, the water remains clear. They were eaten cut across in slices.

4.7. Miscellaneous Products of the Sea

4.7.1. Shellfish Opercula (ḥāfūr)

The larger opercula (kówḥaf) were seen by the islanders as the 'leg' of the shellfish, used by it to move from place to place.[149] There was a steady demand for these large opercula: boats from the Yemeni mainland as well as from Oman were very ready to

---

firmed). Benthic, living on bottom sediments. Caught by free diving to a maximum of 10m. Mainly sold fresh (in wet form) to the main buyer in Hadiboh who then boils, cleans and dries them, and then sells them to exporters on the mainland."

[147] On Samḥa island ḥabšítin 'rolled up'.

[148] But in the early 2000s they were sold on Soqoṭra to a trader at a price of ten Yemeni riyals for two medium-sized specimens or one large [MJM].

[149] And indeed, in some conches, the elongated and sickle-shaped operculum is used to dig into the sand to enable a leaping type of locomotion.

buy any available, and they were also traded to East Africa. Sold by the *raṭl* weight,[150] at the height of demand, they achieved as good a price as did the valuable civet musk (*zibād*) collected by the islanders. The strongest divers would seek the shellfish with the biggest opercula in deeper waters, generally conches and tritons, while women and non-divers would collect opercula removed from shellfish gathered at low tide or washed ashore after storms.

The opercula of different shellfish had different names. The most valuable were the opercula of the conches and tritons (*ḳówḥaf*,[151] 'little scoop', or *ṭifherítin di-ḥánṣ̌ə*, 'toe-, fingernails of the *ḥánṣ̌ə*'). The operculum of the *t̓úbur ʔíbəhān* was called *ḳánfər* (the name for the disc at the flower end of a date, or the kernel of a *Zizyphus spina-christi* pip); that of the *ʕábš̌ər~ʕáfš̌ər* was *sígədə* ('prostration in prayer'), and children would stick one of these on their forehead to mimic the mark left on the forehead of the devout by their repeatedly touching it to the ground in prayer;[152] that of the *míririhin~mirəmíro* was *mətənīyo*

---

[150] Equivalent approximately to 16oz, about 1lb according to Serjeant (writing in 1967, cited in Doe 1992, 178).

[151] Any shellfish with a valuable *ḳówḥaf*-type operculum was called *ḥánṣ̌ə*.

[152] "*ʕáfš̌ər* have an operculum that looks like a prayer mark on a human forehead: we wet this operculum with our tongue and stick it on our forehead." (Aḥmad Saʕd Taḥki)

('tooth'), and that of the *ṭahakāno* was *ṣīʿəfo* ('fish scale'), a thin and transparent operculum.[153]

Opercula were an important ingredient in the fumigant incense mixtures (*baxxūr*) made on the mainland, as well as by a small number of women of 'Arab' origin (*ʿarabiyyāt*) on Soqoṭra.[154] On the island, the opercula of conches and tritons were also used medicinally: they were charred at the fire, pulverised and the powder used as a wound dressing.

4.7.2. Ambergris (*ʿámbəher*)

This hard, waxy material produced in the intestines of the sperm whale, *Physeter microcephalus*, is sometimes found cast up on the shores of the south coast and on the islands of Samḥa,

---

[153] Across the sea in Dhofar, the smaller opercula were played with as 'toy money' (in the Śḥerēt dialect of al-Ḥallāniyyah island, *bēsə ʿaṣfirīn*, 'shell money'; elsewhere *kerś frens*, pl. *ēkerós frens*, 'silver dollars'). It was said that if a boy swallowed one of these, he would not be able to pass urine.

[154] See Serjeant (writing in 1967, cited in Doe 1992, 178): "A shell, here called *jawḥāf*, is exported to al-Mukalla where a *raṭl* of it sells for about 4 shillings. It was said that it is called *ẓufur* in south Arabia, but if this is the same as *ẓufrī*, which I saw at Khawr ʿUmayrah in 1940, it is part of the flesh of a shell-fish of an entirely different shape. It also goes to Aden where it is thought to be ground and used as a sort of perfume. In fact, the Arabic translator of Dioscorides knows *aẓfār* as a perfume made from the shards of shells found in an island off the Sea of India. In Socotra it seems this shell is burnt, ground and put into something (oil?) which women use on their hair." As well as in Arab culture, opercula were used as incense material in Jewish tradition and in China and Japan.

Darsa and ʿAbd al-Kūri.[155] Throughout the Middle East it is highly valued as a cure for many serious conditions, and in other parts of the world for its ability to fix and intensify perfumes. Soqoṭran and visiting traders were always prepared to buy ambergris, and the islanders would scour the shoreline for it. Those who found ambergris preferred to sell it to a trader from outside rather than internally, as this always meant a better price,[156] but they would be wary of asking too high a price in case the sultan got to hear of it and demanded that it be given to him. On the islands it was seen as a marvellous windfall, a most valuable source of 'good luck and blessings' and a medicinal cure-all. Powdered, it was considered to be especially effective in disorders of the stomach and digestive system, as well as treating urinary retention and a wide range of other ailments of the kidneys, liver and spleen. It was taken for a painful and infected throat and was fed in tiny amounts to a person who was very thin and sickly to help them put on weight. It was prepared by grinding a small fragment to a powder and taking this in a little melted butteroil.

---

[155] In 1834 Hulton (2003, 97) writes of ʿAbd al-Kūri: "We were told that considerable quantities of ambergris are found on its shores, and turtle are taken in great abundance for the shell, which is sold. The island belongs to Kissein [Qishn MJM], and the Sultan sends annually to extract as much ambergris and turtle-shell as possible from his subjects."

[156] Serjeant (writing in 1967, cited in Doe 1992, 179) reports that ambergris was sold by the *tawlah* (tola) weight, equivalent to the weight of one silver rupee.

Three kinds of ambergris were distinguished on Soqoṭra: a dark coloured one, a greeney-brown one, and a pale coloured one, the palest being the best quality and the darkest the worst. In popular tradition, ambergris was said to come from the 'ambergris tree' which grew on the floor of the deepest ocean. It was closely guarded by many powerful jinn. Giant whales—of a kind unseen by man because such creatures never rise from the deep—are said to have a passion for ambergris. In their attempts to get hold of some, they dive right down to the sea-bed and swoop past the 'tree', mouths wide open to scoop up as much as possible, flashing past at a speed too fast for any guardian jinn to catch them. Broken fragments of the 'tree' float to the surface where they are eaten by other sea creatures. This is the very best kind of ambergris, fresh and pale green. Darker green-brown ambergris is said to be the vomitus of the giant whales and is the next best kind, and the worst kind is their excrement. Other wondrous sea creatures (*wəḥūš di-rínhem*) which inhabit the deepest seas sometimes rub their bodies against the 'tree', snapping bits off and it is these small pieces that generally end up on the shore.

Someone catching sight of something that might be a piece of ambergris, or who finds even the smallest lump, must, according to island tradition, quickly say *bismillāh*, 'In the name of God', to protect himself and to give thanks to God for his good luck. If he finds a large quantity, he must then walk straight past it to the sea and ritually purify himself in seawater. Then, turning his back on the ambergris, he must perform two *rakʿahs* 'prostrations', say *bismillāh* again, and only then, on the completion of this ritual, can he go and pick it up. To avoid attracting the Evil Eye, the sensible finder of ambergris breaks his find in two, hiding one piece and admitting publicly only to the other.

Most would keep their find a secret, wrapping the ambergris in cloth and burying it in a clay pot, or would bury a piece under the floor of the home to 'bring God's blessing upon the home',[157] and so that, as and when needed, small pieces could be broken off for private use. Secrecy was necessary because if word of such a find got out, everyone would come and beg for a fragment—a request difficult to refuse according to Soqoṭri custom. Another reason for secrecy was that the ruling family claimed the right to any ambergris washed up on the island, so, in theory at least, the finder should straightaway hand any ambergris found over to them.

4.7.3. Ray Tails

Before the days of metal files, the central strip of the long, barbed tail of the ḳiréʿe and ṭabbāḳət 'whiptail stingrays' was used as a sandpaper or file (mə́brid) by island blacksmiths and carpenters. The skin of the tip provided the finest sandpaper. Other Soqoṭrans used ray-tail 'sandpaper' to smooth the goatshorn handles (ḳān) of the homemade knives carried by every

---

[157] ʿámbəher: di-yəkís men ʿámbəher d-íyhé yíkkin wə-yəšṓʾomš tyóʾo ʿégib. wə-šín ʿádə: nədófənš bə-ḳáʿar. yəʿṓmər idā́laḳ ʿek māl, "Ambergris: whoever finds ambergris takes it as his own property to sell as he wishes. And we have a custom: we bury it inside the home—it is said that all that you own will prosper (as a result)." (Aḥmad Saʿd Taḥkí)

adult male. After softening at the fire, the horn was filed smooth with the 'sandpaper', and then trimmed to the exact size of the base of the knife blade. If no ray tail were available, fine dead coral (ḥśōbə) could be used instead, but this was prone to leaving unsightly scratches on the horn.

4.7.4. Conch Shells as Horns

An unmodified conch or triton shell (especially the *Charonia tritonis* triton and the *Strombus gigas* conch) could be played as a musical instrument. It gives out a loud blast like a horn, the sound improved by cutting the tip of the shell across the apex, making a hole to serve as a mouthpiece. The pitch could be altered by moving the hand in and around the main aperture of the shell—the further the hand penetrates the shell the lower the note. The sound was called ʿárho di-ḥánṣə 'the voice of the ḥánṣə'. At sea, it was used by returning sailing ships to signal and celebrate their safe arrival. On land, it was blown by the nəkīb di-tímiher, 'guardian of the communal date palm garden', to announce the opening up of the date palm garden to gleaners. He would blow another blast when the permitted time for gleaning came to an end.

4.7.5. Fish as Feed for Household Herds

At times of drought, some coastal people fed fish and fish debris to their household herds, or gave them the water in which fish had been cooked. However, they never gave the flesh,[158] skin or

---

[158] Friedhelm Krupp (pers. comm.): "Dried shark given as a supplementary livestock feed on its own can be dangerous, either due to its

water in which shark, the small ṣaṭiʿo ray or the larger kə́dəhe ray had been cooked, as this could make goats and camels extremely sick. On Soqotra there seems to have been no tradition of using small fish and fish debris as a fertiliser, as done on the mainland opposite.[159]

4.8. Diving for Pearls and Pearlshell

Soqoṭri fishermen say that diving for pearls has long been practised on the island, the demand for pearlshell coming later. In 1876 Ravenstein reported that there were pearl fisheries with Omani divers around Tamarida (Ḥadibo; Ravenstein 1876, 124), and Forbes (writing in 1899, cited in Forbes 1903, xxvii), described diving for pearlshell and pearl oysters as being widely practiced on Soqotra's north coast and around ʿAbd al-Kūri.[160] Serjeant mentions that pearling was still being done at Di-Ḥamṣ

---

high salt content, or because when fed without additional high energy feed like grain, it causes ammonia toxicity."

[159] Though after learning about its potential use as a fertiliser, Mubārak experimented very successfully with it in his extremely productive garden (See Pietsch and Morris 2010, 375–86).

[160] Forbes (1903, xxvii) writes of ʿAbd al-Kūri: "It seems that the chief occupation of the people is as divers for mother of pearl shell on the Bacchus Bank to the north-east of the island, on the boats of shellers who come probably from Zanzibar, Arabia or India. The diver descends to the sea floor holding to a line weighted by a heavy stone on which he stands, his nostrils being closed by a small wooden springclamp or pincers. At the end of his 'turn' he drops the stone and is pulled to the surface."

when he was there in 1967[161] and that the Somali divers at Ġúbbah had been forbidden to use glass-bottomed face masks, as this would clear out the oyster beds. Diving for pearls used to be important for the island's fishermen, but when pearls started to be cultured and synthetic alternatives became available, the demand for natural pearls declined.

Diving for pearlshell was widespread in the lifetime of Mubārak's grandfather, but halfway through the life of Mubārak's father it came to an end. Pearl oyster beds were worked mainly in the summer months (*ḳéyaṭ* and *dōtə*), the pearlshell oysters at any time of the year. Pearl oysters were found in shallower waters than the pearlshell oysters, closer inshore and in more restricted areas. Pearlshell oysters could be found in deeper waters in many areas of the seas around the island, as well as in lagoons.[162]

---

[161] See Serjeant (writing in 1967, cited in Doe 1992, 177). Mubārak remembered hearing about this ban and said it was because (a) wearing the mask made any oyster look big enough to take, so the immature ones were not left undisturbed; (b) since the eyes of a diver wearing a mask were protected from the salt and the stirred up silt and sand, he could stay down in the same place longer, and thereby potentially clear an entire area of oysters in one diving session.

[162] Nichols (2002, 9.7.2.): "*Pinctada margaritifera* occurs in lagoons, bays and sheltered reefs down to 40m. depth; they are attached to the rocky substrate by byssal threads. They are non-selective filter feeders, highly sensitive to water quality (intolerant of high turbidity and fresh water runoff).... The main fishing grounds are on the north coast between Raʾs Qadamah and Raʾs Ḥawlaf as well as around ʿAbd al-Kūri and the Brothers. The main use is for shell buttons and jewelry; the nacre is also ground up and added to metallic paints."

Somalis hired for the season came to the islands to dive for both kinds of oyster, arriving in large wooden boats carrying 10–12 dugout canoes. It is remembered that they needed an interpreter to interact with the islanders, Arabic- or Soqoṭri-speaking. Some Soqoṭri divers left with the trade boats to travel to ʿAbd al-Kūri or to the al-Ḥallāniyyāt islands (formerly Kuria Muria) in Oman, to dive for pearls and for pearlshell oysters. They left at the end of summer before the sea grew rough as the monsoon winds began to blow. Although many divers came to Soqoṭra from Somalia and elsewhere on the East African coast to dive for pearlshell, it is said that few divers came from the Gulf or from Oman for this purpose.[163]

Islanders say that they never bothered to dive for pearlshell oysters as food. However, once there was a commercial demand for the pearlshell, people began to eat the flesh, scraping it from the shell and cooking it with its red coral or roe (called by the fishermen the 'ear'). In larger specimens, the coral was removed and the flesh put on a skewer and hung in the sun to dry. The dried oyster could be chewed just like that or softened by beating against a rock surface before cooking, as was done for octopus.

4.9. Diving for Pearl Oysters, *Pinctada radiata* (*bílbil*)

The best pearl oyster beds were said to be on the east and north coasts: in the east, around Qábho in Ḥállah and at Di-ʿAféro at

---

[163] See Huntington and Wilson (1995, 2): "It is understood that there are still around 60–100 specialist pearl divers in Socotra and Abdu l-Kuri, although many are reaching retirement age."

Raʔs Mōmi; in the north, around Di-Līyə in Ḥéybaḵ, between Dílli (east of Ḥéybaḵ) and Ḥadibo, and at Ḥáwlef, Dilíšə and ʕArírihun. Pearl diving was done mainly when the sea was calm: in the summer season of ḵéyaṭ and dōti, roughly February to early June, and again in the di-ṣerébhen[164] season, at the very end of the monsoon before the sea is churned up once more by winter storms. There were no restrictions as to place, anyone could dive anywhere. At the beginning of the summer, the wooden sailing boats arrived, bringing traders and pearl divers (ġuwwās, pl. ġuwwāsīn, from Arabic), from the Gulf, Oman and Somalia. The mariners lived on their boats, purchasing items such as butteroil, water, firewood and the occasional animal for meat from the islanders. Some men from the island fishing communities joined these divers and the rowing crews, and in this way learned pearl-diving skills (as is clear from much of the vocabulary associated with pearl diving which is Arabic or Arabic-influenced).

4.9.1. Method

As carried out by Soqotrans, pearl diving was done from dugout canoes, the smaller canoes taking two people, the larger ones four. They loaded their dugouts with equipment such as cooking pot, firewood, firebrand and water, and, as half the crew fished while the other half dived, fishing gear. On the north coast, the pearl divers usually set up camp on the shore close to

---

[164] dōti and ṣerébhən: transitional periods between the two monsoons, a lull of some six weeks during which clouds pile up and disperse repeatedly, and the winds fluctuate.

the oyster beds. They left to dive in the morning and opened their oysters in the afternoon, placing any pearls they had found in a half shell. Some divers used the *merāyə* 'glass magnifying box' (see 4.10.1. below) and some the *fə́ṭām~fíṭəham* 'nose-clip' which was placed over the nostrils to keep them shut when diving. This was made from the notched tip of a cow horn or from any piece of washed-up plastic (ʿag), bent or slit to shape. They might also take an iron spike with a curved tip (*máḥwaš*) to dislodge any tightly attached oysters. Even if lying agape, as soon as the oysters sense the least unnatural movement, they snap shut and cling tightly to their rocky base.

The diver had a rope around his chest and a cloth bag called *díngal*. When he dived down, the straps of the *díngal* were clasped between the big and first toe of one foot, while a weight of six or more *raṭl* of lead was held between the big and first toe of the other. One end of the rope bearing the weight had a running noose which was looped over a thick wooden pole or plank (ʿárṣa) laid across the dugout, one end of which protruded beyond the side of the dugout for the diver to hang on to when he came up to breathe and rested between dives. When ready to dive, he removed the slipknot from the ʿárṣa and tied it around a big toe, holding the rope taut against his chest as he jumped in, feetfirst. On touching the sea bottom, he lifted the loop holding the weight off his big toe and laid it on the ground. As soon as he let go of this rope, his partner in the dugout (the *ṣayyāb*, 'rower') would haul it up and loop it once more over the ʿárṣa 'plank'. The diver would then remove the *díngal* 'oyster bag' from his foot, hang it around his neck, and get to work on the oyster bed. When he began to run out of air he would tug on the rope and, holding onto the *díngal* 'oyster bag' with its oysters, would be pulled up to the *ʿárṣa*. He would rest there and then go down again. When he was exhausted, his partner would take over.

Diving continued from around 8am until midday—even on a Friday they would dive until it was time to get ready for Friday prayer. At midday, the divers came ashore, each placing their oysters in a separate pile and, if there were no shade, covering it with sailcloth or sacking. They would then go off to pray, have lunch and rest. After *ʿaṣr* prayer it was time to open (*fəlk*) the oysters, looking carefully for any pearls. The flesh was discarded unless wanted for bait. If they saw a trader approaching, the divers would do their best to conceal any pearls they had found and would instead put out an empty oyster shell to make it appear that they had been unsuccessful.

4.9.2. The Pearl Trade

Any pearls were sold to traders (*ṭawwāš*, pl. *ṭawāwīš*).[165] These were mostly from the Bāṭinah in Oman, with some coming from Abu Dhabi, Dubai, and Raʾs al-Khayma. Some traders stayed on

---

[165] Islanders say that this name comes from the verb *yəṭāwiš~yəṭūš*, 'to go round and round (after pearls)', but some suggest it comes from the Arabic *ṭawwaša* 'to castrate, emasculate', so *ṭawāšī*, pl. *ṭawāšiya* 'eunuch', and was a term of disapprobriation. In the Gulf, the *ṭawwāš* was the merchant involved in funding diving operations, or the middleman who bought pearls from divers or those they worked for and sold them to the wholesale merchants (*tājir*) (see Al-Salimi and Staples 2019, 550).

the island for the whole summer season, some married local women and returned to the island year after year, and some settled down permanently on Soqoṭra. The right to deal in pearls and pearlshell was either retained by the sultan for himself or was given by him to various favoured people.[166] The traders and merchants would walk up and down the shore encampments to see what the divers had found and make offers for any pearls they were shown. Some traders operated the ʿarbún system whereby they gave the divers money in advance to buy food and other necessities in return for first refusal on any pearls they found. Divers who were not bound to a trader could either sell their pearls directly from the beach or take them home and hang on to them in the hopes of a better price at a later date.

The shells of the pearl oysters sometimes provided additional material of value, and some people processed them to try and find any pearls embedded in the nacre lining, an operation called gəḥōlə. They gathered up the discarded shells and spread them out to dry. Then they crushed them and sifted the frag-

---

[166] This was quite usual: men favoured by the sultanic family classes, such as the *Sayyids, Shaḥra* and *Shuyūkh,* could buy or rent various sorts of monopoly from the sultan. In addition to pearling products, there were monopolies for the right to import grain, export butteroil, transport goods, and so on. Ambergris, however, was reserved for the sultan alone. The Shaḥra (Soqoṭri Śḥaró) were a tribe of mainland origin close to the sultans. The Shuyūkh (Soqoṭri Šyūx, *not* meaning 'shaykh') were another tribe, of uncertain origin, but possibly originally Mashāyikh, another group of people from the mainland accredited with special powers, also close to the sultans. For the Sayyids, see above, footnote 2.

ments for any tiny seed pearls that had been concealed within the shell lining. Women made a glittering cosmetic by further grinding the crushed shells to a fine powder.

Different kinds of pearl each had their own name: "We call the pearls *lūl* or *gówhərə*. On the way back from the diving grounds, one will row while the other opens up (*ifōlaḥ*) the shells. Small pearls the size of finger-millet grains (*ḥabbə di-bombə*) we call *ḥóyhi*, 'dust, soil' or *saḥṭīṭ*, 'sweepings': these are worth very little. Those that reach the size of the eyeball of a small fish (*gəlmə́mo di-ḥoṭ di-kīhən~gə́lməmo di-ṣódə*) are regarded as proper *lūl* pearls. We measure the size of a pearl with our fingers: if it can be pressed into the flesh between two finger joints until it is invisible, it is not worth much. If it remains visible, it is worth something." (Aḥmad Saʿd Taḥkí)

Misshapen or damaged pearls were called *mḵárrat*, 'discoloured and lumpy', and pearls of a good size but dark in colour and with only a very thin coating of mother-of-pearl were called *xárśə*,[167] the name given to the few pearls found in the pearlshell oysters.[168]

---

[167] From √ḥrš~√xrš, 'to be, look dirty, unappetising; to be slightly off, strange tasting (especially water, dates).'

[168] "Some *lūl* or *gówhərə* are bigger, the size of a knuckle, but they are not from the sea. They are from a great snake (*bəkīli*) which carries the *lūl* or *gówhərə* on its head and sometimes puts it down on the ground to light up the area while it browses the trees at night. There are said to be much larger pearls in the sea, but no one can ever get at them as they are guarded (*ḥegīro*) by two giant fish (*ḥóṭi*). These pearls are to be found in giant mother-of-pearl shells and have been glimpsed by divers when the oyster gapes (*tyóʔo śaḥ*). Any pearl of any real size

4.10. Diving for Pearlshell Oysters, *Pinctada margaritifera* (*móṣəliḥ*, Ar. *ṣádaf*)

There was no special season for pearlshell diving, it could be done whenever the state of the sea allowed. There were no restrictions on diving for pearlshell oysters: anyone could dive anywhere. Fishermen say that the best diving sites were around Qāṣeb, Mūri, Sírihin and Šik on the north coast, and in the east, in the seas near the freshwater spring at ʿÁrher d-Ífke, and around Raʾs Mōmi. The diving sites at Mūri, ʿÁrher d-Ífke and Ḥáwlef were fairly close inshore, but in the Ḥadibo area divers had to row some 12 *bāʿ* from shore.

The diving was done from dugouts, but these were constantly on the move, rather than being anchored over a single oyster bed as when diving for pearl oysters. Work continued from around 8am until midday, some returning to the sea after the *ʿaṣr* afternoon prayers. Most divers could only bring up two of these large shells at a time, so for a diver working full time, two diving sessions a day were necessary to gather enough pearlshell to make it worthwhile.

---

must be reported to the sultan and sold to him (*lāzim ṣ́úwlaʿ bis ε-sáṭəhān w-itōgir tos*). He then sells it on to the traders (*ṭawāwīš*) for a good price. It is said that the best pearls went to the Queen of England, and to Iran and India." (Aḥmad Saʿd Taḥkí)

4.10.1. Method

To make pearlshell diving profitable, full-time divers always tried to have the magnifying device, the *merāyə*,[169] on board to help them study the sea floor. This was a box, often a cut-down aluminium container (*tankə*), open at one end, and with a piece of glass sandwiched between two wooden frames at the other.[170] The glass was fixed in place with a glue made of *Euphorbia arbuscula* latex mixed with shark liver oil (*ṣífə*), boiled down to a thick black paste. The longer the glue was left to dry before being used in the sea, the stronger it became. Lumps of tar (*ḳār* or *dámer*) that floated ashore were sometimes used as glue instead. The wooden frames too were packed with cotton fibre soaked in latex glue, making the *merāyə* as watertight as possible. The open end had a loop at top and bottom, held in place by sticks of *Croton socotranus*, glued on and waterproofed by more latex glue. To use the device, the man put his head inside the box and then positioned the glass end on the sea's surface to scan the seabed.

The man who owned a *merāyə* was normally the only one to use it: it was his special area of expertise (*yəréyyis bə-merāyə*

---

[169] In the Gulf, Yemen and the Red Sea called *jāma*. See Al-Salimi and Staples (2019, 511): "a glass-bottomed box or bucket, approximately 2 feet long and 8 inches wide, used to look for pearls on the seabed in shallow waters."

[170] The modern face mask (*kísmə*) worn over the eyes and nose arrived in the 1970s. The traditional *merāyə* could only be used on the surface of the sea. See description in Moser (1918, 267–68).

'he's in charge with the *merāyə* glass'). He was called the *mətaréyyis* or sometimes the *nōxədə* ('captain').

To dive for pearlshell oysters, two men went out in a dugout, one to dive and one to use the *merāyə*. The one with the *merāyə* sat to one side of the bow, both elbows on the padded gunwhale or rubbing strake, holding the glass to the surface of the sea. The pearlshell oysters were usually buried under weed or lay under ledges, making them practically invisible except to the expert eye.[171] When the man with the *merāyə* saw a pearlshell oyster he would signal to the rower by tapping on the *merāyə* rim. He would then guide the diver/rower to the exact place, and the diver/rower would dive down with his *máḥwaš* 'iron spike' and dislodge the oyster. These divers rarely used the cow-horn *fə́ṭām~fíṭəham* 'nose-clip' of the pearl oyster divers as they rarely stayed underwater for long. Guided here and there by the *merāyə* man, the diver would keep going until he was too cold and tired to continue. After lunch and a rest, the two would shuck their oysters. In general, the *ṭawāwīš* 'traders' had little interest in their activities: although some of these oysters do have pearls, even of a respectable size, they are generally of poor quality and of little value.

---

[171] Inexperienced divers were trained to familiarise themselves with the appearance of pearlshell oysters: when a pearlshell oyster was sighted by the *merāyə* man, he lowered a *buld* (a rock tied onto a length of rope) to sit directly on top of the shell to indicate to the learner diver where he should go.

4.10.2. The Care and Sale of Pearlshell

Two qualities of pearlshell were recognised. The smaller shells (that is, those of immature oysters) sold for the best price because their mother-of-pearl was pure white and not 'streaked', while that of the larger, more mature shells had a tendency to develop ridges and wrinkles which lessened their value. The shells were sold by weight. This meant that to get the best price it was imperative to try and to sell them as quickly as possible, while they were still damp and therefore heavy. They were sold by the *raṭl* (about 1 lb.) or *fərāsilə* (about 28 *raṭl*), and divers remember a *raṭl* of pearlshell selling for a *raṭl* of dates or cereal.

If an immediate sale were not possible, the heavy shells were taken back home, cleaned, and then stacked in layers in a pit dug in the sand, outer shell uppermost and mother-of-pearl side face down. They were then covered with a layer of date palm fibre matting (*ḥāṣir*) or sacking (*gūnīyə*), and the pit was watered weekly to keep the shells damp. They were left there until the price was right or until the seasonal trade boats arrived, when they were packed into sacks and sold by the *fərāsilə* weight.

If the shells had been kept damp, they were easy to pack in neat layers, but if they had been allowed to dry out they had a tendency to fracture. Even if carefully watered, the edges of the shells sometimes broke off, damaging the mother-of-pearl and lessening its value. If a buyer had not been found by the time the trade boats were getting ready to leave, the shells were bagged up into *ṣōṭəli* sacks (the large thick ones in which the maize from East Africa was packed) and sent with the captain to sell for whatever price he could get. Like all exports, pearlshell was subject to the standard 5% export tax.

5. The Craft of Soqoṭra

5.1. The Raft (*rēmuš*)

In the days of the grandparents of old men alive today, the majority of Soqoṭri fishermen relied on rafts.[172] They rarely strayed beyond the shallower inshore waters and could not use the raft out at sea to try and catch the larger fish or shark there.[173]

---

[172] Forbes (1903, xxvii) describes seeing a man on ʿAbd al-Kūri fishing "astride a poor catamaran of three narrow logs of wood lashed together, with his legs dangling in the water, by which to paddle himself about the bay." And in 1836 Hulton (2003, 30) writes of Tamarida (Ḥadibo): "the scene was enlivened by numerous catamarans dancing over its bright waters." Mubārak himself remembered two operational rafts in Ḥadibo, three in Sírihin, two in Dišhilinítin and two at Šiḵ (Suḵ). There were also others here and there in other fishing settlements of the north coast.

[173] See Agius (2002, 128): "Regarding catamarans, the *ramath* (pl. *armāth*, *rimāth* or *rawāmith*) was the most popular among the Socotrans, on the west coast of India, and particularly around the island of Sri Lanka. They are still in the memory of many old Omanis in Muscat and the Al-Batinah region, who recall the islanders of Socotra calling at their ports during the fishing season…. Unquestionably these primitive craft are survivals from antiquity." And Agius again (2002, 129): "We have no information on how the *ramath* was built; I assume that the techniques were fairly universal in the maritime culture of the Indian Ocean, and both Edye's (1835, 4) description of a Sri Lankan catamaran off Cape Camorin, and Hornell's (1920, 153), of a boat catamaran off the Tinnevelly coast, would suffice to give us a general pic-

5.1.1. Manufacture

A raft was made by lashing logs together, date palm trunks,[174] large branches of *Sterculia* (*bōhīn*), *Ficus vasta* (*ṭiḵ*), *Commiphora ornifolia* (*íkšə*), *Zizyphus* (*ṣ́óʔod*), or any other light wood available on the island—even driftwood. Date palm trunks, *Sterculia* or *Ficus* were considered to make the best rafts, but these were not available everywhere, and sometimes the wood of *Euphorbia socotrana* or *Cryptolepis socotrana* (both called *dōḵəš*) had to be used instead. Lengths of wood with a natural curve at one end were preferred, as the raft should curve upwards at the bow to improve its performance in heavy surf conditions. The green wood was left to dry out and was then carried down to the shore for trimming and assembly. Four logs were needed. Three were laid parallel to one another and roped together at the extremities, commonly with strips of *Croton socotranus* (*mítrer*) underbark. Further strips were set aside for attaching the fourth

---

ture of this primitive craft. The raft is formed of 3 logs of timber, some 20 to 25 feet in length and 2 to 3 feet in breadth, secured together by means of spreaders and cross-lashings; the central log is larger than the side ones. Hornell explains how these logs are held in position 'by a transverse two-horned block of wood at either end whereto the logs are lashed securely by coir ropes passed through grooves cut in the sides of the logs.' It was navigated by one or two men, and we are told that the catamaran was good for surfing on the beach. In the monsoon a light bamboo yard of 34 feet was placed, balanced with a small outrigger at the end of two poles, and using a mat or a triangular cotton cloth sail. It was paddled by a double oar."

[174] On the south coast they are remembered as having been made principally from date palm trunks (*gōdiˤ*, pl. *egdóˤo*).

log once the raft was floating in the sea—a four-log raft would normally be too heavy to drag up and down the beach. Slimmer poles or spreaders were laid across the logs and strapped on, their ends protruding from each side to provide handles for moving the raft around. It was said that, looked after carefully,[175] a raft could outlast a dugout canoe.

5.1.2. Paddles (mə́ḵdef, pl. mḵādif)

The best wood for the shaft (ṭarb di-mə́ḵdef) was hard *Ziziphus* wood, as this floats if dropped overboard (*Croton* and *Zygocarpum* sink). The circular or square blade (ṣaf di-mə́ḵdef) had a protruding tongue or flange and was shaped from planking or cut from sheets of plywood, usually driftwood. Four holes were bored through the tongue, and this was then laid across the shaft and bound in place with cord twisted from locally grown cotton, date palm material or imported coir (benj or kəmbēri).

5.1.3. Use

The rafts were basically platforms from which to fish, to set or recover fish traps, or to dive for oysters or other valuable shellfish. They were also used as lighters to unload cargo from larger boats,[176] especially cargo such as metal drums, kerosene tins[177]

---

[175] Mubārak knew a man, ʿAbd Allāh Ḥadīd, who had a raft which he used all his life before passing it on to his son ʾAdīb, and it was still in perfect condition.

[176] See Serjeant (writing in 1967, cited in Doe 1992, 171), where he describes lighterage dues for dugout canoes in Qalansiyah.

or timber which would not be damaged by a wetting. Children used rafts to practise working the sea: they were not allowed to use a precious dugout or any other fishing gear in workable condition in case they damaged it.

A raft normally took only one fisherman and at least two baskets, one for bait and one for fishing gear. Some fishermen took a third basket for the catch; others just threw any catch onto the lowest point of the raft. The fisherman would sit on the middle two logs, well back at the flat stern, his legs doubled beneath, heels tilted, and toes bent back on themselves. His basket of bait sat behind him, and the baskets of fishing gear and for the catch in front, at the bow, where the raft curves upwards. Recovering a fish trap was done from the bow: he would haul it in to lie directly below the raft and would then walk slowly up to the front, causing the bow to sink beneath the water. He then manoeuvred the raft so that the bow lay just beneath the waterlogged and heavy trap. Walking slowly backwards brought the bow back up again, bringing the trap up with it. He could then empty out any fish and set the trap again.

5.2. The Dugout Canoe (*hūri*, pl. *hwāri*)

The *hūri* was a double-ended canoe hollowed out from a single tree trunk. It was seen as female, like all seagoing craft. Those who owned one—or more commonly a share in one—were con-

---

[177] Villiers (1940, 56) writes of "ghee in kerosene tins" among the cargo taken on board at al-Mukallā to go to Africa, and (1940, 94) of "ghee in Standard Oil Co.'s rejected containers" being taken on at Aden.

sidered fortunate indeed.[178] The dugouts, often leased out by their owners, were used principally by full-time fishermen in the permanent fishing settlements of the north coast.[179] They were also used as lighters to transport goods and passengers to and from the trade boats.[180] The smaller ones, the most common dugouts on the island, were some 12 feet long and crewed by two fishermen; the larger ones (such as those that came with the visiting pearling dhows) were 18 feet or more in length and

---

[178] Numbers were limited even in Mubārak's lifetime: his father at ꜤEyro owned two (but he was regarded as 'a rich man'), the fishermen of Di-Ḥámri had four, those of ꜤArírihun and Qáriyah three or four, the main fishing area of Qāṣeb 10–12, in each of the village settlements of the Dīḥamṣ area there were one or two, Ḥadibo had six and Sírihin three. His father purchased his first dugout from Di-Sélməho, and it cost him five Maria Theresa silver thalers. Compare this with Brown (1966, 28) who counted 116 *hūri* in the main settlements of the north coast, but only eight on the south coast, and Huntington and Wilson (1995, 3.3), who estimated "350 traditional wooden skiffs on the island as a whole."

[179] The principal north coast fisheries were seen as extending from Di-Ḥámri in the east to Di-ꜤAféro at RaʾMūri in the west.

[180] Serjeant (writing in 1967, cited in Doe 1992, 171–72) reports that a third of the fee for lighterage went to the owner of the dugout, and two thirds to the sailors and the *muqaddam* of the ship. He also writes that: "Lighterage from the vessel to the shore is 2 *kaylah* measures, a *kaylah* being about 9 *raṭls* or pounds, on each bag of maize, and another two from the shore to the house or shop, making four *kaylahs* in all. The bag of maize is 210 *raṭls*, equivalent to 190 *qurṣ* approximately. I noted in 1967 that the lighterage on a bag of grain would cost about two shillings East African."

were crewed by four to six fishermen.[181] Whatever the craft, the catch was divided: one share for each fisherman and a share for the boat. Thus the catch for a small two-man dugout was divided into three: one third for the boat, and one third for each of the two fishermen. This meant that if the owner was also one of the fishermen, he received two thirds of the catch.[182]

5.2.1. Purchase

The majority of the dugouts are said to have come from Malabar (*benēbār*) in India, reaching the island via Muscat and the Gulf.[183] A small number were purchased directly from trade

---

[181] Jansen van Rensburg (2016, 116) in his study of the Soqotra dugout, writes that those he recorded "varied between three to nine meters in length with a beam of one to one and half metres."

[182] Those who worked on the larger wooden fishing dhows (the *sádak*, with a sail but no engine, and the *wārra*, with an engine) of the larger fishing settlements, such as Qalansiyah, had their share calculated differently. The crew usually consisted of the captain and five or six crew (one of whom was the cook). First, each member of the crew (*báḥari*) had the cost of his food (*serkāl*: dates, bread, rice, coffee, cooking oil—the crew caught and shared their own fish) deducted from his share. Then the profit from the catch was divided equally among all (the captain receiving the same share as his crew), with one share again going to the boat for the gear, fuel, lubricants, salt and so on.

[183] Jansen van Rensburg (2016, 101) took samples of the wood of a number of dugouts for analysis and records that they were all made of teak, *Tectona grandis*, from India. Mubārak remembered the dugouts that came from Africa: he said they were "very heavy, red in colour, extremely strong and lasted for a long time."

boats[184] coming from East Africa, or from visiting pearlers. Dugouts could also be ordered in advance from one of the trade boats that visited the island, the purchaser instructing that "the shell of the dugout should be fully watertight (wəšár) and not crooked (ʿáwəj)." Before a new dugout was launched or any work done on it, it was customary to slaughter a goat and sprinkle some of its blood inside the dugout. Its skin was then tied around the prow and left there until it rotted away.

5.2.2. Modification on Soqoṭra

Once on the island, the bare shell was modified by local craftsmen.[185]

Ribs (šilmān). V- or U-shaped ribs were added to brace and strengthen the basic shell. The best timber to use was *Ziziphus* or *Tamarindus* wood. The ribs were shaped by hand and nailed into position to the sides of the dugout—sometimes quite thin—with nails or with cylindrical plugs of wood or bamboo

---

[184] Villiers (1940, 289) writes about seeing in Muttrah, Oman, a dhow from Qeshm Island loaded with 30 dugout canoes from the Malabar coast for onward sale. He also mentions that the same ship carried "teak logs" and that it was not uncommon for ships' carpenters to make dugout canoes on board to sell en route.

[185] In Mubārak's father's lifetime there were a limited number of skilled craftsmen (ʾustād, pl. ʾasātidə): one in Suḵ~Šiḵ, four in Qāṣeb and four in Ḥadibo. Each ʾustād had his own tools: ránda, 'hand plane', ḵedṓm, 'adze', mə́ḵdaḥ, 'bow-drill' and mínšar, 'saw'.

(bómbwə). The ribs had the added effect of widening the dugout by forcing the sides further apart.[186]

Keel runner (ferár~biskīn). A runner was nailed to the outside of the hull, running from one end of the keel to the other. This protected the hull and bore the brunt of the wear and tear of dragging the dugout up and down the beach. The best material for this was bamboo, which was imported in culms, each culm making four or five keel runners. If no bamboo were available, a slim trunk or a branch of a wood such as *Croton* (mítrer) or *Zygocarpum* (ḥímiher) was used, split along its length, shaped and then nailed to the bottom of the boat with treenails of wood or bamboo. The holes for the treenails were drilled out with the bow drill (məḳdaḥ), imported from Muscat or the Gulf. The runner for a smaller dugout needed 15–20 treenails. Once *in situ*, the keel runner was called biskīn.

Thwarts or crossbeams (ḳāriyə, pl. ḳarāri~ḳəwāri). For the two-man dugout, two planks (lōḥ, pl. əlwáḥ, from Arabic) were shaped to run from one side of the dugout to the other: one in the middle and one at the stern. For the larger four- to six-man dugout, four thwarts were made: one at each end, one in the middle, and one halfway between the middle and the stern. This last had a hole in the centre to take a mast.

---

[186] Jansen van Rensburg (2016, 117) writes about some large dugouts of African origin whose hull had been expanded by "cutting two parallel gaps along the hull, and then forcing the gap wider using floor-framing elements. Several pieces of planking were then hammered into place and caulked with cloth or cotton." My informants did not mention this.

Gunwhale. The sides of the dugout were often built up by nailing lengths of wood, usually planking, to the upper rim of the dugout to make a rough gunwhale. This meant that the internal *šɨlmān* bracing ribs had to be cut back a little.

Running strake. A length of wood was nailed to the outside of the gunwhale to protect the lip of the hull from the damage caused by the rubbing of ropes and lines when fishing.

Rollers (*lēsīyə*, pl. *ləwāsi*). To protect the keel of the boat as it was pulled to and from the sea or dragged right up above the tideline, a set of rollers, usually three, was made. These were generally branches of a local hardwood such as *Ziziphus* or the more widely available *Ficus salicifolia*. When the dugout was beached for the monsoon, it was pulled right up the shore, turned upside down, and laid across the rollers. This raised it above the ground and allowed air to circulate.

Paddles (*məḳdef*, pl. *mḳādif*). These were similar to those used for the raft (see 5.1.2. above).

Mast (*dɨḳal*). To support the sail in the larger dugout (the two-crew dugout did not normally use a sail), a mast of 4–4.5 *durūʕ* (the distance from the elbow to the tip of middle finger, a cubit) was cut and shaped from a straight piece of any good island timber: *Zygocarpum, Chapmannia gracilis, Grewia, Maerua, Croton* or *Ziziphus*.

Sail (*śéraʕ*). Sails were usually made from the strong, unbleached calico (*mərēkān~bərēkān*) imported for clothing and shrouds. Triangular in shape, it was cut and stitched, the edges doubled over and hemmed with thread teased from the calico itself or with coir[187] twine.

Anchor (*íngəher* or *barrūsi*). This was usually a rock, one with a hole for the anchor rope to go through, or a square-shaped one around which the anchor rope could be securely bound.

Protective lining (*zəfāyər*). Lengths of wickerwork, similar to the wicker gates made for the home or fold, were made from the petioles or leaf-ribs (*mízərud*) of date palm fronds. These were cut to the same length, laid out on the ground and then bound at the top, middle and bottom with date-leaf twine (*aḥtimí di-ḥéṣə*). The lengths of completed wickerwork were then slung from one side of the dugout to the other, covering the wood beneath. This provided a protective lining for the inside of the dugout and made a more comfortable surface to sit on. It could easily be removed when necessary, and if damaged, was straightforward to replace.

Bailer (*məgāraʕ*~*məgārah*). A bailer was made from half a coconut or a hollowed-out knot of wood.

Other equipment. As well as fishing gear, most dugouts carried a stout club for stunning larger fish and shark, a gaff, and one or more date palm fibre baskets for bait, fishing gear and to hold the catch.

---

[187] Villiers (1940, 289) writes of seeing dhows at Muttrah, Oman, laden with ropes and coils of coir for onward sale.

5.2.3. Later Modifications on Soqoṭra

Rudder (*sukkān*). Within the lifetime of Mubārak's father, a stern-mounted rudder was added. This was made by local boat-builders and carpenters and came in two sections, one *únṭāʔ* 'female', the other *ḏikr* 'male' (Arabic terms). The 'female' part was fixed to the dugout and went down into the water. The 'male' part, the tiller, was fitted to drop down inside the 'female', and was the part held by the man at the helm.

Figure 7: Modified dugout, on rollers, with outboard engine wrapped in sacking, Mōmi

Photo © Miranda Morris, 1990s

Outboard engine (*məkīnə*). When 15hp. outboard engines became available, the dugout had to be further modified to bear its weight. A solid block of hard wood was added to the stern, giving the dugout a squared-off appearance at the back. The outboard engine sat on top of this, and an additional trapezium of wood (šínṭə) was fitted into the stern. The fisherman sat on this to steer the boat and work the engine.

5.2.4. Repairs

A major crack or split in the wood of a dugout usually meant that the owner had to take it to a specialist for repair, as only he was likely to have the necessary tools to cut and shape a wooden patch and nail it into place. However, a small split or crack could be dealt with by the fishermen themselves, caulking it by packing it with cotton or imported coir. The fibres were twisted (ḥówṣak) into twine which was then plied until a rope of the thickness of the crack was achieved. This was then soaked in shark liver oil and hammered into the crack until none of it was visible from inside or out.[188] An alternative caulking mixture was made from the latex extracted from *Euphorbia arbuscula* (dūr di-ʾímtəhe) mixed with shark liver oil and boiled to make a thick paste. The length of rope was tamped firmly into the crack, and then the latex and oil paste was smeared over and around the filling until the cotton wadding could absorb no more. It was then left to set hard: the more oil in the mixture the longer it took to harden.

A minor dent was generally ignored, but a serious one was treated by leaving the dugout in water, or repeatedly soaking the dented area in water to soften the wood. Once the dented area was sufficiently swollen and soft, it was tapped inside and

---

[188] The mixture of fat and sheep wool used for caulking in Hadhramaut was not used on Soqoṭra.

out with a stone or blunt piece of metal until the dent was considerably reduced.

If a dugout sprung a leak, some shark liver debris (*ṭáḥalə*, see 5.2.5. below) was scraped from beneath the oil in the shark liver drum and rubbed all over the area of the leak to seal it. If holed, a piece of hard wood a little larger than the hole was cut and shaped until it could be hammered into the hole and firmly tamped down. Any gaps were packed with one of the caulking mixtures described above.[189]

5.2.5. Shark Liver Oil (*ṣífə di-léḥḥīm~ṣífə di-láxīm*) for Caulking and Treating Wood

Experienced fishermen recognised that certain shark had livers of the *šíbdə* type, while others had livers of the *ṭáḥalə* type (sometimes called *kídwəhe* 'dark-coloured').[190] Only the *šíbdə* type of liver was used to make edible oil, while the oil from the *ṭáḥalə* type was regarded as inedible.[191] It was, however, valuable for more general marine use: for caulking, waterproofing and for protecting wood from wood-boring organisms. The liv-

---

[189] Jansen van Rensburg (2016, 117–18) mentions repairs being stitched in the Ġúbbah area. He reports that along the east coast repairs were nailed and caulked, and in Ḥadibo and Qalansiyah both stitching and nailing/caulking were practised.

[190] It took expertise to differentiate between a *šíbdə* and a *ṭáḥalə*. To the non-expert, one apparent difference is that a *ṭáḥalə* placed in hot sun 'dries out and wrinkles' (*təzˁíbib*), whereas a *šíbdə* 'melts' (*ímhi*). *ṭáḥalə* is also the term for the shark liver debris that sinks to the bottom of the drum in which the shark liver oil was made.

[191] For edible shark liver oil, see 6.1.6. below.

ers of sharks such as the tiger shark or blacktip reef shark were not considered suitable for making oil: they were too small, 'black' (ḥə́wro) and 'lacked fat' (daḥámo).

To make the oil, the livers were cut up (nəḳā́ṣəlsən 'we cut them in slices'), put in an old oil drum (drēm), covered, and left in the sun.[192] They were not cooked in any way: if they were, the resulting oil would dry out very quickly when applied to wood so would be of little use. It takes at least a month for the livers in the drum to produce oil. After the top-quality oil has been removed, what remained (also called ṭáḥələ) was left in the drum year after year, and just added to as and when fresh livers become available. The producers sold the best quality oil by the aluminium lidded container called tánkə.[193]

---

[192] ṣī́bdə di-léḥḥim nəʿāmər mēs ṣifi. nərōgəm ʿis wə-nəʿāḳals bə-šīhum śéher, śhéri. ímhi men šīhum di-ḳānə di-drām. ki ḥə́rotk əl-ḥūri bə-ṣīfi wə-ʿə́ḳalk tos śéhər, lal kēbur ʿis, tkósəs ʿafərίro wə-škɛ́ro, "We make ṣīfi shark liver oil from the livers of shark. We cover them (shark livers) over and leave them for a month, two months. They melt from the heat of the sun inside the drum. If you rub a dugout with shark liver oil and leave it for a month or so (i.e., in the monsoon), when you go to check on it, you find it turned a beautiful red colour." Aḥmad Saʿd Taḥkí.

[193] Serjeant (writing in 1967, cited in Doe 1992, 179) reports that the aluminium tin (tankah) used for measuring out sharkoil for sale held 2.5 raṭl.

Figure 8: Dugout recently treated with shark-liver oil, east coast

Photo © Miranda Morris, 1990s

At least once a month during the fishing season, fishermen would rub the dugout inside and out with a wad of cloth dipped in the *ṭáḥalə* oil. Before the onset of the monsoon, the oiling had to be very thorough or the wood might dry out and crack from the months of harsh, drying winds: *k-al ḥarótk diɛ́ əl-hūri bə-ṣífi, tištíʔirən*, "If you don't oil your dugout with shark liver oil, it will crack." (Aḥmad Saʕd Taḥkí) Two weeks or so after a successful oiling, the wood turns red-brown and oozes droplets of oil.

Shark liver oil was also used for lighting. A fire normally provided adequate illumination at night, but to honour visitors, to sit up with the seriously sick or to deal with the dead, additional lighting was needed. Both *ṣífə* shark liver oil and *ḥámʔī* butteroil were used for this.[194] A wick (ftílə) was twisted from loosely spun fibre (ímdid) of local cotton or sheep wool. This was wound round and round inside a large butteroil storage pot (ḳṓmə), one end protruding from the narrow mouth through a plug of pressed dates. As the wick burned down and the date paste plug dried out and peeled away, the wick was gently pulled through, any gap in the paste being plugged with damp date paste scooped up from below. The smell of shark liver oil is unpleasantly strong, especially indoors, and those who could afford it much preferred butteroil. Simpler and quicker lighting was produced by filling a shallow clay saucer with shark liver oil, coiling a wick around inside it, with one end passing through a plug of date paste on the lip (or dampened finger-millet flour, dəḳī́ḳ di-bómbə, but this dries out very quickly). This was the kind of lighting fishermen often took with them when going out to sea at night.[195]

5.2.6. Care of the Dugout

A brand-new dugout had to be coated with a thick layer of shark liver oil inside and out before being launched for the first

---

[194] On ʿAbd al-Kūri, the islanders made ṣífə from turtle fat as well as from shark livers. This oil was also used for lighting, the lampblack providing a koḥl cosmetic for their eyes.

[195] Shark liver oil was also used to treat the very infectious disease of livestock, sarcoptic mange, gɛrb. Distressingly, it was also used to cauterise the stump when the hand of a persistent livestock thief had been publicly cut off as a deterrent. The hand was then suspended in a place where it would be seen by anyone passing.

time. The very best shark liver oil of all for this first coating was ṣifə ṣal 'pure filtered oil'; the oils made from sardines or from the livers of other fish were of no use for this. Only shark fishermen had ṣifə, and in the lifetime of Mubārak's father, it was a very valuable and essential commodity and the main reason for hunting shark.

During the fishing season a dugout had to spend some time in the water every day, and in addition had to be thoroughly soaked in water (tašrīb, from Arabic) at regular intervals to soften the wood and make it swell so that any dents or cracks could be treated. This was especially important when the craft had been standing idle during the long months of the monsoon. For a good soaking, the dugout had to be left in water for up to four days at a time.

At the end of summer, before the seas grew rough, signalling the approach of the monsoon, the dugouts were dragged up the beach and housed either in specially built stone boathouses or under the protection of date palms—anywhere that offered maximum shade and shelter from the driving sand and spray.[196] They were left to dry out, and then were thoroughly oiled inside and out to protect the wood against the dessicating winds of the monsoon. They remained under shelter until the winds changed again at the end of the monsoon, and futūḥ 'the opening (of the sea)', arrived and fishing could start up once more. The dugouts were given another good oiling before being taken down to sea.

---

[196] In areas with access to date palms, the monsoon quarters were made of palm logs with date palm roofing; the rollers too were made of palm logs.

Figure 9: Dugout shelter among date palms, north coast

Photo © Miranda Morris, 1990s

When not in use, dugouts were normally pulled up on the shore rather than being left tied up in the water. However, if an accumulation of barnacles (*dōser*), algae (*eṣerīʿo*) and other marine organisms on the bottom of the dugout was making it sluggish and unwieldy, this layer was scraped off (*íšrir*) with a piece of iron. A careful owner would then smear the scraped area all over with shark liver oil.

5.3. Sewn Rowing Boats (*śérḥa~śérxa*)

The few sewn rowing boats whose remains were still to be seen until recently, rotting on the foreshore, were said to have been an import from Oman. They were of different sizes and came with the pearling dhows, taking eight, ten or twelve divers and eight, ten or twelve oars (*sībə*, pl. *sībāt*), the number of divers being equal to the number of rowers. Soqoṭran divers say they liked working on the sewn boats because there was much more space in them. However, they rarely had the chance to do so, as the pearling boats tended to bring their own sailors and divers with them. Some of the sewn rowing boats which had become too damaged to be of any further use were left behind on the island, and a few were purchased by island merchants from the mainland. Local fishermen made use of them until they wore out, but they found them heavy, slow and unwieldy, and no one properly understood how to maintain or repair them.

Islanders say that in the days of the PDRY, after 1967, a few sewn boats were introduced into the south of the island as an experiment. According to Jansen van Rensburg (2016, 115), these might have been of a different and lighter make than those from the Gulf and Oman, and he was told that a few island fishermen did know how to maintain them, having learned how to do this on the Yemeni mainland. However, in the end, these sewn boats too were discarded in favour of the dugout.[197]

---

[197] Jansen van Rensburg (2016, 113–14) refers to reports of a date palm frond craft, like the šāša of Oman, seen by Bent in operation on the island. Bent (2010, 347–48) writes in 1897 of watching 'boatbuilding' at Kalenzia (Qalansiyah) "accomplished by tying a bundle of bamboos together at each end and pushing them out into shape with wooden stretchers," and (2010, 357) of seeing 'catamarans' in Kadhoup [Qāṣeb], and (2010, 394) of fishermen at Hawlaf going out "on little rafts made of bundles of palm-leaf ribs to drop the traps for fish." However, during his research, Jansen van Rensburg was unable to learn anything further about this on Soqoṭra, and no one ever recalled such a craft to me.

Figure 10: Old stitched boat, south coast

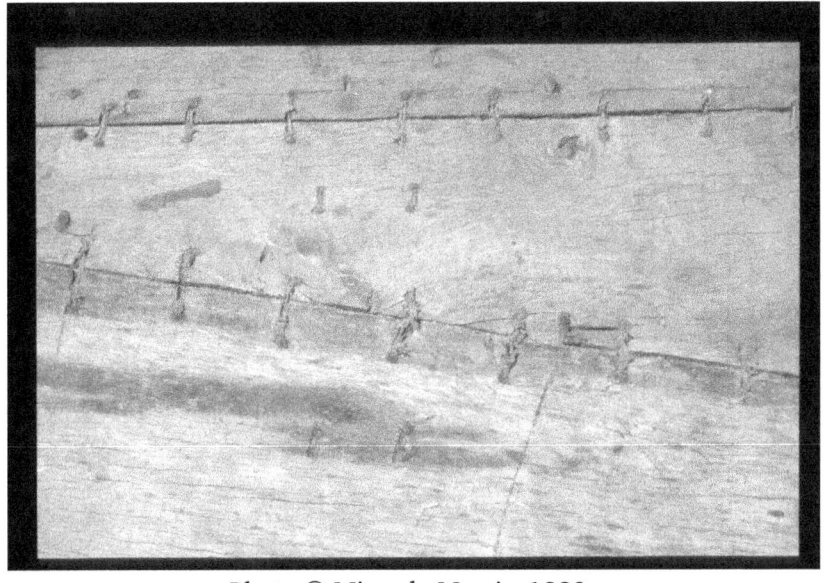

Photo © Miranda Morris, 1990s

After 1967, modern fishing skiffs replaced the dugout: fiberglass (GRP, glass reinforced plastic) made on the mainland at Shiḥr and al-Mukallā, powered by 15hp (or occasionally 25hp) Yamaha or Suzuki petrol engines.

6. Sea Products for Consumption and for Export

6.1. Sea Products for Local Consumption

Traditionally many islanders of the interior never ate fish. They regarded sea creatures and those who ate them with disdain: fish stank; they were not properly (i.e., ritually) slaughtered, nor were their eyeballs decently removed before cooking as was the custom with livestock. This dislike of fish was particularly widespread among livestock herders of the western half of Soqoṭra, in the central Ḥágher mountains and by those from the plateau areas behind. Herders who lived closer to the coast and had patrons (máḥrif, pl. máḥruf) there, or who regularly moved down to the coast in the dry season in search of food, were more accustomed to this food (though they were still usually reluctant to eat shellfish).

6.1.1. Distribution and Sale of Fish

Fresh fish were cooked as quickly as possible after being caught and were then covered and set aside until it was time to eat. In most parts of the island, fish were given away or bartered.[198] In the capital area, however, women—the womenfolk of the fishing families or any poor woman—would go down to the beach at dawn to meet the returning boats. They would be given fish on condition that whatever they managed to get for them in exchange (məkdɛ́rə 'maize', támer 'dates', bəṭā́ṭ 'sweet potatoes', də́bbə 'squash', or other foodstuffs), they would hand over three quarters of it to the fishermen, retaining a quarter share for themselves.[199] Needy Ḥadibo women would walk to the other nearby coastal villages to try and persuade fishermen there to give them fish to sell, and would then walk the alleyways of

---

[198] See Brown (1966, 27): "There is no cash market for fresh fish, which is, if surplus, almost given away... internal trade is wholly barter; ranging from the firewood-for-fish-offal level at Kallansiyah to long established agreements to provide so many pieces of fish against a delivery of ghee or dates. As the inland people can get most of their protein requirements from their own flocks, however, this is limited."

[199] This stopped with the arrival of the PDRY government when a central fish-market was established in Ḥadibo, where the fish were sold by men.

Ḥadibo crying their wares: *ɛɛ! ɛɛ! ṣódə! ṣódə!* "Hey! Hey! Fish! Fish!"

Throwing dead fish or parts of dead fish into the sea was frowned on.[200] It was seen as polluting and was also said to frighten live fish away from the area.

6.1.2. Fresh Fish

Fish were eaten roasted, boiled, or cooked slowly in a pit lined with hot stones. They were always cooked well away from the usual cooking area, often at some distance from the settlement. The pots for cooking fish (*məkíśo di-ṣódə* or *ṣáflaḥa di-ṣódə*) were likewise kept separately from other cooking pots. The water in which fish had been cooked was valued: it was always drunk or added to other foods. If fresh water were in short supply, this cooking water was used again and again.

Fish cut in half along their length were described as *núsfi*, i.e., 'providing two portions', and when each of these halves was further cut in two, *ribáʿi*, i.e., 'providing four portions'. The prime parts were considered to be the head and any fat. As for the head: "We split it open into two halves (*nənāṣer*). It is given to the senior person present or to the guest to suck (*mə́kmək*),

---

[200] On ʿAbd al-Kūri the rules were very strict: they say that the fish around their island feed in 'caves' very close to their rocky shore and would swim away from any such pollution. All fish must be cleaned on the beach rather than in the sea, and any dead fish or fish debris had to be heaped in a pile and then burned or buried. For this reason, fishermen here never used fish to bait their fish traps, only seaweed (see 3.11.5.).

gnaw away at (*mə́šməš*) and chew over (*mə́šməṣ*), so that he can savour (*šṭāʿam*) the cheeks (*gélyud*) and the eyes (*ʿáyni*)." (Aḥmad Saʿd Taḥkí) The livers of many fish were highly prized; indeed parrotfish (*ʿābə* or *mišḥālə*) were always cooked with their liver as otherwise they were considered to be rather flavourless. The livers of the triggerfish (Balistidae) and leatherjacket (Monacanthidae) were considered delicious enough to be eaten on their own as a treat.

Some fish were actively avoided. It was generally agreed that one of the worst was the *šilā́ḳə* (a 'fish with an extremely large head and pointed nose that can open its mouth extremely wide').[201] Other disliked fish were the *ḳášš́o* silversides and various *bóhum* surgeonfish (Acanthuridae), which were considered to have a truly awful smell both raw and cooked.[202] Although seen as marginally preferable to the *šilā́ḳə* fish, these were only eaten when there was nothing else. Many fishermen threw back immature triggerfish and leatherjackets, scorpionfish (*di-ḳáʿnhen di-rínhem*) (Scorpaenidae), most *zaʿmṓmə* 'puffer fish' (Tetrao-

---

[201] Friedhelm Krupp (pers. comm.): "This might refer to a lizard fish, which has an extremely wide mouth. In some areas it is eaten, in others not." On the island it is caught by net or line but is generally discarded or used as bait if nothing else is available. However, *šilā́ḳə* is also a name for the houndfish (Belonidae) or cornetfish (Fistulariidae), so this is a puzzle that remains to be solved.

[202] Uwe Zajonz (pers. comm.): "Many fish which feed on microalgae and turf algae do not taste good because of material decomposition soon after catch, i.e., if not cooled or immediately gutted (with gutting and scaling having anyway a limited 'tradition' in Yemeni and Soqotri fish cooking)."

dontidae), gɛm 'sea catfish' (Ariidae) with their venomous spines[203] and the sənduḳi 'trunkfish' (Ostraciidae).[204] Interestingly the sultanic family and the Sādah were said to have refused to eat the śéʔher~śéʕher 'barracuda' (Sphyraenidae) on the grounds, or so it is said, that it too closely resembles a penis. It was quite happily eaten by other islanders.

6.1.3. Preserved Fish: Making mə́ḳədid

Some fish was preserved by sun-drying to make mə́ḳədid. The fish was gutted, and the head and backbone removed, leaving the tail in place. The fillets were then lifted off, still attached to the tail. If it were a very fat fish, the flesh was scored to allow the heat of the sun to penetrate. The fillets were then turned back to back, skin side together, and hung by the tail in the sun. No salt was added, nor was the fish washed in sea water before being processed.[205] mə́ḳədid fish kept well and were eaten when fresh fish were scarce.

---

[203] Nowadays there is a demand for these fish. Friedhelm Krupp (pers. comm): "They have venomous spines, but are edible, though not good and often discarded."

[204] Friedhelm Krupp (pers. comm.): "They are not suitable for human consumption, because of their bony carapace. Some species of trunkfishes secrete ostracitoxin, poisonous to other fishes."

[205] This was a popular method of treating the bóhim 'surgeonfishes', as when dried the reddish flesh no longer smells so bad.

6.1.4. Salt (mílḥo)

Salt was essential for preserving fish, but also for other food, for cereal dishes[206] and for making the valuable butteroil. Butteroil was the islanders' main trade commodity and both flavour and keeping qualities were greatly improved by adding salt when clarifying the butter. There were substitutes for salt which could be used to flavour meat[207] if far from home or temporarily without salt, and some living close enough to the coast even used seawater in desperation, even though this gives food an unpleasantly bitter flavour. However, for making high quality butteroil, real salt was absolutely necessary.

The greatest demand for salt on the island was from the fishing community: for preserving fish and shark, only sea salt would do.[208] Large quantities were used, both to preserve fish to eat when the sea was too rough for fishing, and to salt the fish which were traded with the boats that plied the East African and Arabian coasts.[209]

---

[206] Like fresh fish, the locally grown finger millet needed little salt. However, meat and the staple diet of imported maize (and, later on, rice), were considered to be tasteless (ríbaḥ) if cooked without salt.

[207] See Miller and Morris (2004, 17).

[208] As an example of the amounts used and the cost to those living in areas without suitable salt: fishermen of the east coast had to fetch salt from Qalansiyah or Śʸáʿab, and fetching this used up half a drum of petrol. Ḥsan Khamīs Taḥkí would buy 28–30 sacks of salt at a time to last him three to four months.

[209] Mubārak: "At the end of summer and up to the start of the monsoon gales, boats would arrive from East Africa (swāḥil), principally bringing cereals. They would purchase fish and salt. At the beginning

Most sea salt was produced in areas with a flat, rocky foreshore (*ṣīṣáʿa*), pocked with shallow depressions. The most prolific salt-producing areas were around Di-Ḥamṣ, Ḥeybaḳ and Di-Ḥámri on the north coast, and at Niyt and Śʸáʿab in the south-west.[210] Small amounts could be made by simply carrying seawater to one of these, leaving it to evaporate in the heat of the sun and then scraping up the salt crystals.[211] Another meth-

---

of the summer, boats from Arabia and the Gulf would stop off at Soqotra on their way to East Africa. They generally arrived empty, and they would load up with salt fish and shark and would usually also purchase salt." See also Serjeant (writing in 1967, cited in Doe 1992, 164): "At Quṣayʿar when we were there in 1964, probably about late February, there was a Dubai *jālibūt* which brings the shaykh from Socotra to Quṣayʿar and takes salt from Socotra to it. The salt is sold by the *gūniyah* bag and would cost about 15 to 16 shillings." And (Doe 1992, 169) about Qalansiyah: "Salt is brought from the area of Rās al-Shaʿb cape and lies on the shore in bags. Fish is salted here and disposed of locally or sold to the vessels arriving in the port."

[210] Within living memory, on ʿAbd al-Kūri, the large amounts of salt needed for processing their fish was always imported, mostly from Śʸáʿab in Soqotra. The trade boats on their way to East Africa, laden with Soqotri salt to sell there, would bring it when they called in at ʿAbd al-Kūri and trade it for fish. In later years, when the people of ʿAbd al-Kūri developed closer relations with the mainland, they imported salt from Aden. Smaller amounts of salt for everyday use were scraped from rock pools and seaward-facing caves.

[211] Aḥmad Saʿd Taḥkí about harvesting salt on the east coast: *mílḥo? šīn mílḥo yíkən šīn men éʾmed di-ḥorf lal ʿáruš géʾerə di-rínhem lə-ríʾ di-ḳéśrīn bíhin eḳālit. nəbúhud híhin ʿaf l-iḳśíʿ wə-ʿaf l-igmíd wə-lāṭ nəḥúmur mílḥo se men ḥalf*, "Salt? We have salt where we live. With us, it's to be found during the monsoon season when the waves splash right up

od, said to be very slow but to produce a superior salt, was to tip seawater into one or more large wide-mouthed clay pots, cover them and leave them in the sun. Over a period of three to four days the liquid progressively thickened and finally dried to a crust. This method produced more salt than simply evaporating seawater in rock pools. Salt harvesters say: "The rock drinks some of the salt."

In areas where salt harvesting was a major commercial activity, it was carried out mainly by women, each of whom had rights over one or more rock pool (*kaṭ*, pl. *iḳāliṭ*)—a heritable property. Production was heavily influenced by the phases of the moon: at times of full moon the pools sometimes overflowed, but on moonless days they barely filled. The best time to make sea salt was in the hot summer months before the monsoon, when it took only two days or so for the heat of the sun to evaporate the seawater; at other times of the year, it could take two weeks or more. At the end of summer, the tides are at their highest and even the pools on the foreshore fill. However, when the demand for salt was high, people would go to gather it at almost any time of the year. The producers bagged the salt in sacks and took it to market by camel or donkey (except for the Śʸáˁab salt, which was delivered by dugout), and bartered it for dates (especially), cereals and butteroil.

---

over areas of rock which have holes (lit. 'rock pools') in them. We wait until these dry out and (the salt) hardens, and then we scoop it up from where it lies."

Figure 11: Rubbing salt into slashed fish, eastern tip of Soqoṭra

Photo © Miranda Morris, 1990s

In some areas of the island, the salt deposited by high tides, winter storms or monsoon winds could be scraped directly from rocks and sea cliffs. The salt that crystalised around the rim of the many brackish lagoons could also be harvested. For example, on the east coast, salt was gathered from the upper end of the large lagoon at Qáriyah, while on the north coast, the people of the Ġúbbah area collected salt from the Di-Kíbšib lagoon, whose water level fluctuates daily with the tides. In the absence of other salt, pieces of saline crust were pulverised and the powder added to water and left to stand until the silt had sunk to the bottom of the pot. The salty water was then poured off into another pot and was used for cooking fish or meat (though never cereals). In the east, this salt was called *mílḥo di-ḳárḳəher* 'salt of reddish infertile ground.'

Different grades of sea salt were distinguished. From Śyáʿab in the west came a very hard and discoloured salt; from the rock pools at Di-Ḥámri and Bit ʿAbūdəh a good clean salt of a quality good enough for human consumption; from Di-Ḥamṣ came a very discoloured salt, contaminated by silt and other impurities; and from Ḥéybaḳ on the north coast, a good clean salt, but this was only available in the monsoon months.

6.1.5. Fish Fat and Fish Oils (śabḥ di-ṣodə)

In fish, as with livestock, it was the fat that was the most highly valued by the islanders: fish oils are an excellent source of vitamins A and D. Fish fat, equivalent to the śēśiyo 'mesentery fat' in an animal, as well as being called śabḥ di-ṣodə, lit. 'fish fat', was also called ḥōmə, a diminutive of hámʔi 'butteroil'. In a fish in good condition, the fat is said to be of a greyish colour, while in a fish in poor condition it is much darker, almost black.

The best fish for fat were the samōmə 'groupers' (Serranidae). The maʿrēmə 'jobfish' (Lutjanidae) too were said to have plentiful fat in the belly, around the liver, in the operculum (śówkibi di-ḥot) and around the intestines (míʔhóytin ~míʿhóytin). The fat was put on a dish and set on the fire to melt, and the oil that resulted was eaten with maize, finger millet or dates. Other line-caught fish with good fat were the zēkə 'sweetlips' (Haemulidae), said to have 'two strips of fat between the belly and the intestines' as well as belly fat. The di-ḳéntəhur 'snappers' (Lutjanidae) are described as being 'all fat'. As well as being heated to produce oil, fish fat was prepared in other ways: cut up small, stuffed into the fish's stomach (ʿángəher

~ʿámgəher in small fish, ḳā́dəl in larger fish and shark), the stomach tied or skewered shut. It was then cooked on its own or added to the water in which the rest of the fish was cooking.[212]

Many considered that the oil extracted from the fat that lies just beneath the skin of a leatherjacket (Monacanthidae) or closely related triggerfish (Balistidae) was the most nutritious food of all, especially for feeding to sickly children. To make it, a number of livers were collected[213] and cooked over a slow fire. The oil that resulted was filtered and kept in a clay pot. Added to the dish of pounded shark foetus (ribī́s, see 6.1.14. below), it was considered to be a good enough dish to offer the most exacting guest. At times of hardship, the livers of many other types of fish were cooked in the same way, but only produced a small amount of oil, and this was usually sucked from the fingers there and then, a vital dietary supplement.

For the islanders of ʿAbd al-Kūri who owned few livestock, fish fat was very important. The rich fat (ímyid) of

---

[212] Aḥmad Saʿd Taḵhkí: ʿámgəher di-ṣódə: nəʿágub ʿámgəher di-ṭárnik wə-di-zī́hnin wə-di-ráʾha wə-ʿámgəher di-ṣódə fáḥerə. ʿámgəher ḵúwder toš dhí kə-ṣódə. korúmma ḵī́hen nəṣóʿobš wə-nənōsirš, wə-ki ʿángəher éʾeb, nəḥáṣalš, "The fish stomach: we like the stomachs of the ṭárnik 'kingfish', the zī́hnin 'tunas' and the ráʾha 'trevallies'—the stomachs of all kinds of fish. The stomach is cooked in water along with the fish. If it's a small one, we bite it, nibble away at it with our teeth, and if it is a large one, we cut it up with a knife."

[213] Fishermen of the north coast said that if you had an ʿídi-type fish as bait you could catch any number of ḵarbṓbə in the daytime. The reddish-coloured kind of ḵarbṓbə especially were regarded as good eating and were said to have particularly rich livers.

maʿsām 'emperors', *silb* and *samōmə* 'groupers' and *ṭáʿami* 'snappers' was carefully melted down and a little salt added. The strained oil was stored in a glass or metal container and was used sparingly to flavour the basic cereal dish or fed in droplets to the weak or sickly to promote good health. Kept in this way the islanders say it lasts for a full year.

6.1.6. Edible Shark Liver Oil for Consumption and Medicinal Use (*ḥámʔi di-léḥḥīm~xáymi di-láxīm*, 'shark butteroil')

The shark livers used to make edible or medicinal oil were called *šíbdə*, like livestock livers, rather than *ṭáḥalə* (see 5.2.5.). The livers of immature *dígil* 'pigeye', 'blacktip reef and sandbar shark', or of immature *nékkə* 'grey reef shark' and 'spottail shark' were preferred, as these produce a pure and palatable oil which has little unpleasant smell.

To make the oil, the livers were cut up and put in a clay pot on a slow fire (with no water). They were left to cook down until all the oil had risen to the top. The residue was eaten[214] and the strained oil was stored in covered clay pots. It was used to flavour the main cereal dish (a porridge of *məḳdḗrə* 'maize' or *bómbə* 'finger millet': *nəḥóṣərin bis əḳəníyo*, "we flavour the basic foods with it"). The oil could also be made in the stomach of the shark itself: *ḳā́dəl di-léḥḥīm yəʿúmur biš šíbəd di-léḥḥīm kor*

---

[214]A perfectly palatable oil could be made from the livers of the dangerous *nímərhən* 'tiger shark' or *dī́bə* 'shortfin mako', but what was left after extracting the oil was discarded, not eaten.

tímhi wə-tíkkən ṣifi. sinɛ́mo. w-iśā́rˤaš bə-ṭarb wələ bə-ˤábəher kor indélilin wə-ˤa təmṭá?š záˤdihim wə-ḥanśí?o; wə-sā́ˤa śīnən ímhe u-ber šiš tərí gúmˤati, nā́kafš wə-níṣīlel méyh dhí ṣifi id məngīto wələ bíli, "People put the livers of the shark in the shark stomach to melt them down and make *ṣifi* shark liver oil. It has a terrible smell. It (the stomach with the livers inside) is suspended from a stick or crossbeam and left to swing there, out of the reach of rodents and crabs. Once we see that (the contents) have melted, after about two weeks, we take it down and strain the oil it has produced into a small clay pot." (Aḥmad Saˤd Taḥkí)

Fishing families who had few livestock and for whom butteroil was a rare luxury, would dip dates into this oil and use it to flavour cereal dishes. The oil was especially precious when times were hard or in the monsoon months when the longing for the taste of fish or meat fat was very great.

6.1.7. Shark Livers

Like the livers used to make shark oil, edible shark livers were called *šibdə* to differentiate them from the inedible *ṭáḥalə* livers. The livers of very small shark however were more commonly called *ˤángəher~ˤámgəher*, like those of smaller fish. The livers were prepared for eating by being placed inside the shark stomach and simmered in water. Pieces of these small, pale livers were much liked and were given to sickly children to build up their strength.

6.1.8. Roasting Sardines, Anchovy and Other Baitfish (kíbhib di-ʿídi)

The small fish were laid on a layer of dry date palm foliage (fériʿ) or other date palm debris (símilihin). This was set alight and, as the fish cooked, they were flicked off the fire (háfśən 'we flick them off') with a palm-leaf rib (mížərid) and eaten straight away. Any leftovers were put in a leather bag or date palm fibre basket and hung from the rafters or cave ceiling to be smoked. Cooked in this way they were said by Mubārak to keep for up to a month: w-al tośól id śéhər, "And they don't spoil for up to a lunar month."

6.1.9. Cooking Fish Underground (mínbihir or níbihir)

If a lot of good-sized fish had been caught—or just for a treat—a pit would be dug and a number of fish cooked in this. As this takes some time to prepare, a family planning a mínbihir would forewarn those they wanted to invite to share their meal.

    A pile of pebbles was collected and an oval pit of a size suitable for the number of fish was scooped out and lined with a tightly fitting layer of pebbles. Small fires were lit all across the base of the pit and left to burn down to ash. Then the whole fish—entire, not even gutted—were laid across in a single layer, and that layer covered with another thick layer of pebbles. More small fires were lit across the top of this layer and then the pit was left alone. Fishermen said that even left all night the fish would not spoil. The best fish for this sort of cooking were good fat ráʔha~ráʿha 'trevallies' (Carangidae); the second best were zíhnin 'tunas' or tānik 'Spanish mackerel'; the third best were *šéysino* 'rabbitfish' (Siganidae) or *ktif* 'sicklefish' (Drepanidae) and 'spadefish' (Ephippidae). Fish with thick, tough skins such as the *rá^ʔḥa~rá^ʕha* 'trevallies' or the *hangəlōlə~ haglōlə* 'pompano' could be cooked in layers of sand or fine gravel instead of pebbles.

A similar method was used to cook small baitfish and was called *níbihir di-ʕídi*. A date-frond rib or petiole was sharpened at one end and used to spit the fish through the eyes. This was then laid across a layer of red-hot pebbles. These small fish cook very quickly.

6.1.10. Wet-Salted Fish (*māliḥ*)[215]

To make *māliḥ*, the fish were filleted, and the fillets cut into pieces the size of the hand (called *ṣōdə nʸáʕasə*). A layer of sea salt was laid in the base of a clay pot or a lidded aluminium *tánkə* container. A single layer of fillet pieces was laid on top of the salt, then came another layer of salt, and so on until the container was full. It was then covered and left for at least a month before being opened. To eat the fish, the salt was washed off and the fish eaten just like that or cooked in a sauce.

The best fish for this sort of preparation were *ṭānik* 'Spanish mackerel', *zíhnin* or *śərə́whin* 'tuna', and various trevallies. Shark of less than an arm's length were treated in the same way, but after removing the gills (*láʕnhin*) and stomach (*ḳādəl*).

---

[215] The name *māliḥ* was given to any salted fish: the whole fish, fillets, or fish trunks.

6.1.11. Smoking Raw Fish (serídān)[216]

Raw fish were rarely smoked on Soqoṭra. However, divers shivering with cold after a session at sea used to huddle round a fire and smoke leatherjackets or triggerfish: these have a thick, leathery skin which protects the flesh inside during smoking. A few sticks were broken up and set alight and then cow dung (kṓbə) was put on top. When all was red-hot, the fish were propped on top, not touching the red embers, and left to cook in the heat and smoke. They were turned over and over until cooked through and were then peeled and eaten. Certain érəḥe 'pompano', ʿírho 'halfbeaks' (Hemiramphidae), 'cornetfish' (Fistulariidae) and 'houndfish' (Belonidae) and ḥárəbo 'mullet' could also be smoked in this way. Fish smoked like this were always eaten straight away: they do not keep.

6.1.12. Smoking Cooked Fish

When fish were especially plentiful, the surplus was often cooked and preserved by smoking. The cooked fish were opened out flat and placed inside a small wicker box (a small and more closely woven version of the fish trap) or wicker food-cage (ṣərámbīl). This was suspended high above the three-stone fireplace (míśkel), well out of reach of rodents, crabs or birds, and left there for the flesh to harden in the heat and smoke. The smoke also protected the fish from flies (idbíbo), maggots (taʿálə), hornets (ʾídbəhir), beetles (di-ʾísto~dísto) and the dikeśʿāmo and gišáʿmihin 'beetles'. When they wanted to eat some,

---

[216] Also, the term for the onboard fireplace (see 3.15.1.).

people just took a fish out of the cage and broke off a *níbihil* 'tiny piece' or a *náʿasə* 'chunk' and chewed away at the hard flesh. The flesh could also be pounded with a stone and the softened fibres mixed with cooked cereal.

6.1.13. Fish Roe (*íbḳəhal di-ṣōdə*,[217] 'fish eggs', *mínḳəhil* or *nḗḳil*)[218]

Fish roe was liked by many fishing families. Most preferred the roe of small fish, but those of larger fish such as *érəḥe* 'pompano', *sínsul* 'marlin' and other 'billfish' (Istiophoridae) or *maʿrḗmə* 'jobfish' were also eaten. The roes were boiled or roasted in hot ash. The pale fatty tissues often found next to the roe, *ráḥal*, were not eaten, though it was noticed that when they were boiled in water the water turned white.

6.1.14. Cooking Shark Foetus (*ribīs*)

A much-liked dish was made from a shark foetus or a newly born shark of one to two days with its navel cord still attached. Such young shark are rich in fat and are called *rḗśi*. The head, fins and tail were removed, and the trunk cut into pieces. These were boiled and, once cooked, the skin and bones were removed, and the flesh rubbed to a rough paste in a little water. This was then squeezed as dry as possible and added to a pot in which some of the shark's liver had been set to melt (but not

---

[217] The eggs of birds, reptiles and turtle are *ḳaḥélihin*, pl. *ḳaḥélahān*.

[218] *mínḳəhil di-ṣōdə di-ḳīhen šker meš taʿm mən ṣōdə di-éʾeb*, "The roe of small fish tastes particularly good, better than that of large fish." Aḥmad Saʿd Taḥkí.

too much liver, or the flavour of shark oil would be too strong). The contents of the pot were mashed and pounded together and then served. If no liver were to be had, the paste was added to whatever cereal was available.

6.1.15. Cooking Immature Rays and Parrotfish

Immature (one or two weeks old) *ṣaṭíʿo* 'whiptail stingrays' (Dasyatidae) and parrotfish (*ʿábə* or *mišḥálə*) came to fish traps in great numbers in the summer months, and they were prepared in a particular way. They were gutted, skinned, the head removed, and the liver set aside. The flesh was added to cold water, brought to the boil, and mashed against the side of the pot as it cooked. Once cooked, the contents of the pot were strained (saving the water), salted, and then squeezed hard until as dry as possible. The liver was then cooked slowly on a slip of pottery, and the oil that oozed out was added to the dry flesh and stirred in before eating.

6.1.16. Spiny Lobster (*šeríḥo~šírah̬*, pl. *šériyah̬~šírxa*, pl. *šírax*)

Sometimes caught in fish traps, spiny lobsters were eaten by many fishing families, either roasted or boiled. However, some disliked the idea of eating any sort of crustacean and would only use the lobsters as bait. On the island of ʿAbd al-Kūri they were considered good food and men dived to catch them.

6.1.17. Squid, Cuttlefish (ʿáṭerhe~ʿateráyə) and Octopus (térəbaḥt)

Squid, cuttlefish and octopus were hung up to dry and, once dry, cut into small pieces. These were softened by beating and then cooked in water, with added turmeric (kérkem) if there was any.

6.2. Processing Fish[219] for Export

In earlier times the key export of fishermen was salted fish and shark, mainly traded to the East African markets.

6.2.1. Dried Salted Shark (mālih̬)

In the lifetime of Mubārak, his parents and grandparents, the only fish exported from Soqoṭra were salted and sun-dried ones. These were traded to the East African markets. There were three types: shark; the kánda~gʸaḥš group of fish, mainly emperors and sweetlips (see 6.2.3.); and various tuna and large trevally. When there was a surplus of such large fish, they were

---

[219] Martin and Martin (1978, 51) report that of the 1970 imports into the old port of Mombasa carried on foreign dhows, the principal one was dried salted fish, the second salt, and the third dried shark. They also write: "The dried salted fish comes mostly from Arabian ports such as Sehut, Ghidha, Jazir and Shihr. The next most important place was Aden. Socotra and Kismayu (especially during the months of October, November and December, when other foreign dhows do not come into Mombasa) also supplied large quantities of dried and salted fish for the Mombasa market and Tanzania."

salted and dried for home consumption, rather than set aside until the trade boats arrived.

Once a shark had been brought ashore (and some shark took four or more men to carry them), it was gutted, the fins[220] and head removed, and the trunk opened out flat. The flesh was slashed, salt rubbed in, and the trunk put in a place of shade until it stopped leaking moisture. It was then taken down to the sea, washed, and laid out to dry in the sun. It was opened out flat, skin side uppermost, so that any liquid that seeped out would soak into the ground. Once the upper surface was dry, it was turned over to lie flesh-side uppermost. Once completely dry, the trunks were stacked in piles and kept under cover.

6.2.2. Dried Salted Large Fish (*māliḥ*)

zíhnin 'tunas', *rá'ḥa~rá'ḥa*, *dāfin* and *ṭamákərə* 'trevallies' (Carangidae) were gutted, opened out flat, the flesh scored lengthways, and salt rubbed in. After this, they were folded shut and stacked in the shade, head to tail, or left spread out for a day in the shade before being closed up and stacked. Fishermen say that: 'All fish prepared in this way must never see the sun'.

The valuable *ṭānik~ṭárnāk* 'Spanish mackerel' or kingfish were prepared slightly differently. The gills (*lá'nhin*) and entrails were removed, some fishermen leaving the head on, others cutting it off. The fish were opened out flat along the spine

---

[220] Before the market for them was known on Soqotra, shark fins were discarded. Later, the fins were salted, dried and kept back for the traders, who sorted them into two types: one the dorsal fins and the other the ventral and pectoral fins, each having its own price.

and then stacked under cover, one above the other, the head end higher than the tail end so that any exudate would drip downwards. Once the fish started to ooze a reddish oil, they were folded shut and stacked head to tail, under cover and preferably in a place open to the sea breezes. After about a month they would started to ooze oil again, those at the bottom of the stack becoming saturated with it.[221] If it rained at this stage, the fish came to no harm, but if they got wet before being fully saturated with oil, they had to be taken out one by one, examined carefully, and more salt rubbed into any damp parts. These were very valuable fish and fishermen took great care of them.[222]

6.2.3. Dried and Salted Medium-Sized Fish (kánda or gʸáḥš)

gʸaḥš is the name given to a group of inshore fish described as 'white rock fish with scales', mainly emperors (Lethrinidae) and sweetlips (Haemulidae). These fish were most readily caught late in the day, from the early afternoon (ʿaṣr) to sunset (máʿrib) and later. Fishermen say: "If there is a good moon, these fish feed the night long." Once salted and dried, they were known as kánda, by traders and by many full-time fishermen.

---

[221] Mubārak said that if you peeled a fish from the bottom of the pile it would make a great tearing, sticking sound.

[222] The sweet flesh of these was much liked by children. They would stealthily pick small pieces off the fish to eat, "just as they do with sugar today."

The best of all for salting and drying were the *kteb*, *máʿsam*, *ḥídəher* and *fṣáḥan* 'emperors'. The fish were gutted, the head, tail and backbone removed, and the trunk split from top to bottom. They were then laid out flat, the flesh scored, and sea salt rubbed in. Then the fish were folded shut and stacked head to tail in the shade and left to drip for two or three days, or until they stopped leaking moisture. They were then opened out again and washed in the sea. Afterwards they were laid to dry in the sun, opened out flat. Once dry they were folded up again and stored under cover until the trade boats arrived.

Figure 12: Storing dried and salted fish in shade, Mōmi

Photo © Miranda Morris, 1990s

For eating, the pieces of salt fish were reconstituted in water and then pounded with a cereal to make a nutritious porridge. Alternatively small strips of dried salted flesh were torn from the carcass and eaten with dates.

6.2.4. Cooked Dried Fish (*ḥaniṭ*~*ṣodə máḥniṭ*)

Islanders say that it had long been customary, when there was a surplus of fish but inadequate salt, to preserve fish for home consumption by cutting them into chunks, cooking these and then sun-drying them. Doing so for export only started in Mubārak's lifetime. Such a demand arose for this that even the rich seas around the uninhabited island, Darsa, were visited to catch fish to preserve in this way. In October, and again in April–May, when the seas were calm enough, men would go to Darsa and fish there. They processed their catch into *ḥaniṭ* onshore, but never spent the night on land, due to the high number of rats, the absence of water and the lack of suitable shelter.

The most valuable were the *zíhnin* (called *təméd* by purchasers) and *śəráwhin* (called *sáhwa* by purchasers) 'tuna'. Various of the larger *ṣódə di-ḳéśʔur* 'rock fish', were also processed in this way, *fṣáḥan, kteb, ḥídəher* and *bígəhel* 'emperors'[223] and, of the smaller fish, the *śéysino* 'rabbitfish' (see 6.2.5. below). Other fish such as the *máʕsam* 'emperor', *maʕrēmə* 'jobfish', *samōmə* and *ḥálḥal* 'groupers' and *ṭáʕami* and *ḥínkəhon* 'snappers' were made into *ḥaniṭ* but their trade value was much less.

The fish were gutted, the head, backbone and tail removed, and the trunk cut across into chunks. A metal drum (*bármil* or *drām*) or aluminium pot with a screw-top lid (*tankə*) was set up on the three firestones and filled with seawater or brackish lagoon water. When it came to the boil, the chunks of

---

[223] These fish were said to be 'extremely nervous', quick to dart away at the least movement or if one of them was hooked.

fish were dropped in and left to cook until the fire died down. Then one of the firestones was removed to tilt the cooking pot to one side, so that the cooking water could be poured off. When the chunks were cool enough to handle, the skin was removed, and the chunks of flesh laid out in a single layer on a bed of stones covered with palm-rib wickerwork (*zífənə*) and palm fronds (*fēriˤ*). The pieces had to be turned at regular intervals. Old bits of fishing net were propped up on sticks over the pieces of drying fish to protect them from gulls and other birds, and a child was usually set to guard the fish from cats, chickens, livestock and so on. Only once the chunks developed cracks and started to split open were they considered to be completely dry—if at all damp they would not keep. If the season for the trade boats was near, the pieces of dried fish were stored in sacks in caves. Otherwise, they were stored under cover, layered with ash as an insecticide, the best being that from burning *Croton socotranus* wood. The dried fish were sold by the sackful, not by weight. By the 1990s, dried Spanish mackerel (see 6.2.2.) and shark were fetching higher prices than the ḥaniṭ fish, an unwelcome development for fishermen.

6.2.5. Rabbitfish (*śéysino~śísínə*)

Rabbitfish were caught in fish traps in great numbers during the months of the monsoon and were dried for home consumption. Later on, in Mubārak's lifetime, a demand arose from overseas for dried rabbitfish. The fish were cooked in seawater, split open, the head, tail, innards, and backbone removed, and the fillets dried in the sun with the same care as the ḥaniṭ fish above (see 6.2.4.). They were then stored in sacks under cover to await the arrival of the trade boats.

6.2.6. The Storage of Dried and/or Salted Fish

Processed shark and other fish were stacked inside caves, or in shelters (ʿariš) constructed from date palm or stone, built to be as waterproof as possible. The valuable dried fish were inspected regularly. A major problem was the di-ʾísto~dísto 'beetles', particularly if insufficient salt had been used or if any damp had penetrated the fish shelter. One di-ʾísto~dísto was winged and regarded as relatively harmless, but the other, described as 'bristly and very smelly'—probably maggots or other insect larvae—were said to cause great damage.[224] If any were seen, they were rubbed off with a further application of salt. The problem of rats, however, seems to have been insoluble, and the waste and spoilage caused by them was extensive.

7. Conclusion

It can be seen from the foregoing that the Soqoṭran islanders were diligent and inventive in their harvesting of the sea. Alt-

---

[224] Krupp and Hariri (1999, 3.4) reported that "No bleeding of fish at sea prior to landing is carried out; consequently ammonia levels are high. The preference for large sharks means that mercury and other heavy metals in the meat is a cause for concern. The amount of salt used to desiccate the large shark carcasses is so large that salt penetration into the meat results in an inferior product. The heaps of shark trunks are not well ventilated and storage procedures are such that losses due to infestations by fly maggots and rats are reported to be high."

hough the marine creatures available varied around the island, the methods of harvesting them were similar everywhere. Outside the chief settlements of Ḥadibo and Qalansiyah, where a limited market for their catch existed, fish and other sea products were used as barter or freely given to those in need. Only the fish suitable for salting and drying were kept back for processing to trade with visiting boats. Links were forged with non-fishing islanders: islanders from the interior came down to the coast to live beside fishing families to eat what the sea provided at times when their animals were unproductive, and fishing families reciprocally turned to herding families of the interior for sustenance at times when the sea had little to offer.

With the development of the fisheries sector this picture has changed. Fishermen are now regarded as the fortunate ones, with a valuable product in high demand, while the stockmen of the interior struggle to make ends meet. The former market for livestock products has collapsed, their butteroil, hides and sheep wool cloth replaced by imported vegetable oils, plastic goods, and other factory-made materials.

The seas surrounding Soqoṭra are potentially extremely rich, but fishermen today are faced by new problems of stock depletion. This is due both to local overfishing of key species, and to uncontrolled access to Soqotri waters of commercial trawlers from elsewhere. The fisheries will have to be carefully managed if they are to provide a sustainable livelihood for the islanders.

References

Al-Salimi, Abdulrahman, and Eric Staples. 2019. *A Maritime Lexicon: Nautical Terminology in the Indian Ocean*. Studies on Ibadism and Oman 2. Hildesheim, Zürich and New York: Georg Olmsted Verlag.

Agius, Dionisius A. 2002. *In the Wake of the Dhow*. London: Garnet.

Al-Saghier, O., A. Alsuhaibany, and Peter Symens. 2000. 'The Status of Breeding Seabirds,' In *Marine Habitat, Biodiversity and Fisheries Survey and Management*, edited by Freidhelm Krupp and Khalid Hariri, 97–104. Reports for G. E. F. Conservation and Sustainable Use of Biodiversity of Socotra Archipelago. UNOPS YEM/96/G32 (unpublished report).

Beckingham, C. F. 1983. 'Some Notes on the History of Socotra'. In *Arabian and Islamic Studies: Articles Presented to R. B. Serjeant on the Occasion of His Retirement from the Sir Thomas Adams's Chair of Arabic at the University of Cambridge*, edited by R. L. Bidwell and G. R. Smith, 172–81. London: Longmans.

Beech, Mark. 2003. 'The Development of Fishing in the UAE: A Zooarchaeological Perspective'. In *Proceedings of the First International Conference on the Archaeology of the U.A.E.*, edited by Daniel Potts, Hasan Al Naboodah, Peter Hellyer, 290–308. London: Trident Press.

Bent, J. Theodore. 1897. 'The Island of Socotra.' *The Nineteenth Century* 41 (244): 975–92.

Bent, Mabel. 2010. *The Travel Chronicles of Mrs J. Theodore Bent: Volume III: Southern Arabia and Persia—Mabel Bent's Diaries of 1883–1898, from the Archive of the Joint Library of the Hellenic and Roman Societies, London.* Edited by Gerald Brisch. Oxford: Archaeopress.

Brown, G. H. 1966. *Social and Economic Conditions and Possible Development of Socotra.* Aden: Federal Government Mission Report.

Cheung, Catherine, and Lyndon DeVantier. 2006. *Socotra: A Natural History of the Islands and Their People,* edited by Kay Van Damme. Hong Kong: Odyssey.

Flower, Capt. H. L. 1946. 'Report on Fisheries of April, 1944'. In Admiralty, Naval Intelligence Division. *Western Arabia and the Red Sea.* Geographical Handbook Series. London: Admiralty.

Forbes, Henry O. 1899. 'The English Expedition to Sokotra'. *The Geographical Journal* 13 (6): 633–37.

——. (ed.). 1903. *The Natural History of Sokotra and Abd-el-Kuri.* London: Henry Young & Sons.

Hariri, Khalid I., and Muhamed D. Yusif. 1999. 'Fishing Communities and Status of the Fisheries Sector in the Socotra Archipelago'. In *Marine Habitat, Biodiversity and Fisheries Survey and Management,* edited by Freidhelm Krupp and Khalid Hariri, 161–79. Reports for G. E. F. Conservation and Sustainable Use of Biodiversity of Socotra Archipelago. UNOPS YEM/96/G32 (unpublished report).

Hulton, W. A. (ed.). 2003. *South Arabia: The 'Palinurus' Journals of Jessop Hulton (1832–1836).* London: Oleander Press.

Huntington, T., and S. C. Wilson. 1995. *Coastal Habitats Survey of the Gulf of Aden. Phase 1: Preliminary Habitat Classification and an Assessment of the Coast's Resources, Users and Impacts*. Report to the Ministry of Fish Wealth, Government of the Republic of Yemen. MacAlister Elliott and Partners Ltd, UK, and Marine Sciences Resource Research Centre, Aden, Yemen.

Jansen van Rensburg, Julian. 2016. *The Maritime Traditions of the Fishermen of Socotra, Yemen*. Oxford: Archaeopress.

Krupp, Freidhelm, and Khalid I. Hariri (eds.). 1999. *Marine Habitat, Biodiversity and Fisheries Survey and Management*. Reports for G. E. F. Conservation and Sustainable Use of Biodiversity of Socotra Archipelago. UNOPS YEM/96/G32 (unpublished reports).

Martin, Esmond B., and Martin, Chrysee P. 1978. *Cargoes of the East: The Ports, Trade, and Culture of the Arabian Seas and Western Indian Ocean*. London: Elm Tree Books.

Miller, Anthony G., and Miranda J. Morris. 2004. *Ethnoflora of the Soqotra Archipelago*. Edinburgh: Royal Botanic Garden Edinburgh.

Moser, Charles K. 1918. 'The Isle of Frankincense'. *The National Geographic Magazine* 33 (3): 267–78.

Nichols, P. V. 2002. 'Fisheries Management Plan for the Socotra Island Group'. In *Marine Habitat, Biodiversity and Fisheries Survey and Management*, edited by Freidhelm Krupp and Khalid I. Hariri, 411–36. Reports for G. E. F. Conservation and Sustainable Use of Biodiversity of Socotra Archipelago. UNOPS YEM/96/G32 (unpublished report).

Pietsch, Dana, and Miranda Morris. 2010. 'Modern and Ancient Knowledge of Conserving Soils on Socotra Island, Yemen'. In *Land Degradation and Desertification: Assessment, Mitigation and Remediation*, edited by Pandi Zdruli, Marcello Pagliai, Selim Kapur and Angel Faz Cano, 375–86. Dordrecht: Springer.

Ravenstein, Ernst Georg. 1876. 'Sokotra'. *The Geographical Magazine* 3: 119–24.

Schweinfurth, Georg. 1897. *Recollections of a Voyage to Socotra, 1881*. Translated by E. A. F. Redl. Bombay: Government Central Press.

Serjeant, R. B. 1992. 'The Coastal Population of Socotra'. In *Socotra: Island of Tranquillity*, edited by Brian Doe, 127–80. London: Immel.

Villiers, Alan. 1940. *Sons of Sinbad: An Account of Sailing with the Arabs in their Dhows, in the Red Sea, around the Coasts of Arabia...* New York: Charles Scribner's Sons.

Wranik, Wolfgang. 2003. *Fauna of the Socotra Archipelago: Field Guide*. Rostock: University of Rostock.

Zajonz, Uwe, Sergey Bogorodsky, Fouad Saeed, Miranda Morris, Abd al-Kareem Nasher, Moteah Aideed, M. Al-Jumaily, C. Weiland, and T. Winter. 2020. *Online Atlas to the Commercial Fishes of Socotra*. Frankfurt: Senckenberg Society for Nature Research. Accessed 1 January 2024. https://socotra.senckenberg.de/FishAtlas/.

8. Texts[225]

8.1. Descriptions and Processes

8.1.1. Shoaling of Fish (iʔirífi)

iʔirífi tíkkən šīn men ʕídi ki dilā́ḳo wə-ʕídi mes šem šīn sḗli. sḗli ki dəlā́ḳo igúdiḥin ʕis ṣṓdə tyóʔo ṭā́nik, tyóʔo zíḥnin, ráʔḥa, ṭamā́kərə, śərə́whin, dā́fin. w-ifṓgiś bis. korúmma fə́guś bis bə-rínhem nəʕā́mər ʕis 'iʔirífi'. "ḥar fogś bə-ṭaḥ." nəṭúhur nəšáʕarok.

The *ʔirífi* shoals of small sardine-type baitfish occur with us when there are large numbers of them. This (kind of) sardine-type fish we call *sḗli* 'Gulf herring'. When there are a lot of *sḗli*, large predatory fish such as the *ṭā́nik* 'Spanish mackerel', the *zíḥnin* 'tuna', the *ráʔḥa* and *ṭamā́kərə* 'trevallies', the *śərə́whin* 'tuna' or the *dā́fin* 'trevally' circle around them, herding them into a tight shoal, feeding on them. If there is a great splashing frenzy like this in the sea (*fogś*) we call it *ʔirífi*. "Today there is a *fogś* 'feeding frenzy' close inshore." We set off to sea to fish.

w-iʔirífi ṭiy nəʕā́mər his "gə́doḥo ḥar." wə-korúmma gə́doḥo, korúmma kān fogś wə-širḳóḥo ʕídi ter di-ḥáməhul wə-míʕsilin mes šem iʔirífi gə́doḥo.

And one kind of *ʔirífi* we call *gə́doḥo*: "There's a *gə́doḥo* today." If there is a *gə́doḥo*, if there is a great *fogś* 'feeding frenzy' and the small fish are driven right up above the tideline and around the rocks revealed at low tide, this is called *ʕirífi gə́doḥo*.

---

[225] A = < Arabic.

wə-šem di-gə́doḥo ṣōdəki ṣā́mə wə-ʿídi ki ṣā́mə men nháfs. w-iyhé bíśi d-išaʿríkiš. mes šem "gə́doḥo ḥar iʾirífi." tíkkən šīn iʾirífi men ter di-ṣerébhən. márra tədā́luḳ šīn iʾirífi wə-márra therér.

And the name *gə́doḥo* is (also) given to fish which wash up dead, or to sardine-type fish when they just die of themselves— no one would go to sea to fish for them. It's called *gə́doḥo ḥar iʾirífi* 'today ʿirífi *gə́doḥo*'. With us, the ʾirífi usually arrives at the beginning of the *ṣerébhən* season.[226] Sometimes there are many ʾirífi and sometimes only a few.

8.1.2. Fishing with a Cast Net

nəʿōdif ṣōdə men éʾmed di-ḥorf, di-ṣerébhən, (di)dˁōti... wə-déher nəʿōdif. ṣōdə d-iʿúdof: nəʿōdif tyóʾo kílibə, ḳáššo, gḗšaʿ, ʿafəríro, sḗli, ʿáyho, mírimɘher, kanṣáʿa, ḥərə́bo, di-míḳəhor, ʿaskə́do, ḳarbóbə. wə-ṣōdə fáḥərə ḥálḳeḳ nəʿúdifš.

We use cast nets for fish during the monsoon months, in the *ṣerébhən* season that follows, in the *dˁōti* season in the summer months... we use cast nets all the time. The fish we use cast nets for: we cast for fish such as *kíliba* 'sprats', *ḳáššo* 'silversides', *gḗšaʿ* 'sardines', *ʿafəríro* 'hawkfish', *sḗli* 'Gulf herring', *ʿáyho* 'trevally', *mírimɘher* 'lizardfish', *kanṣáʿa* 'goatfish', *ḥərə́bo* 'mullet', *di-míḳəhor* 'butterflyfish', *ʿaskə́do* 'damselfish' and 'clownfish',

---

[226] After the monsoon ends and before the *ṣɛrb* winter season comes in, around October.

and ḵarbóbə 'triggerfish' and 'filefish'. And we use the cast net for all the ḥálkik inshore kind of fish.[227]

b-ínyəhem nəˤōdifʔ kílibə, ḵáššo wə-gḗšaˤ ṭaṭ méyhin máˤdif wə-ṭiy méyhin ˤayn. ˤayn men ˤāker tyóʔo násfə di-ṭífher əw tyóʔo ṭífher di-míbərhe.

What do we use to net the fish? The net for the kíliba, ḵáššo and gēsaˤ small fish is the same, the same size of mesh: a mesh the size of half a fingernail or a child's fingernail.

sēli wə-ˤafəríro méyhi máˤdif ṭad meyḫ ˤayn, təʔōkib ˤiš íṣəbaˤ. ḵanśáˤa wə-ˤáyho təʔékibo ˤiš tərí iṣbáˤi. ˤáskədo wə-di-sébaḵ biš men ṣōdə de di-kíʔi tōkəbən ˤiš árbaˤ iṣābiˤ.

The net for the sēli and ˤafəríro fish is the same: a mesh size which would take a finger. For ḵanśáˤa and ˤáyho fish the mesh is of a size that would take two fingers. For the ˤaskədo and other similar fish, the mesh is of a size to take four fingers.

wə-máʔdif men ˤáker xams[A] durūˤ meyh ṭūl[A], wə-ˤášera[A] durūˤ wə-ʔīno xamstˤášer[A] dərāˤ. wə-ʔīno ṭinˤášer[A] dərāˤ meyh ráḥabo men fer ˤaf fer. máˤdif kúwnaḥ tuš men ḵaʔ libīni, mes šem ġāzəl líbəhān.

---

[227] ṣōdə ḥálkik: as ḥáyhal 'grouper', míkəhor 'butterflyfish', ˤáskədo 'damselfish' and 'clownfish', ṣáfrer 'butterflyfish', ḵanśáˤa 'goatfish', ˤárẓəb 'ladyfish' (Elopidae) and 'robust silverside' (Atherinidae) and 'small-scale bonefish' (Albulidae), ḥərəbo 'mullets' (Mugilidae), bēher 'Indo-Pacific tarpon' (Megalopidae) and 'milkfish' (Chanidae), mišḥālə 'parrotfish', ḵarbōbə 'triggerfish' and 'filefish', haglḗlə 'largespotted dart' and 'smallspotted pompano' (Carangidae), ṣeymhéro 'Indian threadfish' (Carangidae), širéˤe 'wolf herring', líhun 'grouper'.

wə-ḳúwnaḥ tuš bə-saḳáṭeri w-al fáḥerə éʔefo kʰel: bíśi di-kāl kal fəlān wə-fəlān ṭíḥḥi.

And a cast net is five də́raˁ[228] or ten də́raˁ in length, and there are some of fifteen də́raˁ length. And there are some which are twelve dərá́ˁ wide from edge to edge. A cast net is knotted from white thread called ġāzəl líbəhan 'white cotton'. It is knotted in Soqotra, but not everybody knows how to do it: only so-and-so or so-and-so of the men of the coast know how to do it.

8.1.3. Fishing with a Larger Net (śígihir)

izīˁa dihé mśígəhur wə-lāṭ yímdid túyhin bə-rínhem wə-yəˁāmer híhin barrūsi, ṭad bə-nʸaṣf wə-ṭad bə-nʸaṣf. wə-yəˁāmer keréb ker ḳayd men ˁālə wə-yəśēraˁ śámdə dhí máśgir. wə-lāṭ yəˁā́kal ˁaf ḳarérə. wə-lāṭ kēbur ˁeyh, yaˁtúbər ʔíno ṣōdə wələ bíśi.

He picks up his mśígəhur[229] nets and then he stretches them out in the sea and adds stone weights (i.e., as anchors), one at one end and the other at the other. He puts floats[230] all along the upper rope of the net, and he suspends bait from (the base of) his míśgir net. And then he leaves it until the next day. And then he goes back to check on it, to see if it has caught any fish or not.

---

[228] dərá́ˁ, span from the tip of the elbow to the tip of middle finger, a cubit.

[229] A type of basic drift net laid between the shore and the sea at right angles to the shore.

[230] keréb, usually the stubs of date palm branches.

8.1.4. Going in Search of Fish (ʿígihel)[231]

ḥéyhi... éʾefo šīn w-əmbūriye iḳéʿed ṭaḥ wə-rīʾihin éʾefo: "ʾíno di-ʿə́ṭab men hwēri ḥar?" d-iʿúmur ʾíno wələ bíśi. ki ʾíno irúʾuhon "mān di-ʿə́ṭab?" ʿə́mur: "ʿə́ṭab fəlān^A wə-fəlān^A." iṭóhur w-iḥōgir bə-máʿləhe ʿaf l-igdáḥ ʿaig dé di-ʿə́ṭab rínhem.

A person... with us people and children go down to the coast and ask people: "Did any of the dugouts go to sea today?" They say yes or no. If there have been (dugouts going to sea) they'll ask: "Who has gone out to fish?" They'll say: "So-and-so and so-and-so." They go off and watch from a high vantage point to see when the man who went out to fish comes back.

yəʿágəl ʿiš, yə́wṣal ʿiš bə-dhí bə-hūri, yəʿólə šiš, wə-yənúkiʿin hiš ləwēsi di-ʿúwlə ʿísən hūri. ki ʾíno ṣódə, zúwgud hiš. ki bíśi, yiktínaḥ.

He goes to meet the craft coming in; he helps him with his dugout, pulling it up the beach, or fetching the wooden rollers on which the dugout is dragged up the beach. If there are fish, he will be given some, and if there are none, he goes back home.

zígid hiš ṣódə, ṭaf ʿiš ḥot ki ʾíno ṣódə. ki bíśi ṣódə kal di-ḥerírhən, yəṣálib w-iṭáf ʿiš náʿsə wələ náḥa wələ ʾamt wələ riʾ wə-šébəhur. ki dáləḳ ʿágihul wə-ṣódə šīyur, išódiyin túyhin dhí men ṣódə: kal ṭád naʿsə naʿsə. wə-ki dáləḳ ṣódə, ṭaf ʿíhin men ḥot ḥot, wələ men ʾamṭ ʾamt, wələ men gāšəl gāšəl.

He gives him fish. He gives him a good-sized fish if there are any. And if there are only a few fish, he cuts one up and gives

---

[231] ʿágəl 'to go to meet a fishing boat as it comes back to shore in the hopes of being given some fish'.

him a chunk, or a half, or half a fillet cut lengthways, or the head and the backbone. If there are a lot of people waiting to be given fish and the fish are few, he shares the fish out between them: each gets a piece. And if there are plenty of fish, he gives them each one good-sized fish, or each one half a fish, or half a fillet, or each one more than a half.

di-škεr men ṣōdə? śōḳib ki ˁə́ṭam. wə-ṣōdə al ṭaṭ meyh ṭaˁm fáḥerə: ṭānīk ṭad mes ṭaˁm, rá$^\textit{?}$ḥa ṭad meyh ṭaˁm. wə-fáḥerə ṣōdə šiš dhí ṭaˁm men é$^\textit{?}$eb wə-men ḳīhən. śōḳib škεr meš ṭaˁm, tyó$^\textit{?}$o ṭānik wə-tyó$^\textit{?}$o rá$^\textit{?}$ḥa, tyó$^\textit{?}$o dāfin, tyó$^\textit{?}$o zíhnin, tyó$^\textit{?}$o ṭamákərə, tyó$^\textit{?}$o šmáḥlil.

Which bit of the fish is best? The upper part, if it is a fat fish. And not all fish taste the same: the *ṭānik* 'Spanish mackerel' has one flavour, the *rá$^\textit{?}$ḥa* 'trevally' has another flavour: each fish has its own flavour, be it large or small. The upper part tastes very good in a fish such as a *ṭānik* 'Spanish mackerel' or a *rá$^\textit{?}$ḥa* or *dāfin* 'trevally' or a *zíhnin* 'tuna' or a *ṭamákərə* 'trevally' or a *šmáḥlil* 'rainbow runner'.

korúmmma $^\textit{?}$íno šiy ḥāliṭ wə-ˁēyik əl-šēši tuš, ṭaf ˁiš ri$^\textit{?}$ wə-śōḳib: də́laḳ bíhi ṭaˁm ˁan níbihil d̥áḥśiš.

If I have a guest and want to give him the very best part, I give him the head and the upper part of the fish. They have the best flavour, better than any other part of a fish.

8.1.5. Catching Fish in Lagoons by Stunning Them with *Euphorbia arbuscula* Latex (*šēbir di-ḥor*) (i)

ˁəwyéghən ṭad díkir é$^\textit{?}$efo d-izōnig $^\textit{?}$imēti wə-rí$^\textit{?}$iš, ˁúmur: "idyó$^\textit{?}$o ifōnə d-izínig ˁáṣyub di-$^\textit{?}$imēti?" ˁímir: "šābir bə-di-ḥōr kor išrākaḥ ṣṓdə əd terr." w-ihērihin ʕəwyéghən yaʕtúbur ʔiném d-íkin. ɔ́ḳdem ʕéyhin tyóʔo yəḥósilin wə-yəḳāṣilin bə-ʔíṣerhe dhin ʔímtəhe di-ḳā́nə dhin di-ḥōr.

A boy remembered people carrying loads of *ʔímtəhe* 'Euphorbia arbuscula' on their backs, and he asked, he said: "Where are they taking the branches of *Euphorbia arbuscula* trees off to?" They replied: "They are going to put plant toxins in the lagoon to stupefy fish and bring them out of the lagoon onto the land." The boy followed them to see what would happen. He watched them slashing the branches of their *Euphorbia arbuscula* shrubs (to make the latex flow) and lopping off (the leaflets) with their knives (and dropping them) into their lagoon.

wə-ʕémer ɛ-ṭhíṭšin: "ḳaréə gōdihin fáhere lal šərā́ḳah šā́m." w-iyhé gídaḥ šīhin wə-kisə ṣṓdə, ʔíno di-ṣā́mə wə-ʔíno d-izə́ḳzək wə-ʔíno d-igúttir. wə-díbil éʔefo dhin ṣṓdə w-ízʕim. ʔíno nhɛrhinítin d-ízʕim di-šɛ̄bir dhín bə-ḥōr.

And they said to one another: "We'll all come tomorrow at sunrise." And he went with them and found fish: some already dead, some still flapping about and some behaving as if they were dizzy. And people gathered up their fish and waited. The plant toxins stayed in their lagoon for some days.

w-éʔefo ikḗbur w-ilōkaṭ w-īti dhin ṣṓdə dé di-šibér bih. wə-bíśi bīhin di-gúʕur w-ol ḥúbur ḳéyri w-iyhé ʕəwyéghən ḳeb meš dé ṣṓdə wə-té men ḳíder.

And people came and checked (on the lagoon) and gathered up and ate the fish that had been stupefied by the latex. And none of them fell ill (as a result) and everything was fine. As for the boy, he roasted some of these fish and ate some that had been cooked in water.

wə-šɛ́bir šīn yəʕúmur men éʔemed di-ḥorf wə-rínhem diméro. ṣōdə d-ī́kin šīn bə-rīho ḥā́li wə-bəḳəbəḳ: ʕáberhəm, ḥagléĺə, ḳašbérə, wə-ʔíno ṣōdə di-ol ʕə́rubk meyh šem.

And we do this šɛ́bir 'plant toxin fishing' during the months of the monsoon when the sea is too rough (to go out to fish). We have fish that live in both sweet and saline water: ʕáberhem 'terapon', ḥagléĺə 'pompano', ḥə́rəbo 'mullet', ḳašbérə 'snapper', and other fish whose names I don't know.

wə-ṣōdə al ʕə́ḳar bə-ḥōr: ʔíno dərá ʕ wə-ʔíno tərá šéberi, wə-də́lag tyóʔo šéber ṭad.

And fish don't grow to any great size in the lagoon: some are a dəráʕ 'cubit' length and some two šéber[232] lengths, and many are only about one šéber length.

8.1.6. Catching Fish in Lagoons by Stunning Them with *Euphorbia arbuscula* Latex (*šɛ́bir di-ḥor*) (ii)

šɛ́bir di-ḥor: ṣōdə ki bə-ḥor bis rīho bə́ḳəbəḳ wə-ʕátšəro rīho ḥā́li wə-di-rínhem. yíkkin bih ṣōdə wə-d-iʕúmur his 'ḥor bis ṣōdə'.

Stupefying fish in a lagoon with plant toxins: if there are fish in a lagoon, they are in one whose water is brackish, a lagoon in which sweet water is mixed with sea water. Fish can be found there, and we say: *ḥor bis ṣōdə* 'the lagoon has fish in it'.

---

[232] *šéber*, the span between the thumb and the extended first finger.

korúmma ʿígibən ṣōdə dálaḵ men ḥor, nəšābur bis. núkiʿin šébəhur di-ʾímtəhe meyh ʿáṣiyub, wə-lāt nəḵáṣḵaṣ tuš bə-ṣārə id rīho.

If we want to catch a lot of fish (at one go) from a lagoon, we stupefy the fish with plant toxins. We gather latex from *ʾímtəhe* 'Euphorbia arbuscula trees', from their branches, and then we chop (the leaflets) into little pieces with a knife and (put them) into the water.

wə-nəbúhud ṭiy šām, əw ki ḵālʿan b-aḥté, šəbōrən b-aḥté, ənkābur əl-ʿōśi. wə-ki šəbōrən bə-šām, ənkābur ḵarérə. ki ʾíno bis dis ḥor ṣōdə, ḵarérə nəkōsə ígibib, ḥútšəm men šébəhur dé di-šəbōrən biš. nəzáʿa tuš w-əntékibin tuš dáḥanə wələ míśṭab wələ di-ḵáʾ wələ di-míśkek, w-ənzáʿiš id káʿar.

And we wait for a whole day, or if we put (the latex) in at night, if we stupefied the fish with latex at night, we go to check on the result at sunrise. And if we put the latex in during the hours of daylight we go and check on the result the next day. If there are fish in this lagoon, the next day we find them floating on the surface, stupefied by the latex we put in. We take them and put them in a palm-leaf basket or in a strip of cloth[233] or (we string them) on a cord or skewer them (on a stick), and we take them back home.

ʾíno d-iʿāmer meyh śámdə di-rínhəm ki ʿígib l-aʿṭāb, wə-kal (= ki al) ʿígib l-aʿṭāb w-al-išáʿrek biš, iḵādir ki ʿígib, wə-ki ʿígib íḵəbib w-

---

[233] *míśṭab*, pl. *míśṭob*, a minimal loincloth worn by fishermen or those doing dirty work, a strip of cloth that goes between the legs to maintain decency.

itíš. meš šem di-ṣódǝ 'ṣōdǝ di-ḥor'. wǝ-ṣōdǝ mísbir ṭúwˤum meyh ṭaˤm, wǝ-ʔíno d-iˤúwrǝb ber mísbir wǝ-ʔíno diyál iˤúwrǝb ber mísbir.

Some people use them as bait for fishing at sea when they want to go to sea. If they don't want to go to sea or to use them for fishing, they cook them in water if that's what they like, or if they like to roast them, they roast them and eat them. The fish are called ṣōdǝ di-ḥor 'lagoon fish'. Fish caught with latex have a specific flavour: some recognise that they were caught with latex and some do not.

8.1.7. Lagoon Fish

ˤábrǝhǝm wǝ-ḥárǝbo díki idélako bǝ-ḥor wǝ-tíkkǝn šámdǝ lǝ-ṣōdǝ minṭílhil men ḳéšʔor ǝw men ṭaḥ. tyóʔo ḳarbōbǝ, ḥíyhal, ˤáyho ḳíhǝn, fákǝrǝš, ˤáskǝdo... ṣōdǝ ḥálkek d-íkin bǝ-ṭaḥ. ḥor al íkkin bis ṣōdǝ kal korúmma rīho bákǝbǝk men rínhem.

ˤábrǝhǝm 'terapon' and ḥárǝbo 'mullet': those two are particularly plentiful in a lagoon. They can be used as fish bait when fishing by whirling the line around the head and then casting it, from rocks or from the shore. (For fish) such as ḳarbōbǝ 'triggerfish' and 'filefish', ḥáyhal 'grouper', smaller ˤáyho 'trevally' and ˤáskǝdo 'damselfish' and 'clownfish'... the ṣōdǝ ḥálkik type of fish found close inshore. There are no fish in a lagoon unless its water is brackish rather than saline (i.e., pure sea water).

8.2. Equipment

8.2.1. Making Lures (*rēkuk̄*)

rēkuk̄ yəˁúmer tus men ṣóḥəlo di-šfāniś; ʾíno d-iˁāmer men míśineg di-óʾoz wə-íno d-iˁāmer men ṭálfə di-fólihi.

A lure is made from animal bone: some make it from the fine bone of the lower back leg of a goat and some from the slender bone of the foreleg of a calf.

rēkuk̄ d-əṣəlīˁo di-ˁáṭerhe: korúmma bíśi rēkuk̄ wə-ṣōdə gídaḥ ṭaḥ ifōgiś wə-bíśi šik ˁidi tšáˁrok bis, ʾiful tšōgiʾ? nəṭúher núkiˁin əṣəlīˁo di-ˁáṭerhe wə-lāṭ nəʾōgə mes riʾ ˁaf tíkkən tyóʾo dənub di-ˁídi.

A lure from a length of *ˁáṭerhe* 'Cissus' stem:[234] if we have no (other) lure and a lot of fish have come close inshore in a feeding frenzy and you have no sardine-type fish to use as bait, what can you do? We go and fetch a section of Cissus stem and then we beat it (flat) and fray out one end (lit. 'the head') so that it looks like a sardine tail.

wə-lāṭ nəśōbək ˁékəlhe bə-dāfə di-əṣəlīˁo di-ˁáṭerhe wə-lāṭ nəˁáṣiṣən ˁis. wə-lāṭ nəšáˁrok bis. bas mes máˁrek al tyóʾo ˁidi: al nəkālaˁ wə-nəfānuk̄. korúmma k̄ālˁan wə-fənāk̄an, bíśi d-īti bis. lēzim nəšmēśiʾīn tus. korúmma nəšmēśiʾīn tus, íkkən bə-rího mes kān tyóʾo ˁidi, w-ihālaḥ ˁis ḥot w-īti.

And then we wedge a hook firmly into one side of the Cissus stem and tie it on. And then we go off and fish with it. But fish-

---

[234] The *ˁáṭerhe* 'Cissus plant' has jointed stems. *əṣəlīˁo* is a section of stem lying between two joints.

ing with it is not the same as fishing with a sardine-type fish (as bait): we don't let it (the baited line) just lie there while we sit and wait. If we leave it like that and just sit and wait, nothing will go for the bait. We have to wiggle and swirl it back and forth. If we wiggle it around it looks like a sardine-type baitfish (swimming along) in the water, and a big fish will pounce on it and take it in its mouth.

8.2.2. The Short Stabbing Spear (*múšʿiḳ*)

múšʿiḳ ṭarb d-iṭífən meyh riʔ ʿaf l-ékkən tyóʔo riʔ di-máhyiṭ. ḳor šáʿḳiḳ biš bíli tyóʔo bikīli, tyóʔo gírbaḳ wə-tyóʔo ṣōdə. íkkin men šírməhim fáḥerə. múšʿiḳ íkkin kə-lhɛ́ tšáḥaḳən ker ṭaḥ, ḳor ki kísə ṣōdə ə́kub di-ḳānə di-šíṣəhur di-ḳaṭ əw šíṣəhur di-ḳɛ́šʔor išáʿaḳs w-irāḳaḥs. əw korúmma ṭad šīni bikīli ikɛ́bo id ḥalf, šáʿḳiḳs di-ḳānə. wə-korúmma ʔíno gírbaḳ ikɛ́bo maḥrɛ̄rə wələ mártəmə wələ mínṣab.

The *múšʿiḳ* is a stick with one end sharpened to a point so it looks like the tip (lit. 'head') of a bodkin. It is for spearing something such as a snake, a wild cat, a fish. It can be made from all sorts of trees and shrubs. The *múšʿiḳ* is for those (women) who go along the shore at low tide looking for shellfish, so that if they find a fish which has slipped into a crevice or a hole in a rockpool or into a cleft in a rock, they can spear it and extract it. Or if someone sees a snake going into a place somewhere, he stabs at it repeatedly inside (its den). Or if a wild cat has gone into a (homemade) stone trap[235] or an (imported metal) trap, or a (homemade) trap of sticks.[236]

8.2.3. The Fishing Knife (ʿátfə di-ṣōdə)

ʿátfə di-ṣōdə ṣúwlub bis ṣōdə wə-léḥḥīm. ʾíno áʾam men di-šéber, di-šéber wə-nasfə, wə-ʾíno tərá šébiri. wə-iʿúwreb tos ber ʿátfə di-ṣōdə: bis ṭayʾ di-ṣōdə.

The ʿátfə[237] knife is used for cutting up fish and shark. Some are longer than a šéber span, a šéber span and a half, and some are two šéber spans long. It is recognised as a fish knife because it smells of fish.

---

[235] maḥrērə, a trap made especially for the wild cat. A small, circular stone pen with a narrow opening at the top is constructed and the bait, impaled on a stick, is placed inside on the ground. The other end of the stick supports a broad slab of stone balanced carefully on the rim of the pen. When the cat climbs in and yanks at the bait it pulls down the stone slab and blocks the exit.

[236] mínṣab, a trap made by balancing three sticks in a wigwam shape with a single long stick, with bait attached to one end, placed inside. When the cat yanks at the bait it pulls the trap down over itself.

[237] ʿátfə, pl. ʿátif: some Soqotrans see this term as being Arabic, and say hébkə, pl. hēbek, instead. hébkə refers to any thin blade or small-bladed knife used by women to shear sheep, often made by the woman herself beating out an old (piece of) blade on a rock. It is flexible and is regarded with disdain: 'a woman's knife'.

8.2.4. Fish Traps (ḳérḳor, pl. ḳarāḳir) (i)

ḳérḳor yəʕúmur tuš men ṭirub əw gərāyid di-mítrer. ḥúwre men gərāyid wə-ḳōṣan wə-yaḥśikíkin túsən wə-śuwḥāsən. wə-ruwḥúnən ʕaf tərhōnən. wə-lāṭ igúdihin dé di-kāl l-íḳinaḥ ḳérḳor.

A fish trap is made from pieces of wood, or from the stems of a *mítrer* 'Croton socotranus tree'. (Suitable) stems are searched out, lopped off, whittled and split lengthways. Then they are put to ret down (in water) until they are soft and supple. Then the person who knows how to weave a fish trap comes.

iḳānaḥ árbaʕ ḳəṭáʕ di-ḳérḳor. yəʕámer ḥáwiye di-ḳérḳor wə-yəʕámer dəfféti: ṭiy men léhe u-ṭiy men ʕālə. wə-yəʕámer ḳār di-ḳérḳor əw ter di-ḳérḳor əw fəḳəríro di-ḳérḳor. wə-lāṭ sēbiḳin túyhin bə-ṭhítšin.

He weaves four sections of the trap. He weaves the *ḥáwiyə* of the trap: the long thin strip which joins the top section to the bottom section; he weaves the two main sections, the *dəfféti* 'sides' (i.e. top and bottom): one for the base of the trap and one for the top; and he weaves the *ḳār* 'throat' or *ter* 'door' or *fəḳəríro* 'neck' of the trap. And then he knits all these parts together.

ʔíful sēbiḳin túyhin? yəʕāḳal ṭabḳə di-dḗfə di-ḳérḳor berr, wə-lāṭ núkiʕin ḥáwiye wə-yəʕāḳal tos men ʕālə. wə-lāṭ nukiʕin ṭabḳə əw dḗfə diš, wə-lāṭ yəʕāḳal men ʕāle. wə-lāṭ iḳānaḥ ker gébo dihé di-ḳérḳor.

How does he knit them together? He puts one *dḗfə* section of the trap flat on the ground and then he brings the long, narrow *ḥáwiyə* strip and lays it on top. Then he brings that other *dḗfə* section and places that on top of the other parts. Then he weaves all around the rim of his trap (i.e., joining the top and bottom main sections together with the long, narrow strip).

wə-ki títe kínih, kōb kār dihé di-kérkor, mes šem kār əw fəkəríro. wə-lāṭ iʿáṣəms w-ikānahs. wə-lāṭ núkiʿin ḥōz di-ʿášer mikāliʿ,[238] wə-lāṭ sēbikin túsən b-ídfof dhí di-kérkor, w-ikānaḥ túsən əw iʿáṣəm ʿísən. úste nāfaʿ di-kérkor.

When the weaving is finished, he inserts the 'throat' of the trap: this is called the 'throat' or 'neck'. He ties that on and weaves it in (to the rest). Then he brings about ten short sticks and places them at intervals along the sides of his trap (to strengthen it), weaving or tying them in. The work of making the trap is now complete.

izégud dihé kérkor əl-tādaʿ id ṭaḥ, w-iʿákal dihé kérkor bə-fəṣíyə di-rínhem w-iyhé iṭúhur yáhṭəṭ men ḥalf biš kéšʾor wə-ʾíno bih ḥalf məšíṭihin. w-idābəl ʾíbəhān men ḥa wə-ḥá di-ḥá dé di-ḥalf. wə-lāṭ íʿud dhí-l kérkor.

He picks up his trap, puts it on his back, and goes down to the shore. He sets his trap down on the wet sand at the tide line, and then goes to look for a place with plenty of rocks, suitable for setting a fish trap. He then collects rocks from here and there and brings them to this place (where he intends to set the trap). Then he goes to fetch his fish trap.

---

[238] mikāliʿ~məkāliḥ, short, strong sticks which are placed at intervals around the trap in the ḥáwiyə to strengthen and support the trap.

*wə-lāṭ yáʕihiṣ biš dé di-ḥalf, ḥalf šə́ṭənhən. w-irā́ṣaf ʕiš dhí bə-
ʔíbəhān l-ídfof wə-lə-ḳanʕáti dhí di-ḳérḳor ʕaf l-išmɛ̄lik ber ʔə́ṭar dhí
bə-ʔíbəhān dhí di-mérṣif. iṭóher. išrā́ḳaḥ ter.*

Then he dives down with it to that place, the suitable place. He piles his rocks over it, around the sides and at the corners of his trap until he is quite sure that it is securely weighed down and held firmly in place by his stones. He leaves. He goes back to the shore.

*zúʕum w-ol kɛ̄bur hiš ḥōz di-^Aʕášerət ayyām^A. lúʔu al kɛ̄bur hiš físaʕ?
ḳérḳor ʕad ṣáʕbeb wə-bíśi biš eṣərīʕo. ṣōdə al igúdiḥin di-ḥalf bíśi biš
eṣərīʕo. ikōsə ṣōdə biš wələ al ikōsə. korúmma ʔíno ṣōdə dé bə-ḥalf,
rā́ḳaḥ dhí ḳérḳor w-intégifin meyh ṣōdə ter.*

He stays put and doesn't go to check on his trap for about ten days. Why doesn't he go and inspect his trap earlier (lit. 'quickly')? The trap is still very pale in colour; it has no green algae or weed on it. Fish won't come to a place without algae or weed. Either he finds fish in it, or he doesn't. If there are fish in that place, he lifts up his trap and shakes the fish out of it onto the ground.

*ʔíful irṓḳaḥ men ḳérḳor? korúmma də́laḳ, nʸúwfur ḳaʔ əl-ḳánʕa di-
ḳérḳor, wə-lāṭ intégifin ṣōdə ter. wə-lāṭ ikōlə ḳánʕa ʕis dsé ḳaʔ. wə-
korúmma ṣōdə šīyur yúwkub ʕiš ʕíid əl-ter di-ter di-ḳérḳor.*

How does he get the fish out of the trap? If there are a lot of them, the cord which holds one corner of the trap (to the other parts) is untied, and the fish are shaken out onto the ground. Then he ties up the corner again with its cord. And if there are only a few fish, he puts his hand inside the trap through the 'door' of his trap (and gets them out in that way).

wə-lāṭ ikōlə dhí ḳérḳor dhí di-ḥalf. w-irāṣaf ʿiš tyóʾo ber ráṣaf fānə. ki bíśi bih di-ḥalf ṣōdə yəʿārum hiš ḥalf dʸáḥṣiš. ʾíful baʿš kēbur dhí ḳérḳor? íʿud w-isābaḥ diš wə-lāṭ yáʿihiṣ di-gʸēmə.

Then he returns his trap to its place and covers it over with stones as before. If he gets no fish from that place, he moves to another place. How does the owner inspect his trap? He goes in the morning and dives down and looks inside the trap down there on the seabed (lit. 'below').

wə-lāṭ yaʿtúbur əl-ter di-xaléf dhí di-ḳérḳor. iḳādum bə-ḳāne ṭad wə-tərá ḥóti wələ dálaḳ wələ bíśi. ḥalf di-rúwṣaf bih ʾíno təlāta bəwáʿ, ʾíno bāʿēn, ʾíno xámsa.[A] bas al rúwṣaf w-al kúwber hiš ki ḥalf míšlul kal zem šiḥāḳo rínhem.

Then he looks through the gaps in the weaving of his trap. Inside he sees one or two fish, or a lot of fish, or none at all. The place where he weighs down his trap with stones is three, two or five $bāʿ$ deep. He doesn't cover over the trap with rocks or go out to inspect it if the place is in deep water—only when the tide is out.

ḳérḳor yəʿúmurš éʾefo fáḥerə: dé d-iḥódim ṭaḥ wə-dihé ṭaḥ ʾíno biš ḳéśʾor wələ eṣəlíʿo wələ šíśéʿe.

Everyone uses a fish trap: the man who works the sea if his part of the coast is rocky, or if it has outcrops of large rocks out at sea with patches of sand in between, or if (the seabed is) an area of stone pavement.

8.2.5. Fish Traps (ḳérḳor, pl. ḳərāḳir) (ii)

yəkōnaḥ ḳérḳor: yəʿúmur meyh ḥáwiyə. ḳérḳor biš ḥáwiyə, u-biš tərí dəfféti, u-biš fəḳəríro, ter di-ḳérḳor. wə-yəʿúmur hiš məḳāliʿ di-šə́rəhām. lal itítə, yəzēgud toš báʿš walə dé di-ʾimer heh iṭóher id rínhem.

He weaves a fish trap: he makes the ḥáwiyə 'long, narrow strip' that goes right around the trap (joining the top to the bottom section). A fish trap has a ḥáwiyə 'long, narrow strip' and two dəfféti 'sides' and a fəḳəríro 'neck': the entrance into the fish trap. And he makes wooden sticks for it (inserted around the circumference of the trap to strengthen it). When he's finished, its owner, or the man who commissioned it, picks it up and goes down to the sea.

walə yəʿāḳal fəṣ́íyə w-íyhe yəṭúher yəḥōrə heyh men ḥalf. wə-núkiʿin ʾə́bəhān w-iḥōṣ̌əfin heyh ḥalf. íʿúd dhé ḳérḳor wə-yáʿiḥiṣ biš toḳ di-gʸēmə. wə-lāṭ yərāṣ́af hiš bə-ʾə́bəhān, dār-mā-dār.

Or he lays it down on the wet sand of the tide line while he goes off to look for a (suitable) site for it. And he fetches rocks and clears a space to set (his trap). He goes to fetch his trap and he dives down with it down there to the bottom. And then he weighs it down with the rocks and (builds a low wall with them) all around it.

wə-lāṭ yəṭúher. korúmma gədīd^A, yəʿáḳalš w-al kēbur ʿiš ḥōz ^Aʿišrīn yōm^A. wə-lāṭ kēbur ʾiš. yaʿtúbər: ki ʾíno ṣōdə nʸāgifīn ʾiš wə-yəkōliš yərā́ṣ́əfš. wə-korúmma bíṣ́i, yəʿáḳal.

And then he goes off. If it is a new trap, he leaves it alone and doesn't go to check on it for about twenty days. Then he goes to inspect it. He looks (inside): if there are fish they are tipped out, and then he puts it back and weighs it down with rocks once more. And if there is nothing in it, he leaves it (there).

8.3. Craft

8.3.1. The Dugout and Dugout Equipment

šilmāyə iʕúmur tos men ṣ́áʔad wələ men ṣúbəhur. yiṭífən ṣ́áʔad wə-śúwḥas tus wə-ʕímidən mes di-kā́nə di-xan di-hūri. iʕúmur his di-xan wə-di-mer men kā́nə. wə-kúwdaḥ bis wə-lúwsok̞ bis šilmāyə se bə-mer di-hūri. lúʔu lúwsok̞ wə-lúʔu iʕúmur his šilmāyə? kor hūri ʕa tšḥós men rínhem wə-men dikdḗkə di-ḥot di-kā́nə, wə-ʕan šīhum wə-hūri táwṭar w-al bíro (tə)ṭóhom.

The *šilmāyə* 'ribs' are made from *ṣ́áʔad* 'Ziziphus' or *ṣúbəhur* 'Tamarindus' wood. The *ṣ́áʔad* wood is shaped and split in half and made to fit the inside of the bottom of the dugout. The ribs are for the bottom, the belly of the dugout, inside. Holes are bored in them, and they are attached to the belly of the dugout. Why are they attached, and why do people make ribs for the dugout? So that the dugout doesn't split open from the (pounding of the) sea, and from the flapping of the fish inside, or from the heat of the sun. (It is done) to strengthen the dugout and prevent it becoming worn out before its time.

ləwāsi iʕúmur tósən men ítʔib k̞úwṣan, wə-mes rīmo dáraʕ wə-nus. hūri ṭiy yəʕúmur his təlāta ləwāsi kor iʕúwlə ʕisən hūri men rínhem id barr id riʔ di-ḥáməhul. w-iʕúwk̞al ʕis hūri men léḥe ṭiy bə-wāraʔᴬ dié hūri wə-ṭit bə-ʕamk̞ wə-ṭiy bə-kúddām men léḥe. wə-ṭaʰ ki gifíʔo hūri. hūri ʕa iʕúwk̞al tos w-al ʕúwlə tus bə-ḥóyhi kal bə-ləwāsi.

The *ləwāsi* 'beach rollers' are made from *ítʔib* '*Ficus cordata*' wood, cut from it to a length of one and a half *də́raˁ*. Three rollers are made for each dugout which is placed on them when the dugout is dragged from the sea to land, up to the dry area above the tideline. They are placed beneath the dugout: one at the back of your dugout, one in the middle, and one at the front. The same is done when the boat is turned upside down. The dugout is never put down or dragged up over the ground without rollers.

məkādif iˁúmur túyhin men śáʔad. məkādif iˁúmur túyhin men ṭarb d-íṣṭib w-al ilɛ̄buk bɛ́nɛ men ˁarṣóno. w-iˁúmur hiš bə-riʔ ġāduf.[239] *ġāduf iˁúmur tuš wə-yiṭífin tuš men luḥᴬ. wə-ġāduf íkkin gáˁləhal wə-nikíˁin riʔ di-ṭarb wə-sōbak biš wə-ḳúwdaḥ biš arbaˁa məkādih. wə-lāṭ śúwrog ˁiš wə-ḥébišin ˁiš bə-kaʔ di-śúʔhur wələ bə-kaʔ di-mə́ṣiyaˁ ˁaf l-iṭār.*

The *məkādif* 'paddles' are made from *śáʔad* '*Ziziphus*' wood. The shafts of the paddles are made from any straight piece of wood, but they shouldn't be much thicker than a wrist. Attached to one end is a *ġāduf* 'blade'. A *ġāduf* 'blade' is made and whittled to shape from a piece of planking. The blade is rounded. (When you have made this,) you bring it and the tip of the shaft together, and put the two together. Then four holes are bored, and then they (the two parts: shaft and blade) are stitched together with big stitches and bound tightly together, round and

---

[239] *ġāduf~ġādif*, blade of a paddle, usually circular. There are two kinds of *ġāduf*: (i) a simple circle, or (ii) a circle with a projection. *ġāduf* can also refer to a stern paddle used like a rudder to steer.

round, with fishing twine or with cord made from the green leaflets of the date palm, until it is held really firm.

mínzek wə-də́ḳəhal di-śīraʿ iʿúmur túyhin men ʿáṣbə di-ṣ́áʔad wə-men ḥímihər ḳaṭāni. mínzek íkkin men ṭarb d-iʿúmur meš ṭarb di-ġāduf, bas rīyum meš marrətēn.[A] *wə-meš bə-riʔ sōbaḳ biš mínzek. mínzek yúwkob tus id riʔ di-ṭarb di-mínzek wə-lāṭ məḥégigin tus se bə-ṭarb. wə-mínzeḳ bis ʿágəl di-durg di-śúʔhur. wə-zúwʿa tus w-iʿúwṣam tus durg lə-mínzek id ʿamḳ di-ṭarb di-mínzek.*

The *mínzek* 'harpoon' and *də́ḳəhal* 'mast' for the sail are made from a branch of *ṣ́áʔad* 'Ziziphus' or from a slim *ḥímihər* 'Zygocarpum' tree (i.e., a sapling). A *mínzek* 'harpoon' (shaft) is made from the same sort of wood used for the shaft of the dugout paddle, but is twice as long. The metal harpoon head is attached to one end. The wooden shaft is placed inside the (hollow) base of the harpoon head and then screwed down hard onto its shaft. A harpoon has a metal ring to which is attached a length of fine chain and length of fishing twine. It is picked up and (the length of chain) is attached to the harpoon by a ring in the middle of the shaft.

durg íkkin men sīm wə-men ʿamḳ di-mínzek. lāṭ śúʔhur di-ʿíṣimo id durg. w-əmbáʿad śúʔhur ḳayd di-másfi men aḥtīmi di-tímihər. meš riyémo ḳayd ʔíno míʔa wə-xamsīn baʿ, wə-ʔíno míʔa kor lal núwzok léḥḥim. wə-léḥḥim zéʿe wə-fírud, fúwraḥ hiš men ḳīyud il bə-másfi.

The *durg* 'chain' is of (?)galvanised iron[240] and lies in the middle of the shaft, tied to the shaft with fishing twine. After the fish-

---

[240] *sīm* usually refers to copper wire.

ing twine comes the length of rope which is kept coiled in the *másfi* 'basket' woven from palm fronds. The rope is a hundred and fifty *bāʿ* long, and some are a hundred *bāʿ*. This is for when a shark is harpooned: the shark takes it (i.e., the harpoon and rope) and swims off as fast as it can, the rope that is kept coiled in the *másfi* 'basket' being paid out behind it.

ḳayd di-másfi ʿímer toš wə-ḳīfaʿ toš men ḥiṣ il-tímihər. wə-másfi yəʿúmur hiš másfi di-ḳīyud di-hūri. wə-másfi iʿúmur toš men ḥiṣ di-tímirə iʿúmur ḳāfaʿ wə-lāṭ ḥōṣen ʿaf l-ékkən másfi. al ṭad másfi íkkin bə-hūri. íkkin tərá, təlāṭ, árbaʿ məséfi. ṭad d-iʿúmur hiš másfi di-mínzek wə-ṭad múḳunhim.

The rope kept in the *másfi* 'basket' is made and worked from date palm fronds. The *másfi* 'basket' is made especially to hold (all) the ropes of a dugout. It is made from palm fronds which are firstly woven into long strips and these are then stitched together to make a *másfi* 'basket'. There is not just one *másfi* 'basket' in the dugout, but sometimes two, three or four. One is used for the *mínzek* 'harpoon' and one is for the large chunks of shark bait.

ġāduf wə-də́ḳəhal di-śīraʿ lhé iʿúmur túyhin men šə́rəhām di-yíśtib tyóʔo ḥímihər, śáʔad, ʿéraṭ, ki ʔíno mīṣeṣ di-škér, ki ʔíno íšḥib wə-ki ʔíno šírəhām di-ʔéṣal wə-ríyum wə-ḳə́ṭəhān wə-mə́ṣṭib wə-gɛd.

The *ġāduf* 'steering paddle' and the *də́ḳəhal* 'mast' for the sail are made from a tree or shrub which is straight limbed, such as *ḥímihər* 'Zygocarpum', *śáʔad* 'Ziziphus', *ʿéraṭ* 'Grewia', or if there is a well-grown *mīṣeṣ* 'Ballochia' or 'Trichocalyx', or an *íšḥib* 'Maerua', or any tree of good wood which is tall, slim, straight-growing and of hard wood.

máʿrif di-ḥūri iʿúmur tuš men ʿáṣbə di-šírəhām. ḳúwlof tuš wə-gúwḥur tuš wə-núwkar tuš ʿaf l-ékkən tyóʾo ḳaḥf.[241] *men ʿāker éʾeb men ḳaḥf w-al lāzim l-ékkən škɛr.*

The *máʿrif* 'bailer' is made from a branch of a tree or shrub. This is debarked, scraped and hollowed out until it is the shape of a bowl, like a *ḳaḥf* measure. In size it is larger than a *ḳaḥf* measure, and it doesn't have to be made well or look good.

hīrab di-ḥūri: hīrab di-ḥūri iʿúmur tuš nḥaṭ hūri. śówḥus šírəhām ḳáṭəhān, yéṭifin tuš w-iʿímidən tuš dhí-l-ḥūri. wə-ḳúwdaḥ biš wə-lúwsoḳ dhí bə-ḥūri men léḥe kor íkif ʿan hūri ʿa təḳtérah lal iʿúwla w-izúwḥur. lúwsoḳ bis bə-mə́smār, yúwge ʿaf l-íkeb mā-bēn hīrab wə-hūri. wə-ki ə́kub mə́smār id hūri di-ḳānə di-xan di-hūri, gúwnaṭ tuš.

The *hīrab* 'keel runner': the keel runner is made to run right along the base of the dugout. A slim tree or shrub is cut in half; then he whittles it and shapes it to the length of his dugout. Holes are bored through it and it is attached to the base of his dugout. This is to stop the boat being scraped and damaged when it is being dragged from the sea to the beach or from the beach to the sea. It is attached with nails which are tapped in to lie between the runner and the bottom of the boat. If the (tip of

---

[241] *ḳaḥf*, a measure used mostly for cereals, salt and dried droplets of *Dracaena* resin; four *ḳaḥf* are equivalent to one *ḳurs* (the Arabic /ṣ/ realised as /s/, as is often the case in Soqoṭri). One *ḳurs* is roughly equivalent to a kilogram.

a nail) goes right through and appears inside the bottom of the dugout, it is bent back (and hammered) flat.

8.3.2. Repairs to Boats

díkərk ʿag ə́nkaʿ bə-maʿállim d-ilókəd hūri. wə-lə́kud ə́lwaḥ bə-ṯhítšin bə-kaʔ di-ṣef wə-bə-śúʔhur di-kə́llun wə-b-íʿiśhur. lə́kud bə-ḥalf śáḥṣó hūri mes dḗfə wələ śébə. wə-keb hes luḥ^A wələ bínis wələ kōlə hūri tibéro. 'hūri wəššā́r': bíśi bis mərkīʿo, bíśi bis śḥayís, bíśi bis mizbīḵo, bíśi bis śéʔer.

I remember a man who brought an expert who knew how to stitch a boat[242] (i.e., to repair it). He stitched planks together with cord made from sheep wool, or from fishing twine made from imported cotton, or from cord (twisted from) locally grown cotton. He stitched together the part that had split or sprung apart on a side of the dugout or on its rim (lit. 'lip'). And he inserted a piece of planking into it (i.e., a crack), or built up the sides (i.e., to increase the height or to make a gunwhale or washstrake), or made good a boat that was damaged (in some way). A *hūri wəššā́r* is a dugout in perfect condition: no patch, no split or crack, no dent and no breach.

---

[242] I.e., a *hūri* was not necessarily only a dugout: in the early days anything that took people out to sea was called a *hūri*, except for dhows or other large sailing boats.

8.3.3. Rafts (*rēmuš*) (i)

hōhən hēmˤak mən éʔefo yəˤúmur fānə ol ṭad rēmuš, yəˤúmur tərá rēmuši kə-ṭhítši, sébəḳen túyhi wə-ˤə́wṣam wə-ḥébišin ˤéyhi mən nōsə wə-aḥtīmi.

I have heard people say that before, it was not only a single raft that was used, but two rafts joined together side by side, tied together and bound round and round with (cordage) made from the leaf sheaths that grow around the trunk of the date palm, or with cordage made from date palm fronds.

korúmma ˤígib l-áˤmer hūri núkiˤin tərə gōdiˤi wə-sébiḳin túyhi diyál ṭhítši. wə-lāṭ núkiˤin erkāyiz di-šírəhām mišṭibhítin wə-lāṭ irāḳal ṭhar ṭhítšin ˤaf l-ékkən ḥōz dirāˤ, dirāˤ wə-nus. wə-ṭaʰ šōgi bə-nʸaṣf id dig. wə-meš rə́həbo ḥōz d-izʸúˤum biš ˤaig bə-ḳānə.

If he wanted to make a craft to go out to sea he'd fetch two tree trunks and attach them together. And then he'd fetch poles of wood from some tree or shrub that grew straight, and he'd arrange them side by side one on top of the other until it was about a *dərāˤ* or one and a half *dərāˤ* in length. And he'd do the same with the other side. And it was wide enough to take a man sitting down inside it.

lékin yōkəb rīho w-ol yaˤmírir w-ol yiḳtúlub. wə-ki ḳoṭílib igōsir l-iḳiléʔš tyóʔo di-fānə. bas gōdiˤi wələ əgdóˤo mən léhe íkkin líbiyeḳ ˤan ṭírob lhé mən ˤálə, tyóʔo tímərə, dʸōgəš, ʔíkšə, ʔišḥib w-ítʔib, wə-ʔíno d-iˤāmer mən ṣ́áʔad diyal libéḳo bénɛ.

Even though water could get in, it wouldn't sink right down or tip over. And if it did tip over, he could (easily) set it upright again, just as before. But the two trunks, or more than two, the ones below, had to be thicker than the lengths of wood above, (the trunks of trees) such as date palm, dʸōgəš 'Cryptolepis socotrana' or 'Euphorbia socotrana', ʔíkšə 'Commiphora ornifolia', íšḥib 'Maerua angolensis' or ʔítʔib 'Ficus cordata'. And some would make it from a ṣáʔad 'Ziziphus spina-christi tree' if it (i.e., the trunk) wasn't too thick.

8.3.4. Rafts (rēmuš) (ii)

rēmuš d-iʕúmər tuš men igdóʕo il-tímiher fānə. ʔamma náʕa, ʔíno méyhin d-iʕúmur bə-drāmāt. nəkaṣ igdóʕo il-tímiher méyhin rīmo árbaʕ dərūʕ, xámsaᴬ dərūʕ, wə-lāṭ nəzōnig túyhin ṭaḥ wə́lə nəḥōmilin b-aḥmīri wə́lə b-ə́bʕar ṭaḥ. wə-lāṭ nərākal árbaʕ əgdóʕo wə-lāṭ nəʕáṣəm túyhin bə-thítšin b-aḥtōyhim əw bə-kayd d-aḥtīmi. aḥtīmi iʕúmur tus men ḥaṣ di-hə́ggub di-tímiher.

A raft was made from the trunks of date palms before, but nowadays some of them make one from fuel drums. We'd cut date palm trunks to a length of three dəráʕ, five dəráʕ, and then we'd carry them down to the beach, or load them onto donkeys or baggage camels as far as the beach. And then we'd lay four date palm trunks in a row on the ground and tie them together with cord or rope made from date palm fronds. The aḥtīmi 'cord' was made from the palm fronds of young date palms.

ʕaṣāmən wə-təté ʔin, nəzúhur dihán rēmuš. nəzúhur tuš id rínhem kor nəšáʕrok ṣōdə. erēmuš al šəʕówrok bih léḥḥīm, kal ṣōdə. w-áʕihiṣ wə-múṣaliḥ. wə-ṭúwrob biš wə-diš tyóʔo bíli diyal tə́ṣṣol ki ləhámis rího, tyóʔo tənāk, drāmāt, ləwáḥᴬ. rēmuš iyhé dhi nāfaʕ.

Once we'd tied them together and finished, we'd drag our raft down the beach. We'd drag it into the sea so we could fish from it. The raft wasn't used for fishing for shark, only for fish, or for diving down for pearlshell oysters. Or it was used for unloading (i.e., from other craft) and transporting things that wouldn't be damaged by getting wet, such as lidded aluminium pots, fuel drums, planking. A raft? That's how it was made and used.

8.3.5. Rafts (*rēmuš*) (iii)

wə-fānə bíśi šīhin éʔefo hwēri kal rēmuš. rēmuš iʕúmur tuš men əgdóʕo di-tímiher wə-men šermihīn di-ʔígbib. rúwkal túyhin təlāt walə árbaʕ men léḥe wə-təlāt walə árbaʕ men ʕālə tyóʔo túyhin. wə-yəʕúṣəm əl-tərá ṯhár ṯhítši wə-zúwhur tuyh id rīho wə-šəʕúwrok biš.

And in earlier days people didn't have dugouts, just rafts. A raft was made from the trunks of date palms or from any type of tree or shrub that would float. They would place three or four (poles) side by side at the bottom and three or four in the same way on top. And they'd tie them together, the one on top to the one below. Then it was dragged down to the sea and used for fishing.

8.4. Some Fish

8.4.1. Blennies, Gobies, Jawfish, and Mudskippers (*kibíʔihin*, pl. *kibíʔihon*; *iʔikídhin*, pl. *iʔikídhan*)

kibíʔihin íkkin bə-ṭaḥ u-bə-míʔsilin il-ḳéśʔor wə-ki šḥáḳo nəkósihin bə-ḳəlēto il-šḥáḳo ʕīhin wə-b-eṣərīʔo di-rínhem w-ihālaḥ men ḥalf di-ḥalf. wə-ki śīni tok ifúrid wə-ṭāridš kor túwduf ʕiš. wə-ki gāmaḥš ih-ālaḥ də-rīho.

kibíʿihin are to be found along the shore and on the rocks uncovered at low tide. And if the tide is right out, we find them in the rock pools left by the receding tide, or on the green algae. And it jumps from place to place, and if it sees you, it runs away, and you have to chase after it to get hold of it. And if you grab hold of it, it leaps (back) into the water.

wə-ḥánhen nəʿágub nədéf ʿiš kor nəʿāmerš ṣ́ámdə. bas o yə́wle biš wə-yə́fṯhoš ki kēbiʾik ʿiš wə-ʾə́dofk ʿiš. yə́fṯhoš tyóʾo mḗrə mek men ı̄́ʿid. ki ʿigı́bən nədéf əl-də́laḳ ol nəgōsir, kal ṭad wələ tərá. iʾikı́dhin al yə́wte tyóʾo ṣódə, tyóʾo šáḥaḳ. al nəʿágub nətéš.

And we (i.e., we children) would want to catch it to use it as bait.[243] But it can't be got hold of properly: if you manage to creep up on it and make a grab for it, it slips out of your hand. It slips away like a (piece of a) mirror (i.e., it is like glass) from your hand. If we wanted to catch them, we couldn't catch many, only one or two. The *iʾikı́dhin* fish is not eaten like fish and shellfish—we don't want to eat it.

8.4.2. Sprats (*kíIibə*)

kíIibə šīn nəʿāgəb his bɛ́nɛ men sēli wə-ʿafərı́ro wə-ḳə́ššo. lal nəʿāgəb náḳder, nərāḥaṣ́ tus bə-rı̄ho di-rínhem wələ bə-rı̄ho di-ḥāli men šīmi wələ men ṣóʿofo wələ men ḥóyhi. wə-lāṭ nəʿāfuś bis bə-rı̄ho bə-ṣ́áflaḥa ʿaf l-ihōb wə-ʿaf l-eʿfés.

kíIibə 'sprats': we like them more than the *sēli* 'Gulf herring' or the *ʿafərı́ro* 'hawkfish' or the *ḳə́ššo* 'silverside'. When we want to

---

[243] Children use these to practise fishing: no adult fisherman would use them as bait.

cook (them), we wash the sand or scales or dirt off them with sea water or with sweet water. Then we put it (i.e., water) to boil in a clay cooking pot until it grows warm and comes to the boil.

wə-lāṭ nəˁāṭub dihán kíliba wəla dihán ˁídi di-rīho d-ináḥa wə-nəmāliḥ mílḥo wə-nəbúhud heyh ˁaf l-éˁfeś ˁíntə, ˁíntə, ḥōz dəkīkəᴬ. wə-lāṭ nənētug.

Then we put our sprats or our sardine-type baitfish into the very hot water, add salt and wait for it to come back to the boil—just for a very short time, only a short time, around one minute. Then we take (the pot) off the fire.

ímmaᴬ néṣəlil di-rīho korúmma ˁígibən rīho nínśəz wəla nəˁākal ˁiš šfāniś il-ˁégibən rīho. nənōgif tuš id mérḳəhel əw náḥəṣəṣ tuš.

Either we strain off the water if we want to drink it,²⁴⁴ or we put it out for a thirsty domesticated animal (to drink). We pour them out (i.e., the fish) onto an area of stones laid side by side, or we make a layer of pebbles (to put) them on.

korúmma kíliba wəla ˁídi entéˁeró,²⁴⁵ nəšáˁfuś la-rīho ˁaf l-éˁfeś siwé wə-lāṭ nənōgif dihán ˁídi. wə-korúmma al entéˁero, nəḳādər tus bə-rīho heb korúmma al éˁefśən bə-rīho.

If the sprats or sardine-type fish have become a bit soft (i.e., are not absolutely fresh), we add them one by one to the water until it comes to the boil properly, and then we tip our small fish

---

²⁴⁴ nínśəz: lit. 'take small sips of a hot liquid'.

²⁴⁵ entéˁeró, 'to be(come) rather soft, friable, crumbly; to be rather high, a bit smelly (especially fish)'.

out (onto the ground). And if they haven't become rather soft, we cook them in water even if we haven't brought the water to a boil.

8.4.3. The Stingray (ḳiréʿe)

ḳiréʿe bis dánub wə-naʿāgub nəḳṣáṣ tuš w-íkkin šīn b-íʾid tyóʾo mérḳaḥ ḳor nənáḥag biš wə-yəʾúwge biš. wə-naʿāmer ɛ-ṯhídin: "ʿa təgɛʾ bis máxluḳ!" wə-d-iʾígi bih máxluḳ yəʿúmur hiš: "ɛ́hen kɛ̄fir!"

The ḳiréʿe type of stingray has a tail and we (i.e., we, children) like to cut it off and hold it in the hand like a herding stick and play around with it and hit things with it. And we say to one another: "Don't hit people with it!" And if someone does hit a person with it, he's told: "You're an unbeliever!"

dánub di-ḳiréʿe bis ḥáśbob tyóʾo mínšer. wə-ḳúwṣaṣ meš íʾint tyóʾo šɛ̄bir ḳor igúḥur[246] bih ḳān di-ʾíṣerhe ki iḳerén. ki gúḥurk biš iṭáḥaḳ.

The ḳiréʿe tail has sharp points on it like a saw. A length of it can be cut off—about a šɛ̄bir length—and used to rub smooth the goat-horn sheathe for the knife set, when someone is working (goat) horn. If you rub away with it (i.e., the stingray tail), it (i.e., the horn sheathe) becomes smooth.

8.5. Dangers of the Sea

némiro təṣúʿub máxluḳ, íʾid wələ śab.

A *némiro* 'moray eel': it bites people, on the hand or on the leg.

---

[246] √gḥr, 'to scrape a surface steadily, slowly; to rub smooth'.

gáḥban: ki śaḥḥ wə-bíluk(ək) (= bílugk) díɛ́ aṣābiˁ wə-śab tékizin w-ol ˁad ibúlug ˁaf tə́sme wələ ˁaf tə́kṣəṣ díɛ́ aṣābiˁ.

A *gáḥban* 'conch': if it opens wide and you put your fingers or foot in it (i.e., when diving), it clamps shut and won't let go until you die or until you cut off your fingers.

ṣafáḳa: ki lehémutk íśfif mek gad wə-gilído.

A *ṣafáḳa* 'jellyfish': if it touches you, your whole body feels as if it's on fire and your skin peels.

térəbaḥt āʔam tyóʔo méraḥt. diš nāṣəṣ~náʔṣuṣ tuš korúmma láhamk tos wə-miṭóʔtik ṭiy b-íṣbaˁ ol təgōsir təghúz mes.

There is an octopus which is as big as a circular palm fibre mat. We are really frightened of this one: if it touches you or stretches one of its tentacles (lit. 'finger') out at you, you can't escape from it.

gízihel wə-gizélhen: ol nítiš, nəˁāmer biš sem w-ol ˁirōbən ki ʔíno wə-ki bíśi. zaˁmāmə ḳáḳa di-gizélhen.

The full-sized and the smaller *gízihel* 'elongate puffer fish': we don't eat them. We say it's poisonous, but we don't know if it really is or not. The *zaˁmāmə* kinds of puffer fish are related to (lit. 'brother to') the *gízihel* 'elongate puffer fish'.

dəgág: ol nítiš al nəˁāgub biš wə-meyh kān tyóʔo míśərak mōtirig.

The *dəgág* 'lionfish': we don't eat it and we don't want it for anything. It looks like a comb with some of its teeth missing.

ḥelīmi: ˤa yúwte. korúmma ṣaˤdútk təʔāṣaḥ wə-ʔíṣərir mek gad tyóʔo korúmma ríkutk əl-ḥádḥed dé ḥáher.

The ḥelīmi 'sea urchin' (*Diadema setosum*):[247] it's not eaten. If it pricks you, it causes you a lot of pain. Your whole body (lit. 'skin') hurts, just as if you had stepped on a ḥádḥed 'sea urchin', that black kind (which has very long spines).

dībé wə-śīṣé:[248] tərá ləḥīmi díki náʔṣuṣ túyhi bénɛ. dībé təʔāraḥ hūri wə-təʔōkib di-kānə. śīṣé korúmma káno bə-ṭaḥ walə míbrəhe ber śīṣé wə-śīni mek mihlóˤo l-aʔāmt di-géʔerə yḥālaḥ ṭhárək.

The *dībé* 'shortfin mako shark' and the *śīṣé* shark: we are very afraid of those two. The mako shark comes right up to a dugout and gets inside it. The *śīṣé* kind of shark, when close inshore or immature, if it sees your shadow in the water beside a wave, it attacks you (lit. 'leaps on top of you').

8.6. Uses of Shark

8.6.1. Non-Edible Shark Liver Oil

ṣīfi: šibdə di-léḥḥīm naˤāmer mes ṣīfi. nəzēgud šibdə di-léḥḥīm id dram wə-lāṭ nəkāṣalsən ˤaf l-imléʔ wə-nərōgəm ˤiš wə-nəʔākals bə-šīhum. śéher, śhéri.

---

[247] Wranik (2003, 480) about *Diadema setosum*: "the spines are very thin, long, needle-like and have backward-facing barbs. They can form irritating wounds and inflict severe pain because they readily puncture human skin, penetrate deeply before they fracture and release a venom from their hollow shafts."

[248] *śīṣé*: variously grey reef shark, sicklefin lemon shark, whitetip reef shark, blacktip shark and blacktip reef shark.

Shark liver oil: we make ṣīfi oil from shark liver. We take the shark liver(s) to an (old) fuel drum and then we cut them up (and put them in) until the drum is full. Then we cover it and leave it in the heat of the sun. For a month, two months.

ímhe men šíhum di-ḳānə di-drām. nəʿərəf meš kor ənḥārot əl-ídfof di-hwēri men ḳānə u-men terr. men éʔemed di-ḥorf ḥúwrof biš hwēri. bíśi nāfaʿ bisən, rínhem diméro. wə-sen b-áʿariš wə-hə́wrot ʿísən.

Inside the drum they melt down from the heat of the sun. We scoop (the contents) out of the drum to oil the sides of the dugout, inside and out. When the monsoon arrives, the dugouts are moved to their monsoon quarters: nothing useful can be done with them as the sea is too rough. They are moved to the shelters specially constructed for them and are oiled.

wə-ʿuwḳālən túsən hwēri ʿaf di-ṣerébhən. ki ḥárotk əl-hūri bə-ṣīfi wə-ʿə́ḳalk tos śéher, lal kēbur ʿiš, tkósəs ʿafəríro wə-škéro wə-tkósəs tyóʔo yənāṭaf mes ṣīfi. kal ḥarótk dié əl-hūri bə-ṣīfi, tštíʔiren.

They are left there until the ṣerébhən season (the end of the monsoon before ṣéreb 'winter'). If you oil your dugout and leave it for a whole month, when you go to check up on it you find it gleaming red and in excellent condition—almost dripping shark liver oil! If you don't oil your dugout with shark liver oil, it (the wood) will crack and split.

8.6.2. Edible Shark Liver Oil (i)

dígil wə-nékkə nəʿāmer tos hámʔī wə-nəḥóṣirin bis eḳəníyo. hámʔī di-dígil wə-nékkə škéro. nərāḳaḥ šíbdə w-enḥarér tuš wə-nəʿāḳal tuš bə-šādihir kor nəhóṣirin bis ker éʔemed.²⁴⁹ korúmma śāḵer, ʔéyyəᴬ ṣōdə di-ḵīhen nəzīʿa meš šíbəd w-enḥarér tuš wə-nə́mṣeṣḥ.

We make pure oil²⁵⁰ from the *dígil* 'blacktip reef shark', 'pigeye shark', and 'sandbar shark', and the *nékkə* 'grey reef shark' and 'spot-tail shark'. We use it as a relish to flavour food. The pure oil from the *dígil* and *nékkə* sharks is delicious. We remove the liver and heat it in a dish over the fire (on its own, no added water), or we set it (to melt) in a clay pot, so that we can use it as a relish to flavour food throughout the season. If there is a period of drought, we take the liver from any small fish and heat it (to extract the oil) and then we dip our fingers into (the oil) and suck them.

8.6.3. Edible Shark Liver Oil (ii)

šíbdə di-nékkə wə-di-nímerihun yəḥóṣirin bíhi wə-yəʿə́wgub bíhi bénɛ. korúmma ksōwi túyhi wə-ṣílibo, zúwʿa méyhi šíbdə wə-ḵeśélen šíbdə. wə-múwha túyhi bə-śéyaṭ. wə-lāṭ ṣówlal méyhi ḥámʔī id ḵōmə wələ id šādihir wə-yəʿúwḵal. wə-zúwmaʿ kor yḥóṣirin meyh. w-ol bíro tə́śśol.

The liver of the *nékkə* 'grey reef shark' and 'spot-tail shark' and the *di-nímerihun* 'tiger shark' are used as a relish. They are much sought after. If we come across these two shark and butcher

---

[249] *ker éʔemed* 'for the season' (*ker šām* 'for the whole day~all day'; *ker aḥté* 'all night'; *ker dʸōtə* 'all during the summer rains', etc.).

[250] This kind of shark oil is especially liked in hard times or during the monsoon when the basic diet is dates and the longing for any taste of fish or meat is very great.

them, we take the liver and cut it up small. The pieces are put on the fire to melt down (to extract the oil). Then the pure oil is strained into a small-mouthed clay storage pot or into a wider-mouthed clay cooking pot and set aside. It is put somewhere safe and kept to be used as a flavouring and relish. And it doesn't spoil or go off.

8.6.4. Shark Fins

nōfʿan ḥśés(s)ən. kaṣāṣənsən men ḥot. wə-mēsən šem ṣəfríro di-ṭādaʿ wə-təri ṣəfrirúti di-ʾídəhān wə-ṭey ṣəfríro di-dɔ́nub. kaṣāṣən ṣəfríro di-ṭādaʿ wə di-ʾidḗni wə-di-dɔ́nub. w-al tikébən tósən kal ḥśés(s)ən, w-al śoʾōmən kə-ṣōdə, kal ḥśés(s)ən. kīmi di-ṣōdə aḥśíś wə-di-ṣəfrér aḥśíś. nádul ṣəfrér wə-lāṭ nəʿákal tyóʾo ʿigíbən. mḗsən kīmi.

We work them separately. We cut them away from the big fish (i.e., the shark). Each has its own name: *ṣəfríro di-ṭādaʿ* 'dorsal fin'; *ṣifrirúti di-ʾídəhān* 'two pectoral fins', and one *ṣifríro di-dɔ́nub* 'tail fin'. We cut off the dorsal fin, the pectoral fins and the tail fin and we collect them up separately. We don't sell them along with the big fish, but separately. The price for the shark is one thing and that for the fins is another. We weigh the fins and then we set them aside wherever we want. They have their own price.

8.6.5. Shark Stomach and Shark Livers (i)

kādəl di-léḥḥīm yəʿúmur biš šíbəd di-léḥḥīm kor tímhi wə-tíkkən ṣifi—sinɛ́mo. w-iśāraʿš bə-ṭarb wələ bə-ʿábəher kor indélilin wə-ʿa təmṭáʾš záʿdihim wə-ḥansīʾo. wə-sāʿa śīnen ímhe u-ber šiš tərí gúmʿati, nāḳafš wə-níṣīlel méyh dhí ṣīfi id ténkə.

He puts shark livers into a shark stomach[251] so that they liquify and turn into shark liver oil. It stinks. And he hangs it from a wooden pole or from a roof-supporting beam so that it swings back and forth there, out of the reach of rodents and crabs. And once we've seen that it has liquified—after about two weeks—we take it down and strain off its oil into an aluminium lidded pot.

8.6.6. Shark Stomach and Shark Livers (ii)

"ɛ-bébɛ, bíśi bis ṭáʾhal ṣīfi?" "bíśi bis w-ol íkkin bis. śíbdə di-léḥḥīm yəʿúmur hes ṭáḥalə korúmma ḳiṣaṣ mes bíli."

"Oh father, isn't there oil (to be made) from ṭáʾhal livers?" "No, there isn't. It doesn't have any. They call a shark liver ṭáḥalə if part of it has been cut off."

nyem ṭáḥalə di-ṣīfi? ṭáḥalə tíkkən men śíbdə di-léḥḥīm. wə-ṭáḥalə tíkkən tyóʾo hanɛ́kɛ. wə-korúmma ʿigíbin nóḥrit lə-hūri ʿan šīhum ʿa tśḥós wə-ʿa l-ikébs rīho, wələ hūri di-ḥarifo, ḥə́wrot ʿes bə-ṭáḥalə di-ṣīfi. nəḥúmurs b-íʾid wələ bə-luḥᴬ men nḥáṭ hámʾi.

What is ṭáḥalə di-ṣīfi? ṭáḥalə is from a shark liver. When it has liquified and become pure shark liver oil, the ṭáḥalə (i.e., that which is left over and is not oil) is like hanɛ́kɛ[252] (i.e., it has

---

[251] ḳādəl, pl. ḳúdəhul, 'stomach and stomach contents of shark'; also 'swim-bladder of some kinds of fish'.

[252] hanɛ́kə 'solidified boiled buttermilk': the buttermilk is put on the fire and brought to the boil without stirring. It is then taken off the

sunk to the bottom of the drum). If we want to oil a dugout to protect it from the sun and stop it splitting and developing a leak, or if the dugout has been pulled up out of the sea for the monsoon months, it is rubbed with the *ṭáḥələ* from making shark liver oil. We scoop it from below the oil that lies above, by hand or with a flat piece of wood.

ʿángəher[253] *di-ṣōdə wə-ḳādəl: ol nəʿāmer hiš ḳādəl kal korúmma léḥḥīm. nəʿāgub ʿángəher di-ṭárnīk wə-di-zíhnin wə-di-ráʾḥa, ʿángəher di-ṣōdə fáḥerə. ʿángəher ḳúwder toš dhí kə-ṣōdə. korúmma kīhen nəṣóʿobš wə-nənōsirš, wə-ki ʿángəher éʾeb, nəḥāṣalš.*

An *ʿángəher* stomach of a fish and a *ḳādəl* of a shark: we only call it *ḳādəl* if it is (the stomach) of a shark. We like the stomach of *ṭərnāk* 'Spanish mackerel' and of *zíhnin* 'tuna' and of *ráʿḥa* 'trevally'—indeed the stomach of any fish. The stomach and its contents are cooked in water along with the fish it came from. If it is a small one, we bite into it and eat it bit by bit just like that. If it is a large stomach, we cut it up into pieces (like meat).

8.6.7. Cooking Shark Young (*ḳídihir di-ribīs*)

ribīs: nəḳāderš men embūriye di-léḥḥīm. ʾiful nəkósə embūriye di-léḥḥīm? al nəkósa kal ki šaʿrókən léḥḥīm, ki lúwi léḥḥīm. nəkósh bə-ṭaṭ men ləḥáḥum ʾíbiš, meš šem ʿážə di-léḥḥīm. nəkósh bə-mer di-léḥḥīm.

---

fire and left to cool. It separates out into (i) *rīho di-ḥálob* 'whey', and (ii) *ḥanέkə* 'solidified chunks' that sink to the bottom of the pot.

[253] *ʿángəher*, pl. *ʿangírhān*, 'stomach and/or entrails of fish (non-shark)'; also *ʿámgəher* or *ʿámžəher*.

ribīs: we cook shark young in water. How do we get hold of shark young? We only get them if we are fishing for shark, if a shark is caught. We find them in one or other of the pregnant sharks, called 'the female or wife of a shark'. We find them in a shark's belly.

nékṣaṣ ríʔ wə-ṣəfrér dihán di-réʔeś²⁵⁴ wə-lāṭ nəkāṭabš éḳṭab. wə-lāṭ nəʿáfoś ʿeyh bə-rīho ʿaf l-ibəhúl. ənrāḳaḥ ter dihán ḳetéb, dihán mírśi, dihán di-rēśi. nəbúhud ʿaf l-íḳṣum. wə-lāṭ nərāḳaḥ ḳérišo. nəḳālaʿ bis wə-nərāḳaḥ šébəhur.

We remove the head and fins of our creature (i.e., the shark foetus) and then we cut it into sections. Then we cook it in water until it is done. We take our pieces out, of our animal, of our creature. We wait until they have cooled down, and then we remove the skin and throw it away. Then we remove the backbone.

ikéʔe níbihil. nəfúʿuṣ əw nəmúss bə-rīho wə-nəʿáṣərəš men rīho. núkiʿin šíbdə di-léḥḥim wələ dihé di-šēbəd kor yíkif. wə-nəbōləg id ṣáflaḥa ᴬmárra ṯānīyəᴬ. wə-lāṭ nəhárer tuyh əl ṭhítši. wə-nəʿáṣəd wə-nəḳādif tuyh bə-ṭhítši.

What's left are small pieces. We squeeze (them) in water and rub (them) between our fingers and then we wring the water out. We get the liver of the shark, or their own livers (i.e., those of the baby shark), to make enough (for everyone). And we put everything in the cooking pot once more. Then we stir the two

---

²⁵⁴ *réʔeś~rēśi*, pl. *erśóʔo*, 'creature', usually referring to a variety of creatures seen as vermin (certain ants, spiders, snakes and other reptiles, scorpions, the giant centipede etc.).

(i.e., the livers and the flesh) together: we mash and pound them together with a stick.

ḥámʔī di-šíbdə al idōlaḵ lə-ribīs lal tōkəb ṭeyʔ di-ḥámʔī di-šíbdə se b-ínʕis. wə-ʕatəṣədó siwɛ́. nōtug tuyh wə-nəḵōḥuf wə-náte. wə-nəʕágub rīho l-āḵən šīn kor níte wə-nároi.

Not a lot of pure shark liver oil is added to the *ribīs* or the pieces will have too much of the flavour and smell of shark liver oil. The two are all well mixed together, and then (the pot) is taken off the fire and we serve it out and eat it. We must have water to hand to drink as we eat (as this dish makes you thirsty).

8.7. Whales (and Ambergris)

8.7.1. Whales (*śíḥāṭə*) and a Whale Story

śíḥāṭə al tíkkən kal bə-ġúbbə w-al tšóʔiki maʕrérə. śíḥāṭə náʔṣaṣ tos korúmma šíkido wələ šíʔiki tan wə-tšālaḥ wə-tšéliḥin. təḵtəlōbən hwēri mes men ḵalḵālə se diš šíliho. korúmma šínen tos šíʔiki, nəḵáḥkaḥ ʕis hwēri wə-tfōrid.

Whales are only to be found in the deeper seas, they do not come inshore to where fish shoal. We are afraid of a whale if it suddenly appears or comes close to us or broaches: leaping out of the sea, leaping here and there all around. Dugouts can be overturned as a result of the splashing and turbulence caused by this leaping. If we see one nearby, we bang on the sides of the dugouts, and it swims off.

śínək ṭiy márra hōhən śíḥāṭə nehéro ʕīn nhaṭ dihán hwēri. hūri diš əl-ʔáwwaliyyə[A] śínó mes əgsíso wələ mes mihilīʕo wə-ʔālaḥ mes. kērhe hēmáʕan meyh ʕérho ʕag d-išímtil tan. ʕúmur: "ʔīno əgsíso nhaṭ *toʔ, ḥáwro!" wə-tyóʔo fədōrən di-gʸḗmə men baʕd ʔínṭe šínən bíli ḥáwro d-irigāmo se rīho.*

Once I saw a whale passing underneath our dugouts. The dugout in front saw its black shape or its shadow and he shouted out about it. We could barely hear the man's voice and what he said to us. He said: "There's a dark shape beneath me, a black shape!" As we raced back towards the shore, after a while we saw something dark-coloured, covered by water.

wə-nəhéro ʕin wə-ʕə́do mes šíl ʕe aw gísso kə-ʕag d-il-ʔə́wwəli^A. wə-ʔíno ḥōz di-ʔínṭe nəšgúhud di-gʸḗmə wə-se al əstóʔo tinhér ʕin. əstóʔo wə-ʕíffo. ḥánhən nəʕāmər šīḥāṭə aw kefʕānə aw waḥš di-rínhem. al šínən al šímʔhil w-al ímʔhil kal əgsīso ḥáwro.

It passed right by us, and its shadow or dark shape was still visible beside that man in front. And even after some time of us staring down into the water it was still passing beside us, so great was its length. Finally it came to an end and disappeared from sight. We say this (i.e., a huge dark shape seen in the water) is a *šīḥāṭə* 'whale' or a *kefʕānə* 'giant manta ray' or 'sea monster'. To left and right we saw nothing but a dark-coloured shape.

šīḥāṭə nəhāmaʕ mes fonś lal fēnisin wə-nəkādum nísas di-ʕiś mes men fonś íhikɛ id səmáʔ. wə-ʔíno iʔārah hūri mes fonś di-rīho wə-iʕúwrub ber fonś di-šīḥāṭə: kefʕānə al fēniśin.

We hear the breath of a whale when it comes up to breathe, and we can see the fine spray that arises when it spouts, shooting up into the sky. Sometimes the water from this spouting reaches a

dugout and is recognised as being the breath of a whale: a
ḳefʿānə 'manta ray' does not (come up to) breathe (like this).

8.7.2. Whales (śíḥāṭə) and Whale Shark (kɛr)

kɛr wə-śíḥāṭə ki šərḳóho al nəšōgi bíki bíli. lúʔu? wə-ḥánhən ʿigíbən nəšgé: nəṣəléb wə-nəgəzél kor naʿtúbur nyem bi-mer kal ʔíno ʿámbəher. bas al nəgōbi meyh gad: ʿíśś wə-ḳeśbub biš.

If a whale shark or a whale are beached, we don't do anything with them. Why? We would like to do something: slaughter it and cut it up to see what's in its belly, to see if there is any ambergris. But we can't cope with its hide: it's too tough and it's all spikes (i.e., covered in barnacles).

ʔíno d-inkáʿ bə-fɛs wə-ʿāṭer wə-múśərih̬ wə-ṣārə wə-gúzur w-al gíbi l-ifláh̬ meyh mer. mer ráʿaś men ṭādaʿ w-al gibíʔin.

People would bring an axe or a long sharp knife or a mattock or a billhook, but they couldn't cut its belly open. Its belly is softer than its back, but (still) they couldn't manage it.

8.7.3. Ambergris (ʿámbəher) (i)

ʿámbəher al íkkin kal men śíḥāṭə. w-iʿúmur wə-hēmʿak mítilin ʿámbəher bíśi di-gʸōsir hiš l-áʿad ʿiš dihé men h̬alf kal śíḥāṭə.

Ambergris comes only from a whale. It is said, and I have heard people say, that ambergris is a thing that no creature dares to venture to where it is found, except a whale.

wə-ʿámbəher šírəhām di-ʔéśa bə-gəháyo di-ḳáʿ di-rínhem. w-iʿúmur śíḥāṭə sáʿa di-ʿigɛ́bo títe ʿámbəher al steš tyóʔo taʿgób: tšābaṭ ʿanš.

təgódiḥins tyóʔo birk il-xāṭif wə-tṣúʿurš. šíṣʿir his meš. fōtíṣad kens yígbib w-išrākah ter w-ikósʔiš éʔefo.

Ambergris is a tree which flourishes in a deep valley at the very bottom of the sea. It is said that when the whale wants to eat ambergris it cannot just go and eat it whenever it wants to: it is afraid of it. It rushes at it like a streak of lightning and takes a bite from it. (Chunks) are bitten off it (i.e., the ambergris tree). Broken up fragments of it float to the surface, and (finally) reach the shore where people find them.

wə-meš kān ṣáʿbeb al té tuš. wə-ʿámbəher dé d-išrākah mes ḥáher dé di-táʿbibš. wə-iʿúmur ʔíno wəḥūš di-rínhem išḥánin bə-ʿámbəher w-al ítiš. wə-ki išḥánin biš wə-ḳōtíṣaʿ, išrākah.

Some of it is pale-coloured: this kind has not passed through the gut of the whale. The kind that floats ashore is dark-coloured: this is the kind which has been excreted by the whale. It is also said that there are sea monsters which rub their bodies against the ambergris (tree), but they don't eat it. And when they rub their bodies against it, bits get broken off, and these (too) reach the shore.

ḥágiher di-ʿámbəher: ʿámbəher iʿúmur ləʿámihe al maḥrūz išrākah ter bénɛ. w-iʿúmur ʿámbəher iḥúgur ʿiš gyūn, wə-íno d-iʿāmer ᴬmeléʔikə il-baḥrᴬ.

The 'guardian of the ambergris tree': it is said that if ambergris were not closely guarded it would come ashore in great quantities. It is said that jinn guard the tree, though some say it is the 'angels of the sea' (who do so).

8.7.4. Ambergris (ˤámbəher) (ii)

ˤámbəher: d-ikōsə men ˤámbəher díyhe yíkkin wə-yəśōʔomš tyóʔo ˤágib. wə-šīn ˤādə: nədófənš bə-ḳaˤr. iˤówmer idālaḵ ˤek māl. bíśi šik di-yōtəm šik biš.

Ambergris: if someone finds ambergris, it becomes his property and he can dispose of it as he wishes. And we have a custom: we bury it in our home. It is said that your possessions will multiply. Nobody has any (right to a) share of it with you (i.e., only you and yours profit from the ambergris if you manage to keep it secret).

korúmma himōwaˤ bik ber kísək ˤámbəher, yímkin sáṭəhān l-irīʔihin meš, ʔímmā kor ṭāf ˤiš wələ śōm ˤiš.

If word gets out that you have found ambergris, it is possible that the sultan will try to find out about it, (with the result that) either you have to give it to him as a gift or you have to sell it to him.

ˤámbəher meyh féydi šīn: di-gʸúˤur yəˤúmur meš íʔinṭ di-rīho kor inḗśuṣ meš kor itōrif diš men bíli eśáḥis əw šḥabílis əw ibdíds.

Ambergris is of great value to us: if someone is ill he takes a tiny bit of it and adds it to (hot) water and sips it to cure himself of the pain or whatever he is feeling or whatever is hurting him.

8.7.5. The Whale Shark (*kɛr*) (i)

ṭiy márra šə́rkaḥ šīn kɛr[255] *wə-néheg biš təlātə ʿiyug bə-ṭādaʿ tyóʾo korúmma inéheg bə-mīdān miskído. wə-ṣ́ə́baṭ béyhin fáḥerə. wə-rīyum ḫōz* ᴬ*xams wə-təlātīn*ᴬ *dərá.ʿ wə-ḳáṣa ṭad bə-riʾ di-ʿāḳaf wə-mid dhí tʿídi id ʿāḳaf diš w-al míṭa men riʾ di-ʿāḳaf ʿaf riʾ di-ʿāḳaf.*

One time a whale shark beached where we live and three men danced around on its back, just as they would dance around in the arena at a circumcision. And it held them all (i.e., it was so big)—its length was some thirty-five *dəráʿ*![256] One man stood on the tip of one side of the caudal fin and stretched out his hands towards the other tip but couldn't reach to touch one tip from the other!

8.7.6. The Whale Shark (*kɛr*) (ii)

kɛr íkkin bə-rínhem wə-iʿúwrub tuš wə-nəʿāmer hiš kɛr di-ś́kef. wə-biš məḥóḳiḳ əl-ḥāṭer dihé men śédaḳ di-ḥá ʿaf ʿārib. wə-nəʿāmer kɛr al ilúhum máxluḳ l-ínnə ś́kef. al tyóʾo śīḥāṭə. wə-kɛr meyh kān ʿábdəher wə-di-ʾínḳaṭ wə-di-ḥáśyuḳ. kɛr ʾíno ʾēb wə-ʾíno ḳīhen.

A whale shark lives in the sea and is well-known: we call it *kɛr di-ś́kef* 'bridled whale shark'.[257] It has curved score marks mak-

---

[255] That year it is said that some nine or ten whale sharks floated ashore between Ras Mōmi and Ḥadibo. The sultan of the time heard of this and sent a number of slaves to try and carve it open to get at the ambergris he thought would be inside, but they didn't succeed in finding any.

[256] For *dəráʿ*, see footnote 228 above.

[257] I.e., it has lines extending from the corners of its mouth like a goat kid wearing the weaning peg to stop it suckling its dam.

ing lines and streaks around the corners of its mouth and extending to the back of its neck. And we say that the whale shark doesn't harm (lit. 'touch') a human being because it is 'bridled'. Not like a whale. The whale shark has blotches and spots and circular bars. There are large whale shark and there are small ones.

díkerk wə-hōhən ʿəwyéghen šérḳaḥ šīn kɛr dihán bə-ḥalf bə-ḥállə wə-meš šem dé ḥalf šérḳaḥ bih zīmhítin. wə-dé bə-zə́man símak díkerk ʿímer ínhi ber šérḳaḥ ᴬḥwāli sábaʿᴬ wə-íno kɛr wə-ʾíno šúwəre kɛr.

I remember that when I was a boy, a *kɛr* 'whale shark' was beached where we live in Ḥállə (on the east coast), and the name of the place where it was beached is Zīmhítin. And at that time I remember being told that about seven had come ashore, some of them whale shark and some creatures that looked like a whale shark.

šérḳaḥ bə-díbəni wə-ḥówlef wə-ḳáriyə wə-di-ḥámri wə-bə-ṣáḳerə wə-di-fōnə iríssey ḥalf iʿúmur ʿiš ḳábəho. wə-ʾímben toš dé zéman kōnīyə di-wəḥūš di-rínhem. dé ḥot, dé kɛr di-šérḳaḥ šīn wə-hōhən šínək tuš, šínək ʿággi ináḥago meyh bə-ṭādaʿ tyóʾo ki ináḥago mīdān di-miskído di-ḥówtən bis.

They beached at Díbini and at Hówlef and at Ḳáriyə and at Di-Ḥámri and at Ṣáḳerə and at a place by (the headland of) Irísseyl called Ḳábəho. And we gave that period the name *kōnīyə*[258] *di-*

---

[258] *kōnīyə*: (i) an epidemic leading to many livestock and/or human deaths; (ii) an unknown disease which sweeps though livestock and

wəḥūš di-rínhem 'the year of disaster for the sea monsters'. That fish, that whale shark that came ashore where we live and which I myself saw: I saw two men dancing along its back just as they would dance in the arena where (young men) are circumcised.

wə-men śādaḳ ʕaf śādaḳ dāraʕ ʕaig təlātīn dərá ʕ nāḳaṣ śéber. wə-men ʕāḳaf ʕaf ʕāḳaf, men rīʔ di-ʕāḳaf ʕaf riʔ di-ʕāḳaf, men riʔ di-səfríro di-də́nub ʕaf di-səfríro di-də́nub al yāraḥ ʕaig tərí məḳəlimōti ʕaig d-iḳālim. wə-ʕaig šīn dé d-iḳālim iḳālim təmāniyəᴬ durūʕ wə-ʕášerəᴬ durūʕ. wə-səfríro di-ṭādaʕ šəmāṭa ʕaig w-al miṭéʔis.

And a man measured from one corner of its mouth to the other corner and it was thirty *dəraʕ*-spans less one *šéber*. And from one side of its tail to the other, from one tip of the caudal fin to the other, from one tip of the tail fin to the other, was a distance that a man could not cross with two leaps. And with us a man who is famous for his leaping can leap a distance of eight or ten *dəráʕ*. A man tried to touch the tip of the dorsal fin (i.e., from the whale's back) but he couldn't reach it.

wə-ḥot əl-dḗfə ḳōtílib. w-iyhé rīyum ḥōz di-árbaʕ məḳālihim, ḥōz di-arbaʕīnᴬ durūʕ. hēmaʕ sátəhān dé bə-kɛr šérḳaḥ ímta diyál éʔefo, wə-bílug dihé embúʕile. w-embúʕile ʔíno bīhin ʕásker ker ṭad ʕa l-inṣérihin wə-kor lal nʸōṣir kúwse ṭad men lhé bəlégihin di-sátəhān kor izáʕa meyh ʕámbəher. šības sátəhān ʔíno bīhin ʕámbəher. di-hēmʕak bíśi bih ʕámbəher.

---

people; (iii) when all a man's animals die after his death (because with his death, his *baraka*, 'blessings', come to an end).

And the fish was washed up lying on its side. Its length was about four *məkālihim* leaps: some forty *dərá*ˤ. The sultan heard about this whale shark that had washed ashore, and he sent his slaves (to see it). And the slaves had a soldier with them to make sure than no one would cut it open by himself (i.e., in secret), and to ensure that, when it was cut open, there would be someone among those the sultan had sent who could take charge of the ambergris. The sultan believed that there might be ambergris in them. But from what I heard, there was no ambergris in it.

ʔíno níṣer wə-ʔíno diyál gíśér hiš. ki inkíˤo ṣārə taˤtətáf. w-ínkaˤ ˤútəhur w-ínkaˤ məsāmīr w-ínkaˤ miśīraḥ kor nʸūṣar biš w-al šínṣir: meyh gad fáḥərə zə́ko ťúˤud fáḥerə.

Some were cut open, but there were some that could not be managed: if a knife were brought (and used) it would bend and buckle. Great machetes were brought to split it open with, and metal rods were brought and mattocks were brought, but it could not be cut open! Its hide was all rock oysters (i.e., barnacles)!

8.7.7. The Whale Shark (*kɛr*) and a Whale Shark Story

ṭiy márra kāno íʔrīfi wə-ˤə́ṭab hwēri. wə-ˤəṭábki hōhən wə-dihó nínhin ˤalí bə-hūri mes šem ġarībi. menál šeˤrēko k-éʔefo ḥánʔé śérḳaḥ kɛr bə-ˤamḳ dihé di-maˤrērə. wə-lāṭ tśāḥ wə-lāṭ təʔōkib di-ˤidi meyh di-ḥá tyóʔo korúmma śáˤab tənāṭaḳ əl-gēḥi, təḳúˤud əl-gēḥi.

One time there were great shoals of fish with larger fish feeding on them, and the dugouts went out. I went out with my elder brother ˤAli, in a dugout called Ġarībi. Where we were fishing with the others, a whale shark surfaced, right there in the middle of the feeding frenzy. And then it opened its mouth wide and the sardines went down into its mouth like a riverbed filled with water, cascading down a wadi, flooding down a watercourse.

wə-ʾə́ḳdəmk meyh əl-śáʿnhun tyóʾo šərāḳaḥ ʿídi sé wə-tsé (= di-sé) rīho ter, wə-se ʿə́do bə-ʿid w-al ḥebéro ḳéyri. éʾefo išíʿir əl-ṯhítšin hwēri "ʿa tšéʾkin kɛr!" ʾiṣṣ lal yaʿmírir ker təgúdiḥin géʾerə wə-ḳalḳā́lə di-rīho wə-təḳtəlṓbin hwēri.

And I saw its gills when the sardines and the water they had been swimming in came back out: they were still alive and quite unharmed! People were shouting back and forth between the dugouts: "Don't go near the kɛr 'whale shark'!" They were scared that when the whale shark dipped its head under the water (again) a wave would come and a great wake, and the dugouts would be tipped over.

menál ḥánʾé ḳeṣáʿiki wə-šeʿrēko té hiš ḥot dihó nínhin. w-iyhéhən ber yəʿāmer ínhi kor éʿemed: "ɛ́hen ʿa tšáʿrək! bērīn hūri ʿan maʿrērə!" bas al ṭōmʿak tuš kor bērīyin hūri ʿan maʿrērə.

Exactly where we were standing up to fish, a large fish took the bait of my elder brother. And he had already told me: "Don't you fish! Steer the dugout away from the feeding frenzy!" But I wouldn't do as I was told and row the dugout away from the feeding frenzy.

šíśərik ho éʾero l-əšáʿrek. diš bə-sáʿa té hiš ḥot ho éʾero té ínhi ḥot. hṓhən ízʿumk bə-ḳērīyə w-iyhéhən ḳə́ṣaʿ bə-riʾ di-ḳērīyə wə-hūri *təktəʿílən. tyóʔo símak té hiš ḥot wə-kéddiš, ḳtáʿalo hūri. wə-ki bíki šiʔkéki kɛr w-al ʿak śīnək kal aʿág bə-rīho.*

I was keen to fish too. At the same time that a big fish took his bait, a big fish took my bait as well. I was sitting on a thwart of the dugout and he was standing on the bow thwart, and the dugout was rocking from side to side. When the big fish took his bait and he was working hard with it (i.e., to land it), the dugout tipped right over to one side. We two were already right by the whale shark and I saw no more until there he was! The man was in the water!

*ləʿámihi ḥot al té ínhi wə-ṭaḥáro hūri d-ifónə ḥot sōri ho wə-se meyh id ḳādəl, id ḥá. ḥot d-ité ínhi ṣəḥób toʔ əl-nʸaṣf. ʿak išʔāṣiyin dihó ḥot ékdumk dihó əl-nínhin meyh bə-ḳeśeríbo*²⁵⁹ *di-ʿāreb di-kɛ́r w-išūʔur w-ikólibin w-iḳārə* ᴬʔ*āyyah b-il ʿaks*ᴬ*, al ḳeréʔes tyóʔo ḳúwre. men tyóʔo ʿiṣ wə-yəʿāmer:* "ᴬ*yā mərsāha wə-yā məgrīha!*ᴬ"

If a big fish hadn't taken my bait and gone swimming off, the dugout would have gone towards the great fish (i.e., the whale shark), and I and it (i.e., the dugout) would have disappeared down into its belly, into its mouth. But the fish that had taken my bait dragged me off to one side. I was still pulling in my fish when I saw my brother on the back of the neck of the whale shark, on the huge dome of its head. He was screaming and cursing and reciting the verse of the Qurʔān back to front. He

---

²⁵⁹ *ḳáśəribo*, pl. *ḳáśrəb~ḳaśīribhítin*, the back of the top of the head; sth. just surfacing above the sea; the whole of the domed top of the skull, but especially at the back.

didn't recite it as it ought to be recited, but out of his great fear he said (instead): "yā mərsāha wə-yā məgrīha!"[260]

wə-ʔámma hōhən, tyóʔo hēmʕak tuš yəʕāmer ṭaʰ, ṣāmək b-éṣ́hak. wə-ḥɛ̄rə l-íṣ̌ʕur ḥey kor núkiʕin hiš hūri. hōhən al ʕād fī ʕid men aṣ́áḥak, hōhən míbərhe. ʕémer heš éʔefo: "tsābaḥ di-fōnə diɛ́ bə-hūri. múgšəm ʕa l-énkaʕ bə-hūri dek ʕan ḳəlḳālə di-kɛ́r!" sābaḥ dihé id hūri wə-ʕam išrāḳaḥ dəhí di-hūri, dəhí íʔidi, ʕarṣənōti wə-dihé erbəbōti dūr men zíko wə-ḳeśeríbo di-ḥot. wə-dihé kɛr al ṣ̌hábiliš.

And as for me, when I heard him saying that, I nearly died laughing. He was doing his best to shout to me to bring the dugout towards him, but I was quite insensible from laughter—I was just a boy. The others said to him: "Swim in the direction of your dugout. The boy can't bring the dugout to you, the whale shark is making too much wake." He swam to his dugout. When he got out of the water into his dugout, his hands, forearms, and thighs were bleeding from the rock oysters (i.e., the barnacles) of the huge domed head of the fish. And the whale shark hadn't even realised (lit. 'sensed') that he was there!

w-iyhé kɛr al ilúhum máxluḳ w-al hūri kal korúmma šinhórk ʕiš. nyem meš šenḥɛ̄rə? korúmma núhur ʕik bə-ġúbbə wə-śīnək tuš nḥaṭ hūri ʕa l-áśəraṭ ʕiš. ki ṣ̌arāṭək ʕiš, ki ber wə-śínḥir ʕik, yəʕāmer dəhí bə-ṭal wələ bə-ʔídəhen yəʕāmer ʕis ḥāsīyə di-rīho kor iḳálḳal diɛ́ hūri

---

[260] Q 11 (Hūd):41 wa-qāla rkabū fīhā bi-smi llāhi majrāhā wa-mursāhā. inna rabbī la-ghafūrun raḥīm ('And [Noah] said: "Embark therein; in the name of Allah is its course and its anchorage. Indeed, my Lord is Forgiving and Merciful'.) Many thanks to Orhan Elmaz for these details.

wə-tək̇təlub. wə-ʾíno diyal tək̇təlub. wə-ʾíno d-iḥōli his k̇áḥadə ʿaf l-izgúts men rīho. bas al iti tuk. nəʿāmer hiš állah śkof tuš ʿa l-ité máxluk̇.

And the whale shark doesn't harm (lit. 'touch') a human or a dugout unless you give it cause. What makes it angry? If it passes by you out at sea, or if you see it beneath the dugout, don't let off a loud fart at it. If you let off a loud fart at it, if it wants to demonstrate its anger with you, it uses its flukes or its pectoral fins to produce a great swirl in the water so that your dugout tips from side to side and capsizes. Some don't capsize. And some (whale shark) put the great hump of their back beneath it (i.e., the dugout) and lift it right out of the water! But it won't attack you (lit. 'bite, eat'). We say of it: "The Lord bridled it so that it wouldn't attack and kill a human being."

8.8. Turtle and Remora

8.8.1. Turtles (*ḥōmis*) (i)

men éʾemed di-dímiher al tšrāk̇aḥ ḥōmis,[261] *wə-ki šərk̇óho al dilāk̇o, ṭiy ṭiy. šə́rk̇ah men ḥorf əl-ter di-ṣerébhən, tšrāk̇ah kor táʿyig wə-təbōrə bə-ṭaḥ. tədālak̇ bə-nōgəd wə-k̇áʿara wə-bə-śʲáʿab. tədālak̇ bə-ʿayn di-méde wə-tḥarér bə-ʿayn di-ṣérbihi.*

When the sea is rough, the female turtle does not come ashore, or if it does, not many, only one or two. They come ashore during the monsoon, at the beginning of the post-monsoon *di-ṣerébhən* season, before *ṣɛrb* winter. It comes ashore to have its

---

[261] *ḥōmis* is the generic term for turtle, but usually refers to the female.

young, to give birth on the shore. There are a lot of them on (the south coast of) Nōged and at Kaʿara (at the western end of the south coast) and at Śʸáʿab (on the western tip of the island). They come in great numbers when the wind is from the south, but only a few come when the wind is from the north.

éʔefo lhɛ́ di-šíʕiki ṭaḥ ki ʿígib ḥōmis, ʔíno méyhin d-išmēriyin ṭaḥ. ki kísə məšḥībo di-ḥōmis, yúwihur ʿaf l-iksé menól kīro mes míhiba. ikōsə tos wələ ikōsə mes ḳaḥélihan. ki ksɛ́ʔs menól ksɛ́ʔs ki kḗrhe šərḳóḥo wə-ki kḗrhe kətínḥo, iḳālibs əl-ṭādaʿ.

Those people who live close to the shore, if they want a turtle, they go down to the beach in the evening. If he sees the tracks of a turtle dragging herself up the beach he follows the tracks until he finds where it has hidden itself (lit. 'hidden its shape'). He finds either it or its eggs. If he finds it, wherever he finds it—just recently emerged from the sea or only recently turned round to make her way back (to the sea)—he turns it upside down on its back.

ki gísur l-aḥəzés (= l-aḥəzézs) yáḥzis (= yáḥzizis), wə-ki al gísur, yəʿāḳals tse (= di-sé) bə-ḥalf w-iyhé iṭóhur iṣālaʿ e-éʔefo. wə-se al ʿído tšḥáylin se men ḥalf ʿaf ígdaḥ éʔefo. ʿábəhan al yəšrāḳaḥ. ḳúwdum ʿiš~ʿeyh bə-rínhem k-aḥśíš. ʔíno di-ʿərub ber ʿábəhan wə-ʔíno diyál ʿerḗbiš.

If he can manage to cut its throat, he does so. If he can't, he leaves her where it is and goes off to tell others. And it doesn't move from where it has been left until people arrive. The male turtle doesn't come ashore. It's seen out at sea on his own. Some recognise a male turtle when they see one and some don't.

korúmma śinōwi rə́tkəbo, ḥōmis wə-ˁabəhan, yəˁúmur hīhi 'rəkkḗbi': ˁábəhan rə́kub əl-ḥōmis. wə-ˁábəhan ki rə́kub əl-ḥōmis al ber iṭārib w-al ber iśíziyun heb korúmma fizóˁo men máxluḳ wələ men hūri w-iyhé bə-rīho. yáˁihiṣo kə-ṭhítśi. wə-bíśi di-ˁə́rub díful waḳt záˁamo kə-ṭhítśi.

If they are seen mating, a female and a male turtle, they are called *rəkkḗbi* 'the two riders'; that is, a male turtle on top of a female one. And once the male is on top of the female, it won't get off her and they will not separate, even if startled by a human being or by a dugout in the water. They dive down still attached one to the other. No one knows how long they remain like that, stuck together.

korúmma ʔíno di-ksé ʔeš bə-rínhem wə-ʔēkis ˁiš wə-ləʹṭiš men ḥérhen wə-íbṭiš wə-íbṭə tus, yə́šxaf tus mə́šxaf.

If someone comes across one out at sea and can creep up on it, come at it from behind, catching a male or female unawares, he gaffs it with a hooked gaff.

8.8.2. Turtles (*ḥōmis*) (ii)

korúmma ənkáˁans w-al šərḳóho men rīho, nəˁāmer ˁis kəllāb wə-náˁnən bis ˁaf išōʔiki tan. šíʔiki tan, nərté ʔhən wə-nəróbən wə-niftikérən: "ʔíful nəšōgi? nəḳāters? wələ nāgahs id hūri?" ki gáhan tus id hūri, nəḳālibs əl-ṭādaˁ. wə-ki ḳətārəns, nəḳōtifs əl-ṭiy men ʔidbíti wələ əl-fəḳəríro. któfən əntúher, nəḳādif bar ˁaf nəšə́rḳah. šərḳáhan, nərāḳahs ter wə-nəḳālibs.

If we come across one and it is not on the shore, we use the grappling hook on it, and pull it in close (i.e., to the dugout).

When it is close by, we ask one another, we discuss what to do and we think long and hard: "What should we do (now)? Tie it on (i.e., to the dugout, to be dragged behind us)? Try and get it into the dugout?" If we get it into the dugout, we turn it upside down on its back. If we tie it (on to the dugout), we bind it either by one of its flippers or around its neck. Once we've attached it, we set off rowing back to shore. Once we're ashore, we get it out onto dry land and we turn it upside down.

wə-lāṭ núkiʿin dihán b-íṣərhe. išōfin d-išōfin wə-ṭad yáḥziz tos əl ḳār. nərāḳaḥ ḳɛrf id ter wələ śéḳeḳ wə-rāḳaḥ ḳɛrf. wə-lāṭ nəgāzəls wə-nərāḳaḥ mes ḳɛrf di-ḳhó áḥśiš wə-nərāḳaḥ mes te^h men ḳéśəribo di-ḥōmis. nəḳāder wə-nəšōdiʿīn.

And then we fetch our knives. Whoever needs to sharpen his blade does so, and someone cuts it across the throat. We remove the plastron and put it down on the ground, or the plastron is sawn around and around and removed (like that). Then we butcher it. We remove the plastron at the sternum by itself and remove the meat that lies behind the back of the turtle's head. We cook (it) in water and we share it out.

ámmā ḳɛrf di-ḳíhən, nəʿāmer biš ṣōdə wə-nəḳtíni bis. ámmā ḳéśerə di-ḥōmis dé éʔeb, nəgōfiʔš əl-ṣōdə wə-nərōgimš əl bíli, nəʿāḳalš men ʿālə. wə-nərūd bis ḳánəho wələ mišírud.

As for the smaller shell, the plastron, we put fish on it and eat off it. As for the carapace of the turtle, that big shell, we use it to cover fish or we use it as a lid to cover something: we put it right over it. Or we use it (as a trough) for watering livestock or anything else that comes to drink.[262]

8.8.3. Remora (*lēmi*) and Turtles (*áḥmis*) (i)

lēmi ki šaʕrókən tuyh wə-buʔúrənš al nəlātʕaš, nəʕāḳalš ḥayy bə-rīho. korúmma śīnən ḥōmis nəkōtifš bə-dánub bə-śóʔhor wələ nəʕāmer hiš ʕéḳəlhe d-ʸáḥśiš bə-śéba di-ʕālə wə-nəbúlugš. ki búlugən, nəfāraḥ hiš śóʔhor w-iyhé iṭúher d-is w-ilāsək ʕis.

If we go fishing and catch a remora, we don't kill it, but instead put it alive into some water (inside the dugout). If we see a turtle, we tie a length of fishing line to its (i.e., the remora's) tail or insert a hook into its upper lip, and we let it go (down into the sea). Once we've let it go, we pay out the fishing line behind it and it goes straight for it (i.e., the turtle) and attaches itself to it.

ki lásak ʕis, náʕnən wə-nišmērišin bə-śóʔhor wə-se tfōrid. tfōrid diᵍʸēmə w-ol déhər: iḳtiṭār ʕis fonś wə-tšrāḳaḥ. wə-lal tšrāḳaḥ náʕnən bis bénɛ se wə-tsé (= di-sé) lēmi. w-al ibúləg tus ʕaf l-énkaʕs. wə-korúmma lásak bə-láḥḥim, ṭaʰ nəšōgi ʕaf l-énkaʕš wələ ʕaf təbṣaḳ dié śóʔhor.

If it has attached itself to it (i.e., the turtle), we pull it in hand over hand, and it tries to get away. It tries to escape by diving down, but it can't (stay there) for ever: it runs out of breath and has to come up again. And when it surfaces, we pull it in and pull it in with all our strength, it and its remora. We don't let it go until we've brought it right in. And if it (i.e., the remora) at-

---

[262] The carapace is also used as a pen for young kids.

taches itself to a shark, we do just the same to bring it in or until it breaks your line.

8.8.4. Remora (*lēmi*) and Turtles (*áḥmis*) (ii)

ki ʾíno lēmi w-ol ṣā́mə wə-śīni ḥōmis ibōləg dhí lēmi id rīho w-iyhé iʿúmur biš ʿékəlhe. ki śīni tos, iṭābuḵ bis se bə-ḳáśerə. išmḗśiyīn tus dhí bə-śúʾhur ʿaf l-érḳahs súwətsé (= sé wə-di-sé) lēmi. lal išōʾikis wə-sé šíʾiki hūri, yíšxaf tus bə-míšxaf.

If there is a remora and it is alive, and he (i.e., the fisherman) sees a turtle, he looses his remora into the sea, after inserting a hook into it. If it (i.e., the remora) sees it (i.e., the turtle), it latches onto it, onto its carapace.[263] He (i.e., the fisherman) plays it on the line until he manages to bring it up (i.e., to the surface), it and its remora. When he has brought it close, when it is right by the dugout, he gaffs it with the hooked gaff.

wə-ʾíno korúmma tərá bə-hūri wələ təlāta, ʾíno di-yáʿnən ʿaf tšíʾiki ḥōz di-bāʿ. wə-ṭad yáʿihiṣ míšxaf w-íšxaf tus wə-dé ilúi bə-śúʾhur kor ʿal ʿə́do túḵʿud di-gʸḗmə. lúʾu yáʿihiṣ? dé di-áʿihiṣ ʿes?

And sometimes, if there are two men in the dugout, or three, one will pull it in until it is about a *bāʿ* distance away from them. Another will dive down with the gaff and gaff it, the first holding tight onto the line so that it (i.e., the turtle) can't dive back down to the bottom. Why does he dive down? That man who dives down to it?

---

[263] Saying: *ṭibāḵo tyóʾo lēmi!* "She stuck (i.e., to a person or action) like a remora!" and *yɛ! kān ṭābeḵ tyóʾo lēmi!* "Hey, he stuck like a remora!"

korúmma śīni dihé śúʔhur təbāṣ̌aḳ w-ol ṭār máḥdišo di-ḥōmis lal tšrākaḥ wə-tígbib bə-rīho wə-lāṭ śównə hūri wə-śównə máxluḳ ṯḥādiš wə-táʕihiṣ.

(He does so) if he sees that his line might break, or that the hook is not embedded in the turtle firmly enough to stop it getting away. When it comes up and lies there on the surface of the water, and sees a dugout or sees people, it will break free (i.e., with the extra strength lent it by its terror) and dive right back down again.

ki ʔə́duf ʕis wə-béʔeris ki bə-ṭaḥ wə-ki bə-rínhem ṭad mes ḥazíz. ḥówzuz tus men ḳār. mes ḳaḥélahan ḳúwdur túyhin bə-rīho ʕaf l-íbihel wə-lāṭ fōḳeš túyhin. wə-ʔíno d-ifākiš ḳaḥélahan w-iḥarír ʕiš ʕaf l-ibhúl. wə-meš kan íkkin tyóʔo kēfə.

If he manages to get hold of it and catch it, the cutting of its throat is the same whether on shore or out at sea: it is cut across the throat. Its eggs are boiled in water until cooked and ready to eat. They are then broken open. Some people break open the (raw) eggs and heat them on the fire until they are cooked (i.e., like scrambled eggs). They look a bit like cooked colostrum.

ḳáśerə igúwfə biš əl-bíli tyóʔo ṣōdə, tyóʔo ʕífif. yəḥófer nōgir wə-d-ibúləg ʕífuf di-ḳānə, wələ bíli tyóʔo ṣafláḥa wə-lāṭ d-igōfi dis əl-bíli.

The carapace is turned upside down over something, fish for instance, or a young kid. He digs a hole and puts a young kid inside, or something such as (food in a) clay cooking pot. Then he puts it (i.e., the carapace) upside down over this thing.

8.8.5. Turtle and Fish Eggs

ḥōmis tšrā́ḳah men rínhem lol tə‘égib təbrέ. tšrā́ḳah id ḥáməhal wə-lā́ṭ təḥōfir wə-té‘yig. wə-təkōtilin se əl-ḳaḥélahan wə-təktə́naḥ id rínhem. sá‘a tféḳiś, išrōḳah dhin men ‘abgḗrə wə-yəḥóbiyən id rínhem. korúmma ná́ḥziz ḥōmis, nəṭúher nəḥōri ṭah wə-na‘túbur men məshī́bo.

A female turtle comes out of the sea when it wants to give birth. It comes out onto the dry foreshore and then digs a hole and gives birth. It covers its eggs over (with sand) and goes back to the sea. When they hatch (lit. 'break open'), they (i.e., the baby turtles) leave their hole and crawl to the sea. If we kill a female turtle we go along the beach and look for signs of it having dragged herself out onto land.

korúmma śínən məshī́bo, nəkā́bur ri’ di-məshī́bo: korúmma ol ksé’ən ḥōmis, nəḥōfer wə-nərā́ḳah ḳaḥélahan. korúmma ksé’ən ḥōmis, nəḳā́libs wə-ná́ḥzizis. ki ksé’ən ḳaḥélahan, nəzá‘ihin wə-nəfṣá‘ihin wə-nəḳā́dirhin bə-śā́dihir bə-ṭhidítš wə-lā́ṭ íkkin tyó’o kḗfə. wə-lā́ṭ níti.

If we see such tracks, we follow them to see where they come to an end. If we don't find the turtle, we dig down and remove the eggs. If we find the turtle, we turn it over on its back and cut its throat. If we find eggs we take them, crack them open and cook them on their own in water in a clay pot: they look rather like cooked colostrum. And then we eat them.

bə́ḳəhāl di-ṣōdə ḳúwbeb bə-śéyāṭ wə-yúwte. korúmma ḳíder ibťó‘ug.

The eggs of fish are roasted on the fire and eaten. If they're cooked in water, they crumble away to nothing.

8.9. Dolphin (ʿílǝho)

ʿílǝho nítiš, ǝnḥárḥer meyh teh wǝ-níti. wǝ-meyh teh ḥámʔī fáḥerǝ, ímhe tyóʔo ḥámʔī. wǝ-korúmma tuyk meyh dǝ́laḳ wǝ-hōhǝn ṣǝ́ṭʿak, āṣ́aḥ mǝ́nhi mer w-ǝš́ǝ́fǝl meyh.

We eat a dolphin. We heat its flesh and we eat it. And its flesh is all fat—it melts just like butter oil. And if I eat a lot of it when I'm really hungry, I get a belly ache and severe diarrhoea as a result.

ʿílǝho ol iʔōkib id ḳérḳor w-al íti bǝ-śúʔhur, ol nǝgōbiš kal mínzek. wǝ-nǝnōzik tuš korúmma iʿud ǝl-dēfǝ dhí di-bīyo. w-al nǝnōzik ʿílǝho dé éʔeb, nǝnōzik di-ḳíḥǝn. lúʔu al nǝnōzik dé éʔeb? izáʿa ʿin dihán ḳīyud w-al nǝgōsir hiš, yáʿṣ́iṣ́ ʿin.

A dolphin doesn't go into a fish trap nor does it take the bait on a fishing line. We can only catch it with a spear: we stab it if we see it going along beside its mother. We don't spear the adult dolphin, only the little one. Why don't we spear the adult one? It will go off with our rope-lines and we can't manage it—it's much stronger than we are.

ʿílǝho nǝṣālib tus tyóʔo léḥḥīm wǝ-tyóʔo ṣōdǝ, bíśi ṣalb di-ʿíreb tuš. nǝnōzik tuš wǝ-náʿnǝn diyál núfuš ʿaf l-igdáḥ. wǝ-lāṭ iʔúwge mǝḳǝláʿa ʿaf l-iṣmé.

We slaughter a dolphin just like a shark or a fish—there's no special way to slaughter it. We spear it and drag it towards us until it's close by. Then it is beaten to death with a heavy club.

fānǝ yǝʿúwgub hiš. náʿa dé bǝ-zámān di-šīn al ʿād yǝʿúwgub hiš tyóʔo di-fānǝ. ki ksōwi ʔǝ́kub id šábak[A] ǝw id míśgir ǝw šǝ́rḳaḥ, bíśi *d-ínihaḥ biš tyóʔo di-fānə. fānə bíśi šábak^A wə-bíśi míśgir, kal nízik wə-śúʔhur.*

In earlier times it was highly prized. Now, in these times we live in, it's no longer prized as it used to be. If it's found trapped in a *šábak* or *míśgir*[264] net, or if it's stranded on shore, there is no great rejoicing as there used to be. Before there were no large *šábak* nets and no *míśgir* nets, just a spear or a fishing line.

8.10. Harvesting the Sea: Non-Fish

8.10.1. Low Tide and Gathering Shellfish (*šáḥak*)

rínhem šīn təmōlə wə-tədōmir men ḥorf u-men ṣērəb. wə-tə́šḥak šīn bénɛ men éʔemed di-ḍʸōti wə-men ṣerébhən. tə́šḥak šīn ʿaf náʿmer: "rínhem sféro wə-tə́šḥak šīn!" nəʿāmer šḥā́ko wələ kērhe nikā́ṣo, kērhe milóʔo.

Where we live, the sea comes far in and is very rough during the summer monsoon and in the winter. You go in search of shellfish a lot during the season of *ḍʸōti* 'the end of the summer (just before the monsoon)', and at *ṣerébhən* 'the end of the monsoon (just before *ṣēreb* 'winter')'. With us, you go off in search of shellfish when we say: "The tide has gone right out, so come and look for shellfish with us." We say *šḥā́ko* 'the tide has gone out', or *kērhe nikā́ṣo* 'the tide is nearly out', *kērhe milóʔo* 'the tide is nearly in'.

---

[264] *míśgir*, a type of small drift net with a mesh finer than the *ṣīni* 'cast net'. It was used along the north coast around Ḥadibo, where it is also called *ḳáṭabə*. It was made of *ġazəl* 'cotton' and was set between the shore and the sea, at right angles to the shore.

wə-ínihaḥ éʔefo sāʿa di-šḥāḳo rínhem wə-sféro ḳor nəšáḥiḳin wə-nəkōsə kə-šáḥaḳ ṣōdə di-ʿotírir b-eḳəléṭo.

And people are very happy when the tide has gone out or is really low so that we can go and look for shellfish, and find fish flapping around in the pools left by the receding tide.

8.10.2. Edible Shellfish: Cowries (ḳáḥəbə~ḳaḥbōbə)

ḳaḥbōbə ḳúwbub w-ol ḳúwdur w-ol yúwte tus né[2A]. wə-ʔíno d-iḳādir ḳaḥbōbə. ḳáḥəbə əw ḳaḥbōbə nəʿāgub his ḳor nənáḥag bis ki bíśi bis eḳənīyo. wə-ki ʔíno bis eḳənīyo níti tus.

ḳaḥbōbə 'cowries' are roasted and not boiled in water. No one eats them raw. Some cook them in water. We like to play with ḳáḥəbə or ḳaḥbōbə 'cowries' if they're just empty shells. But if they are still alive, we like to eat the flesh inside them.

wə-nətōbers wə-nəḳāder mes eḳənīyo wələ nékəbib. korúmma nékəbib tus, nékəbib tus se bə-ḳaḥf. wə-korúmma dálaḳ wə-ʿigíbən nəḳāder, nətōbər túsən wə-nəzáʿ mésən ḥáṣəhal wə-nəḳāder.

We break (the shells) open and we either cook the meat in water or we roast it. If we roast it, we do so in its shell. If we have a lot of them and we want to boil them in water, we break them open and take out the pieces of flesh and boil (them).

wə-korúmma nənáḥag bísən, nəzáʿa dis āʔam wə-nənēśurs óʔorəm wə-nəʿāmer his: "íyhin íləhe." wə-yúwihurs disé 'mánḳaʿ' wə-yúwihurs disé 'fólihi'. wə-nəʿáḳalsən ber əl-fānə ḥīn. wə-ṭa[h] nəšōgi wə-ṭa[h] nənáḥag bísən.

And if we want to play with them, we take the largest one and make it go along and say to it: "You're a cow." And following behind it is its 'year-old heifer', and following behind this is its 'new calf'. And we put them down on the ground in front of us (i.e., as if we were herding them). That's what we do and that's how we play with them.

8.10.3. Different Edible Shellfish (ʿáfšer, di-meriméro, ṭəhákəhān, di-ṣíʾəfo)

ʿáfšer yúwge ki kíder tuš kor tšrákaḥ meš ekəniyo wə-yúwte tuš. wə-korúmma kíhen, nəʿákal tuš aḥśíš kor ki bíśi biš ekəniyo nəʿákalš kor əntákibinš kə-šáḥak, kə-di-meriméro wə-kə-ṭəhákəhān wə-kə-tṣíʾəfo (= di-ṣíʾəfo) kor nəʿāmerhin aḥnāko.

ʿáfšer 'turban shells': if they're to be boiled in water, they're broken open to get at the flesh inside and this is eaten. If they're small shells, we put them to one side, so that once they're emptied of food we can add them to the other (emptied shells) of the shellfish collected at low tide: with the di-meriméro 'dark-coloured periwinkles' and the ṭəhákəhān 'black and white periwinkles' and the periwinkle with the di-ṣíʾəfo 'very fine operculum' (lit. 'fish scale'), so that we can make a necklaces out of them.

nəʾōgíhin wə-nənōfíhin wə-niśkik túyhin id kaʾ, wə-lāṭ nəʿāmer ḥank. wə-nənáḥig bíhin ṭhídin. wə-ináḥig bíhin embūriye, w-inkáḥəkaḥ bíhin.

We knock them (to the shape we want), bore a hole in them and thread them on a piece of twine to make a necklace. We play together with them. Children play with them and rattle and clash them together.

ʿáfšer biš bíli tyóʾo sígidə di-máxluḳ. ki biš sígidə men ṣəlá, əntōri tus bə-líššin wə-lāṭ nəlēsuks bə-fíʿo.

ʿáfšer 'turban shells' have something (i.e., an operculum) that looks like the prayer mark on a human (forehead). If it has (this) 'prayer mark', we wet it with our tongue and stick it on our forehead (i.e., to look like a prayer mark).

8.10.4. Conch or Triton (ḥánṣ̌ə) and Clam (gáḥbān) (i)

ʾíno šáḥaḳ di-ḳúwbub wə-ʾíno di-ḳúwder. ḥánṣ̌ə wə-gáḥbān iḳúbəbo wə-lāṭ fuwṣ́óʿo bə-ʾōbən kor itébero wə-yúwte méyhi ekəniyo. kuwsóʾo ki ešḥāḳo rínhem wə-kuwsóʾo lal ʿə́wihaṣ əl-múṣəliḥ.

Some shellfish are roasted and some are boiled in water. The ḥánṣ̌ə 'conch' or 'triton' and gáḥbān 'clam' are roasted. They're struck one hard blow with a stone to break them open to get at the meat inside to eat it. They are found at low tide or when (people are) diving for pearlshell oysters.

ʾíno ḥánṣ̌ə núwbe tus ḥánṣ̌ə əw ʿárho di-ḥánṣ̌ə ki šīʿer bis. w-īʿúwrub ber ʿárho di-ḥánṣ̌ə. ḥánṣ̌ə tíkkən kə-nəkīb di-tímiher, yəhōger tímiher kor éʾefo ʿa l-ílḳaṭ ḥálhul wə-bíšera diš d-iṭārib men tímera kal bə-rúxsa[A].

There is a type of conch or triton called ḥánṣ̌ə or 'the voice of the ḥánṣ̌ə' if a loud trumpeting sound is made through it. It is well known by everyone as the 'the voice of the ḥánṣ̌ə'. A conch or triton like this is to be found with the guardian of the communal date palm plantation, the man who guards the date palms to stop people gleaning the half-and-half dates[265] and the fully ripe ones that have fallen from the palm, except at permitted times.[266]

ḥánṣə núwfaḥ tus men dánub ḥōz di-kérṣə[267] d-íṣəbáˤ kōr lal ināfaḥ tos dhí əl-xálfə təˤāmer ˤárho men ter dig əw dsí men ter.

The *ḥánṣə* is blown into across (an aperture) at its tip, about a finger-joint's distance from it, so that when he blows across the hole he's made, it makes a loud trumpeting sound from this opening or from its own mouth.

8.10.5. Conch or Triton (*ḥánṣə*) and Clam (*gáḥbān*) (ii)

ḥánṣə nəˤágub his bénɛ ˤan šáḥak, wə-mes ekənīyo diláko wə-škēro. w-ol yə́wte néʔ w-al bénɛ ḳúwbub. ḳúwdur w-áḥsan ki ḳidíro. wə-ḥánṣə tirí ḥanšíti: ḥánṣə d-iṣābi ol nəˤāmer bis xálfə kor nəšúˤur bis. nəˤāmer xálfə bə-ḥánṣə diž. wə-diž gáˤalhil wə-nəˤāmər hes ḥinbōbə.

We like the *ḥánṣə* 'conch' or 'triton' best of all the shellfish gathered at low tide. It has a lot of flesh and is really delicious. It's not eaten raw nor is it often roasted. It is cooked in water. It's best when cooked in water. And there are two kinds of *ḥánṣə*: the one 'with fingers' which we don't pierce to make a

---

[265] *ḥálhul*, dates one half of which is yellow and crisp, the other half ripe, brown and soft, seen as very delicious.

[266] He blows into the conch at fixed times of the day to signal the opening and closing of the communal date palm plantation to gleaners.

[267] *kérṣə* 'the gap between two finger joints'.

loud trumpeting noise. We make a hole in the other kind of
ḥánṣə. This kind is round and fat and we call it ḥinbōbə.

*wə-bis išúʿur nəḳīb l-əməṭārih. ḥánṣə diž mes šem d-iṣābiʿ al šuʿúr
bis lə-ḥārif. bas ṭiy méyhi eḳənīyo, wə-ṭad méyhi ṭaʿm wə-ṭiy méyhi
šīḥiḳo. w-al təlásko bə-ḳéśʾor, kəwsóʾo ṭabihíto əl-šīmi w-əl-rúʿud di-
rīho.*

The *nəḳīb* 'guardian of the communal date palm plantations' trumpets through it (as a signal for gleaners to enter or leave). The kind of conch 'with fingers' isn't the one used to make a signal to those harvesting the dates. But the two kinds provide the same kind of food: they taste the same and the way of collecting them is the same. They don't stick on rocks, but are found crawling (lit. 'stretched out flat') over areas of white sand or sea grass.

8.10.6. Chiton (*śéyḥino*) (i)

*śéyḥino bis líššin iʿúmur his 'líššin di-śéyḥino'. śéyḥino yúwte néʾ wə-
ki ḳidíro wə-ki ḳibíbo. wə-rúwḳah mes məḳáṣihi d-íkkin mes bə-
ṭādaʿ. wə-se məḳáṣihi al yúwten: ʿiś tyóʾo mēsən ʿáṣiyaś tyóʾo
óʾōbən.*

The chiton has a tongue (of flesh) which we call the 'tongue of the chiton'. The chiton is eaten raw or boiled or roasted. The shell plates are removed, those that lie along its back. The shell plates are not eaten: they're hard, some of them as hard as stone.

8.10.7. Chiton (śéyḥino) (ii)

śéyḥino təlēsuk bə-ḳéśʔor wə-ʕa śúwnə tus kal ki šḥāḳo. wə-nəʕāgub his kor nə́ḳbibs wə-nəḳādirs wə-níti néʔ mes líššin. se mer líššin, wə-di-kíʔi dɛr-mā-dɛr śíbihe. wə-mes ṭādaʕ ṭifherítin wə-ʕáṣ̌iyaṣ̌ tyóʔo óʔōbən, wə-bíśi d-itīhin.

The chiton sticks onto rocks and can only be seen when the tide is out. We like to roast it or cook it in water, or we eat the fleshy part (lit. 'tongue') raw. What lies inside (i.e., beneath the shell plates) is the 'tongue', and what remains, that part which goes around the circumference of the shell, is śíbihe 'the lips' (i.e., the girdle). And on its back are 'fingernails' (i.e., the overlapping shell plates) and they are as hard as stone. No one eats them.

śéyḥino sté tos ki ʕīyək néʔ wə-ki ʕīyək ḳādər wə-ʕa yəʕúwḳal tos sáʕte. éʔefo ki ṣə́ṭaʕ šáḥaken kor yəḳtōnə w-iśōbaʕ.

A chiton is eaten either raw or cooked in water—as you like. But it mustn't be left for long (i.e., as it goes off quickly). When people were hungry,[268] they'd go to gather shellfish at low tide to have something to eat and to fill their bellies.

8.10.8. Rock Oyster (zōkə)

zōkə yúwge tus se bə-ḳéśʔor. yúwge tos id riʔ. wə-yəʔōgiz dé diyál kāl l-igé kor ʕa təfṣ̌áʕ. dé di-kāl, lal iʔōgə, yišḳúʕi mes ter wə-tḳéʔe mes ekəniyo bə-ḳānə al fiṣ̌óʕo w-al nətə́ṣəro. wə-rúwḳaḥ tos bə-bíli ḳino.

---

[268] According to Aḥmad Saʕd Taḥkí, in times of hunger people eat especially śéyḥino 'chiton', ʕáfšer 'turban shell', ḥfoš 'sea-slug', ḥánṣ̌ə 'conch' or 'triton' and məḳhīro 'limpet'.

núwkar tos men ḳānə wə-tšrāḳaḥ id ter. yúwte tos néʔ. wə-mes ʕāḳer tyóʔo mer di-šíbdə wə-mes kān libíni.

The *zōḳə* 'rock oysters' are struck off the rock to which they are attached. It (i.e., a chunk of rock oysters) is struck directly on the top (lit. 'on the head'). The person who doesn't know how to do it properly can't knock them off without smashing them to pieces (i.e., and spoiling them). The expert, when he strikes a blow, manages to unlock its 'door', keeping the flesh inside entire, uncrushed and still whole. It (i.e., the flesh) is then removed (from the shell) with something small. It is poked from inside and brought out. It's eaten raw. Its size is something like the small lobe of the liver (lit. 'the stomach of the liver') and it's pale in colour.

8.10.9. Limpets (*məḵḥīro*)

məḵḥīro yúwte tos néʔ w-iḳúwbub w-iḳúwdur. məḵḥīro yúwte ṭaʰ, w-iḳúwdur kə-šáhak əw aḥṣiš. wə-ḳúwbub. wə-məḵḥīro diš bíśi bis ekəniyo əw ber tōwi ekəniyo, zúwmaʕ bísən kor ḳúwḥur bísən ḥirórə di-məḳdērə wələ di-bómbə wələ sāro.

məḵḥīro 'limpets' are eaten raw, roasted or cooked in water. *məḵḥīro* are eaten just like that (i.e., as you find them, raw), boiled along with other shellfish gathered at low tide, or (cooked) on their own. And they can be roasted. Those *məḵḥīro* which have no meat or from which the meat has already been removed are kept to be used as scrapers to scrape away the food burned on to the bottom of the cooking pots: burned-on maize or finger millet or what remains after clarifying butter to make butter oil.

8.10.10. Nerites (*ṭʸúbər ʔə́bəhān*)

ṭʸúbər ʔə́bəhān šáḥakan tuš kə-šáḥak wə-ḳúwdur tuš wələ ḳúwbub, wə-bíśi d-itīš néʔ.

We gather *ṭʸúbər ʔə́bəhān*[269] 'nerite topshells' along with other edible shellfish at low tide. They are cooked in water or roasted. No one eats them raw.

8.10.11. Cone Shells (*fáʕrhur*)

fáʕrher bíśi d-īti meyh ekənīyo. bas nəʕágub hiš kor nənáḥag biš bə-ḥāṣir wələ bə-gād wələ bə-ṣ̌iṣ̌áʕa. nəfōduḳš b-iṣbéʕi w-iyhé yəḥélin.

No one eats the flesh of the *fáʕrher* 'cone shell', but we like to play with it: on an oblong date palm floor mat, on a tanned hide, or on an area of flat rock. We give it a sharp pinch between two fingers (i.e., like a top) and it spins round and round.

8.10.12. Abalone (*iʔīdānə*)

iʔīdānə: al dálaḳ šīn ʔidəhántən, al tyóʔo məḳáḥir. wə-ʔidānə šker mes šáḥak ʕan šáḥak di-məḳhīro. wə-ʔidānə ikōsə tos korúmma šḥáḳo ḳúwlub ʕans ʔə́bəhān wə-təkósəs nhaṭ ʔə́bəhān lísko tyóʔo məḳhīro wə-tyóʔo śeyḥíno. ḳúwbub wə-ḳúwdur w-al yúwte néʔ tyóʔo śeyḥíno wə-məḳhīro. wə-mes məḳhīro di-ʔidānə bíśi d-iʕágub his.

The *iʔīdānə* 'abalone': we don't have many abalone where we live, not like limpets. Gathering abalone is better (i.e., easier) than gathering limpets when the tide is out. Abalone can be

---

[269] *ṭʸúbər ʔə́bəhān* 'stone breaker' because it is such a hard shell to crack open.

found at low tide by turning over rocks: you find it under rocks, sticking to them like limpets or chiton. (The abalone) is roasted or cooked in water, but it's not eaten raw like the chiton and the limpet. And as for the shell of the abalone, no one bothers about it or wants it.

8.11. Harvesting the Sea: Other Sea Creatures

8.11.1. Brittle Star (*di-ḥaṣáhan di-rínhem*)

di-ḥaṣáhan di-rínhem: ksé⁷es wə-śínis. bíśi di-śí⁷iš. kúwse tus bə-ṣīṣá⁵a di-keśərīn di-bíhin rīho. w-al déher tšḥák ⁵is, tə⁵águb tíkkən bə-rīho. ki šḥáko ⁵is wə-šḥabílo šīhum, tə⁵águb l-ósiri id rīho. u-bíśi bis bíli di-škéro əw l-ínihaḥ bis ḥéyhi ki ksé⁷es. embūriye diyál ⁵érebis ya⁷ṣáṣis.

The *di-ḥaṣáhan di-rínhem*[270] 'brittle star': it's to be found and it's seen, but no one bothers about it. It's found on flat areas of rock where there's water. You don't always see it at low tide because it likes to be in water. If the tide goes out, leaving it behind, and it feels the heat of the sun, it tries to go down into water. There is nothing good or useful about it and no one's happy should he come across it. Children who don't know about it are scared of it.

8.11.2. Starfish (*négəmə di-rínhem*)

négəmə di-rínhem tyó⁷o di-ḥaṣáhan: ṭaʰ mes ⁵agébihin tyó⁷o di-ḥaṣáhan.

---

[270] *di-ḥaṣáhan di-rínhem* 'giant centipede of the sea' (*di-ḥaṣáhan* 'Scolopendra').

The starfish is like the *di-ḥaṣáhan* 'brittle star': feelings towards it are the same as those towards the *di-ḥaṣáhan* 'brittle star'.

8.11.3. Sea Cucumber (*fáḥal di-rínhem*)

fáḥal di-rínhem kúwse bə-ríḥo wə-tə́šḥaḳ ʿis, wə-bíśi d-iʿágeb his. bas ḥánhən nəʔáṣiṣin bis ṭḥídin wələ ḥéyhi gélbihi. u-bíśi bis féydə u-bíśi tos d-īti u-bíśi bis d-išʿárik.

The *fáḥal di-rínhem*²⁷¹ 'sea cucumber' is found in water when the tide has gone out, but no one wants it. We just used to scare one another with it, or we'd frighten a mountain person (i.e., one who is ignorant of sea matters) with it. It's useless: no one eats it and no one fishes with it (i.e., as bait).

náʿa dé bə-zámān di-náʿa, gídaḥ ṭad men əl-ʿāli wə-śīnis šīn bə-sakáṭeri wə-ʿúmur: "ʿēyək mēsən. táʿihiṣ ʿísən wə-təḳōdersən wə-nēgib túsən ʿaf təḳśíʿan wə-təʿúmur ʿísən id bíli wə-núkiʿin ínhi wə-hōhun ətōger."

Now, in this time, a man arrived from the Gulf and saw it here with us on Soqotra and said: "I want some of them. Dive for them and cook them in water; spread them out in the sun to dry, and then put them in something and bring them to me and I'll buy (them)."

8.11.4. Sea Urchins (*úʔiriʿ~úʔiriḥ*, pl. *iʔiráḥan~íʔiraḥ*)

úʔiriḥ al tə́šḥaḳ ʿiš w-íkkin bə-śíṣərhin əl-ḳéśʔor. w-úʔiriḥ ki rə́kutk ʿiš iṣúʿud wə-yaḥṭímim mek di-ḥalf dé di-ṣaʿādək. wə-təʔáṣaḥ tyóʔo

---

²⁷¹ *fáḥal di-rínhem* 'sea penis'; smaller versions are called *míḳəliz di-rinhem* 'sea penis of a child'.

*korúmma ʔéṣaḥk men síkərát.*²⁷² *wə-nəfōrid ˤanš ki eḳdúmən ˤiš w-al nənéher dé bə-ḥalf w-al nərōkit id ḥalf biš íʔiráḥan. wə-bíśi biš féydə dʸáḥṣiš.*

You don't go along the rocks and search for the *úʔiriḥ* 'sea urchin' (*Diadema setosum*) at low tide. It's found in cracks and crevices in rocks. And if you tread on the *úʔiriḥ* 'sea urchin', (its spines) stick right into you and break off in your skin right there. And it's as painful as the final pains of death. We keep well away from it if we see it. We don't walk about in that place and we don't step anywhere where there are *iʔiráḥan~íʔiraḥ úʔiriḥ* 'sea urchins'. It is of no use at all.

8.11.5. Sea Urchins (*di-kōriz*, pl. *il-kōriz*) (i)

il-kōriz nəˤágub his wə-nəzáˤas menól nəksés. wə-nəkōsis bə-śíṣərhin di-rínhem wə-nḥaṭ rīho kúwse. w-al kúwse kal ki nəḳāṣo rínhem di-šáḥak. nəzáˤas wə-nənāṣers wə-nīti mes ḳaḥélǝhān lhé nəkósihin mes bə-ḳaḥf.

We like the *il-kōriz* 'sea urchins' and we take them wherever we find them. We find them in cracks and crevices in the rocks in the sea and under water. They are only foound when the tide has gone out, at low tide. We take it and we split it in half and we eat its eggs (i.e., gonads or 'sea coral'), those that we find in its shell.

---

²⁷² *síkərát* (*əl-mōt*) 'death throes: shaking and trembling before death' < Arabic *sakrat al-maut*, 'agony of death'.

méyhin kān kerkə́mhān wə-hínhən ḳíhun wə-réˤeṣ́ tyóʔo lúḳəmə di-məḳdɛ̄rə libɛ́ko. il-kōriz al fáḥerə éʔefo yəˤágib his. ˤag rínhi wə-ṭéyḥḥi iyhé d-iˤágub his. éʔefo gə́lbəho al yəˤágub his.

They (i.e., the gonads) are yellowish in colour and small and soft like a fat kernel of maize. The *il-kōriz* 'sea urchins' are not liked by everyone: a fisherman and a man of the coast likes them. People from the mountains don't like them.

8.11.6. Sea Urchins (*di-kōriz*, pl. *il-kōriz*) (ii)

ʔíno il-kōriz wə-ʔíno fʔiraḥ ḥāher wə-fʔiraḥ ˤāfer. ki rə́kutk ˤiš əw láhamk toš b-íʔid iṣúˤud, yaḥtímim mek di-gad ˤaf išérḳaḥ mek dur.

There are the *il-kōriz* sea urchins and the *fʔiraḥ* sea urchins: one black kind and one reddish kind. If you step on it or touch it with your hand its (spines) pierce your skin and break off in it and make you bleed.

il-kōriz al təṣúˤud w-al taḥtímim wə-yúwte mes eḳəníyo diš bə-ḳā́nə. wə-mes eḳəníyo kérkəhim tyóʔo se kɛ̄fə. rúwḳaḥ tus id terr wə-lāṭ núwḳab tus men riʔ b-óʔobən wələ tfāṣ́ˤas tse (= di-sé) míˤsil ˤaf taˤmér ḳáḥyif wə-tftílim. wə-lāṭ təḳóhor wə-sté.

The (spines of the) *il-kōriz* 'sea urchins' do not pierce the skin or break off in it. They contain edible material inside, yellowish like cooked colostrum. It (i.e., this kind of sea urchin) is removed (from where it was) and then the top is cracked open with a stone, or tapped hard against a rock uncovered by the receding tide to make a half-shell that breaks away. And then you scrape out (the edible part) and eat it.

8.11.7. Sea Cucumber (ḥfoš)

ḥfoš ḥə́wre meš b-aḥté wə-ḥə́wre meš bə-šām korúmma rínhem šḥā́ḳo wə-sféro. ki kísək ḥfoš tíśkek tuš míśkek. míśkek íkkin men ʔáyyəᴬ ṭarb. yə́ṭifin riʔ di-míśkek kor lal tíśkek diɛ́ ḥfoš yəšíśkek. ʔíno d-ikósə də́laḵ wə-ʔíno diyál ikósa wə-ʔíno d-ikóse ṣ̌íyur.

The sea-slug is hunted by night and by day at low tide, when the tide is far out. If you find a sea-slug, you thread it on a skewer: a skewer of any kind of wood. The tip of the skewer is whittled to a point so that when you want to spit your sea-slug on it it slides on easily. Some people find lots of sea cucumbers, some find none at all, and some find only a few.

zúwˤa ḥfoš id ḳáˤar wələ id mə́sṭaḥ wələ id máhger[273] wələ id mə́sxan.[274] wə-lāṭ ḳúwdur ˤaf l-ibəhúl. wə-lāṭ rúwḳaḥ wə-šódiyin éʔefo. ʔíno d-iṣ̌úˤubš wə-ʔíno d-iḥə́sal wə-ʔíno d-imáˤaš b-íʔid. wə-yúwte.

The sea cucumbers are taken to the house or to the date-drying ground or to the hut in the date palm garden or to the monsoon shelter. Then they are boiled in water[275] until ready to eat. They are removed from the cooking pot and shared out amongst everyone. Some bite into it there and then, some cut it into strips and some pull bits off with their hands. And it's eaten.

---

[273] máhger, a cleared area or hut built in a date palm garden, lived in while working the dates.

[274] mə́sxan, a small hut built to shelter people from the strong monsoon winds.

[275] The sea-slug usually has to be cooked twice: the first time the water turns green, the second time it remains clear.

8.11.8. Crabs (ḥansĩʔo, pl. ḥánsə) (i)

ḥansĩʔo: ʔíno ḥansĩʔo di-yúwte wə-ʔíno diyál yúwte. ḥansĩʔo di-men rīho ḥāli wə-ḥansĩʔo men ḥángəgo di-ḳéśʔor wələ di-šírəhām men bar, wə-ḥansĩʔo tíkkən bə-ḥalīlo di-šīmi, ḥansĩʔo libīni, al yúwte. ḥansĩʔo ṭey tíkkən bə-ḳéśʔor mes šem mĩʕsil bə-rīho di-rínhem.

The crab: there are crabs that are eaten and crabs that are not eaten. Crabs of sweet water, crabs of the rockpools or of the seashore vegetation, and crabs that are found on the shore on sand—white crabs—are not eaten. One kind of crab is found on rocks called *mĩʕsil* 'rocks splashed by the sea or revealed at low tide'.

ḥansĩʔo ṭiy mes šem ḳśébeb wə-ṭiy al mes šem ḳśébeb. u-méyhi kān ḥəwrōti yuwtēyo. wə-yəʕúwgub béne ḥansĩʔo mes šem ḳśébeb. lúʔu mes šem ḳśébeb? bis málḳaz di-ʕə́ḳār wə-líbək, wə-málḳaz ṭad ḳíhən. w-íkin bis te^h də́lak ʕan diš bíśi bis málḳaz. íful yúwte túyhi? yəʕāgəb l-íḳbib tósən w-al iʕāgəb l-əḳdórən bə-rīho. ṭáʕm bis ki ḳibíbo al tyóʔo ki ḳedíro bə-rīho.

One kind is called *ḳśébeb* and another is not called *ḳśébeb*. The two kinds that are very dark in colour are both eaten. The crab called *ḳśébeb* is much liked. Why is it called *ḳśébeb*?[276] It has one claw which is large and fat and one claw which is small.[277] It has a lot more meat than the kind without the (large) claw. How are they both eaten? They are liked when roasted but not

---

[276] *ḳśébeb*, of terrain: 'spiky, pitted and very hard': these crabs have a hard and prickly shell.

[277] A fiddler crab.

when boiled in water. The roasted one has a quite different flavour from the one boiled in water.

wə-sehən iʿúwgub his kor šəʿúwrok bis ṣōdə, iʿúmur mes śámdə. se śámdə al təntəbul tyóʾo śámdə dʸáḥśiš, tyóʾo ʿídi. wələ níbihil wələ ḥanśíʾo intíbul físaʿ. wə-šənēbur ki nibériš ṣōdə. térəbaḥt inōbirs tyóʾo ṣōdə w-al tšnēbul, w-al bíro təntəʿérən.

And this kind is wanted for catching fish: it's used as bait. As bait, it doesn't fall apart like some other baits, such as a sardine-type baitfish. A bait of a chunk of fish or of a crab does not disintegrate and fall off the hook quickly. They (i.e., these crabs) can be cooked underground between hot stones if you're cooking fish in this way. Octopus (too) can be cooked underground between hot stones, like fish, and it doesn't disintegrate or crumble away to nothing.

8.11.9. Crabs (*ḥanśíʾo*, pl. *ḥánśə*) (ii)

ḥanśíʾo libíni tíkkən bə-rího ḥáli wə-tímiher w-egḥáyo. ḥanśíʾo libíni tíkkən bə-ṭaḥ di-šími. wə-thōfer ḥangə́go w-al təgōsir taḥfér ʿis ki ʿíyək his. al tyóʾo ḥanśíʾo tíkkən bə-rího ḥáli. ḥanśíʾo tíkkən bə-rího ḥáli al nəʿágəb his nəśáʿrok bis, al tyóʾo ḥanśíʾo libíni tíkkən bə-ḥáməhul bə-ṭaḥ: iti bis ṣōdə ki tšáʿrok bis. ḥánhən ol níti ḥanśíʾo libíni tíkkən bə-ṭaḥ wələ tíkkən bə-rího ḥáli.

A pale-coloured crab is found in sweet water and among date palms and in riverbeds. A pale-coloured one is also found on the shore in areas of white sand. It digs itself a hole and you can't dig it out, even if you want to. It's not like the one found in sweet water. We don't use the kind found in sweet water as bait for fishing, not like the white shore crab found above the high tideline: if you fish with this kind it's taken by fish. We don't eat either the white crab of the shore or the one of sweet water.

wə-ʔíno tərí ḥanśiyōti tkə́no bə-míʕsilīn di-rího di-rínhem w-al tšrā́ḳoho ṭaḥ wə-ter. díki méyhi šem ṭiy: ḥanśíʔo ḥə́wro. wə-ṭiy yəʕúmur his ḥanśíʔo di-ḳśébeb. ḥanśíʔo di-ḳśébeb mes kān wə-mes ʕā́ker al tyóʔo ḥanśíʔo ləhég. málḳaz bis ṭad líbek wə-ṭad ḳáṭəhān. nəʕā́gub his, nitís.

There are two kinds of crab found on the rocks out at sea and neither of these come ashore or onto dry land. They have the same name: ḥanśíʔo ḥə́wro 'black crab'. And there is one called the ḥanśíʔo di-ḳśébeb. The ḥanśíʔo di-ḳśébeb crab doesn't look like those other crabs, either in appearance or size. It has one large fat claw and one that is thinner and smaller. We like this kind, we eat it.

ḥanśíʔo diž ḥə́wro nəʕā́gub his, bas al bénɛ tyóʔo di-ḳśébeb. wə-mes kān al tyóʔo di-ḳśébeb w-al tyóʔo ḥanśíʔo bə-ṭā́ḥ wə-bə-rīho ḥā́li. ḥanśíʔo dé bə-ṭaḥ mes kān tyóʔo ḥanśíʔo di-rīho ḥā́li, bas ol ṭad méyhi ʕā́ker. ḥanśíʔo dé bə-ṭā́ḥ śə́rəhān bis rīmhítin wə-riyāmo lol tūʕud u-mes ḳā́śerə. ḥanśíʔo dé bə-rīho ḥā́li tíkkən ḳī́no wə-kī́ri mes śə́rəhān wə-sə́ṭḥiḥ. u-bíśi d-īti túyhi díki ḥanśiyōti libiníti. wə-ḥanśíʔo ʔíno ṭiy ʕaféro wə-tíkkən bə-rīho ḥā́li w-al ʕaféro bénɛ. bíśi d-īti tus.

That ḥanśíʔo ḥə́wro 'black crab' is all right but we don't like it as much as the di-ḳśébeb crab. The black one doesn't look like the di-ḳśébeb crab or like the shore crab or the sweet water crab. That shore crab looks like the sweet water crab but they're not the same size. That shore crab has long thin legs and it looks long and thin as it moves around: it stands high off the ground.

That sweet water crab is small, has short legs and is squat and low to the ground. No one eats these two kinds of pale crab. There is another reddish one found in sweet water. It's not very red. No one eats it.

ʾíno kśébeb w-al dilāḵo b-áḥlef fáherə kol bə-fídənhin wə-níḵihel korúmma ʾíno bə-tīri déher wə-šəḵaḵ déher. ʾíno bih ḥanśíʾo nəʿāmer hes kśébeb. al ṭad méyhi kān sūʷsə (= sé wə-se) ḥanśíʾo diž.

There is another kind of kśébeb crab, but it is not common and is not found everywhere. It is only found in the high mountains and in deep holes where it is always damp and cold. This is where the (other) crab we call kśébeb is found. It looks quite different from that other (di-kśébeb) crab.[278]

8.11.10. Octopus (térəbaḥt, pl. terébaḥ) Ink

térəbaḥt: térəbaḥt núwdəf ʿis l-əriʾ kor nərāḵaḥ mes híber, dəwé di-kówtub meš wə-kor nəšáʿrok bis. nəḥōləbs tsé (= di-sé) men šériś wələ tsé (= di-sé) men ḵādəl. kúwse tos lal tóšhaḵ míʿsəlīn.

The octopus: we grab an octopus by the head, to extract its ink to write with, and also to use it (i.e., the octopus flesh) to fish with (i.e., as bait). We 'milk' its ink from its šériś ('stomach', for humans and mammals) or from its ḵādəl ('stomach', for shark). It (the octopus) is found when you're looking for shellfish around the rocks revealed at low tide.

---

[278] This is *Socotra pseudocardiosoma* which is caught and eaten by those living in the mountain areas where it occurs.

kor śínək tus kibīyən ʕis ʕaf tədéf ʕis lə-ʕāreb wə-lə-riʕ. wə-lāṭ máʕaṣ̌ tos fīsaʕ wə-bínə. wə-di-zēgud id ter ʕa təʕákals ber: ber tsáḥam se dəwé wələ se ekəniyo diž di-ʕīyək ʔɛ́hən mes.

If you see it, you creep up on it until you can grab it by the back of the neck or by the head. Then very quickly you give a great yank. And when it's out (i.e., of its crevice) don't put it down on the ground: on the ground it will disgorge (lit. 'urinate') its ink or its food, that which you want to get from it.

zēgud ter wə-ḥóli his bíli. ṭhōlub diɛ́ dəwé. wə-ḥágirin ʕis ʕaf tə́kši ʕ wə-ʕaf l-érahs menol ʕīyək. sáʕa di-ʕīyək téktəb mes, təʕāmer bis: záʕa īʔinṭ dəwé wə-təʕāmer bis īʔinṭ di-rího. wə-lāṭ núkiʕin diɛ́ kelém, wə-karúḥul ʕaf l-ékkən tyóʔo mədéd. wə-lāṭ kōtəb biš di-ʕīyək.

Take it out (i.e., of its hiding place) and put something under it, then 'milk' your ink from it. Be very careful with it (i.e., the ink) until it's dried out and you've got it where you want it. When you want to write with it, use it: take a little of the ink and add a small amount of water. Then fetch your writing instrument and stir the mixture until it is thick and viscous (lit. 'stretchy'). And then write whatever you want to with it.

8.12. Pearls and Pearlshell[279]

8.12.1. Pearls (*lūl*[A])

lūl wə-gōherə ṭad méyhi šem šīn. díkerk hōhən əʕə́wihaṣ əl-móṣəliḥ. wə-lal téte men ʕíhiṣ, éʔefo yəšrōkaḥ ter w-ifōlaḥ dhin móṣəliḥ w-

---

[279] *Pinctada radiata* for pearls and *Pinctada margaritifera* for pearlshell (nacre).

iḥə́wrə men lūl. íful iḥə́wrə mes lūl? ʾíno ḥalf di-ʿireb bə-ǵāṭer móṣəliḥ. ki bíro, tíkkən ḥá dé bə-ḥalf, ki āʾam wə-ki ḳīno. ʾíno d-ifōlaḥ bə-hūri. dihí al šərḳóḥo: ṭad iḳādif wə-ṭad ifōlaḥ dihí móṣəliḥ.

Lūl 'pearls' and gōḥerə 'jewel' have the same name with us. I remember diving for pearlshell myself. When the diving was finished, people would go back to the shore and open up their oysters to look for pearls. How did they look for pearls? There is a well-known place in the flesh of the oyster. If there is one (i.e., a pearl), large or small, it will be there in that place. Some open up their oysters while still in the dugout. The two of them don't go ashore: one rows while the other opens up their oysters.

korúmma kíse lūl ḳīno tyóʾo ḥábbə di-bómbə iʿúmur hiš 'ḥóyhi'. w-iyhé al ḥóyhi di-ḳérḳəher, bas nʸúwbe tus ḥóyhi, korúmma ʾíno tyóʾo míyə, xamsīn^A, ṯəlāṯīn^A. kōsáʾan b-íʾid. mēsən ḳimi al dəlak, wəlākin iʿúwgub hísən. di-ʿekāro mésən tyóʾo gelmə́mo di-ʿayn di-ṣōdə di-ḳīhən, áḥsən men ḥóyhi mēsən ḳīmi.

If he finds a small pearl, the size of a grain of finger millet, it is called ḥóyhi 'earth, dirt'. This is not the ḳérḳəher 'red earth' kind of ḥóyhi, it's just called ḥóyhi, whether there are some hundred, fifty, thirty. They can just be felt (lit. 'found') with the fingers (lit. 'hand'). They're not worth much, but there is a demand for them. If one of them is as big as the eyeball of a fish, a small fish, it's better than the ḥóyhi pearl and has more value.

wə-korúmma ksέʾen āʾam men gelmə́mo di-ḥot di-ḳīhən, nōḳiḥins diḥán bə-ḳerśíti. korúmma ekḗbo id ḳérśíti wə-ʿa śinōwi, ḳīmi diyál dilāko. wə-korúmma šərḳóho men ḳerśíti wə-śinōwi tus, mes ḳīmi dilāko. wə-korúmma āʔam men ḳerśíti se ḳīmi ġeyr.

And if we find one bigger than the eyeball of a small fish, we test it between the pads of the tip of the thumb and the tip of the first finger. If it sinks into the two pads until it's no longer visible, then it's not worth very much. But if it protrudes from the two pads of flesh and is clearly visible, then it's worth a lot. And if it's bigger than the two pads of flesh, then its price is quite other.

ʔíno āʔam tyóʔo ḳérśə wə-íno āʔam tyóʔo ḳérməhem wə-ʔíno āʔam tyóʔo ṣáʕt. bas al hīmʕak kíse tyóʔo ṣaʕt kal ʕag ṭad mítilin biš ʕag ṭad men mōmi.

There are some as big as the pad at the top of the finger, and some the size of a knuckle, and some as big as a fist. Though I've never heard of one as big as a fist, except for one man in Mōmi they used to talk about.

wə-ʔíno lūl al men rínhem, men bar, men bəkīli di-ḳiləhúts bə-ḥalf mes šem ḥoḳ di-ḥāllə[280] wə-ʕaḳālo tus kor ṣāyiḥ his wə-sté ʕis šérmihim b-aḥté.

And there are pearls which do not come from the sea but from the land. From a snake which spits it out in a place called Ḥoḳ di-Ḥāllə ('the Ḥoḳ cave in the eastern coastal strip of Ḥāllə'). It puts it down on the ground to light its way as it feeds on the bushes at night.

---

[280] See story in 8.15.6.

8.12.2. The Story of the Guardians of the Giant Pearls

lūl di-rínhem korúmma āʔam śúwnə tus w-al-gúwsir l-úʕud ʕis korúmma ḥigíro. ḳúwdum əl-lūl bə-ḳānə di-móṣaliḥ tyóʔo śaḥ. wə-biš bə-ḳānə lūl əw gōḥerə. w-iḳúwdum ḥot ṭad bə-nʸaṣf wə-ṭad bə-nʸaṣf tyóʔo iḥégero dihí móṣaliḥ. bíśi d-iḳúʕud dis, iʕúwrub ber móṣaliḥ ḥiger dé di-biš lūl.

A really large pearl has been seen in the sea, but no one can get close to it because it is guarded. The pearl has been seen inside the oyster when it gaped: inside there was a pearl or a jewel. And one large fish can be seen on one side of it and another on the other side of it, guarding their oyster. No one can go down (i.e., dive) to it: it's well known that there is this oyster containing a pearl, but that it's well-guarded.

márra ṭiy kśóʔo ʕággi tərá móṣaliḥ biš lūl wə-ḥiger. wə-śídido ʕággi. ʕumur ṭad méyhi: "ā-ḳāḳa! hōhun áʕihiṣ wə-ṭārid díki ḥóti di-ḥigíro dé móṣaliḥ. ʕasé igōsir l-izʕá dihó móṣaliḥ dihé wə-dihé gōḥerə!" ʕúmur hiš: "lā, al śínkek (= al śínək hek) wálmə táʕihiṣ ʕiš." ʕúmur: "hōhən áʕihiṣ walākin di-kān!" wə-ʕihaṣ wə-zíʕi kə-nhafš dihé máḥwaš, wə-tyóʔo gídaḥ dihé ʔə́šaḳ dé wə-ʔə́šaḳ dé. wə-zígid dihí móṣaliḥ.

One time, two men found an oyster with a pearl but it was guarded. The two men discussed what they should do. One of them said: "Oh brother, I'll dive down and chase off those two big fish that are guarding that oyster. Perhaps I'll be able to grab that oyster of mine, it with its jewel!" He said to him: "No, I don't think you'll be able to dive all the way down to it." He said: "I'll dive down happen what may!" And he dived down and took with him his *máḥwaš* 'iron rod' with the hooked tip'. When he reached them (i.e., the two guardian fish) he stabbed first one and then the other. And he picked up their oyster.

tyóʔo zígid dihí móṣəliḥ, bídum móṣəliḥ dihé əl-lūl w-išə́rḳaḥ. tyóʔo símak zíʕi ḥōz di-bāʕ kor išrāḳaḥ, gídaḥ hiš ḥówlihin u-butílig dihé móṣəliḥ. áʕihiš śfáʕ hiš bə-miśfiʔo. wə-"ɛ́ḥɛn álĺah séllim ínhi dihó ḳáḳa!" wə-ʕīhaṣ ʕiš. ʕīhaṣ l-áʕhaš wə-érḳahiš ter. wə-ʕáṭeb biš id dihí hūri w-al ḥúbur ḳéyri.

When he picked up their oyster, the oyster clamped tight shut over its pearl. He started to come up. When he had come up about one *bāʕ* depth he was overcome with dizziness and he let go of his oyster. His brother made a vow that he would slaughter such-and-such if only his brother were to survive, and (said:) "Oh Lord! Save my brother!" And he dived down to him. He dived down to where his brother was and brought him up out of the sea. He got him back into their dugout and everything was alright.

kōtinaḥ áʕhaš bə-ḥórḳa dihí-l-móṣəliḥ. tyóʔo ékdem ʕiš dihé bə-ḥalf ḳōtílib wə-bíli di-higériš. wə-érḳahiš. níḥo ʕággi dihí móṣəliḥ dé di-ṭíbo biš dihí lūl. wə-ḳedéfo dihí hūri wə-šərḳóḥo id bar. filóḥo dihí móṣəliḥ w-iyhí níḥo diš bíli di-ksóʔo tos. wə-tyóʔo filóḥo dihí móṣəliḥ, ksóʔo tos dihí lūl kāno tyóʔo ḥámhim.

His brother went back, driven mad by his desire for their oyster. When he saw it in its (former) place, he saw that the oyster had tipped over on one side and that nothing was standing guard over it. He got it up and out. The two men were overjoyed about that oyster of theirs: they were quite certain that it had their (huge) pearl inside. And they paddled off in their dugout and went ashore. They opened up their oyster, and were overjoyed about this thing they had found. And when they opened up their oyster they found a pearl as big as a lump of charcoal!

lūl šīn korúmma ʿekāro šərḳóho men kérśə wə-di-ʿalá, lāzim ṣ́úwlaʿ bis ɛ-sáṭəhān w-itōgir tos. w-iyhéhən ḳáddəmuw tuš kor itōgirs ʿan ṭawāwiš wə-ʿan tāgir. w-itōgir tos siwé.

With us, if a pearl the size of the the pad at the top of a finger joint or larger is brought up, the sultan has to be informed so that he can buy it. And they offered it to him to buy rather than to the traders who came to the island from overseas or to a (local) merchant. And he gave a reasonable price for it.

8.12.3. Fishing for Pearlshell Oysters (móṣəliḥ) (i)

korúmma ʿīn dayn, dayn di-móṣəliḥ, nəṭúher náʿihiṣ men éʾemed di-ḳéyaṭ wə-šwār. ʾíful náʿihiṣ? naʿāṭeb bə-hūri wələ nəšʿāṭəb bə-hūri, wə-nəzīʿa dihán mərāyə yaʿtúbur id rínhem. korúmma yəśīni móṣəliḥ yəʿéyin tuš id dihé məšáʿṭihib (wələ dihé ḳākaʿ wələ dihé nínhin wələ dihé ḥaléla wələ dihé dído, dihé móʿo, dihé bɛ́bɛ, dihé sáherᴬ, dihé máḥrif, dihé múgšəm, dihé ʿəwégəhən).

If we are in debt, 'the debt of the pearlshell oyster', we go off in the summer to work at the diving, when the sea is flat calm. How to we dive? We go out to sea in a dugout, or we get a ride in someone else's dugout, and we take our mərāyə instrument to magnify and study the sea(bed). If he (i.e., the mərāyə user) sees a pearlshell oyster he points it out to his companion (or his brother or his elder brother or his maternal uncle or his paternal uncle or his grandfather or his father or his brother-in-law or his son or his boy).

yəṭúher yáʕihiṣ ʕiš di-gʸēmə. ʔímmā^A yəʕāmer fə́ṭəham[281] wələ al yəʕāmer, wə-méyhin yáʕihiṣ bə-risāsə. yəʕúmer fə́ṭəham id náḥrer kor al ikéb rīho, kor al fānuś. yəʕámer fə́ṭəham men ḳān di-šfāniś wələ men ʕāg men rínhem. d-iʕámer heh ḳaʔ w-ikōtif biš wə-d-iʕámer tuš id ḳār.

He (the other one in the dugout) sets off to dive down to the bottom for it. He might wear a nose clip or he might not, and some of them dive down carrying a lead weight. He attaches a nose clip to his nose to stop water getting in and go stop him breathing (underwater). He makes the nose clip either from animal horn or from a piece of plastic washed up ashore. He makes a cord and ties it on, wearing it around his neck.

di-yáʕihiṣ bə-rəsāsə korúmma búlbul. wə-di-yáʕihiṣ móṣəliḥ yáʕihiṣ lə-riʔ. ʔímmā^A yəzáʕa k-ənháfš máḥwəš wələ al yəzáʕa bíli. korúmma móṣəliḥ héləhə yəzʸúʕa tuš b-íʔid. korúmma móṣəliḥ bə-śíṣəhor wələ mitigémi, yərōḳaḥ tuš máḥwəš.

The one that dives for pearl oysters does so with a lead weight (attached to his feet). But those diving for pearlshell oysters dive down headfirst. They take either the short máḥwəšʸ[282] 'iron rod with a hooked tip' with them or they take nothing at all. If the pearlshell oyster is just lying there on the seabed it can be

---

[281] fə́ṭəham nose clip (i) from the tip of cow horn with a notch made in one side; (ii) from a piece of plastic (ʕāg) bent or slit to hold the nostrils shut.

[282] máḥwəš (i) metal rod with a hooked tip; (ii) the a stump of a knife.

picked up by hand. If it is deep in a crevice in the rocks or wedged into a crack, he has to hook it out with the *máḥwaš* rod.

ʿáwihuṣ ʿiš móṣaliḥ bə-ḳaśʔíri di-ruš. dé di-áʿihiṣ bə-ḳaśʔíri di-ruš men xamsa^A wələ təmāniyə bəwáʿ. wə-dé di-áʿihiṣ bə-férifer di-ḳaśʔíri men xamstʿašer^A wələ sitʿašer^A bəwáʿ. móṣliḥ éʔeb tkósə tuš bə-ḥalf míšlol. íʿud dihé ḥalf móṣəliḥ wə-ḳəfərómš wə-yəšrāḳaḥ bis ʿalé.

The pearlshell oyster is dived for in an area called Ḳaśʔíri Di-Ruš, 'The Skerry of Ruš',[283] at a depth of five or eight *bāʿ*. And those that dive around the base of the rocks of the skerry go down fifteen or sixteen *bāʿ*. The larger pearlshell oysters are found in the deepest waters. He goes to where the pearlshell oyster lies and levers it off (i.e., with the *máḥwəš*) and carries it up to the surface.

yəʔāgaḥ dihí di-hūri yəḳālaʿ dihí móṣəliḥ id xan dihí di-hūri wələ id kélʔé dihí di-hūri, wələ id ḳoddām dihí di-hūri. ikínaḥ yaʿtúbur di-g^yēmə dihí bə-mərāyə. wə-tyóʔo d-iśáne iṭārib ʿiš ṭad méyhi. korúmma ḥéber ṭad, yəṭāreb iyhé. w-iṭá^h šəgóʔo ʿaf l-iḥebéró, ʿaf l-išēkəkó.

He gets back into their dugout and puts their pearlshell oyster in the bottom of the dugout, in the middle. Or (he puts it) at the very back or at the very front. He goes back to studying the seabed with their *mərāyə* magnifying instrument. And as soon as one is seen, one of them dives down for it. If one of them gets

---

[283] Ḳaśʔíri Di-Ruš 'The Skerry of Ruš': *ruš* 'deep sea, area of the sea where sharks are to be found'; *ḳaśʔíri* 'underwater rocks whose tops are visible above the sea'.

too cold the other one goes down. And so they continue until they are both too cold, until they're too chilled to continue.

yəšrāḳohó yəkēdəfó dihí məkādif, ṭad men ḥérhən wə-ṭad men fānə ˤaf l-irīḥó bar. yəˤāləyó dihí hūri ləwēsi ˤaf təráḥ ḥáməhul. korúmma al ˤígib li-yúˤlə dhin hwēri yəˤúmur hísən bárrūsi, wələ ʔíngəhir men óʔobən wələ ḥádīd, wə-yərōḳaḥ dhín məṣāliḥ. yəˤúmur w-iṭéher ifōlaḥ. d-ifɛ́laḥ ifōlaḥ bə-ṣārə dhin məṣāliḥ.

They come out (of the sea) and paddle away with their paddles, one at the back and one at the front, until they reach shore. They drag their dugout on rollers up to the dry foreshore. If they don't want to drag their dugouts up to the dry foreshore they let down an anchor instead, or a lump of rock or metal which they use as an anchor. They take their oysters out (of the dugout). They do this and off they go to open up their oysters. Those who are doing the opening do so with a knife.

yaˤtúbur w-īful[284] bə-réfɛ men lūl, wə-tékəbin dhin ġāter dhin móṣəliḥ. ḳúwdur wə-yúwte ki ˤígib. móṣəliḥ dáwle tuš korúmma ʔíno d-itōger náˤa. korúmma bíśi d-itōger, šúwḥan toš id gwāni ˤaf təmlɛ́ʔ. wə-lāṭ nəśūreg túsən wə-lāṭ nəroṣṣ (= nərṣəṣ) tósən thar thítsən wə-nəˤāḳal ˤaf ḥōz mōsəm. lal gídihin mōsəm, nədōʔi d-ikíʔi dihán men dayn dé d-ifān tuš ɛ-ləhɛ́ d-iḥéʔil tan.

He studies and picks over (the oysters) carefully for pearls, and he collects the oyster meat into a pile. This is cooked in water and eaten if they want. The pearlshell is weighed if there is anyone there to buy them there and then. If there isn't anyone to

---

[284] *iful*, √fly, usually 'to pick over someone's scalp for headlice'.

buy them (at that time), they're packed into sacks until the sacks are full. Then we stitch them closed with big stitches and stack them one on top of the other and leave them until the trade boats arrive. When the trade boats arrive we send what remains of our former debt to those who have to be repaid.

8.12.4. Pearlshell Oysters (*móṣəliḥ*) (ii)

móṣəliḥ ʾíno d-īti meyh ġáter w-íno diyál īti. fánə ol īti kal ki ḳérim men ḥorf. w-iyhé al kúwse men ḥorf. rínhem diméro. al kúwse kal men éʾemed di-rínhem ki ṣóʾo wə-ḥalóʾo. nəfálaḥš men lūl. ki ʾíno wə-ki bíśi biš lūl, nəkālaʿ bə-ġáter.

móṣəliḥ pearlshell oysters: some eat its flesh and some don't. Before, no one used to eat it unless he was longing for the taste of flesh during the monsoon (i.e., when the dates were being harvested and were the main food). But they're not (easily) found during the monsoon when the sea is rough. They can only be got when the sea is calm and clear. We'd open them up to look for pearls. Whether there were pearls or not, we'd throw the flesh away.

wə-šīn fánə yəʿúwgub ḥiyh~ʿiyh béne móṣəliḥ wə-ki ʾíno di-kísə biš lūl ínihaḥ béne w-ikósi bis ḳími dəláḳo. móṣəliḥ nəkōniz tuš id gwāni wə-ki milóʾo gōniyə nəśōrig ʿis wə-láṭ igúdihin d-itōgir. wə-diyál tíger dúwʾɛ tuš id swāḥil kor śówʾum wə-nikíʿin hik meš bə-ḳími eḳəníyo wələ fíḳəhe.

With us before, the *móṣəliḥ* pearlshell oysters were highly prized. If someone found a pearl in one he was overjoyed because he might get a really good price for it. The *móṣəliḥ* pearlshell itself we'd stuff into sacks. Once a sack was full we'd sew it shut with rough stitches until such time as a trader arrived. And if they were not sold to a trader, they would be sent away with the trade boats to East Africa to be sold there, and they'd bring you back its value in food or cloth.

ḥánhen náʿihiṣ li-móṣaliḥ sāʿa di-ḥalóʾo rínhem. w-áḥlef di-ʿúwihaṣ bīhin tyóʾo ḥówlef wǝ-di-ḥámiri wǝ-śíṣǝhur wǝ-ḥállǝ wǝ-fídǝhan di-ruš wǝ-níssem wǝ-tə́rbak w-irísseyl: lhɛ́ áḥlef bīhin móṣaliḥ šīn.

We'd dive for pearlshell oysters when the sea was clear. The places where people used to dive were places such as Ḥówlef, Di-Ḥámiri, Śíṣǝhur, Ḥállǝ, Fídǝhan di-Ruš, Níssem, Tə́rbak and Irísseyl.[285] These are the places that have pearlshell oysters in our area.

móṣaliḥ ol yǝʾāṣaʿ kol bǝ-ḥalf biš eṣǝrīʿo wǝ-ḳéśʾor. yíkin bǝ-šīmi lɛ́kin ol idɛ́luḳ. wǝ-náʿihiṣ men ḳéyaṭ wǝ-men ṣerébhǝn. korúmma ʿīn dayn, dayn di-móṣaliḥ, nǝṭúher náʿihiṣ men éʾemed di-ḳéyaṭ wǝ-šwār.

Pearlshell oysters only grow in rocky areas where there is green algae. They can be found in sandy places, but not many. We dive in the summer and in the period at the end of the monsoon before winter comes in. If we're in debt, 'pearlshell oyster debt', we set off to dive in the summer when the sea is calm.

korúmma táʿihiṣ rínhem wǝ-bíśi šik fíḳǝhe wǝ-ʿə́ṭalk wǝlǝ ṣə́ṭʿak, záʿa kǝn tāger ʿarbún. ʿarbún šīn ʿal ihúʾulk tāger ʿaf táʿihiṣ wǝlǝ ʿaf thádǝm wǝ-tšáʿarek rínhem. wǝ-sāʿa di-tšáʿarek wǝ-ʾīhaṣk ʾōfi diɛ́

---

[285] All places along the east coast of the island, the speaker's home area.

máḥrif. wə-ki ʔíno di-gídaḥik kor yətōger, təˤāmer: "hōhun zaˤk ˤarbún kən fəlān, w-ol iśōʔom ˤak w-ol əzáˤa kənk ˤarbún."

If you go diving and you don't have any clothes, only worn-out rags, or if you're very hungry, you go and take on an *ˤarbún* loan from a wealthy man.[286] Where we live, having an *ˤarbún* means that the rich man won't ask for the debt to be repaid until you've gone diving, or until you've worked at some (other) sea work, or gone fishing. Once you've caught fish or gone diving, then you repay your patron. And if someone (else) comes to buy (what you've harvested), you say: "I took on an *ˤarbún* loan from a wealthy man, so I can't sell to you or take on a loan from you."

8.12.5. Pearl Oysters (*bílbil*) and Pearlshell Oysters (*móṣəliḥ*)

bíśi šin bílbil: bílbil íkkin bə-di-sírihin wə-šiḳ wə-ḥádibo wə-ḥēbaḳ wə-men ḥēbaḳ ˤaf ḳalansíyə: half di-bílbil ḥá. ḥalf béhele bílbil íkkin bih móṣəliḥ; ḥalf béhele móṣəliḥ dálaḳ ol íkkin bih bílbil. móṣəliḥ ol yəʔāṣaˤ kol bə-ḥalf biš eṣərīˤo wə-ḳéśʔor. yíkin bə-šimi lékin ol idéluḳ.

We don't have any pearl oysters (lit. 'a pearl oyster') here where we live. They're to be found at Di-Sírihin or Šiḳ or Ḥádibo or Ḥēbaḳ, and from Ḥēbaḳ right to Ḳalansíyə: the places for pearl oysters are there. Where there are pearl oysters there are (also) pearlshell oysters, but where there are a lot of pearlshell oysters there aren't any pearl oysters. Pearlshell oysters only grow in a

---

[286] *ˤarbún* is a system of advancing goods against future produce.

place with a lot of green algae and underwater rocks. They can be found on a sandy bottom, but rarely.

8.13. Preparing Fish

8.13.1. Salting Fish

nəmālaḥ ṭānĭk wə-zíhnin wə-rá'ḥa wə-dāfin wə-ṭamákərə. lhɛ́ nəmālaḥ bíhin. kor dɔ́laḵ ṣōdə wə-tun wə-ś́bá'an, nəmālaḥ bíhin. níṣrer méyhi ér'iš id ter. kal ṭānĭk, al ṣɔ́wrur mes ri'.

We salt *ṭānik* 'Spanish mackerel' and *rá'ḥa*, *dāfin* and *ṭamákərə* 'trevallies': these are the ones we salt. If there are a lot of fish and we have eaten our fill, we salt them. We cut off and discard their heads, all except for the Spanish mackerel: its head is not cut off.

nāfa' di-emlóḥo, emlóḥo di-ṭānĭk. nərāḵaḥ mes ḵād id ter wə-nəśāters əl-merr 'af tíkkən tərá 'ámti. wə-lāṭ nəšōri'ins wə-nərāḵaḥ mes šébəhur. 'íno d-irāḵaḥ šébəhur wə-'íno diyál irāḵaḥ šébəhur. nə'ā́ḵalš bə-'amḵ sɔ́bāḵ bə-ri' wə-sɔ́bāḵ bə-dɔ́nub.

How to salt fish: the salting of Spanish mackerel.[287] We remove the fatty *ḵād* material[288] and we cut it along its belly to make two halves. And then we slash the flesh in vertical parallel lines and remove the backbone. (Some remove the backbone and some don't). We leave the middle (i.e., we do not separate the two halves): it is joined at the head and tail.

---

[287] The method for salting shark is the same.
[288] *ḵād* 'a white "strand" in the stomach which is very fatty and does not absorb salt well'.

šōri⁽ins ⁽af tšēri⁽ wə-lāṭ nəmālaḥ bis. emlóḥo: nə⁽ākal lə-⁽āmtən gūnīyə mílḥo wə-nəfési⁽ən dihán ḥot dé di-ṣəlōbins kor nəmālaḥ bis.

We slash the flesh in parallel lines until it has all been done, and then we salt it. The salting: we place a sack of salt beside us and we spread the fish we've killed out flat so that we can salt it (thoroughly).

nəṣá⁽aṭ b-í⁽id mílḥo wə-nə⁽ērif b-í⁽id wə-nəzēgud w-ənfétitin ṭáher dihán ḥot. wə-lāṭ ənkób mílḥó dihán bə-ṣōdə dé di-šōri⁽inš ⁽af əl-tētə. nəṭārif ṭáher ṭhidítš wə-ṭaʰ nəšōgi ⁽af əntētə.

We grab the salt in fistfuls, scooping it up by hand. We take it and sprinkle it all over our fish. And then we rub the salt into the fish we have slashed until it's done. We fold it in half, one side on top of the other. And we do that (with the rest of the fish) until we've finished.

néṣəninš ⁽af tkébš mílḥo men ṭhar[289] ṭiy šām wələ tərí šāmi. nəgúdihin w-ənkēbur ⁽iš dihán ṣōdə dé di-⁽ímlaḥ biš. wə-lāṭ nintégifin meš mílḥó wə-nəráḥaṣ tuš bə-rīho di-rínhem men mílḥo wə-men tə⁽ālə.

We stack them up one on top of the other for one or two days to allow the salt to penetrate the flesh thoroughly. We come regularly to check on our salted fish. Then we knock off any salt still adhering to the fish and wash them in sea water to get rid of excess salt and any grubs.

---

[289] *men ṭhar* 'then, next, after(wards)'.

wə-lāṭ (nə)nēgubš ḥáṣḥiṣ ḳéśaʿ wə-(nə)nēgib tuš əl-merr. wə-lāṭ
nəḳōliʿiš əl-ṭādaʿ wə-nəḳālibinš ʿaf l-íḳśiʿ. ḳor ki ḳéśaʿ nətéḳibin
túyhin ṭáher ṭhítšin wə-nəḥósibin: kúllə kórgih[290] áḥśiš.

And then we spread them out on dry pebbles, belly side down.
And then we turn them on their backs. We keep on turning
them from one side to the other until they are completely dried
out. When they are quite dry, we pile them up in a stack, one
above the other. And then we make our calculations: each lot of
twenty fish (is counted) by itself.

wə-nəzēgud men ṭaḥ id ḥalf mihlóʿo w-al iʾāraḥš mése wə-nəʿākal
ḥánʾéh ʿaf l-igdáḥ mōsəm wələ d-itōger wələ d-iḳāfəd biš ḳor śə́wōm.

And we take them from the shore to a place of shade, where no
rain will reach them. We leave them right there until the trade
boats arrive or until someone comes to buy them or until someone goes down to (the coastal markets) to sell them.

8.13.2. Preparing and Cooking Fish

nəṣāləb ḥot. ṣə́wirur riʾ di-ḥot, wə-nərāḳaḥ meyh śáʿnhun wə-ḳādəl.
wə-níniyaḥ tuš korúmma ḥot éʾeb. wə-nərāḳaḥ áʾamti wə-nərāḳaḥ
šébəhur. wə-lāṭ nínyiḥ áʾamt, nəʿāmer náḥa.

We kill the fish. The head of the fish is cut off and we remove
the gills and the stomach~swim-bladder.[291] And we are very
pleased if it is a large fish! We remove the two halves and we

---

[290] kúrgə~kórgi[h], pl. kwārig, a measure for timber, shark, Spanish mackerel and other valuable salted whole fish, equal to twenty pieces.

[291] For ḳādəl, see footnote 251 above.

remove the backbone. Then we cut each half into two—each half (i.e., of a half-fish) is called *náḥa*.

wə-lāṭ nəḳāṣafs wə-nəʿāmer ínʿis. šərākah náʿsə ṭiy di-šʲōḳib wə-ṭiy di-gídəni wə-dánub. w-əlhɛ́ il-kíʔi mésən šem ínʿis.

Then we cut it (i.e., the *náḥa*) across into sections to make *ínʿis* pieces. One *náʿsə* piece, the *di-šʲōḳib*, goes from below the gills (to halfway down the fish), and one *náʿsə* piece, *di-gídəni wə-dánub*, goes from the lower belly (i.e., from mid-fish) down to the tail. These pieces are called *ínʿis*.

wə-yəʿōgib šīn ṣōdə bénɛ, wə-šté men éʔemed di-ḥorf bénɛ bénɛ. riʔ di-ḥot nənāṣerš tərá náṣeri. riʔ di-ḥot yəʿúber tuš ḥéyhi šíbəb wəla ḥālət kor mékəmek wə-mášməš wə-šṭáʿamš meš gélyud²⁹² wə-ʿáyni. ber šker wə-ʿāṭem. mes šíbdə wə-ḳādəl ḳúwdur túyhi. wəla ḳúwbub šíbdə wə-ḳúwdur ḳādəl.

Fish is greatly liked by us in our area, and a lot of it is eaten, especially during the months of the monsoon. The fish head we divide into two halves (through the middle of the skull to the tip of the nose). The fish head is given to an old person or to a guest so that they can suck away at it and chew over it to extract all the flavour from the two cheeks and the two eyes. It (i.e., the head) is very good and full of fat. Its liver and stomach~swim-bladder is cooked in water, or the liver is roasted and the stomach~swim-bladder is cooked in water.²⁹³

---

²⁹² *gílyid*, pl. *gélyud*, 'cheek of a fish'; also a diminutive form of *gād*, 'skin'.

²⁹³ Because the *ḳādəl* disintegrates if roasted.

8.13.3. Preparing Fish for Eating

ṣə́wirur riʾ di-ḥot wə-nərā́kaḥ meyh ṣáʿnhun wə-nínyiḥ tuš: náḥa ṭiy di-ʾídəhen wə-náḥa ṭiy di-ṭādaʿ. wə-náḥa ṭiy di-šə́bəhur korúmma al rə́kaḥ šə́bəhur. korúmma ḥot kī́hən, ʿal rúwkaḥ meyh šə́bəhur.

The head of the fish is cut off and we remove the gills. We cut it into *náḥa* sections: one section is the bottom half of the fish (lit. 'of the ear', the pectoral fins), and the other section is the top half of the fish (lit. 'of the back'). There is another section, 'of the backbone', if the backbone has not been removed: in a small fish the backbone is not removed.

nərā́kaḥ meyh áʾamti wə-nərā́kaḥ šə́bəhur. wə-lāṭ nínyiḥ áʾamt, nəʿā́mer náḥa. wə-lāṭ nəkā́ṣaf wə-nəʿā́mer ínʿis. šərā́kaḥ naʿsa ṭiy di-kṓšəb²⁹⁴ wə-ṭiy di-də́nub. w-əlhɛ́ il-kíʾi mésən šem ínʿis di-gídəni korúmma di-ṭādaʿ wə-korúmma ínʿis di-náḥa di-bímér, ḳā́dəl.

We remove the two halves from it, and we take out the backbone. And then we cut (each half) into two further halves to make *náḥa* sections. And then we cut these *náḥa* sections across to make pieces called *ínʿis*. One *náʿsə* is cut across just beneath the gills and is called *di-kṓšəb*, and another *náʿsə* is cut across from beside the tail and is called *di-də́nub*. What remains is *ínʿis* pieces: *ínʿis di-gídəni*, if it is the (larger) one from the top (lit. 'back') of the fish, or *ínʿis di-náḥa di-bímer*, if it is (the smaller one) from the lower half (lit. 'belly') of the fish.

---

²⁹⁴ *kṓšəb*, lit. 'to trim the tips of twigs, slim branches' (as when lopping foliage to feed livestock); in fish: 'a slice made across the top half of a fish, beneath the pectoral fins'.

8.14. Methods of Cooking Fish

8.14.1. Cooking in a Trench (níbihir)[295]

nənōber ṣōdə korúmma iʔirīfi. nəḥōfer taḥk wə-nəṣākaˤ bə-śéyāṭ di-gʸēmə ˤaf l-inḥá. wə-lāṭ niśkik ḥot, nərākaḥ meš bímér ki ˤigíbən. wə-lāṭ nəbōləg di-gʸēmə tərá, təlātə... dálak.

níbihir: we use the níbihir method if we have a great number of fish from an ʔirīfi shoal. We dig down into the coarse gravel and sand and light a fire in the bottom (of the trench) and let it burn. Then we cut the fish open along the belly and, if we want to, we remove the entrails. And then we lay the fish in the bottom (of the trench): two, three... many.

wə-lāṭ nərākal ˤiš dihán taḥk. wə-lāṭ nəṣākaˤ men ˤālə wə-lāṭ nəˤākal hánʔéh ˤaf l-íkṣam. sáˤa di-ˤigíbən, nəkēbur. nənōber dihán nōber, dihán múnbəhur.[296] nərākaḥ ḥot men ḳānə, nəkōsə kān tyóʔo ḳān. dé nāfaˤ di-ḳíbhib bə-ṣōdə dálak.

And then we put some of our coarse gravel and sand on top of them (i.e., the fish), and then we light (another) fire on top of that. We leave it just like that until the fire dies down. When we want to, we go and check up on it. (We say:) nənōber dihán nōber, dihán múnbəhur 'we are cooking in our nōber method, in our trenches.' We take a big fish out of the trench (i.e., to test its readiness), and we find it as hard as horn (i.e., done to a turn). This is the method we use to roast a lot of fish at once.

---

[295] níbihir, pl. núbəhur, 'pit, trench; method of cooking in a trench or pit'.

[296] múnbəhir, pl. múnbəhur, 'trench, pit'.

8.14.2. Cooking Small Sardine-Type Fish in a Trench (*níbihir di-ˤídi*)

ámmā[A] *ˤidi, nískik tos id girīdi di-tímərə əl-ˤayn ˤaf tíkkən tyóʔo səlsálə, wə-lāṭ nənōbers tyóʔo nəbōrən ṣodə.*

As for the small sardine-type baitfish, we spit them through the eyes along a skewer made from the stem of a date palm frond, making something like a chain. And then we cook them in a trench just as we do with (bigger) fish.

8.14.3. Roasting Small Sardine-Type Fish (*ḳíbhib di-ˤídi*)

núkiˤin fēriˤ wə-nərāḳalhin. wə-lāṭ nəféśˤən ˤidi wə-lāṭ nərāḳal men ˤālə fēriˤ wə-símilihin. wə-lāṭ nəlōṭiʔ śéyāṭ bīhin dihán fēriˤ. sté śéyāṭ dsi fēriˤ tyóˤo kān. wə-ḥánhən kul ṭad dhí míźərid ḥáfśən men nʸaṣf wə-yərāḳaḥ ˤidi di-béhelo ter.

We fetch dry date palm fronds and we spread the small sardine-type baitfish out on them. And then we lay more dry date palm fronds and other dry date palm debris on top. Then we set our dry date palm fronds alight. The fire steadily eats away at all the dry fronds. Each of us has a date-frond palm stem we use to flick the fish that are cooked and ready to eat off the fire onto the ground.

wə-ṭa[h] *nəšōgiʔ ˤaf əntētə. dé ḳíbhib di-ˤídi. nīti. tʸun mes, wə-diyol tūyən mes, nəˤāmers id igzíri wələ id dáḥanə wə-nəṣārˤas. wə-d-izōnəg yəzōnəg mes d-əl-éʔefo. w-al toṣṣol id śéher.*

And we continue like this until they are all done. That's the *ḳíbhib di-ˤídi* 'roasting small sardine-type fish'. We eat. When we've eaten (as many as we want to), we put any we haven't eaten into leather bags or a palm-frond basket and we hang it up high. Anyone who wants can take from it to give to others. And they don't go off for (up to) a month.

8.14.4. What Is Done with the Inshore ḥálkek Fish (nāfaʿ di-ṣódə ḥálkek)

korúmma ṣíʿəfo, ṣúʿəf. wə-nəṣáʿafš wə-lāṭ nəkáṭabš, nərākaḥ meš bímér tyóʾo šíbdə wə-ḳādəl wə-miʾḥóytin. korúmma ʿígibən nəkbébš nəkbébš, wə-korúmma ʿígibən nəḳdɛ́rš nəḳdɛ́rš bə-rího. nəḳādərš bə-rího ḥāli wə-nəmōlaḥ biš.

If they have scales, these are removed. We descale them and then we cut them across in half and gut them, removing such things as the liver, the stomach and the intestines. If we want to roast them, we roast them, and if we want to cook them in water, we cook them in water. We cook them in fresh water to which we add salt.

ʾífúl ḳādərš? núkiʿin dihán məkī́šo, mes šem məkī́šo di-ṣōdə:[297] al ṭad méyhi šem: məkī́šo wələ ṣáfləḥa di-ṣódə wə-məkdḗrə. ṣáfləḥa di-məkdḗrə škéro men ṣáfləḥa di-ṣódə, tkōsi ṣáfləḥa di-ṣódə, tkōsis ḥidɛ́ko wə-tkōsi bis emtḗrek dáləḳ bis.

---

[297] *məkī́šo* 'clay cooking pot'. Pots used for cooking fish are kept separately from other cooking pots, and fish are cooked well away from the living quarters and from where other sorts of cooking take place. The water in which fish is cooked has to be fresh: fish cooked in seawater becomes *murr* 'bitter'. The cooking water is saved and used again and again in areas short of fresh water.

How do you cook them in water? We bring our pot called *məḳíśo di-ṣə́də* 'fish clay cooking pot'. The two (clay cooking pots) don't have the same name: a *məḳíśo* or a *ṣáflǝḥa* for fish, or (a *məḳíśo*) for finger millet. The *ṣáflǝḥa* for finger millet is better looking than the *ṣáflǝḥa* for fish. The *ṣáflǝḥa* for fish is encrusted with dirt and has a lot of accumulated soot burned onto it.

ḳədōren dihán ṣə́də. nəʿáṭub. nəbōdə riʾ dé di-ṣə́də di-gʸḗmə di-ḳā́nə di-ṣáflǝḥa. nǝḥōliś ínʿis wə-lāṭ nəʿā́ḳal ínʿis ṭáheriś. wə-nəṭékidin wə-nəṣā́ḳaʿ bə-ṭīrub śéyāṭ ʿaf l-íbǝhul dihán ṣə́də. nǝnḗtug dihán ṣáflǝḥa əw məḳíśo, nǝnḗtugs men míśkel id ter.

We cook our fish in water. We put it in the pot. We begin by putting the head of that fish into the bottom of the cooking pot. Under this we put chunks of cleaned fish, and then (more) chunks of cleaned fish on top. We push sticks under the pot and set them alight. We let them burn until our fish is cooked and ready to eat. We take our *ṣáflǝḥa* or *məḳíśo* pot off the fire: we lift it off the three stones (of the fireplace) and put it down on the ground.

wə-korúmma ʿād ṣə́də diyál béhǝl, wə-ʿā́dən ʿígibən nǝkdér biś di-rího, ḳədōrǝn biś ṣə́də. nǝrā́ḳaḥ dihán ṣə́də bə-tərá ṭárbi wələ tərá lōḥi[A]* men ḳā́nə dihán ṣáflǝḥa, men náʿsə naʿsə. wə-lāṭ nəʿā́ṭub ṣə́də dé di-itkíʾi. lúʾu nǝḳāder ṣə́də d-itkíʾi? bə-rího dé di-ḳidḗr biś, nǝḳāder biś korúmma bíśi ʿād śīn rího wələ mílḥo.*

And if there are some chunks not yet fully cooked, and we want to cook them more in the water, we do so. We take our (cooked) fish out of the pot with two sticks or with two bits of flat wood, piece by piece, and then we put in any (uncooked) fish that remains. Why do we cook the (raw) fish that remains? We reuse the water the fish were cooked if we can't (easily) get hold of any more water or any more salt.

8.14.5. Smoking Fish

korúmma tun diḥán ínʿis wə-kíʔi, wələ korúmma ʔíno ṣōdə dálaḵ, nəzēgud diḥán ínʿis w-ənkúbsən sərámbīl[298] wələ ḵárḵor.[299] wə-lāṭ nəśérʿaś ṭáher mískel di-śéyāṭ. lúʔu nəśérʿaś ṭáher mískel? kor ʿa tígdaḥ idbíbo wələ di-ʿə́ssó wələ təʿálə wələ di-ḵeśʿámo wələ giśʿámihin wələ ʔídbəhir wələ ʔéyyə[A] nóyhir.

If we have eaten our chunks of fish and there are still some left, or if there are a lot of fish, we take our chunks of fish and put them in a woven cage or a fish trap and hang it above the three firestones of the hearth. Why do we hang it up over the three firestones? So that idbíbo 'flies' don't get at it, or little di-ʿə́ssó 'beetles'[300] or təʿálə 'maggots' or di-ḵeśʿámo 'beetles'[301] or giśʿámihin 'weevils' or ʔídbəhir 'hornets' or any bird of prey.

nəʿákalš ṭáher śéyāṭ wə-lāṭ nəśárif men náʿsə náʿsə, níbihil níbihil. mes šem, nəšōmi tuš níbihir, mánḵas. ṭaʰ nəšōgi tuš ki ʔíno šīn ṣōdə dálaḵ. nəzīʿa men níbihil w-ənḵárṣabš w-ənmāṣ́ʿaš w-ənḵeríṣab. wə-diyál tímaʿ l-imṣ́áʿ wələ l-iḵárṣabš ṭḵíḵənš b-óʔobən wə-yəʔōgi b-óʔobən.

---

[298] sərámbīl (i) wooden bedframe (in town); (ii) cage for hanging food.

[299] ḵárḵor: the fish trap can be made in many sizes; some very small ones are made for storing food.

[300] Not yet identified.

[301] Not yet identified.

We put it above the fire(place). We use it sparingly, chunk by chunk, broken off piece by broken off piece. It's called… we call it *níbihir* 'cooked till hard', (or) *mə́nḳas* 'jagged fragment'. This is what we do if we have a lot of fish. We take a small piece and we tear strands of it with our teeth, or we (just) gnaw away at it. And the person who can't tear off strands with his teeth or gnaw away at it (because it's too hard), grinds it up with a stone or beats it with a stone.

8.14.6. Fish Fat (*śabḥ di-ṣōdə*)

śabḥ di-ṣōdə: əmbaʿd əl-fālaḥan, nərākaḥ toš ḥśiš. wə-lāṭ nəfālaḥ meš ḳādəl. wə-nərākaḥ meš mírher wə-nərākaḥ meš miʔḥóytin ʿaf l-iḳéʿe śabḥ. wə-lāṭ ənḥárher tuš bə-šādihir wələ bə-naḥf.

Fish fat: after we've cut (the fish) open, we take it out (i.e., the fat), and put it to one side separately. Then we cut open the belly; we remove the gallbladder, and we remove the intestines so that the (belly) fat is revealed. Then we heat this (fat) over the fire in a clay pot or on a slip of clay pottery.

wə-lāṭ nəḥóṣirin biš wələ nə́mṣəṣ. wə-šker meyh ṭaʿm wə-mahiro biš. ṣōdə di-ʿāṭem tyóʔo samōmə wə-ʔílmi wə-līhan wə-zɛ́kɛ wə-maʿrḗmə wə-di-ḳənā́ṭirihin wə-ráʔha fáḥere śabḥ. wə-śéysino təʿā́ṭum mes mer.

Then we use it to flavour a cereal dish, or we dip our fingers in it and suck them. It tastes lovely and it's very good for you. Fish with (plentiful) fat are those such as the *samōmə*, *ʔílmi* and *līhan* 'groupers', the *zɛ́kə*, *maʿrḗmə* and *di-ḳənā́ṭirihin* 'snappers', and the *ráʔha* 'trevally': they are all full of fat. And the *śéysino* 'rabbitfish' has a lot of fat in its belly.

śabḥ di-ṣṓdə kúwnuz id ḳā́dəl di-ḥot. wə-lā́ṭ nəʿúgum wələ nəʿáṣəm ʿeyh bə-śúʔhur wələ bə-kaʔ. w-ənḳā́ders kə-ṣṓdə. śabḥ di-ṣṓdə yíkkən kə-šíbdə wə-kə-miʔḥóytin w-ilḗsuk áʔamṭ śówḳibi³⁰² di-ḥot. al íkkən śabḥ kal bə-mer di-ḥot, bdan.

The fat from a fish is (also) stuffed into the stomach of a large(r) fish. We then tie off the opening (of the stomach) with fishing twine or with thread, and we cook it in water along with the fish. Fish fat is found in and around the liver and intestines, and sticking to the lower half of a fish (i.e., not along the backbone). You only find fat inside a fish, nowhere else.

8.15. Stories

8.15.1. A Man in Search of Salt (ʿag ṭad yəḥórə men mílḥo)

ʿag ṭad yəḥórə men mílḥo wə-ḳúʿud dihé men ḥalf wə-dhí ḥalf šérḥaḳ men rínhem di-bis mílḥo. ṭáher w-ol ʿad bálug ʿaf igúdiḥin ṭaḥḥ. kóḥob wə-fśé w-áʿamid ʿaf əmbáʿad təṣímo³⁰³ ʿúmur: "ṭaf ḥiy mílḥo, ʿēyək l-əšárḳaḥ wə-l-úṭhur l-úkber dihó embūriyə wə-dihó ḳánəho." ṭaf hiš ḥōz ᴬxámsa áḳrasᴬ mílḥo. ʿésam bə-dhí bə-nakf wə-ʿə́kal bə-máʿṣad w-iyhé kōtínaḥ di-ḳā́nə d-il-ʿīyug wə-téḳi.

A man was on the lookout for salt so he went down from his place: where he lived was far from the sea where salt was to be found. He kept going until he reached the coast. He rested at

---

³⁰² ś͗ṓḳib ~ śṓḳib, du. śówḳibi, pl. śéḳeb, the lower belly-half of a fish; the fish beneath the head (from the pectoral fins or gills down to midfish).

³⁰³ √ṭlm.

midday, had lunch and spent the evening (with people) until after the evening meal, he said: "Give me some salt. I want to go back up and check on my children and my livestock." They gave him about 5 ḳurs measures[304] of salt. He tied it up in his waistcloth and put it on one of the doorposts and went back inside to where the men were and had a smoke.

gídaḥ lhɛ́ šíḳwə. igído mílho wə-nigífo di-ḥalf d-ʸaḥśiš w-íyhin kíli hiš šīmi. wə-ʿag téki w-émraʿ éʾefo: "l-émraʿkən állah! l-óṣim ʿánkən! ber ṭáfkən ḥiy mílho dəlāḳo! tíkkan ínhi iʿiśíro dɔ́laḳ!"

Some of these people who are keen on practical jokes arrived. The salt was taken and tipped out somewhere else and replaced with white sand. And the man had his smoke and made his farewells to people: "Fare you well! Bless you! (lit. 'I would die for you!') You've given me a lot of salt! It will last me a long time (lit. 'many tens')!"

kɔ́lə lə-ʿārib dhí zeng di-mílho wə-ráʿ śígəri w-ol ʿad bə́lug ʿaf igúdiḥin dhí di-ḳáʿr diš di-bíśi bis éʾefo w-iyhéhən bə-maṭʿino. naʿ ʿégib l-inḳáṣ dhí men mílho dhí bə-ḳáʿr diš di-bíśi bis éʾefo kor lal igúdiḥin men maṭʿíno ikósi mílho dhí bə-ḳáʿr. wə-tyóʾo ḳéʿe dhí zing, kísə šīmi di-rínhem wə-ḥaṣé ber ʿiyug il-šíḳwə hīn ṭaʰ di-šigéʾiš.

He slung his load across the back of his neck and went straight up the pass. He didn't stop to rest until he reached his home. There were no people in it: they had transhumed elsewhere. But he wanted to lighten his load of salt and leave some in his deserted home, so that when they came back from transhuming

---

[304] ḳurs (the Arabic /ṣ/ realised as /s/, as is often the case in Soqoṭri). Locally one ḳurs is roughly equivalent to a kilogram.

they'd find salt already there at home. And when he opened up his pack, he found white sand from the sea! And he knew that it was those people who like to play practical jokes who had played the trick on him.

wə-kōlib inōṣirin ṭaʰ w-inōṣirin ṭaʰ: "ya ber ṭaʰ wə-ya ber ṭaʰ...!" wə-ʿīyug lhɛ́ di-šígi ṭaʰ ṣéme bə-ṣaḥák wə-yáḥtəfer bə-śérʔhān. wə-ḳarérə ṭáher ṭad w-ə́nkaʿ heh dhí mílḥo.

And he cursed and swore: "You son-of-a-whatsitname and you son-of-a-whatsitsname!" And the men who had played that trick on him nearly died laughing, digging a hole in the ground with their feet (i.e., they were laughing so much)! And the next day one of them went and brought his salt up to him.

8.15.2. The Man Who Was Taken Out to Sea by a Turtle

ʿaig ṭéyḥḥi bə-zə́mān kísə ḥōmis bə-ṭaḥ təbōrə ḳaḥélǝhun. gídaḥ dis kor iḳālibs wə-sēhən símak táʿyig disé ḳaḥélihun. ʿúmur: 'ṣ́ābis kor təbōdə táʿyig disé ḳaḥélihun wə-lal téte əḳālibs'. tyóʔo šíno tuš ḥōmis ḥegéris ektə́nəho id rího. gídah wə-keb íʔid əl-ḳaḥélihun dé, ṣeméṭo ʿiš. wə-ṣeméṭo meš l-íʔid. wə-girēśutš wə-eshābo tuš id rínhem.

A man of the coast once found a turtle on the shore laying its eggs. He went up to it to turn it upside down (i.e., to disable it). At that time she was in the process of laying her eggs. He said (to himself): 'Leave her to lay her eggs, and then when she's finished I'll turn her upside down'. When the turtle saw him standing guard over her she turned back and went down to the sea. He went up to her and put his hand inside this place from which she lays her eggs (i.e., to get some), but she clenched (her muscles) down on it, braced her muscles hard over his hand, and dragged him after her right down to the sea.

wə-ekɛ́bo biš nḥaṭ fídəhān wə-bə-nḥaṭ fídəhān ʔíno bar. w-erkuḥútš. wə-bíro disé kíʔi men ḵaḥélihun wə-šərḵóho íʔid di-ʕaig. kíʔi ʕag búḵnáʕa də́nʕa b-ə́ṣ̌əhim. wə-kíʔi ʕag ḥoz ᴬsə́bʕat ʔayyāmᴬ bə-ḵānə b-ə́ṣ̌əhim mī di-állah! wə-fútkur ʕag: "ʔifúl l-išgé'. wə-bit ber ʕag al išrāḵaḥ men ḥá kol korúmma ʔíduf əl-ḥōmis lal tšrāḵaḥ men ḥá, yɛ ʔímmaᴬ yáḥye wə́lə yə́ṣam.

And she took him down far below the escarpment, beneath which there was land (i.e., a deep cave). She dragged him out (i.e., out of the sea into the cave), and laid the rest of her eggs. The man's hand came out, and there the man was, in that dark place! And he stayed there for some seven days in total darkness—facing death. And he thought and thought: 'What can I do?' And the man realised that he would not get out of there unless he grabbed hold of the turtle when she herself left the place. Either he'd live or he'd die (in the attempt)!

éʔefo fíḵid dhin ʕaig wə-tímed ʕiš. ted ʕaig ʕaf tyóʔo hīmaʕ ʕárho wə-śíʔifo di-ḥōmis ṭā́ʔif ʕaf ikōsis. wə-lāṭ búḥuš mes id ḵéśərə. wə-tyóʔo šḥábilo bíli men ṭádaʕ təktə́nəho id ríḥo. w-iyhé ʕaf tšrāḵaḥ. wə-tyóʔo šərḵóho wə-fēnišo, ə́ḵdəm əl-ṣiyḥ. bálug dhí ḥōmis w-iyhé sābaḥ id ber. wə-gə́daḥ id dihé di-ḵáʕr wə-dihé ḵáʕr al šərḥóḵo, l-áʔamt dihé ṭaḥ. ʕímer: "ḗ fl. al ṣāmək? šibíʕin tok ʕatéskik wə-ṣāmək!" ʕúmur: "al ṣāmək." wə-ṣā́laʕ ʕíhin bə-dé kān šiš. ʔíno di-šéʔimin tuš wə-íno diyal šéʔimin!

People thought the man was lost and they held the funeral feast for him. The man waited until he heard the sound of the turtle scrabbling around. He felt around here and there blindly until he found her, and then he flung himself right on top of her shell and hung on, crouched there. And as soon as she felt something on her back she went back into the sea. And he hung on until she swam up (to breathe). When she came up to breathe, he saw the shore. He let go of his turtle and swam ashore. He went to his home: it wasn't far away, it was in the middle of the shore. They said: "Oh so-and-so, you aren't dead?! We thought you had gone so far out you weren't able to see (your way back) and had died." He said: "I didn't die." And he told them what had happened to him. Some believed him and some didn't!

8.15.3. The Son Who Lost a Fish through Ignoring His Father's Advice

ṭaháro ʿággi, ʿag wə-dihé múgšəm, zihɛ́ro di-hūri, iṭéhero išʿériko ṣódə. wə-ṭībo éʔefo bə-kaʿr ṣə́ṭaʿ wə-ʿégib ekənīyo. šā́ker šīhin w-ənḥámšilo ʿīhin.

Two men went along, a man and his son. They dragged their dugout down to the sea and went off fishing. They both knew that people at home were very hungry and badly needed something to eat. It was a time of drought where they lived, and everything was unproductive, on land and on sea.[305]

šeʿériko ʿággi. menol išʿériko, té iyhí ḥot meš šem samṓmə. té ɛ-múgšəm, meš šem di-ḥézirhən. gid di-ḥézirhən dihí bə-samṓmə, wə-ʿen bis kor irā́ḳah dhí id hūri. tyóʔo gídəho samṓmə kor irā́ḳah mes

---

[305] √n-ḥmšl: 'to be a time of hardship and lack of food, when livestock, date palms and the sea are all unproductive'.

riʔ men rīho, ʕúmur śíbeb ɛ-dhí múgšəm, ʕúmur: "ɛ̄ di-bɛ́bɛ! kə́llub ʕis múklib!"³⁰⁶

The two men fished. In the place where they were fishing, a *samōmə* 'grouper' took their bait. It took the bait of the son, who was called Di-Ḥézirhən. Di-Ḥézirhən jerked the line hard to get the hook firmly stuck into their *samōmə* and he pulled it in towards him to get it into their dugout. As the *samōmə* came towards them and it was time for him to pull its head out of the water, the old man said to his son: "Oh son, hook it with a gaff!"

al tōmiʕ múgšəm l-íklib ʕis. šúʕur śíbeb, ʕúmur: "ʕa tízgud samōmə disé men ḥalf, ber tintúʕub!" ʕúmur: "ɛ bɛ́bɛ! škānaʕ ḥiy, al tighúz toʔ samōmə!" ḥɛ̄rə l-išʕúr śíbeb, ʕúmur: "al ṭaf ḥiy śúʔhur?" ol ṭaf múgšəm dihé-l-bɛ́bɛ. entə́wḥo ʔíntə śíbeb wə-dihé múgšəm. zígid di-ḥézirhən dihé śúʔhur. tyóʔo zígid, íbʔir mes riʔ, wə-tyóʔo símak ḳerīb ikób tus di-ḳānə id ḳārīyə dihí id hūri, nətáʕabo samōmə wə-gihézo.

The son wouldn't do as he was told, he wouldn't gaff it. The old man shouted at him: "Don't yank the *samōmə* up from where it is now: it will snap the line!" He said: "Oh father, have some faith in me! The *samōmə* won't get away from me!" The old man kept on shouting at him, trying to persuade him, saying: "Won't you hand your line over to me?" But the boy wouldn't hand it over to his father. They struggled together for a time over it, the old man and his son. Di-Ḥézirhən grabbed his line and when he got hold of it, the head (of the fish) appeared (above the sur-

---

³⁰⁶ More commomly *kəllāb ~ kullāb*.

face). Just as he was about to get it into bottom of their dugout, the *samōmə* snapped the line and got away.

kōlə šíbeb, ˤúmur: "ɛ-di-ḥézirhən, óʔo samōmə!" ˤúmur: "ɛ-bɛ́bɛ, gihézo samōmə." ˤúmur: "al ˤúmuk hek šēbuk ˤis wə-gēnaṭ ˤis míšḥaf?" ˤúmur: "ɛ-bɛ́bɛ! nyem bis? daḥámo! daḥámo!" ˤúmur: "ɛɛɛɛɛɛ! izˤék ḥāṭer di-állah![307] *u-míṭá éhɛn fálaḥk di-ḥézirhən ˤaf l-óḥṣi ber daḥámo! níti ḥánhən daḥámo. al tōmˤak ménhi di-ḥézirhən!" ˤémido šam wə-šə́rḳoḥo ˤággi di-bal meyh!*

The old man responded with: "Oh Di-Ḥézirhən, where is the *samōmə* 'grouper'?" He replied: "Oh father, the *samōmə* 'grouper' got away." He said: "Didn't I tell you to get your hook well and truly into it and to gaff it with the gaff?!?" He said: "Oh father, what was it worth? It was terribly thin! Nothing but skin and bones!" The father replied: "Ayeee! God strike you! And just when, Di-Ḥézirhən, did you cut it open to know that it was all skin and bones?!? We eat even skin and bones! You wouldn't listen to me, Di-Ḥézirhən, and do as you were told!" The sun sank down and they went ashore, empty-handed!

8.15.4. The Spanish Mackerel and the Wolf Herring: The Stealing of the Teeth (*ṭānik wə-širéʔe*)

bə-zámān dé di-fānə yəˤúmur éʔefo ḥá ṭānik al díʔse, kal ḥá di-širéʔe. [A]*yōm men əl-ʔayyām*[A] *ˤatə́gəlito ṭānik wə-širéʔe di-ˤamḳ di-maˤrērə di-ṣōdə, ṣōdə wə-di-ˤídi wə-di-sēli. gídəho ṭānik diyál širéʔe wə-ˤiméro his: "ah ḳáḳa! al túwzəm toʔ dié ḥá l-əkhāb biš kə-tsúwləhal*

---

[307] *ḥāṭer di-állah ~ xāṭer di-állah* 'anything catastrophic, as a falling meteor; a lightning strike; a landslide; a really heavy flood after a storm'.

(= di-súwləhal)." wə-di-súwləhal di-sēli. ʿiméro: "tkóli ínhi toš lal təḳéheb kə-tsúwləhal wə-šígzə hiš?" ʿaméro "əkōli." ʿiméro: "ḥaš!"

People here say that in days long ago the teeth (lit. 'mouth') of the ṭānik 'Spanish mackerel' were not actually hers, but those of the širéʿe 'wolf herring'. One day the Spanish mackerel met up with the wolf herring in the middle of a huge shoal: fish, small sardine-type fish and larger Gulf herring. The Spanish mackerel went up to the wolf herring and said: "My dear sister, won't you lend me your teeth so I can spend the midday splashing around and playing with the di-súwləhal 'Gulf herring'?" di-súwləhal are di-sēli Gulf herring. She replied: "You'll return them to me when you've spent the midday hours with the di-súwləhal 'Gulf herring' and have had enough?" She replied: "I'll give them back." She said: "Here you are then!"

zíʿi dsé ḥá wə-lāṭ ṭahéro tənáḥag wə-tšélihin ʿaf tərāzaḥ. fināḳo širéʿe kor təgúdihin ṭānik tkōlə his tsé (= disé) ḥá. al gidóho wə-šíno təʿōmid šām. ʿiméro: "úʿud diyal eʿḥíyti ṭānik kor dēkurs. yímkin níšo. bíro ʿemido hey šām wə-ʿéyək l-əḳār." ʿiméro: "yɛ! al tíʾtiš? w-al šígzə hiš?"

She (the ṭānik) took her (the širéʿe's) teeth and then went off to play and leap around until she was exhausted. The wolf herring waited for the Spanish mackerel to come and return her teeth to her. She didn't come and the wolf herring saw that the sun was beginning to set. She said: "I'll go to my sister the Spanish mackerel and remind her: perhaps it has slipped her memory. The sun is going down and I want to go back home." She said: "Hey! Haven't you finished? Haven't you had enough yet?"

ˁiméro: "mínʸəhem al šígzə ínhi wə-ʔínyəm ˁēyiš wə-l-ínʸəhem gídaḥš?" ˁiméro: "naˁ níšiš?" ˁiméro: "níšək ʔínyem?" ˁiméro: "dihó ḥá. al tkōli ínhi?" ˁiméro: "túwkif wə́lə-l-əkātabš wə-l-əgúrəmš." wə-lāṭ ʸhə́ləho. wə-tyóʔo ʸhə́ləho, ferēdo širéˁe. w-əmbōwi tos lāṭ ṭānīk lal tšālaḥ iˁúmur his: 'l-ité lafš!' dé men waḳt ˁaf də waḳt.

She (the Spanish mackerel) replied: "What do you mean 'Haven't I had enough?' What do you want? Why have you come?" The wolf herring said: "Have you forgotten now?" She said: "Forgotten what?" The wolf herring said: "My teeth! Aren't you going to give them back to me?" She said: "Be quiet, or I'll bite you in half or take a great chunk out of you!" And then she leaped high into the air. And when she leaped high in the air, the wolf herring turned tail and fled. Now, when the Spanish mackerel leaps high into the air, she is called: 'l-ité lafš!' "May the Lord kill (lit. 'eat up') your strength and vigour!" From that very day until this day.[308]

ṭānīk ímbe[309] nhafs. ˁiméro: "hōhən bíśi tyóʔo toʔ." ˁimer his: "b-ínʸəhem bíśi tyóʔo tuš?" ˁiméro: "hōhən šərót məhók." kōlə bis zíhnin, ˁúmur: "b-ínʸəhem īhin šərót məhók?" ˁiméro: "hōhən bíśi bíli di-ḳówlaˁ ménhi lal yūte toʔ. heb dihó íśʔḥal il-šébəhur." śáḥak

---

[308] The ṭānīk 'Spanish mackerel' is known for its terrible sawlike teeth, while the širéˁe 'wolf herring' is said to have only one tooth on each side of its mouth. di-súwləhil and sēli di-súwləhal are nicknames for the sēli 'Gulf herring'. súwləhil, pl. súwləhal refers to 'tiny hairs, threads', or to 'threads of mould growing on a surface'. The sēli 'Gulf herring' is called this because as it swims along, the fins on each side of its head flutter.

[309] ímbe < √nby.

mes zíhnin, ʿúmur: "hōhun áḥsanᴬ meš." ʿiméro: "b-ínʸəhem?" ʿúmur: "hōhən ḱáṭabə ménhi tə́rwi ʿášerə!" ʿiméro: "b-ínʸəhem tə́rwi ʿašerə? wə-b-ínʸəhem śəbáʿihin?" ʿúmur: "hōhən bíśi d-īti ménhi náʿsə w-iyhe al rī ḥey rīho." ʿiméro: "ʔēmunk!"

The Spanish mackerel gave herself a nickname. She said: "There is no one like me!" They said to her: "What do you mean, there is no one like you?" She replied: "I am *šəróṭ məhók*."³¹⁰ The *zíhnin* 'tuna' said to her: "How are you *šəróṭ məhók*?" She said: "When they come to eat me, absolutely nothing of me is left over, even the bones of the backbone." The *zíhnin* 'tuna' laughed at her and said: "I'm much better than you!" The Spanish mackerel said: "How so?" He said: "One half of me quenches the thirst of ten!" The Spanish mackerel said: "What do you mean, 'quenches the thirst of ten'? And what do *you* have to satisfy them and fill their bellies?" He replied: "No one can eat a morsel of me without having to drink water afterwards!" She said: "You're right!"³¹¹

---

³¹⁰ *šəróṭ* 'to swallow at a gulp without chewing' (i.e., every single part of me is edible); *məhók* 'anything delicious that slips down without having to be chewed (as butter oil, hot milk, ripe dates pulped in water)'.

³¹¹ The flesh of the *zíhnin* is said to be very hard and dry and anyone eating it needs to drink a lot to wash it down.

8.15.5. The Mountain Man Who Didn't Realise Fish Go Off

ˤaig ṭad ḳúˤud dhí men ṣándəhal³¹² wə-ˤaig al rínhi. wə-kísə iʔirīfi gidóho bə-ṭaḥ. wə-ˤúmur: "ṭaf ḥiy dihó ʔíməhen di-mízgud!" wə-ˤīmer: "záˤa nhafk ˤaf tədáḳ."³¹³ wə-ˤīmer: "túˤud ṣ̌ālaˤ éʔefo bə-bēdīyə ber ʔíno šīn ḥar iʔirīfi diláḳo."

There was a man who went from the lip of the ridge (where he lived) down to the coast, a man who knew nothing about the sea and fishing. He found that a huge shoal of fish had come right in close to shore, and he said: "Give me my share, as much as I can carry!" And they said: "Take as much as you can manage!" And they said: "Go and tell the people in the interior that we have masses of fish today!"

izáˤa di-ˤígib w-izōnig di-ˤígib. zéˤe ˤaig wə-tāḳib id ḥōr ˤaf təmōləʔ. wə-tyóʔo milóʔo dhí ḥōr ṣōdə, ṭáher wə-zíˤi d-ikíˤi men dhí zing w-ol ˤad búlug ˤaf igúdihin dhí di-ḳáˤr. ˤīmer: "men óʔo énkaˤk ṣōdə?" ˤúmur: "énkaˤk men ṭaḥ, wə-ˤə́kalk híkin tin ʔíməhen. əl-ˤōśi d-īˤud šiy igúdihin kor núˤud dé d-ikíˤi."

He picked up as many as he wished and carried off as many as he wanted on his back. He took the (the fish) off and poured them into a small goat pen until he had filled it right up. When his goat pen was full of fish, he set off. He picked up what was left of his load (of fish) and didn't stop until he reached his

---

³¹² ṣ́ándəhil, pl. ṣ́índəhol 'end, tip, extremity; tip of a ridge where it overlooks the sea; area above the anus, the very tip of the backbone'.

³¹³ < √ʔdḳ: ʔédaḳ iʔúwdaḳ l-idáḳ 'to be heavy; to have too much to carry, to be overburdened, overloaded'.

home. They said: "Where did you get fish from?" He said: "I brought them up from the coast, and I've left your share for you. Tomorrow at dawn anyone who wants to can come with me to fetch the fish that remain."

ᶜamǝd éʔefo ᶜaf ǝl-ᶜōśi w-ǝl-ᶜōśi śhalíf wǝ-śhalúf šiš éʔefo lhɛ́ d-fᶜid dhín l-iʔirīfi di-ṣōdǝ. wǝ-tyóʔo gídaḥ wǝ-ḳéᶜe dhí ḥōr kísǝ sǝ́nǝhum wǝ-tǝ́lo men ṣōdǝ d-ibtáʔar wǝ-nutíṣar.

People spent the evening together, chatting until dawn. When the sun rose, he set off, and those who wanted their share of the great shoal of fish went with him. But when he arrived and opened up his small goat pen, he was met with a terrible smell, the stink from the fish that had been caught but had decomposed (lit. 'leaked').

ᶜúmur: "ol ṭebk ṭaʰ tuš ᶜam aᶜákalš ḥá." ᶜīmer: "ya mǝnḳéynaᶜ! ṣōdǝ ki ᶜīḳel tuš ʔínṭe intéᶜirin men šīhum wǝ-men mahgḗgǝ di-šéhed!"

He said: "I never thought that this is what would happen to them when I put them there!" They said: "You madman! Fish rot if you leave them for any time in the heat of the sun and in a place with no air!"

ᶜaig ol ᶜǝ́rub wǝ-men solk w-ol ᶜǝ́rub ṭabīᶜaᴬ di-ṣōdǝ. ol tyóʔo naᶜ: éʔefo ᶜǝ́rub fáhǝrǝ ṭabīᶜa di-rínhem wǝ-ṭabīᶜa di-bēdīyǝ wǝ-ṭabīᶜa di-solk wǝ-ṭabīᶜa di-ḳǝ́nǝho. fānǝ ṭéḥḥi d-iḥúdum rínhem o yǝᶜúrub ṭabīᶜa di-šfāniś, wǝ-dé d-iḥúdum šfāniś o yǝᶜúrub ṭabīᶜa ṭéḥḥi.

The man knew nothing about this. He was from the mountains and knew nothing about the characteristics of fish. Not like today: today everyone knows about sea matters and about life in the interior and about livestock management. Before, the man of the coast who worked the sea knew nothing about looking after livestock, and the man who worked livestock knew nothing about the way of life of the man of the coast.

wə-ʾíno men ṭaḥ, w-ol dálak, d-iʿúrub ṭabīʿa di-šfāniś, tyóʾo óʾoz wə-téʾe yəʿúreb mes ṭabīʿa. wə-íno bédəwi d-iʿúrub ṭabīʿa ṭéḥḥi wə-dirínhem w-ol fáḥerə.

But there were some on the coast—not many—who knew about managing livestock, goats for instance or sheep, they knew about looking after them. And there were people from the interior who knew about the way of life of the people of the coast and about the sea, but not all of them.

8.15.6. The Glowing Jewel of the Serpent (gówherə di-bəkīli)

gídaḥ ʿaig men mōmi, ḳúʿud ṭaḥ yəʿágal men ṣōdə, iḥūrə men ṣōdə. tyóʾo ʿégib l-iktínaḥ, kutínaḥ lə-ḥalf di-ʿúmur hiš ḥoḳ. wə-nḥaṭ ḥoḳ ḥalf d-iʿúmur hiš fídəhān l-áʾamt ṣáḳerə di-Ḥállə. búʿur ʿaig tyóʾo ṣánnəfət šiš men báʿd təśímo. tyóʾo ʾéraḥ ʿamḳ di-óʾorəm d-ifōnə mōmi, wə-ḥalf d-išárḳaḥ hiš biš sēbir w-áḥarif wə-šérmihin, menól ťʿud śīno ṣayḥ d-áśga bə-ʿamḳ di-gēḥi əmbēn ʿōbir wə-ʿōbir.

A man came from Mōmi (the eastern end of Soqoṭra). He went down to the coast hoping to be given some fish; he was in search of fish. When he was about to go back (up), he went by way of a place called Ḥoḳ. And beneath Ḥoḳ is a place called Fídəhān, beside Ṣáḳerə di-Ḥállə. After the evening meal, he insisted on setting off and walking through the night. When he was halfway there, on his way to Mōmi—and the path he had chosen to go up was through thick undergrowth, with cliff faces and trees—as he was going along he saw a light glowing in the middle of the watercourse, between one bank and the other.

íftig. ʿúmur: "ʾínyem diš? gəlólə di-kḗfir?" wə-ʿúmur: "diš al gəlólə, ḥá bíśi kḗfir." wə-ʿag məṭḗmə. ʿud w-íʿtur di-fṓnə dihé bə-ṣayḥ. wə-tyóʾo śíʿiki, śíni diš bíli d-ihḗbaḥ men kesf ʿaf kesf ker šérmihin. wə-ʿə́rub wə-šəmālik ber bikīli. w-iyhé ber iʿúmur fā́nə éʾefo imṓtilin iśṓni ṣayḥ dé bə-ḥalf, w-al ʿə́rub ínʸəhem. méyhin iʿúmur ḥalf di-ginn.

He was amazed. He said to himself: "What on earth is this? A *gəlṓlə di-kḗfir*, 'an infidel's light'[314]?" And he said: "This can't be a *gəlṓlə*, there is no unbeliever here!" And he was an extremely curious man. He walked forward towards the light he'd seen (lit. 'his light'). When he got close, he saw this thing among the trees and shrubs, stretched out from side to side (of the watercourse). And he realised and recognised that it was a serpent. He'd been told, he'd heard people before talking about a light seen there at night, but they didn't know what it was. Some of them said the place belonged to the jinn.

zígid ʿaig dihé śéḳaʿ wə-ṭerḗfis árbaʿ məṭérif wə-lā́ṭ kḗbi wə-ʿud əl-mer ʿaf irṓgim ʿis wə-ʿaf yáʿṭiṭ ʿis. wə-lā́ṭ ṭḗbil dihé śéḳaʿ wə-dihé gówherə. wə-lā́ṭ ʸhālaḥ d-ifṓnə bis wə-seré ʿis kor séhen lal tšéḳidin tkōl riʾ d-ifónə bis. w-iyhéhen ləṭṭ séris d-ifṓnə ʿalé. ləʿámihe fə́rud di-gʸḗmə túwḳamš bə-šérmihin wə-bə-ʾíbəhān lal tintiśáḥan śímihel wə-ʾímihel.

---

[314] Visiting merchant ships always had lights on board which were widely known as *gəlṓlə di-kḗfir*.

The man took his shoulder wrap and folded it in four and then he crept forward, going along on his belly, until he was able to throw (the wrap) over it (i.e., the glowing jewel), covering it completely. Then he gathered up his wrap with the glowing jewel inside and made a great leap from in front of it (i.e., the serpent), right over it, so that, taken by surprise, it would turn its head round to look for it (i.e., its jewel). But he went around behind it (i.e., out of sight) and upwards. If he had fled downwards, it would have battered him with trees and rocks as it thrashed around to the left and right (searching everywhere for its jewel).

wə-tyóʔo šḥabílo éṣ̌əhim, nəháḳo ʕaf ihōmaʕ éʔefo di-ṣáḳerə wə-di-fídəhān wə-di-ḳábho. wə-ḥerégo bə-tēbə men boḳ men ʕálə se men ḥalf, wə-téʔes állah rínhem. wə-bíśi di-ḥúbur ḳéyri mes se men óʔorəm diš nihéro ʕis. ʕág záʕa dihé gówḥerə wə-ṭáher bis id riʔ d-irísseyl, wə-ḳárə tus w-al śálaʕ bis ɛ-ḥíy.

And when it sensed (nothing but) darkness, it let out a great shriek, so loud that the people of Ṣáḳerə and Di-Fídəhān and Di-Ḳábho heard it. And off it slithered, wailing and moaning (lit. 'mooing'), down from above: God sent it right to the sea and nothing and no one was harmed by it as it went. The man took his glowing jewel and went with it to Riʕ D-Irísseyl (at the very eastern tip of the island). He hid it and told no one anything about it.

ᴬyōm men al-ʔayyāmᴬ tyóʔo śíni mərākib tənéherən l-əriʔ d-iġális d-irísseyl ʕúmur nhafš rāmuš wə-difériš wə-ṭáher biš id ġúbba. wə-ted bə-ġúbba dé bə-ḥalf tənéherən ʕiš mərākib wə-yēnifin w-išúʕur w-iśáʕaḳ. ʔíno mərākib tənéherən ʕiš w-al tid hiš. bə-ʕamḳ di-éʕemed, tádo hiš márkab wə-ṭireb diš wə-ˁimer ˁiš: "nyem ˁēyək?" wə-márkab diš ṭerébo yímkin éʔefo lhέ il-bis ˁígib l-ihoríḳiš.

One day, when he saw sailing ships passing by the headlands of D-Irísseyl, he made a raft for himself and pushed it (down to the sea). He went right out to sea in it, and sat and waited there in the depths where the sailing ships were bound to pass by. He waved at them, and he screamed and shouted out to them. The ships went past him but did not stop for him. After some time a ship did stop for him. It turned aside to come towards him and asked: "What do you want?" And this ship that had turned side for him, perhaps the people in it hoped to steal something from him.

wə-tyóʔo gídaḥ diš u-bɛ-l-rəwúʔuš "nyem ˁēyək," śəné dihé gówḥerə. bítiš ˁag, dé núxədə diš márkab ber ˁag ol gídaḥ di-ḥá kal əl-bíli, ʔímməᴬ iśōʔum wələ ʔíno šiš bíli dʸáḥṣiš. ˁúmur hiš: "nyém ˁēyek wə-ṭaf ḥiy diέ gówḥerə." zígid ḳérməhim dihé d-íʔid wə-ˁúmur hiš: "hōhun ˁēyək ṭaʰ wə-ṭaʰ." wə-ḳáhəḳaḥ dihé fíʔo dihé bə-ḳérməhim. ˁúmur: "ˁēyək mékkə w-əmdīni." zígid kεfir dihé íʔid wə-ˁə́kal dihé íʔid bə-riʔ, riʔ di-kεfir. bit wə-ˁə́rub ˁaig ber maḥrūz wə-bíli ˁiš al tíkkən.

And when they reached him and before they could ask: "What do you want?", they saw his jewel. The man understood him: the captain of this ship realised that he hadn't come all this way out here without a good reason, either to sell something or for some other purpose. He (i.e., the captain) said to him: "What do you want for giving me your jewel?" He (i.e., the Soqoṭri) took him by the knuckles of his hand and said to him: "I want such and such," knocking his forehead again and again with his knuckles.[315] He said to him: "I want Mecca and Medina." The unbeliever grasped his hand and put it on his (own) head, the unbeliever's head. He (the Soqotri) understood him and knew that (now) he had been taken under the captain's protection, and that nothing bad would happen to him.

wə-gaḥ tuš dihé di-márkab. wə-zíʕiš nōxədə iyhé wə-di-šiš, w-al ʕad bílug biš ʕaf igúdiḥin biš gíddə. w-ínkaʕ hiš mətárgim^A w-ízʕim šiš. wə-kēfir mətárgim dé d-ínkaʕ hiš ʕárabi wə-múslim. wə-ʕúmur hiš: "díful ʕēyək men diréhəm l-āṭaf ʕek wə-ɛ́ḥɛn thagíg biš dé bə-ʕag wə-təméddən biš ʕaf l-itītə ḥag wə-tkōləʔiš ínhi ídəbóh. wə-ɛ́ḥɛn masʔōl^A ʕiš korúmma kāno ʕiš bíli." wə-ḳəbə́l ʕag wə-zíʕi dihé ʕag wə-ḥag biš wə-máddən biš ʕaf itītə wə-kilíʔo. w-iʕúmur dé men waḳt d-ifíḳad biš ʕaig ʕaf igúdiḥin ʔíno ^Asíttat áshur^A.

And the captain had him taken up into his ship. He took him with him, he and what he had with him, and he didn't stop until they reached Jeddah. He fetched a translator and sat with him. And the translator brought by the unbeliever was an Arab and a Muslim. (The captain) said to him (i.e., the translator): "What money do you want from me for going on the Ḥajj with this man, and (then) going with him to Medina, (staying with him) until the Ḥajj is completed, and then bringing him back to me, to right here? And you would take full responsibility for anything that might happen to him?" And the man (i.e., the translator) accepted. He took the man he was responsible for (lit. 'his man') and accompanied him on the Ḥajj and went with

---

[315] I.e., striking his forehead with his knuckles to signify that he wanted to pray.

him to Medina until everything was done. Then they both went back. And it is said that from the time that the (Soqoṭri) man went missing until he came back (to the island) was six months.

wə-tyóʔo símak úste waḳt di-ḥag wə-kōnaḥ, ʿúmur hiš: "nyem ʿḗyək l-itgér hek?" ʿúmur: "bíli al ʿḗyək. ʿḗyək tkəlḗ toʔ dihó di-ḥalf." ʿúmur hiš: "bíli al ʿḗyək stəgér? hōhən əkōlək dié di-ḥalf wə-bíli ʿek al tíkkən. ᴬməʿáziz mḥárrəmᴬ." ʿúmur: "ʿḗyək lə-stəgér ínhi ṭad kitábᴬ." ʿúmur: "óʔo ṭaʰ? óʔo ṭaʰ śówʔum?" ʿúmur: "bilád." ṭērub kḗfir w-il-šiš, wə-zíʿi k-ənháfš ʿag dé saḳóṭeri.

And when the time for the Ḥajj had come to an end and they had come back, he (i.e., the captain) said to him: "What do you want me to buy for you?" He said: "I don't want anything. I just want you to take me back to where I came from." He said to him: "You really don't want to buy anything? I'll take you back to your place and you can be sure that nothing (bad) will happen to you: you are esteemed and untouchable." He said: "I would like you to buy one book for me." He said: "What book is that? What book and where is it for sale?" He said: "In town." The infidel and those with him disembarked, and he took that Soqoṭri man with him.

wə-ṭerēbo id suḳ wə-ríʿiš, ʿúmur: "óʔo śówʔum kútubᴬ?" ʿímer: "ɛ́hɛ əl-fānə hek." ksóʔo máktəbəᴬ milóʔo əw dákkānᴬ mīli di-kútub wə-ḳurʔān. ʿúmur kḗfir ɛ-ʿaig di-béhelə dəkkān di-kútub, ʿúmur: "kam tśóʔom dié kútub?" ʿúmur: "díful ʿḗyək?" ʿúmur: "ʿḗyək hīhin fáherə. tšrākaḥ ter dié men máktəbəᴬ." wə-šə́rḳaḥ ʿaig id ter men baʿd əl-ṭɛf ʿiš kam səndūḳ di-dərɛ́həm. w-iyhéhin ʿúmur: "ṭḗbilin di-kisíʿkin bə-ḳānə ʿaf ziké, wə-ʔōgaḥ id márkab!"

They went down to the market and asked around. He said: "Where are books sold?" They said: "Right there in front of you." They found a bookshop, a shop full of books and (copies of the) Qurʾān. The infidel said to the man who owned the bookshop: "How much will you sell your books for?" He replied: "How many do you want?" He said: "I want them all. Leave your shop!" After he (i.e., the infidel) had given him I don't know how many chests of money, the man (i.e., the bookshop owner) went out. He (i.e., the infidel captain) said: "All of you, gather up whatever you find inside until there is nothing left, and then go back on board!"

wə-kilíʿiš dihé bə-ḥalf wə-tyóʿo iróḥo dihé di-ḥalf éṭerbiš wə-éṭerib hiš dihé kútub lhé tīgur hiš. wə-ʿād méyhin lhé kútub dé di-ʿag dé bə-zə́mān di-símak di-ínkiʿihin, ʿād náʿa bə-saḳóṭeri. wə-ʾíno kútub méyhin d-inḳānaʿ méyhin éʾefo ʾēm[316] *iḳeríʿiš!*

And he (i.e., the captain) took him back to his home. And when the two of them reached his place (i.e., Soqotra), he helped him disembark and he unloaded his books, those that he had purchased for him. And some of those books that he brought at that time are still to be found on Soqotra to this day. And some of the books drive some of those who read them mad!

8.15.7. The Men Who Ate ṣáfrer Fish

ṣáfrer ḥot ḳíhən o išābaʿ tərá, lékin bih ʿáṣṣub. iyhéhin ʿan ṣódə ʿáṣṣub bih wə-sínəhum bih. korúmma ḳúdurk tuš wə-tuyk toš dié b-íʿid, təráḥaṣ di-ʾídi meyh bə-ríḥo yōmēn[A] *wə-ʿād al ṭáher meyh ṭayʾ!*

---

[316] Lit. 'the day'.

The ṣáfrer 'butterflyfish' or 'coralfish' is a small one, not even enough to fill two people, but it causes the ʿáṣṣub sickness. More than any other fish it causes the ʿáṣṣub sickness. Also, it smells bad: if you cook it and eat it with your hand, you can wash your hands in water for two days afterwards and the stink of it still won't have gone away!

korúmma šṭālimk tuš wə-bíśi ekəníyo kal íyhe wə-lāṭ ʿiśk men dēmi, túʿud əw tšárkaḥ śígirə, tə́nṭəṭən mɛk śírəhān wə-bīrok. ki ʾíno śīni tok túʿud wə-tə́ʿáṣaf wə-ɛ́hen ṭíbəb tok al gúʿurk wə-lāfi, ḥówṣeʾ bik ɛ́hən ber tuyk ṣṓdə w-enʿáṣibk, wə-ɛ́hən bə-nḥáfk ḥóṣi ber enʿáṣibk diɛ́ men ṣáfrer di-tuyk tuš.

If you ate one for the evening meal, if there was nothing to eat but this fish, and then you got up and set off or climbed a pass, your legs and knees would tremble and shake. If anyone saw you going along, but (being forced) to stop and rest, and if it were known that you were not ill but were a strong and fit person, people would realise that you had eaten a fish and developed the ʿáṣṣub sickness. And you yourself would realise that you had become sick with the ʿáṣṣub sickness from eating the ṣáfrer 'butterflyfish' or 'coralfish'.

íno tərá ʿággi di-gədə́ho ʾekāro, al ʿaggi ṭeyhó wə-ʿággi men fídəhān. wə-ṭālimiyhí ṣáfrer. wə-šiṭə́lmo ʿággi bə-ṣáfrer wə-dəmāyo ʿaf əl-ʿṓśi. w-əl-ʿṓśi ṣ̌hálifo ektínəho dihi di-ḥalf. fānə ʾɛ́rəho dihi di-ḥalf fisaʿ ki išḥálifo: əl-ʿṓśi lə-šərkóho di-šām, iʾɛ́rəho men ṣalāti əw igəhémo. kol dé šām tiyéyo bis ṣṓdə. ṣ̌hálifo wə-kērhe ʾekāro. iʿādo wə-iʿā́ṣəfo ḥówʷhá!

Once there were two men who arrived at dusk. They were not men from the coast but from the mountains above. And they (i.e. their hosts) gave them both *ṣáfrer* 'butterflyfish' or 'coralfish' for their evening meal. And the two men ate the *ṣáfrer* fish and slept until dawn the next day. In the early morning, they set off to go back up home. Before, if they set off in the early morning, they would reach their place quickly: (if they left) at sunrise, they would get there between the two prayers (i.e., mid-morning) or at noon. Except for that day that they ate that fish: they set off in the early morning and they barely got home at dusk! They would go along but then had to sit down to rest, here and there and everywhere!

INDEX

abalone, 11, 189, 284, 288, 312, 320, 343, 346–47, 352–54, 359–61, 365–68, 370–72, 381, 526, 668–69

algae, 93–94, 101–3, 105, 217–18, 222, 230 n. 12, 242, 461–62, 487, 492, 569, 574 n. 202, 616, 628, 688, 690

al-Ġayḍah, 11, 275, 342, 347, 351 n. 5, 352, 354, 375, 417–18

al-Ḥallāniyyāt islands, 2, 4, 542

al-Mahrah, 2, 5, 8–9, 12, 341–42, 344–49, 351

al-Qaṭīf, 118 n. 5, 445 n. 22

anchovies, 131, 465, 475, 476 n. 71, 477, 584

angelfish, 47, 56, 58, 62, 74, 481

Arabia / Arabian, 1–7, 11–14, 16, 18, 31 n. 1, 32, 35, 46, 53, 55, 57–58, 64, 67–68, 71, 79, 81, 107–10, 112–13, 115, 117 n. 5, 123, 132, 134 n. 16, 147 n. 26, 155, 158, 171, 174, 179, 254, 341–42, 355, 358, 362, 433, 440 n. 14, 442, 446 n. 24, 448–49, 452 n. 32, 469 n. 59, 482 n. 77, 496 n. 94, 520, 535 n. 154, 540 n. 160, 576, 577 n. 209, 589 n. 219

Arabic / *ārabī* (Ar.), 2–3, 5–6, 9, 12–15, 22, 31 n. 1, 33, 36, 38 n. 2, 41, 47, 52–61, 64–85, 107–12, 118–20, 122, 125, 131–35, 136 n. 20, 139–40, 141 n. 23, 142–43, 145–48, 151, 154–58, 169–70, 180, 184, 246, 247 n. 19, 253, 255–56, 322 n. 61, 333–34, 351, 355, 358, 373 n. 18, 378 n. 21, 393, 429, 438, 443–44, 447 n. 26, 459, 467–68, 504 n. 111, 535 n. 154, 542–43, 545 n. 165, 548, 559, 562, 568, 601, 613 n. 237, 623 n. 241, 671 n. 272, 702 n. 304

Gulf Arabic (GAr), 23, 31 n. 1, 41, 61, 65–66, 70–74, 76, 78, 80, 83, 85, 110, 112, 119 n. 7, 120, 131, 133–34, 136, 139, 142, 146, 147 n. 26, 156–57

Khuzestani Arabic, 131 n. 13

Musandam Arabic (MusAr), 7, 13–14, 16, 22–23, 31 n. 1, 53–54, 57, 59–61, 63, 65–67, 69–74, 77–80, 82–84,

109–10, 112, 118, 119 n. 6, 120, 123, 126 n. 12, 130, 137–39, 142–43, 156–57
Omani Arabic, 124–25, 155, 211
Sanaa Arabic, 123
Shihhi Arabic, 110
Arabism, 21–22
Bahrain, 118 n. 5, 120, 136 n. 20, 428
Balochi (Bl.), 12, 31–32 n. 1, 65–67, 70–82, 84–85, 130
Bandari (Bn.), 12, 31–32 n. 1, 65, 67, 73, 75, 80–82, 85
barnacles, 93–94, 101–2, 210, 218, 569, 641, 647, 650
barracuda, 14, 460, 478, 501 n. 106, 504, 575
Baṭhari (B.), 2, 4, 6, 10, 13–15, 19, 31–32 n. 1, 67, 72–77, 82–84, 134 n. 16, 169–71, 173–75, 176 n. 5, 179–80, 184, 186, 192, 198, 209, 211, 236, 243–45, 249, 253–56, 273, 314 n. 58, 334, 342
Bedouin dialects, 110, 132
Bəṭāḥira, 169, 171–76, 178–80, 182–83, 185, 187, 195, 197, 203, 206, 210–11, 214, 219, 222, 224, 226, 228, 230 n. 12, 232, 234, 236 n. 16, 240, 242–43, 247, 249, 251–52, 254–56, 284 n. 45, 290
Bəṭaḥrēt, *see* Baṭhari
billfish, 357, 359, 587
bream, 15, 44, 46–49, 56–57, 59, 61–62, 64, 70, 72, 74, 76, 81, 204, 215, 287, 297, 299, 351, 355, 358, 460, 472 n. 65, 480–81, 492
bull, 46, 52–53, 64, 71, 73, 80, 183, 236, 355, 406–7, 420
butterflyfish, 15, 47, 58, 62, 66, 74, 82, 495, 501, 602, 603 n. 227, 720–21
Btahret, *see* Baṭhari
camels, 127, 133–36, 141, 149, 172, 174, 179, 187, 194, 221, 225, 231, 237, 248, 260, 262, 264–66, 290–96, 321, 333–34, 336, 349, 356, 358, 362, 412, 415–16, 500 n. 105, 512 n. 118, 528, 540, 578, 626
cardinalfish, 44, 46, 48, 52, 57, 71, 81, 83
casting of lots, 240, 242
catfish, 52, 65, 73, 299, 497, 575
cephalopod, 42, 51, 58, 70, 221, 224, 479, 530–31
chiton, 189, 220, 224, 288, 312, 320, 360, 380–84, 386, 523, 525, 665–66, 669

climate, 9, 99, 252, 342, 344–45
cod, 409, 500 n. 103
coir, 211, 362, 403, 445, 462 n. 45, 502, 553 n. 173, 554, 561 n. 187, 563
crabs, 42, 181, 202, 204, 214–15, 218, 239, 381, 480–81, 492, 529–30, 583, 586, 636, 674–77
croaker, 355
cuttlefish, 41–42, 51, 58, 64, 70, 214, 220, 287, 290, 447–48, 461, 479, 530–1, 589
Daba, *see* Dibba
Dhofar, 2, 4, 9, 11–12, 14, 17, 23, 169–74, 248, 254, 288, 341–42, 344, 346–47, 349, 351, 359, 398, 416, 535
Dibba / Daba, 32, 98, 110, 118
diver, 346, 354, 361, 368–70, 372, 428, 451, 498, 499, 534, 540–46, 547 n. 168, 548–51, 569–70, 586
diving, 110, 222, 258 n. 25, 327, 343, 346, 353–54, 365–66, 371–72, 451, 474–75, 488, 506, 526 n. 137, 530, 533, 540–45, 547–49, 627, 631, 655, 663, 679, 683–84, 689

dolphin, 42, 50, 65, 73, 75, 223, 264, 288, 434, 517–20, 659
dolphinfish, 47, 62, 66, 70, 74, 459
drum, 116, 215, 237–38, 351, 355, 358, 374–75, 396, 451, 453, 456, 481, 495, 554, 564–65, 576, 593, 626–27, 633, 637
Dubai, 313, 409, 416, 545, 577 n. 209
dugout canoe, 178–79, 188, 211, 218, 237, 250, 308, 321, 347, 406, 432 n. 4, 436, 452 n. 33, 466, 468, 471–72, 485, 488–89, 498, 502, 505–8, 511–16, 518, 520, 542–44, 550, 554–64, 565 n. 192, 566–71, 578, 605, 619–24, 632–33, 637, 640–41, 647–51, 653–57, 679, 682–86, 705–7
East Africa, 13, 179, 192, 241, 303, 350, 430, 433, 441 n. 17, 443–44, 446, 451 n. 30, 462 n. 45, 502–3, 514 n. 120, 534, 551, 558, 576 n. 209, 577 nn. 209–10, 688
ecosystems, 1–3, 35, 113
Emirates, *see* United Arab Emirates
emperor, 44–47, 55, 61, 63, 73–74, 78–80, 83, 204, 215–

16, 234, 287, 297–99, 351, 357, 409, 457, 460, 472, 480, 482, 490, 492, 582, 589, 591–93

ethnobiology, 34–36, 38–39, 41

fat, 206, 214, 216, 221, 223–26, 231, 234–36, 238–39, 241, 244–45, 252, 260, 283, 287, 299, 328–30, 332, 399, 477, 496, 500–1, 512 n. 118, 516–17, 519, 563 n. 188, 565, 567 n. 194, 573, 575, 580–81, 583–84, 587, 606, 659, 665, 672, 674, 676, 693, 700–1

fin, 14, 53–54, 73, 76, 84, 206–7, 304–5, 309, 320, 350, 355–56, 374, 379, 483, 491, 497, 502, 587, 590 n. 220, 635, 638, 644, 646, 651, 694, 701, 709 n. 308

fish, 5–6, 8, 10–14, 16–17, 31, 33–85, 97–98, 112, 126, 130–31, 133–35, 148–50, 155, 158, 176, 178, 180–82, 184–86, 189, 191, 194, 196, 202–6, 210, 212–17, 219–20, 223–24, 228–31, 234, 236–37, 239–43, 245, 246 n. 17, 247, 249, 251–52, 256, 258 n. 26, 260–61, 263–64, 268–70, 277, 280–83, 285–87, 289, 291, 296–300, 302, 304, 306–7, 312, 314, 323, 327, 334, 342–45, 347, 349–63, 386–88, 390–98, 400–3, 408–13, 417–18, 421, 429–31, 433, 435 n. 7, 443–44, 446, 449–50, 452 n. 33, 453–54, 455 n. 35, 456–62, 465–68, 469 n. 59, 470–80, 482–85, 487–97, 499–501, 502 n. 108, 503 n. 110, 504, 506, 509, 513 n. 120, 514, 517, 517 n. 122, 518, 522, 526, 530–32, 535, 539–40, 547, 552, 554–55, 557 n. 182, 561, 568, 570 n. 197, 571–76, 577 nn. 209–10, 579–81, 583–96, 601–19, 621, 626–29, 631, 634, 635, 636 n. 251, 637, 639, 646–50, 654, 657–62, 675–77, 679–82, 689–701, 705–6, 708, 711–13, 719–21

fisheries, 10, 36, 429, 452 n. 32, 454, 458, 540, 556 n. 179, 596

fishermen / fishers, 5, 8–12, 14, 17, 31, 36–37, 50, 91, 97, 150, 203–4, 209, 211–12, 216, 222, 231, 235, 241–42, 325, 342–45, 353–54, 359, 363, 372, 391, 429–33, 449–50, 452, 454, 457–58, 460–63, 465–69, 473, 475, 477 n. 73, 478, 482, 484–85, 491 n. 88, 492 n. 90,

496, 498 n. 100, 499, 502, 505–8, 511–15, 518–21, 524 n. 131, 530, 540–42, 548, 552, 555–56, 557, 563–64, 566–68, 570, 572, 573 n. 200, 574, 576 n. 208, 581 n. 213, 584, 589–91, 594, 596, 609 n. 233
fishing, 3, 5, 8–10, 12, 16, 34, 38–40, 50, 57, 96–99, 104, 107–8, 110–12, 114, 121, 126–27, 135, 137, 140, 142, 145, 156–58, 172, 179, 181, 183, 187, 190, 203–4, 206, 212–13, 216–17, 240–42, 245, 247–48, 261 n. 29, 268 n. 33, 270, 280, 290, 303, 306, 320, 324, 330, 342–47, 352, 358, 360, 363, 373 n. 17, 428–32, 434, 437, 445, 446 n. 24, 449–50, 452 nn. 32–33, 453–55, 456–58, 460–61, 465–69, 471–73, 476, 480, 483–84, 494, 496, 502, 503, 509, 511, 513–14, 520, 522, 541 n. 162, 543, 552 nn. 172–73, 555–56, 557 n. 182, 560–61, 566, 568, 571–72, 576, 583, 587–88, 594, 596, 602, 604, 605 n. 231, 608, 610–13, 621–22, 624, 627, 628 n. 243, 638, 647, 655, 659–60, 675, 683, 689, 701, 705–6, 711
flap, 118, 152, 156
flatfish, 79, 466 n. 53
flippers, 328, 332–33, 335–36, 366, 511, 513–14, 516, 654
flora, 394 n. 25
flounder, 51, 63, 68, 79
Ġayḍah, *see* al-Ġayḍah
glide, 18, 20–23
goatskin, 102, 188, 207, 212–13, 218, 269, 275, 307–8, 315, 321, 444 n. 22, 494
grazing, 178, 293, 295, 345, 449 n. 28, 451, 511, 513
grouper, 14, 46, 51, 56–57, 59, 61–62, 66, 68, 71, 75, 77–78, 84, 204, 234, 236, 297, 351, 354, 457, 460 n. 43, 461, 472, 480, 482, 490, 492, 501 n. 106, 580, 582, 593, 603 n. 227, 610, 700, 706–7
grunter, 14, 66, 78, 81, 480–81
guitarfish, 14, 43, 47, 53, 57–58, 79, 81, 357–58, 407, 520
Gulf, 12–13, 22, 32, 36, 48–49, 55–56, 76, 91, 93, 95–97, 102–3, 107–8, 110–12, 117, 119, 123–24, 130, 132, 135–39, 152, 156–58, 179, 241, 350, 427, 430, 433, 439, 443–44, 446 n. 24,

447, 452 n. 33, 468, 472, 476–77, 496 n. 94, 501, 542–43, 545 n. 165, 549 n. 169, 557, 559, 570, 577 n. 209, 601–2, 628, 670, 708–9

Habalayn, 109, 111, 113–14, 158

Ḥadbīn, 353, 363, 398, 400

Ḥallāniyyāt, *see* al-Ḥallāniyyāt islands

Ḥarsūsi / *ḥərsə́yyət*, 6, 169, 254

Ḥāsik, 12, 173, 176, 179, 243, 343, 346–47, 372, 380, 382, 384, 400, 403, 410

Ḥawf, 11, 417

ḥərsə́yyət, *see* Ḥarsūsi

Hobyot / *hobyōt* (H.), 6, 10, 15, 19, 31–32 n. 1, 67, 72–73, 75, 78, 80, 83–84, 134 n. 16, 254, 342, 375 n. 19

hooks, 203–4, 216, 218, 222, 242, 245, 263, 267–69, 276–77, 280, 285–86, 312, 325–28, 331, 347, 360–61, 373 n. 17, 408, 431, 455, 457, 468–73, 475–76, 480–81, 482 n. 77, 483, 489, 503–6, 511–13, 516, 518, 520, 532, 611, 653, 655–57, 675, 685, 706–7

Hormuz, Strait of, *see* Strait of Hormuz

Indian Ocean, 58, 84, 114, 433

Iranic languages, 67, 109

jellyfish, 42, 183–84, 497, 523, 631

Jufa, 343, 383

kawakawa, 45, 58, 75, 84, 131, 356

Khasab, 32, 35–36, 53, 59, 61, 69, 72, 91, 110, 118–19, 135 n. 18

khor (fjord), 97, 114

kingfish, 46, 50–51, 62, 64, 75, 77–78, 85, 108, 114, 126–27, 130–31, 138, 140, 146, 155, 203, 205, 210, 277, 280–82, 287, 297–98, 314, 358, 456, 459–60, 470, 479, 590

Korea, 409

Kumzari / *kumẓāri* (K.), 3–8, 10, 12–14, 16, 22, 31–50, 52–56, 58–85, 91, 93, 96–98, 100, 102–4, 109, 112, 130–31, 137

lagoons, 177, 208, 219, 247, 305–6, 309, 387, 457 n. 39, 466, 479, 481, 485 n. 82, 486, 493–95, 511, 514, 529, 541, 579, 593, 606–10

latex, 493–95, 549, 563, 606–10

lexicography, 34

lexicon / vocabulary, 7–8, 10, 31 n. 1, 33–34, 40, 49–50, 58, 60, 62–64, 65 n. 10, 66

n. 11, 67, 69, 115, 128, 130, 133, 139, 151, 154, 156, 171, 429, 543
lionfish, 85, 497 n. 96, 631
lobster, 42, 45, 47, 53, 55, 83, 131 n. 14, 202, 214, 220, 287, 361, 390–92, 532, 588
longlining, 373 n. 17
lures, 216, 277, 280, 457, 461, 471, 482–83, 611
mackerel, 13, 75, 77–78, 85, 130–31, 205, 210, 298, 356, 434, 465, 475–76, 478, 501 n. 106, 506, 584–85, 590, 594, 601, 606, 637, 690, 692, 707–10
Mahrah, *see* al-Mahrah
Mahri / Mehri (M.), 6, 9–10, 13–15, 19, 31–32 n. 1, 53 n. 8, 67, 70, 72–76, 78, 80–83, 134 n. 16, 169–70, 254–56, 334, 341–44, 346–50, 351 n. 5, 355–63, 365, 400–1, 403, 411, 417–18, 430 n. 2
Mahriyōt, 349, 354, 356–57, 360–61, 417
Makran coast, 12
marine, 4–6, 8, 10, 13, 16–17, 91, 133 n. 15, 178, 180, 202, 215–16, 220–21, 359, 428–29, 432–33, 469 n. 59, 482 n. 77, 490, 493 n. 91, 496 n. 94, 499 n. 101, 564, 569, 596

marlin, 77, 238, 357–59, 434, 587
Mehri, *see* Mahri
Middle Persian (MP), 31–32 n. 1, 59, 64, 68, 72, 76, 82, 85
milkfish, 48–49, 51–52, 60, 83, 298, 357, 481, 495, 603 n. 227
Minabi, *see* Minowi
minnow, 76–77, 84
Minowi / Minabi (Mn.), 31–32 n. 1, 52, 65–68, 70–82, 84–85, 392
Mirbāṭ, 12, 343, 346, 361, 383–84, 386, 393, 415
Modern South Arabian languages (MSAL), 3, 6–7, 12–15, 18, 19 n. 1, 20, 31–32 n. 1, 53, 67, 134 n. 16, 171, 174, 254 n. 22, 255, 341–42, 429
monsoon, 9, 11–12, 183, 185–87, 189, 197, 206, 215, 218–19, 222, 230 n. 12, 240–42, 245, 257, 259, 263–64, 283, 285, 296, 304–5, 310–11, 319–20, 341, 344–45, 348, 353, 366, 415, 434–35, 440 n. 15, 443–44, 447 n. 26, 454, 457–58, 460 n. 43, 461, 465, 466 n. 52, 468 n. 58, 473, 477, 484, 493, 503 n. 109, 509, 511–13, 520,

522–23, 542–43, 553 n. 173, 560, 565 n. 192, 566, 568, 577 n. 211, 578–80, 583, 594, 602, 608, 633, 634 n. 250, 637, 651, 660, 673, 687–88, 693

moray eel, 14, 189, 284–85, 312, 470, 490, 495–96, 501 n. 106, 630

mullet, 66, 71, 204, 223, 229–31, 234, 241–42, 252, 286, 297–98, 300, 357, 412, 457 n. 39, 480, 495, 501, 586, 602–3, 608, 610

multilingual, 11, 112, 345

Musandam, 2–6, 8–9, 12, 16, 23–24, 32–33, 35, 37, 60, 68, 91, 96–97, 105, 107–14, 117–19, 132, 133 n. 15, 135, 147 n. 26, 155–57, 344–45

Muscat, 12, 35, 416, 427, 442–43, 445–47, 455 n. 34, 468 n. 58, 552 n. 173, 557, 559

navigation, 93, 103, 553 n. 173

net, 44, 50, 63, 126, 155, 185, 203, 207, 209, 214, 216–18, 228, 242, 246 n. 17, 247, 252, 257–58, 261, 263, 267, 269, 271, 274–75, 278–79, 290, 306–9, 312–16, 319–20, 322–23, 345, 347–49, 351, 357–58, 360–63, 367–68, 373–74, 378, 390–92, 403, 404 n. 26, 405–6, 410–14, 417, 431, 445 n. 23, 451, 452 n. 33, 454–57, 462–68, 476 n. 72, 477, 479, 485, 492, 502–3, 508, 513, 520, 574 n. 201, 594, 602–4, 660

oil lamps, 351, 398

Oman, 4–6, 12, 32, 35–36, 43, 56, 74, 81, 91, 107, 111, 117–18 n. 5, 119, 131–32, 135, 147 n. 26, 151, 170, 173, 179–80, 216, 241, 254, 256, 271–72, 294 n. 47, 350, 430, 433, 440 n. 15, 443–44, 496 n. 94, 502 n. 109, 517 n. 123, 533, 542–43, 545, 558 n. 184, 561 n. 187, 569–70

oral literature / oral tradition / oral texts, 4, 7–8, 34, 39, 103, 107–8, 110–11, 113–14, 174, 255, 435

oysters, 93–94, 101–2, 189, 220, 312, 320, 360, 384–86, 451, 469 n. 59, 482 n. 77, 492, 524, 526, 540–42, 544–48, 550–51, 554, 627, 647, 650, 663, 666–67, 679, 681–89

parrotfish, 15, 58, 62, 64, 84, 354, 359, 499 n. 101, 500 n. 103, 574, 588, 603 n. 227

pearl, 110, 428, 436 n. 9, 447, 469 n. 59, 482 n. 77, 484 n. 79, 498 n. 98, 526, 540–48, 549 n. 169, 550–51, 678–84, 686–87, 689

Persian (P.), 31 n. 1, 33, 41, 57, 59, 61, 64–66, 68, 70–75, 77–85, 130, 433

pompano, 15, 206, 215–16, 223, 242–43, 245, 287, 297, 358–59, 409, 481, 495, 585–87, 603, 608

prawns, 49, 58, 80–81

Qaṭīf, *see* al-Qaṭīf

queenfish, 49–50, 58, 64, 66, 76, 82, 184, 283 n. 44, 355

rabbitfish, 14, 45, 58, 64, 71, 73, 82, 241, 244–45, 286–87, 297–98, 300, 349–50, 357, 359, 361, 387–90, 393, 396, 412, 466, 490–91, 585, 593–94, 700

Ras al-Khaimah, 95–96, 99

ray, 43–44, 51, 64–65, 68, 79–80, 314, 344, 356–57, 434, 480, 497, 504, 515, 520–21, 538–40, 588, 640–41

Raysūt, 349 n. 4, 362–63

remora (suckerfish), 13, 63, 77, 513–16, 651, 655–56

Sadḥ, 343, 352–53, 355, 358, 360–61, 365, 384, 386, 393–94, 402, 415

Salalah, 12, 170–71, 254, 347, 357–58, 416

salt, 202, 207, 210, 212, 218–21, 224, 228, 230, 232, 233 n. 13, 235, 247, 305–6, 309–10, 316, 329–30, 374, 376, 378–79, 439 n. 13, 444, 446, 456, 476 n. 72, 481, 493 n. 91, 499, 540 n. 158, 541 n. 161, 557 n. 182, 575–80, 582, 585, 589 n. 219, 590–93, 595, 623 n. 241, 629, 690, 691, 697, 699, 701–3

sardine, 11, 50, 64, 76, 84, 185, 205, 213, 216, 267–68, 277, 300 n. 50, 304, 316, 318, 320–21, 345–50, 358–59, 361, 410–16, 434, 465–66, 471, 474–79, 481 n. 76, 483–84, 492, 506, 530, 568, 584, 601–2, 611–12, 629, 648, 675, 696, 708

Saudi Arabia, 118 n. 5, 445 n. 22

sawfish, 14, 55, 82, 236, 238, 288–89, 314, 358

scad, 43, 53, 61, 66, 72, 74, 80, 357, 358, 412, 466, 476

scales, 128, 151, 155, 351, 396, 476 n. 72, 535, 591, 603, 629, 662, 697

sea cucumber, 42, 220, 222, 532, 670, 673

sea lemon, 221, 288, 360, 380–83
sea snake, 53, 78, 496
sea urchin, 312–13, 523, 528–29, 632, 671–72
seahorse, 52, 70
seaweed, 200, 208, 210, 215, 218, 223, 228, 230, 249, 301–2, 310, 488, 491–92, 496, 512, 550, 573 n. 200, 616
Semitic, 5, 18, 60, 109
shark, 12–14, 24, 43, 45–46, 48–55, 60–62, 64–65, 67–68, 70–81, 83–84, 176 n. 5, 178, 180–81, 183–85, 194, 202–13, 216–19, 224, 226–28, 231–34, 236–38, 243, 246 n. 17, 252, 258, 264, 268, 272, 274, 276, 279, 291, 296, 299, 302–11, 314–24, 344–46, 349–52, 355–56, 358–59, 361, 372–77, 379, 398–400, 403, 405–7, 434, 443, 453, 456, 460, 467–68, 470, 472, 474, 478, 480, 485, 498, 502–8, 514, 519, 530, 539 n. 158, 540, 549, 552, 561, 563–69, 576, 577 n. 209, 581–83, 585, 587–90, 594–95, 613, 622, 627, 632–39, 641, 644–51, 656, 659, 677, 685 n. 283, 690 n. 287, 692

Shehret / Śḥerēt (Sh.), 6, 9–10, 13–15, 19, 20, 24, 31–32 n. 1, 53, 67, 70, 72–78, 82–85, 134 n. 16, 174 n. 4, 314 n. 58, 342, 348, 349 n. 4, 351, 361, 365, 372, 376 n. 20, 380, 383, 387, 393, 456, 535 n. 153
shell, 102, 183, 193, 202, 221, 224–25, 236–37, 239, 259, 278–79, 330, 333, 360, 381–82, 383 n. 24, 384, 386, 436 n. 9, 462 n. 44, 464, 469 n. 59, 481–82, 498, 510, 512 n. 118, 514 n. 120, 516, 518 n. 124, 521–28, 535, 536 n. 155, 539, 540 n. 160, 541 n. 162, 542, 544–48, 550 n. 171, 551, 558, 654, 661–63, 665–69, 671–72, 674 n. 276, 705
shellfish, 42, 177, 181, 189, 220–21, 231, 302, 313, 320, 343–44, 355, 360, 370, 383–86, 450, 455 n. 35, 482, 491, 517, 521–23, 524 n. 132, 524 n. 134, 525–26, 533–34, 554, 572, 612, 628, 660–64, 666–68, 677
shelter, 97–98, 132, 176, 195–97, 199–201, 253, 271, 453, 458, 568–69, 593, 595, 633, 673
Shihuh, 33, 110

shrimp, 42, 45, 49, 65, 74, 77, 80
sicklefish, 15, 481, 585
snails, 214, 220, 278, 287, 312, 343, 383, 385–86, 522–23, 525, 528
snake, 53, 78, 359, 481 n. 76, 490, 496, 547 n. 168, 612, 680
snake-eel, 53, 60, 78, 82
snappers, 15, 45, 48, 57, 64, 71, 78–79, 82–83, 204, 215, 409, 457, 460 n. 43, 472, 480–81, 495, 501 n. 106, 580, 582, 593, 608, 700
sɔ̄ḳóṭri ~ sāḳáṭri, see Soqoṭri
sole, 79, 446 n. 24
Soqoṭra, 2, 4–6, 10, 344, 427–29, 430 n. 2, 432–33, 435 n. 6, 436–37, 439 n. 13, 440 n. 14, 443, 451, 454, 455 n. 34, 455 n. 37, 457, 467, 478, 491, 496, 501, 505 n. 112, 510, 514, 529, 533 n. 148, 535, 537, 540, 542, 546, 552, 557–58, 562, 563 n. 188, 570 n. 197, 571, 577 nn. 209–10, 579, 586, 589, 590 n. 220, 596, 604, 670, 713, 719
Soqoṭri / *sɔ̄ḳóṭri ~ sāḳáṭri* (Sq.), 6, 10, 14–15, 20–21, 24, 31–32 n. 1, 67, 72–74, 76, 78, 80, 82–84, 427–30, 430 n. 2, 431–32, 435 n. 6, 436–37, 439, 440 n. 15, 444, 446 n. 24, 458, 477, 503, 504 n. 111, 509, 519 n. 125, 531, 538, 540, 542, 546 n. 166, 552, 574 n. 202, 577 n. 210, 596, 623 n. 241, 702 n. 304, 716–18
Southwestern Iranic (Iranian) (SwIr), 31 n. 1, 52, 65–66, 68, 73
spirits of the dead, 243, 248–49
squid, 42, 64, 70, 214, 220, 461, 479, 530, 589
squirrelfish, 55, 62, 77
stingray, 74, 183, 239, 356–58, 520–21, 538, 588, 630
storms, 95–97, 99–100, 104–5, 183, 186, 219, 244, 247, 283, 435, 437, 458, 534, 543, 579, 707 n. 307
Strait of Hormuz, 12, 32, 91, 100, 108
supernatural, 9, 102–3
Ṣūr, 12–13, 180, 256, 503 n. 109
surgeonfish, 72, 500 n. 106, 574, 575 n. 205
swordfish, 357, 359
trade / traders, 10, 110, 169, 179–80, 184, 187–89, 205–6, 208–11, 232, 241, 252, 259, 311, 352–53, 371, 427, 429, 433, 437–42, 444, 445

n. 23, 446, 447 nn. 25–26, 448, 451 n. 30, 459, 462 n. 44, 468, 502, 520, 526, 531, 533 n. 148, 536, 542, 545–46, 551, 556–58, 572 n. 198, 576, 577 n. 210, 590, 592–96, 687–88, 692

translanguaging / *trawsieithu*, 7, 11–13, 23, 112, 158

trevally, 15, 53, 66, 72, 82, 85, 203, 244, 298, 356–57, 457, 459–61, 472, 478–79, 504, 506, 581 n. 212, 584–85, 589–90, 601–2, 606, 610, 637, 690, 700

triggerfish, 47, 49, 51, 67, 73, 79, 236, 459, 471, 473, 504, 511, 515, 574, 581, 586, 603, 610

tulchan, 359, 419–21

tuna, 45, 50, 63, 66, 73, 75–76, 82, 84, 234, 298, 356, 357–58, 434, 459–60, 468, 470, 474–75, 478–79, 501 n. 106, 504, 506, 530, 581 n. 212, 584–85, 589–90, 593, 601, 606, 637, 710

turtle, 42, 204, 216, 222–23, 229, 231, 234–35, 243, 264, 287, 291, 324–28, 330–31, 333 n. 64, 334–36, 344, 462 n. 44, 491–92, 509–17, 518 n. 124, 520, 536 n. 155, 567

n. 194, 587 n. 217, 651–58, 703–5

United Arab Emirates (UAE), 158

vocabulary, *see* lexicon

water, 1, 63, 74, 92–96, 101, 158, 177, 191, 194, 212, 216–19, 221, 226, 228, 230–34, 250, 262, 264–65, 277, 279, 281, 288–94, 315, 330–31, 333, 362, 378, 384, 388, 395–96, 405, 430, 449, 451, 457, 459, 464 n. 49, 465, 472–75, 476 n. 72, 480, 484, 486, 488, 493 n. 91, 494–95, 498–99, 501, 504, 506–7, 511–13, 515, 519, 521, 531 n. 144, 533, 539–40, 541 n. 162, 543, 547 n. 167, 552 n. 172, 555, 562–63, 568–69, 573, 575, 579, 581–83, 587–89, 592–94, 608–10, 612, 614, 617, 625, 628–30, 632, 634, 637–40, 643, 648–51, 653–55, 657–58, 661–64, 666–67, 669–71, 673 n. 275, 674–78, 684, 686, 691, 693, 697, 698–99, 701, 706, 710, 720

weather, 9, 95, 97–98, 104, 178, 186, 209, 435

whale, 14, 42, 48–49, 55, 67, 76, 83, 434, 478, 508, 518,

535, 537, 639–42, 644, 645–51
winkles, 360, 383, 525
Yemen, 4–5, 9, 12, 283, 342, 347 n. 1, 357, 417–18, 435 n. 6, 448, 454, 456, 549 n. 169

About the Team

Geoffrey Khan and Alessandra Tosi were the managing editors for this book.

Krisztina Szilagyi performed the copyediting of the book in Word. The fonts used in this volume are Charis SIL and Scheherazade New.

Cameron Craig created all of the editions — paperback, hardback, and PDF. Conversion was performed with open source software freely available on our GitHub page at https://github.com/OpenBookPublishers.

Jeevanjot Kaur Nagpal designed the cover of this book. The cover was produced in InDesign using Fontin and Calibri fonts.

www.ingramcontent.com/pod-product-compliance
Lightning Source LLC
Chambersburg PA
CBHW052007290426
44112CB00014B/2155